PEARSON   ALWAYS LEARNING

Personal and Business Development for Advertising Sales 1 and 2

SALE10373/SALE19240

Custom Edition for Sheridan College

Taken from:
Selling Today: Creating Customer Value,
Fifth Canadian Edition
by Gerald L. Manning, Barry L. Reece, Michael Ahearne,
H.F. (Herb) MacKenzie

What Every Student Should Know about Study Skills
by Enid Leonard

Professionalism: Skills for Workplace Success,
Second Edition
by Lydia E. Anderson and Sandra B. Bolt

*What Every Student Should Know about
Preparing Effective Oral Presentations*
by Martin R. Cox

What Every Student Should Know about Researching Online
by Dave Munger and Shireen Campbell

Cover Art: Courtesy of Stockbyte, Purestock, Digital Vision/Getty Images.

Taken from:

Selling Today: Creating Customer Value, Fifth Canadian Edition
by Gerald L. Manning, Barry L. Reece, Michael Ahearne, H.F. (Herb) MacKenzie
Copyright © 2010, 2007, 2004, 2001, 1998 by Pearson Education Canada
Published by Prentice Hall
Upper Saddle River, New Jersey 07458

What Every Student Should Know about Study Skills
by Enid Leonard
Copyright © 2007 by Pearson Education, Inc.
Published by Allyn & Bacon/Longman
Boston, MA 02116

Professionalism: Skills for Workplace Success, Second Edition
by Lydia E. Anderson and Sandra B. Bolt
Copyright © 2011, 2008 by Pearson Education, Inc.
Published by Prentice Hall

What Every Student Should Know about Preparing Effective Oral Presentations
by Martin R. Cox
Copyright © 2007 by Pearson Education, Inc.
Published by Allyn & Bacon/Longman

What Every Student Should Know about Researching Online
by Dave Munger and Shireen Campbell
Copyright © 2007 by Pearson Education, Inc.
Published by Longman
New York, New York 10036

This special edition published in cooperation with Pearson Learning Solutions.

Pearson Learning Solutions, 501 Boylston Street, Suite 900, Boston, MA 02116
A Pearson Education Company
www.pearsoned.com

Printed in Canada

1 2 3 4 5 6 7 8 9 10 V084 16 15 14 13 12 11

000200010270788226

SD

ISBN 10: 1-256-34008-1
ISBN 13: 978-1-256-34008-9

Brief Contents

Contents

Taken From: *Selling Today: Creating Customer Value*, Fifth Canadian Edition by Gerald L. Manning, Barry L. Reece, Michael Ahearne, H.F. (Herb) MacKenzie

Chapter 1
Study Skills for Personal Development

Confidence Building and Goal Setting

STEPS TO INCREASED SELF-CONFIDENCE

SELF-ESTEEM CAN BE DEFINED AS HOW YOU FEEL ABOUT YOURSELF. IT IS YOUR self-image. If you have high self-esteem, you have a positive self-image and feel that you are a worthwhile and deserving person. You have faith in your abilities and trust that you make the right decisions for yourself. If you have low self-esteem, you have a low opinion of yourself and a negative self-image. You tend to trust and have faith in other people more than you do yourself. How can you build self-esteem and change a negative image into a positive one? One way is to develop confidence in your own abilities. This may seem like it is an insurmountable task if you already feeling bad about yourself, but the good news is that you can change an old pattern of negative beliefs and build confidence to achieve success in school and in life.

Where do the ideas we have about ourselves come from? We begin to develop our self-image in childhood, depending on the messages we receive from our parents and people around us. As children, we believe what people tell us about ourselves. Depending on the message, the effects are positive or negative. If we hear that we are lazy and that we can't do anything right, or that we'll never amount to anything, we feel bad inside and can carry these feelings into adulthood. The task then is to change the message to one that is positive and self-empowering.

When you feel successful, you feel more confident, which opens the way to more success. It's a positive, self-affirming cycle. Here are some tips and some ideas to consider. Some of the suggested tips may be difficult to follow at first, but with practice, positive, successful changes will occur. Remember that you can take action immediately.

- Don't let others define you. Well-intentioned friends and family may have preconceived ideas about you. For various reasons, they think they know what you can, can't, and should do. The *only* person who can define you is you. You are your best resource.

- Avoid negative people. Some people always see the negative side of a situation. They will not help you increase your self-confidence; in fact, they can undermine it. Their behavior can alter you mood and affect you emotionally. You end up feeling worn down. Positive people, on the other hand, are easy to be around and will be encouraging and uplifting. They want to see you confident and successful.

- Accept the small successes. Although we are often successful in our daily lives, we often ignore or minimize "little successes." Here's an example: A student participates

"You have to believe in yourself in spite of what other people believe."
Whoopi Goldberg

in a class discussion and earns a compliment from the instructor; he pretends that it doesn't mean anything. Another student is tired and doesn't feel like attending class, but he pushes himself to get there and takes good notes for the day. Don't gloss over the little successes, because they help you build your confidence. They do add up to bigger successes.

- Write a short daily list of several things that you can do each day to build your self-esteem. Keep the list with you and look at it as a reminder of what is important in building your confidence.

- Follow through on tasks. Accomplishing what you've set out to do is a great success builder. Do what is designated on your time management schedule. Staying on task to reach a goal gives you confidence to move to something more challenging.

- Take care of yourself physically, mentally, and emotionally. This book has many suggestions for creating your well-being.

POSITIVE SELF-AFFIRMATION: WHAT TO SAY WHEN YOU TALK TO YOURSELF

AFFIRMATIONS ARE STATEMENTS USING POSITIVE LANGUAGE. IF YOU HAVE HEARD someone answer a question with "Affirmative!" instead of a simple yes, you know the power of that word. It seems charged with energy. There isn't any doubt in that response. *Self-affirmations* are positive statements that you say to yourself. Most people don't think that they talk to themselves, but we do it all of the time. Stop yourself during the course of your day and pay attention to what's going on in your mind. What do you say to yourself? Is it, "I'll never have enough time to complete this assignment," or "This is so hard," or "I'm going to be late for class—I'm always late." When we talk to ourselves (mind chatter), we give messages to a deep part of our mind, the subconscious. We are not aware of this part of the mind, yet it accepts what we say and believes our statements to be true. The subconscious mind is discussed in more detail later, but for now, think of it as a receptacle. What do you want to put in it? Positive thoughts or negative ones? It makes sense to think positively when we know that what we say to ourselves does have an impact. It really does matter! How can we change negative statements like the ones previously discussed to positive ones? "I'll never have enough time to complete this assignment" could be changed to, "I have enough time to complete this assignment." "This is so hard" could be changed to, "This is getting easier every day." Are you too familiar with negative mind chatter? Changing how you think might be a challenge, but it's one that will put you on a direct path to success. Practice putting your thoughts into positive language.

Negative Thought	Positive Affirmation
I never have enough money.	I always have enough money for what I need.
I can't concentrate on my work.	Every day my concentration is improving.

GOAL SETTING: ANOTHER PART OF SUCCESS

A GOAL REPRESENTS SOMETHING YOU WISH TO ACHIEVE IN LIFE. IT IS WHAT YOU MAKE happen. Remember that along with good time management skills, "successful" people have goals. Success means different things to different people, whether having a 4.0 GPA, getting a dream job after college, having a spouse and family, or traveling around the world, success and goals go hand in hand.

Why are goals important? If you answered that they help you reach your dreams, you are correct. The next question is, "How will you know you've arrived if you don't know where you're going?" or put another way, "How will you know if you're *there* if you don't know where *there* is?" Creating goals gives you the arrival destination and the plan of action that will get you there.

People tend to believe what they read more than what they hear. Reading what you have written is powerful; it makes sense to put your goals down on paper. It's easy to fantasize about all of the wonderful things that you want to have or to be, but those thoughts will just linger as thoughts. Writing a goal down makes it more real and helps you focus on the daily and weekly tasks needed to make it a reality. It can help keep you stay focused when you feel overwhelmed.

When you have decided on a goal, the next step is having a plan for achieving it. This requires writing down each step that will put your plan in action. When you do this, you are on the way to achieving your personal success.

Tips for Creating a Goal

- Write your goal in short sentences. Keep the language simple. For example, "I will complete my Writing 121 paper by Friday evening," or "I will complete my prenursing requirements by June 15 of next year." Put a specific date in your written statement.

- Write a goal that is both challenging and realistic. This takes a bit of practice, so don't worry if your goal doesn't come out exactly the way you thought it would on the first try.

- Number each step in your plan of action. Write down the date by which you will complete the step. Target dates keep you motivated and focused.

- Use brightly colored pens to write your goals. If you like, use a different color for each goal.

- Keep your written goal in a highly visible place. Post it on your refrigerator, bulletin board, or bathroom mirror. Look at it every day as a reminder of what you need to do to get where you want to be.

- Break down your plan of action into manageable steps. A plan that is unrealistic can be a set-up for failure, and that is the opposite of what you want to accomplish.

- Use positive language; your subconscious mind is taking in every word.

- Visualize yourself achieving your goal. Pretend that you have already accomplished it. This is an important step in realizing your goals. What do you see? How do you feel?

SHORT- AND LONG-TERM GOALS

There are two kinds of goals to consider: short- and long-term. A short-term goal can be daily or weekly. An example of a short-term goal is to complete an assignment by a certain date or to receive a particular grade in a class. For example, if you want to get an A on a psychology exam, write your goal statement first: I will receive an A on my psychology midterm exam.

Next, write the steps in your plan for achieving the goal.

1. I will put in 3 hours of study each day.
2. I will make flash cards for each chapter.
3. I will unplug my telephone while I am studying.
4. I will ask Judy to study with me.
5. I will quiz myself every evening on the material I have been reviewing.

The process is the same for all of your goals.

If you tend towards procrastination, a daily list is helpful. If you need to, break down the goal into steps and check off each one as you reach it. Remember that "baby steps" usually work when nothing else will. As you spend more time in your classes, you will be able to gauge how much time you will need to complete an assignment. This information will help you write manageable goals.

Use long-term goals for future planning. An example of a long-term goal is to earn a college degree or to get accepted into a professional program. Your goal statement could be: I will be accepted into the nursing program by September of (200X).

The next step is to write the steps in your plan for achieving this goal.

1. I will take all of the prerequisite classes required for entrance into the nursing program by (date).
2. I will look into the availability of financial aid by (date).
3. I will apply to the nursing program by (date).
4. I will interview people who are in the nursing profession to get additional information by (date).

Because everyone has his or her own concept of time, what constitutes a long-term goal is different for each person. For one student, a goal that takes three months to achieve may be short-term; for another, the same goal might fit the long-term category.

MEASURING GOALS: USING TIME LIMITS

Having a target date for achieving your goals is important. It lets you know if your time line is realistic, and whether you've given yourself enough time to complete the goal. It's like the finish line in a race; you want to reach it, but not at the expense of hurting yourself. When you achieve your target date, you feel successful and are motivated to accomplish new goals. If you don't reach your target date, don't panic. Adjust it to a more appropriate time.

REWARDING YOURSELF: DEVELOPING A SYSTEM

REWARDING YOURSELF FOR REACHING A GOAL IS A POSITIVE BEHAVIOR. CHOOSE AN ACTIVITY that you enjoy doing but that you don't always have time to do, such as seeing a film or reading your favorite magazine. If you're low on funds, check your college newspaper for free films shown on campus. Local theatres have inexpensive afternoon showings, or check out a free DVD at your public library. Your school library has magazines and news-papers to read, also free. Going out to lunch or dinner with friends is a great reward. Check the local listings for inexpensive restaurants and student discounts.

Even though you may feel great after accomplishing a goal, don't reward yourself with a big-ticket item like a vacation, compliments of your credit card. Getting into debt will create stress, and that is not relaxing. College students are always busy; taking the time for a relaxing walk or drive is a reward in itself. Often it is the small things in life that are the best rewards. Be creative. Catch up on e-mails and phone calls, or play your favorite sport. Only you know which is the best reward reward system for you.

YOU'RE MORE THAN YOUR I.Q. SCORES

"The best way to get a good idea is to get a lot of ideas."
Linus Pauling, Nobel Prize–winning chemist

AT ONE TIME OR ANOTHER, EVERY STUDENT HAS TAKEN AN IQ (INTELLIGENCE QUOTIENT) test. These tests do not always measure or recognize the sum talents and abilities of an individual. Today's educators know that IQ reaches beyond test scores and that students have different ways of being "smart." Each student brings innate abilities, resources, experience, and potential to the classroom. One way in which you can reach your potential is to know your preferred learning method or style. This means knowing the way that you learn best. As you know, learning involves accessing, processing, and retaining information.

The three main learning styles are visual, auditory, and kinesthetic. Although most learners use a combination of styles, one may emerge as dominant. Understanding the way in which you learn can make studying and remembering easier. The following inventory will help you identify your preferred style.

Learning Styles Inventory

Answer the questions to the best of your ability. Mark a yes or no response.

		Yes	No
1.	I prefer watching a video to reading.	___	___
2.	When I sing along with my CDs or the radio, I know the words to the songs.	___	___
3.	I have athletic ability.	___	___
4.	I can picture the setting of a story I am reading.	___	___
5.	I study better with music in the background.	___	___
6.	I enjoy hands-on learning.	___	___
7.	I'd rather play sports than watch someone play them.	___	___
8.	Reading aloud helps me remember.	___	___
9.	I prefer watching someone perform a skill or a task before I actually try it.	___	___
10.	I color-coordinate my clothes.	___	___
11.	I'm good at rhyming and rapping.	___	___
12.	I use phrases like "I've got a handle on it," "I'm up against the wall," or "I have a feeling that . . ."	___	___
13.	I need to look at something several times before I understand it.	___	___
14.	I prefer having having instructors give oral directions rather than written ones.	___	___
15.	I have difficulty being still for long periods of time.	___	___
16.	I use phrases like "I see what you're saying," "that looks good," or "that's clear to me."	___	___

	Yes	No
17. I'm good at figuring out how something works.	___	___
18. I can understand a taped lecture.	___	___
19. It's easy for me to replay scenes from movies in my head.	___	___
20. I enjoy studying foreign languages.	___	___
21. I would rather conduct my own science experiment than watch someone else do it.	___	___
22. I would rather paint a house than a picture.	___	___
23. I enjoy studying in groups.	___	___
24. I prefer to have written directions to someone's home.	___	___
25. I can look at an object and remember it when I close my eyes.	___	___
26. I have musical ability.	___	___
27. When I study new vocabulary, writing the words several times helps me learn.	___	___
28. I can imagine myself doing something before I actually do it.	___	___
29. I use phrases like "that rings a bell," "I hear you," or "that sounds good."	___	___
30. I enjoy building things and working with tools.	___	___

Scoring Your Inventory

Tally your responses by adding up only the Yes answers. Put the number of the question in the appropriate box. For example, if you answered #9 with a yes, write 9 in the Visual box. If you answered #11 with a yes, write #11 in the Auditory box. If you answered #7 with a yes, write 7 in the Kinesthetic box. Add up the number of questions in each box and write a total for each one. This will determine your preferred learning style. Don't worry if a dominant mode doesn't emerge. You're a versatile learner! Use the knowledge you gain to create excellent study tools, the ones that are right for you. Chart your answers below.

Visual Style: Questions 1, 4, 9, 10, 13, 16, 19, 24, 25, 28
Auditory Style: Questions # 2, 5, 8, 11, 14, 18, 20, 23, 26, 29
Kinesthetic Style: Questions # 3, 6, 7, 12, 15, 17, 21, 22, 27, 30

Visual	**Auditory**	**Kinesthetic**
___	___	___
___	___	___
___	___	___
___	___	___
___	___	___
Total:	Total:	Total:

The highest score indicates your preferred learning style. If you have a high score in more than one area, you're using additional modalities. Remember that there are no wrong answers to this inventory. Everyone is an individual and their own style of learning.

CHARACTERISTICS OF VISUAL, AUDITORY, AND KINESTHETIC MODES

- *Visual learners* need to *see* information. If your preferred style is visual, you have strong visualization skills and can remember objects, shapes, and pictures. You learn by reading and watching films, DVDs, and demonstrations. You can see pictures in your mind.
- *Auditory learners* need to *hear* information. If your preferred style is auditory, you have a "good ear" and can hear differences in tones and rhythm. Reading out loud will be beneficial. You can remember what you hear in a lecture.
- *Kinesthetic learners* need to be physically active and doing things. If your preferred style is kinesthetic, you are a hands-on learner. You have good coordination and learn by doing. You generally have an active approach to learning.

USING MULTI-SENSORY LEARNING

Now that you know your learning style(s), you have an idea of the important role your senses play in the learning process. The best strategy is to combine modalities whenever possible. Incorporate visual, kinesthetic, and auditory learning into your study plan. Using combinations will strengthen your ability to retain information. Be creative. Add your own ideas. Here are some strategies:

Visual Learners

- Create mind maps, flowcharts, and diagrams using bright colors. Put them where you can view them frequently.
- Practice building your visual memory. Refer to the exercises in "Developing Your Photographic Memory".
- Rewrite your notes using different colors.

Auditory Learners

- After you read a page in your textbook, summarize the information out loud in your own words.
- Tape your instructor's lecture and if you are a commuter, listen to the tape on the way home, either in your car, or on the bus or subway.
- Discuss with a friend or study group the material that you have been learning.

Kinesthetic Learners

- Use your hands. Cut up charts and diagrams. Create flash cards and move them around with large, sweeping movements.

- Walk and talk the information. Recite as you move.
- Type on a computer keyboard. You are using your muscle memory.

DEVELOPING YOUR STYLE: COMBINING V, A, AND K MODES

Additional Ways You Can Use Multi-Sensory Learning

- Use background music (with no lyrics to distract you) when you study. Choose a piece of music for a particular subject. Every time you study that subject, play the music. You are creating an association for your subconscious mind. You may be surprised to discover how much of the information you remember when you play the music by itself. You are combining V and A modes.
- Use rap or rhyme to memorize information. To add kinesthetic to this A mode, walk, dance, or clap when you sing.
- If you are athletically inclined, dribble a basketball while you recite information. You are combining A and K modes.
- Study with a partner or in a group. Discuss the information. Hold up flash cards, diagrams, hierarchies, and mind maps to test each other. This combines V and A modes.
- Put yourself in the picture. You can do this with a subject like history; participate in a battle or a significant meeting such as the signing of the Declaration of Independence. Ask yourself how you feel. This combines V and K modes.

Make up your own strategies. Incorporate multi-sensory learning into your studies.

Additional Strategies

- If you are learning a new vocabulary word or math formula, write it in the air using large, sweeping movements. Close your eyes and see it in your mind's eye. Say the word out loud. You are combining V, A, and K modes.
- Use the sense of smell. One student created olfactory (smell) associations by using scented pencils for studying. He used a grape pencil for one subject and a chocolate pencil for another. When taking an exam, he used the appropriate pencil to help him recall information. He combined V and K and added an additional sensory mode.
- Use 5 × 7 flash cards to self-quiz. Use different and bright colors for each side. Lay them on a desk or table. Move them around and put them in different places as you study, or create a game with them. Place them into different categories in a hierarchical fashion such as "don't know," "review," and "need to study more."
- Create your own auditory notes using a tape recorder.

MANAGING YOUR TIME: WHY IT'S IMPORTANT

"Time is life."
Alan Lakein, author

WE NEVER SEEM TO HAVE ENOUGH TIME. IT'S THAT ELUSIVE THING THAT SLIPS FROM our grasp, causing us to ask the same question over and over again: "Where did the time go?" Each week has 168 hours, no more, no less, yet we always crave more time, complaining that we don't have enough hours in the day to get everything done! Managing our time is important because it gives us authority over our lives and ourselves. We can't control time, but we can control ourselves by deciding what we do in those 168 hours every week.

In the many books written about success and how to achieve it, two main points emerge. "Successful" people manage their time well, and they set goals for themselves. (Refer to "Goal Setting: Another Part of Success".) "Successful" students also manage their time well. They get good grades because they are prepared, know when assignments are due, know what is expected of them, and most importantly, know what they need to do to succeed.

MAKING YOUR TIME COUNT: DETERMINING YOUR NEEDS

THE FIRST STEP IN ACQUIRING GOOD TIME MANAGEMENT SKILLS IS TO DETERMINE your needs. You find out what they are by taking an honest look at how you are *actually* spending your time. Begin with the following exercise.

Step 1. For one week, keep track of everything you do with your time. Be honest with yourself. No one is judging you. The process should give you a realistic picture of how you spend your time.

Step 2. When you have completed step 1, add up the hours and divide them into categories such as family, recreation, class hours, chores, commuting time, social activities, and work. Create categories that fit your lifestyle. Perhaps you have an ongoing weekly meeting, doctor's appointments, or a religious service that you regularly attend. You will want to include all of your activities.

Step 3. Look carefully at your completed information. What can you say about the way you spend your time? What decisions will you make based on what you have written? After doing this exercise, some people make radical changes in the way they manage their time; others discover that they like things the way they are. Your determination is exactly that—yours! What works for you may not work for your friend. Don't compare your life to anyone else's; trust that you know what's best for you. You are now ready to take the next step in managing your time successfully—creating a time management schedule.

SETTING UP A SCHEDULE: HOW TO FOLLOW IT

USING YOUR PERSONAL SCHEDULE IS EFFECTIVE BECAUSE IT ALLOWS YOU TO CREATE a realistic approach to managing time and because it gives you flexibility, an important asset to have while going to college. When you have set aside time for a particular activity, you know what you need to accomplish in that time block. Because periods for recreation and socializing as well as studying are scheduled, you can focus your concentration on the activity at hand. It's a relatively guilt free system. When you're spending time with your family, you don't feel guilty for not studying because you've set aside time for both important activities. Here are the steps for creating a workable time schedule:

Step 1. Determine how many hours you will need to study for each class. If you do not know how many hours you may need for each class, use the following rule: For each hour that you spend in class, set aside two for studying. In other words, if you have a class that meets three hours every week, designate six hours for studying. You may discover that you don't need that many hours for one class, or you may need more. You can adjust your schedule as needed. This rule is simply a guideline.

Step 2. On your schedule, write in the times of your classes and other activities that *will not change throughout the term*. One example might be your work schedule or picking up the kids from day care. Now mark the times you will use for studying. Be specific. Write in "History 101" rather than "Study Hour."

Step 3. Fill in the schedule with meal and family time as well as time that you plan to socialize, exercise, or engage in any other activity. Check your category list.

Step 4. Create *flextime*. Flextime is a block of time that is open in your schedule. You can block out one hour or an afternoon. You decide how much time you can afford and what you want to do in that time period. It could be used for studying, family time, or doing absolutely nothing! You can trade flextime as needed. Perhaps you have a midterm exam coming up; use your flextime for studying.

Additional Tips for Creating a Time Schedule

- Color-code your schedule: use bright colors—the brighter, the better. Choose a different color for each class and activity. Make copies of your schedule to keep in your notebook or dayplanner. Putting a copy on your refrigerator or bulletin board acts as good visual reminder.

- Create a schedule on your computer. This allows you to make changes when you need to, as well as print additional copies. A time management schedule is not "written in stone." It may take some time to discover what works for you and what doesn't.

- Trade time—don't lose it. Use your flextime or any free period to trade activities. The concept of trading time encourages a different way of thinking. Instead of feeling that time is lost, we gain it by trading one scheduled period for another. A regular Friday night out with friends might turn into a needed study evening as it gets close to exam time. As studying becomes the priority, students often give up TV time, computer games, or talking on the phone.

- Schedule in weekend study hours. It's easy to forget about studying on the weekend, especially if you have been out of school for a while and have been working at a full-time job. Being a student doesn't end when classes are over; in fact, the work is just beginning. Another advantage to studying on the weekend is that it keeps information current. Repetition is needed to get information stored in your long-term memory.

Now that you've created your schedule, you will need to follow it for approximately three weeks. This will provide a test period to determine whether your time frames are workable and realistic. During the early weeks of the term, you're likely to have less homework. Remember to adjust your schedule as the term progresses, because you'll be carrying a heavier assignment and study load. Following a schedule can be challenging, especially if you've never done it before; its function is to help you manage time well and to minimize stress, not create more of it. Be realistic and you *will* create good study habits.

THE WEEKLY SCHEDULE AND DAILY LIST

USE WEEKEND TIME TO CREATE YOUR SCHEDULE FOR THE COMING WEEK. YOU MIGHT not have much of a change in your routine until you approach exam time. Because you already have scheduled times for studying, you can add additional hours. Getting up an hour earlier to study is a way to gain time. Write in the extra hour on your schedule, and don't forget to set your alarm. Be creative; move activities around when you have a busy or unusual week. *Always* add study time when you are preparing for an exam. Plan your week ahead of time.

A daily list helps you stay on track with tasks and goals. Make a list of what you would like to accomplish for the day. When you complete a task, check off the item. This is a great way to see what you've actually accomplished for the day. If you have difficulty in getting things done, a daily list is perfect for you. Use both daily and weekly schedules for effective time management.

Time Tips

■ Ask yourself this question: "What is the best use of my time right now?" The answer may surprise you.

Week of _____

Time	Monday	Tuesday	Wednesday	Thursday	Friday	Saturday	Sunday
6–7	Sleep ———————————————————————→						
7–8	Breakfast & commute ————————————→					Sleep	Sleep
8–9	History 101	Spanish 101	History 101	Spanish 101	History 101	Breakfast	
9–10	Psych 201	↓	Psych 201	↓	Psych 201	Part-time job	
10–11	Study Hist.	Study Spanish	Study Hist.	Study Spanish	Study Hist.		Breakfast
11–12	Volleyball	Swimming	Volleyball	Swimming	Volleyball		
12–1	Lunch ———————————————————————→					↓	↓
1–2	Study Psych.	Study Hist.		Part-time job	Study Spanish	Lunch	Flex
2–3	Writer's Club	↓	Writer's Club		Study Psych.	Laundry	
3–4	Flex Time	Flex time	Study Psych.		Read/Study English	Cleaning	Finish Eng. paper
4–5	↓	↓	Flex	↓	Flex	Study Hist.	
5–6	Dinner ——————————————————————————→					Study Psych.	Study Spanish

Figure 1.1 Weekly Schedule.

- Use small blocks of time that you might normally waste to review your class material. Do you spend ten minutes waiting for your friend in the cafeteria? How about the twenty-minute wait at the doctor's office or the ten-minute wait at the post office or bank? Three 10-minute periods equal a half-hour of study time. It's a good idea to always have study material with you. You never know when you may be able to take advantage of a small block of time.

Scheduling takes more time in the beginning, but the payoffs are great—good grades and accomplishing your goals. Here is an example of a weekly schedule.

PROCRASTINATION: DEALING WITH DEADLINES

PROCRASTINATION IS PUTTING SOMETHING OFF UNTIL A FUTURE TIME. POSTPONING tasks or assignments that need to be completed can create anxiety, especially when the task keeps getting delayed. If you are a procrastinator, consider yourself a creative person; after all, it does take some creativity to keep coming up with excuses. The trick is to take that creative energy and put it to work for you. People who procrastinate seem to like working under deadlines, which creates a kind of stress that would drive others mad. Whether you procrastinate regularly or on occasion, here are some helpful tips:

- *Stop* thinking about the assignment that you need to do and just begin to do it. For example, if you have a thirty-page reading assignment and you find yourself sitting and staring at the textbook, *take action*. Open it up and start skimming. Turn the pages and let your eyes skim over the material. Now tell yourself that you will read five pages. After you have read five pages, tell yourself that you will read five more and then do it. The trick is to break down large tasks into manageable smaller ones. Imagine a large sandwich you're about to eat. You couldn't possibly put the whole thing in your mouth and consume it at one time; however, you can manage it by eating one bite at a time. An assignment that feels overwhelming can surely trigger procrastination. It is important to begin. Think of a popular shoe company's slogan and "Just Do It!"

- Set a realistic goal for yourself. (Refer to "Goal Setting: Another Part of Success".) If you are tackling a difficult subject, allow extra time for the task.

- Acknowledge the work that you have accomplished. Don't "beat yourself up" for what you haven't done.

- Work when you have the highest level of energy. If you are most productive in the morning, tackle the most difficult subjects at that time. If you are a "night person" or you experience a "second wind," take advantage of the time to do your work.

- Try not to cram. Cramming is an ineffective way to study and can inhibit storage of information in your long-term memory. Learning over a period of time using repetitive practice is a more efficient tool for retaining information.

- Eliminate external distractions. (Refer to "Developing Concentration".)

- Change activities if you are tired or begin to lose concentration. Instead of studying history for one hour followed by an hour of psychology, divide the time into half-hours. This will help keep you focused when studying becomes difficult. "Mixing it up" can be highly productive. Use a timer to keep you on track.

	Standard Schedule	"Mixing It Up" Schedule
1:00	Study History 101	Study History 101
1:30		Study Psychology 101
2:00	Study Psychology 101	Study History 101
2:30		Study Psychology 101
3:00		

PRIORITIZING: THE BALANCING ACT

LIFE FOR MANY STUDENTS IS A BALANCING ACT. ATTENDING CLASSES TAKES UP only part of the day. Family obligations, work, friends, exercise sessions, recreation . . . the list goes on. It is clear that today's college students need to be good at "multi-tasking" and setting priorities. Priorities are defined as what is most important to you. Everyone's are different. Although family and church might be a priority for one person, sports and socializing might be a priority for another. Identifying your priorities assists you in accomplishing your goals and in achieving success.

Developing Concentration

Concentration is the ability to focus without distraction. Have you ever noticed that you seem to have amazing powers of concentration when you're not trying to concentrate? Sometimes, the more you try, the harder it becomes. Think of a time when you were immersed in a favorite activity. The time seemed to fly by; concentration was effortless. Unfortunately, this doesn't always happen when we are reading textbooks. Most students have had the experience of reading the same paragraph over and over again, wondering if any information is sinking in at all. Wouldn't it be great if we could transfer the focused concentration we have when we're doing something we love, to our textbook reading and studying? The key to accomplishing this feat is to *practice* the following concentration techniques. Create your plan and follow it.

> "What we learn with pleasure, we never forget."
> Alfred Mercier

- Get into a routine; this will help you concentrate. Study at the same time and place every day, if possible. Your time management schedule is a good reminder.

- Study when you are most alert. Studies show that people are most alert one hour after waking up. If you're not rushing off to school or to a job, use that hour to study.

- Create good study habits in the beginning of the term. Remember that we are creatures of habit, and because it's easier to make a habit than break one, it's better to start out with positive behaviors.

- Use affirmations. Affirmations are positive self-statements. Every time you read or study, tell yourself—or affirm—that you have excellent concentration. Keep repeating this affirmation. Even if you don't believe it, your subconscious mind will! You are working with a powerful part of your mind.

- Use the index card technique. Keep an index card next to your text or notebook. Every time that you begin to lose concentration, mark a check on the index card. By the end of the study period, count up the number of checks. At the next study session, work at minimizing the number of checks you make.

- Increase your attention span. The trick is to *pretend* that the material you are studying is the most exciting and interesting you've ever read. If this sounds silly, remember that you are working not only with the conscious part of your mind, but with the subconscious part, which can be tricked into believing this is true.

TIPS AND TRICKS FOR DEVELOPING YOUR CONCENTRATION

- Use relaxation techniques. When you are relaxed, your concentration is better. Use deep breathing. This technique will alert your subconscious mind that you are ready to concentrate.

- Read with a pen in your hand to help focus your concentration.

- Listen to music. Soft music without lyrics (words) can enhance learning. Certain classical pieces of music (e.g., those by Bach or Mozart) can actually change brain wave activity to help you learn better.

- Create a study area and use it for studying *only*. This is important because you are creating a positive habitual behavior. Every time you sit down to study, your mind knows that it's time to concentrate and learn. Excellent concentration becomes automatic.

- Have a desk in your study area (no couches here). Students have come up with creative ideas for desks, including putting a door across two low file cabinets or sawhorses. Used desks can be found at furniture stores and garage sales, or through ads in the local papers.

- Sit in a comfortable chair. Put a pillow behind your lower back for support, if needed. Be sure to have all of your materials on your desk. This includes textbooks, yellow markers for highlighting, notebooks, pens and pencils, calculators, and computers.

- Be sure your study area has adequate lighting. You don't want to have shadows on your reading material.

The goal here is to create an environment that is conducive to excellent concentration. Some students prefer to study in the school library for the sake of quiet and proximity to materials. If you live in a house that is filled with noise and distractions, consider using the library for your study area. If you do use the library, try and sit in the same place every time. When you are ready to study, whether it is at home or on campus, take a deep relaxing breath, tell yourself that you're going to have an excellent session, sit down, and begin. If, while studying, your mind begins to wander and you feel that you are losing concentration, *immediately* get up and do something else for a couple of minutes. Drink a glass of water or go outside for some fresh air. Go back to your desk and start the process over. Soon your mind and body will know that you are serious about concentration. Remember that these techniques require practice. Have patience and don't give up.

Some Don'ts

Don't study in bed, where you sleep, or at the table where you eat. Remember that you are creating a perfect study area, one in which the only thing you do is study.

ELIMINATING INTERNAL AND EXTERNAL DISTRACTIONS

Two kinds of distractions can affect concentration: internal and external. The external ones are easier to eliminate. They happen in your environment or "outside of yourself." Outside influences can certainly detract from your ability to concentrate. What are the external distractions in your life? Examples are the telephone ringing constantly, loud music blaring through the neighbor's wall, dogs barking, horns honking, or roommates wanting to share their ongoing problems. What are the external distractions in your life? Here is one student's list of external distractions and her plan to eliminate them.

Internal distractions come from within. Examples are feeling tired from lack of sleep, experiencing hunger, illness, or constantly thinking about personal problems.

If you have a serious problem that is getting in the way of your ability to concentrate, make an appointment with a professional counselor. Your college may offer free counseling

External Distraction	Plan to Change
1) Telephone ringing	1) Turn on answering machine or turn off phone
2) Family member always wanting to talk to me while I'm studying	2) Ask politely not to be disturbed or go to the library to study
3) Children wanting my attention	3) Keep children busy with creative project Trade babysitting or child care with another student who has children Spend an extra hour at school studying
4) TV is too loud	4) Ask person watching TV to wear headphones or turn down the sound Go to the library to study

services. Check your local telephone directory or the Internet for names of local counselors who may offer a sliding scale fee. Many student service groups on campus can provide information. Talking with a counselor or teacher doesn't mean that there is anything wrong with you; it simply means that you are taking care of yourself because you value yourself. It's a stressful world, and no one is problem free. You can't always eliminate a problem, but you can learn strategies for minimizing the pain.

Hunger is another internal distraction. When you are hungry, you may experience low blood sugar, which can affect your ability to think clearly. Students often grab a candy bar or donut and coffee for breakfast. Because this breakfast consists of sugar and caffeine, a great feeling of energy occurs; however, forty-five minutes later, when blood sugar levels drop, fatigue sets in. Students complain of having headaches, not being able to concentrate, and feeling hungry for "real" food. What you eat can affect your health as well as your ability to retain information. Here are some healthy breakfast suggestions: toasted cheese on a bagel, toast with peanut butter, whole grain cereal with milk, eggs, and yogurt. Add nuts and seeds for protein.

When you're tired, it's difficult to concentrate. Every task seems to take longer to do. Determine how many hours of sleep you need, and then do your best to get them. Every person has different sleep requirements. One person may do fine with six hours, while another needs eight or nine to function during the day. Your body restores itself in deep sleep cycles, so it's important to give your body what it needs. Remember that it takes more energy to concentrate when you are tired than when you are rested.

Worry is a common internal distraction. Although some people worry once in a while, others are constant "worriers." How can you have good concentration when worry invades your thought process? Here's a great trick. It sounds ridiculous, but it really does work. Nagging thoughts are like little children who always want our attention. Pick a time that you set aside specifically for worrying. Take about five minutes (or more time if you need it), and worry about everything! Give those thoughts your full attention. Consciously worry, but only one time per day. Try this and be surprised at how it works.

GETTING ASSISTANCE FROM THE PEOPLE IN YOUR LIFE: HELPING OTHERS WHILE YOU HELP YOURSELF

The people in your life can be hindering your concentration and not know it. If you are studying at home, you are perceived to be available, and therefore you can be interrupted. It's your responsibility to let the people in your life know that school and studying are a priority for you. This is not as easy to do with children, of course. Here are some ideas for limiting interruptions:

- Create a system for letting others know when you are not available. Put a symbol on your door, a picture or cutout to indicate that you don't wish to be disturbed. When the symbol comes down, you're available. One student put up a paper clock indicating the time he would be ready to join the rest of his family. A creative parent devised a system for his children. He drew a stoplight with red, yellow, and green lights and taped it to his door. Red meant don't bother dad, green meant that it was ok to knock on the door, and yellow meant that the children needed to wait ten minutes before coming in.

- If you have school age children, arrange quiet projects for them to do. If they want to watch television or DVDs, give them headsets to wear. If they have homework of their own, create a family study time.

- If parents or friends call you constantly, turn off the phone or tell them that your study time is important and that you won't be answering your phone. This is sometimes difficult to do, but when you are assertive with the people in your life, you're helping them help you.

- Tell the people in your life that you are working toward specific goals or grades. Share more information about your goals. Often family members want to support you, but they don't know how.

- Enlist the support of other friends and family.

Practice the techniques presented in this book. Patience will be a virtue; remember that taking time to build your concentration is a good use of your time.

Memory: How It Works

When you are a college student, it is essential to develop your memory. For some, remembering information and learning facts seem effortless, but for others, the task is a constant struggle. Memory is certainly mystifying. We can remember odd details from our past, yet we can't remember what we had for lunch a couple of days ago. One thing is certain—developing your memory will help you achieve success in college. Getting the good grades that you want requires doing well on exams, and that means being able to remember the information that is in your textbooks and notes.

Our minds are like computers; information gets programmed in and stored for use at a later date. When you work on a computer, you store information in a particular file for a period of time; when you need access to it, you click the mouse on the appropriate icon, and it appears on the screen. Your memory works much the same way. It is your job to get information (programmed) from the *short-term memory* into *the long-term memory* (stored). The process by which you do this is called *Rehearsal* or *meaningful repetition*. Think of actors in a play. First they learn their lines; they rehearse them over and over until they know them "by heart." As they rehearse, they are *personalizing*; in other words, they are understanding the character, they are making it their own. What they've memorized (learned) is stored in their *long-term memory*, and when it is time for the performance, they feel confident and ready to go on stage. A college student's job is not unlike that of an actor. The same techniques apply.

SHORT- AND LONG-TERM MEMORY

THE *SHORT-TERM MEMORY* (STM) IS LIMITED BECAUSE IT DOES NOT STORE INFORMATION. Here's an example of how it works. You're at a party and your friend introduces you to someone. You exchange hellos and chat briefly, but the following day when you run into her on campus, you have completely forgotten her name. You feel embarrassed. Blame it on the short-term memory. Here's another example. You are taking a telephone message. You have part of the phone number written down when your roommate walks in the door and starts talking to you. The number in your head completely disappears.

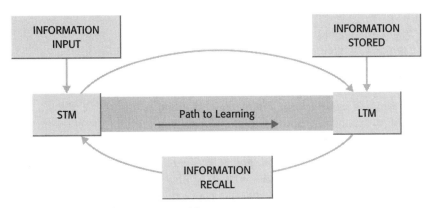

Figure 1.2 Short- and Long-term Memory.

Memory is like a chain link fence. Each link (thought) connects to another and creates a body of knowledge. This knowledge is stored in the *long-term memory (LTM)*, which can hold an infinite amount of information. A student must store the material he is learning in the LTM to retain it and retrieve it on exam day. How is this formidable task accomplished? The answer is through *recitation*. Reciting aloud is a powerful learning tool. When you recite the material in your own words, you are, like the actor, making it your own. In other words, you're not just memorizing the information, you understand it as well.

Additional Tips

■ Study in groups or with a study partner. As you explain (recite) the material to each other, you begin to develop a deeper understanding of it. There might be gaps in your knowledge that can be filled in by your study partner or a member of the group, or you may be able to clarify the issue. Perhaps you discover that you need to review certain sections of your textbook. Each of you is processing the information through the filter of your own mind. Remember that recitation is important and helps you to truly know your subject.

■ Personalize the material. This means putting your own personal stamp on information by effectively using study techniques that work for you. Because everyone processes information differently, a technique or skill that helps you may not be right for your study partner. Flash cards and mind maps might appeal to you, while outlines and copying class notes appeal to your study partner.

TIPS AND TRICKS: DOING WHAT THE EXPERTS DO

■ Use the principle of *association*. We remember things with which we have an association. A song from our past comes on the radio, and suddenly, we are singing along, remembering the words and experiencing memories. Emotions fill us and we're transported back in time. You will remember information if you create associations. Connect the new material with something that you already know. For example, if you have a geology class and you are studying rock formations, think back to the school field trip that gave you hands-on experience. What associations can you make? What do you remember? How did you feel when you were on that trip? *Emotions and feelings are directly connected to memory.* Use this knowledge to your best advantage. *Associations are memory links.* Connect the old knowledge to the new!

■ Use the principle of *background building*. A subject that is familiar is easier to study than one that isn't. As a student, you will be introduced to many new and unfamiliar concepts. If the subject material is unfamiliar to you, brush up on the basics. Begin with the glossary at the back of the book. Look up unfamiliar terms and write down their definitions. Check the Internet for basic facts related to the subject. Go to the library and check out materials that will help you get background information and build your knowledge base.

■ Use the principle of *divided practice*. It is easier to learn and remember when your study time is divided into short blocks rather than long ones. Use the suggestions in the time management section "Getting Control of Your Time and Life" to help you create a schedule that divides your study time into appropriate periods.

- Use the principle of *selection*. Make good choice about the parts of your material that are important to study. You can't possibly memorize every word that you read, nor do you want to. Begin by identifying the main ideas of each paragraph or section of the chapter. Think of a main idea as an umbrella. It covers supporting details, examples, opinions, and statistics, all of which expand the main idea. As you practice the principle of selection, you will be able to decide which pieces of information need to be stored in your LTM.

- Use the principle of *visualization*. When you use pictures and symbols to remember information, you are accessing the visual or spatial side of your brain. Visualization is one of the most powerful tools for memory. Learning visual techniques can improve your ability to remember, and the effects can be long-lasting. Creativity plays an important part in visual learning, and it can actually make memorizing fun.

An instructor shared the following true story with her students. The incident occurred during her high school drama class many years before. One day, a substitute teacher entered the room. Instead of taking attendance, as the regular teacher did, he asked each student to say his or her name aloud. This was a large class consisting of thirty-five students. When everyone had spoken their names, the room became uncomfortably quiet. The teacher then named each student, beginning with the first. The students were astounded by this feat of memory and wanted to know how he was able to do this. The teacher then explained the memory trick. He used a visualization technique. As each student stated his or her name, he created a ridiculous visual image and associated it or connected it to the student. For example, if the student's name was Ben Waters, he might visualize "bending waters" and see a stream of water bending around the student. The water might be rainbow colored because color aids memory. The point is to create an image that is as silly or ridiculous you can imagine. The more outrageous, the better! You are on your way to building visual memory. What images can you come up with for the name Carla Washington? How about *Carla* washing her car with a map of Washington state in her hand? Do you remember the famous picture of the first U.S. president, George Washington, with his wide brimmed hat? Fill up the brim with funny looking cars. You get the idea. Using creative and outrageous images will help you remember.

USING YOUR WHOLE BRAIN

USING YOUR WHOLE BRAIN MEANS UTILIZING BOTH THE RIGHT AND LEFT HEMISPHERES of your brain. The two sides function differently, and learning how to incorporate both can create new options for understanding and for maximizing learning ability.

Left Side	Right Side
Logical	Intuitive
Linear	Non-linear
Mathematical	Visual
Language	Spatial
Analytical	Creative
Reasoning	Subconscious Mind
Conscious Mind	

Although we do use both sides of our brain to varying degrees, some people are more dominant in one hemisphere. Consider the artist who creates beautiful paintings, but can't balance a checkbook or keep track of his money. He sees the world in symbols and pictures and is highly intuitive about people. Would you say that he is left or right brain dominant? What about the accountant who is logical and rational and writes down every penny he spends? He won't make a decision without thoroughly researching a topic, and he would never make a decision based solely on his intuition. His home is organized, and he has a particular place for everything in it. Do you think he is right or left brain dominant? Of course these examples are extreme, but they illustrate differences in the way people think, and this has important implications for learning.

Traditionally, students have been taught using left brain techniques. The teacher writes information on the board, the student copies it, and later, there is a test. Somewhere between copying the information from the board and taking the test, the information gets lost; it doesn't get stored in the LTM. This is a frustrating experience. By incorporating visual right brain techniques, the problem can be minimized, perhaps even solved.

Making an emotional connection to information is a way to use the right side of the brain. We tend to remember experiences that involve our emotions. Everyone remembers where they were and what they were doing on September 11, 2001, the day of the terrorist attacks, but they would have to look at their calendars to tell you what they were doing on September 11 of the previous year.

When you are trying to learn new material, get excited about it, even if you have to pretend. Remember that the subconscious mind doesn't know the difference and will believe that you are excited. Creating emotion and excitement is a way to remember and retain information.

HIERARCHIES, MIND MAPS, AND CREATING PICTURES

HIERARCHIES—VISUAL MEMORY AIDS—ARE ALSO CALLED FLOWCHARTS AND TREE diagrams. The information you want to learn is categorized in a holistic way and is processed in the right side of the brain. You can make a hierarchy for a paragraph or a chapter in a textbook, or you can use it to brainstorm ideas. The beauty of a hierarchy is that there is no wrong way to make one. You are personalizing the information through your own processing system, your mind. Your hierarchy will look different than your friend's. Trust your instincts and you will create a perfect one.

Because a hierarchy shows the relationships between main ideas and their supporting details, it is an excellent study tool. In a hierarchy, the most important ideas are written on the top levels (tree branches) while the supporting ideas get placed on the lower ones.

Begin your hierarchy for a textbook chapter by placing the main heading of your chapter on the top line. Use the next level for the subheadings. Under each subheading or branch, write information that supports the main idea. The trick is to be brief. Write key words and short phrases, which you will use to recall the material. Too much information will defeat the purpose of the hierarchy. Recite the material, working from the top levels down. If can't recite the information, go back to the text. Remember that *recitation* is the key to retention. You can create as many levels as you feel are necessary, but college exams usually do not ask test questions based on information lower than *five* levels down. When

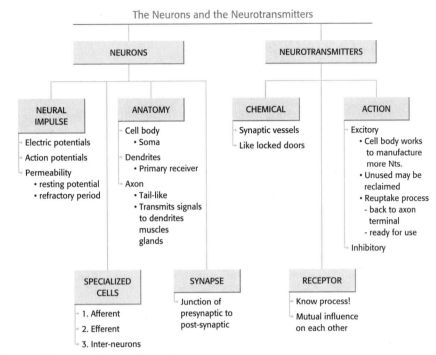

Figure 1.3 Example of hierarchy.

you study from a hierarchy, you get the big picture. All of the information is presented in one visual representation. Here is an example from a college psychology text.

Tips for Creating Hierarchies

- Use bright colors. Choose a different color for each level or color code in your personal way.

- Limit information to five to seven items on one branch. The STM is limited in its capacity and learning no more than seven items at a time will make it easier to get the information stored in your LTM.

- Use one hierarchy for this chapter. If you can't fit all of the information on one page, tape two pieces of paper together. You want to be able to visualize the entire picture.

- Create a large hierarchy and tape it to your wall. Study it often. Use posterboard or blank newspaper. Newspaper offices as well as supply and discount stores sell inexpensive roles of blank paper. Students have come up with creative ways to use recycled materials, including using cut up cardboard from boxes and brown paper bags.

Mind maps are similar to hierarchies in that they are a visual display of information. The can be used for notetaking, for generating ideas (brainstorming), or as a study tool. In mind mapping, symbols, colors and pictures are used to enhance right brain learning. It is a less structured form than the hierarchy. The main ideas are written in the center of the page, while the supporting details branch off in the direction you choose. A mind map enables you to bypass the linear, logical, critical left side of the brain, which can inhibit your creativity. Traditional notetaking is a left brain process, while mind mapping gets

THE NEURONS AND THE NEUROTRANSMITTERS

The Neurons: The Nervous System s Messenger Cells

All our thoughts, feelings, and behavior can ultimately be traced to the activity of **neurons**—the specialized cells that conduct impulses through the nervous system. Most experts estimate that there may be as many as 100 billion neurons in the brain (Swanson, 1995). This would mean that you have about 17 times as many neurons as there are people living on the earth right now.

Neurons perform several important tasks: (1) Afferent (sensory) neurons relay messages from the sense organs and receptors—eyes, ears, nose, mouth, and skin—to the brain or spinal cord. (2) Efferent (motor) neurons convey signals from the brain and spinal cord to the glands and the muscles, enabling the body to move. (3) Interneurons, thousands of times more numerous than motor or sensory neurons, carry information between neurons in the brain and between neurons in the spinal cord.

Anatomy of a Neuron: Looking at Its Parts   Although no two neurons are exactly alike, nearly all are made up of three important parts: the cell body (soma), dendrites, and the axon. The **cell body** contains the nucleus and carries out the metabolic, or life-sustaining, functions of the neuron. Branching out from the cell body are the **dendrites**, which look much like the leafless branches of a tree (*dendrite* comes from the Greek word for "tree"). The dendrites are the primary receivers of signals from other neurons, but the cell body can also receive signals directly. And dendrites do not merely receive signals from other neurons and relay them to the cell body. Scientists now know that dendrites relay messages backward—from the cell body to their own branches (a process called *back propagating*). These backward messages may shape the dendrites responses to future signals they receive (Magee & Johnston, 1997; Sejnowski, 1997).

The **axon** is the slender, tail-like extension of the neuron that sprouts into many branches, each ending in a bulbous axon terminal. The axon terminals transmit signals to the dendrites or cell bodies of other neu-

Figure 2.1

The Structure of a Typical Neuron

A typical neuron has three important parts: (1) a cell body, which carries out the metabolic functions of the neuron; (2) branched fibers called dendrites, which are the primary receivers of the impulses from other neurons; and (3) a slender, tail-like extension called an axon, the transmitting end of the neuron, which sprouts into many branches, each ending in an axon terminal. The photograph shows human neurons greatly magnified.

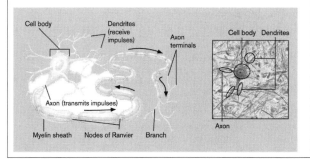

Figure 1.4 Pages from a College Textbook

(*Source*: From Ellen R. Greenwood and Samuel E. Wood. The World of Psychology, 4th ed. Published by Allyn and Bacon, Boston, MA. Copyright © 2002 by Pearson Education. Reprinted by permission of the publisher.)

processed on the right side. The little voice inside that says, "This is the wrong way to do it," or "This will never work," is quieted. Using mind-mapping techniques can feel awkward at first, but you may discover that they provide a valuable missing piece of your learning process. It's also a great idea to use a mind map when you feel "stuck" or unmotivated. It gets you started.

rons, and to muscles, glands, and other parts of the body. In humans, some axons are short—only thousandths of an inch. Others can be up to a meter long—39.37 inches—long enough to reach from the brain to the tip of the spinal cord, or from the spinal cord to remote parts of the body. Figure 2.1 shows a neuron s structure.

The Synapse   Remarkably, the billions of neurons that send and receive signals are not physically connected. The axon terminals are separated from the receiving neurons by tiny, fluid-filled gaps called *synaptic clefts*. The **synapse** is the junction where the axon terminal of a sending (presynaptic) neuron communicates with a receiving (postsynaptic) neuron across the synaptic cleft. There may be as many as 100 trillion synapses in the human nervous system (Swanson, 1995). And a single neuron may synapse with thousands of other neurons (Kelner, 1997). A technique that has recently been developed to monitor the action at the synapses may soon enable researchers to visualize the activity of all the synapses of a single neuron.

If neurons are not physically connected, how do they communicate? How do they send and receive their messages?

The Neural Impulse: The Beginning of Thought and Action
Researchers have known for some 200 years that cells in the brain, the spinal cord, and the muscles generate electrical potentials. These tiny electric charges play a part in all bodily functions. Every time you move a muscle, experience a sensation, or have a thought or a feeling, a small but measurable electrical impulse is present.

How does this biological electricity work? Even though the impulse that travels down the axon is electrical, the axon does not transmit it the way a wire conducts an electrical current. What actually moves through the axon is a change in the **permeability** of the cell membrane. This process allows ions (electrically charged atoms or molecules) to move into and out of the axon through ion channels in the membrane.

Body fluids contain ions, some with positive electrical charges and others with negative charges. Inside the axon, there are normally more negative than positive ions. When at rest (not firing), the axon membrane carries a negative electrical potential of about -70 millivolts (70 thousandths of a volt) relative to the fluid outside the cell. This slight negative charge is referred to as the neuron s **resting potential.**

When the excitatory effects on a neuron reach a certain threshold, ion channels begin to open in the cell membrane of the axon at the point closest to the cell body, allowing positive ions to flow into the axon. This inflow of positive ions causes the membrane potential to change abruptly, to a positive value of about $+50$ millivolts (Pinel, 2000). This sudden reversal of the resting potential, which lasts for about 1 millisecond (1 thousandth of a second), is the **action potential.** Then the ion channels admitting positive ions close, and other ion channels open, forcing some positive ions out of the axon. As a result, the original negative charge, or resting potential, is restored. The opening and closing of ion channels continues segment by segment down the length of the axon, causing the action potential to move along the axon (Cardoso & Sabbatini, 2000).

The action potential operates according to the "all or none" law—a neuron either fires completely or does not fire at all. Immediately after a neuron fires, it enters a *refractory period,* during which it cannot fire again for 1 to 2 milliseconds. But this rest period is often very short: When stimulated, neurons can fire up to 1,000 times per second.

Figure 1.4   (*continued*)

Tips for Creating Mind Maps

▪ Use different colors for main ideas and supporting details, as you did in your hierarchy. When you study, close your eyes and see the map. This will enhance visual memory skills.

▪ Draw as many pictures as you dare. Remember that a picture is worth a thousand words. The right side of your brain holds this picture in your memory.

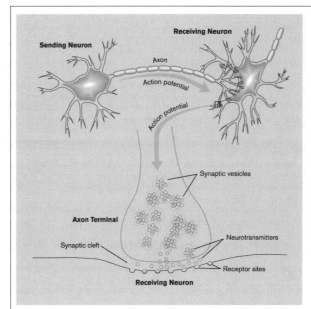

Figure 2.2
Synaptic Transmission

Sending neurons transmit their messages to receiving neurons by electrochemical action. When a neuron fires, the action potential arrives at the axon terminal and triggers the release of neurotransmitters from the synaptic vesicles. Neurotransmitters flow into the synaptic cleft and move toward the receiving neuron, which has numerous receptors. The receptors will bind only with neurotransmitters having distinctive molecular shapes that match their enclosed volumes. Neurotransmitters influence the receiving neuron only to fire or not to fire.

Neurotransmitters: The Chemical Messengers of the Brain

Once a neuron fires, how does it get its message across the synaptic cleft and on to other neurons? Messages are transmitted between neurons by one or more of a large group of chemical substances known as **neurotransmitters.**

Where are the neurotransmitters located? Inside the axon terminal are many small, sphere-shaped containers with thin membranes called *synaptic vesicles*, which hold the neurotransmitters. (*Vesicle* comes from a Latin word meaning "little bladder.") When an action potential arrives at the axon terminal, synaptic vesicles move toward the cell membrane, fuse with it, and release their neurotransmitter molecules. This process is shown in Figure 2.2.

The Receptor: Locks for Neurotransmitter Keys   Once released, neurotransmitters do not simply flow into the synaptic cleft and stimulate all the adjacent neurons. Each neurotransmitter has a distinctive molecular shape, and **receptors** on the surfaces of dendrites and cell bodies also have distinctive shapes. Neurotransmitters can affect only those neurons that have receptors designed to receive molecules of their particular shape. In other words, each receptor is somewhat like a locked door that only certain neurotransmitter keys can unlock (Cardoso & Sabbatini, 2000; Restak, 1993).

However, the binding of neurotransmitters with receptors is not as fixed and rigid a process as keys fitting locks or jigsaw puzzle pieces interlocking. Receptors in the brain are living matter; they can expand and contract their enclosed volumes. Consequently, the interaction where

Figure 1.4 Pages from a College Textbook   (*continued*)

▪   If you are using mind mapping to take class notes, add in textbook information. If you are using mind mapping to take notes from your textbook, add in class notes. Don't worry if it seems as though you are putting in an enormous effort. These techniques require more work in the beginning for a great payoff in the end. Here's an example of a mind map using the same information from the psychology text.

the neurotransmitter and the receptor meet is controlled not by the direct influence of one on the other, but by their *mutual* influence on each other. In such a dynamic interplay, a certain neurotransmitter may be competing for the same receptor with another neurotransmitter of a slightly different shape. The receptor will admit only one of the competing neurotransmitters—the one that fits it most perfectly. Thus, a receptor may receive a neurotransmitter at one time, but not at other times if another neurotransmitter molecule is present whose "affinity with the receptor is even stronger. As in dating and mating, what is finally settled for is always a function of what is available" (Restak, 1993, p. 28).

The Action of Neurotransmitters   When neurotransmitters bind with receptors on the dendrites or cell bodies of receiving neurons, their action is either excitatory (influencing the neurons to fire) or inhibitory (influencing them not to fire). Because a single neuron may synapse with thousands of other neurons at the same time, there will always be both excitatory and inhibitory influences on receiving neurons. For the neuron to fire, the excitatory influences must exceed the inhibitory influences of neurotransmitter substances by a sufficient amount (the threshold).

For many years researchers believed that each individual neuron responded to only one neurotransmitter. But it is now known that individual neurons may respond to several different neurotransmitters, suggesting a greater flexibility of response, even at the level of a single neuron (Pinel, 2000).

You may wonder how the synaptic vesicles can continue to pour out neurotransmitters, yet have a ready supply so that the neuron can respond to continuing stimulation. First, the cell body of the neuron is always working to manufacture more of the neurotransmitter substance. Second, unused neurotransmitters in the synaptic cleft may be broken down into their component molecules and reclaimed by the axon terminal to be recycled and used again. Third, by an important process called **reuptake**, the neurotransmitter substance is taken back into the axon terminal, intact and ready for immediate use. This terminates the neurotransmitter s excitatory or inhibitory effect on the receiving neuron. Figure 2.3 illustrates the reuptake process.

The nature of synaptic transmission—whether it is primarily chemical or electrical—was a subject of controversy during the first half of the 20th century. By the 1950s, it seemed clear that the means of communication between neurons was chemical. Yet, at some synapses, what was termed "gap junction," or electrical transmission, occurred between the neurons. Recent research has shown that this electrical transmission may be more frequent than neuroscientists once believed (Bennett, 2000). Even though synaptic transmission of information between neurons is primarily chemical, some electrical transmission is known to occur at synapses in the retina, the olfactory bulb (sense of smell), and the cerebral cortex, which we will discuss later in the chapter (Bennett, 2000).

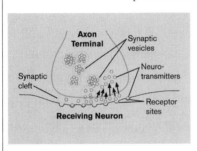

Figure 2.3

The Process of Reuptake

Through the process of reuptake, neurotransmitter molecules are taken back into the axon terminal, intact and ready for immediate use.

Figure 1.4

DEVELOPING YOUR PHOTOGRAPHIC MEMORY

THIS IS THE ABILITY TO READ OR VIEW SOMETHING ONCE AND FULLY REMEMBER IT. Only a small segment of the population has this gift, but everyone can increase their visual, or photographic, memory. Your visual memory is working all of the time. For example, think of pictures, sayings, or magnets that you have on your refrigerator door. If you close your eyes, you will most likely be able to remember what's on the door. That is because every time you go to your refrigerator, your visual memory (right brain) is taking a picture of it. These pictures get stored without your conscious awareness. Think of what you could

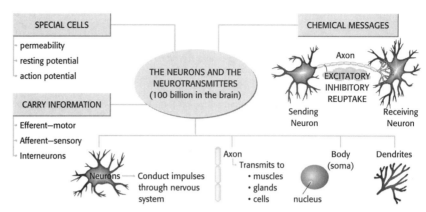

Figure 1.5 Mind Map.

remember if you practiced using your photographic right brain. The following exercises will help you develop this skill.

- Choose an ordinary object and look carefully at it. Notice *everything* you can about it including shape, color, texture, and size. When you feel ready, look away from it and view it with your eyes closed. Does the picture in your mind look like the actual object? Keep practicing until you see an exact picture. Once you master simple objects, you can move on to more complicated pictures.

- When you are reading a short story or novel, create a movie of it in your mind. See the characters and watch the action.

- Study Tip: Close your eyes and visualize yourself taking an upcoming exam. Take a few deep breaths and relax. Imagine that the instructor is passing out the exam. Now visualize yourself answering the questions correctly and happily handing in your paper. *Mental rehearsal* builds photographic images. Feel your success.

- Do what the athletes do. Did you know that visualizing is part of an athlete's training? Have you ever watched an Olympic figure skater before a performance? As she waits patiently to go on the ice, she stands still with her eyes closed while her head is moving and bobbing around. She is imagining a perfect performance. This picture and a feeling of success are imprinted on the visual side (right) of the brain. Because visualization techniques work, they are an important part of sports psychology.

- As you read textbooks, begin making color pictures of the information in your mind. For example, if you are reading about stem cell research in a biology text, visualize the process by which the cells create new cells. Create a video of it in your mind. Add music. Make the cells colorful and watch them change. Use your imagination. This is a complex skill, so do not worry if it is difficult at first. The way to develop your photographic mind is to think in pictures.

TRICKING THE SUBCONSCIOUS MIND

THE CONSCIOUS MIND IS THE PART OF YOUR MIND THAT YOU ARE AWARE OF; IT IS the thinking and problem solving part, the one that busies itself with decision making and "mind chatter." At any time, you can know what you are thinking. Your subconscious, on the other hand, is the part of the mind that you are not aware of, yet it plays an important role in your life; it motivates everything you do, and that makes it powerful! What follows is an example of how your mind works.

You are driving in your car and realize that soon you will need to make a left hand turn. You *consciously* turn on your left signal and execute the turn. You're driving along and soon you are pulling into your driveway, but you don't remember driving there. Your thoughts were somewhere else. You were thinking about your vacation or your last date or remembering what you need to pick up at the grocery store. Your conscious mind was free to drift off while your subconscious mind became more active and got you home. When you realize that you're home, your awareness shifts and your conscious mind takes over.

Self-talk is speaking directly to your subconscious mind, which takes in information and processes it literally. In other words, it believes whatever you tell it. Talking to the subconscious mind is like talking to a six-year-old child. Think of a time when you have called someone, and a young child answers the phone. You ask politely, "Is your mother home?" You hear a resounding yes and then you hear nothing. The phone hasn't gone dead; your question has been answered with a one-word answer, and the child has responded quite literally. If an adult had answered the phone, the response might have been different, "Yeah, she's here. Wait just a minute and I'll get her."

Because the subconscious mind believes what we tell it, it's vital to be positive when we talk to ourselves. Our minds are active and busy. We're always thinking. What do you say when you talk to yourself?

Understanding how the subconscious works can help create a positive learning environment. Sometimes you'll have to take a class that is not your first choice. Perhaps the class meets too early, or you don't like the way the instructor lectures. The trick is to turn a negative situation into a positive one by using the power of your mind. You do it by *pretending*. Tell yourself that the instructor is the most dynamic you've ever had, that the material is simply fascinating, that this is the most interesting class you've ever attended. Get the idea? You're tricking your subconscious. Remember that it is taking in information literally, and it believes what you tell it. If you enjoy your experience, you'll learn more. There is power in self-affirmation. Use what you know about the subconscious mind to your advantage.

ACTIVE LISTENING: A GREAT BEGINNING!

SUCCESSFUL NOTETAKING REQUIRES THE ABILITY TO LISTEN. IF YOU ASK SOMEONE if he considers himself a good listener, you'd probably get a "Yes" response. The truth is that people don't always listen well. We might hear the words that someone is speaking, but we don't always pay attention to the meaning. Our thoughts drift to our own concerns, we may "tune out" and come back to the conversation, or even be accused of not listening. Clearly, there is a difference between hearing and listening. This can happen during class as well. Many students sit in class and take notes on the instructor's lecture only to realize that they've been "somewhere else" for a while. They quickly realize that they've missed some important points. They now know that they haven't really been paying attention, even though they've heard the instructor's voice. Remember that what you pay attention to is also what you miss!

Successful notetaking requires active listening. *Active listening* means listening with awareness and intent. It is listening to understand the lecture and to think about what is being said. Every instructor has her own organizational pattern for giving a lecture, and it's your job to discover it. It will assist you in taking good class notes.

Generally, a lecture will begin with a main topic followed by supporting information, which expands and explains the main idea. When you listen actively, you get the whole picture. At first, it might seem difficult to listen and take notes at the same time, but ongoing practice will make it easier to do. Active listening and successful notetaking are skills that can be developed.

Tips for Becoming an Active Listener

- Sit as close to the instructor as you dare. Remember this tip from "Developing Concentration", on concentration, and keep your eyes on the speaker. It will help you keep distractions to a minimum.

- Listen for main ideas and think about how the supporting details fit for each one.

- Be alert. Recognize when a new idea is being introduced.

- Keep an open mind. Becoming emotionally upset or angry will not work to your advantage. Keep taking notes. If you find yourself in disagreement with the instructor, make an appointment to talk with him during his office hours. Be honest with your instructor, and let him know your feelings.

- Aim for excellent concentration. Engage in self-talk. Tell yourself that you are "getting" all of the information.

- Test your active listening skills. Practice with a friend. When you are engaged in conversation, listen actively and don't talk for a while. You may be surprised at the outcome.

- Be sure that you've had enough sleep the night before class. It's difficult to listen and take good notes when you are tired.

- Don't come to class hungry. Low blood sugar can affect your ability to concentrate.

- If you are bored in class, add your own ideas to your notes. Think about the material your are learning.

Listen for *cue words* that move the lecture along. Your instructor is constantly giving you hints to help you take good notes. Listen for cue words and you will be able to follow the direction of the lecture, as well as discover which ideas the instructor thinks are important. Here are some examples:

- Cue words for *examples*
  For example, for instance, to illustrate
- Cue words for *organization* or *steps in order*
  The six steps are, . . . next, finally, first, second, third
- Cue words for *additional points*
  Furthermore, in addition, also, moreover
- Cue words for *opposing ideas*
  On the other hand, in contrast, although, however
- Cue words for *similar ideas*
  Likewise, similarly, to compare
- Cue words for *exceptions*
  However, nevertheless, but, yet, still
- Cue words for *emphasis*
  Above all, finally, more important
- Cue words to for *understanding*
  In other words, in essence, briefly
- Cue words for *summarizing*
  In conclusion, to sum up, for these reasons, in a nutshell
- Cue words for *exams*
  Remember this, this is important, this could be on the test

Pay attention to these words and phrases when you are reading your texts, as well as when are you listening to take notes.

PREPARATION FOR EXCELLENT NOTETAKING

IT IS A MYTH THAT SITTING IN CLASS AND JUST LISTENING WILL EARN YOU GOOD grades. Taking class notes is necessary for learning and remembering. Remember that the short-term memory doesn't store information; taking notes will help you make the transfer into the long-term memory. It can also help you concentrate and focus on material in the lecture.

Tips for Preparing to Take Notes

- Read homework assignments before you come to class and take notes. It is always easier to learn material when it is familiar. Keep current with your reading assignments.
- Have all of your supplies ready to use. Open your notebook to a blank page or have your laptop ready to go. Bring colored pens or pencils to class for notetaking. You can

miss important information when you are digging into your purse or backpack to look for a pen.

- Don't let yourself feel overwhelmed by the notetaking process. Practice is required for improvement. Over time, it will become easier. Do breathing or visualization exercises before each class session. Use positive self-talk and affirmations.

- Arrive to class early and get a good seat away from distractions. Could these distractions be your friends?

- Remember to use active listening skills.

TAKING NOTES

EXCELLENT NOTETAKING CONSISTS OF (1) ACTIVE LISTENING, (2) FOCUSED ATTENTION, and (3) the intention to understand.

Here are Some Valuable Tips for Taking Notes:

- Come to class mentally prepared to take notes for the entire period.

- Begin to take notes as soon as the instructor begins lecturing. Don't wait until you think you've heard an important idea. Everything is important!

- Write down key words, main ideas, and supporting details. Keep in mind that exams are comprehensive. You will not have sufficient information if you only write down main ideas. Write down explanations, facts, terms, and definitions.

- Pay attention to cue words. Memorize the list in this chapter.

- Write down everything that your instructor writes on the board. If it's important enough for her to write it, it's important enough to be on a test.

- Write down everything that is emphasized on an overhead projector. This is possible test exam material.

- When revising your notes, color-code them. Use different colored pens for main ideas, supporting details, and examples. For example, use yellow for main ideas, blue for supporting details, and pink for examples.

- Take notes in the instructor's words, but when you study, recite them in your own to *personalize* the information.

- Leave blank spaces if you can't get all of the information down. You can fill the page later with notes from another student. Ask your instructor for a copy of her notes. Check your textbooks, too.

- Leave white space between the main ideas and the supporting details. This will help you determine the organization of the lecture.

- Pay attention to your instructor's lecturing style. Some instructors are organized and easy to follow, while others may quickly switch topics or tell a story before getting back to the original point. If you need to, leave room in your notes and catch up later. Discovering your instructor's lecturing style will help you make adjustments in your notetaking.

- Check to see whether the instructor's lecture comes directly from the textbook. If the lecture does come straight from the text, you can refer to the book and add necessary or additional information to your class notes. If the lecture material is not from the text, take notes from your book and compare them to the information in the lecture.

- Take notes until the end of the class period, even if everyone else is getting ready to leave. An instructor wants to make sure that all of the material is presented, and an important idea can come at the very end of class. If you're packing up your books, you can easily miss the information.

- Remember that notetaking skills improve with practice. Practice at home by taking notes from a TV documentary, DVD, or videotape. Use material that is organized and instructional.

- Pay attention to the instructor's "pet" or favorite ideas. Any ideas that an instructor finds worth repeating are important enough to be on a test.

- Write legibly. You can't learn from your notes if you can't read them. It's OK to write in phrases when you take notes, but you need to be able to understand what you've written. If you can't, then try writing in complete sentences.

- Use an adjusted writing style. This style combines cursive writing and printing. It enables you to write rapidly in a style that is legible.

Enid Leonard	cursive
Enid Leonard	printing
Enid Leonard	adjusted

Figure 1.6 Styles of writing.

- Use a tape recorder in class if you are still having trouble taking notes (however, this is generally not recommended). Becoming dependent on a tape recorder won't build your confidence for in-class notetaking. It certainly can be useful if you are an auditory learner, a commuter, or a non-native speaker. If you know that you're going to be absent from class, you can have someone tape the lecture for you (with permission from the instructor). The ideal is to take your own excellent notes.

Figure 1.7

ESTABLISHING YOUR CONSISTENT SYSTEM

CONSISTENCY IS A VITAL COMPONENT OF EFFICIENT NOTETAKING. IT MEANS TAKING notes the same way each time. Having a consistent system enables you to understand your notes. Once you have established a pattern for notetaking that works, don't change it. One student looked at her notes years after having a class and was amazed at how clear and understandable they were.

Tips for Creating a Consistent Notetaking System

- Develop your own shorthand method. Use symbols and abbreviations as much as possible. Once you've established a symbol for something, use it consistently.

- Shorten words by omitting vowels. This is the same concept used in creating designer car license plates.

    prblem—problem   bkgd—background   histry—history
    vwl—vowel

- Use standard abbreviations in place of words.

    w—with   w/o—without   b4—before   + or &—and
    =—equals   %—percent   c—with   ∴—therefore

- Use the first part of a word for the full word.

    info—information   psych—psychology   est—estimate
    symb—symbolic

- Create your own symbols. If you are taking a sociology class, you could use:

    soc—sociology/sociological   O—family
    soc-N—social norms   S.Inst—social institutions
    SD—social density   (K)—kinship

    For general notetaking, use:

    B.C—because   (m)—most importantly   c→—compared to
    Ex—example

- Add symbols, pictures, and drawings to your notes as you review. Make them different sizes and colors. This is a great right brain activity.

| Arrows | |
| Brackets | [ ]   ***Important ⟶ |

Write notes to yourself.

Example: *See page 21 of text for notes from date . . .*

SHORTCUTS FOR STRESSFUL TIMES

STRESS CAN AFFECT YOUR ABILITY TO TAKE COMPLETE NOTES. HERE ARE SOME suggestions for those days when you're not "up to speed."

- Take the best notes that you can under stressful conditions. Ask a classmate if you can look at his notes. Establishing a relationship with another student can be mutually beneficial. Exchange phone numbers.

- If you know you will not be attending class, call a friend and ask her to make copies of her notes. When you return to class, ask the instructor if he has any additional information for you.

- If you are suffering emotional stress and you feel that your concentration is too poor to take notes, ask the instructor if you may tape the lecture. Then take notes from the tape in a less stressful environment. The important thing is to always have class notes, whether you take them yourself or get them from someone else.

- See a drop-in counselor at your school. Don't put off getting help. Try to keep up with your assignments. Study someone else's notes.

- Sit in a different seat. Create a new association for learning.

- Ask questions; it will keep you alert in class.

THE CORNELL NOTETAKING SYSTEM

MANY DIFFERENT NOTETAKING SYSTEMS HAVE BEEN DEVELOPED THROUGH THE years. Choosing one that fits your learning style will build confidence in your ability. Knowing different systems can provide flexibility. The instructor's style of lecturing may be a consideration when choosing a style.

The Cornell System was developed at Cornell University more than forty years ago and continues to be popular with college students.

Guidelines for Taking Cornell Notes

- Take notes on one side of the page only.

- Draw a 2.5-inch margin down the left side of the page. This is called the cue column. College bookstores often sell notetaking paper with the margin already printed on each page. Check your campus bookstore or art supply shop. You may also leave several inches of space on the bottom of each page for writing a summary. Some students prefer to have a separate page for summarizing their notes after each class session.

- Include the date and class name on each page. You may also include the instructor's name and the time of the class.

Steps in the Cornell System

Step 1. Take notes on the right side of the paper only. Remember to leave the 2.5-inch margin blank. You will fill that in at a later time. Be as comprehensive as possible in getting the information from the lecture.

Step 2. *After* the lecture, while the information is still fresh in your mind, use the cue column to write study questions as well as key words or phrases that are related to the notes that you took on the right side of the page. You will use these as cues to test yourself on the material in your notes. Filling in the cue column while you are taking notes defeats the system. When you have completed the cue column, you are ready for the next step.

Step 3. Cover up the notes on the right side of the page and use the cue column to test your knowledge of the material. Use the key words and phrases to help you remember the main ideas and supporting information from the lecture. If you wrote study questions, try to answer them. Recite out loud and in your own words. If you cannot answer your questions or do not know the material at this point, go back and study your notes and begin the process again. This important step will provide feedback for you. It lets you know if you're learning and understanding the material.

Step 4. Write a summary of the information on the bottom of each page or use one sheet for each notetaking session. A summary clarifies the main ideas for you.

Step 5. Review your notes immediately and continue with regular review periods. Reviewing your notes on a daily basis helps store the information in your long-term memory.

Step 6. Study the information using flash cards, outlines, hierarchies, and mind maps. Think about the material and make connections to what you already know. Remember what you learned in "Memory: How It Works" on memory. This step involves integrating the material so you can understand it at a deep level. You're not just memorizing it, you know it.

```
                                                          Health 101Ł
                                                          date _____
                        Lecture on Stress                 prof. _____

 What factors             Many things contribute – reactions,
 contribute to stress?    family, environ, health status,
                          personality – need support systems

                          Means diff. things to diff. people

 What is the defin.       Stress – phys + mental response in
 of stress?               bodies to changes + challenges.

 What is a stressor?      Stressor – physic, social, psych event
                          causes body to have to adjust
 Kinds of stress            ① tangible – angry parent
                            ② intangible – mixed emotions

 What is adjustment?      Adjustment – attempt to cope
 What is strain?          Strain – wear and tear on body & mind
 *difference between 2
                          Eustress = positive str. = personal growth
 What is Eustress?              new        getting
 Give ex.                      friendship   married

 What is Distress?        Distress = negative str. debilitative→   Can't
 Give examples            prevent/ pt. of life/ death of loved one/ finan. prob.
                          – train ourselves to recognize events
                          – anticipate reactions
                          – develop-managmt tech.   coping skills

     Stress is the mental and physical response of our bodies to challenge and change.
 Many things contribute to how we respond to a stressful event. We experience
 stressors and relate with adjustment and strain. Eustress is positive while Ł
 distress is negative.
```

Figure 1.8 Cornell Notetaking System.

THE LEONARD NOTETAKING SYSTEM

THE LEONARD SYSTEM COMBINES NOTETAKING WITH STUDY FLASH CARDS. NOTES are taken on 5 × 7 cards. It is preferable to use spiral bound cards, which are easy to carry in your backpack or notebook. They keep your notes organized and in one place. Before you begin taking notes, write your name, the instructor's name, and the name and time of your class on the front flap cover. If your note cards get lost, they can be returned to you.

Steps in the Leonard Notetaking System

Step 1. Take notes on one side of the card. You may want to leave a few cards blank to add information from your textbook or handouts at a later time.

Step 2. Turn the card over and write study questions and key words that are related to the material on the front side. Add symbols and pictures to incorporate right brain learning. Color-code as previously suggested. One idea is to use one color for class notes and one for study questions and symbols.

Step 3. Use the questions, symbols, and pictures on the back of each card to test yourself on the material. Use it as a flash card. If you can't answer a question, put the card in a separate stack and ask the question again later. Keep testing yourself until there are no cards stacked.

```
                                            Psych 101Ł

                                            Instr. _____

              Emotional Intelligence        date _____


    Em. Int. = set of capabilities separate from I.Q. but necessary for success
             in life; workplace, personal relationships, social interactions.
        Personal components
   ① Awareness of one's — emotions — recognize feelings
        — acknowledge as they happen
        — aware of thoughts + moods
        — monitor feelings — can manage emotions
   ② Managing one's emotions — balance feel.
        — feel. has value/significance — regulates moods/managed by activts.
           — challenge unwanted thoughts.
   ③ Self motivation — controlling impulses
        — strength of emotional self-control — postponing immediate gratif. for
           success. — resists impulse behavior
        — can persist toward a goal.
```

Figure 1.9 Example of Leonard system of notetaking.

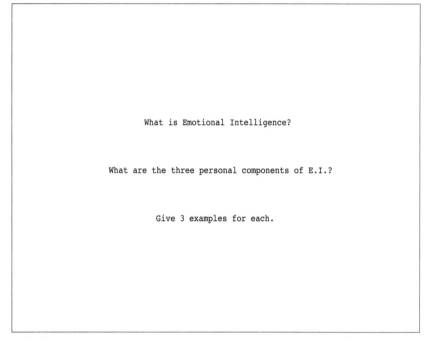

Figure 1.10 Another example of Leonard system of notetaking.

Textbooks: Reading, Highlighting, and Notetaking

READING TEXTBOOKS

READING A COLLEGE TEXTBOOK REQUIRES DIFFERENT READING SKILLS THAN ONES used to read a novel or magazine. Textbooks are packed with information. Ideas are discussed in great detail, and serious attention is required to learn the information that is presented. The best way to master textbook material is to begin with the initial step of *previewing* or *surveying*. You may notice that this skill has been presented in this chapter. That's because organizing information is an essential part of learning and studying. Before you tackle your first reading assignment, survey the entire text. Begin by learning what you can from the:

> "Tell me, and I'll forget. Show me, and I may remember. Involve me, and I'll understand."
> Author unknown

1. Title page
2. Table of contents
3. *Preface or introduction to the student*
4. Glossary (an alphabetical list of terms)
5. Index (subjects in alphabetical order at the back of the book), which is an excellent tool for finding information quickly
6. Appendix (supplemental material at the back of the text)

SQ3R

THE TASK OF READING TEXT MATERIAL CAN BE OVERWHELMING, AND IF THAT ISN'T enough, there's an exam covering this chapter. Using a multi-step reading system will assist you in mastering textbook material. One such time honored system is SQ3R, which stands for (1) survey, (2) question, (3) read, (4) recite, and (5) review.

Step 1. *Survey*. Surveying or previewing gives you the "big picture." Before you delve into the chapter, spend a few minutes reading headings and subheadings, introductions and summaries. Look at pictures and graphs, and read study questions that follow the chapter. Make mental notes of vocabulary words. Will you need a dictionary to read this text? Surveying provides an overview that will help you become familiar with the material.

Step 2. *Question*. Turn chapter headings and subheading into questions as you read. Your busy left brain (language side) naturally wants to answer the question because it's the problem solving part of the brain. This step helps you focus and identify main ideas. If there are no subheadings to guide you, turn the first sentence of the first paragraph into a question. Write your questions in the margin of the text or in your notebook.

Step 3. *Read*. Read carefully, keeping your questions in mind. Underline the answers to the questions, main ideas, and important supporting details. Think about what you are reading and try to connect the new ideas to ones that you already know.

How do the details support the main ideas? Write down ideas as you read. Become an active reader.

Step 4. *Recite.* "Talk the material." After reading a section, look away from the text and try to recite the material in your own words. You practiced this step in the Cornell and Leonard notetaking systems. Reciting helps you learn and store information in the long-term memory.

Step 5. *Review.* Begin reviewing immediately and continue to review throughout the term. Write summaries of the information in the chapter. Some texts have questions at the end of a chapter for you to answer. Create flash cards, outlines, or mindmaps. Use your time management schedule to designate review and study periods.

Some Additional Tips for Reading Texts

- *Always* read with a pen or pencil in hand and be ready to mark important information. This technique uses hand–eye coordination (visual–kinesthetic modes) and helps you focus on the material. You are developing a positive pattern. Your subconscious knows that when you pick up a pen, you are ready for serious reading and comprehension.

- Look for main ideas that are often the first sentence of a paragraph. Pay attention to when a new idea begins.

- Review often. By now, you know that reviewing is an essential skill for learning and remembering. Studying textbook material is similar to studying class notes; they both require ongoing review. Spend time with your textbooks and notes. The payoff is worth the energy and time.

- Read other sources related to the material. You may be able to find a guidebook that can help you clarify the information. Do a Google search on the Internet to find related materials.

- Pretend that you are having a discussion with the author. Do you agree or disagree with his ideas? This process helps you become an active reader.

- Without looking, recite the information that you have in your summaries.

- If the material is difficult to understand, read it out loud. Hearing the material can help you understand it (auditory learning). Modulate your voice.

HIGHLIGHTING AND MARKING TEXTBOOKS

TEXTBOOK MARKING HELPS YOU SORT OUT THE ORGANIZATION OF THE MATERIAL you are reading, so you can determine which ideas are important. When you know what to study, preparing for an exam becomes easier.

Tips for Marking a Text

- *Preview* before you begin marking the chapter (step 1 in SQ3R). Highlight main ideas, key concepts, numbered items, definitions, and examples. Use a yellow marker, or choose your own color. Some students use several colors to separate main ideas from supporting information. When you highlight, *less is more*. Mark sparingly. Marking everything defeats the purpose.

AIR POLLUTION

Although we often assume that the air we breathe is safe, the daily impact of a growing population makes clean air more difficult to find. Concern about air quality prompted Congress to pass the Clean Air Act in 1970 and to amend it in 1977 and again in 1990. The object was to develop standards for six of the most widespread air pollutants that seriously affect health: sulfur dioxide, particulates, carbon monoxide, nitrogen dioxide, ozone, and lead. Table 21.1 shows the number of Americans still living in counties where air standards are not met.

Sources of Air Pollution

main source

▶ *Sulfur Dioxide* **Sulfur dioxide** is a yellowish brown gas that is a by-product of burning fossil fuels. Electricity generating stations, smelters, refineries, and industrial boilers are the main source points. In humans, sulfur dioxide aggravates symptoms of heart and lung disease, obstructs breathing passages, and increases the incidence of respiratory diseases such as colds, asthma, bronchitis, and emphysema. It is toxic to plants, destroys some paint pigments, corrodes metals, impairs visibility, and is a precursor to acid rain, which we discuss later in this chapter.

non human *human effects*

▶ *Particulates* **Particulates** are tiny solid particles or liquid droplets that are suspended in the air. Cigarette smoke releases particulates. They are also by-products of some industrial processes and the internal combustion engine. Particulates can in and of themselves irritate the lungs and can additionally carry heavy metals and carcinogenic agents deep into the lungs. When combined with sulfur dioxide, they exacerbate respiratory diseases. Particulates can also corrode metals and obscure visibility. Numerous scientific studies have found significant links between exposure to air particulate concentrations at or below current standards and adverse health effects, including premature death.[11]

▶ *Carbon Monoxide* **Carbon monoxide** is an odorless, colorless gas that originates primarily from motor vehicle emissions. Carbon monoxide interferes with the blood's ability to absorb and carry oxygen and can impair thinking, slow reflexes, and cause drowsiness, unconsciousness, and death. Many people have purchased home monitors to test for carbon monoxide.

▶ *Nitrogen Dioxide* **Nitrogen dioxide** is an amber-colored gas emitted by coal-powered electrical utility boilers and by motor vehicles. High concentrations

TABLE 21.1
Percent of Americans Living in U.S. Counties That Meet Air Quality Standards

All pollutants	75%
Ozone standards	80%
Carbon monoxide standards	94%
Particulates	95%
Sulfur dioxide standards	100%
Nitrogen dioxide standards	100%
Lead standards	98%

Source: Health, United States: 1996–97, U.S. National Center for Health Statistics, Washington, DC: USDHHS, Public Health Service.

of nitrogen dioxide can be fatal. Lower concentrations increase susceptibility to colds and flu, bronchitis, and pneumonia. Nitrogen dioxide is also toxic to plant life and causes a brown discoloration of the atmosphere. It is a precursor of ozone, and, along with sulfur dioxide, of acid rain.

▶ *Ozone* Ground-level **ozone** is a form of oxygen that is produced when nitrogen dioxide reacts with hydrogen chloride. These gases release oxygen, which is altered by sunlight to produce ozone. In the lower atmosphere, ozone irritates the mucous membranes of the respiratory system, causing coughing and choking. It can impair lung functioning, reduce resistance to colds and pneumonia, and aggravate heart disease, asthma, bronchitis, and pneumonia. This ozone corrodes rubber and paint and can injure or kill vegetation. It is also one of the irritants found in smog. The natural ozone found in the upper atmosphere (sometimes called "good" ozone), however, serves as a protective membrane against heat and radiation from the sun. We will discuss this atmospheric layer, called the ozone layer, later in the chapter.

IMP.

▶ *Lead* **Lead** is a metal pollutant that is found in paint, batteries, drinking water, pipes, and dishes with lead-glazed bases. The elimination of lead from gasoline and auto exhaust in the 1970s was one of the great public health accomplishments of all time. Although stricter standards for all of the above prevail, almost 1 million children in the United States had elevated blood lead levels in 1997.[12] Lead affects the circulatory, reproductive, and nervous systems. It can also affect the blood and kidneys and can accumulate in bone and other tissues. Lead is particularly detrimental to children and fetuses. It can cause birth defects, behavioral abnormalities, and decreased learning abilities.

Figure 1.11(a) Example of highlighting and textbook marking (*continued*)

(*Source*: Access to Health, 7th ed. by Rebecca J. Donatelle and Lorraine G. Davis. Copyright © 2002, Pearson Education. Reprinted by permission of Pearson Education, Inc.)

Figure 1.11(a)   (*continued*)

- Use brackets [ ] { } to mark longer passages. It's efficient and easy on the eyes.

- Circle key concepts or put boxes or circles around numbered items.

- Mark up your textbooks. Because reading is an active process rather than a passive one like watching TV, you need to be involved. When you're involved, you're learning. Don't be afraid to argue with the author by writing comments in the margin. Get involved. Use your right brain; get emotional and interact with the material. Develop

Acid rain has many harmful effects on the environment. Because its toxins seep into groundwater and enter the food chain, it also poses health hazards to humans. (Will and Deni McIntyre/Photo Researchers, Inc.)

acid and nitric acids, respectively). Small acid particles are then carried by the wind and combine with moisture to produce acidic rain or snow. Because of higher concentrations of sunlight in the summer months, rain is more strongly acidic in the summertime. Additionally, the rain or snow that falls at the beginning of a storm is more acidic than that which falls later. The ability of a lake to cleanse itself and neutralize its acidity depends on several factors, the most critical of which is bedrock geology.

▶ **Effects of Acid Rain**   The damage caused to lake and pond habitats is not the worst of the problems created by acid rain. Each year, it is responsible for the destruction of millions of trees in forests in Europe and North America. Scientists have concluded that 75 percent of Europes forests are now experiencing damaging levels of sulfur deposition by acid rain. Forests in every country on the continent are affected.[13]

Doctors believe that acid rain also aggravates and may even cause bronchitis, asthma, and other respiratory problems. People with emphysema and those with a history of heart disease may also suffer from exposure to acid rain. In addition, it may be hazardous to a pregnant womans unborn child.

Acidic precipitation can cause metals such as aluminum, cadmium, lead, and mercury to **leach** (dissolve and filter) out of the soil. If these metals make their way into water or food supplies (particularly fish), they can cause cancer in humans who consume them.

Acid rain is also responsible for crop damage, which, in turn, contributes to world hunger. Laboratory experiments showed that acid rain can reduce seed yield by up to 23 percent. Actual crop losses are being reported with increasing frequency. A final consequence of acid rain is the destruction of public monuments and structures, with billions of dollars in projected building damage each year.

Indoor Air Pollution

Combating the problems associated with air pollution begins at home. Indoor air can be 10 to 40 times more hazardous than outdoor air. There are between 20 and 100 potentially dangerous chemical compounds in the average American home. Indoor air pollution comes primarily from six sources: woodstoves, furnaces, asbestos, passive smoke, formaldehyde, and radon.

▶ **Woodstove Smoke**   Woodstoves emit significant levels of particulates and carbon monoxide in addition to other pollutants, such as sulfur dioxide. If you rely on wood for heating, you should make sure that your stove is properly installed, vented, and maintained. Burning properly seasoned wood reduces the amount of particulates released into the air.

▶ **Furnace Emissions**   People who rely on oil- or gas-fired furnaces also need to make sure that these appliances are properly installed, ventilated, and maintained. Inadequate cleaning and maintenance can lead to a buildup of carbon monoxide in the home, which can be deadly.

▶ **Asbestos**   **Asbestos** is another indoor air pollutant that poses serious threats to human health. Asbestos is a mineral that was commonly used in insulating materials in buildings constructed before 1970. When bonded to other materials, asbestos is relatively harmless, but if its tiny fibers become loosened and airborne, they can embed themselves in the lungs and cannot be expelled. Their presence leads to cancer of the lungs, stomach, and chest lin-

Figure 1.11(b) Practice sheet for Activity 1.   *(continued)*

(*Source*: Access to Health, 7th ed. by Rebecca J. Donatelle and Lorraine G. Davis. Copyright © 2002, Pearson Education. Reprinted by permission of Pearson Education, Inc.)

a consistent marking system, and you'll have a great study aid that you can always count on.

▪ Write questions in the margin. You can use the margins as recall columns to test yourself.

ing, and is the cause of a fatal lung disease called mesothelioma.

▶ *Formaldehyde*   **Formaldehyde** is a colorless, strong-smelling gas present in some carpets, draperies, furniture, particle board, plywood, wood paneling, countertops, and many adhesives. It is released into the air in a process called *outgassing*. Outgassing is highest in new products, but the process can continue for many years.

Exposure to formaldehyde can cause respiratory problems, dizziness, fatigue, nausea, and rashes. Long-term exposure can lead to central nervous system disorders and cancer.

To reduce your exposure to formaldehyde, ask about the formaldehyde content of products you purchase and avoid those that contain this gas. Some houseplants, such as philodendrons and spider plants, help clean formaldehyde from the air. If you experience symptoms of formaldehyde exposure, have your home tested by a city, county, or state health agency.

▶ *Radon*   **Radon** is one of the most serious forms of indoor air pollution. This odorless, colorless gas is the natural by-product of the decay of uranium and radium in the soil. Radon penetrates homes through cracks, pipes, sump pits, and other openings in the foundation. An estimated 30,000 cancer deaths per year have been attributed to radon, making it second only to smoking as the leading cause of lung cancer.[14]

The EPA estimates that 1 in 15 American homes has an elevated radon level. A home-testing kit from a hardware store will enable you to test your home yourself. "Alpha track" detectors are commonly used for this type of short-term testing. They must remain in your home for 2 to 90 days, depending on the device.

▶ *Household Chemicals*   When you use cleansers and other cleaning products, do so in a well-ventilated room, and be conservative in their use. All those caustic chemicals that zap mildew, grease, and other household annoyances cause a major risk to water and the environment. Avoid buildup. Regular cleanings will reduce the need to use potentially harmful substances. Cut down on dry cleaning, as the chemicals used by many cleaners can cause cancer. If your newly cleaned clothes smell of dry-cleaning chemicals, either return them to the cleaner or hang them in the open air until the smell is gone. Avoid the use of household air freshener products containing the carcinogenic agent *dichlorobenzene*.

Indoor air pollution is also a concern in the classroom and workplace. Studies show that one in five U.S. schools has indoor air quality problems, which affect an estimated 8.4 million students.[15] Poor air quality in classrooms may lead to drowsiness, headaches, and lack of concentration. It may also affect physical growth and development. Children with asthma are particularly at risk for adverse health affects from poor air quality.

Each day, many people who work indoors complain of maladies that tend to lessen or vanish when they leave the building. **Sick building syndrome (SBS)** is said to exist when 80 percent of a buildings occupants report problems. One of the primary causes of sick building syndrome is poor ventilation. Symptoms include eye irritation, sore throat, queasiness, and worsened asthma.[16]

Acid rain   Precipitation contaminated with acidic pollutants.

Leach   To dissolve and filter through soil.

Asbestos   A substance that separates into stringy fibers and lodges in the lungs, where it can cause various diseases.

Formaldehyde   A colorless, strong-smelling gas released through outgassing; causes respiratory and other health problems.

Radon   A naturally occurring radioactive gas resulting from the decay of certain radioactive elements.

Sick building syndrome (SBS)   Problem that exists when 80 percent of a buildings occupants report maladies that tend to lessen or vanish when they leave the building.

Figure 1.11(b) Practice sheet for Activity 1.

TAKING NOTES FROM TEXTBOOKS

TAKING NOTES ON THE MATERIAL THAT YOU'VE HIGHLIGHTED AND MARKED IS necessary for in-depth learning. It would be difficult to have a complete understanding of the material without the notetaking component. When you take notes from your textbook, you add a multi-sensory approach—kinesthetic and visual learning.

Taking notes from printed material is similar to taking notes from a lecture. As you use the SQ3R system, you can write the answers to your questions. Some students like to take notes in a notebook while others prefer note cards or typing on their computer. You can use any notetaking system. Practice to find the right combination.

Chapter 2
Delivering Effective Oral Presentations

- **Maintain a positive attitude.** Franklin Delano Roosevelt once noted that "The only thing we have to fear is fear itself." Although he was talking about a national crisis, the adage also applies to oral presentations. Nervousness becomes compounded when the speaker perceives the oral presentation to be a necessarily frightening and uncomfortable experience. Remember that as a student, you are only one of a group of people who share a common task and experience. Generally speaking, your audience will be in the same proverbial boat as you. Your audience will understand the kinds and amount of preparation required for your presentation. Your relationship with the audience is not adversarial or hostile. Also remember that an oral presentation is usually the most efficient and effective way to demonstrate your mastery of a concept. If you can project enjoyment in the process and in the presentation, your speech will be much more effective.

- **Prepare thoroughly.** The most important factor that will affect your ability to control nervousness is preparation. The more that you can practice the speech prior to the time you have to deliver it for an audience, the more comfortable you will be during the speech itself. Practice may not make the presentation perfect, but it will certainly make you better prepared and make the speech as good as it can be. If possible, and if your instructor has available time, try to perform the speech for your evaluator prior to the day you deliver the speech in class. Your instructor may be able to provide some feedback and additional instruction to help you be sure that you have met the requirements for the assignment. If your presentation assignment includes a time requirement, be absolutely sure to practice the speech using a stopwatch to determine the length of the speech.

TEN COMMON ERRORS TO AVOID

1. **Inappropriate or Distracting Visual Presence.** Although it may seem disagreeable and even silly at some level, the way that we look and the way that we dress affect the way that people perceive us. At a psychological level, we express aspects of our personality in the visual presentation of our selves, but we also assess others based on the characteristics of outward appearance. Be aware of the signals you send based on your choices for attire, hairstyle, jewelry, and so on. For example, good grooming of your hair and clothing sends a message that you took some extra time to prepare yourself for the specific speech situation. Avoid hats or any other facial accoutrements that would distract the audience's attention from your eyes. Be sure that your shirt

does not have large letters or distracting slogans or images. Avoid dangling jewelry such as large earring hoops or items with loud or very mixed colors. Even your shoes can distract the audience's visual focus from your performance. Be aware that visual noise can be a detriment to your effectiveness as a communicator.

2. *Awkward or Imbalanced Physical Stance.* In everyday conversation, we have become comfortable shifting our weight onto one or the other leg, and then shifting from side to side as needed. When speaking in a formal setting, however, that stance can leave the impression of someone who is out of control, nervous, or simply imbalanced. Be sure to balance your physical stance, by distributing your weight evenly across both legs. A general rule of thumb is to square your feet evenly below your shoulders. Balancing your physical stance will help you to avoid swaying or thrusting out your hip.

3. *Closed Gestures.* Hands clasped in front of the speaker or gestures that are delivered directly in front of the torso are called *closed* or *blocking* gestures. Usually, clasped gestures are a sign of nervousness, but clasped gestures can also leave the impression that the speaker is unsure of him- or herself, or possibly even hiding something. Work to keep your gestures open. Openness of gesture carries with it a psychology of open-mindedness, and invites the audience into the conversation rather than blocking the audience out.

4. *Overreliance on Notes.* No matter the guidelines for your specific presentation, whether or not notes are allowed, reliance on note cards, outlines, or even a prepared text decreases your effectiveness as a speaker. The ability to connect directly with the audience, especially with your eyes, is crucial for an effective presentation. The better you know your speech, the better your chances of staying on track with minimal disruption in the flow of the presentation.

5. *Not Looking at the Eyes of Your Audience.* For some speakers, nervousness increases at the very prospect of having to talk directly to other people in a formal setting. To sidestep that nervousness, some speakers work actively *not* to make eye contact with the people in the audience, but rather to look above the audience members' heads. In most presentation settings, there is a relatively small distance between the speaker and the audience, enabling the average audience member to tell when the speaker is making direct eye contact or looking at a spot above the audience. Failure to look directly into the eyes of audience members dramatically reduces the effectiveness of the communication.

6. *Failure to Meet the Time Requirements.* Remember that your presentation will probably have a set time limit, with a maximum allowable time and possibly even a minimum amount of time available. Keep in mind that the logistics of a classroom environment require these maximum time limits. If your speech exceeds the maximum time limit, your presentation will take time away from other presentations. If your speech falls below the time requirement, it will not have been developed sufficiently to explore the content as required. Be sure to time yourself prior to the final presentation by practicing with a stopwatch.

7. *Hiding Behind a Lectern.* A lectern is a useful tool for presentations. It enables the speaker to place reference material and notes within easy view, and may include

controls for presentation aids and voice amplification. However, a lectern also blocks the speaker from the audience, decreasing the connection between the speaker and listeners. Whenever possible, avoid "hiding" behind the lectern. Use wireless control devices or a handheld or clothing attachable microphone if available.

8. **Mispronunciations.** Nothing is more bothersome to an audience than a speaker's unintentional mispronunciation of everyday words, specialized terms, or names. Always remember to look up the pronunciation and meaning of difficult words. Whenever possible, check the pronunciation of names. If it is not possible, choose your pronunciation carefully and *practice* saying a difficult name so that it can be articulated with no verbal break.

9. **General Dysfluency.** *Fluency* refers to the smooth flow of language, devoid of errors or interruptions. A speech that contains the opposite, "general dysfluency," including "ums," "ahs," awkward pauses, misstatements, or lapses in memory, will hinder the effectiveness of both the speaker and the presentation. Practice the speech carefully and work to avoid these verbal interruptions.

10. **Failure to Deal with Unforeseen Circumstances.** It is a near inevitability that something will go wrong during your presentation. Another student will arrive late to the class during your presentation, a multimedia element (such as an overhead or LCD projector lamp) will fail, or you will be forced to sneeze in the middle of an important sentence! You will say a line wrong, skip a sentence, forget a piece of research/support, and so on. Count on an unforeseen circumstance—but do not let the unexpected foil you. If you suffer from a lapse in memory or an interruption, try to get back on track immediately and *without apology*. Always test your technology (preferably in your designated performance space) beforehand, and always have a backup plan.

The best way to avoid all of these errors is to PRACTICE, PRACTICE, PRACTICE, paying careful attention to the details noted previously.

The organization that you choose for your presentation depends tremendously on the purpose of the speech. Presentations that are informative in nature differ greatly in both language and structure from speeches that are persuasive in nature. Once the purpose of speaking is clear to you and the research process is well under way, it is time to make some choices about the organization of the speech, based on the chosen purpose.

All presentations begin with some kind of device to gain the attention of the audience. The introduction establishes the context and tone of the speech, and generally should end with the thesis statement and preview of the speech.

THE THESIS STATEMENT

THERE IS A DIFFERENCE BETWEEN THE GENERAL PURPOSE OF THE SPEECH AND THE thesis statement. The purpose helps to guide your preparation, determining the general tone and direction of your message. The thesis is a single statement that encapsulates that purpose into a central claim from which the rest of the presentation will emerge.

Examples:

Informative Presentation
Topic: Computers
Purpose: To inform the audience about new advances in computer technology
Possible Thesis: Recent advances in the computer industry have revolutionized the way that we live our daily lives.

Persuasive Presentation
Topic: Computers
Purpose: To persuade the audience to reduce reliance on computers for academic research
Possible Thesis: Though very useful, computerized databases have dramatically affected students' abilities to retain information.

Speech to Demonstrate
Topic: Computers
Purpose: To show the audience how to use the World Wide Web
Possible Thesis: Although sifting through all of the information available on the Internet may seem daunting, the use of Internet search engines can make using the Internet nearly effortless.

The thesis is the single most important sentence in the speech, and should make clear to the audience the overall point of the presentation. The body of the speech should be designed to expand upon that central claim.

THE BODY OF THE SPEECH

THE BODY OF THE SPEECH COMPRISES THE MAJORITY OF THE PRESENTATION. It includes all of the information needed to forward your central thesis, including the content of the major ideas, research, and other support materials.

The body of the speech should address the major issues of the speech, including the following major questions:

- What or where is the problem/issue?
- Who is involved?
- Why does it exist?
- Why should your audience care?
- If it is a problem, what can or should be done to solve it?
- What are the implications?

Developing the body of the speech requires that you subdivide major ideas into smaller, more compact units that will allow you to take the audience through the content without overloading your listeners with too much information at once. By and large, most presentations will contain two to three major body areas, with possibly more if absolutely necessary. The reasons for that division are rooted partially in cultural modes of thinking in binaries (on/off; male/female; black/white) and trinities (one-two-three strikes; father/son/spirit Christian precepts; red/blue/yellow primary colors; yes/no/maybe).

The limitation has more to do with psychology and memory. Short-term memory synthesizes knowledge based on meaningful "chunks" of information. The more chunks of information, the less our capacity to remember the information without significant decay or degradation. The members of your audience will retain only the major ideas of the speech, and potentially they will attach some detail to those major ideas, such as specific vocal or visual illustrations, particular modes of proof, or reactions to ideas that are intriguing or that stimulate an emotional response. Determining what that division into two or three major areas will entail depends entirely upon the purpose of the speech.

There are many templates or patterns upon which you may choose to build the structural organization of the speech. In some cases, different strategies from different templates may be employed in the same speech. These templates are not all inclusive, nor will they accommodate each and every specific purpose. They will, however, provide a starting point upon which to build the structure of your presentation.

PATTERNS OF ORGANIZATION

Chronological Patterns

Arrangement of the speech in a time sequence, usually beginning with the past, exploring the present, and moving toward the future. Chronological patterns may also examine different periods of time, such as major historical events in different time periods. As a method of organizing the macro-structure of a presentation, chronological patterns are best used in informative presentations, but may serve as organizational patterns for specific body areas or sub-areas as well. Chronological patterns also work well for speeches of demonstration or those detailing a sequential process (such as a recipe).

Spatial Patterns

Arrangement of the speech according to position. For example, an informative speech dealing with the development of agriculture in separate major geographical regions.

Spatial patterns are also useful in speeches of mechanical demonstration or processes that require the completion of separate stages in different geographical centers (such as a process of textile manufacture), or procedures that require movement in different physical locations (such as a golf swing).

Topical Patterns

Arrangement of the speech by division into sub-topics or classes. Topical arrangements are useful for taking broad concepts or ideas and dividing them into taxonomies. For example, a speech on ethnicity can be topically divided into major ethnic categories. A presentation on learning styles might be divided into the sub-topics of physical learning, aural learning, and visual learning.

Topical patterns are especially useful in informative presentations, but may also be effective in some types of persuasive presentations. For example, separate topical reasons designed to support a central argument or claim, as in:

Speech to Persuade
Topic: The Fed (Federal Reserve Board)
Thesis: The Fed is central to keeping the American economy stable, for three reasons:
    I. Because the Fed controls inflation
    II. Because the Fed controls fluctuations in interest rates
    III. Because the Fed makes policy recommendations to the U.S. Congress

Causal Patterns

Causal patterns are investigative in nature and are designed to explain relationships between causes and effects. The causal design is best for speeches that seek to explore a problem and its causes and its effects without the explicit goal of defining solutions or stimulating action by the audience.

Problem/Cause/Solution Design

The problem/cause/solution (PCS) design is a standard model for persuasive appeals. Like causal patterns, the PCS design is investigative in that it connects a relationship between a problem and its underlying causes. The PCS design goes one step further by offering specific solutions that must be accomplished in order to change future outcomes. A variation on this pattern is a division into the cause/effect/solution (CES) design. The CES variation is effective for problems that are broad in nature or simple to define, and that may be covered in sufficient depth in the introduction.

Pro/Con Division

The pro/con division is a topical pattern designed to show both sides of an issue. Pro/con designs are weak templates for persuasive appeals, but are useful in explaining conflicting or controversial perspectives. The pro/con division shows that a speaker understands opposing viewpoints. The pro/con division is informative in nature.

A more persuasive variation of the pro/con division is the concession/assertion division. In this variation, the speaker concedes the perspective of the opposing view, demonstrating that it is understood, and then presents the speaker's own view, asserting why in comparison the speaker's view is preferable. Concession/assertion demonstrates that the speaker understands and respects both points of view, but that a preference should be made.

The Motivated Sequence

There have been many attempts to formulate effective models of motivational speaking. In the 1930s, Alan Monroe introduced an organizational pattern that takes the audience through a prescribed sequence of steps. Based on the problem/cause/solution design, the motivated sequence goes a bit further by setting the audience up for a single action that may help to start the process of change. The pattern prepares the listener for a persuasive message and compels the audience to respond by fulfilling five steps: (1) gaining attention, (2) establishing a need, (3) satisfying the need, (4) visualizing the results, and (5) requesting action.

You will find the elements of the motivated sequence design in most commercials, and the motivated sequence is the basic model for political stump speeches. In addition, the sequence is particularly effective in motivating an audience to respond to common problems.

Step 1: Gaining the Audience's Attention

When delivering a motivated sequence speech, use the attention getting device as a means to establish concern about the topic and interest in the subject. Often, attention is established by offering a startling statistic or narrative, as in the following excerpt from Karon Bowers's 1990 speech on medical testing of women:

> Trapper John, M.D. has long been relegated to the television graveyard, but Pernell Roberts is still trying to diagnose our ills. We've all seen the commercial: Trapper John advising us that a study shows that aspirin can reduce the risk of heart disease. But there's a twist: Trapper—and many real doctors—haven't learned the difference between a man and a woman. You see, the aspirin study was conducted on 22,071 males . . . and it is unknown if females, who compose 52% of the population, respond the same way to the aspirin regimen.

In her speech, Bowers gains the audience's attention by recalling a familiar image— Trapper John—and offering a startling statistic.

Step 2: Establishing a Need

Establishing a need specifically defines the problem and demonstrates that the problem needs to be dealt with. Need can be established by showing that the audience has something to lose or to gain. Need can also be established by showing the audience that they need to be concerned. This is shown in the next excerpt from Bowers's speech:

> While we can chuckle at Trapper's ignorance, few women are laughing. As Representative Patricia Schroeder argued in testimony before the subcommittee on

Health and the Environment on June 18, 1990, "Sexism in medical practices is a reality, and for some women, there are fatal consequences." Most medical research considers men the "norm." Women are viewed often as more complicated to study due to hormonal and physiological differences. Unfortunately, the results of this research are being applied to women—without any proof of effectiveness—resulting in potentially dangerous side effects, ineffective treatment, and even death. Moreover, men are missing out on potentially life-saving treatments by this lack of attention to women. The September 24, 1990, edition of U.S. *News and World Report* contends that focusing on the implications of the differences between men and women "would surely prove beneficial to both sexes."

Step 3: Satisfying the Need

The third step of the motivated sequence answers the question "What can be done?" The satisfaction step provides a detailed plan of action for solving the problem. It is not enough, however, to simply make suggestions. You must also demonstrate that there is widespread support or a logical basis for your solution. In other words, you must prove that the solution will really satisfy the problem. In her speech, Bowers suggests specific solutions to her problem, and demonstrates that similar approaches have worked in the past:

> In order to provide these benefits, the medical community must strive to provide testing populations composed of both men and women. We need to apply pressure to the government and medical research organizations to ensure that this occurs. To do this, we must launch grassroots campaigns to illustrate that we are aware of the problem and its damaging effects and that we will not tolerate further medical ignorance. The January 7, 1991, edition of *The New York Times explains* that applying pressure has worked. As a result of inadequate breast cancer research, breast cancer advocacy groups formed throughout the nation to lobby for changes in research and legislation—and found that their efforts paid off. The success of these groups indicates that, by acting along with government and industry, we can increase the possibility of further and necessary change taking place.

Step 4: Visualizing Results

Monroe postulated that the proposal of a solution was not enough to motivate the audience to seek change. In the fourth stage of the motivated sequence, the speaker takes the audience beyond the solutions, and details what life will look like after the problem has been solved:

> Only when all medical testing is conducted on both men and women equally can we insure that our health care is safe and sufficient. When the medical community recognizes the viability and the necessity of women's participation in all medical research, we can rest assured that our health and our lives are in good hands.

Step 5: Requesting Action

In the final stage of the motivated sequence, the speaker calls the audience to specific action. Having demonstrated the problem, offered a means of solving the problem, and visualized how different things could be, the speaker now capitalizes on the heightened interest by asking for direct action.

Both the government and private industry need to strive for a balanced research population in all medical tests and trials. We must also take action to protect ourselves. Until change occurs, we must continue to pressure the organizations that control our medical treatment. We must also take precautions by asking our doctors and pharmacists questions about the drugs and tests that are prescribed for us—make sure your treatment is right for your gender. Although Trapper John's limited knowledge about the differences between men and women can be explained easily—he only played a doctor on TV—the ignorance and oversight of the medical community cannot. As biochemist Meira Fields stated in the October 1987 issue of *Omni*, "The sex difference can be a matter of life and death."

Structural Overview of Major Organizational Templates

Applied Concept

Speech to Inform

Designed to teach or inform an audience about an unfamiliar concept.

Structure:

1. Introduction
2. Thesis and preview
3. Definition/background of subject
4. Topic 1
5. Topic 2
6. Topic 3
7. Restatement of thesis and summary of main points
8. Conclusion

Often, informative speeches are structured chronologically (past/present/future) or topically (with parallel classifications).

Applied Concept

Speech to Investigate

Best for speeches of explanation or deduction. Also excellent for problems without existing solutions.

Structure:

1. Introduction
2. Thesis and preview
3. Description of the problem/subject
4. Examination of the causes
5. Investigation of the effects
6. Restatement of thesis and summary of main points
7. Conclusion

Applied Concept

Speech to Motivate

Excellent for speeches requiring a single solution to a broad problem. Also ideal for advertising, promotions, sales presentations, and business model proposals.

Structure:

1. Introduction
2. Demonstration of need (we need this)
3. Description of the solution
4. Visualization of the results (see the future for us)
5. Call to action (do this now)

Applied Concept

Speech to Persuade

Designed to persuade the audience to change their actions or opinions about a narrow or controversial problem.

Structure:

1. Introduction
2. Thesis and preview
3. Description of the problem
4. Examination of the causes
5. Suggested solutions
6. Restatement of thesis and structural summary
7. Conclusion

Applied Concept

Speech to Persuade/Argue

Designed to justify the reasoning for a central claim.

Structure:

1. Introduction
2. Thesis and preview
3. First Reason
4. Second Reason
5. Third Reason
6. Restatement of thesis and summary of main points
7. Conclusion

Using Language Effectively

ORAL STYLE VERSUS WRITTEN STYLE

MANY STUDENTS WRITE WELL. THE DEMANDS OF ACADEMIC LANGUAGE REQUIRE A continual exploration of complex language and syntax. Those complexities do not serve as well in the oral environment. An oral presentation is an interactive process. It is a conversation with an audience. Though in most presentation formats the audience will not respond verbally, the audience will respond non-verbally, either with evident reactions to the speech (*feedback*) or internal response to the content.

Few people speak conversationally with the same language tone and syntax typical of academic writing. Part of the reason for this is the *immediacy* of the speech situation. Speakers are immediately connected to and associated with the content of the speech.

Writers can create a written text that goes on to live a life of its own. A written text gains life only in the mind of the reader or voice of the performer. Reading a text is a much slower process than hearing a speech. A written text can be scanned quickly, or read slowly and deliberately. In either case, the reader has an opportunity to return to the start of a written passage and read it again.

This is not the case for oral presentations, which usually have set time limits and which proceed at a much faster pace than the reading process. This is the reason why structural clarity, previews, transitions, and reviews are so important to oral presentations. The repetition helps to concretize the ideas for the audience.

It is important to remember that when you write a speech, you must use an oral style. In other words, you must learn to write words as you normally would speak. An oral presentation should come across as natural to the speaker. The more conversational the tone and language of the speech, the easier it will be for the audience to engage and interact with the speaker. There is little room in a speech for grandiloquence and complex sentence structures. Your audience must be able to follow your ideas from sentence to sentence and paragraph to paragraph. Complex elements, such as technical terms and difficult concepts, must be presented and then explained in such a way that listeners can keep pace.

TIPS FOR EFFECTIVE LANGUAGE USE

- Define technical terms or complicated concepts in a concise manner.
- Alert your audience to changes in subject matter by incorporating previews, transitions, and recaps.
- Try to write your speech in conversational language. Write your speech as you would talk to a friend.
- Try to simplify sentence structure. Always aim for clarity over complexity.
- Try to make each sentence flow logically from its predecessor.
- Use humor where possible and appropriate.
- Read the text aloud as you complete each section. Make sure that you are comfortable *saying* the text, as well as reading it.

MEMORABLE LANGUAGE

AVOIDING OVERLY COMPLEX LANGUAGE IS NOT THE SAME AS AVOIDING *ELOQUENCE*. Finding ways to create memorable language is a difficult skill, but certainly an important and even necessary one.

There are many ways to create language that when delivered orally can leave a lasting impression on the audience. John F. Kennedy once said, "Ask not what your country can do for you, but what you can do for your country." This linguistic reversal is a moment of eloquence that will be long remembered. Shakespeare uses a similar strategy in *Hamlet*. "To be, or not to be—that is the question."

Martin Luther King's continuing repetition of the phrase "I have a dream" in his famous speech insured that the audience would remember that key concept. It is nearly impossible, now, to separate the phrase from the historical figure.

Writing devices are useful in creating memorable language. Some of the more popular writing devices used in oral presentations are listed here. These and many more writing concepts are developed in detail in the writing handbooks available in the reference section of your library.

Food for Thought

Assonance	Repetition of the same vowel sounds in nearby words; e.g., "No pain, no gain."
Consonance	Substitution of vowels within words that have the same consonant sounds; e.g., "Do you pine for your pain?"
Alliteration	Repetition of consonant sounds, usually at the beginnings of words; e.g., "Particular products purchased by pushy parents."
Simile	Expressed comparison using *like* or *as*; e.g., "Words are like water."
Hyperbole	Purposeful exaggeration in the service of truth; e.g., "He caved in—it was obviously the boldest thing he could have done."
Allusion	Reference to history, art, literature, theatre, etc.
Imagery	Language that refers to sense experience.
Irony	Purposeful discrepancy between what is stated and what is meant; can be either verbal or situational. Irony should be used sparingly and carefully, because it can muddle the meaning of your text.
Oxymoron	The linking together of two words or concepts customarily regarded as opposites; e.g., "A giant of a microbe; a bacterium with true stature."

One of the best ways to create memorable language in your presentation is to incorporate language that already *is* remembered. Collections of quotations are often divided by subject, and can be referenced quickly and easily. Quotations by famous (and infamous) persons are exceptionally useful in reinforcing specific ideas. Quotations can also add color, variety, and vividness to the language of the speech.

Chapter 3
Managing the Information You Find

As your research progresses, you'll begin to access a tremendous amount of material. It's temptingly easy to download everything about a particular topic. Before long, you'll end up with a collection of printouts and files that makes no more sense than the vague ideas you had when you began your project. In order for your research to be effective, you need a plan for managing the information you find.

When you start a project, you'll want to skim a few online sources to get a sense of the broad context of your chosen research topic. As you work, make a note of the sources that you think will be useful later when you begin to learn more about your topic. You can quickly evaluate a source's usefulness by using your browser's *Find* command to look for a few key terms that you know are important.

Later, as you focus and narrow your topic, you will want to go back and read these sources more carefully and follow links within them to new research materials. It's essential to set up a system that will make it easy for you to find these materials again when you need them.

BUILDING A DOCUMENT MANAGEMENT SYSTEM

AS YOU LOCATE SOURCES FOR YOUR RESEARCH, YOU NEED TO BE ABLE TO DO TWO things: access the information you need later, when you need it, and document your sources correctly when you've completed your project. In addition, any system you come up with must be able to accommodate both online and traditional sources.

Saving Information About Your Sources

As you locate potentially useful online sources, you need to keep track of them so you can access them later if you need to. The simplest way to track web sources is to use the **favorites** or **bookmarks** command in your browser. However, a favorite saves only the title, URL, and access date for your source. In academic research, you need to keep all of the following information (when available) about each source you use:

- Author name
- Title (of web page, etc.)
- Title of larger work containing the source (web site, etc.)
- Publication date
- URL

- Access date
- Brief summary of site's contents and relevance to your topic

There are lots of different options for keeping track of this information, from professional software such as Endnote, to simple 3 × 5 note cards. Many people just use a word processor such as Microsoft Word, and for small projects (with fewer than, say, 20 sources), this is probably the easiest solution: you just copy and paste the source information from into your word processor and type up a quick summary for later reference. To save yourself time later, format the information according to the guidelines for your discipline.

You can use a similar method to keep track of print sources, either by copying and pasting citation data from your library's electronic catalog into a text file or using the *save as text* function from the electronic catalog and later transferring the text into the same file as your online sources. Other library catalogs and online databases offer the option of emailing you citation information. If none of these options is available at your library, then print or write down the citation data for the sources you use and type them into your computer file later. Just make sure, when you use any of these methods, that you have *all* the information you need. Three o'clock in the morning before your project is due is a bad time to realize you don't have the publication date of one of your key sources.

Using a Research Blog

When you're working on a larger project, with dozens or even hundreds of sources, you'll need to use a more sophisticated system. It's difficult to work with a single, large Microsoft Word file, and Word's capability of searching in a group of smaller files is limited. One method that has worked well for Dave is keeping a research blog. It's easy to set up a quick blog using the standard templates at **blogger.com** or **livejournal.com.** This is just a personal blog, so you don't need to make it look pretty or worry about phrasing everything perfectly. Many blog services even allow you to make your blog private, only accessible via a password.

Whenever you locate a new source, you can type or copy and paste notes, quotations, and citation information right into the blog, and make a link directly back to the original source. Then, when you're ready to create your final project, you can easily search through your entire blog to find just the information you need—most of the difficult work is already done! If you create categories as you go, then clicking on a category in your blog will quickly display all your notes on that subtopic. One drawback of working with a blog is that if you don't have access to the internet, you won't be able to find your research notes, so you should plan accordingly.

Other Ways to Track Research Sources

Many textbooks (including several published by Pearson Longman), offer web services for their users to help them catalog sources. Or, if you're doing a group research project, you might want to set up a research wiki or a group blog, where all members of your group can post notes. Just make sure everyone in your group agrees on how you're going to keep track of sources before you start.

SAVING YOUR SOURCE MATERIALS

ONCE YOU'VE SAVED THE BACKGROUND INFORMATION FOR YOUR SOURCES, THERE are two ways to save the source material itself. The first method is downloading an entire file to your computer. By choosing the *save as* command from the *file* menu, you can save the actual text of any web page to a computer disk. With blog and forum posts, however, this can be a huge amount of information. You're probably better off just copying and pasting the text of the particular post you're interested in. Saving images and other media is accomplished by clicking and holding the mouse button on the image (Macintosh) or clicking the right-hand mouse button (Windows).

Since web sites can be instantaneously changed by their creators, you'll need to preserve your source in its original form to document it for your research. It's a good idea to save the complete text of every online document you use in your research.

The second method is to print out the documents you need. Since traditional research has always relied on print sources, this can give you a sense of comfort and security as you work. But remember that whether or not a document is printed is no sure measure of reliability.

DOWNLOADING HELPER APPLICATIONS

Some web sites require **helper applications** in order for you to use the diverse media they offer. Most commonly, you may need a helper application to view video or hear audio files, or to view specialized web sites incorporating animation or audio. In many cases, the site itself will provide a link to a site that allows you to download the helper application for free. For example, to hear Parker Posey reading from the F. Scott Fitzgerald story "Benediction," at *http://www.salon.com/audio/fiction/2001/04/25/ fitzgerald/index_np.html,* you need the RealAudio helper application. To download it, you would click on the RealAudio icon, which links you to the RealAudio site at *http://www.real.com/player/index.html,* and then follow the instructions posted at that site.

Generally, files you download will be compressed, meaning they are in a special format that must first be uncompressed with yet another helper application before they can be used. For Windows, most files can be uncompressed with WinZip, available at *http://www.winzip.com.* Macintosh files are generally compressed with Stuffit, available at *http://www.aladdinsys.com/.*

Once you've downloaded a helper application, your browser will look for helper applications in a special folder on your hard drive, usually called Plug-ins.

Tip

Ethics: Printing and saving. When printing your sources, make sure you print only the pages you need. Some web sites contain forty or more printed pages of text. Printing all of a site by mistake wastes paper and ink and often costs you money. To avoid this, use the *page setup* or *print preview* command to make sure you're printing only the pages you need.

Etiquette: When you save files in public computer labs, make sure you put them on your own space, not the computer's hard drive (which may be periodically erased by technical staff). Some schools offer students personal server space, accessible from anywhere on the school network, and sometimes from anywhere on the internet. Learn how to use this space, and you'll be able to have access to your documents whenever you need them, no matter where you are. If such a service is unavailable on your campus, invest in a **USB Thumb drive** or learn how to save files on your iPod or other device.

Chapter 4
Preparing for a Professional Environment

Goal Setting and Life Management

Learning Objectives

- Describe the importance of goal setting
- Identify the impact setting *goals* and *objectives* will have on your life plan
- Set realistic goals to help you reach your full potential in life
- Define goal-setting techniques
- Create *short-term* and *long-term* goals
- Describe the importance of setting priorities
- State the advantages of having a *mentor*

THE IMPORTANCE OF PERSONAL GOAL SETTING

TO REALIZE THE IMPORTANCE OF A GOAL, YOU MUST FIRST KNOW WHAT A GOAL IS. A **goal** is a long-term target. Think of a goal as a reward at the top of a ladder. To reach that reward, you need to progress up each step of the ladder. The degree of your goal will determine how long it will take to get there. Each step on your ladder has to contribute to your achievement of the final reward and support your personal values.

Goals will help you become more focused; help you increase your self-esteem; and help you overcome procrastination, fear, and failure. Setting goals will help you become more successful in your career. By setting and focusing on goals, your career plans will become more clear and meaningful.

INFLUENCES OF GOALS

GOALS HELP YOU KEEP FOCUSED ON WHERE YOU WANT TO BE IN YOUR FUTURE. THEY keep you motivated to continue working to improve yourself. Goals help you achieve, not just hope for, what you want in life.

Take a look at Cory. When twenty-two years old, Cory had only a high-school education. After working as a service clerk since graduating from high school, Cory decided to go to college to become a Certified Public Accountant (CPA). Cory's long-term goal is to finish college in five years. Self-supporting and having to work, Cory set a realistic goal to obtain an associate degree in accounting within three years. After achieving that goal, Cory has found a good job, has a good income, and has more self-confidence. Still committed to becoming a CPA, Cory needs to earn a bachelor's degree and has set a goal to do that within two years. This is motivating Cory to perform well.

In the example with Cory, as one goal is reached, you will be motivated and self-confident enough to set a higher goal. You will continually strive for improvement.

Goals can and should be set in major areas of your life including personal, career, financial, educational, physical, social, and psychological. Goals help you maintain a positive outlook in all aspects of your life. They also help you maintain a more positive perception of yourself and will result in improved human relations with others. If you perceive yourself as doing well and being positive, others will feel your positive attitude.

HOW TO SET GOALS

ACHIEVING SHORT- AND LONG-TERM GOALS IS LIKE CLIMBING A LADDER. Imagine that there is a major prize (what you value most) at the top of the ladder. The prize can be considered your long-term goal, and each step on the ladder is a progressive short-term goal that helps you reach the major prize.

Set short-term and long-term goals, and put them into writing. **Long-term goals** are anywhere from five to ten years, although you should reevaluate your goals each year.

To set goals think of what you want to accomplish in your life. Write down everything you can think of, including personal, career, and educational dreams. Then review the list and choose what items you most value. In reviewing your list, ask yourself where you want to be in five to ten years. These are your long-term goals. Make sure that each goal is realistic and something that you want. Each goal should be challenging enough that you will work toward it, but it should also be attainable. There must be a reason to reach this goal. Identify why each long-term goal is important to you. This is a key step because you are setting yourself up for success. Identify both opportunities and potential barriers toward reaching your goals. For example, remember Cory's goal to be a CPA? Cory has a reason to become a CPA: it represents success. It is important to Cory, and it is a realistic goal that can be reached.

Short-term goals are goals that can be reached within a year's time. Short-term goals are set to help reach long-term goals. Businesses often refer to short-term goals as **objectives** because they are short-term, measurable, and have specific time lines. When creating personal goals, several short-term goals need to be set. These goals can be achieved in one day, a week, a month, or even several months. However, they should be achieved within a year's time and support a long-term goal.

Short-term goals/objectives must be realistic, achievable, and important to you. They need to be measurable so you know that you actually have reached them.

Another example of a long-term goal for Cory is to buy a car in one year after graduation. Cory has set several short-term goals, one being to save a specific amount of money each month. Another supporting goal is to work a specific number of hours each week. Cory also needs to be specific about the type of car, whether to buy used or new, and

Exercise 4-1 Long-Term Career Goal

Fill in the star with your long-term career goal. Identify where you want to be in your career in five years.

Exercise 4-2 Short-Term Goals

Using your long-term career goal from Exercise 4-1, identify short-term goals (objectives) for each step on the ladder.

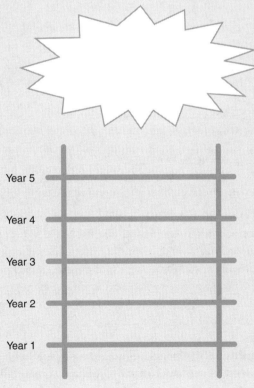

Year 5

Year 4

Year 3

Year 2

Year 1

whether Cory needs to take out a loan. The answers to these questions will determine if the time frame is realistic and how much Cory needs to save per month.

Now that you have a list of goals, there are a few more important aspects of goal setting to consider. These include owning the goals, being in control of the goals, making the goals measurable, and setting a time frame to achieve these goals.

Talk It Out Discuss one goal that can be set for this class.

Owning the goal is important for successfully reaching a goal. Make sure the goal belongs to you. You should be the one to decide your goals, not your parents, spouse, significant other, friends, relatives, or anyone else who may have influence over you. For example, if Cory goes to college because it is a personal dream of being a CPA, it will be accomplished. However, if Cory goes to college to become a CPA because it was Cory's parents' idea for Cory to be a CPA, this would not be Cory's goal, and it could be hard to accomplish this goal.

Know who is in *control of the goal*. Make sure you have the right information to create these goals. This means knowing what resources and constraints are involved. Drawing on the concept of locus of control, not every factor is within your control. Therefore, be flexible and maintain a realistic control of your goal.

Web Quiz Take the online goal-setting quiz to see if you are making the most of your career potential.

http://www.achievebalance.com/data/articles/goalsetting.htm

Set a time frame for reaching the goal. A time frame makes your goal measurable so you will know when you have reached your goal. Write down details. For example, instead of writing "I will become a manager in the future," write "I will become a manager with a top Accounting Firm by the beginning of the year 2014."

Write goals positively and in detail. Include: what you want, when you want to accomplish it, where you will be when you reach the goal, who is involved in helping you reach the goal, and how you will get there. Identify what it will take to meet goals in regard to finances, education, and other matters. Keep your goals realistic so they are achievable.

CREATING A LIFE PLAN

CREATING GOALS WILL HELP YOU WITH YOUR LIFE PLAN. A LIFE PLAN IS A WRITTEN document that identifies goals in all areas of your life, including personal, career, and education. Some of your goals may blend in two or more of these areas.

Consider the following life issues:

- *Social and spiritual:* Marriage, family, friends, religion.
- *Financial:* Home ownership, car ownership, investments.
- *Activities:* Travel, hobbies, life experiences.

Think about the type of personal relationships you want in the future.

Consider where you want to be financially. Many people dream of becoming a millionaire, but you need to be realistic. Think about what kind of house you want to live in and what type of car you want to drive. If a spouse and children are in your future, account for their financial needs as well. Also, identify what outside activities you enjoy. Your personal financial plan will determine your ability to achieve these goals. Think about what results and rewards will come from achieving your goals. Look at both intrinsic and extrinsic rewards.

Talk It Out Share common rewards that are important to you. Identify these rewards as intrinsic or extrinsic.

Intrinsic rewards include such things as self-satisfaction and pride of accomplishment. These come from within you. **Extrinsic rewards** include such things as money and praise. These rewards come from external sources. Intrinsic and extrinsic rewards are needed to achieve satisfaction in your future. Both are equally important and need to be recognized. They motivate and can help you keep a positive outlook when working toward goals.

Planning a career is equally as important as planning your personal life. When planning your career consider:

- Why your selected career is important.
- What resources are needed to achieve your career goals.
- How you will know you have achieved career success.

Choosing the right career is important. People choose careers for different reasons, including earning power, status, intellect, and self-satisfaction. If there is a career center available at your college, take time to visit and see what it offers. Talk to friends and family members about what you do well. There are several personality and career interest tests you can take that will help you determine your potential career. These career assessments are offered at many college career centers or online. They will help you identify interests, abilities, and personality traits to determine what career will suit you best. Use all resources available and gather information to help you make the best career decision. Conduct Internet searches and interview people who are already working in your field of interest.

To be successful in your career, it is important to enjoy what you do. Select a career that supports your short-term and long-term goals.

Education is an important key to achieving your life plan. Just as your personal life goals and career goals are important, education is another contributing factor toward reaching your life plan. Consider:

- Degrees/certificates needed
- Time frame
- Financial resources
- Support network

No one can ever take your knowledge away from you. Make college course choices based upon your desired educational goals. Choose courses that will benefit you and help you explore new concepts.

Take a trip to your college career center or talk to a counselor. An excellent method to use to explore potential careers is through volunteering, job shadowing, and internships.

PRIORITIES

Priorities determine what needs to be done and in what order. Juggling priorities is the key to reaching goals. Not only is it important in your personal life, but it will be necessary at work as well.

You may need to adjust priorities to reach your goals. Before priorities can be put in order, you need to determine what they are. Sometimes your first priority is not necessarily what is most important in life; it is just that a particular activity demands the most attention at a specific point in time. For example, if Cory has a young child, that child will be most important to Cory. However, if Cory is attending college to become a CPA and needs an evening to study for a big exam, the priority will be to study for that test. That does not mean the exam is more important than the child. However, the test is a step to a better future for Cory and the child.

Cory's decision is called a **trade-off**. A trade-off means giving up one thing to do something else. Another example involving Cory is the decision to purchase a car in one year; Cory needs to save a certain amount of money each month. In order to do this, Cory may have to give up going to the coffeehouse each morning and, instead, make coffee at home in order to save enough money to meet the savings goal to purchase the car.

Talk It Out Identify priorities and trade-offs for successfully completing this course.

Be prepared to be flexible in all areas of your life plan. When working toward goals, flexibility is important. Times change, technology changes, and your priorities may change. Reevaluate your goals at least once a year. At times, you may need to update or revise your goals and/or time lines; do not just give them up.

MENTORING

ANOTHER OPPORTUNITY TO IMPROVE YOUR JOB SKILLS AND INCREASE YOUR POTENTIAL for career advancement is to find a mentor. A **mentor** is someone who can help you learn more about your present position, provide support, and help you to grow in your career. In addition, the mentor will help you learn about the culture of the company. The **corporate culture** includes the values, expectations, and behaviors of people at work. Knowing the culture of the company will help you succeed. By understanding a company's corporate culture you will learn about the politics, policies, and how people expect you to act on the job.

A mentor is different than a coach. Although a mentor can be a coach, a coach is not a mentor. A mentor is someone who will help you focus and work toward your career goals. A coach is someone who serves as an advisor that focuses on improving personal performance.

Finding a mentor can be a formal or informal process. Some companies have a formal mentor program. In this instance, you will be assigned a mentor who is able to help you succeed on the job. In addition, he or she will be able to help you to identify and reach your career goals. This mentor may be paid by the company to help you. This allows more time for the mentor to work with you.

If your company does not offer a formal mentor program, try to establish a mentoring relationship with someone who can help you while you are learning about your new job and career. This person may choose you, or you may choose that person. Your mentor should be someone who you can trust, someone who knows the company and industry, and someone who is willing to spend time to help you succeed.

Exercise 4-3 Finding a Mentor

Name at least three qualities you would look for in a person that you would want to be a mentor to you.

1. _____

2. _____

3. _____

What would you say to that person (how would you ask that person to be your mentor)?

_____

_____

_____

WORKPLACE DOS AND DON'TS

Do set goals in writing	*Don't* set goals that are difficult to reach
Do set long-term and short-term goals	*Don't* give up on goals
Do make your goals attainable	*Don't* wait to create goals
Do have measurable goals	*Don't* create unrealistic goals
Do set priorities. Include trade-offs and flexibility when setting goals	*Don't* give up when working to reach your goals
Do try to establish a mentor relationship	*Don't* try to learn about the company culture on your own

CONCEPT REVIEW AND APPLICATION
Summary of Key Concepts

- Goal setting is important in helping you keep focused. It will increase your self-esteem and help you become more successful in all areas of your life

- As goals are reached, motivation and self-confidence will increase

- Goals need to be put into writing. They need to be realistic and measurable. Know who owns the goals and who controls the goals. A time frame is needed to know when you plan on reaching these goals

- Long-term goals are set to be achieved in five to ten years

- Short-term goals are achieved within a year's time and are needed to reach long-term goals

- When creating a life plan, consider all aspects of your life, including personal, career, and education

- Flexibility and juggling priorities are needed to achieve goals

- As you begin your new job, establish a relationship with a mentor

- A good mentor will help you learn more about your position and the company

Key Terms

corporate culture

extrinsic rewards

goal

intrinsic rewards

long-term goals

mentor

objectives

priorities

short-term goals

trade-off

If You Were the Boss

1. Why does an employer need to set goals?
2. Why is it important that an employer ensure that employees set personal and career goals?
3. Why would you establish a mentoring program for your employees? What specific advantages would it provide your company?

Learn More

To learn more about subjects addressed in this chapter take an Introduction to Psychology course

Web Links

http://www.mindtools.com/pages/article/newHTE_06.htm
http://www.topachievement.com/goalsetting.html

http://www.mygoals.com/helpGoalsettingTips.html
http://www.gems4friends.com/goals/index.html
http://www.management-mentors.com

ACTIVITIES

Activity 4-1

List three personal, career, and educational dreams you want to accomplish in your life.

Personal	Career	Education
1.	1.	1.
2.	2.	2.
3.	3.	3.

Activity 4-2

From your Activity 4-1 list, create three long-term goals in each section. Make sure they are realistic.

Personal	Career	Education
1.	1.	1.
2.	2.	2.
3.	3.	3.

Activity 4-3

From Activity 4-2, prioritize the goals you set.

Personal	Career	Education
1.	1.	1.
2.	2.	2.
3.	3.	3.

Activity 4-4

Using the previous activities in this chapter, set long- and short-term goals. The star is your long-term goal. The steps are your short-term goals. Write positively and in detail. Set one personal goal and one career goal. Keep goals specific, measurable, and realistic. Include what (the goal), when (specific time you plan to achieve it), and how to get there (be specific). *Hint:* Refer back to Cory's goal to obtain a car.

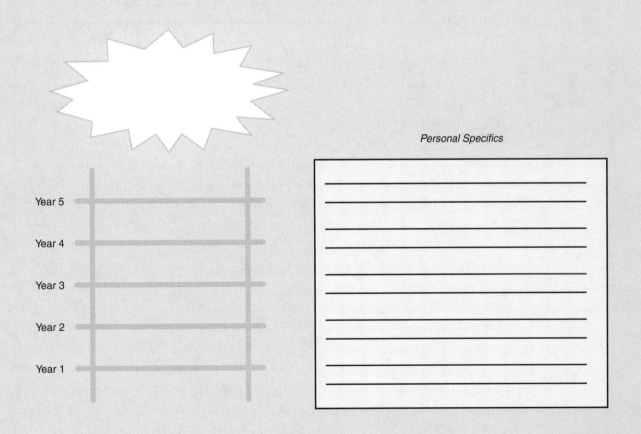

Personal Specifics

Career Specifics

Year 5

Year 4

Year 3

Year 2

Year 1

SAMPLE EXAM QUESTIONS

1. Goals need to be set so you can become _____ _____.

2. Long-term goals are set to be reached after _____ _____.

3. Short-term goals should usually be reached _____ _____.

4. _____ help you reach long-term goals.

5. When setting a goal, there must be a time frame; it must be _____ and _____.

6. _____ will help you decide what needs to be done and in what order.

7. To give up one thing for another is known as a/an _____.

8. Goals should be challenging but _____ _____.

9. It is important to put goals into _____ _____.

10. When creating a life plan, consider the following three areas: _____, _____, and _____.

11. A/An _____ is someone who can help you to develop in your career.

CAREER GOAL SETTING   BY (STUDENT NAME)

This writing assignment guides you through the process of creating goals. Remember that these goals must be realistic, attainable, important to you, and measurable. Be as specific as possible in every paragraph.

Ten-Year Goal

Paragraph 1	*In ten years, I want to be . . .*
	Identify and write your ten-year career goal here. Be specific: Identify what kind of job and what title you want, in what city you want to work, whom you want to work for, and why you chose this goal.

Five-Year Goal

Paragraph 2	*In five years, I want to be . . .*
	Identify and write your five-year career goal here. Be specific: Identify what kind of job and what title you want, in what city you want to work, whom you want to work for, and why you chose this goal.

One-Year Goal(s)

Paragraph 3	*In order to reach my five-year goal, I need to set the following short-term goals . . .*
	Identify necessary steps to reach your five-year goal. Be specific with activities, resources, and time frames.
Paragraph 4	*I am currently . . .*
	What are you currently doing to reach these short-term goals? Be specific with activities, resources, and time frames.
Paragraph 5	*I will know I have reached these goals when . . . .*
	Goals must be measurable. How will you know when you have reached each short-term goal? Be specific with activities, resources, and time frames.
Paragraph 6	*I need the following resources to reach my goal . . . .*
	Identify physical, financial, emotional, and social resources and where they will come from.
Paragraph 7	*My priorities for reaching my goals are. . . . My trade-offs include. . . . I must be flexible. . . .*
	Have priorities set for reaching your goals. Include your trade-offs and the areas where you may need to be flexible.

Ethics, Politics, and Diversity

Objectives

- Define *ethics* and its impact both personally and professionally
- Identify the importance of maintaining *confidentiality*
- Define and identify the appropriate use of *power* and power bases
- Understand the topics of *politics* and *reciprocity* and their appropriate use in the workplace
- Understand the importance of ethical decision making
- Define *workplace diversity* and realize its impact on performance
- State the basic employee rights and legal protection available for workplace diversity issues
- Recognize the negative impact *stereotypes* and *prejudice* have in the workplace and on performance
- Identify *cultural* differences and the positive and negative impact these differences have on business

ETHICS DEFINED

THROUGHOUT OUR SCHOOLING, WE ARE TOLD TO BEHAVE ETHICALLY. IN EDUCATION, ethics typically refers to not cheating on homework and exams. At work, cheating can occur in all areas of a job. From the time we clock in to the time we leave the office—and even extending into the weekend, we must behave in an ethical manner. Ethical behavior is a twenty-four-hour process. Behavior reflects ethical values. In turn, our ethical behavior reflects and represents our company.

Ethics is a moral standard of right and wrong. Although the definition of ethics is a simple statement, it is important to identify who and what determines what is morally right and wrong. Just as your personality is shaped by outside influences, so is your ethical makeup.

Ethical behavior is a reflection of the influences of coworkers, friends, family, religion, and society. For example, if you associate with people who shoplift, you most likely will not view shoplifting as an unethical act. As a result, you may shoplift without remorse. If your family routinely lies about a child's age to pay a lower admission fee to a movie theater or amusement park, the child is being taught to be dishonest. Common religions teach that lying, cheating, and stealing are wrong. Consider the influences our society and culture have on our ethical behavior. Corporate America has been bombarded with ethics-related scandals. Additionally many of the marketing messages we receive on a daily basis influence ethical behavior.

Although the preceding factors all have an enormous influence on the makeup of one's ethics, it is important to note that ethical behavior starts with the individual. As we explore the concept of ethics at work, remember that ethics begins with you.

Talk It Out Discuss recent corporate ethics-related scandals.

INFLUENCES ON ETHICS AT WORK

At work you will be confronted with ethical issues. Many issues must be kept **confidential,** meaning they are matters that should be kept private. These matters include client records, employee information, business reports, documentation, and files. Whether you are told or not told to keep work-related information confidential, you have an obligation to not share information with individuals with whom the business is of no concern. This is called **implied confidentiality.** An example of implied confidentiality would be not sharing customers' personal information with others. Sometimes, you may be tempted or even asked to share confidential information. Do not fall into that trap. If you are uncertain about sharing confidential information with someone, check with your boss. Doing so will demonstrate to your boss that you want to not only maintain the privacy of your department but also behave in a professional manner.

Your ethical behavior extends beyond the professionalism of how you deal with others. It is also reflected in your dependability and how you conduct yourself on company time. Remember that the company is paying you to work when you are on the job. Although at times it may be necessary to conduct personal business on company time, it is inappropriate to consistently spend your time on noncompany activities. The following activities should not be done during work time:

Talk It Out What activities done during class could be considered unethical?

- Surfing the Internet for personal business
- Taking personal telephone calls
- Making personal telephone calls (including family, personal appointments)
- Routinely exceeding allotted break and lunch periods
- Playing computer games
- Using company supplies and equipment for nonbusiness purposes

Web Quiz Test your business ethics.

http://resources.monster.com/tools/quizzes/bizethics

If you must conduct personal business while at work, only do so during your break or lunch hour. Whenever possible, conduct the business before or after work hours and in a private manner.

POWER AND ETHICS

Power is one's ability to influence another's behavior. Whether you recognize it or not, everyone at work has some form of power. Some people understand this ability to influence others' behavior and use it appropriately. Let us first review the different types of power, what they are, and how you can increase this use of power at work. There are seven bases of power: legitimate, coercive, reward, connection, charismatic, information, and expert.

Legitimate power is the power that is given to you by the company. It includes your title and any other formal authority that comes with your position at work. For example, a manager has legitimate power to assign schedules. **Coercive power** is also power that is derived from your formal position. However, the difference between legitimate and coercive power is that coercive power uses threats and punishment. An example of coercive power is if your manager threatens to cut your hours. In contrast to coercive power is **reward power.** Reward power is the ability to influence someone with something of value. For example, a manager has offered you a bonus for meeting a goal. Those with legitimate power can reward others with promotions, pay increases, and other incentives. You do not have to have legitimate power to reward others in the workplace. **Connection power** is based on using someone else's legitimate power. Consider the department assistant that arranges meetings based on his boss's power. This is because the department assistant has a connection to an individual with authority.

Exercise 4-4 Identify What Power Can Do
Identify three ways employees without legitimate power can reward others.
1.
2.
3.

The last three types of power come from within. They are often referred to as types of personal power. **Charismatic power** is a form of personal power that makes people attracted to you. We all know someone who walks into a room and immediately people are attracted to him or her. This is because the individual with charismatic power or charisma shows a sincere interest in others. **Information power** is based upon an individual's ability to obtain and share information. Doing so makes you more valuable to those with whom you interact. For example, a coworker is part of a committee and routinely shares information. **Expert power** is power that is earned by one's knowledge, experience, or expertise. Consider the company's computer repair technician. On the company's organization chart, he or she is not very high in the formal chain of command. However, this individual wields a lot of power because of his or her computer expertise.

INCREASING YOUR POWER BASES

As mentioned earlier, everyone possesses some form of workplace power. The trick is to recognize, utilize, and increase your power. The easiest way to increase your legitimate power is to make people aware of your title and responsibilities. Because coercive power utilizes threats and/or punishment, coercive power should only be used when an individual is breaking policy or behaving inappropriately.

Reward power can be used daily. Whenever possible, dispense a sincere word or note of appreciation to a coworker who has assisted you or has performed exceptionally well. Doing so will develop and enhance relationships not only within your department but also outside your department. Just remember to be sincere. Increase your connection power by strengthening your network. **Networking** means meeting and developing relationships with individuals outside your immediate work area. Network with individuals within and outside of your organization.

Charismatic power is increased when you focus attention on others. Make eye contact, initiate conversation, and focus the conversation on the other individual instead of on yourself. Information power is developed by attending meetings, joining committees, and networking. Whenever possible and without over committing, join committees and attend meetings. Doing so exposes you to other people and issues throughout the company. You, in turn, not only learn more about what's going on within the organization but also increase your connection or network power. Increase your expert power by practicing continual learning. Read books and business-related articles, scan reputable and applicable Internet sites, attend workshops and conferences, and learn new technology when possible. Whenever you learn something new that can assist others at work, share this information. Coworkers will see you as the expert in the respective area.

POLITICS AND RECIPROCITY

WHEN YOU BEGIN TO OBTAIN AND UTILIZE YOUR POWER, YOU ARE PRACTICING POLITICS. **Politics** is obtaining and using power. People generally get a bad taste in their mouth when someone accuses them of being political, but this is not necessarily a bad thing. As mentioned, it is important to recognize, increase, and utilize the various power bases at work. It is when one expects reciprocity that politics at work gets dangerous. **Reciprocity** is when debts and obligations are created for doing something. Suppose you are on a time crunch and must get a report out in two hours but you need help. You ask a coworker to help you. He or she stops what she is doing and assists you with an hour to spare. You have just created a reciprocal relationship with the coworker. When he or she is in a crunch, he or she will not only ask you but expect you to help him or her out. The workplace is comprised of reciprocal relationships. Unfortunately, sometimes the phrase "you owe me" encroaches on our ability to behave ethically.

Cory has a coworker who helps Cory out with special projects when time is short. When the coworker tells Cory she needs help with something, Cory immediately responds, "Sure, no problem." Unfortunately, there is a problem. The coworker wants Cory to attend a meeting for her and tell people at the meeting that she is home sick when Cory knows she plans to take a trip with friends. Cory tells the coworker that it would be unethical to cover for her. "But you owe me!" says the coworker. Cory is unsure what to do. After some thought, Cory tells the coworker that Cory wants to repay the favor and appreciates all the help the coworker provides but Cory's ethics cannot be compromised. Cory should expect some tension between the two, but, in the long run, the worker will respect Cory.

CORPORATE VALUES/CULTURE

EACH COMPANY HAS A CORPORATE CULTURE. A CORPORATE CULTURE IS THE WAY a company's employees behave. It is based upon the behavior of its leaders. This culture can be viewed from a corporate level and also from a departmental level. For example, if all the executives within the company are very laid-back and informal, most employees throughout the company will also be laid-back and informal. If a department supervisor is always stressed out and unprepared, the department members will most likely be stressed out and unprepared as well. This behavior also reflects an organization's ethical behavior. Companies that want to be proactive and decrease any type of unethical temptation will have and enforce an **ethics statement.** An ethics statement is a formal corporate policy that addresses the issues of ethical behavior and punishment should someone behave inappropriately. As Corporate America recovers from its scandals, more companies are placing great importance on ethics statements. Included in most corporate ethics policies will be a statement regarding **conflict of interest.** A conflict of interest occurs when you are in a position to influence a decision from which you could benefit directly or indirectly.

Cory's company needs a flower vendor for an upcoming company event. Cory's uncle owns a local flower shop, and getting this contract would be a big financial boost to his store. Cory wonders if it would be unethical to tell his uncle about the opportunity. After some thought, Cory decides to ask the boss about the dilemma. Cory's boss explains that there is no conflict of interest if Cory does not financially benefit from the contract and encourages Cory to contact the uncle.

If there is ever any possibility that someone could accuse you of a conflict of interest, excuse yourself from the decision-making process. If you are uncertain that there is a conflict, check with your boss or the respective committee. Explain the situation and ask for your boss's or committee's opinion. To avoid a conflict of interest, many companies have strict policies on gift giving and receiving. Many companies do not allow the acceptance of gifts or have a dollar limit on the value of a gift allowed.

Exercise 4-5 Receiving a Gift at Work

Your company has a strict policy on not accepting gifts valued over $15. A key vendor for your company sends you flowers on your birthday. The arrangement is quite large, so you know it clearly exceeds the $15 limit. What do you do?

_____

_____

_____

MAKING ETHICAL CHOICES

As you attempt to make ethical choices at work, use the three **levels of ethical decisions.** _The first level of ethics is the law._ When confronted with an ethical issue, first ask if the action is legal. If the action is illegal, it is unethical.

The second level of ethics is fairness. Your actions/behavior should be fair to all parties involved. If, when making a decision, someone is clearly going to be harmed or is unable to defend himself or herself, the decision is probably not ethical. Note that the concept of "fairness" does not mean that everyone is happy with the outcome. It only means that the decision has been made in an impartial and unbiased manner. Sometimes, a behavior is legal but may be considered unethical. Just because a behavior is legal does not mean it is right. Take the case of an individual who has a romantic relationship with someone who is married to someone else. There is no law that says having an extramarital affair is illegal. However, many consider this behavior unethical.

It is understandable that not everyone agrees on what is right and fair. This is where *the third level of ethics—one's conscience*—must be considered. This is also when an ethical decision gets personal. In the classic Disney movie, *Pinocchio,* there was a character named Jiminy Cricket. He was Pinocchio's conscience. He made Pinocchio feel bad when Pinocchio behaved inappropriately. Just like Pinocchio, each individual has a conscience. When one knowingly behaves inappropriately, most will eventually feel bad about his poor behavior. Some people take a bit longer to feel bad than others, but most everyone at some point feels bad when they have wronged another. Sometimes a behavior may be legal and it may be fair to others, but it still may make us feel guilty or bad. If it does, the behavior is probably unethical.

Cory is responsible for the department's petty cash box. Cory is planning on going to lunch with friends but does not have time to stop by the ATM until later in the afternoon. Cory struggles with the thought of temporarily borrowing $10 from the petty cash box and

Exercise 4-6 Legal Behavior

Based on Cory's dilemma, is Cory borrowing money from the petty cash box legal?

Yes ☐   No ☐

Is this behavior fair?

Yes ☐   No ☐

Whom could it harm and why?

_____

_____

_____

_____

Exercise 4-7 Honesty: Part I

It is 9:00 p.m., it is raining, and you are hungry. You are on your way home from a long workday. You only have $5 in your wallet, so you decide to go to a fast-food drive-through restaurant to get dinner. You carefully order so as not to exceed your $5 limit. You hand the drive-through employee your $5, and he gives you change and your meal. You place it all in the passenger's seat and drive home. When you get home, you discover that the fast-food employee gave you change for $20. What do you do?

_____

_____

_____

_____

Review the scenario; apply the three levels of ethical decision making to the following questions. Is your behavior legal? Is it fair? How do you feel about keeping the money?

Is it legal to keep the money?

Yes ☐   No ☐

Is it fair to keep the money?

Yes ☐   No ☐

How do you feel about keeping the money?

_____

_____

_____

Typically, in the fast-food business, employees whose cash boxes are short or over more than once are at risk of being fired. If you initially were going to keep the money, but now you know the employee who gave you too much cash could get fired because you decided to keep the money, would you still keep the money?

_____

_____

returning the money later in the day (after a visit to the ATM). No one would ever know. Technically, it is not stealing. It is just borrowing. Cory decides the behavior is unethical, does not take the petty cash, and skips going out to lunch with friends.

WHEN OTHERS ARE NOT ETHICAL

THE LAST SECTION DISCUSSED HOW TO BEHAVE ETHICALLY AT WORK. BUT WHAT SHOULD you do when others are not behaving ethically? Let us go back to the three levels of ethical decision making. Everyone must abide by the law. If someone at work is breaking the law, you have an obligation to inform your employer immediately. This can be done confidentially to either your supervisor or the human resource department. Whenever you accuse anyone of wrongdoing, have documented facts and solid evidence. Keep track of important dates, events, and copies of evidence. Your credibility is at stake. Remember, depending on the enormity of the situation, you, as an employee, have three choices: (1) alert outside officials if the offense is illegal and extreme; (2) if the offense is not extreme and is accepted by management, accept management's decision; or (3) if the inappropriate behavior is accepted by management and you are still bothered, decide whether you want to continue working for the company.

Cory finds out that a certain coworker received a laptop computer from a vendor for personal use. No other employee received a laptop. The coworker said the laptop was an incentive for the company's good standing with the vendor and, because he was the employee who made the purchases, it was his right to keep the laptop. Cory thinks this is not fair and is unethical. Cory politely checks with the human resource department, and they tell Cory that the coworker can keep the laptop. Cory must accept the company's policy. Although construed as being unethical in Cory's mind, the company found no conflict with its policies. Cory decides the offense is not extreme; and, because it was accepted by management, Cory accepts management's decision.

Another common ethical issue at work occurs in the area of company theft. Company theft is not always large items such as computers or equipment. More often, it is smaller items such as office supplies. Time can also be stolen from a company. If you use company time to surf the Internet, make personal calls, or take extra long breaks, you are stealing from the company. You may not realize that taking a pen or pencil home is stealing from your company. Office supplies should only be used for business purposes. Although it is heavily influenced by the company and how others view right behavior from wrong, ethical behavior starts with the individual.

DIVERSITY BASICS

This section addresses workplace diversity, cultural differences, and employee rights regarding these differences. Diversity comes in many forms. Although most people think of diversity as a race issue, the topic goes far beyond race. People are different in many aspects, ranging from ethnicity to the way we wear our hair. As we discuss these issues, it is important to note three primary messages regarding workplace diversity:

- No matter what our differences, treat everyone with respect and professionalism.

- Diversity should be used as an asset that utilizes our differences as ways to create, innovate, and compete.

- Workplace diversity should only be an issue when the diversity negatively affects performance.

The following is a common example of workplace diversity: One of Cory's new friends at work has a lifestyle that is not as conservative as Cory's. Although Cory's friend has never openly mentioned his lifestyle, he behaves in a feminine fashion and always talks about various parties he attends. Cory really enjoys the workplace friendship with this co-worker. He is older and watches out for and helps Cory; yet, Cory does not know how to behave around this friend. Cory thinks about talking to coworkers about the new friend and his lifestyle but ultimately decides that personal opinions on one's lifestyle should be kept private. Cory decides it is best to maintain a good working relationship with the new friend regardless of lifestyle differences.

Web Quiz How diverse is your thinking? Take the diversity quiz.

www.augsburg.edu/education/edc210/diversityquiz.html

FORMS OF DIVERSITY

Workplace diversity means there are differences among coworkers. Whenever people address the issue of diversity at work, they primarily address cultural and racial differences. Diversity extends well beyond culture and race. We differ in age, gender, economic status, physical makeup, intelligence, religion, and sexual orientation, among other things.

The Equal Employment Opportunity Commission (EEOC) enforces laws that protect individuals from workplace discrimination in recruiting, hiring, wages, promotions, and unlawful termination. These laws are based upon Dr. Martin Luther King Jr.'s establishment of Title VII of the Civil Rights Act, which prohibits discrimination based on sex, religion, race or color, or national origin. Since that time, additional laws have been made to further protect individuals from discrimination in the area of age (over forty years), physical and mental disabilities, gender, sexual orientation, hate crimes, pregnancy, and military service. If you ever feel you are a victim of discrimination, first contact your human resource department. If you feel you are still experiencing discrimination, contact your state's *Department of Fair Employment and Housing* or the *Equal Employment Opportunity Commission*.

Race is defined as people with certain physical traits. Racial differences include various ethnicities including Hispanics, Asians, African Americans, Native Americans, and Anglo-Saxons. **Culture** is the different behavior patterns of people. Examples of various cultures may include where you live geographically, your age, your economic status, and your religious beliefs. As the workplace becomes more diverse, it is hard to imagine a workplace that does not include various races and cultures.

Look around the room and list at least three differences between you and your classmates.

1.

2.

3.

As we understand how race and culture impact our workplace, we will begin to recognize how these differences influence our values and behavior. Moreover, people look different and have different value systems. Although we may not like one's looks or agree with others' values or religious beliefs, we must respect everyone's differences and treat them professionally.

Digging deeper into the issue of culture, we need to appreciate the various generational differences and its impact on the workplace. Individuals entering the workforce (eighteen- to twenty-two-year-olds) have different needs than those preparing to retire (fifty-five and older). Moreover, these needs reflect priorities, values, and attitudes.

STEREOTYPES AND PREJUDICE

EVERYONE IS A PRODUCT OF PAST EXPERIENCE. INDIVIDUALS USE THESE PAST experiences to form perceptions about people and situations. A perception is one's understanding or interpretation of reality. If we had a positive previous experience, we will most likely have a positive perception of a person or circumstance. For example, if your boss calls you into his or her office, you will either have a positive or negative perception of the upcoming situation. If your boss is a good communicator and you frequently visit his or her office, you will have a positive perception of being called into the office. On the other hand, if your boss only calls you into his or her office for bad news, your perception of reality is that the boss's office only represents reprimands and punishment.

To make situations easier to understand or perceive, we often stereotype. **Stereotyping** is making a generalized image of a particular group or situation. We often take our perceptions and mold groups or situations. These images can be positive or negative, but we generally apply them to similar situations and groups. At work, this can include types of meetings (situations) or members of specific departments (groups). Using the preceding example of the boss and his or her office, one could stereotype that all bosses are good communicators.

It is important to not only know the definition of stereotyping but also to avoid applying stereotypes in a negative manner. Let us use the example of females with blonde hair. A common stereotype is that females with blonde hair are not intelligent. This is not true. Prior to responding to a situation, conduct an attitude check to ensure that you are not basing your reaction on a perception or stereotype rather than responding to the current facts and situation.

Using the previous example of attitudes toward females with blonde hair, if we assume that all females with blonde hair are unintelligent (stereotype), we have just demonstrated prejudice. **Prejudice** is a favorable or unfavorable judgment or opinion toward an individual or group based on one's perception (or understanding) of a group, individual, or situation. Typically, at work, prejudice is a negative attitude or opinion that results in discrimination. Therefore, if we do not hire females with blonde hair because we believe they are not intelligent, we are guilty of discrimination. **Workplace discrimination** is acting against someone based on race, age, gender, religion, disability, or any of the other areas we have discussed in this chapter.

Many people harbor some form of prejudice. Recognize what areas you may be harboring prejudice and begin understanding why. Once you recognize what areas need improvement, begin taking action to decrease your prejudice. One way is to learn about the individual, group, or situation that is causing the prejudice.

Labeling is when we describe an individual or group of individuals based upon past actions. We attach positive or negative labels to groups or individuals, and we frequently have the group or individuals live up or down to these standards. We then watch for supporting behaviors to see if these behaviors live up to or dispel the labels we have attached. For example, if we label a coworker as being the smartest person we know, that person may live up to this expectation by behaving as the smartest person (regardless of if he or she really is intelligent). However, he or she may dispel the label by purposely behaving opposite of a smart person.

Assumptions sometimes are made at work based on people's language differences and accents. These assumptions may include economic status, intelligence, and social customs. In our melting pot society, it is common for individuals to speak a different language (bilingual) when at home. At work, speaking a second language can be a means of attracting and meeting customer needs. Therefore, being bilingual can be a workplace asset.

Do not make fun of people with different cultures or lifestyles or individuals with physical and mental disabilities. Even jokes that we believe are innocent may cause deep wounds. Moreover, they may not only be offensive but violate one's civil rights. Inappropriate comments can be construed as both workplace discrimination and harassment.

For example, Cory is invited to lunch with some new coworkers. During the meal, one of the coworkers tells a joke against a blind person of a certain ethnicity. Cory politely

Talk It Out

What does the Cory story found in the Diversity Basics section have to do with stereotypes and prejudice?

chuckles at the punch line but is actually offended. Cory wonders how to best handle the situation. Should Cory tell the joke teller that the joke was offensive? Should Cory tell the department supervisor? Cory clearly believes that this type of behavior is inappropriate. Cory decides to informally tell the joke teller that the joke was offensive. If Cory continues to see inappropriate or offensive behavior from this employee, Cory has decided to mention the behavior to the department supervisor and request diversity training for the department.

Companies are attempting to better address workplace diversity through several actions. First, they are developing **diversity statements.** These statements remind employees that diversity in the workplace is an asset and not a form of prejudice and stereotyping. Secondly, companies are providing **diversity training** to teach employees how to eliminate workplace discrimination and harassment. This training applies to all employees, customers, and vendors. Thirdly, they are eliminating the **glass ceiling** and **glass walls.** These are invisible barriers that frequently make executive positions (glass ceiling) and certain work areas such as a golf course (glass wall) off limits to females and minorities. A glass ceiling stops females and minorities from advancing up the corporate ladder through promotions. Glass walls are barriers that prevent females and minorities from certain situations. Finally, proactive companies offer formal mentoring programs to assist in identifying and training women and minorities for promotion opportunities. People should not receive special treatment because they are female or a minority, but they should be given an equal opportunity. The employer is responsible for hiring the most qualified candidate.

CULTURAL DIFFERENCES

Our society is a mix of individuals from all over the world. For this reason, it is important to address cultural differences and its impact on the workplace. Cultural differences include, among other things, religious influences and the treatment of individuals based on age, gender, and family influences.

There are many different religions in the world. Although most major U.S. holidays are based around Christian holidays, not everyone who works in the United States is a Christian. Individuals who do not share your religious values are afforded the same rights as you. As mentioned earlier in this chapter, the Civil Rights Act protects individuals from discrimination based on religion. Everyone is entitled to observe his or her respective religious holidays and traditions. Once again, we must be respectful of everyone's individual religious beliefs and not condemn someone for his or her religious difference. Although an individual's religious beliefs may permeate every element of his or her life, as with other issues of diversity, if religion negatively impacts performance, the issue must be addressed.

Some countries have self-centered cultures, while other countries put what is best for society as a priority over personal needs. In some cultures, women and children are often not treated as equals to men. Although we may not agree with this treatment, we have to respect cultural differences. It is important to understand these differences so you do not offend others. For example, some hand gestures that are commonly used in the United States may be offensive to someone who has come from another country. If you feel you may have offended someone based upon a cultural difference, find out what behavior offended the other person, apologize if necessary, and make sure you do not repeat the offensive behavior.

Cultural differences have both a positive and negative impact on business. Learning about other cultures can provide insights into new markets and stimulate creativity. With so much diversity among employees and customers, knowing other cultures will result in improved relationships. Outcomes can be negative when companies do not properly train and address cultural differences; this is when opportunities for prejudice and discrimination may emerge.

WORKPLACE DOS AND DON'TS

Do always behave in an ethical manner	*Don't* behave one way at work and another around your friends
Do keep information confidential	*Don't* break the company's trust
Do recognize and increase your workplace power bases	*Don't* use your workplace power in a harmful or unethical manner
Do know your rights regarding workplace diversity	*Don't* accept defeat in discriminatory situations
Do learn to respect differences in others	*Don't* use your minority status to take advantage of situations
Do be proud of your culture and heritage	*Don't* show prejudice toward others
Do take responsibility for increasing awareness about workplace diversity issues	*Don't* label people

CONCEPT REVIEW AND APPLICATION
Summary of Key Concepts

- Personal ethical behavior is a reflection of the influences of friends, family, religion, and society

- Do not share confidential information with individuals with whom the business is of no concern

- Power and power bases are effective tools to use in the workplace

- Be cautious to not use power and reciprocity in an unethical manner

- A conflict of interest occurs when you are in a position to influence a decision from which you could benefit directly or indirectly

- No matter what our differences, treat everyone with respect and professionalism

- Title VII of the Civil Rights Act prohibits discrimination based on sex, religion, race or color, or national origin

- Diversity should be used as an asset that utilizes our differences as ways to create, innovate, and compete

- Workplace diversity should only be an issue when the diversity negatively affects performance

Key Terms

charismatic power
coercive power
confidential
conflict of interest
connection power
culture
diversity statements
diversity training
ethics
ethics statement
expert power
glass ceiling
glass wall
implied confidentiality
information power

labeling
legitimate power
levels of ethical decisions
networking
perception
politics
power
prejudice
race
reciprocity
reward power
stereotyping
workplace discrimination
workplace diversity

If You Were the Boss

1. You have just been promoted to boss. What are the first five things you should do?

2. What is the best method of dealing with an ethical decision regarding the performance of an employee?

3. What would you do if you noticed an employee treating another employee in a discriminatory manner?

4. What can you do to minimize workplace discrimination and harassment?

Learn More

To learn more about subjects addressed in this chapter take an Introduction to Sociology class and/or a Business Ethics class

Video Case Study: Making Ethical Choices

Two employees are having a conversation at work. This video shows two different ethical perspectives. Go to *MyProfessionalismKit* or your course website, watch this video, and answer the following questions:

1. Are either of the characters in this video demonstrating unethical behavior? If so, what are the specific unethical behaviors?

2. Is Brian's ethical behavior Regina's business? Why or why not?

3. How does the ethics test apply to this scenario?

4. What should the company be doing to address the situation?

Web Links

http://www.discriminationattorney.com/eeocdfeh.shtml
http://www.managementhelp.org/ethics/ethics.htm
http://www.dol.gov

http://www.dol.gov/dol/topic/discrimination/index.htm
http://www.executiveplanet.com

References

Etzioni, Amitai. *Comparative Analysis of Complex Organizations*, 4–6. (New York: The Free Press), 1961, 4–6.

French, John R. P., and Bertram Raven. "The Bases of Social Power." In *Studies in Social Power*, (Ann Arbor: University of Michigan Press, 1959), 150–67.

Kotter, John P. "Power, Dependence and Effective Management." *Harvard Business Review* (July–August 1977): 131–36.

Peale, Norman V., and Kenneth Blanchard. *The Power of Ethical Management*, (New York: William Morrow, 1988).

ACTIVITIES

Activity 4-5

Is it ever ethical to take paper clips, copy paper, and pens home from work?

Yes ☐   No ☐   Sometimes ☐

Support your answer.

_____

_____

Activity 4-6

Research a company's conflict of interest policy.

Name of company: _____

Policy: _____

_____

What would you add to the policy to make it better?

_____

What would you eliminate?

_____

What should you do if you work for a company that does not have a policy?

_____

_____

Activity 4-7

List a time when you overheard confidential information that should not have been shared—for example, sitting in a physician's office or overhearing a private conversation while shopping.

_____

_____

How should this situation have been better handled?

_____

_____

Activity 4-8

Identify at least three potential areas for employee theft on a small scale.

1. _____

2. _____

3. _____

4. _____

Identify at least two potential areas for employee theft on a large scale.

1. _____

_____

2. _____

Activity 4-9

In the United States, the thumbs-up symbol communicates a job well done. Research and identify what the thumbs-up symbol communicates in at least two other countries. What did this activity teach you about various cultures and hand gestures?

Country	Meaning

Conclusion: What did you learn?

_____

_____

Activity 4-10

Identify a recent experience or observed act of prejudice. How would you have handled the situation differently?

Act of Prejudice	How You Would Handle the Situation?

Activity 4-11

With a partner, dialogue what you would say if someone offended you with a joke. Was this dialogue easy? Why or why not? Share your findings with your class.

_____

_____

SAMPLE EXAM QUESTIONS

1. _____ is a moral standard of right and wrong.

2. _____ is your obligation to not share information with individuals with whom the business is of no concern.

3. Everyone at work has some _____. The difference is that some people understand this ability to _____ and use it appropriately.

4. _____ means creating debts and obligations for doing something.

5. A/An _____ occurs when you are in a position to influence a decision from which you could benefit directly or indirectly.

6. The first question for ethical decision making is: Is it _____?

7. The second question for ethical decision making is: Is it _____?

8. The third question for ethical decision making is: How does it _____?

9. Differences among coworkers are referred to as _____.

10. _____ is a group of individuals with certain physical traits, while _____ are different behavior patterns of various groups.

11. Companies provide _____ to teach employees how to eliminate workplace discrimination and harassment.

Etiquette/Dress

Objectives

- Describe and discuss the importance of professional behavior in your career
- State the impact dress can have on others' perception of you
- Demonstrate a professional and correct introduction and handshake
- Demonstrate appropriate professional behavior in business dining situations
- Recognize and apply the appropriate use of technology in business/social situations
- Utilize professional *etiquette* in appropriate business situations

EXECUTIVE PRESENCE

THE WAY YOU LOOK AND BEHAVE IS A REFLECTION OF THE ORGANIZATION FOR WHICH YOU work. **Executive presence** is defined as having the attitude of an executive. Projecting an executive presence is important because one of the biggest concerns employers have when hiring are new employees' lack of knowledge regarding basic workplace behavior.

The purpose of this chapter is to provide basics regarding expected professional behavior on topics including attire, social etiquette, dining, and the appropriate use of technology. There is a reminder of what many of our parents taught us early in life that some have forgotten, such as smiling and saying please and thank-you. You will encounter many of these social situations daily at work, while other situations may not be as common. Knowing how to behave in the social situations presented is important.

Some of this information may be new to you, and you may feel awkward when you first implement these positive behaviors. The purpose of this chapter is to prepare you for many of the social experiences you will face in the workplace. Practice makes perfect.

INFLUENCES OF DRESS IN A PROFESSIONAL ENVIRONMENT

BOTH YOUR MATURITY AND THE IMPORTANCE YOU PLACE ON YOUR JOB ARE REFLECTED IN the way you behave and dress at work. Because impressions are often made in the first few minutes of meeting someone, individuals rarely have time to even speak before an impression is made. The majority of first impressions are made through your visual **appearance**, which is how you look. Coworkers, bosses, and customers form attitudes based on your appearance. Appearance has an impact on how you perform at work. If you dress professionally, you are more apt to act in a professional manner. The more casual you dress, the more casual you tend to behave. Think of your appearance as a frame. A frame is used to highlight a picture. You do not want the frame to be too fancy, because it will take away from the picture. You want a frame to complement the picture. This appearance frame highlights not only your physical features, including your face, but also your attitude, knowledge, and potential.

One of the toughest transitions to make when entering the workplace is appropriate dress. Dressing professionally does not have to conflict with current fashion trends. The trick is to know what is acceptable. A basic rule of thumb is to make it a habit to dress one position higher than your current position (i.e., dress like your boss). Doing so communicates that you are serious about your career and how you represent the company. Dressing professionally will assist you in projecting a favorable image at work and position you for advancement.

Know your workplace dress policies. One of the first steps to determining appropriate attire for work is to identify your company's **dress code.** A dress code is a policy that addresses issues such as required attire, uniforms, hairstyle, undergarments, jewelry, and shoes. Many organizations have policies regarding appropriate workplace attire for customer service, safety, and security reasons. Frequently, these policies are included in the employee handbook. If there is no policy, ask your boss if there is a formal dress code and secure a copy. An important cue to workplace attire is how managers dress. Suits are not always the preferred attire. In some situations, pants are acceptable for women, while in other situations they are not. Note that sweats (shirts and/or pants) are not appropriate for work.

Once you have identified what your organization considers proper attire, begin to create a **work wardrobe.** These are clothes that you primarily wear only to work and work-related functions. You need not invest a lot of money when building a work wardrobe. Start with basic pieces and think conservative. For women, this includes a simple, solid skirt or pantsuit in a dark color and a blazer. Skirts should not be above the knee. Pants should only be worn with a matching blazer. For most office environments, men should select dark slacks, a matching jacket, and a tie. Frequently, these items can be found inexpensively at thrift and discount stores. If these items are purchased at a thrift store, take them to the dry cleaners for cleaning and pressing. You will be surprised how professional these items will look after they are cleaned and pressed. Select items that are made of quality fabrics that will not wear out quickly. Purchase items that fit properly and are comfortable. As you begin to earn money, continue building your wardrobe and develop a style that conforms to both company policy and your taste.

Talk It Out Name local places where you can buy professional attire at a low cost.

TIPS FROM HEAD TO TOE

Regardless of the company's dress code, practice these basic hygiene rules:

- *Shower daily.*

    If needed, use deodorant. If you wear perfume, lotion, or cologne use it sparingly. Scent should not be overpowering.

- *Clothes should be clean and ironed, not torn or tattered, and they should fit properly.*

- *Hair should be clean, well kept, and a natural color.*

    Your hairstyle should reflect your profession. Fad hairstyles and unnatural color are inappropriate in many workplaces.

- *Hands and nails should be well groomed, clean, and trim.*

    Nails that are too long are inappropriate. Women, if you use polish, it should be neat and color/artwork conservative.

- *Jewelry should be kept to a minimum.*

    Jewelry should complement your outfit. Do not wear anything that is distracting or that makes noise.

- *Shoes should be in good condition.*

    Keep your shoes polished and free of scuffs. Flip-flops are not appropriate for the workplace. Men, sock color should match shoe or pant color. Women, heels should be in good condition; if not, get them repaired or replaced. Heels should not be too high. Nylons should be free of runs and snags.

A woman's outfit should be a reflection of her style and personality—within reason. When dressing for work, your goal is to appropriately frame yourself in a manner that draws attention to your face (i.e., your brains and inner beauty). Additional tips for women include the following:

- *Makeup should be for day wear.*

    Makeup is appropriate for work. Makeup that makes people think you are going to a bar after work is not. Do not wear heavy eyeliner, eye shadow in colors that draw attention, or lipstick in bold colors.

- *It is not acceptable to wear suggestive clothing.*

    This means no cleavage or bare midriffs. No matter the current fashion trends, undergarments (bras, panties, and thongs) should not be visible. Remember, skirts should not be above the knee.

Just like a woman's outfit, a man's outfit should be a reflection of his style and personality. For some positions, a suit may not be appropriate. The biggest wardrobe blunder men make is wearing clothing that is not clean and/or pressed. After checking with your company's dress code, heed these unspoken rules regarding professional dress at work for men:

- *Shave and/or trim facial hair, including nose and ear hair.*

- *In an office environment, dress pants are the only pants that are professional.*

    With the exception of casual workdays, jeans are inappropriate. Baggy pants that reveal underwear are also inappropriate. Whenever possible, wear a neutral, plain belt that does not draw attention.

Talk It Out When or when not is it appropriate for a woman to be sleeveless in a professional setting?

What do you have?

Take inventory of your current wardrobe.

_____

_____

List clothing you own that you can use for your professional wardrobe.

_____

_____

List the necessities that you are missing.

_____

_____

- *Shirts should be tucked in.*

  A polo shirt or a dress shirt with a tie is best. Shirts should not display excessive wear (check around the collar line). Shirts with inappropriate logos or offensive phrases should not be worn at work.

- *Hats should not be worn inside buildings except for religious purposes.*

JEWELRY, BODY PIERCING, AND TATTOOS

ALTHOUGH BODY ART, PIERCING, AND BODY RINGS/JEWELRY APPEAR TO BE CURRENT fads, they are offensive to some individuals. For this reason, it is important that you check with your company regarding its policies. However, in general:

- Nose rings, lip rings, and/or tongue rings are not professional and should not be worn in a professional setting.

- Any other body piercing/body jewelry should not be visible at work.

- More than two earrings worn on each ear is considered unprofessional.

- Earrings, chains, and other jewelry should not draw attention. This includes symbols or words that could be considered offensive to others.

- Body art (tattoos) should not be visible at work. If you are thinking about getting a tattoo, consider the long-term consequences. They are painful and expensive to remove and are designed to last a lifetime.

CASUAL WORKDAYS AND SPECIAL EVENTS

MANY COMPANIES ALLOW CASUAL WORKDAYS. THESE ARE DAYS WHEN COMPANIES relax their dress code. Unfortunately, too many employees attempt to stretch the term *casual*. If your company has a casual workday, remember that you are still at work and should dress appropriately. Of course, you can wear jeans if jeans are the preferred attire; just adhere to the *head-to-toe tips* recently presented. Do not wear clothing that is tattered, stained, or torn (even if it is considered stylish). Avoid wearing shirts with sayings or graphics that may offend others.

Your company may also play host or invite you to attend a special function. Holiday parties and receptions are such examples. In these situations, instead of daily work attire, more formal attire may be required. Just as with casual workdays, stick with the basics provided in the *head-to-toe tips*. Women, if appropriate, should wear something in a more formal fabric. Although you have increased freedom and flexibility regarding style and length, this is still a work-related function, so remember to dress conservatively and not suggestively. Men, check ahead of time and see if tuxedos are preferred. Although seldom required these days, if a tuxedo is required, you may need to rent one. For most semi-formal occasions, a suit will suffice.

As a reward for winning Employee of the Month, Cory was invited to attend a one-day conference/luncheon with several managers from Cory's company. Cory had not attended a function like this before and was a little nervous about how to dress and behave in this new business situation. Cory did some preparation and found that dress and behavior are as important in public situations as they are at work. Cory checked with others who had attended these functions and decided dressing more formal would be most appropriate. Cory made sure to shower, clean and trim fingernails, wear polished shoes, and not wear inappropriate jewelry.

Talk It Out Identify people in class who are wearing something appropriate for a casual workday.

BUSINESS ETIQUETTE

IN A MODERN WORKPLACE, HUMAN INTERACTION IS UNAVOIDABLE. OUR SOCIETY HAS A standard of social behavior that is called **etiquette.** Typically, when individuals think of etiquette, they think it only applies to the wealthy, high society. This is not true. Socially acceptable behavior should penetrate all demographic and economic groups. Individuals wanting to succeed in the workplace need to heed this protocol and consistently utilize it not only at work but in all areas of their life.

Before we study common areas of business etiquette, we need to define a few terms. Understanding these terms and integrating them into your daily routine will make it much easier to carry out the desired and appropriate workplace behavior. The first word is **courtesy.** When you display courtesy, you are exercising manners, respect, and consideration toward others. The second word is **respect.** Respect is defined as holding someone in high regard. This means putting others' needs before your own needs. Displaying both courtesy and respect toward others are the keys in becoming ladies and gentlemen at work.

Some of the first words parents teach young children are *please* and *thank-you*. Although they are not used as frequently as they should be, both are extremely powerful words that can actually create power for you at work. Think about it; when someone says "please" and "thank-you" to you, you are more likely to repeat a favor or gesture because your deed was acknowledged. When someone does something nice, verbally say "thank-you." Not doing so makes you appear selfish and unappreciative. When you express thanks, individuals will be more likely to continue performing kind acts for you.

Make it a habit to write a thank-you note when someone does something for you that takes more than five minutes or when someone gives you a gift. Do not wait more than three days to write the thank-you note. Write the note as soon as possible. Always send a thank-you note within twenty-four hours of completing a job interview, and remember to send thank-you notes to individuals who agree to be job references for you.

In addition to saying "please" and "thank-you," do not underestimate the value of a simple smile and eye contact. If you have a positive attitude, it will be reflected in your demeanor. When encountering people in the hallways, elevators, and/or meeting rooms, make eye contact, smile, and greet them.

At times, you will be with individuals who do not know each other. When you are with two people who do not know each other and you know both people, it is your responsibility to introduce the two individuals to each other. Politely introduce the least important person to the most important person. For example, "Roger, this is Tim Wilson, the president of our company." "Tim, this is Roger Hue, my next-door neighbor." Apply this introduction rule to all social situations including dining, meetings, receptions, and parties.

A daily function of business is making and keeping appointments. Sometimes you will be required to work with receptionists and/or administrative assistants to schedule these appointments. Be kind to the receptionist and/or administrative assistant. These individuals are the gatekeepers to their bosses; they control schedules and often wield great power in decisions. When scheduling an appointment, state your name, the purpose of the meeting, and the desired date and time. If possible, avoid scheduling appointments on Monday mornings. Many use Monday mornings to schedule their own week and are less likely to accommodate you. If you will be arriving late to an appointment, call and let the other party know you are running late. If you must cancel an appointment, do so immediately and apologize for any inconvenience. Do not just ignore an appointment. When keeping an appointment, arrive five minutes early. After you enter the office, greet the receptionist and politely introduce yourself. State whom you have an appointment with and the time of the meeting. When entering an office for a meeting, wait to be invited to sit down. After the meeting, extend a handshake and thank the individual for his or her time.

Talk It Out Discuss ways you can be courteous and respectful in class.

HANDSHAKES

A GOOD HANDSHAKE CONVEYS CONFIDENCE. MAKE A HABIT OF GREETING OTHERS IN business situations with a professional handshake and greeting. Approach the individual you are greeting and extend your right hand as you verbalize a greeting. For example, "Hello Ms. Jones, my name is Danielle. We met at last week's meeting. It's nice to see you again." Ms. Jones will extend her right hand. Your two hands should meet at the web (see Figure 4-1). Grip the other person's hand and gently squeeze and shake hands.

- Do not squeeze the other hand too firmly.
- Make certain you shake the entire hand and not just the other person's fingers. Doing so is insulting and implies that you feel you are better than the other person.
- Do not place your hand on top of the other person's hand or pat the hand. Doing so is insulting.
- If your palms are sweaty, discretely wipe your palm on the side of your hip prior to shaking.

Make eye contact and smile while extending your hand. A good handshake takes practice. As mentioned earlier, get into the habit of being the first to greet and introduce yourself to others. At first you may not feel comfortable, but practice makes perfect. The more frequently you initiate a good handshake, the more comfortable and confident you will become.

Figure 4.1 Proper
Handshake

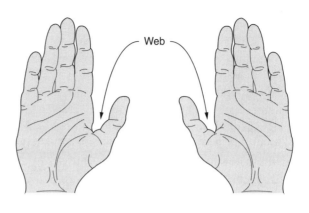

Exercise 4-13 **Shake Hands**

Pair up with a classmate and practice initiating an introduction making sure to include a professional handshake. Rate the quality of the introduction and handshake on a scale of 1 to 5 with 5 being the best. Discuss what improvements should be made.

DINING

In business, you will encounter a variety of dining situations. Some dining experiences will be less formal than others. You will most likely encounter some form of the table setting illustrated in Figure 4-2. Take time to study and review a common place setting to help you understand proper use for utensils, plates, and cups. Apart from fast food, few college students are generally comfortable eating in a formal dining situation. Here are several rules of thumb regarding dining etiquette:

- As soon are you are seated, place your napkin on your lap. If you need to leave the table, place your napkin to the side of your plate instead of on your chair.

- Utensils are set to be used in order of necessity. As your courses are served, start with the outside utensil and work in, toward the plate. The utensils set at the top of the plate are for your dessert.

- When serving coffee, water, tea, or any other beverage available at the table, first offer and serve others at your table.

- Do not order anything expensive or messy.

1	napkin
2	plate
3	salad fork
4	dinner fork
5	dinner knife
6	teaspoon
7	soup spoon
8	salad plate
9	bread plate
10	butter knife
11	dessert spoon
12	dessert fork
13	water glass
14	beverage/wine glass
15	coffee cup and saucer

Figure 4.2 Table Setting

- Do not order alcohol unless others at your table first order an alcoholic beverage. Abstaining from alcohol is the most desired behavior. If you choose to drink, limit consumption to one drink.

- When bread is available, first offer bread to others at your table before taking a piece.

- Place your bread on the bread plate (located at the top left corner of your dinner plate). Place your serving of butter on the bread plate. Do not butter the entire piece of bread at one time. Tear a piece of bread, and butter only that piece of bread before eating.

- Do not take the last piece of bread or appetizer unless it is first offered to others at your table.

- When your meal arrives, do not begin eating until everyone at your table has been served. If everyone receives their meals except you (you are the last to be served), give others at your table permission to begin eating without you so that their food does not get cold. Eat your meal at the same pace as others at the table.

- Do not eat your meal with your fingers unless your main course can be eaten without utensils.

- Burping and slurping are inappropriate while dining. If you accidentally burp or slurp, make sure you immediately apologize and say "excuse me."

- When you are finished eating, place your knife and fork together, with the blade facing in and the tines up. When you are only resting and you do not want the server to take your plate away, cross your utensils with the tines facing down.

- It is inappropriate to use a mobile communication device while dining. If you must take a call or text, excuse yourself from the table.

Talk It Out Share common dining and social situations that make you uncomfortable and identify how best to deal with these situations.

When Cory arrived at the conference, Cory was glad to be dressed professionally. Everyone there was dressed as a business professional. Cory was introduced to many business professionals. Cory was sure to make eye contact, smile, and properly shake hands when meeting new people. Cory was also careful to follow dining etiquette during lunch. At work the next day, Cory immediately wrote a thank-you note to the managers forbeing included in the event. At the end of the day, Cory's manager invited Cory into the office and let Cory know what a great impression Cory made at the conference. Several colleagues had mentioned to Cory's manager how impressed they were with Cory's professionalism. Cory realized that doing a little research and being professional was well worth the effort.

A major area of business involves attending social functions. Many invitations request an RSVP, which is French for *répondez s'il vous plaît* (i.e., please respond). As soon as you receive an invitation, send a reply—whether it is an acceptance to attend or a regret that you cannot attend. Not acknowledging the invitation and failing to respond is rude.

When you attend a social function, remember that you are attending the function to meet and network with other professionals, not to receive your last meal.

Web Quiz Rate your workplace etiquette.

http://www.emilypost.com/business/business_ei_quiz.htm

- Refrain from or limit the consumption of alcohol.
- Serve yourself a small plate of hors d'oeuvres and move away from the food table.
- Hold your hors d'oeuvres in your left hand, leaving your right hand free to shake hands and greet others.
- Do not talk with food in your mouth.

TECHNOLOGY AT WORK

TEXTING, CELL PHONE USAGE, MESSAGES, VOICE MAIL, E-MAILS, PORTABLE ENTERTAINMENT devices—it all gets so confusing! This section provides basic rules for the appropriate use of technology-based communications in the workplace.

Mobile (Portable) Communication Devices

Today's business environment relies on current technologies to improve communication. This is achieved through the use of mobile (portable) communication devices. Common devices include cell phones, personal digital assistants (PDAs), portable music/entertainment devices (e.g., iPODs), and wireless computers. While the use of these important business tools is acceptable in selected business situations, it is important that all employees be aware of the proper etiquette regarding the use of these devices.

Mobile devices should not be seen or heard in public. Therefore, turn off or silence your device when attending a meeting (business or nonbusiness related). If you are anticipating an important call/message, if possible, inform the leader of the meeting and explain that you are expecting an important call or message. When the call or message is received, quietly step out of the meeting to respond to the call/message. It is rude to use your communication device while dining or while attending meetings or performances.

It is not polite to take calls in front of others. Doing so implies that the individuals you are with are not important. When taking a call, excuse yourself and step away for privacy. Finally, when interacting with others, it is inappropriate to use or display portable music/entertainment devices in the workplace unless the device provides quiet background music appropriate for a professional workplace.

Text messaging etiquette is equally as important when using portable communication devices. Many students utilize text slang, text shorthand, acronyms, and codes. The use of these styles is not appropriate for formal and informal business communications. In the workplace, texting should only be used for brief, informal communications, utilizing proper spelling. Just as with other portable communication devices, it is not appropriate and is considered rude behavior to view and send text messages while with others (including discreetly during meetings).

Phone Etiquette

The phone is clearly one of the most common workplace communication tools. Phone etiquette, whether land line or wireless, is one topic that every individual must practice to create and maintain a professional image for his or her company. Because the individual(s) on the other end of the phone cannot see you, it is important for you to communicate properly through the words you choose, your tone of voice, the pitch of your voice, and your rate of speech.

Convey a positive, friendly attitude when speaking on the phone. Smiling when you speak creates a friendly tone. Speak clearly and slowly, and do not speak too softly or too loudly.

Phone calls are for brief interactions. If you expect the discussion to be lengthy, ask the individual on the other end of the line if he or she has time to talk or if he or she prefer you call at a more convenient time. When you are having a phone conversation, do not eat or tend to personal matters.

Speakerphones are useful communication tools for specific situations and require proper etiquette. A speakerphone should only be used when you are on a conference call with other participants in the same room or when you require a handsfree device. Only use a speakerphone when you are in a private room where your call will not be distracting to others in your work area. When you use a speakerphone, ask individuals included in the call for permission to use the speakerphone. If all parties agree, alert those included in the call that others are in the room with you and make introductions. This ensures confidentiality and open communication between all parties. Those using a speakerphone should be aware that any small noise he or she makes may be heard and distracting to those on the other end of the line.

When answering a phone call, answer by the second ring. Taking a call in the presence of others implies that the individual in your presence is not important. When with others let the call go into voice mail. If you are expecting an important call and are in the presence of others, inform those you are with that you are expecting a call and will need to take it when it arrives. When the call is received, politely excuse yourself. If you are in your office, politely ask your office guest to excuse you for one moment while you quickly take the call. If you take a call and need to place the caller on hold, politely tell the individual on the phone that you are placing him or her on hold. If an individual is placed on hold for more than 1 minute, get back on the line and ask if you can return the call.

Voice mail messages are a routine part of conducting business. A voice mail impression is equally as important as how you answer in person. Keep voice mail messages brief. State your name, purpose of the call and return number at the beginning of the message. Speak slowly and clearly. After you have left your message, repeat your name and return number a second time at the end of the call. When you receive voice mail messages, it is proper and important to promptly return all messages left for you. Routinely check and empty your voice mail box.

On both portable and land-line phones, it is important that you keep your voice mail greeting professional. Cute voice mail greetings are not professional. Musical introductions or bad jokes do not form favorable impressions when employers or customers are attempting to contact you.

E-Mail and Computer Usage

In addition to all other workplace tools and equipment, your work computer is the property of the company. Therefore, only use it for company business. This includes Internet use and electronic messaging.

When composing or responding to e-mails, emoticons (faces made and embedded in e-mail messages) are inappropriate. Include the business subject in the subject line to let the receiver know your message is not junk e-mail or a virus. The subject "hello" or "hi" is not appropriate. Check all outgoing messages for spelling and grammar. Do not send e-mail messages with large and colorful letters or all capital letters. This is interpreted as yelling and is considered rude. Carefully proofread and think about a message before you press reply to ensure that it cannot be interpreted improperly.

If you receive a work-related message that requires a reply, respond to the message. Ignoring a message is rude; it communicates to the sender that you do not care. You also run the risk of being excluded from future messages. Do not forward messages that do not involve work-related issues. Routinely clean and empty your e-mail box.

Talk It Out Do you agree with the technology communication rules of etiquette? Why or why not?

OTHER ETIQUETTE BASICS

- *Knock before entering an office.*

   Do not enter an office until you are invited. If the individual you want to see is with someone else, politely wait your turn. If the matter is urgent, apologize for interrupting.

- *Put others first.*

   When you are with colleagues and you are taking turns (in line, to order, etc.), allow your colleagues to go first.

- *Interruptions.*

   In today's society, we have so many inputs trying to attract our attention. As a result, we often get anxious to share our point of view in a conversation and fail to allow others in the conversation to complete their sentence. Show others respect by not interrupting conversations. If you accidentally interrupt someone, immediately apologize and ask him or her to continue his or her statement.

- *Apologies*.

    Everyone is human. Therefore, everyone makes mistakes. When you realize that you may have said or done something hurtful to someone, apologize immediately. Apologizing is not a sign of weakness; it is a sign of strength and maturity. Even if you are not sure whether you have offended someone, apologize to avoid any potential misunderstandings. However, do not unnecessarily and continually apologize. Doing so not only gives you the appearance of being needy and insecure, more importantly you are not being assertive and possibly not standing up for your rights in an unoffending manner.

- *Profanity*.

    This type of language does not belong in the workplace. Do not assume others are comfortable with profanity. Conversations should be professional and respectful.

- *Dominating a conversation*.

    There is a key to carrying on a successful conversation. The key is listening. Listening means that you value the information the other individual is providing. Too frequently, individuals dominate a conversation with their own personal accounts. In general, this is not appropriate. This behavior becomes annoying to the listener when you turn the conversation to yourself. Next time you are in a conversation, listen to how many times you state the words *me*, *I*, and *my*. Try to minimize the use of these words in your conversation.

WORKPLACE DOS AND DON'TS

Do wear professional clothes to work	*Don't* wear sweats, tennis shoes, or suggestive apparel at work
Do shower and make sure you are always clean	*Don't* overdo the cologne (or any body sprays)
Do make eye contact and offer a gentle but firm handshake	*Don't* grasp just the fingers when shaking hands
Do follow formal dining etiquette at work-related functions	*Don't* reach, grab, or overload your plate at the hors d'oeuvres table
Do say "please" and "thank-you" when appropriate	*Don't* assume that the other person knows you are thankful for his or her act of kindness

CONCEPT REVIEW AND APPLICATION

Summary of Key Concepts

- Projecting an executive presence is important in demonstrating knowledge of basic workplace behavior

- The majority of first impressions are made through visual appearances

- Both your maturity and the importance you place on your job are reflected in the way you behave and dress at work

- Begin to create a work wardrobe today

- Visual body art/piercing and body rings/jewelry are offensive to some individuals and are not appropri-ate in a professional work environment. Consider the long-term consequences of getting a tattoo or piercing

- Follow business etiquette protocol and consistently utilize it in all areas of your life

- Make a habit of thanking individuals either verbally or in writing

- Appropriate etiquette at social functions and while dining is as important as professional behavior at work

Key Terms

appearance

casual workdays

courtesy

dress code

etiquette

executive presence

respect

work wardrobe

If You Were the Boss

1. As the manager of a bank, one of your employees comes in on a Monday morning with a pierced tongue and purple hair. What should you do?

2. You have just hired a new employee who clearly has no concept of business etiquette. What specific steps would you take to teach your new employee how to behave professionally?

Learn More

To learn more about subjects addressed in this chapter attend a workshop on Business Etiquette.

Video Case Study: Dress for Success

This video presents expert advice on how to dress professionally at work. Go to *MyProfessionalismKit* or your course website, watch this video, and answer the following questions.

1. What specifically are Franchesca and Brad wearing that makes their appearance professional?

2. What four items make Patricia's and Brian's appearance unprofessional?

3. What specific advice does the expert provide for looking professional regarding make-up, tattoos, jewelry, jeans, hair, and shoes?

Video Case Study: Business Lunch Etiquette

This video addresses a common business lunch sales meeting. Go to MyProfessionalismKit or your course website, watch this video, and answer the following questions:

1. Name three things Brian did right or wrong?
2. What advice would you give Brian?
3. Midway through this lunch, how should Karen have handled this situation?

Web Links

http://www.ravenwerks.com/practices/etiquette.htm
http://www.youngmoney.com/careers//onthejob/149

http://www.letstalk.com/promo/unclecell/
unclecell2.htm

Reference

Post, Peggy, and Peter Post. *The Etiquette Advantage in Business: Personal Skills for Professional Success*. New York: Harper-
Collins Publishers, 1999.

ACTIVITIES

Activity 4-12

Assume you are starting a new job as an accounting clerk next week. You need a work wardrobe and are limited to a $50 budget. Make a list of what you need and could buy to get you through your first week of work. Include the cost.

What You Need to Buy	Cost
	$
Total Cost	**$50**

Prior to being faced with this scenario, what items can you purchase today to begin building your professional wardrobe?

Activity 4-13

Pretend you are at a business reception and you do not know anyone else in the room. Role-play formal introductions with a classmate, and then evaluate your partner's performance by identifying strengths and weaknesses.

STUDENT NAME	
Strengths	Weaknesses
STUDENT NAME	
Strengths	Weaknesses

Activity 4-14

Visit a (non-fast-food) restaurant to practice proper dining etiquette. While you are doing so, identify five acts of inappropriate behavior others are exhibiting.

Inappropriate Behavior	Why Behavior Is Inappropriate
1.	
2.	
3.	
4.	
5.	

SAMPLE EXAM QUESTIONS

1. The majority of first impressions are made by _____ _____.

2. One of the first steps to determining appropriate attire for work is to identify _____ .

3. Give five tips for women for dressing professionally from head to toe. _____, _____, _____, _____, _____.

4. Give five tips for men for dressing professionally from head to toe. _____, _____, _____,

5. A standard of social behavior is called _____ _____ .

6. When someone does something nice for you, you should _____.

7. A good handshake conveys _____ _____ .

8. Give five rules of thumb regarding dining etiquette. _____, _____, _____, _____, _____

_____, _____.

Chapter 5
Personal Selling and the Marketing Concept

Learning Objectives

After studying this chapter, you should be able to

1 Define *personal selling* and describe the three prescriptions of a personal selling philosophy

2 Describe the contributions of personal selling to the information economy

3 Discuss personal selling as an extension of the marketing concept

4 Describe the evolution of consultative selling from the marketing era to the present

5 Define *strategic selling* and name the four broad strategic areas in the Strategic/Consultative Selling Model

6 Describe the evolution of partnering and the nature of a strategic selling alliance

7 Explain how value-added selling strategies enhance personal selling

 Reality Selling Today Video Series

Successful salespeople who sell financial services products—such as those employed by Manulife Financial, London Life, Sun Life Financial, or State Farm—are masters of consultative selling. Marcus Smith (see page 105), one of the most productive sales representatives of Liberty Mutual (**www.libertymutual.com**), uses the consultative selling approach exclusively. He believes that excellence in selling starts with an in-depth understanding of what customers value most and working closely with customers to satisfy their needs.

Founded in 1912, Liberty Mutual is an important player in the highly competitive insurance market. The three pillars of the company's culture consist of behaving with integrity, treating people with dignity and respect, and providing superior products and services. Smith is a strong believer of those corporate values. Yet implementing this relationship-oriented selling approach represents a challenge, given the constraints of resources and the competitive intensity of the insurance market. Smith's strategy is simple yet effective: placing emphasis on tracking and forecasting market information, focusing on identifying profitable customers, and directing resources to those customers.

Smith does not start conversations with his new customers with a sales pitch. Instead, he spends time building rapport with the customer—for example, finding some areas that he and his customers have in common. These icebreakers go a long way toward making the customers comfortable sharing with Smith what their actual needs are. Then he presents a balanced comparison between his offers and those of competitors. Being empathetic and honest with the customer lies at the heart of consultative selling.

PERSONAL SELLING—A DEFINITION AND A PHILOSOPHY

PERSONAL SELLING OCCURS WHEN A COMPANY REPRESENTATIVE INTERACTS DIRECTLY WITH a customer or prospective customer to present information about a product or service.[1] It is a process of developing relationships; discovering needs; matching the appropriate products with those needs; and communicating benefits through informing, reminding, or persuading. The term **product** should be broadly interpreted to encompass information, services, ideas, and issues. Increasingly, personal selling is viewed as a process that adds value. In an ideal situation the salesperson diagnoses the customer's needs and custom-fits the product to meet those needs.

Preparation for a career in personal selling begins with the development of a personal philosophy or set of beliefs that provides guidance. To some degree this philosophy is like the rudder that steers a ship. Without a rudder the ship's direction is unpredictable. Without a personal philosophy the salesperson's behaviour also is unpredictable.

The development of a **personal selling philosophy** involves three prescriptions: adopt the marketing concept, value personal selling, and assume the role of a problem solver or partner in helping customers make buying decisions. These three prescriptions for success in personal selling are presented here as part of the Strategic/Consultative Selling Model. This model is expanded in future chapters to include additional strategic steps in the selling process.

personal selling Involves person-to-person communication with a prospect. It is a process of developing relationships; discovering customer needs; matching appropriate products with those needs; and communicating benefits through informing, reminding, or persuading.

product Should be broadly interpreted to encompass physical goods, services, and ideas.

personal selling philosophy A salesperson's commitment to value personal selling, adopt the marketing concept, and become a problem solver and partner to help customers make better buying decisions.

THE STRATEGIC/CONSULTATIVE SELLING MODEL

WHEN YOU STUDY A VALUE-ADDED APPROACH TO PERSONAL SELLING THAT COMBINES strategic planning, consultative selling practices, and partnering principles, you experience a mental exercise that is similar to solving a jigsaw puzzle. You are given many pieces of information that must form a complete picture. Putting the parts together isn't difficult, however, if you can see the total picture at the beginning. Therefore, a single model has been developed to serve as a source of reference throughout the entire text. Figure 5.1 shows this model.

Strategic/Consultative Selling Model*	
Strategic step	Prescription
Develop a personal selling philosophy	• Adopt marketing concept • Value personal selling • Become a problem solver/partner
Develop a relationship strategy	• Adopt win-win philosophy • Project professional image • Maintain high ethical standards
Develop a product strategy	• Become a product expert • Sell benefits • Configure value-added solutions
Develop a customer strategy	• Understand the buying process • Understand buyer behaviour • Develop prospect base
Develop a presentation strategy	• Prepare objectives • Develop presentation plan • Provide outstanding service

* Strategic/consulative selling evolved in response to increased competition, more complex products, increased emphasis on customer needs, and the growing importance of long-term relationships.

Marketing Concept:
• coordinate all activities
• to create satisfied customers
• and achieve company goals.

Figure 5.1 The Strategic/Consultative Model is an extension of the marketing concept.

The Strategic/Consultative Selling Model features five steps, each based on three prescriptions. The first step involves the development of a personal selling philosophy. Each of the other four steps relates to a broad strategic area of personal selling. Each step makes an important and unique contribution to the selling process.

Developing a Relationship Strategy

Success in selling depends heavily on the salesperson's ability to develop, manage, and enhance interpersonal relations with the customer. People seldom buy products or services from someone they dislike or distrust. Harvey B. Mackay, founder of Mackay Envelope Corporation, says, "People don't care how much you know until they know how much you care." Most customers are more apt to discuss their needs and wants openly with a salesperson with whom they feel comfortable.

A **relationship strategy** is a well-thought-out plan for establishing, building, and maintaining quality relationships. This type of plan is essential for success in today's marketplace, which is characterized by vigorous competition, look-alike products, and customer loyalty dependent on quality relationships as well as quality products. The relationship strategy must encompass every aspect of selling, from the first contact with a prospect to servicing the sale once this prospect becomes an established customer. The relationship strategy is an integral dimension of **relationship selling**. Relationship selling is a form of personal selling that involves securing, developing, and maintaining long-term relationships with customers.[26] Increased support for relationship selling recognizes the growing importance of partnerships in selling. The primary goal of the relationship strategy is to create rapport, trust, and mutual respect, which ensures a long-term partnership. To establish this type of relationship, salespeople must *adopt a win-win philosophy— that is, if the customer wins, I win; project a professional image; and maintain high ethical standards* (see Fig. 5.1). Chapters 7, 8 and 9 provide important information on development of the relationship strategy.

Some people think that the concept of *relationships* is too soft and too emotional for a business application; these people think that it's too difficult to think about relationships in strategic terms. In fact this is not the case at all. Every salesperson can and should formulate a strategic plan that builds and enhances relationships.

Developing a Product Strategy

Products and services represent problem-solving tools. The **product strategy** is a plan that helps salespeople make correct decisions concerning the selection and positioning of products to meet identified customer needs. The three prescriptions for the product strategy are *become a product expert, sell benefits, and configure value-added solutions*. The development of a product strategy begins with a thorough study of one's product (see Fig. 5.1) using a feature–benefit analysis approach. Such product features as technical superiority, reliability, fashionableness, design integrity, or guaranteed availability should be converted to benefits that appeal to the customer. Today's high-performance salespeople strive to become product experts. Chapter 10 focuses on company, product, and competition knowledge needed by salespeople.

Product knowledge is not the only important element of a product strategy. In fact, salespeople who are too focused on selling products often fail to identify complete solu-

relationship strategy A well-thought-out plan for establishing, building, and maintaining quality relationships.

relationship selling A form of personal selling that involves securing, developing, and maintaining long-term relationships.

product strategy A well-conceived plan that emphasizes acquiring extensive product knowledge, learning to select and communicate appropriate product benefits that will appeal to the customer, and configuring value-added solutions.

tions to the customer's problem. Stephen Covey, author of the best-selling book *The 7 Habits of Highly Effective People*, says, "Diagnose before you prescribe." If the salesperson does not deeply engage the customer and fails to diagnose the problem correctly, chances are the solution recommended may not be the best one.[27]

The development of a product strategy often requires thoughtful decision making. Today's more knowledgeable customers seek a cluster of satisfactions that arise from the product itself, from the manufacturer or distributor of the product, and from the salesperson. The "new" product that customers are buying today is the sum total of the satisfactions that emerge from all three sources.

Developing a Customer Strategy

Patricia Seybold, author of *The Customer Revolution*, says we are in the midst of a profound revolution—the customer revolution. And it's bigger than the Internet revolution:

> Customers have taken control of our companies' destinies. Customers are transforming our industries. And customers' loyalty—or lack thereof—has become increasingly important. . . .[28]

Customers have become increasingly sophisticated in their buying strategies. They have come to expect value-added products and services, and long-term commitments. Selling to today's customer starts with getting on the customer's agenda and carefully identifying his or her needs, wants, and buying conditions.

customer strategy A carefully conceived plan that will result in maximum responsiveness to the customer's needs.

A **customer strategy** is a carefully conceived plan that will result in maximum responsiveness to the customer's needs. This strategy is based on the fact that success in personal selling depends, in no small measure, on the salesperson's ability to learn as much as possible about the prospect. It involves the collection and analysis of specific information on each customer. When developing a customer strategy, the salesperson should *develop an understanding of the customer's buying process, understand buyer behaviour, and develop a prospect base* (see Fig. 5.1). The first two parts of the customer strategy are introduced in Chapter 11. Suggestions concerning ways to develop a solid prospect base are discussed in Chapter 12.

The customer strategy is dictated by the needs of the customer. For example, it's best to consider relationship formation from the customer's perspective. When a *consultative* selling approach is required, the customer strategy will usually encompass a long-term relationship and ongoing collaboration. If a *transactional* approach is required, the customer strategy would not, in most cases, emphasize need assessment, problem solving, relationship building, and sales follow-up.[29]

Developing a Presentation Strategy

Typical salespeople spend about 30% of their time in actual face-to-face selling. However, the sales presentation is a critical part of the selling process. The **presentation strategy** is a well-developed plan that includes *preparing the sales presentation objectives, preparing a presentation plan that is needed to meet these objectives, and renewing one's commitment to provide outstanding customer service* (see Fig. 5.1).

The presentation strategy usually involves developing one or more objectives for each sales call. For example, a salesperson might update personal information about the customer, provide information on a new product, and close a sale during one sales call. Multiple-objective sales presentations, which are becoming more common, are discussed in Chapter 13. Presale presentation plans give salespeople the opportunity to consider those activities that take place during the sales presentation. For example, a salesperson might preplan a demonstration of product features to use when meeting with the customer. Presale planning ensures that salespeople are well organized during the sales presentation and prepared to offer outstanding service.

Interrelationship of Basic Strategies

The major strategies that form the Strategic/Consultative Selling Model are by no means independent. The relationship, product, and customer strategies all influence development of the presentation strategy (see Fig. 5.2). For example, a salesperson might develop one relationship-building tactic for use during the initial face-to-face meeting with the customer, and another for use during the negotiation of buyer resistance.

presentation strategy A well-developed plan that includes preparing the sales presentation objectives, preparing a presentation plan that is needed to meet these objectives, and renewing one's commitment to provide outstanding customer service.

Figure 5.2 The major strategies that form the Strategic/Consultative Selling Model are by no means independent of one another. The focus of each strategy is to satisfy customer needs and build quality partnerships.

Another relationship-building method might be developed for use after the sale is closed. The discovery of customer needs (part of the customer strategy) will greatly influence planning for the sales presentation.

EVOLUTION OF PARTNERING

PARTNERING BECAME A BUZZWORD IN THE 1990S, AND IN THE 2000S IT BECAME A BUSINESS reality.[30] Partnering has been driven by several economic forces. One is the demise of the product solution in several industries. When products of one company are nearly identical to those of the competition, the product strategy becomes less important than the relationship, customer, and presentation strategies. By contrast, some partnerships grow out of the need for customized products or services. Many manufacturers have formed partnerships with companies that offer flexibility in terms of product configuration, scheduling of deliveries, or some other factor.

Today's customer wants a quality product *and* a quality relationship. Salespeople willing to abandon short-term thinking and invest the time and energy needed to develop high-quality, long-term relationships with customers are greatly rewarded. A strong partnership serves as a barrier to competing salespeople who want to sell to your accounts. Salespeople who are able to build partnerships enjoy more repeat business and referrals. Keeping existing customers happy also makes a great deal of sense from an economic point of view: experts in the field of sales and marketing know that it costs four to five times more to get a new customer than to keep an existing one. Therefore, even small increases in customer retention can result in major increases in profits.[31]

partnering A strategically developed, long-term relationship that solves the customer's problems.

Partnering is a strategically developed, long-term relationship that solves the customer's problems. A successful long-term partnership is achieved when the salesperson is able to skilfully apply the four major strategies and, thus, add value in various ways (Fig. 5.3). Successful sales professionals stay close to the customer and constantly search for new ways to add value.

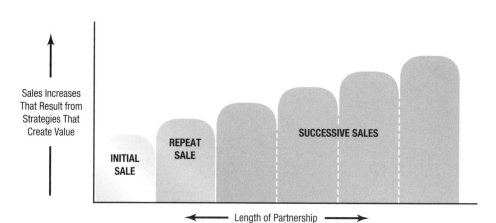

Figure 5.3 Partnering is a strategically developed, long-term relationship that solves the customer's problems. A successful partnering effort results in repeat sales and referrals that expand the prospect base. The strength of the partnership increases each time the salesperson uses value-added selling strategies.

The salespeople at Mackay Envelope Corporation achieve this goal by making sure they know more about their customers than the competitors know. Salespeople who work for Xerox Corporation are responding to a sales orientation that emphasizes postsale service. Bonuses are based on a formula that includes not only sales but also customer satisfaction.

Strategic Selling Alliances—The Highest Form of Partnering

Throughout the past decade we have seen the growth of a new form of partnership that often is described as a **strategic selling alliance**. The goal of strategic selling alliances is to achieve a marketplace advantage by teaming up with another company whose products or services fit well with your own.[32] Alliances often are formed by companies that have similar business interests and, thus, gain a mutual competitive advantage. It is not uncommon for a company to form several alliances. Corning, a maker of glass products, has formed partnerships with several companies that need innovative glass technology. For example, Corning formed an alliance with Samsung, a Korean manufacturer of television screens. Burlington, Ontario–based Jenex Corporation formed a strategic selling alliance with U.S.-based Competitive Technologies, giving that company the right to sell Jenex's Thermapik® in specified geographic territories around the world. Competitive Technologies must guarantee a specified sales volume of the product—designed to relieve pain and itch caused by insect stings and bites—in order to maintain its exclusive rights to sell the product.[33]

Strategic alliances have created a new selling environment. The first step in building an alliance is to learn as much as possible about the proposed partner. This study takes place long before face-to-face contact. Alliances that are formed between companies that vary greatly in such areas as customer focus, financial stability, or ethical values will likely

strategic selling alliance
Alliances that are achieved by teaming up with another company whose products or services fit well with your own.

Customer Relationship Management with Technology

Introducing Salesforce.com CRM Software

Today, many sales professionals use computers to help them better perform the tasks associated with successful personal selling. Various software programs are used, including e-mail, electronic spreadsheets, word processors, configuration systems, presentation packages, fax managers, and **customer relationship management (CRM)** systems. A basic CRM system consists of a database containing information about the people with whom a company maintains relationships, such as customers, prospects, coworkers, and suppliers. For your use with the CRM studies in this text, you will be provided with access to Salesforce.com, an Internet-based CRM system. You can learn the fundamentals of CRM with this application, including searching for customer and product-related information, managing time and priorities, communicating, and forecasting sales. (See CRM Instructions for Assessing Salesforce.com in Appendix 2 on p. 420 and the CRM Application Exercise Introducing Salesforce.com CRM Software on p. 24. Also go to **www.salesforce.com** and view introductory and sales demonstration videos.)

fail.[34] The second step is to meet with the proposed partner and explore mutual benefits of the alliance. At this point the salesperson (or account manager) is selling advice, assistance, and counsel, not specific products. Building win-win alliances requires the highest form of consultative selling. Very often, the salesperson is working with a company team made up of persons from such areas as research and development (R&D), finance, and distribution. Presentations and proposals usually focus on profit impact and other strategic alliance benefits.[35]

Partnering Is Enhanced with High Ethical Standards

In the field of selling there are certain pressures that can influence the ethical conduct of salespeople, and poor ethical decisions can weaken or destroy partnerships. To illustrate, let us assume a competitor makes exaggerated claims about a product. Do you counteract by promising more than your product can deliver? What action do you take when there is a time management problem and you must choose between servicing past sales and making new sales? What if a superior urges you to use a strategy that you consider unethical? These and other pressures must be dealt with every day.

Although Chapter 9 is devoted entirely to ethical considerations in personal selling, it should be noted that ethics is a major theme of this text as a whole, with the topic interwoven throughout several chapters. The authors believe that ethical decisions must be made every day in the life of a salesperson, so this important topic cannot be covered in a single chapter.

Partnering Is Enhanced with Customer Relationship Management

customer relationship management (CRM) The process of building and maintaining strong customer relationships by providing customer value.

Many companies have adopted some form of customer relationship management. **Customer relationship management (CRM)**, sometimes referred to as *sales automation*, is the process of building and maintaining strong customer relationships by providing customer value.[36] A modern CRM program relies on a variety of technologies to improve communications in a sales organization and enhance customer responsiveness. A variety of CRM applications will be discussed throughout the text.

VALUE CREATION—THE NEW CUSTOMER IMPERATIVE

WE HAVE DEFINED VALUE-ADDED SELLING AS A SERIES OF CREATIVE IMPROVEMENTS WITHIN the sales process that enhance the customer experience. The *information economy* will reward those salespeople who have the skills, the knowledge, and the motivation to determine how to create value at every step of the sales process.

As Figure 5.4 shows, value creation begins with an understanding of the customer's value needs. Salespeople can create value in many ways: by establishing a relationship based on trust; by carefully identifying the customer's needs; and by identifying the best

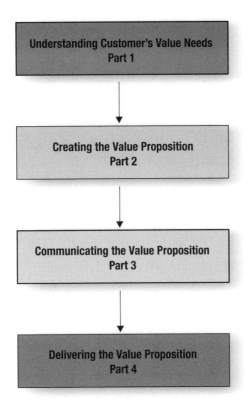

Figure 5.4 Creating and delivering customer value model.

The salesperson's role in value creation is illustrated in this figure.

Adapted from Figure 1.2, Making and Delivering Value, Solomon, Marhsall, and Stuart, *Marketing: Real People, Real Choices*, Prentice Hall, Upper Saddle River NJ, 2008, Page 23.

possible product solution. In the case of a complex sale, understanding the customer's value needs may take a great deal of time and may involve bringing in team members who have specific technical expertise.

Creating an appealing value proposition (Part 2) requires a detailed study of the customer's value needs. If you discover that timely delivery of your product is of critical importance, you must give the customer what they want. And if you promise on-time delivery, you must back up your claims.

Communicating the value proposition (Part 3) presents another major challenge. Traditional selling has too often emphasized communicating only the value that lies in the product. The focus of the sales call has too often been the product, not creating value for the customer.[37]

Delivering value (Part 4) can be very challenging. It may require coordination of credit approval, training, installation, service, and other aspects of the sale. Of course each element of the selling process provides an opportunity to add value.

REVIEWING KEY CONCEPTS

- Define personal selling and describe the three prescriptions of a personal selling philosophy.

  Personal selling occurs when a company representative interacts directly with a customer or prospective customer to present information about a product or service. Salespeople are encouraged to develop a personal selling philosophy based on three prescriptions: adopt the marketing concept, value personal selling, and assume the role of a problem solver or partner.

- Describe the contributions of personal selling to the information economy.

  Restructuring from an industrial economy to an information economy began in the 1950s. We now live in an age in which the effective exchange of information is the foundation of most economic transactions. Salespeople use a variety of information technology tools to gather and process information of value to the customer.

- Discuss personal selling as an extension of the marketing concept.

  The *marketing concept* is the belief that a firm should dedicate all its policies, planning, and operations to the satisfaction of the customer. Salespeople today are problem solvers who obtain the participation of buyers in identifying their problems, which can then be translated into needs.

- Describe the evolution of consultative selling from the marketing era to the present.

  The *marketing era* that began in Canada in the 1950s looked first at customer needs and wants and then created goods and services to meet those needs and wants. *Consultative selling* emerged in the late 1960s and early 1970s as an approach that emphasizes the identification of customer needs through effective communication between the salesperson and customer. The evolution of selling continued with the development of *strategic selling* and *partnering*.

- Define strategic selling and name the four broad strategic areas in the Strategic/Consultative Selling Model.

  Strategic selling evolved in the 1980s and involves the preparation of a carefully conceived plan to accomplish sales objectives. Strategic selling is based on a company's *strategic market plan*, which takes into consideration the coordination of all the major functional areas of the business—production, marketing, finance, and personnel. The four broad strategic areas in the Strategic/Consultative Selling Model (after development of personal selling philosophy) are developing a relationship strategy, developing a product strategy, developing a customer strategy, and developing a presentation strategy.

- Describe the evolution of partnering and the nature of a strategic selling alliance.

  Partnering is a strategically developed, long-term relationship that solves the customer's problems. The long-term partnership is achieved when the salesperson is able to skilfully apply the four major strategies and therefore add value in various ways. The *strategic selling alliance* is the highest form of partnering. The goal of this type of alliance is to achieve a marketplace advantage by teaming up with another company whose products fit well with your own.

- Explain how value-added selling strategies enhance personal selling.

  Value-added selling has emerged as a major response to the customer economy. This approach to personal selling is defined as a series of creative improvements that enhance the customer's experience. The information economy rewards those salespeople who have the skills, the knowledge, and the motivation to determine how to create value at every step of the sales process.

Key Terms

adaptive selling **106**

customer relationship management (CRM) **112**

customer strategy **108**

partnering **110**

personal selling **105**

personal selling philosophy **105**

presentation strategy **109**

product **105**

Review Questions

1. Explain how personal selling can help solve the problem of information overload.

2. According to the Strategic/Consultative Selling Model, what are the three prescriptions for developing a successful personal selling philosophy?

3. How is peddling or "pushing products" inconsistent with the marketing concept?

4. What is consultative selling? Give examples.

5. Diagram and label the four-step Consultative Sales Presentation Guide.

6. List and briefly explain the four broad strategic areas that make up the selling process.

7. Briefly describe the evolution of partnering. Discuss the forces that contributed to this approach to selling.

8. Provide a brief description of value-added selling. What economic forces have motivated companies to adopt value-added selling?

9. Briefly explain why some organizations are developing strategic selling alliances.

10. Explain why the ethical conduct of salespeople has become so important.

Application Exercises

1. Assume that you are an experienced professional salesperson. A professor who teaches at a nearby university has asked you to speak to a consumer economics class about the benefits of personal selling. Make an outline of what you will say.

2. A friend of yours has invented a unique and useful new product. This friend, an engineer by profession, understands little about marketing and selling this new product. She does understand, however, that "nothing happens until somebody sells the product." She has asked you to describe the general factors that need to be considered when you market a product. Prepare an answer to her question.

3. When Brenda Fisher received her B.Ed., she thought she would like to teach. However, a pharmaceutical firm offered her a sales position that would require her to call on doctors and pharmacists to explain her firm's product line. Describe the similarities and differences between personal selling and teaching.

4. To learn more about industry-based global sales training programs, access **www.wilsonlearning.com.** Click on the "Sales Effectiveness" link and examine the content of the various sales courses offered throughout the world by this company. From this review, describe the similarities between what this company offers and the material in this chapter.

5. One of the topics frequently debated among salespeople and sales managers is whether men or women are better suited to sales positions. Where do you stand on this issue? Find support for your position and then be prepared to defend your views in class.

⟳ ROLE-PLAY EXERCISE

The purpose of this role play is to provide you with an opportunity to engage in a basic need identification exercise. You will be meeting with someone (a class member) who is preparing for an important job interview and needs a pen and/or pencil. Prior to the meeting, make a list of the questions you will ask. Then pair off with the class member and ask your questions. Be sure to take notes. At the end of the interview, be prepared to recommend the most appropriate pen and/or pencil.

CRM Application Exercise Introducing Salesforce.com CRM Software

The CRM system that is available for you to install is a demonstration version of Salesforce.com, the best-selling Internet-based CRM application. See Appendix 2 on page 418 for instructions on how to login to and use the Salesforce.com CRM software. Using your Salesforce.com login you will access a database of information about prospective customers for a company selling network systems. In the case study and exercises ahead, you will assume the role of a salesperson who is selling these network systems. The emphasis in these exercises is customer relationship management. No prior experience or prior knowledge of networking systems is required to complete these exercises.

Salesforce.com is a database program, which means that it uses records and fields. *Records* are the screens that contain information about each person. *Fields* are the boxes on the records for entering and displaying data,

such as the name of the person (e.g., Bradley Able). Salesforce.com also functions as a contact management program because it maintains a record for each contact (person). In Salesforce.com, this contact (person) is always associated with a company or organization.

You can experiment with Salesforce.com without concern about damaging the application. To get acquainted with the Salesforce.com version of CRM, click on the various menu items and icons and observe the functions that are available to you. Experimenting with this software gives you a feel for the potential power of using technology to enhance your sales career. Test Salesforce.com's reporting capabilities by looking at a mailing list: select Reports then Mailing List.

As you experiment with Salesforce.com you can obtain help at any time by pressing the Help and Training button.

Reality Selling Today Video Case Problem

At the beginning of this chapter, you were given an introduction to Marcus Smith, employed by Liberty Mutual, a successful insurance company. Smith is responsible for introducing a very large number of products and services and he must always keep one eye on the competition. He must be prepared to answer questions about his own products and services and those of the competition. He must also be prepared to discuss the intricacies of the insurance terms and possible bundles of insurance policies in order to offer his customers the best value.

Like every other professional salesperson, Smith is constantly involved in learning. We now know that the principles of selling can be learned and applied by people whose personal characteristics are quite different. Most successful salespeople spend considerable time acquiring product knowledge, keeping up to date in their industry and related industries, and learning more about their customers. Smith acquired his formal training in professional selling from the Program in Excellence in Selling while

he attended university. In the insurance industry, salespeople often go through industry-related training and a formal exam to acquire a license to sell personal and property insurance. Smith also undergoes Liberty Mutual's rigorous training program, which provides courses in four concentrations: products and services, company, competition, and quoting.

Smith realizes the importance of a relationship strategy that is built on a win-win philosophy. In addition to building a strong relationship with the customer, he must be able to work effectively with others who directly or indirectly influence the sale. He shares market information with his peers periodically because a broad view of the market as a whole is crucial in the highly competitive insurance industry. The salesperson who is honest, accountable, and sincerely concerned about the customer's welfare brings added value to the sales. (See chapter opener on page and Reality Selling Today Role-Play 1 in Appendix 1 on page 405 for more information.)

Questions

1. Does it appear that Smith has adopted the three prescriptions of a personal selling philosophy? (See Strategic/Consultative Selling Model.) Explain.

2. What prescriptions of the relationship strategy (see Strategic/Consultative Selling Model) have been adopted by Marcus Smith?

3. Value-added selling is defined as a series of creative improvements in the sales process that enhance the customer's experience. Describe the various ways that Marcus Smith can create value for his customers.

4. Let's assume you are considering a career in personal selling. Describe how you strike a balance between information collection (i.e., information about the market, about the competitor, about the customers in your assigned market and in other markets) and information utilization (i.e., using the information gathered to close sales).

Figure 6.1 How salespeople spend their time during an average 46-hour workweek (approximate).

A professional selling position encompasses a wide range of tasks (see Fig. 6.1), and therefore salespeople must possess a variety of skills. A salesperson representing Federal Express (FedEx) will make numerous sales calls each day in an attempt to establish new accounts and provide service to established accounts. There is a wide range of potential customers who can use FedEx delivery services. A salesperson working for a Caterpillar construction equipment dealer may make only two or three sales calls per day. The products offered by the dealer are expensive and are not purchased frequently.

Just as selling occupations differ, so do the titles by which salespeople are known. Their titles reflect, in part, the variety of duties they perform. A survey of current job announcements indicates that companies are using such titles as these:

Account Executive	Sales Consultant
Account Representative	Relationship Manager
Sales Account Manager	Sales Associate

Business Development Manager   Marketing Representative
District Representative   Territory Manager

Two factors have contributed to the creation of new titles. First, we have seen a shift from "selling" to "consulting." When salespeople assume a consulting role, the value of the relationship exceeds the value of the transaction. Second, the new titles reflect a difference in education and skill sets needed for sales positions.[12]

Salespeople, regardless of title, play an important role in sustaining the growth and profitability of organizations of all sizes. They also support the employment of many non-selling employees.

Rewarding Aspects of Selling Careers

From a personal and an economic standpoint, selling can be a rewarding career. Careers in selling offer financial rewards, recognition, security, and opportunities for advancement to a degree that is unique compared with other occupations.

Above-Average Income

Studies dealing with incomes in the business community indicate that salespeople earn significantly higher incomes than most other workers. Some salespeople actually earn more than their sales managers and other executives within the organization. The high level of compensation—whether from a base salary, a bonus, or incentives—is justified for good performance. Compensation varies according to years of experience in sales. The compensation range for junior salespeople in Canada ranges from $33 800 to $55 900 per year; for intermediate salespeople, from $42 500 to $76 000 per year; and for senior sales-people, from $55 200 to $133 200 per year.[13]

In recent years we have seen new ways to report compensation for salespeople. Hay Group's Sales Force Effectiveness Practice, working with C&C Market Research Inc., developed a reporting method that tracks earnings for different types of sales approaches. Research indicates that salespeople involved in transactional sales earned the lowest compensation. Sales personnel involved in value-added sales earned the highest level of compensation. These highly paid salespeople created improvements in the sales process that enhanced the customer experience.[14]

Above-Average Psychic Income

Two major psychological needs common to all people are recognition and security. **Psychic income**, which consists of factors that provide psychological rewards, helps satisfy these important needs and motivates us to achieve higher levels of performance. The need for recognition has been established in numerous studies that have examined human motivation. Workers from all employment areas indicate that recognition for work well done is an important morale-building factor.

In selling, recognition will come more frequently and with greater intensity than in most other occupations. Because selling contributes so visibly to the success of most business firms, the accomplishments of sales personnel will seldom go unrecognized. Most people want to achieve some measure of security in their work. Selling is one of those occupations that usually provide job security during both good and bad times.

psychic income Consists of factors that provide psychological rewards; it helps to satisfy the need for recognition and security, and motivates us to achieve higher levels of performance.

Opportunity for Advancement

Each year, thousands of openings appear in the ranks of supervision and management. Because salespeople work in positions of high visibility, they are in an excellent position to be chosen for advancement to positions of greater responsibility. The presidents of many of today's companies began their careers in the ranks of the sales force. Theodore Kinni, in *Selling Power*, notes, "Today's C-suites are literally bursting with sales professionals."[15] Of course, not every salesperson can become president of a large corporation, but, in the middle-management ranks there are numerous interesting and high-paying positions in which experience in selling is a prime requisite for advancement.

Opportunities for Women

Prodded by a growing awareness that gender is not a barrier to success in selling, business firms are recruiting qualified women in growing numbers. The percentage of women in the sales force has increased considerably. Although women are still relative newcomers to industrial sales, they have enjoyed expanded career opportunities in such areas as real estate, insurance, advertising services, investments, and travel services. Women are turning to sales employment because it offers excellent economic rewards and in many cases a flexible work schedule. Flexible schedules are very appealing to women who want to balance career and family.

At Pitney Bowes, a major provider of corporate mail services, about 24 percent of the top employees are women. Many of the top salespeople are women who were formerly teachers.[16] About 20 percent of all financial advisers are women.[17]

EMPLOYMENT SETTINGS IN SELLING TODAY

inside salesperson
A salesperson who performs selling activities at the employer's location, typically using the telephone.

CAREERS IN SALES INCLUDE BOTH INSIDE AND OUTSIDE SALES POSITIONS. AN INSIDE **salesperson** is one who performs selling activities at the employer's location, typically using the telephone. Many manufacturers and wholesalers have developed inside sales forces to take orders, make calls on smaller customers, and provide support for outside salespeople. In some cases the inside salespeople are called customer service representatives and provide a number of support services on behalf of outside salespeople.

Inside sales can be either *inbound* or *outbound*. *Inbound* inside salespeople respond to calls initiated by the customer. **Telemarketing** is a common form of outbound inside sales that serves several purposes including sales and service. In some cases this includes technical support personnel who provide technical information and answer questions. Some companies utilize sales assistants to confirm appointments, conduct credit checks, and follow up on deliveries.[18] The use of telemarketing has grown rapidly as businesses use this method to contact potential new customers and to follow up on current small customers or customers in distant areas.

Unlike inside sales, an **outside salesperson** travels to meet prospects and customers in their place of business or residence. Information technology companies such as Hewlett-Packard and Dell employ thousands of salespeople to sell computer systems, peripherals, and integrated technology solutions to other companies, large and small. Wholesalers across Canada, such as Sysco Canada and Acklands-Grainger, employ outside salespeople who, in addition to selling products, offer a variety of services to their customers, such as maintaining inventories, merchandising, providing promotional support, gathering and interpreting market information, extending credit, and distributing goods. In addition, many direct-to-consumer salespeople, such as interior designers, engage at least partially in outside sales, e.g., financial services, life insurance, direct sales.

Inside and outside salespeople for the same company often work together and rely heavily upon each other. For example, inside salespeople often prospect, generating and qualifying leads for outside salespeople to call on personally. Also, once an initial sale is made by an outside salesperson, inside salespeople are asked to provide ongoing customer contact and service, taking responsibility for meeting customer needs while being alert for opportunities to sell additional products or services.

telemarketing A common form of outbound inside sales that serves several purposes including sales and service.

outside salesperson A salesperson who travels to meet prospects and customers in their place of business or residence.

SELLING THROUGH CHANNELS

MANY TIMES PEOPLE MISTAKENLY THINK OF SELLING JOBS AS BEING LIMITED TO THE interaction between the company and the end user of a good or service. However, goods and services flow from manufacturer to end user through a **channel of distribution**, which includes all of the intermediaries that exist between them, such as various types of retailers or wholesalers.

As can be seen in Figure 6.2, sales jobs exist throughout this distribution chain.[19] In fact, many of the most promising sales careers in terms of career advancement and compensation exist in the beginning of the channel flow in the form of business to business, or "B2B," sales. **Trade selling** refers to the sale of a product or service to another member of the channel of distribution. For example, a manufacturer of household goods may employ sales representatives to sell its products to retailers. It may instead (or also) sell its products to wholesalers that warehouse the product and in turn the wholesaler employs sales representatives to sell these and other products to retailers that the manufacturer does not want to service directly.

channel of distribution Includes all of the intermediaries that exist between the manufacturer and the end user, such as various types of retailers or wholesalers.

trade selling Refers to the sale of a product or service to another member of the channel of distribution.

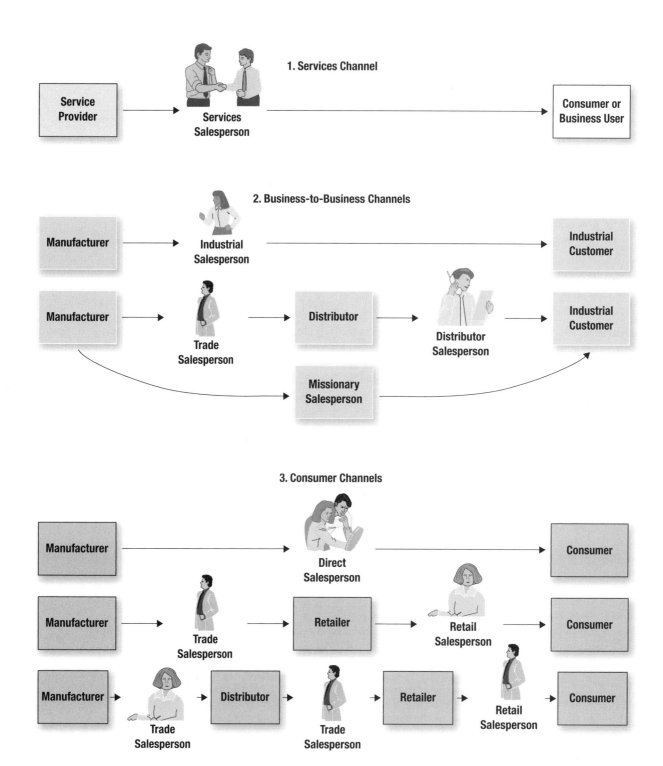

Figure 6.2 Salespeople in different channels

Similar scenarios exist with industrial products where the end user is a business rather than an individual consumer and with services where the end user is either a consumer or business user. Another example of B2B sales is detail, or missionary, sales. Rather than selling directly to the end user, the detail salesperson attempts to generate goodwill and stimulate demand for the manufacturer's product among channel members.

As you can see, selling careers may be classified in several ways. One of the most useful classifications is based on the sales channels depicted in Figure 6.2. Three major channels exist—service sales channels, business goods channels, and consumer goods channels.

CAREER OPPORTUNITIES IN THE SERVICE CHANNEL

SALES CAREERS IN SERVICE SALES INCLUDE BOTH BUSINESS-TO-BUSINESS AND BUSINESS-TO-consumer sales. Today approximately 80 percent of the Canadian labour force is employed in some capacity in the service sector of the economy. The growth rate for the service industry is much higher than the growth rate for product companies. Service companies provide career opportunities in a variety of settings.

- **Banks and financial services.** This is one of the hottest areas of sales growth. There are more than 3000 firms that provide financial services in Canada, directly employing more than 550 000 people.[20] Banks, brokerage firms, and other businesses are branching out, selling a broader range of financial planning and investment services. More and more bank employees are involved in personal selling activities, developing new accounts and servicing existing ones. Bank personnel are completing sales training courses in record numbers these days.

- **Media sales.** Revenue from advertising supports the radio, television, newspaper, and magazine industries and is also a major source of profit for the Internet. Both local and national advertising supports each of these and each must sell advertising to remain in business. In fact, newspapers and magazines generate far more revenue from the sales of advertising than from subscriptions. The wide variety of client needs and the task of meeting these needs make the work of media sales representatives interesting. Additionally, the requirement for the members of the media sales staff to develop or to help the client develop commercials makes this work very interesting.

- **Hotel, motel, and convention centre services**. Each year, thousands of seminars, conferences, and business meetings are held throughout Canada. Most of these events are hosted by hotels, motels, or convention centres. The salespeople employed by these firms play an important role in attracting clients to utilize these facilities. Salespeople diversify markets and upgrade services to sell room space, food, beverages, entertainment, and other services to create an attractive atmosphere for potential clients.

Samantha Cheuk and Erin Munro are part of the sales team at The Westin Grand in Vancouver. Samantha is a sales and catering coordinator. She works with customers to establish their meeting and food service needs when they also plan to book sleeping accommodations as part of their meeting or conference package. Erin is a catering manager. She works with customers who do not have accommodations needs, but who require the hotel's meeting or dining facilities. Both Samantha and Erin must communicate effectively with customers, completely understand their specific needs, and then ensure the hotel delivers on any promises made. Salespeople at The Westin Grand understand the importance of customer satisfaction. Customers who are completely satisfied often return; dissatisfied customers do not.[21]

- **Telecommunications services.** The deregulation of telephone service resulted in considerable fragmentation within the industry and the creation of numerous new communications companies. This has led to an increased need for telecommunications salespeople. These individuals must have a thorough knowledge of their system and a good understanding of competing telecommunications systems.

- **Real estate.** The purchase of a home is usually the single largest expenditure in the average person's lifetime. The purchase of commercial property by individual investors or business firms is also a major economic decision. Therefore, the thousands of Canadian real estate salespeople assume an important responsibility. Busy real estate salespeople often hire sales associates to conduct open houses or perform other tasks. Real estate salespeople must obtain listings, advertise the properties, conduct visits with potential clients, and sell properties. Pearl Paul moved to Canada from Trinidad in 1972. She decided to get into real estate sales when her husband wanted to return to his hometown—Winnipeg—in search of work. In 2008, after only three years in sales, Pearl Paul became the top-selling salesperson among approximately 150 salespeople in her Royal LePage office. Honesty helped Pearl establish trust and build good relationships. The backside of Pearl's business card states, "The referral of your friends and family is the greatest compliment you can give me."[22]

- **Insurance.** Selling insurance has always been one of the most rewarding careers in sales. Common forms of insurance sold include fire, liability, life, health, automobile, casualty, homeowner, and business. There are two broad groups of insurance salespeople. Employees of major companies such as Manulife Financial, London Life, Sun Life Financial, or State Farm make up one group. Independent insurance agents who

The sales team at The Grand Westin in Vancouver—including Erin Munro and Samantha Cheuk—understand the importance of satisfying customers.

serve as representatives for a number of companies make up the second group. The typical independent agency will offer a broad line of personal and business insurance services.

- **Business services.** Michael Davidson is Vice President, Marketing and Business Development, at Arnold Worldwide Canada, a full-service marketing communications agency. He is responsible for leading new business initiatives for the agency. In a typical week, Michael spends time cultivating relationships with prospects and introducing them to the agency. He spends considerable time with prospects, getting a solid sense of their needs, assessing the opportunity, and then assembling and leading the right agency team for the client. Michael Davidson says, "Successful selling comes down to your ability to truly understand client needs and building trust and respect. Ultimately, people hire people that they want to work with in this business."[23]

Chapter 7
Creating Value with a Relationship Strategy

Learning Objectives

After studying this chapter, you should be able to

1 Explain the importance of developing a relationship strategy

2 Discuss how thought processes can enhance your relationship strategy

3 Identify and describe the major nonverbal factors that shape our sales image

4 Describe conversational strategies that help us establish relationships

5 Explain how to establish a self-improvement plan based on personal development strategies

 Reality Selling Today Video Series

The salespeople who work for CB Richard Ellis (**www.cbre.com**) understand the importance of developing relationship strategies. This successful commercial real estate services company, with 14 Canadian sales offices from Halifax to Vancouver and more than 300 offices in some 50 countries, strives to build a long-term partnership with each customer.

Susana Rosas (see page 127), a real estate broker at CB Richard Ellis (**www.cbre.com/usa/us/tx/houston+galleria**), places a great deal of emphasis on building rapport during the first contact. She, like most other real estate professionals, knows that rapport with commercial real estate clients is of critical importance. She knows that to build relationships with clients, a good knowledge of the market is necessary but not sufficient. She has to master a multitude of skills, among which keeping an open and empathetic conversation with her clients is the key. Above all, listening closely to everything that prospects say helps a salesperson to accurately identify their wants and needs. Furthermore, she works closely with her team members in the same collaborative manner to make sure all of those identified needs are met.

DEVELOPING A RELATIONSHIP STRATEGY

DEVELOPING AND APPLYING THE WIDE RANGE OF INTERPERSONAL SKILLS NEEDED in today's complex sales environment can be challenging. Daniel Goleman, author of the bestselling books *Emotional Intelligence* and *Working with Emotional Intelligence*, notes that

there are many forms of intelligence that influence our actions throughout life. One of these, **emotional intelligence**, refers to the capacity for monitoring our own feelings and those of others, for motivating ourselves, and for managing emotions well in ourselves and in our relationships. People with a high level of emotional intelligence display many of the qualities needed in sales work: self-confidence, trustworthiness, adaptability, initiative, optimism, empathy, and well-developed social skills.[1]

Goleman and other researchers state that there are widespread exceptions to the rule that IQ predicts success. In the field of personal selling and most other business occupations, emotional intelligence is a much greater predictor of success.[2] The good news is that emotional intelligence can be enhanced with a variety of self-development activities, many of which are discussed in this chapter.

Information age selling involves three major relationship challenges. The first major challenge is building new relationships. Salespeople who can quickly build rapport with new prospects have a much greater chance of achieving success in personal selling. The second major challenge is transforming relationships from the personal level to the business level. Once rapport is established, the salesperson is in a stronger position to begin the need identification process. The third major challenge is the management of relationships. "To achieve a high level of success salespeople have to manage a multitude of different relationships."[3] Salespeople must develop relationship management strategies that focus on four key groups. These groups are discussed later in this chapter.

In this chapter we introduce the win-win philosophy and discuss the importance of projecting a professional image. Chapter 8, on adaptive selling, explains how an understanding of our own communication style and that of the customer can help us better manage the relationship process. Chapter 9 focuses on the importance of maintaining high ethical standards in order to build long-term relationships with the customer. (See Fig. 7.1.)

emotional intelligence The capacity for recognizing our own feelings and those of others, for motivating ourselves, and for managing emotions effectively in ourselves and our relationships.

Relationships Add Value

Ron Willingham, author of *Integrity Selling For The 21st Century*, says there is a relationship between the salesperson's achievement drive and their view of personal selling. Salespeople who feel a professional responsibility to create as much value for customers as possible exhibit more energy, a stronger work ethic, and a greater eagerness to ask customers for decisions.[4]

Strategic/Consultative Selling Model	
Strategic step	Prescription
Develop a personal selling philosophy	✓ Adopt marketing concept ✓ Value personal selling ✓ Become a problem solver/partner
Develop a relationship strategy	• Adopt win-win philosophy • Project professional image • Maintain high ethical standards

Figure 7.1 Every salesperson should have an ongoing goal of developing a relationship strategy that adds value to the sale.

The manner in which salespeople establish, build, and manage relationships is not an incidental aspect of personal selling; in the information age it is the key to success. In the information economy, business is defined by customer relationships and sales success depends on adding value (see Fig. 7.2). Daniel Pink, author of *A Whole New Mind*, says we are moving from the information age to the conceptual age. He predicts that one of the major players in the conceptual age will be the **empathizer**. Empathizers have the ability to imagine themselves in someone else's position and understand what that person is feeling. They are able to understand the subtleties of human interaction.[5]

empathizer Someone who has the ability to imagine themselves in someone else's position and understand what that person is feeling.

We have defined value-added selling as *a series of creative improvements in the sales process that enhance the customer experience*. Customers perceive that value is added when they feel comfortable with the relationship they have with a salesperson. A good relationship encourages customers to feel that, if a problem arises, they will receive a just and fair solution. A good relationship creates a clear channel of communication about issues that might surface during each step of the sales process. Len Rodman, CEO of a large engineering and construction company, recalls a problem in one particular region: earnings were minimal and the person in charge could not sell to high-tier clients. Len put a different salesperson in charge whose strength was building relationships and, within an 18-month period, that region became one of the most profitable.[6]

The salesperson who is honest, accountable, and sincerely concerned about the customer's welfare adds value to the sale. These characteristics give the salesperson a competitive advantage—an advantage that is becoming increasingly important in a world of "look-alike" products and similar prices.

Partnering—The Highest-Quality Selling Relationship

Salespeople today are encouraged to think of everything they say or do in the context of their relationship with the customer. They should constantly strive to build a long-term partnership. In a marketplace characterized by increased levels of competition and greater product complexity, we see the need to adopt a relationship strategy that emphasizes the "lifetime" customer. High-quality relationships result in repeat business and important

Partnering is a strategically developed, high-quality, long-term relationship that focuses on solving the customer's buying problem. Partnering involves establishing, re-establishing, and maintaining relationships with customers.

referrals. A growing number of salespeople recognize that the quality of the partnerships they create is as important as the quality of the products they sell. Today's customer wants a quality product *and* a quality relationship. One example of this trend is the J. D. Power and Associates customer satisfaction studies. J. D. Power conducts customer satisfaction research in several different industries; for example, the Domestic Hotel Guest Satisfaction Study measures guest satisfaction among frequent business travellers.[7]

In Chapter 5 we defined partnering as a strategically developed, high-quality, long-term relationship that focuses on solving the customer's buying problems.[8] This definition is used in the sales training video entitled "Partnering—The Heart of Selling Today." Traditional industrial-age sales training programs emphasized the importance of creating a good first impression and then "pushing" your product. Partnering emphasizes building a strong relationship during every aspect of the sale and working hard to maintain a quality relationship with the customer after the sale. Today, personal selling must be viewed as a process, not an event.[9]

Larry Wilson, noted author and founder of Wilson Learning Worldwide, identifies partnering as one of the most important aspects of strategic thought processes needed by salespeople. He points out that the salesperson who is selling a "one-shot" solution cannot compete against the one who has developed and nurtured a long-term, mutually beneficial partnership. Wilson believes there are three keys to a partnering relationship:

- *The relationship is built on shared values.* If your client believes that you both share the same ideas and values, it goes a long way toward creating a powerful relationship.

- *Everyone needs to clearly understand the purpose of the partnership and be committed to the vision.* Both the salesperson and the client must agree on what they are trying to do together.

- *The role of the salesperson must move from selling to supporting.* The salesperson in a partnership is actively concerned with the growth, health, and satisfaction of the company to which she or he is selling.[10]

Salespeople willing to abandon short-term thinking and invest the time and energy needed to develop a high-quality, long-term relationship with customers are rewarded with greater earnings and the satisfaction of working with repeat customers. Sales resulting from referrals also increase.

Relationship Strategies Focus on Four Key Groups

Establishing and maintaining a partnering-type relationship internally as well as with customers is a vital aspect of selling. High-performance sales personnel build strong relationships with four groups (see Fig. 7.2):

1. *Customers.* As noted previously, a major key to success in selling is the ability to establish working relationships with customers in which mutual support, trust, and goals are nurtured over time. Research suggests that salespeople who maintain regular contact with their customers and develop sound business relationships based on mutual trust are able to drive up sales productivity.[11] Cisco Systems is one of many companies that now measure themselves by the quality of their relationships with their customers. Salespeople earn their bonuses in large part based on customer satisfaction instead of gross sales or profit.[12]

2. *Secondary decision makers.* High-performance salespeople understand the importance of building relationships with the people who work with customers. In many selling situations, the first person the salesperson meets is a receptionist, a secretary, or an assistant to the primary decision maker. These persons can often facilitate a meeting with the prospect. Also, the prospect may involve other people in making the buying decision. For example, the decision to buy new office furniture may be made by a team of persons including the buyer and the persons who will actually use the furniture.

3. *Company support staff.* The maintenance of relationships internally is a vital aspect of selling. Support staff may include persons working in the areas of market research, product service, credit, training, or shipping. Influencing these people to change their priorities, interrupt their schedules, accept new responsibilities, or fulfill any other request for special attention is a major part of the salesperson's job. At UPS, the drivers are the eyes and ears of the sales force, so the most successful UPS salespeople nurture a relationship with the drivers in their sales territory.[13]

4. *Management personnel.* Sales personnel usually work under the direct supervision of a sales manager, a department head, or some other member of the firm's management team. Maintaining a good relationship with this person is important.

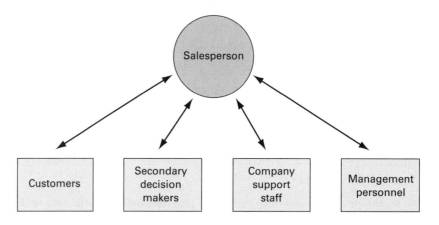

Figure 7.2 An effective relationship strategy helps high-performing salespeople build and maintain win-win relationships with four key groups.

Communicating Through CRM

Customer relationship management (CRM) software can be used to enhance the quality of your relationships. A good example is the software's ability to enhance communications between you and your contacts. With Salesforce.com, for example, you can quickly prepare and send a letter, fax, or e-mail to one or more people in the database. Recipients of your appointment confirmations, information verifications, company or product news, or brief personal notes recognize and appreciate your effort to keep them informed. The written word conveys consideration and helps avoid misunderstandings and miscommunications. CRM empowers you to easily use the written word to advance your relationship building. (See the exercise Preparing Letters with CRM on page 146 for more information.)

Adapting the Relationship Strategy

Ideally, the relationship strategy should be adapted to the type of customer you are working with. The three most common types of selling situations are: transactional selling, consultative selling, and strategic alliance selling. Transactional buyers are usually aware of their needs and often stay focused on such issues as price, convenience, and delivery schedules. They usually know a great deal about the products or services they wish to purchase. In the transactional sale, the relationship strategy is often secondary.

In the consultative sale, however, the impact of relationships on the sale is quite important. A consultative sale emphasizes need identification, which is achieved through effective communication and a relationship built on mutual trust and respect. The consultative salesperson must display a keen ability to listen, define the customer's problem, and offer one or more solutions. The opportunity to uncover hidden needs and create custom solutions is greatly enhanced by a well-conceived relationship strategy.[14]

In terms of relationship building, strategic alliance selling is often the most challenging. Very often the salesperson is working with a company team made up of people from such areas as research and development (R&D), finance, and distribution. The salesperson must build a good working relationship with each team member. Forming an alliance with another company involves building relationships with several representatives of that buying organization.

We will revisit these three types of selling situations later in Chapter 9 when we discuss the trust factor. In the meantime, keep in mind that customers almost never buy products from someone whom they dislike. A salesperson who is not viewed as helpful and trustworthy will not succeed in any type of selling situation.

THOUGHT PROCESSES THAT ENHANCE YOUR RELATIONSHIP STRATEGY

INDUSTRIAL-AGE FOLKLORE CREATED THE MYTH OF THE "BORN" SALESPERSON—A dynamic, outgoing, highly assertive individual. Experience acquired during the age of information has taught us that many other factors determine sales success. Key among these factors are a positive self-image and the ability to relate to others in effective and productive ways. With the aid of knowledge drawn from the behavioural sciences, we can develop the relationship strategies needed in a wide range of selling situations.

Self-Concept—An Important Dimension of the Relationship Strategy

Your **self-concept** is the bundle of facts, opinions, beliefs, and perceptions about yourself that are present in your life every moment of every day.[15] The self-concept you have today reflects information you have received from others and life events that occurred throughout childhood, adolescence, and adulthood. You are *consciously* aware of some of the things you have been conditioned to believe about yourself. But many comments and events that have shaped your self-concept are processed at the *unconscious* level and continue to influence your judgments, feelings, and behaviours whether you are aware of them or not.[16]

Phillip McGraw, author of *Self-Matters*, says we often sabotage our own success by adopting limiting beliefs. These are the specific things we think about that cause us to conclude that we are not capable of achieving success. These beliefs restrict our thinking and our actions.[17] McGraw, better known as "Dr. Phil," has developed a one-sentence guide to understanding the importance of your self-concept: *The past reaches into the present, and programs the future, by your recollections and your internal rhetoric about what you perceived to have happened in your life.*[18] Past experiences and events, which McGraw describes as "defining moments," can influence your thinking for a lifetime.

How can you develop a more positive self-concept? How can you get rid of self-destructive ways of thinking? Bringing your present self-concept out into the open is the first step in understanding who you are, what you can do, and where you are going. Improving your self-concept will not happen overnight, but it can happen. A few practical approaches are summarized as follows:

1. *Focus on the future and stop being overly concerned with past mistakes or failures.* You should learn from past errors, but they should not immobilize you.

2. *Develop expertise in selected areas.* By developing "expert power" you not only improve your self-image but also increase the value of your contributions to your employer and your customers.

3. *Learn to develop a positive personal attitude.* To develop a more positive outlook, read books or listen to audio presentations that describe ways to develop a positive personal attitude. Consider materials developed by Jack Canfield, Stephen Covey, Brian Tracy, Dale Carnegie, and Phillip McGraw.

Later in this chapter you will learn how to develop and initiate a plan for self-improvement. If you want to improve your self-concept, consider adopting this plan.

The Win-Win Philosophy

The marketing concept is a philosophy that leaves no doubt in the mind of every employee that customer satisfaction is of primary importance. Salespeople who work closely with customers are in a position to monitor customer satisfaction.

Relationships Are Important for Fund Development

Brenda Lockyer is the director of fund development at the Dr. H. Bliss Murphy Cancer Care Foundation, a not-for-profit organization that depends partly on public and private donations for its support. Brenda recently completed a university course in professional selling and sales management and was surprised how much of the course was applicable to her job.

Brenda Lockyer says, "A key to our success is how we approach, engage, and steward our donors. Many donors start with small donations but continue to support charities with increasing commitment. We have stewardship plans in place for different giving levels and monitor increased gifts from one appeal to the next. When a donor is identified as a major gift prospect, he or she is visited personally by a volunteer or staff person. Once a donor has donated cumulatively to a major gift level ($5000 or more), the next obvious giving vehicle is through a planned gift—the most popular being a bequest from the donor's estate. We value and foster our relationships with these donors because they are so important to us. The cost of losing such donors and having to replace them can be very significant, just like losing a major customer [is] for a sales organization."[a]

Adopting the win-win philosophy is the first step in developing a relationship strategy. Stephen Heiman and Diane Sanchez, authors of *The New Conceptual Selling*, describe the "win-win" approach as follows:

> In Win-Win selling, both the buyer and seller come out of the sale understanding that their respective best interests have been served—in other words, that they've both won. It is our firm conviction, based on thousands of selling situations, that over the long run the only sellers who can count on remaining successful are the ones who are committed to this Win-Win philosophy.[19]

The win-win strategy is based on such irrefutable logic that it is difficult to understand why any other approach would be used. The starting point to the development of a win-win philosophy is to compare the behaviours of persons who have adopted the win-lose approach with the behaviours of persons who have adopted the win-win approach (see Fig. 7.3).

Win-lose people	Win-win people
• See a problem in every solution	• Help others solve their problem
• Fix the blame	• Fix what caused the problem
• Let life happen to them	• Make life a joyous happening for others and themselves
• Live in the past	• Learn from the past, live in the present, and set goals for the future
• Make promises they never keep	• Make commitments to themselves and to others and keep them both

Figure 7.3 The starting point to developing a win-win philosophy is to compare behaviours of win-lose salespeople with those of win-win salespeople. (Adapted from a list of losers, winners, and double winners in *The Double Win* by Denis Waitley.)

Empathy and Ego Drive

We have described the growing importance of the *empathizer*, the ability to imagine yourself in someone else's position, to understand what that person is feeling. A salesperson simply cannot sell well without the invaluable ability to get critical feedback from the client through empathy. When you sense what the customer is feeling, you can change pace and make whatever modifications in your sales presentation are needed.[20] Fortunately, the ability to relate to and connect with customers can be learned.

Ego drive is another basic quality that is of critical importance in personal selling. **Ego drive** is an inner force that makes the salesperson want and need to make the sale. Closing the sale provides a powerful means of enhancing the salesperson's ego. Research indicates that top salespeople have both the motivation to make the sale and the empathy that gives them the connecting tool with which to do it. Therefore, empathy and ego drive reinforce each other.[21]

ego drive An inner force that makes the salesperson want and need to make the sale.

Character and Integrity

Shoshana Zuboff, contributing columnist for *Fast Company* magazine, sees widespread acceptance of wrong as normal. She points to acceptance in some industries of the belief that "It's not wrong because everyone is doing it."[22] Employees working for prominent companies such as Merck, WorldCom, Putman Investments, Tyco, and Edward D. Jones & Company have been involved in ethical lapses.[23] Most white-collar crime is committed by persons who lack character and integrity.

Character is composed of personal standards, including honesty, integrity, and moral strength. It is a quality that is highly respected in the field of personal selling. **Integrity**, the basic ingredient of character, is exhibited when you achieve congruence between what you know, what you say, and what you do.[24] Toronto-based clinical psychologist Barbara Killinger says, "Integrity is built one small step at a time, yet it can slip away seemingly overnight."[25] In a world of uncertainty and rapid change, integrity has become a valuable character trait. Salespeople with integrity can be trusted to do what they say they will do. One way to achieve trustworthiness in personal selling is to avoid deceiving or misleading the customer. More will be said about this topic in Chapter 9, which examines the ethical conduct of salespeople.

character Your personal standards of behaviour, including honesty and integrity. Your character is based on your internal values and the resulting judgments you make about what is right and what is wrong.

integrity Part of your character; what you have when your behaviour is in accordance with your professed standards and personal code of moral values.

VERBAL AND NONVERBAL STRATEGIES THAT ADD VALUE TO YOUR RELATIONSHIPS

THE FIRST CONTACT BETWEEN A SALESPERSON AND A PROSPECT IS VERY IMPORTANT. During the first few minutes—or seconds, in some cases—the prospect and the salesperson form impressions of each other that will either facilitate or detract from the sales call. Malcolm Gladwell, author of the best selling book *Blink*, says that when two people meet for the first time, both will make very superficial, rapid judgments about the other person. This decision-making process, he argues, usually happens subconsciously in a split second (in the blink of an eye).[26]

Every salesperson projects an image to prospective customers, and this image influences how a customer feels about the sales representative. The image you project is the sum total

This salesperson's clothing and facial expression project a professional image. A pleasant smile and eye contact convey friendliness to the customer.

of many verbal and nonverbal factors. The quality of your voice, the clothing you wear, your posture, your manners, and your communication style represent some of the factors that contribute to the formation of your image. We discuss several forms of verbal and nonverbal communication in this chapter. Communication style is examined in Chapter 4.

Nonverbal Messages

When we attempt to communicate with another person, we use both verbal and nonverbal communications. **Nonverbal messages** are "messages without words" or "silent messages." These are the messages—other than spoken or written words—that we communicate through facial expressions, voice tone, gestures, appearance, posture, and other nonverbal means.[27]

nonverbal message A form of communication that has been defined as "messages without words" or "silent messages."

Research indicates that when two people communicate, *nonverbal messages convey much more impact than verbal messages*. Words play a surprisingly small part in the communication process. Every spoken message has a vocal element, coming not from *what* we say, but from *how* we say it. The voice communicates in many ways: through tone, volume, and speed of delivery. A salesperson wishing to communicate enthusiasm needs to use a voice that is charged with energy.

As we attempt to read nonverbal communication, it is important to remember that no *one* signal carries much meaning. If the person you meet for the first time displays a weak grip during the handshake, don't let this one signal shape your first impression. Such factors as posture, eye contact, gestures, clothing, and facial expression must all be regarded together.[28]

Nonverbal messages can reinforce or contradict the spoken word. When your verbal message and body language are consistent, they give others the impression that you can be trusted and that what you say reflects what you truly believe. When there is a discrepancy between your verbal and nonverbal messages, you are less apt to be trusted.[29]

Entrance and Carriage

As noted earlier, the first impression you make is very important. The moment a salesperson walks into a client's office, the client begins making judgments. Susan Bixler, author of *The Professional Image* and *Professional Presence*, makes this comment:

> All of us make entrances throughout our business day as we enter offices, conference rooms, or meeting halls. And every time we do, someone is watching us, appraising us, sizing us up, and gauging our appearance, even our intelligence, often within the space of a few seconds.[30]

Bixler says that the key to making a successful entrance is simply believing—and projecting—that you have a reason to be there and have something important to offer the client. You can communicate confidence with a strong stride, good posture, and a friendly smile. A confident manner communicates to the client the message, "This meeting will be beneficial to you."

Shaking Hands

An inadequate handshake is like dandruff: no one will mention it, but everyone will notice it. The handshake is an important symbol of respect and, in most business settings, it is the proper greeting.[31] In the field of selling, the handshake is usually the *first* and frequently the *only* physical contact you make during a sales call. The handshake can communicate warmth, genuine concern for the prospect, and an image of strength. It can also communicate aloofness, indifference, and weakness to the customer. The message we communicate with a handshake is determined by a combination of five factors:

1. *Eye contact during handshake.* Eyes transmit more information than any other part of the body, so maintain eye contact throughout the handshaking process and display a pleasant smile.

2. *Degree of firmness.* Generally speaking, a firm handshake communicates a caring attitude, while a weak grip (the dead-fish handshake) communicates indifference.

3. *Depth of interlock.* A full, deep grip communicates friendship to the other person.

4. *Duration of grip.* There are no specific guidelines to tell us what the ideal duration of a grip should be. However, by extending the duration of the handshake we can often communicate a greater degree of interest and concern for the other person. Do not pump up and down more than once or twice.

5. *Degree of dryness of hands.* A moist palm not only is uncomfortable to handle but also can communicate the impression that you are quite nervous. Some people have a physiological problem that causes clammy hands, and they should keep a handkerchief within reach to remove excess moisture.[32]

The best time to present your name is when you extend your hand. When you introduce yourself, state your name clearly and then listen carefully to be certain you hear the customer's name. To ensure that you will remember the customer's name, repeat it. In some cases you will need to check to be sure you are pronouncing it properly.

Remembering Names

In the field of personal selling remembering a person's name is very important. To improve your ability to recall names, use one or more of these memory aids.

- *Verify the spelling.* After hearing the name ask, "Is that Reece with a 'c' or an 's'?" Repetition helps you remember the name.

- *Ask how the person wants to be addressed.* Ask, "Should I call you Miss Thomas, Ms. Thomas, or Mrs. Thomas?" This is another opportunity for repetition.

- *Relate the name to something easy to remember.* If the person's last name is park, connect this name with

"Central" in your mind. Some aspect of appearance (hair style, eyeglasses, etc.) might serve as a connecting reference.

- *Use the name quickly.* Work the person's name into the conversation right away: "Ms. Thomas, may I ask you a few questions?"

- *Use the name frequently.* During and at the end of the meeting, work the name into the conversation: "Ms. Thomas, thank you for meeting with me."[b]

Facial Expressions

If you want to identify the inner feelings of another person, watch facial expressions closely. The face is a remarkable communicator, capable of accurately signalling emotion in a split second and capable of concealing emotion equally well. You can tell in a blink of an eye if your customer's face is registering surprise, pleasure, or skepticism (see Fig. 7.4). Facial expressions are largely universal, so people around the world tend to "read" faces in a similar way. It is worth noting that the smile is the most recognized facial signal in the world and it can have a great deal of influence on others. George Rotter, professor of psychology at Montclair University, says, "Smiles are an enormous controller of how people perceive you." People tend to trust a smiling face.[33] Get in the habit of offering a sincere smile each time you meet with a prospect.

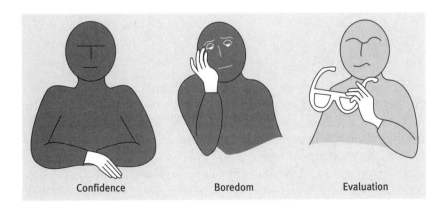

Confidence   Boredom   Evaluation

Figure 7.4 Our subtle facial gestures are continuously sending messages to others.

Eye Contact

When the customer is talking, eye contact is one of the best ways to say, "I'm listening." If you are looking across the room or at papers in your briefcase, the customer will assume you are not listening. However, prolonged eye contact can send the wrong message. A prolonged direct stare can be threatening. To avoid the prolonged stare, take fleeting glances at your notes. As the customer speaks, nod occasionally to indicate agreement or interest.[34]

THE EFFECT OF APPEARANCE ON RELATIONSHIPS

WE FORM OPINIONS ABOUT PEOPLE BASED ON A PATTERN OF IMMEDIATE IMPRESSIONS conveyed by appearance. The clothing we wear, the length and style of our hair, the fragrances we use, and the jewellery we display all combine to make a statement about us to others—a statement of primary importance to anyone involved in selling.

unconscious expectations
Certain views concerning appropriate dress.

We all have certain views, or **unconscious expectations**, concerning appropriate dress. In sales work we should try to anticipate the expectations of our clientele. The clothing worn by salespeople does make a difference in terms of customer acceptance because it communicates powerful messages. The clothing we wear can influence our credibility and likeability.

Most image consultants agree that there is no single "dress for success" look. The appropriate wardrobe will vary from one city or region to another and from company to company. However, there are some general guidelines that you should follow in selecting clothing for sales work. Three key words should govern your decisions: simplicity, appropriateness, and quality.[35]

Simplicity

The colour of your clothing, as well as the design, will communicate a message to the customer. Some colours are showy and convey an air of casualness. In a business setting we want to be taken seriously, so flashy colours should usually be avoided.

Appropriateness

business casual Clothing that allows you to feel comfortable but looks neat and professional.

Selecting appropriate clothing for sales work can be a challenge. We must carefully consider the clients we serve and decide what will be acceptable to them. Many salespeople are guided by the type of products they sell and the desired image projected by their employers. Deciding what constitutes appropriate attire in today's business-casual world begins with an understanding of what it means to "dress down." **Business casual** is clothing that allows you to feel comfortable but look neat and professional. Pay close attention to the clothing your clients wear.[36] If a client is wearing a nice sport coat, a collared long-sleeved shirt, and dress slacks, don't wear khaki trousers and a short-sleeve polo shirt. In recent years, the casual dress trend has reversed at many companies, and workplace dress codes have become more formal.[37]

Quality

The quality of your wardrobe will also influence the image you project to customers. A salesperson's wardrobe should be regarded as an investment, with each item carefully selected to look good and fit well. Susan Bixler says, "If you want respect, you have to dress as well as or better than your industry standards."[38]

Visual Integrity

Visual presence must have a certain amount of integrity and consistency. The images you project are made up of many factors, and lack of attention to important details can negate your effort to create a good impression. Too much jewellery, a shirt that does not fit well, or shoes that are not shined can detract from the professional look you want to project. People are often extra alert when meeting someone new, and this heightened consciousness makes every detail count.[39] Many young people today have tattoos or body piercings. While these may be considered fashionable among friends, they may be problematic for salespeople as some customers will hold other views. Like dandruff on your collar or stale tobacco on your breath, they may not be mentioned, but they will most certainly be noticed, and they are likely to have a negative impact on your sales. Keep in mind that customer contact often takes place in several settings. The first meeting with a customer may take place in his or her office, but the second meeting may be on the golf course. And the third meeting may take place at a nice restaurant. The clothing you wear in each of these settings is important.

EFFECT OF VOICE QUALITY ON RELATIONSHIPS

As noted previously, every spoken message has a vocal element. What we hear is greatly influenced by the speaker's tone of voice, vocal clarity, and verbal expressiveness. On the telephone, voice quality is even more important because the other person cannot see your facial expressions, hand gestures, and other body movements. You cannot trade in your current voice for a new one; however, you can make your voice more pleasing to others. How? Consider these suggestions.

1. *Do not talk too fast or too slowly.* Rapid speech often causes customers to become defensive. They raise psychological barriers because a "rapid-fire monologue" is associated with high-pressure sales methods. Many salespeople could improve their verbal presentation by speaking more slowly. The slower presentation allows others to follow, and it allows you, the speaker, time to think ahead—to consider the situation and make judgments. Another good tip is to vary the speed of your speech, leaving spaces between thoughts. Crowding too many thoughts together may confuse the listener.[40]

2. *Avoid a speech pattern that is dull and colourless.* The worst kind of voice has no colour and no feeling. Enthusiasm is a critical element of an effective sales presentation. It is also contagious. Your enthusiasm for the product will be transmitted to the customer.

3. *Avoid bad speech habits.* Kristy Pinand, a youthful-looking 23-year old, routinely used "teen speak." For example, she described a recent promotion as "so cool." Her

supervisor felt she not only looked young, but sounded very young, and this image could potentially hurt her ability to win the respect of clients. She urged Ms. Pinand to select her words more carefully. Ms. Pinand heeded the constructive advice and now rehearses her remarks aloud before she calls a client.[41]

Some speech habits can make us sound poorly educated and inarticulate. At age 22, Mike White learned that his unique regional accent and colourful speech patterns created problems at work. He recognized this was a "turnoff" to some of the image-conscious people he worked with. One day his sales manager asked him if he had his racquetball equipment with him, and White replied, "Yeah, I brung it." Fortunately, White's supervisor was willing to tactfully correct his grammatical problems and help him communicate with greater clarity. Today, Mike White is CEO of a successful company and a frequent speaker at trade shows.[42]

EFFECT OF ETIQUETTE ON YOUR RELATIONSHIPS

THE STUDY OF ETIQUETTE (SOMETIMES CALLED MANNER OR PROTOCOL) REVEALS A number of ways to enhance your relationship strategy. Salespeople who possess knowledge of the rules of etiquette can perform their daily work with greater poise and confidence. Think of etiquette as a universal passport to positive relationships and respect.

With practice, anyone can develop good etiquette without appearing to be "stiff" and at the same time win the respect and admiration of others. Space does not permit a complete review of this topic, but we cover some of the rules of etiquette that are especially important to salespeople.

1. *Avoid the temptation to address a new prospect by first name.* In a business setting, too much familiarity too quickly can cause irritation.

2. *Avoid offensive comments or stories.* Never assume that the customer's value system is the same as your own. Rough language, off-colour stories, or personal views on political issues can do irreparable damage to your image.

3. *Recognize the importance of punctuality.* Ann Marie Sabath, owner of a firm that provides etiquette training for business employees, says, "we teach people that if you're early, you're on time, and if you're on time, in reality, you're late." Showing up late for an appointment will be viewed as rudeness by most clients.[43]

4. *When you invite a customer to lunch, do not discuss business before the meal is ordered unless the client initiates the subject.* Also, order food that is easily controlled, and avoid such items as ribs, chicken, or lobster.

5. *When you use voice mail, leave a clear, concise message.* Do not speak too fast or mumble your name and number.

6. *Avoid cellular phone contempt.* Turn off the cell phone ringer any time you are with a client. Never put your phone on the table during a meal.

It has been said that good manners make other people feel better. This is true because good etiquette requires that we place the other person's comfort ahead of our own. One of the best ways to develop rapport with a customer is to avoid behaviour that might be offensive to that person.

CONVERSATIONAL STRATEGIES THAT ENHANCE RELATIONSHIPS

THE FOUNDATION FOR A LONG-TERM RELATIONSHIP WITH THE CUSTOMER IS frequently a "get acquainted" type of conversation that takes place before any discussion of business matters. Within a few minutes it is possible to reduce the relationship tension that is so common when two people meet for the first time. This informal visit with the customer provides the salesperson with an opportunity to apply three guidelines for building strong relationships featured in *How to Win Friends and Influence People*, the classic book written by Dale Carnegie.

- *Become genuinely interested in other people.* Tim Sanders, Chief Solutions Officer at Yahoo!, says, "How we are perceived as human beings is becoming increasingly important in the new economy."[44] When you become genuinely interested in the customer, you create an experience that is long remembered.

- *Be a good listener; encourage others to talk about themselves.* Stephen Covey, the noted author and consultant, recommends empathetic listening. This requires listening with your ears, your eyes, and your heart.[45] We live in a culture in which empathic listening is quite rare. Interrupting has become all too common as people rush to fill every gap in the conversation.

- *Talk in terms of the other person's interests.*[46] When you are initiating a conversation with a customer, don't hesitate to use small talk to get the conversation started. This may involve current events, business, or sports. Be sure to focus on topics that the customer is interested in.

The length of this conversation depends on your sense of the prospect's reaction to your greeting, how busy the prospect appears to be, and your awareness of topics of mutual interest. In developing conversation the following three areas should be considered.

Comments on "Here and Now" Observations

Observant salespeople are aware of the things going on around them. These observations can be as general as unusual developments in the weather or as specific as noticing unique artifacts in the prospect's office. These observations often provide the basis for *small talk*, which can break the ice and speed up the building of a relationship.

Compliments

When you offer a *sincere* compliment to your prospect, you are saying, "Something about you is special." Most people react positively to compliments because they appeal to the need for self-esteem. Your admiration should not be expressed, however, in phony superlatives that will seem transparent. Jack Canfield, author of *The Success Principles*, reminds us that everything we say to a customer produces an effect: "Know that you are constantly creating something—either positive of negative—with your words."[47]

Search for Mutual Acquaintances or Interests

A frequent mode for establishing rapport with a new prospect is to find friends or interests you have in common. If you know someone with the same last name as your prospect, it may be appropriate to ask whether your friend is any relation. Anything you observe in the prospect's office or home might suggest an interest that you and your prospect share. A strong bond often develops between two persons who share the same interest or hobby. Estate planner Frances Carlisle says her love of animals lands her many clients. Some of these clients wish to include provisions for the care of pets in their estate plans. Sometimes an unusual hobby (skydiving, mountain climbing, auto racing, etc.) is the perfect way to stand out and cultivate relationships with clients.[48]

STRATEGIES FOR SELF-IMPROVEMENT

ORSON WELLES, A WELL-KNOWN AND HIGHLY RESPECTED ACTOR, ONCE SAID, "Every actor is very busy getting better or getting worse." To a large extent, salespeople are also "very busy getting better or getting worse." To improve, salespeople must develop an ongoing program for self-improvement (see Chapter 18). It is important to keep in mind that all improvement is self-initiated. Each of us controls the switch that allows personal growth and development to take place.

At the beginning of this chapter, when we introduced the concept of emotional intelligence, we noted that it can be increased with the aid of self-development activities. Would you like to develop a more positive self-concept? Improve your ability to develop win-win relationships? Develop effective nonverbal communication skills? Improve your speaking voice? These relationship-building strategies can be achieved if you are willing to follow these four steps:

Step one: Set goals. The goal-setting process begins with a clear, written statement that describes what you want to accomplish. If your goal is too general or vague, progress toward achieving that goal will be difficult to observe. Next, you must identify the ways in which you plan to achieve your goal. Perseverance is the key to goal achievement.

Step two: Use visualization. To **visualize** means to form a mental image of something. The power to visualize (sometimes called guided imagery) is in a very real sense the power to create. If you really want to succeed at something, picture yourself doing it successfully. For example, spend time developing mental pictures of successful sales presentations or visualize yourself as one of the top salespeople in your organization. Once you have formed a clear mental picture of what you want to accomplish, identify the steps needed to get there and then mentally rehearse them. The visualization process needs to be repeated over and over again.[49]

visualize Form a mental image of something.

Step three: Use positive self-talk. People with a strong inner critic will receive frequent negative messages that can erode their self-esteem. It helps to refute and reject those negative messages with positive self-talk. **Self-talk** takes place silently in the privacy of your mind—a series of personal conversations you have with yourself continually throughout the day. Just like statements from other people, your self-talk can dramatically affect your behaviour and self-esteem.[50]

self-talk An effort to override past negative mental programming by erasing or replacing it with conscious, positive new directions.

Step four: Reward your progress. When you see yourself making progress toward a goal, or achieving a goal, reward yourself. This type of reinforcement is vital when you are trying to change a behaviour. There is nothing wrong with taking pride in your accomplishments.

Self-improvement efforts can result in new abilities or powers, and they give us the motivation to draw more fully on the talents we already have. As a result, our potential for success is greater.

This salesperson has set a fitness goal. Physical fitness can be an important part of a self-improvement program.

REVIEWING KEY CONCEPTS

- Explain the importance of developing a relationship strategy.

  The manner in which salespeople establish, build, and maintain relationships is a major key to success in personal selling. The key relationships in selling include management personnel, company support staff, secondary decision makers, and customers.

    The concept of *partnering* is revisited and discussed in detail. Partnering emphasizes building a strong relationship during every aspect of the sale and working hard to maintain a quality relationship with the customer after the sale. Partnerships can be strengthened when salespeople use value-added relationship strategies.

- Discuss how thought processes can enhance your relationship strategy.

  An understanding of the psychology of human behaviour provides a foundation for developing relationship strategies. In this chapter, we discuss the link between self-concept and success in selling. Self-imposed fears can prevent salespeople from achieving success. The relationship strategy is built on the win-win philosophy, empathy and ego drive, and character and integrity.

- Identify and describe the major nonverbal factors that shape our sales image.

  We describe several factors that influence the image we project to customers. The image others have of us is shaped to a great extent by nonverbal communication. We may choose the right words to persuade a customer to place an order, but aversive factors communicated by our clothing, handshake, facial expression, voice quality, and etiquette miscues may prejudice the customer against us and our product or service.

- Describe conversational strategies that help us establish relationships.

  The various conversational strategies that enhance relationships are reviewed. These include comments on "here and now" observations, compliments, and the search for mutual acquaintances. Dale Carnegie's guidelines for building strong relationships are discussed.

- Explain how to establish a self-improvement plan based on personal development strategies.

  We discussed the importance of adopting strategies for self-improvement. A four-step, self-improvement plan is the key to relationship building.

Key Terms

business casual   **138**

character   **134**

ego drive   **134**

emotional intelligence   **127**

empathizer   **128**

integrity   **134**

nonverbal message   **135**

self-concept   **132**

self-talk   **143**

unconscious expectations   **138**

visualize   **143**

Review Questions

1. List the three prescriptions that serve as the foundation for development of a relationship strategy.

2. How important are establishing, building, and maintaining relationships in the selling process? List the four groups of people with whom sales personnel must be able to work effectively.

3. Why is *partnering* described as the highest-quality selling relationship? Why has the building of partnerships become more important today?

4. Defend the statement, "Successful sales relationships depend on a positive self-concept."

5. Describe the win-win approach to selling.

6. How is our self-concept formed? Why is a positive self-concept so important in personal selling?

7. Describe the meaning of the term *emotional intelligence*.

8. Identify three conversational methods that can be used to establish relationships.

9. Describe the meaning of *nonverbal messages*. Why should salespeople be concerned about these messages?

10. List and describe each step in the four-step self-improvement plan.

Application Exercises

1. Select four salespeople you know and ask them if they have a relationship strategy for working with customers, management personnel, secondary decision makers, and company support staff. Ask each salesperson to give you two or three specific examples of steps they have taken to build and maintain a positive relationship with their customers.

2. The partnering style of selling is emphasized throughout the book. To gain more insight into the popularity of this concept, use an Internet search engine of your choice and key in the words "partnering + selling." Notice the large number of documents related to this query. Click on and examine several of these documents to learn more about this approach to selling.

3. Complete the following etiquette quiz. Your instructor will provide you with answers so you can check your responses.

   a. On what side should you wear your name tag?

   b. Is it appropriate to drink beer from a bottle at a reception?

   c. When introducing a female salesperson to a male prospect, whose name should be spoken first?

   d. At the table, when should you place your napkin in your lap?

   e. Is it ever proper to comb, smooth, or touch your hair while seated at a restaurant table?

4. In October, people of the Hindu religion celebrate Diwali, the festival of lights. The festival of lights is one of the most important and most beautiful Indian festivals. Rick Saulle, a pharmaceutical sales representative employed by Pifzer, knew that one of the most important physicians he called on was Indian and would celebrate Diwali. He also knew that it is commonplace to provide sweets to Indians who celebrate Diwali. Saulle visited an Indian grocery store and purchased a plate of Indian sweets to celebrate Diwali. When he presented the sweets to the physician, the response was very positive. The doctor grabbed Saulle's hand, shook it forcefully, and sincerely thanked him for honouring this important holiday.[51]

   Canada is host to a kaleidoscope of the world's cultures, and the trend toward greater diversity will accelerate in the years ahead. Reflect on the gift given by Mr. Saulle and then answer these questions.

   a. Is it appropriate for a salesperson to give a gift to someone who is celebrating a religious holiday?

   b. In addition to giving a gift, what are some other ways to recognize a religious festival or holiday?

   c. List and describe three religious holidays or festivals celebrated by denominations other than Christian.

5. Move quickly through the following list of traits. Use a check mark beside those that fit your self-image. Use an *X* to mark those that do not fit. If you are unsure, indicate with a question mark.

   —— I like myself.

   —— I trust myself.

   —— People trust me.

   —— I often do the wrong thing.

   —— I usually say the right thing.

   —— People avoid me.

   —— I dislike myself.

   —— I enjoy work.

   —— I waste time.

   —— I control myself.

   —— I put up a good front.

   —— I enjoy nature.

   —— I use my talents.

   —— I am dependent on others for ideas.

   —— I feel hemmed in.

   —— I am involved in solving community problems.

   —— I use time well.

   —— I do not use my talents fully.

   —— I enjoy people.

   —— I do not like myself.

   —— I usually say the wrong thing.

   —— I do not like to be around people.

   —— I am discouraged about life.

   —— I have not developed my talents.

   —— People like to be around me.

   Now look at the pattern of your self-assessment.

   a. Is there a pattern?

   b. Is there a winner or loser pattern?

   c. What traits would you like to change? List them.

   d. Pick the trait you would like to change the most and prepare a plan to achieve this change. Your plan should include specific goal statements.

6. It is pointed out in this chapter that clothing communicates strong messages. In this exercise you will become more aware of whether your clothes communicate the messages you want them to communicate.

a. Make a chart like the one that follows:

Item of clothing being analyzed	What I want my clothes to say about me to others	What others think my clothing says about me

b. In the first column, list the clothing you are now wearing (e.g., dress slacks, dress shoes, and sweater; athletic shoes, jeans, and T-shirt; or suit, dress shirt, and dress shoes).

c. In the middle column, describe the message you would like the clothes you have chosen to say (e.g., "I want to be comfortable," "I want people to trust me," or "I want people to take me seriously.").

d. Have somebody else fill in the third column by describing what they think your clothes say about you.

e. Compare the last two columns. Do your clothes communicate what you want them to? Do the same exercise for social dress, casual dress, business attire, and hair style.

Note: If you are currently employed, analyze the clothing you wear at work.

ROLE-PLAY EXERCISE

This is a two-part role-play exercise. Part one involves preparation for a sales call on a new prospect you have not met previously. The primary objective of this meeting is to get acquainted with the prospect and begin the process of building a long-term relationship. You anticipate that this prospect will become a very good customer. Review the text material on thought processes that will enhance your relationship strategy, nonverbal strategies that add value to your relationships, and conversational strategies that enhance relationships. Prepare a written outline of what you plan to say and do during the first five to ten minutes of the meeting. Think of this outline as your "strategic plan." Part two involves a role play with a class member who will play the role of the prospect. Throughout the role play, try to say and do everything that was part of your plan. At the end of the role play, give your strategic plan outline to the prospect and request feedback on your performance.

CRM Application Exercise   Preparing Letters with CRM

The Salesforce.com application demonstrates how customer relationship management (CRM) programs are designed to be used by people in a hurry or without extensive typing skills. Menu choices can be made with the mouse, by typing simple key combinations, or by selecting an icon. This means that a procedure, such as sending an e-mail to a contact (Dottie Smith) can be started by: (1) searching for the Dottie Smith contact record; (2) clicking the Send E-mail button in Activity History; (3) clicking the Select Template button and selecting the Park Inn New Contact template. A professional e-mail with contact and customer names in the appropriate places appears. The e-mail already has the date, salutation, closing line, your name, and your title on the screen. All you need to do is begin typing the body of the e-mail and press Send. Note that after you send the e-mail it is part of Dottie Smith's permanent activity history.

Search for the Brad Able contact record. With Brad Able's record on the screen, click the Mail Merge button and select the Confirm Appointment template. Make the necessary changes to the letter to confirm an appointment to meet at Brad Able's office next Thursday at 9:00 a.m. to discuss his training needs. Your letter should feature the win-win approach discussed in the chapter.

Reality Selling Today Video Case Problem

The commercial real estate services industry is highly competitive. CBRE, the firm featured at the beginning of this chapter, offers a wide variety of services such as industrial and logistical services, real estate consulting, investment properties services, and global corporate services.

When clients want to find an office space, they hold their realtor to high standards. After all, the term of a lease contract is a long-term one, and the stakes are high. CBRE salespeople understand the magnitude and trend of the commercial real estate market. They know that the customers are anxious to partner with someone who can be trusted to look after their best interests.

When new salespeople join the CBRE sales force, they usually work under a senior broker. The mentor helps these recruits form a professional image that appeals to the type of clientele served by the company. In the end, there is a direct link between the image projected by the salespeople and the success of the company. CBRE also adopts a team-based selling approach to ensure that the client is in the good hands as the relationship between CBRE and the client develops. Susana Rosas, an experienced CBRE broker, believes that working under a mentor to learn how to process a deal with a relationship orientation is invaluable. That mentality is part of CBRE's culture and success. Susana works closely with her team members through several stages of the relationship with CBRE clients, from prospecting to post-sales follow-up. When working with new recruits and her team members, she emphasizes the following points:

- Customers notice even the little details such as the firmness of a handshake or simply the properness of an introduction.

- Salespeople at CBRE must be able to build rapport with a variety of personality types. Some customers are quiet, reserved, and somewhat guarded when expressing their views. Others are more impulsive and express their views openly. Salespeople are encouraged to alter their communication style to increase the comfort level of the customer. Susana believes that it is always important for a salesperson to gauge how his or her communication style impacts the prospect. A positive attitude is another important aspect of the relationship-building process at CBRE.

- Susana is a strong believer that salespeople should find out what customers value. Most of the time, a salesperson must come up with innovative solutions to seemingly irreconcilable needs, such as the need to have a large space to accommodate cyclical ups and downs of the customer's industry and the need for efficiency. What is the most important aspect of commercial real estate sales? Most customers do not open up and share important information until they trust the salesperson. (See chapter opener on p. and Reality Selling Today Role-Play 2 in Appendix 1 on page for more information.)

Questions

1. Does it appear that the CBRE salesperson supports the three prescriptions that serve as a foundation of the relationship strategy? (See Strategic/Consultative Selling Model in Figure 7.1.) Explain your answer.

2. Why should real estate salespeople spend time developing a relationship strategy? What might be some long-term benefits of this strategy?

3. Is it ever appropriate to touch your client other than with a handshake? Explain your answer.

4. How would you behave differently when dealing with a return client versus a new client?

5. What are some precautions to take when preparing for a meeting with a foreign-born prospect?

Chapter 8
Communication Styles:
A Key to Adaptive Selling

Learning Objectives

After studying this chapter, you should be able to

1   Discuss how communication style influences the relationship process in sales

2   Identify the two major dimensions of the communication-style model

3   Explain the four communication styles in the communication-style model

4   Learn how to identify your preferred communication style and that of your customer

5   Learn to achieve interpersonal versatility and build strong selling relationships with style flexing

 Adaptive Selling Today Training Video Series

COMMUNICATION STYLES—A KEY TO ADAPTIVE SELLING

Communication styles—or behaviour styles, as they are sometimes called—form the basis of some of the most popular training programs in sales and management.

In the two-part Adaptive Selling Today training video that is available with this book, you'll meet Lana, a senior salesperson. While working with Ron, one of her top customers, Sandra, her sales team member, and Raymond, her marketing manager, she shares what she has learned about building selling relationships with communication styles. We will learn how Lana and her team take a "No, this won't work" response from Ron and, with the adaptive selling "Platinum Rule," attempt to build a mutually rewarding relationship.

Every year publications such as *Canadian Business, Business Week, Fortune,* and *Fast Company* feature profiles of well-known business leaders. These articles often focus on the communication styles of the executives who provide leadership in companies across North America. Who can forget Al "Chainsaw" Dunlap, who was described as aggressive, frank, opinionated, and impatient? He earned his nickname by ordering huge layoffs when he was the CEO responsible for restructuring companies such as Scott Paper and Sunbeam

We form impressions of others by observing their behaviour. Jeff Bezos, founder of Amazon.com, is often described as the happy extrovert who frequently displays spontaneous, uninhibited laughter. By contrast, Microsoft's Bill Gates is described as a quiet, reflective person who often seems preoccupied with other matters.

Corporation. Deborah Hopkins earned the nickname "Hurricane Debby" for the way she conducted business while holding leadership positions at Unisys, GM Europe, Boeing, and Lucent Technologies. Her demanding, ambitious, and sometimes emotional style occasionally created personality clashes. By contrast, Bill Gates is described as a quiet, reflective person who often seems preoccupied with other matters. And then there is Jeff Bezos, the founder and CEO of Amazon.com, who is often described as the happy extrovert. He seems to enjoy being with other people and often displays spontaneous, uninhibited behaviour.[1]

We form impressions of people by observing their behaviour. The thoughts, feelings, and actions that characterize someone are generally viewed as their **personality**.[2] Communication style is an important aspect of our personality.

personality The thoughts, feelings, and actions that characterize someone.

COMMUNICATION STYLES—AN INTRODUCTION TO MANAGING SELLING RELATIONSHIPS

ALMOST EVERYONE HAS HAD THE PLEASANT EXPERIENCE OF MEETING SOMEONE FOR THE first time and developing instant mutual rapport. There seems to be something about some people that makes you like them instantaneously—a basis for mutual understanding that is difficult to explain. On the other hand, we can all recall meeting people who "turn us off" almost immediately. Why do these things happen during the initial contact?

The impressions that others form about us are based on what they observe us saying and doing. They have no way of knowing our innermost thoughts and feelings, so they make decisions about us based on what they see and hear.[3] The patterns of behaviour that others observe can be called **communication style**. *Behaviour style* and *social style* are additional terms frequently used to describe these patterns of behaviour.

communication style Patterns of behaviour that others observe. Voice patterns, eye movement, facial expression, and posture are some of the components of our communication style.

Adaptive selling is defined as altering sales behaviours in order to improve communication with the customer. It relates to a salesperson's ability to collect information regarding the customer's needs and respond appropriately. Adaptive selling frequently requires complex behavioural adjustments.[4] Adjusting one's communication style in order to fit individual customer needs and preferences is an important element of adaptive selling.

Communication-Style Bias

Bias in various forms is quite common in our society. In fact, governments at all levels have passed many laws to curb blatant forms of age, ethnic, religious, and gender discrimination. We also observe some degree of regional bias when people from various parts of Canada meet.

The most frequently occurring form of bias is not commonly understood in our society. What has been labelled **communication-style bias** is a state of mind that almost every one of us experiences from time to time, but we usually find it difficult to explain the symptoms. Communication-style bias can develop when we have contact with another person whose communication style is different from our own. For example, a purchasing agent was overheard saying, "I do not know what it is, but I just do not like that sales representative." The agent was no doubt experiencing communication-style bias but could not easily describe the feeling.

Your communication style is the "you" that is on display every day—the outer pattern of behaviour that others see. If your style is very different from another person's, it may be difficult for the two of you to develop rapport. All of us have had the experience of saying or doing something that was perfectly acceptable to a friend or co-worker and being surprised when the same behaviour irritated someone else. However, aside from admitting that this happens, most of us are unable to draw meaningful conclusions from these experiences to help us perform more effectively with people in the future.[5]

In recent years, thousands of sales professionals have learned to manage their selling relationships more effectively through the study of communication styles. Books such as *I'm Stuck, You're Stuck* by Tom Ritchey, *People Styles at Work* by Robert Bolton and Dorothy Grover Bolton, and *The Versatile Salesperson* by Roger Wenschlag serve as good references. Many training companies offer seminars that provide enrollees with a practical understanding of communication-style theory and practice. Wilson Learning (**www.wilsonlearning.com**) offers a program entitled *The Versatile Salesperson*. This program helps salespeople develop the interpersonal skills necessary to work effectively with customers whose communication style is different than their own. Over 7 million people worldwide have completed Wilson Learning programs that focus on communication styles.[6]

Communication-Style Principles

The theory of behavioural- or communication-style bias is based on a number of underlying principles. A review of these principles will be beneficial before we examine specific styles.

1. *Individual differences exist and are important.* It is quite obvious that we all differ in terms of such physical characteristics as height, shoe size, facial features, and body

This Dentist Communicates

Most people feel some apprehension before going to a new dentist for the first time. But patients of Dr. Steve Bajura in London, Ontario, grow increasingly comfortable after each visit. That's because he talks to his patients—and not just about recommended dental procedures. He asks about their work, their children, their hobbies, and anything they wish to discuss. When they return for a second visit, they are pleasantly surprised to find that he remembers everything from their previous conversation. If they tell him that another patient referred them, he makes sure to thank that patient during their next visit.

Steve Bajura carefully manages his patient information, and this enables him to build better relationships with them, resulting in greater customer satisfaction, increased loyalty, and frequent referrals. He claims his business format just evolved naturally, but adds, "It seems to me that the way I manage patients is or should be the way all business is handled. I feel that, when the patient is in the chair, he or she deserves my full attention. That may or may not include 'small talk' which I feel is comfortable for me and probably for the patient. As time has gone on, the practice has continued to grow—far exceeding any expectations that I may have had."[a]

build, but the most interesting differences are those patterns of behaviour that are unique to each of us. Voice patterns, eye movement, facial expressions, and posture are some of the components of our communication style. Additional characteristics are discussed later in this chapter. Research by Swiss psychoanalyst Carl Jung and others has helped us understand the importance of individual differences.

2. *A communication style is a way of thinking and behaving.* It is not an ability, but instead a preferred way of using the abilities one has. This distinction is very important. An ability refers to how well someone can do something. A style refers to how someone likes to do something.[7]

3. *Individual style differences tend to be stable.* Our communication style is based on a combination of hereditary and environmental factors. Our style is somewhat original at the time of birth; it takes on additional individuality during the first three to five years of life. By the time we enter elementary school, the teacher should be able to identify our preferred communication style. While an individual's communication style tends to remain fairly constant throughout life, adapting to different communication counterparts or the ability to "flex" can be enhanced.

4. *There are a finite number of styles.* Most people display one of several clusters of similar behaviours, and this allows us to identify a small number of behavioural categories. By combining a series of descriptors, we can develop a single "label" that describes a person's most preferred communication style.

5. *To create the most productive relationships, it is necessary to get in sync with the communication style of the people you work with.*[8] Differences between people can be a source of friction unless you develop the ability to recognize and respond to the other person's style.

The ability to identify another person's communication style, and to know how and when to adapt your own preferred style to it, can afford you a crucial advantage in dealing with people. Differences between people can be a source of friction. The ability to "speak the other person's language" is an important relationship-management skill.[9]

Group sales presentations can be very challenging because, in most cases, you are attempting to adapt to several different communication styles.

Improving Your Relationship Selling Skills

Anyone who is considering a career in selling will benefit greatly from the study of communication styles. These concepts provide a practical method of classifying people according to communication style and give the salesperson a distinct advantage in the marketplace. A salesperson who understands communication-style classification methods and learns how to adapt them can avoid common mistakes that threaten interpersonal relations with customers. Awareness of these methods greatly reduces the possibility of tension arising during the sales call.

The first major goal of this chapter is to help you better understand your own most preferred communication style. The second goal is to help you develop greater understanding and appreciation for styles that are different from your own. The third goal is to help you manage your selling relationships more effectively by learning to adapt your style to fit the communication style of the customer. This practice is called **style flexing**.

style flexing The deliberate adjustment of one's communication style to accommodate the needs of the other person.

COMMUNICATION-STYLE MODEL

THIS SECTION INTRODUCES YOU TO THE FOUR BASIC COMMUNICATION STYLES. ONE OF THESE will surface as your most preferred style. The communication-style model that defines these styles is based on two important dimensions of human behaviour: dominance and sociability. We look at the dominance continuum first.

Dominance Continuum

dominance Reflects the tendency to influence or exert one's will over others in a relationship. Each of us falls somewhere on this continuum.

Dominance can be defined as the tendency to control or prevail over others.[10] Dominant people tend to be quite competitive. They also tend to offer opinions readily and to be decisive, opinionated, self-assertive, and vocal. Each of us falls somewhere on the dominance continuum illustrated by Figure 8.1.

Low High

Figure 8.1 The first step in determining your most preferred communication style is to identify where you are on the dominance continuum.

A person classified as high in dominance is generally a "take charge" type of person who makes a position clear to others. A person classified as low in dominance is usually more reserved, unassertive, and easygoing. Dominance has been recognized as a universal behavioural characteristic. David W. Johnson developed the Interpersonal Pattern Exercise to help people achieve greater interpersonal effectiveness. He believes that people fall into two dominance categories:

1. *Lower dominance:* These people have a tendency to be quite cooperative and let others control things. They tend to be lower in assertiveness.

2. *Higher dominance:* These people tend to like to control things and frequently initiate demands. They are more aggressive in dealing with others.[11]

The first step in determining your most preferred communication style is to identify where you fall on the dominance continuum. Do you tend to rank low or high on this scale? To answer this question, complete the Dominance Indicator form in Table 8.1. Rate yourself on each scale by placing a check mark on the continuum at the point that represents how you perceive yourself. If most of your check marks fall to the right of centre, you are someone who is higher in dominance. If most of your check marks fall to the left of

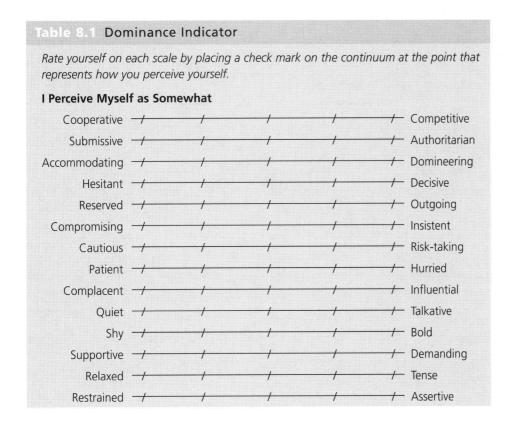

Table 8.1 Dominance Indicator

Rate yourself on each scale by placing a check mark on the continuum at the point that represents how you perceive yourself.

I Perceive Myself as Somewhat

Cooperative	Competitive
Submissive	Authoritarian
Accommodating	Domineering
Hesitant	Decisive
Reserved	Outgoing
Compromising	Insistent
Cautious	Risk-taking
Patient	Hurried
Complacent	Influential
Quiet	Talkative
Shy	Bold
Supportive	Demanding
Relaxed	Tense
Restrained	Assertive

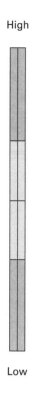

High

Low

Figure 8.2 The second step in determining your most preferred communication style is to identify where you are on the sociability continuum.

sociability Reflects the amount of control one exerts over emotional expressiveness. People who are high in sociability tend to express their feelings freely, while people who are low on this continuum tend to control their feelings.

centre, you are someone who is lower in dominance. Is there any best place to be on the dominance continuum? The answer is no. Successful salespeople can be found at all points along the continuum.

Sociability Continuum

Sociability reflects the amount of control we exert over our emotional expressiveness.[12] People who are high in sociability tend to express their feelings freely, while people who are low in this dimension tend to control their feelings. Each of us falls somewhere on the sociability continuum illustrated in Figure 8.2.

Sociability is also a universal behavioural characteristic. It can be defined as the tendency to seek and enjoy interaction with others. Therefore, high sociability is an indication of a person's preference to interact with other people. Lower sociability is an indicator of a person's desire to work in an environment where he or she has more time alone instead of having to make conversation with others. The person who is classified as being lower in the area of sociability is more reserved and formal in social relationships.

The second step in determining your most preferred communication style is to identify where you fall on the sociability continuum. To answer this question, complete the Sociability Indicator form shown in Table 8.2. Rate yourself on each scale by placing a check mark on the continuum at the point that represents how you perceive yourself. If most of your check marks fall to the right of centre, you are someone who is higher in sociability. If most of your check marks fall to the left of centre, you are someone who is

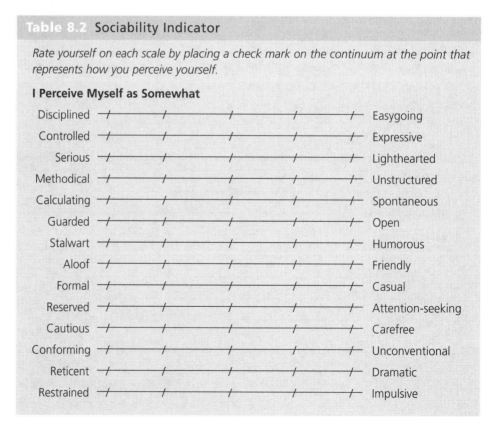

Table 8.2 Sociability Indicator

Rate yourself on each scale by placing a check mark on the continuum at the point that represents how you perceive yourself.

I Perceive Myself as Somewhat

Disciplined	Easygoing
Controlled	Expressive
Serious	Lighthearted
Methodical	Unstructured
Calculating	Spontaneous
Guarded	Open
Stalwart	Humorous
Aloof	Friendly
Formal	Casual
Reserved	Attention-seeking
Cautious	Carefree
Conforming	Unconventional
Reticent	Dramatic
Restrained	Impulsive

lower in sociability. Keep in mind that there is no best place to be. Successful salespeople can be found at all points along this continuum.

As you reflect on your dominance and sociability ratings, keep in mind that self-ratings can be misleading. Many people do not see themselves in the same way that others see them. Friends and co-workers who frequently observe your behaviours may be in a better position to identify your communication style.

With the aid of the dominance and sociability continuums we can now discuss a relatively simple communication-style classification plan that has practical application in the field of selling. We will describe the four basic styles: Emotive, Directive, Reflective, and Supportive.

Four Styles of Communication

By combining the two dimensions of human behaviour—dominance and sociability—we can form a partial outline of the communication-style model (Fig. 8.3). Dominance is represented by the horizontal axis, and sociability is represented by the vertical axis. Once the two dimensions of human behaviour are combined, the framework for communication-style classification is established.

The Emotive Style The upper right-hand quadrant of Figure 8.4 defines a style that combines higher sociability and higher dominance. We call this the **Emotive style** (see Fig. 8.5). Emotive people are expressive and willing to spend time maintaining and enjoying

Emotive style A communication style that displays the following characteristics: appears to be quite active, takes the social initiative in most cases, likes to encourage informality, and expresses emotional opinions.

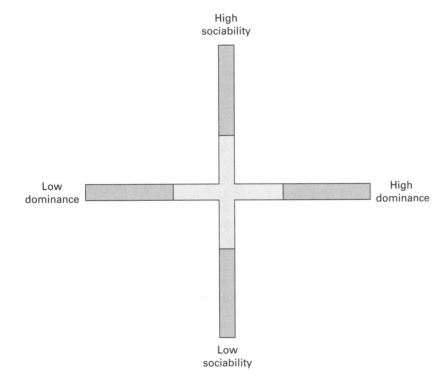

Figure 8.3 When the dominance and sociability dimensions of human behaviour are combined, the framework for communication-style classification is established.

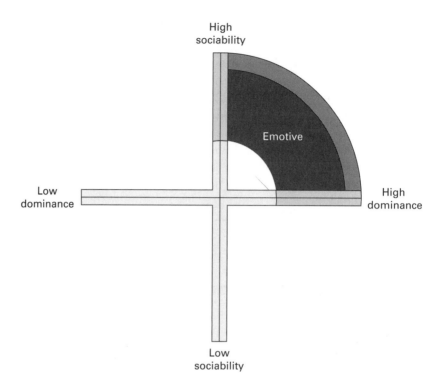

Figure 8.4 The Emotive style combines high sociability and high dominance.

a large number of relationships. Television personalities Rick Mercer, Ben Mulroney, and comedian Shaun Majumder provide excellent models of the Emotive communication style. Sports personality Don Cherry, actors Jim Carrey and Mike Myers, and Richard Branson, the founder of Virgin Atlantic Airways, also project the Emotive communication style. They are outspoken, enthusiastic, and stimulating. The Emotive person wants to create a social relationship quickly and usually feels more comfortable in an informal atmosphere. Some of the verbal and nonverbal clues that identify the Emotive person follow:

1. *Appears quite active.* This person gives the appearance of being busy. A person who combines higher dominance and higher sociability often displays spontaneous, uninhibited behaviour. The Emotive person is likely to express feelings with vigorous movements of the hands and a rapid speech pattern.

2. *Takes the social initiative in most cases.* Emotives tend to be extroverts. When two people meet for the first time, the Emotive person is more apt to initiate and maintain the conversation as well as to initiate the handshake. Emotives rate higher in both directness and openness.

Sociable	Unstructured
Spontaneous	Excitable
Zestful	Personable
Stimulating	Persuasive
Emotional	Dynamic

Figure 8.5 Key words for the Emotive style

3. *Likes to encourage informality.* The Emotive person moves to a first-name basis as soon as possible (too soon in some cases). Even the way this person sits in a chair communicates a preference for a relaxed, informal social setting.

4. *Expresses emotional opinions.* Emotive people generally do not hide their feelings. They often express opinions dramatically and impulsively.

Emotive people like Oprah Winfrey are enthusiastic, outspoken, and stimulating. By contrast, persons who display the Reflective style like Tiger Woods are more reserved and tend not to express dramatic opinions.

The Directive Style The lower right-hand quadrant of Figure 8.6 defines a style that combines higher dominance and lower sociability. We will call this the **Directive style** (see Fig. 8.7).

To understand the nature of people who display the Directive communication style, picture in your mind's eye the director of a Hollywood film. The person you see is giving orders in a firm voice and is generally in charge of every facet of the operation. Everyone on the set knows this person is in charge. While this common image of the Hollywood film director is probably exaggerated, this example will be helpful as you attempt to become familiar with the Directive style.

Directive style A communication style that displays the following characteristics: appears to be businesslike, displays a serious attitude, and voices strong opinions.

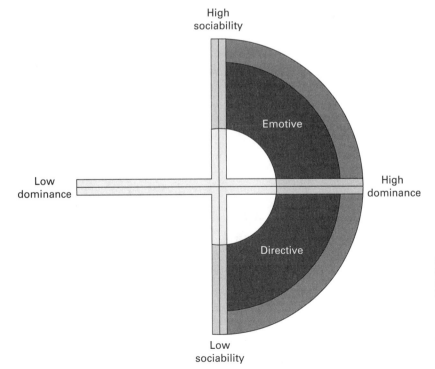

Figure 8.6 The Directive style combines high dominance and low sociability.

Aggressive	Determined
Intense	Frank
Requiring	Opinionated
Pushy	Impatient
Serious	Bold

Figure 8.7 Key words for the Directive style

Judith Sheindlin, better known as Judge Judy, uses a brash "take no prisoners" approach to handling disputes on the *Judge Judy* television show. She is frank, assertive, and very focused.

Reflective style
A communication style that displays the following characteristics: controls emotional expression, displays a preference for orderliness, tends to express measured opinions, and seems difficult to get to know.

Many senior executives of large corporations project the Directive style. Other examples include Prime Minister Stephen Harper and *American Idol*'s Simon Cowell. They may be described as frank, demanding, assertive, and determined.

In the field of selling you will encounter a number of customers who are Directives. How can you identify these people? What verbal and nonverbal clues can you observe? A few of the behaviours displayed by Directives follow:

1. *Appears to be quite busy.* The Directive generally does not like to waste time and wants to get right to the point. Judy Sheindlin of the *Judge Judy* television show displays this behaviour.

2. *May give the impression of not listening.* In most cases the Directive feels more comfortable talking than listening.

3. *Displays a serious attitude.* A person who is lower in sociability usually communicates a lack of warmth and is apt to be quite businesslike and impersonal. Mike Wallace, former star of the popular *60 Minutes* television show, seldom smiles or displays warmth.

4. *Likes to maintain control.* The person who is higher on the dominance continuum likes to maintain control. During meetings the Directive often seeks to control the agenda.[13]

The Reflective Style   The lower left-hand quadrant of the communication-style model features a combination of lower dominance and lower sociability (Fig. 8.8). People who regularly display this behaviour are classified as having the **Reflective style** (see Fig. 8.9).

The Reflective person tends to examine all the facts carefully before arriving at a decision. Like a cautious scientist, this individual wants to gather all available information and weigh it carefully before taking a position. The Reflective type is usually a stickler for

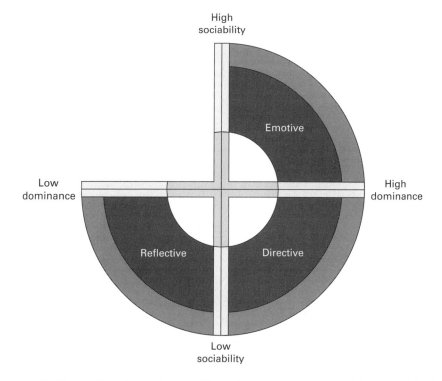

Figure 8.8 The Reflective style combines low dominance and low sociability.

Precise	Scientific
Deliberate	Preoccupied
Questioning	Serious
Disciplined	Industrious
Aloof	Stuffy

Figure 8.9 Key words for the Reflective style

detail.[14] The late physicist Albert Einstein fits the description. Rex Murphy, the journalist who hosts CBC's *Cross Country Checkup*, and David Suzuki, the scientist who hosts CBC's *The Nature of Things*, also display the characteristics of the Reflective type.

The Reflective communication style combines lower dominance and lower sociability; therefore, people with this classification tend to be reserved and cautious. Some additional behaviours that characterize this style follow:

1. *Controls emotional expression.* Reflective people tend to curb emotional expression and are less likely to display warmth openly. Bill Gates displays this personality trait.

2. *Displays a preference for orderliness.* The Reflective person enjoys a highly structured environment and generally feels frustration when confronted with unexpected events.

3. *Tends to express measured opinions.* The Reflective individual usually does not express dramatic opinions. This communication style is characterized by disciplined, businesslike actions.

4. *Seems difficult to get to know.* The Reflective person tends to be somewhat formal in social relationships and therefore can be viewed as aloof by many people.

In a selling situation the Reflective customer does not want to move too fast. This person wants the facts presented in an orderly and unemotional manner and does not want to waste a lot of time socializing.

Persons with the Reflective style, such as David Suzuki, tend to control their emotions and examine all the facts when making a decision.

The Supportive Style The upper left-hand quadrant shows a combination of lower dominance and higher sociability (Fig. 8.10). This communication style is called the **Supportive style** (see Fig. 8.11) because these people find it easy to listen and usually

Supportive style
A communication style that displays the following characteristics: appears quiet and reserved, listens attentively to other people, tends to avoid the use of power, and makes decisions in a thoughtful and deliberate manner.

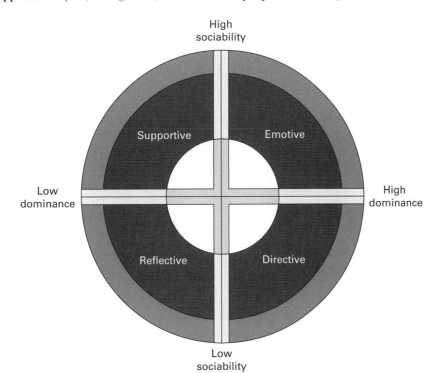

Figure 8.10 The Supportive style combines low dominance and high sociability.

Lighthearted	Patient
Reserved	Sensitive
Passive	Relaxed
Warm	Compliant
Docile	Softhearted

Figure 8.11 Key words for the Supportive style

People with the Supportive communication style are usually quiet and unassuming.

do not express their views in a forceful manner. Actress Julia Roberts, singer Anne Murray, and *American Idol*'s Paula Abdul display the characteristics of the Supportive style.

Low visibility generally characterizes the lifestyle of Supportive people. They complete their tasks in a quiet, unassuming manner and seldom draw attention to what they have accomplished. In terms of assertiveness, persons with the Supportive style rank quite low. Someone who ranks higher on the dominance continuum is likely to view the Supportive individual as being too easygoing. Other behaviours that commonly characterize the Supportive person follow:

1. *Gives the appearance of being quiet and reserved.* People with the Supportive communication style can easily display their feelings, but not in the assertive manner common to the Emotive individual.

2. *Listens attentively to other people.* In selling, good listening skills can be a real asset. This talent comes naturally to the Supportive person.

3. *Tends to avoid the use of power.* Whereas the Directive may rely on power to accomplish tasks, the Supportive person is more likely to rely on friendly persuasion.

4. *Makes decisions in a thoughtful and deliberate manner.* The Supportive person usually takes longer to make a decision.

Popularity of the Four-Style Model

We are endlessly fascinated by ourselves, and this helps explain the growing popularity of the four-style model presented in this chapter. To satisfy this insatiable appetite for information, many training and development companies offer training programs that present the four social or communication styles. Figure 8.12 features the approximate equivalents of the four styles presented in this chapter. Although four-style programs were initially

Supportive (Manning/Reece/Ahearne/MacKenzie) Amiable (Wilson Learning) Supportive-Giving (Stuart Atkins Inc.) Relater (People Smarts) Steadiness (Personal Profile System) Supportive (DiSC)	Emotive (Manning/Reece/Ahearne/MacKenzie) Expressive (Wilson Learning) Adapting-Dealing (Stuart Atkins Inc.) Socializer (People Smarts) Influencing (Personal Profile System) Influencing (DiSC)
Reflective (Manning/Reece/Ahearne/MacKenzie) Analytical (Wilson Learning) Conserving-Holding (Stuart Atkins Inc.) Thinker (People Smarts) Cautiousness/Compliance (Personal Profile System) Conscientious (DiSC)	Directive (Manning/Reece/Ahearne/MacKenzie) Driver (Wilson Learning) Controlling-Taking (Stuart Atkins Inc.) Directive (People Smarts) Dominance (Personal Profile System) Dominance (DiSC)

Figure 8.12 The four basic communication styles have been used in a wide range of training programs. For comparison purposes the approximate equivalents to the four communication styles discussed in this chapter are listed.

created and marketed in the United States, they have become a global phenomenon, according to staff at the Wilson Learning Corporation.[15] Inscape Publishing, the company that developed the DiSC learning instrument over three decades ago, reports that more that 40 million people worldwide have completed DiSC workshops.[16]

Determining Your Communication Style

You now have enough information to identify your own communication style. If your location on the dominance continuum is right of centre and your position on the sociability continuum is below the centre mark, you fall into the Directive quadrant. If your location on the dominance continuum is left of centre and your position on the sociability continuum is above the centre mark, then your most preferred style is Supportive. Likewise, lower dominance matched with lower sociability forms the Reflective communication style, and higher dominance matched with higher sociability forms the Emotive communication style.

An Online Assessment of Your Communication Style

You can gain further insight into your communication style by accessing the **www.pearsoned .ca/manning** website and clicking on the Online Assessment of Your Communication Style link. After completing the assessment, you will be supplied with a profile indicating your most preferred communication style. You will also be presented with a profile of your secondary style. See application exercises 1, 2, 3, and 4 on page 170 for more ways to use this online assessment tool.

Of course, all of us display some characteristics of the Emotive, Directive, Reflective, and Supportive communication styles. However, one of the four styles is usually predominant and readily detectable.[17] Some people who study the communication-style model for the first time may initially experience feelings of frustration. They find it hard to believe that one's behavioural style tends to remain quite uniform throughout life. People often say, "I am a different person each day!" It is certainly true that we sometimes feel different from day to day, but our most preferred style remains stable.

The Supportive person might say, "I sometimes get very upset and tell people what I am thinking. I can be a Directive when I want to be!" There is no argument here. Just because you have a preferred communication style does not mean you will never display the behavioural characteristics of another style. Some people use different styles in different contexts and in different relationships.[18] Reflective people sometimes display Emotive behaviour, and Emotive people sometimes display Reflective behaviour. We are saying that each person has one most-preferred and habitually used communication style.

MINIMIZING COMMUNICATION-STYLE BIAS

SALESPEOPLE OFTEN MAKE THE MISTAKE OF FOCUSING TOO MUCH ON THE CONTENT OF THEIR sales presentation and not enough on how they deliver their message.[19] When information is presented ineffectively, salespeople miss the opportunity to add value. Communication-style bias is a barrier to success in selling. This form of bias is a common problem in sales work simply because salespeople deal with people from all four quadrants. You cannot select potential customers on the basis of their communication style. You must be able to develop rapport with people from each of the four quadrants. When people of different styles work together but don't adapt to one another, serious problems can develop.[20]

How Communication-Style Bias Develops

To illustrate how communication-style bias develops in a sales situation, let us observe a sales call involving two people with different communication styles. Lana Wheeler entered the office of Ron Harrington, one of her large accounts, with a feeling of optimism. She was sure that her product would save Ron's company several thousand dollars a month. She was 99 percent certain that, this being her third call on Ron, the sale would be closed. Ten minutes after meeting Ron, she was walking out of his office without an order. What went wrong?

Lana Wheeler is an engaging type who is an Emotive in terms of communication style. Her sales calls are typically fast-paced. She entered Ron's office and immediately began to close the sale. Ron interrupted and told Lana he couldn't commit to her proposal. Lana appeared to ignore Ron's response and told him she could put some more figures together on pricing and then used another trial close. Ron finally told Lana, "Look you don't understand the way I do business. We have bigger issues than additional figures. As I said, this is a 'no go' project."

Ron's communication style is Directive. He feels uncomfortable when someone is making a decision for him. He wants to maintain control and be in charge of making his own decisions. He felt tension when Lana tried to get him to make a decision on her terms. If Lana had spent more time asking questions, listening more closely, and allowing Ron to feel like the decision was his—she may have found out what "the bigger issues" were. The approach she used would have been more appropriate for the Supportive or Emotive communication style.

A salesperson who is highly adaptable can usually build rapport with customers regardless of their communication style. Style flexing is a sales strategy that can be learned.

In the training video *Communication Styles: A Key to Adaptive Selling Today,* Lana, Ron, Raymond and Sandra all moved into their excess zones before learning about the platinum rule and developed communication-style bias. After learning flexability and versatility, salespeople can adapt to the style of others, and then build the kind of rapport that adds value to the sale.

Rich Goldberg, CEO of Warm Thoughts Communications, a marketing communications company, sensed he was about to lose an important client. He met with his staff, and together they created a profile based on their knowledge of the client's communication style. It soon became apparent that there was a mismatch between the client and the salesperson who called on that person. The customer was low in sociability but high in dominance. The customer was also described as someone who needed facts and figures. The salesperson was working on relationship building, and this approach was agitating the client. Goldberg counselled his staff to keep conversations with this customer brief, use facts and figures frequently, and clearly spell out the company's commitment to the client.[b]

ADAPTIVE SELLING REQUIRES VERSATILITY

PERSONAL SELLING HAS BECOME MORE CUSTOMER-FOCUSED THAN EVER BEFORE, SO EVERY effort should be made to reduce the tension between the salesperson and customer. Dr. David Merrill, one of the early pioneers in the development of communication-style instruments and training programs, uses the term **versatility** to describe our ability to minimize communication-style bias.[21] Roger Wenschlag, author of *The Versatile Salesperson*, describes versatility as "the degree to which a salesperson is perceived as developing and maintaining buyer comfort throughout the sales process." *Adapting* to the customer's preferred communication style can enhance sales performance.[22]

versatility Our ability to minimize communication-style bias.

Mature and Immature Behaviour

There is a mature and an immature side to each behavioural style. Let us examine the Emotive style to illustrate this point. People with this style are open, personable individuals who seem genuinely friendly. The natural enthusiasm displayed by the mature Emotive is refreshing. On the other hand, an Emotive person who is too talkative and too emotional may have difficulty building rapport with some customers; this is the immature side of the Emotive communication style.

You will recall that we used the words "industrious" and "precise" to describe the Reflective style. These are words that apply to the mature side of the Reflective person. We also used the words "aloof" and "stuffy." These words describe the immature side of the Reflective.

The good news is that we all have the potential for developing the mature side of our communication style.

Strength/Weakness Paradox

It is a fact of life that your greatest strength can become your greatest weakness. If your most preferred style is Reflective, people are likely to respect your well-disciplined approach to life as one of your strengths. However, this strength can become a weakness if it is exaggerated. The Reflective person can be too serious, too questioning, and too inflexible. Robert Haas, former CEO of Levi Strauss & Company, is known for extraordinary—some say obsessive—attention to detail. Those who work with him say an offhand conversation can sound like a lecture. This Reflective, however, has the ability to flex his style. Levi's employees are fiercely loyal to Haas and describe him as compassionate to a fault.[23]

People with the Directive style are open and frank. They express their true feelings in a direct manner. In most cases we appreciate candour, but we do not like to be around people who are too straightforward or too blunt in expressing their views. Steven Ballmer, CEO of Microsoft, was known as a very demanding executive during his early years with the company. His explosive temper was legendary and he often put the fear of God into his staff members. He once needed throat surgery because he yelled so much. Later he became more diplomatic and less domineering.[24] When people come across as opinionated, they tend to antagonize others. We should avoid pushing our strengths to the point of unproductive excess.[25]

To illustrate how strengths become weaknesses in excess, let us add more detail to our communication-style model. Note that it now features three zones that radiate out from the centre (see Fig. 8.13). These dimensions might be thought of as intensity zones.

Zone one. People who fall within this zone display their unique behavioural characteristics with less intensity than those in zone two. The Emotive person, for example, is moderately high on the dominance continuum and moderately high on the sociability continuum. As you might expect, zone one communication styles are more difficult to identify because there is less intensity in both dimensions (dominance and sociability).

Zone two. Persons who fall within this zone display their unique behavioural characteristics with greater intensity than persons in zone one. The zone two Reflective, for example, falls within the lowest quartile of the dominance continuum and the lowest quartile of the sociability continuum. The boundary line that separates zone one and zone two should not be seen as a permanent barrier restricting change in intensity. Under certain circumstances we should abandon our most preferred style temporarily. A deliberate move from zone one to zone two, or vice versa, is called style flexing.

Excess zone. The excess zone is characterized by a high degree of intensity and rigidity. When people allow themselves to drift into this zone, they become very inflexible, which is often interpreted by others as a form of bias toward their style. In addition, the strengths of the inflexible person become weaknesses. Extreme intensity in any quadrant is bound to threaten interpersonal relations.

Customer Relationship Management with Technology

Being Prepared

Customer relationship management (CRM) software empowers a salesperson with information essential to continue a relationship. The software can be used to record, retain, and produce personal information including such factors as marital status, names and ages of children, and individual preferences. Before placing a call, the salesperson might review the database information to refresh his or her memory about the prospect. This can be especially helpful when preparing to talk with someone with a specific communication style. (See the exercise Identifying Communication Styles on p. 95 for more information.)

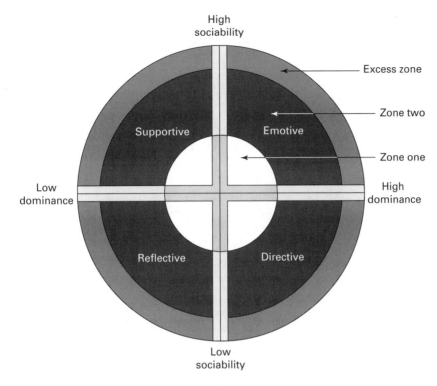

Figure 8.13 The completed communication-style model provides important insights needed to manage the relationship process in selling.

We are apt to move into the excess zone and exaggerate our style characteristics under stressful conditions. Stress tends to bring out the worst in many people. Here are some of the behaviours that salespeople and customers may display when they are in the excess zone:

Emotive style
Expresses highly emotional opinions
Stops listening to the other person
Tries too hard to promote own point of view
Becomes outspoken to the point of being offensive

Directive style
Gets impatient with the other person
Becomes dictatorial and bossy
Does not admit being wrong
Becomes extremely competitive

Reflective style
Becomes stiff and formal
Is unwilling to make a decision
Avoids displaying any type of emotion
Is overly interested in detail

Supportive style
Agrees with everyone
Is unable to take a strong stand
Becomes overly anxious to win approval of others
Tries to comfort everyone

The excess zone is characterized by a high degree of intensity and rigidity. We are more apt to move into the excess zone under very stressful conditions.

ACHIEVING VERSATILITY THROUGH STYLE FLEXING

STYLE FLEXING IS THE DELIBERATE ATTEMPT TO ADAPT ONE'S COMMUNICATION STYLE TO accommodate the needs of the other person. You are attempting to communicate with the other person on his or her own "channel." Ron Willingham, in his book *Integrity Selling*, reminds us that "people are more apt to buy from you when they perceive you view the world as they view the world."[26] In a selling situation you should try to determine the customer's most preferred style and flex your own accordingly. If your preferred communication style is Directive and your customer is a Supportive, try to be more personal and warm in your presentation. Once you know the customer's style, flexing your style can make the difference between a presentation that falters and one that exceeds your expectations.[27] Style sensitivity and flexing add value to the sales process.

Throughout the preapproach, you should learn as much as possible about the customer and try to determine his style. Once you are in the customer's presence, do not become preoccupied analyzing the person's style. If you are trying hard to analyze the person's style, you may not listen closely enough to what she is trying to tell you. If you are truly tuned in to the customer, you can absorb many clues that will help you determine her style. After the sales call, analyze the communication and record your findings. Use this information to plan your next contact with the customer.[28] Listen closely to the customer's tone of voice. A Supportive person sounds warm and friendly. The Reflective customer's voice is more likely to be controlled and deliberate. Pay particular attention to gestures. The Emotive individual uses his hands to communicate thoughts and ideas. The Directive also uses gestures to communicate but is more controlled and less spontaneous. The Reflective person appears more relaxed, less intense. The Emotive individual is an open, impulsive communicator, while the Reflective person is quite cautious. The Supportive type is personal and friendly, while the Reflective person may seem difficult to get to know. To avoid relationship tension, consider the following suggestions for each of the four styles.

Selling to Emotives

If you are attempting to sell products to an Emotive person, keep in mind the need to move at a pace that will hold the attention of the prospect. Be enthusiastic and avoid an approach that is too stiff and formal. Take time to establish goodwill and build relationships. Do not place too much emphasis on the facts and details. To deal effectively with Emotive people, plan actions that will provide support for their opinions, ideas, and dreams.[29] Plan to ask questions concerning their opinions and ideas, but be prepared to help them get "back on track" if they move too far away from the topic. Maintain good eye contact and, above all, be a good listener.

Selling to Directives

The key to relating to Directives is to keep the relationship as businesslike as possible. Developing a strong personal relationship is not a high priority for Directives. In other words, friendship is not usually a condition for a good working relationship. Your goal is to be as efficient, time disciplined, and well organized as possible, and to provide appropriate facts, figures, and success probabilities. Most Directives are goal-oriented people, so try to identify their primary objectives and then determine ways to support and help with these objectives. Early in the sales presentation, ask specific questions and carefully note responses. Look for specific points you can respond to when it is time to present your proposal.

Selling to Reflectives

The Reflective person will respond in a positive way to a thoughtful, well-organized approach. Arrive at meetings on time and be well prepared. In most cases it is not necessary to spend a great deal of time building a social relationship. Reflective people appreciate a no-nonsense, businesslike approach to personal selling. Use specific questions that show clear direction. Once you have information concerning the prospect's needs, present your proposal in a slow, deliberate way. Provide as much documentation as possible. Do not be in too big a hurry to close the sale. Never pressure the Reflective person to make quick decisions.

Selling to Supportives

Take time to build a social relationship with the Supportive person. Spend time learning about the things that are important in this individual's life—family, hobbies, and major interests. Listen carefully to personal opinions and feelings. Supportive individuals like to conduct business with sales personnel who are professional but friendly. Therefore, study their feelings and emotional needs as well as their technical and business needs. Throughout the presentation, provide personal assurances and support for their views. If you disagree with a Supportive person, curb the desire to disagree too assertively; Supportive people tend to dislike interpersonal conflict. Give them the time to comprehend your proposal. Patience is important.

As you develop your communication-style identification skills and become more adept at style flexing, you are better able to manage the relationship process. With these skills, you should be able to open more accounts, sell more to established customers, and more effectively meet the pressures of competition. Most important, your customers will view you as a person better able to understand and meet their needs.

A Word of Caution

It is tempting to put a label on someone and then assume the label tells you everything you need to know about that person. If you want to build an effective sales partnership with a prospect, you must acquire additional information about that person. Stuart Atkins, a respected authority on communication styles and author of *The Name of Your Game*, says we should be careful not to use labels that make people feel boxed in, typecast, or judged. He believes we should not classify *people*; we should classify their *strengths* and *preferences* to act one way or another under certain circumstances.[30] You must also be careful not to let the label you place on yourself become the justification for your own inflexible behaviour. Try not to let the label justify or reinforce why you are unable or unwilling to communicate effectively with others.

REVIEWING KEY CONCEPTS

- Discuss how communication style influences the relationship process in selling.

  Many sales are lost because salespeople fail to communicate effectively with the prospect. Communication-style bias contributes to this problem. Every salesperson who is willing to develop style sensitivity and engage in appropriate style flexing can minimize one of the most common barriers to success in selling.

- Identify the two major dimensions of the communication-style model.

  The communication-style model is based on two continuums that assess two major aspects of human behaviour: dominance and sociability. By combining them as horizontal and vertical continuums we create quadrants that define four styles of communication. We have called these the Emotive, Directive, Reflective, and Supportive styles.

- Explain the four communications styles in the communication-style model.

  The Emotive style combines high sociability and high dominance whereas the Directive style combines high dominance and low sociability. The Reflective style combines low dominance and low sociability whereas the Supportive style combines low dominance and high sociability.

- Learn how to identify your preferred communication style and that of your customer.

  With practice you can learn to identify your preferred communication style. The starting point is to rate yourself on each scale (dominance and sociability) by placing a check mark at a point along the continuum that represents how you perceive yourself. Completion of the dominance and sociability indicator forms will help you achieve greater awareness of your communication style. This same approach can be used to identify the customer's preferred style.

- Learn to achieve interpersonal versatility and build strong selling relationships with style flexing.

  A third dimension of human behaviour—versatility— is important in dealing with communication styles that are different from your own. You can adjust your own style to meet the needs of others—a process called *style flexing*. Style flexing is an attempt to change or alter your style to meet the needs of the customer.

Key Terms

adaptive selling   **150**

communication style   **149**

communication-style bias   **150**

Directive style   **157**

dominance   **152**

Emotive style   **155**

personality   **149**

Reflective style   **158**

sociability   **154**

style flexing   **152**

Supportive style   **159**

versatility   **163**

Review Questions

1. What is the meaning of the term *communication style*?
2. Describe the five major principles that support communication-style theory.
3. What are the benefits to the salesperson who understands communication style?
4. What two dimensions of human behaviour are used to identify communication style?
5. Describe the person who tends to be high in sociability.
6. What are the four communication styles? Develop a brief description of each of the styles.
7. What is the reaction of most people who study communication styles for the first time? Why does this reaction surface?
8. Define *style flexing*. How can style flexing improve sales productivity?
9. Explain the statement, "Your greatest strength can become your greatest weakness."
10. What suggestions would you give to a salesperson who is planning to meet a new prospect who displays the Reflective communication style?

Application Exercises

1. Communication, or Behaviour, Styles is one of the most popular training programs. Worldwide, 47 million people have participated in Wilson and DiSC programs. An understanding of communication styles assists us in building better personal and business relationships. As indicated in this chapter, the first step in applying what you have learned about communication styles is to identify and understand your own style. Using the Online Communication Style Assessment tool at **www.pearsoned.ca/manning**, assess your communication style.

   a. Do you agree with your assessment of your most preferred style? How about your results on your secondary style?

   b. Referring back to the material presented in this chapter, identify the strengths and weaknesses of your style.

   c. Identify the styles you enjoy working with best. Identify the styles you enjoy working with least.

   d. Referring to the behaviours listed on page 154, can you identify those behaviours you tend to exhibit when you feel stressed?

   e. Explain why you think so many individuals and companies have participated in these programs. From Figure 8.12 on page 160, list the names of other training programs you could use to identify your most preferred style.

2. Self-awareness is important in personal selling. As we get to know ourselves, we can identify barriers to acceptance by others. Once you have identified your most preferred communication style, you have taken a big step in the direction of self-awareness. We have noted that self-ratings can sometimes be misleading because some people lack a high degree of self-awareness. They do not see themselves as others see them. Consider asking four or five people, co-workers for example, to assess and print the profile of your communication style using the online assessment. Then compare these ratings with your self-rating.

3. Many salespeople, after being introduced to communication-style concepts, attempt to categorize each of their customers. They report that their relationships become mutually more enjoyable and productive. Select four people whom you know quite well (e.g., supervisor, subordinate, customer, teacher, friend, or member of your sports team). Using the two behavioural continuums in this chapter, determine these people's communication styles. Using your own descriptive terminology in conjunction with terminology in this chapter, develop a descriptive behavioural profile of each of these people. Explain how this information could improve your relationship with each of these people.

4. To develop your observation skills and your ability to identify communication styles, watch two or three television shows and attempt to identify the style of individuals portrayed on the screen. To develop your listening and observation skills, try this three-step approach:

   a. Cover the screen with a towel or newspaper and try to identify the style of one or two persons using voice only.

   b. Turn down the volume, uncover the screen, and attempt to identify the style of the same persons using visual messages only.

   c. Turn up the volume and make another attempt to identify the communication style of the persons portrayed on the screen. This time the identification process should be easier because you will be using sight and sound.

   These practice sessions will help you learn how to interpret the nonverbal messages that are so important in identifying another person's communication style. When you select television shows, avoid situation comedies that often feature persons displaying exaggerated styles. You may want to watch a talk show or a news program that features interviews.

5. Myers-Briggs Personality Types and Jungian Personality Types are two very popular descriptions of the material in this chapter. Using your search engine, access the Internet sites that refer to these concepts. Type in "Jungian" + personality profiles to access the Jungian personality types. To access the Myers-Briggs types, type in "Myers-Briggs" + personality profiles. Does the number of hits indicate anything about the validity and popularity of these theories? Examine specific queries about both of these theories. Do you see the relationship between the theories and the material in this chapter? Each year about 2.5 million North Americans complete the Myers-Briggs Type Indicator (M.B.T.I.). Why is this psychological-assessment instrument so popular?

ROLE-PLAY EXERCISE

For the purpose of this role play, assume the role of Ray Ito, who is described in the case problem below. Ray is described as a quiet, amiable person who displays the Supportive communication style. You will meet with Vera Maynard, who is also described in the case problem.

For the purpose of this role play, assume that Vera displays the characteristics of the Directive communication style. Prior to the role play, study the chapter material on style flexing and information on how to sell to persons who have the Directive communication style.

CRM Application Exercise Identifying Communication Styles

The previous salesperson carefully recorded the communication styles of most of the people in the Salesforce.com CRM database and identified the prospects as Emotive, Directive, Reflective, or Supportive. If you feel like talking to an Emotive, you can find them by running the report "contacts by communication style" in the reports tab of the Salesforce.com system. Using the information you have learned in this chapter, explain how you would use style flexing when working with these four contacts.

Case Problem

Ray Ito has been employed at CanTrust Real Estate for almost two years. Prior to receiving his real estate licence, he was a property manager with a large real estate agency in another community. During his first year with CanTrust, he was assigned to the residential property division and sold properties totalling $3 875 000. He then requested and received a transfer to the commercial division.

Three months ago, Ray obtained a commercial listing that consisted of 10.5 hectares (26 acres) of land near a growing residential neighbourhood. The land is zoned commercial and appears to be ideally suited for a medium-sized shopping centre. Ray prepared a detailed prospectus and sent it to Vera Maynard, president of Consumer Growth Corporation, a firm specializing in development of shopping centres. One week later he received a letter from Vera requesting more information. Shortly after receiving Ray's response, Vera called to set up an appointment to inspect the property. A time and date were finalized, and Ray agreed to meet her plane and conduct a tour of the property.

Ray is a quiet, amiable person who displays the Supportive communication style. Friends say that they like to spend time with him because he is a good listener.

Questions

1. If Vera Maynard displays the characteristics of the Directive communication style, how should Ray Ito conduct himself during the meeting? Be specific as you describe those behaviours that would be admired by Vera Maynard.

2. If Vera wants to build rapport with Ray Ito, what behaviour should she display?

3. It is not a good idea to put a label on someone and then assume the label tells us everything about the person. As Ray attempts to build rapport with Vera, what other personal characteristics should he try to identify?

Chapter 9
Ethics: The Foundation for Relationships in Business

Learning Objectives

After studying this chapter, you should be able to

1 Describe how ethical decisions influence relationships in selling

2 Discuss factors that influence character development

3 Describe the factors that influence the ethical conduct of sales personnel

4 Discuss guidelines for developing a personal code of ethics

5 Describe ethical and legal issues in international business

Herbert Schulte, a veteran sales representative for Prudential Insurance (**www.prudential .com**), was forced to make a difficult ethical decision. His sales manager gave him a list of his middle-aged customers and sales literature that described a Prudential life insurance policy as nursing home coverage. He contends that his manager was implicitly recommending an insurance-industry practice called "churning," a practice by which agents pressure customers to use built-up cash value in an existing policy to buy a new, more expensive one. In some cases information is withheld so that customers fail to understand the negative aspects of the buying decision. Herbert realized that the sales approach recommended by his sales manager would require that he mislead his established customers and he refused to go along with the plan.

Herbert Schulte was one of hundreds of Prudential sales representatives encouraged to use misleading sales practices. Soon after the Prudential problems made headlines, the company began to reform its sales practices and meet its legal obligations. More than a thousand agents and managers were fired and a fine of $35 million was paid. The company purchased full-page newspaper ads to apologize for "intolerable" deceptive sales practices. Later, Prudential agreed to a class-action settlement of $2 billion that involved 650 000 policyholders.[1] Unethical sales practices encouraged by management personnel pose a major dilemma for salespeople. In some cases the motivation to engage in unethical sales practices may increase when companies provide incentive structures that entice salespeople to go over the line.[2]

MAKING ETHICAL DECISIONS

BUSINESS ETHICS COMPRISE PRINCIPLES AND STANDARDS THAT GUIDE BEHAVIOUR IN the world of business. They help translate your values into appropriate and effective behaviours in your day-to-day life. Whether a specific behaviour is right or wrong, ethical or unethical, is often determined by company leaders, customers, investors, the legal system, and the community.[3] Of course, the views of various stakeholders may be in conflict. Kickbacks and secret payoffs may be acceptable practices to the vice president of sales and marketing, yet may be viewed as unethical by members of the sales force, the board of directors, investors, and the general public.

There is no one uniform code of ethics for all salespeople. However, numerous business organizations, professional associations, and certification agencies have established written codes. The Canadian Professional Sales Association (CPSA), requires all persons seeking to become a Certified Sales Professional to agree to abide to the CPSA Sales Institute Code of Ethics (see Fig. 9.1).

business ethics Comprise principles and standards that guide behaviour in the world of business. They help translate your values into appropriate and effective behaviours in your day-to-day life.

The CPSA Sales Institute Code of Ethics is the set of principles and standards that a certified sales professional will strive to adhere to with customers, organizations, competitors, communities and colleagues.

The Certified Sales Professional pledges and commits to uphold these standards in all activities.

I will:

1. Maintain honesty and integrity in all relationships with customers, prospective customers, and colleagues and continually work to earn their trust and respect.
2. Accurately represent my products or services to the best of my ability in a manner that places my customer or prospective customer and my company in a position that benefits both.
3. Respect and protect the proprietary and confidential information entrusted to me by my company and my customers and not engage in activities that may conflict with the best interests of my customers or my company.
4. Continually upgrade my knowledge of my products/services, skills and my industry.
5. Use the time and resources available to me only for legitimate business purposes. I will only participate in activities that are ethical and legal, and when in doubt, I will seek counsel.
6. Respect my competitors and their products and services by representing them in a manner which is honest, truthful and based on accurate information that has been substantiated.
7. Endeavor to engage in business and selling practices which contribute to a positive relationship with the community.
8. Assist and counsel my fellow sales professionals where possible in the performance of their duties.
9. Abide by and encourage others to adhere to this Code of Ethics.

As a certified sales professional, I understand that the reputation and professionalism of all salespeople depends on me as well as others engaged in the sales profession, and I will adhere to these standards to strengthen the reputation and integrity for which we all strive. I understand that failure to consistently act according to this Code of Ethics may result in the loss of the privilege of using my professional sales designation.

Source: www.cpsa.com/institute.html. Reprinted with permission.

Figure 9.1 The CPSA Sales Institute Code of Ethics

Today, we recognize that character and integrity strongly influence relationships in personal selling. As noted in Chapter 7, character is composed of your personal standards of behaviour, including your honesty and integrity. Your character is based on your internal values and the resulting judgments you make about what is right and what is wrong. The ethical decisions you make reflect your character strength.

We are indebted to Stephen Covey, author of *The 7 Habits of Highly Effective People*, for helping us to better understand the relationship between character strength and success in personal selling. In his bestselling book, Stephen Covey says there are basic principles that must be integrated into our character. One example is to always do what you say you are going to do. "As we make and keep commitments, even small commitments, we begin to establish an inner integrity that gives us the awareness of self-control and courage and strength to accept more of the responsibility for our own lives."[4] Fulfilling your commitments builds trust, and trust is the most important precondition of sales partnering.

CHARACTER DEVELOPMENT

COLLEGES AND UNIVERSITIES ARE BEGINNING TO PLAY A MORE ACTIVE ROLE IN character development, now commonly offering courses that focus on ethics. When a new ethics course was developed at the University of Virginia, the faculty indicated that the purpose of the course is not to point out what is right and what is wrong. Rather, the course is designed to help students understand the consequences of their actions when they face an ethical dilemma.[5]

Despite growing interest in business ethics, unethical behaviour has become all too common. A survey conducted by *Newsweek* suggests that the current generation of workers may be more tolerant of deception. Many of those involved in the survey did not view lying and cheating as unacceptable.[6] Employees who are involved in unethical behaviour often report that they were under pressure to act unethically or illegally on the job.

The Erosion of Character

As the past decade unfolded, many large inflexible corporations were transformed into smaller, more nimble competitors. "New economy" thinking prevailed as business firms, large and small, worked hard to become lean, innovative, and profitable. We witnessed an almost unrelenting emphasis on earnings that was driven, in many cases, by executive greed. During this period, some of the most respected companies began to cross the ethical divide.[7]

A company cannot enjoy long-term success unless its employees are honest, ethical, and uncompromising about values and principles. Yet many employees engage in dishonest practices that erode character. The collapse of Lehman Bros., one of the largest U.S. corporations, can be traced to a culture that emphasized risk-taking, personal ambition over teamwork, and earnings growth at any cost. The new economy depends on innovation and aggressive development of markets, but actions that weaken the moral contract with employees, customers, and shareholders can have serious consequences. Let's examine some half-truths that have influenced the erosion of moral character in business settings.

◼ *We are only in it for ourselves*. Some critics of today's moral climate feel that the current moral decline began when society's focus shifted from "what is right" to "what is right for me." In personal selling, this point of view can quickly subtract from rather than add value to a customer relationship. Fortunately, there are many salespeople for whom integrity and self-respect are basic values. Darryl Ashley, a pharmaceutical representative for Eli Lilly Company, suspected that a pharmacist (a customer) was diluting chemotherapy drugs in order to increase profit margins. Darryl shared his suspicions with one of the cancer doctors who was purchasing the drug from the pharmacist. Tests indicated that the drug had indeed been diluted.[8]

■ *Corporations exist to maximize shareholder value.* In the past, corporations were often viewed as economic and social institutions—organizations that served a balanced group of stakeholders. In recent years, analysts, stock traders, CEOs, and the media have too often focused on a single standard of performance—share price.[9] Marjorie Kelly, editor of *Business Ethics*, says, "Managing a company solely for maximum share price can destroy both share price and the entire company."[10]

Pressure to increase "numbers" led to sales abuses at WorldCom Incorporated. Some salespeople double-booked accounts in order to make their quota and collect increased commissions. The false reporting was identified by an internal company probe and the guilty sales representatives were fired.[11] The same pressure led financial executives at Canada's Nortel Networks to report forecast revenues and earnings that were "out of touch with reality"; as a result, the company's CEO and a number of senior financial executives were fired.[12]

■ *Companies need to be lean and mean.*[13] Downsizing has become a common practice even when the economy is strong. After the layoffs, companies must deal with serious problems of low morale and mistrust of management. Those employees who remain after a company reduces its ranks often feel demoralized, overworked, and fearful. The stress of long hours and a faster pace can result in losses in quality and bad service that alienate customers. Richard Sennett, author of *The Corrosion of Character*, says that the decline of character strength can be traced to conditions that have grown out of our fast-paced, high-stress, information-driven economy. He states that character strength builds as we display loyalty, mutual commitment, and the pursuit of long-term goals.[14] These are the qualities needed to build strong buyer–seller relationships.

Today many business firms are struggling to align their values, ethics, and principles with the expectations of their salespeople and their customers. The process of negotiating ethical standards and practices must be ongoing. Citigroup Incorporated, the world's largest financial services firm, is working hard to move beyond regulatory scandals. Charles Prince, Citigroup CEO, wants the company to better balance its "delivering-the-numbers" culture with a long-term attention to reputation. He readily admits that "at times, our actions have put at risk our most precious commodity—the trust of our clients, the patience of our employees, and the faith of our shareholders."[15]

Can moral behaviour be taught? The National Business Ethics Survey, conducted annually by the Ethics Resource Center (**www.ethics.org**) found that 90 percent of employees said that ethics training is useful or somewhat useful to them. A growing number of students are completing business ethics courses as part of their business programs.[16]

FACTORS INFLUENCING THE ETHICS OF SALESPEOPLE

IN THE FIELD OF PERSONAL SELLING, THE TEMPTATION TO MAXIMIZE SHORT-TERM GAINS by some type of unethical conduct is always present. Salespeople are especially vulnerable to moral corruption because they are subject to such temptations. Here are a few examples:

The competition is using exaggerated claims to increase the sale of its product. Should you counteract by using exaggerated claims of your own to build a stronger case for your product?

You have visited the buyer twice and, each time, the person displayed interest in your product. During the last visit the buyer hinted that the order might be signed if you provide a small gift. Your company has a policy that gifts are not to be given under any circumstances. What do you do?

Your sales manager is under great pressure to increase sales. At a recent meeting of the entire sales staff, this manager said, "We have to beat the competition no matter what it takes!" Will this emotional appeal change your way of dealing with customers?

During a recent business trip, you treated a good friend who is not a customer to lunch. You paid for the entire bill and left a generous tip. Do you put these non–business-related expenses on your expense account?

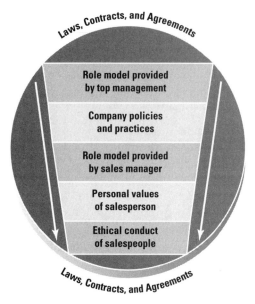

Figure 9.2 Factors determining ethical behaviour of salespeople

These ethical dilemmas arise frequently in the field of selling. How do salespeople respond? Some ignore company policy, cast aside personal standards of conduct, and yield to the pressure. However, most salespeople are able to resist. They are aided by numerous factors that help them distinguish right from wrong. Figure 9.2 outlines the forces that help them deal honestly and openly with prospects at all times. We will discuss each of these factors.

Top Management as Role Model

Ethical standards tend to filter down from the top of an organization. Employees look to company leaders for guidance. The organization's moral tone, as established by management personnel, is the most important single determinant of employee ethics. Richard Schulze, Best Buy founder and chairman, is the person who must put ethics concerns on the front burner and make sure that employees stay focused on that priority. The most influential ethics spokesman at Timberland is CEO Jeffrey Swartz, a third generation CEO whose grandfather founded the company. With pride, he points out Timberland's slogan: "Boots, Brand, Belief."[17]

In recent years, top management has often been guided by advice from professional service firms such as McKinsey & Company and Arthur Anderson. Too often these firms are recommending strategies that result in quick, short-term gains. Alan M. Webber, who has been studying professional service firms for 20 years, notes, "They want the money right now." He says, "to make the most money, you actually have to believe in the product or service you offer and care for the customers or clients whom you serve."[18]

Company Policies and Practices

Company policies and practices can have a major impact on the ethical conduct of salespeople. Al Rosen, who taught accounting at York University for 30 years, says that once you are hired, you become a product of your company and its ethics drift through you. He says, "People are telling you to forget this and that—it becomes a birds-of-a-feather atmosphere."[19] Many employees do not have well-developed moral sensitivity and, therefore, need the guidance of ethics policies. These policies should cover distributor relations, customer service, pricing, product development, and related areas.[20]

Developing policy statements forces a firm to "take a stand" on various business practices. Distinguishing right from wrong can be a healthy activity for any organization. The outcome is a clearer philosophy of how to conduct business transactions. Furthermore, the efforts of salespeople can be compromised by the unethical actions of their companies. Selling products for a company that condones unethical practices is very difficult for the salesperson who maintains high ethical standards.[21]

Sun Life Financial—headquartered in Toronto, with offices in 22 countries serving millions of customers—provides its employees with a carefully worded document entitled "Code of Business Conduct." Employees must affirm annually their commitment to these values. Several of these values form the foundation for a corporate culture that encourages ethical behaviour:[22]

- **Integrity** We are committed to the highest standards of business ethics and good governance.

- **Customer Focus** We provide sound financial solutions for our customers and always work with their interests in mind.

- **Value** We deliver value to the customers and shareholders we serve and to the communities in which we operate.

Most marketing companies provide salespeople with guidelines in such areas as sharing confidential information, reciprocity, bribery, gift giving, entertainment, and business defamation.

Sharing Confidential Information Personal selling, by its very nature, promotes close working relationships. Customers often turn to salespeople for advice. They disclose confidential information freely to someone they trust. It is important that salespeople preserve the confidentiality of information they receive.

It is not unusual for a customer to disclose information that may be of great value to a competitor. This might include development of new products, plans to expand into new markets, or anticipated changes in personnel. A salesperson may be tempted to share confidential information with a representative of a competing firm. This breach of confidence might be seen as a means of gaining favour. In most cases this action will backfire. The person who receives the confidential information will quickly lose respect for the salesperson. A gossipy salesperson will seldom develop a trusting relationship with a customer.

Reciprocity **Reciprocity** is a mutual exchange of benefits, as when a firm buys products from its own customers. Some business firms actually maintain a policy of reciprocity. For example, a manufacturer of commercial sheets and blankets may purchase hotel services from firms that use its products. Is there anything wrong with the "you scratch my back and I'll scratch yours" approach to doing business? The answer is sometimes yes. In some cases the use of reciprocity borders on commercial blackmail. Salespeople have been known to approach firms that supply their company and encourage them to buy out of obligation. The firm may be forced to buy products of questionable quality

reciprocity A mutual exchange of benefits, as when a firm buys products from its own customers.

Personal selling, by its nature, promotes close working relationships. It is important that salespeople preserve the confidentiality of information they receive. Violation of this ethical responsibility will quickly erode a relationship with the customer.

at excessive prices. A business relationship based on reciprocity often has drawbacks, such as the ever-present temptation to take reciprocal customers for granted. A customer who buys out of obligation may take a back seat to customers who were won in the open market.

Ethics: Increasingly Becoming Front and Centre

Customers today are more likely to demand proof of integrity, particularly when choosing important vendors that must be capable of providing long-term support. Many salespeople simply try to refer customers to their company Web sites, where they can find statements of company values and ethics practices. However, many customers are now demanding more. Requests for proposals are increasingly requiring vendors to sign documents that explicitly outline their good ethical practices.

Experts in business ethics suggest four things common to vendors that follow "best practices":

1. *A top-level business executive responsible for ethics, business conduct, and compliance.* These executives are increasingly responsible for reporting directly and regularly to company boards of directors.

2. *The ability for all employees to be able to report, anonymously and confidentially, any suspected wrongdoing.* At Nortel Networks, employees are now able to call a confidential advice line, e-mail the business ethics department, or communicate directly with anyone in the organization, including individual members of the board or the board as a whole.

3. *The ability to monitor and assess their ethics program effectiveness.* Vendors need more than simple statements of ethical conduct and values.

4. *Ethics training for all employees, including senior executives.* Sun Microsystems provides a basic online ethics training program for all of its 35 000 employees worldwide, and requires that they take ongoing training. In addition, about 1200 top executives and some staff members are required to participate each year in a two-day workshop. Before Brian Conlon, Chief Information Officer at Howrey, Simon, Arnold & White, a large international law firm, awarded a contract to Sun Microsystems to overhaul his company's IT infrastructure, he carefully scrutinized Sun's business conduct and compliance programs. As justification, he says, "The things we are doing with Sun are not one-offs. It will be our partner for a long time, and we need to make sure it will stay in business."[a]

Bribery The book *Arrogance and Accords: The Inside Story of the Honda Scandal* describes one of the largest commercial corruption cases in North American history. Over a 15-year period, Honda officials received more than US$50 million in cash and gifts from dealers anxious to obtain fast-selling Honda cars and profitable franchises. When the bribery became public, 18 former Honda executives were convicted of obtaining kickbacks; most went to prison.[23] In some cases, a bribe is wrong from a legal standpoint. In almost all cases, the bribe is wrong from an ethical point of view. However, bribery does exist, and a salesperson must be prepared to cope with it. It helps to have a well-established company policy to use as a reference point.

Salespeople who sell products in foreign markets need to know that giving bribes is viewed as an acceptable business practice in some cultures. However, bribes or payoffs may violate federal government legislation. Canada has the Corruption of Foreign Public Officials Act, and for Canadian salespeople who work for U.S. companies, the U.S. Foreign Corrupt Practices Act (FCPA) may also be relevant. Lucent Technologies dismissed two high-ranking executives in China after it found potential violations of the FCPA.[24]

Gift Giving Gift giving is a common practice in Canada. However, some companies do maintain a "no gift" policy. Many companies report that their policy is either no gifts or nothing of real value. Some gifts, such as advertising novelties, planning calendars, or a meal, are of limited value and cannot be construed as a bribe or payoff.

There are some grey areas that separate a gift from a bribe. Most people agree that a token of insignificant value, such as a pen imprinted with a company logo, is an appropriate way to foster goodwill. A bribe, on the other hand, is an attempt to influence the person who is receiving the gift.

Are there right and wrong ways to handle gift giving? The answer is yes. The following guidelines will be helpful to any salesperson who is considering giving gifts to customers:

1. Do not give gifts before doing business with a customer. Do not use the gift as a substitute for effective selling methods.

2. Never convey the impression you are "buying" the customer's business with gifts. When this happens, the gift becomes nothing more than a bribe.

3. When gift giving is done correctly, the customer will clearly view it as symbolic of your appreciation—a "no strings attached" goodwill gesture.

4. Be sure the gift is not a violation of the policies of your firm or of your customer's firm. Some companies will not allow employees to accept gifts at all; others place a dollar limit on a gift's value.

In summary, if you have second thoughts about giving a gift, do not do it. When you are sure some token is appropriate, keep it simple and thoughtful.

Entertainment of Customers Entertainment is a widespread practice in the field of selling but may be viewed by some people as a bribe. The line dividing gifts and entertainment from bribes is often quite arbitrary. Salespeople must frequently decide how to handle entertaining. A few industries see entertainment as part of the approach used to obtain new accounts. This is especially true when competing products are nearly identical. A good example is the cardboard box industry. These products vary little in price and quality. Winning an account may involve knowing who to entertain and how to entertain.

Entertainment of customers is a highly individualized process. One customer might enjoy a professional football game while another might be impressed most by a quiet meal at a good restaurant. The key is to get to know your customer's preferences. How does the person spend leisure time? How much time can the person spare for entertainment? You will need to answer these and other questions before you invest time and money in entertainment.

Business Defamation Salespeople frequently compare their product's qualities and characteristics with those of a competitor during the sales presentation. If such comparisons are inaccurate, are misleading, or slander a company's business reputation, such conduct is illegal. Competitors have sued hundreds of companies and manufacturer's representatives for making slanderous statements while selling.

What constitutes business defamation? Steven M. Sack, co-author of *The Salesperson's Legal Guide*, provides the following examples:

1. *Business slander.* This arises when an unfair and untrue oral statement is made about a competitor. The statement becomes actionable when it is communicated to a third party and can be interpreted as damaging the competitor's business reputation or the personal reputation of an individual in that business.

2. *Business libel.* This may be incurred when an unfair and untrue statement is made about a competitor in writing. The statement becomes actionable when it is communicated to a third party and can be interpreted as damaging the company.

3. *Product disparagement.* This occurs when false or deceptive comparisons or distorted claims are made concerning a competitor's product, services, or property.[25]

Use of the Internet Use of the Internet offers salespeople many advantages, but it can also create a number of ethical dilemmas. For example, e-mail abuse has become a modern-day problem because some employees forget that their employer owns the e-mail system. E-mail messages that contain inflammatory or abusive content, embarrassing gossip, or breaches of confidentiality can lead to legal liabilities. A growing number of companies are developing policies that define permissible uses of their e-mail system.[26]

Some resourceful salespeople have created their own Web sites to alert, attract, or support clients. The rise of these "extranets" has created some problems because they often

---

Selling in Action
When the Competition Uses Negative Practices

Negative selling practices create two problems for companies with integrity. First, the salesperson must use valuable time correcting misinformation presented by the competition. Second, a sale may be delayed until the customer rejects the untruth. Jim Galtan, Director of Sales for Schick Technologies, Inc., the leading manufacturer of digital dental X-ray technology, often learns that the competition has said something negative about his product. When this happens he looks the customer in the eye and says, "Having the best product often frustrates our competition." He also tells customers that if the competition is honest in their assessment, they should be willing to prepare a letter outlining their concerns. Galton says documentation is the easiest way to cope with negative selling because no one's going to document untruth.[b]

function outside of the company's jurisdiction. What should top management do if a salesperson encourages her customers to participate in a special Web auction for a backlogged product? What if the salesperson makes exaggerated claims about a new product? Every marketing firm needs to carefully monitor the development and use of extranets.[27]

The effectiveness of company policies as a deterrent to unethical behaviour depends on two factors. The first is the firm's attitude toward employees who violate these policies. If violations are routinely ignored, the policy's effect soon erodes. Second, policies that influence personal selling need the support of the entire sales staff. Salespeople should have some voice in policy decisions: they are more apt to support policies they have helped develop.

The Sales Manager as Role Model

The salesperson's actions often mirror the sales manager's behaviour and expectations. This is not surprising when you consider the relationship between salespeople and their supervisors. They look to their supervisors for guidance and direction. The sales manager is generally the company's closest point of contact with the sales staff. This person is usually viewed as the chief spokesperson for top management.

Sales managers generally provide new salespeople with their first orientation to company operations. They are responsible for interpreting company policy. On a continuing basis the sales manager monitors the salesperson's work and provides important feedback regarding conduct. If a salesperson violates company policy, it is usually the sales manager

Customer Relationship Management with Technology

Exercising Care with CRM Data

Customer relationship management systems enable you to collect information about people with whom you maintain relationships, using methods including the taking of notes. It is a good practice to record more than basic transaction information, such as personal details about your customers. Reviewing your observations about their behaviour and recording their statements can help you understand them and their needs. Re-reading their comments about ethical issues can assist you in assessing the value of maintaining a business relationship with them.

To be fair, it is important to record only the facts regarding your observations, not necessarily your conclusions. Information in an electronic database can last a long time and, as a result of such circumstances as litigation or company acquisitions, can be "mobile." This means that others may form an opinion about your customer based on your recorded observations, with potentially detrimental consequences for your customer. Not being aware of the existence of the information in your database, your customer does not have a fair opportunity to correct any erroneous conclusions. Another reason to record only facts is the possibility that the information may be read by the customer. For example, there have been instances in which a customer has later joined the sales organization and gained access to the CRM system.

Most CRM systems contain scheduling functions, which means that you can set aside time on your calendar to attend meetings, make phone calls, and perform tasks. The scheduling tools usually include alarms, which will remind you that a deadline is approaching. The disciplined use of these features can help you get things done on time. Taking advantage of the system's reminder tools can be especially important when it involves fulfilling your commitments. The system can help you build trust by reminding you always to do what you said you would do. (See the exercise Preparing Mailing Lists with CRM on page 189 for more information.)

Sales managers influence the ethical behaviour of salespeople by virtue of what they say and what they do.

who is responsible for administering reprimands. If the moral fibre of a sales force begins to break down, the sales manager must shoulder a great deal of responsibility.

Sales managers influence the ethical behaviour of salespeople by virtue of what they say and what they do. From time to time, managers must review their expectations of ethical behaviour. Salespeople are under continual pressure to abandon their personal ethical standards to achieve sales goals. Values such as integrity and honesty must receive ongoing support from the sales manager.

The Salesperson's Personal Values

Ann Kilpatrick, a sales representative in the transportation industry, encountered something unexpected when entertaining a potential client. The client said, "Let's go to Johnny's." She was not familiar with Johnny's but, on arrival, discovered it was a raunchy bar. Kilpatrick related that she sat there for five minutes and then said, "This is not what I was expecting. This is a sleazy place. Let's go somewhere else where we can talk." She was not willing to compromise her personal values to win a new account.[28]

values Your deep personal beliefs and preferences that influence your behaviour.

Values represent the ultimate reasons people have for acting as they do. **Values** are your deep personal beliefs and preferences that influence your behaviour. To discover what really motivates you, carefully examine what it is you value.[29] Values serve as a foundation for our attitudes, and our attitudes serve as a foundation for our behaviour (see Fig. 9.3).

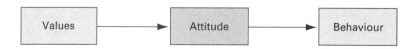

Figure 9.3 The relationship of values, attitudes, and behaviour

Salespeople must avoid misleading sales claims. To stretch the truth is not only unethical, but also illegal.

We do not adopt or discard values quickly. In fact, the development of values is a lifelong process.

Customers have a very negative view of salespeople who lack integrity. Yet, the temptation to lie about a product's features or benefits grows when you are trying to meet sales quotas. Pharmacist John Craig describes a meeting with a pushy sales representative employed by a pharmaceutical company. The salesperson emphasized the wonders of a powerful, expensive painkiller but failed to describe its side effects. Craig said, "He was very pushy at the beginning," and this behaviour revealed a character flaw.[30]

Values Conflict

Values help us establish our own personal standards concerning what is right and what is wrong. Ron Willingham, author of *Integrity Selling for the 21st Century*, says, "Selling success is more an issue of who you are than what you know."[31] A salesperson's ethics and values contribute more to sales success than do techniques or strategies. Some salespeople discover a values conflict between themselves and their employer. If you view your employer's instructions or influence as improper, you have three choices:

1. Ignore the influence of your values, and engage in unethical behaviour. The end result will likely be a loss of self-respect and a feeling of guilt. When salespeople experience conflicts between their actions and values, they also feel a loss of confidence and energy.[32] Positive energy is the result of creating value for the customer. Negative energy emerges when salespeople fail to honour and embrace their ethical values.

2. Voice strong opposition to the practice that is in conflict with your value system. Take a stand, and state your beliefs. When ethical infractions occur, it's best to bring them up internally and try to influence decisions made by your peers or superiors. In some cases, doing the right thing may not be popular with others. Price Pritchett, the

author of *The Ethics of Excellence*, says, "Not everybody will be on your side in your struggle to do the right thing."[33]

3. Refuse to compromise your values and be prepared to deal with the consequences. This may mean leaving the job. It may also mean that you will be fired.

Salespeople face ethical problems and decisions every day. In this respect they are no different from doctors, lawyers, teachers, or any other professional. Ideally, they will make decisions on the basis of the values they hold.

LAWS, CONTRACTS, AND AGREEMENTS

TAKE ANOTHER LOOK AT FIGURE 9.2 AND NOTICE THAT ALL OF THE KEY ELEMENTS, personnel, and policies are influenced by laws, contracts, and agreements. Everyone involved in sales and marketing is guided by legal as well as ethical standards. We live in a society in which the legal system plays a key role in preventing people from engaging in unethical behaviour.

Laws

The specific obligations imposed by government on the way business operates take the form of statutes. In Canada, it is necessary for salespeople not only to know federal statutes but also to recognize that there are many provincial and territorial statutes, and that important differences exist between provinces and territories. The *Competition Act* is the major federal legislation in Canada that defines illegal practices, including price fixing, bid rigging, price discrimination, predatory pricing, double ticketing, resale price maintenance, bait and switch selling, and pyramid selling.

All Canadian provinces and territories have passed legislation that establishes a cooling-off period during which the consumer may void a contract to purchase goods or services. While the provisions of **cooling-off laws** vary from jurisdiction to jurisdiction, their primary purpose is to give customers an opportunity to reconsider a buying decision made under a salesperson's persuasive influence. In most jurisdictions, this legislation is referred to as either *The Direct Sellers Act* or *The Consumer Protection Act*.

cooling-off laws Provincial and territorial laws that give customers an opportunity to reconsider a buying decision made under a salesperson's persuasive influence.

Contracts and Agreements

The word *contract* may bring to mind the familiar multipage, single-spaced documents that few people seem able to understand. A **contract** is simply a promise or promises that the courts will enforce. Oral contracts are enforceable, but written contracts are preferable, as they reduce the possibility of disagreement; courts give written contracts great weight in a lawsuit. A written contract can consist of a sales slip, a notation on a cheque, or any other writing that offers evidence of the promises that the parties made.[34]

Salespeople are sometimes the legal representatives of their company and, therefore, must be careful when signing written contracts. They often oversee contracts with customers, suppliers, and resellers. A salesperson may be asked to sign an employment contract at the time he or she is hired. Most of these agreements include a noncompete

contract An oral or written promise enforceable by law.

clause. One of the most common clauses, a noncompete clause prohibits salespeople from joining a competing firm for a year after they leave. Most clauses are legally binding even when an employee's position is cut. Employers see employment contracts as an effective way to protect intellectual property, customer lists, and other resources an employee might take to a competing firm.[35]

Many companies are learning that resolving legal disputes can be very costly and time-consuming. Resolving a dispute in the courts can sometimes take several years. A serious effort to prevent unethical activities can prevent costly litigation.

Ethics beyond the Letter of the Law

Too often people confuse ethical standards with legal standards. They believe that if they are not breaking the law, then they are acting in an ethical manner.[36] A salesperson's ethical sense must extend beyond the legal definition of what is right and wrong. To view ethics only in terms of what is legally proper encourages the question, "What can I get by with?" A salesperson must develop a personal code of ethics that extends beyond the letter of the law.

Bruce Weinstein, a professional ethicist who is often introduced as "The Ethics Guy," offers sound advice on living an ethical life. He says we should do the right thing simply because it's the right thing to do. The only way you can build a loyal and growing client base is to demonstrate that you have the customer's own best interests at heart. You are trying to make things better for them: "Here is where ethics differs from the law. It demands more of us," says Weinstein.[37]

A PERSONAL CODE OF ETHICS THAT ADDS VALUE

MANY PEOPLE CONSIDERING A CAREER IN SELLING ARE TROUBLED BY THE THOUGHT that they may be pressured into compromising their personal standards of right and wrong. These fears may be justified. The authors of *The Ethical Edge*, a book that examines organizations that have faced moral crises, contend that business firms have given too little thought to the issue of helping employees to function ethically within organizations.[38] Many salespeople wonder if their own ethical philosophy can survive in the business world. These are some of their questions:

"Can a profitable business and good ethics coexist?"
"Are there still business firms that value adherence to high ethical standards?"
"Is honesty still a valued personal trait in the business community?"

In the field of athletic competition the participants rely heavily on a written set of rules. The referee or umpire is ever-present to detect rule violations and assess a penalty. In the field of personal selling there is no universal code of ethics. However, some general guidelines can serve as a foundation for a personal code of business ethics.

1. *Personal selling must be viewed as an exchange of value.* Salespeople who maintain a value focus are searching for ways to create value for their prospects or customers. This value may take the form of increased productivity, greater profit, enjoyment, or security. The value focus motivates the salesperson to carefully identify the prospect's wants and needs.[39] Salespeople who accept this ethical guideline view personal

selling as something you do *for* customers, not something you do *to* customers. The role of the salesperson is to diagnose buyer needs and determine whether value can be created. Always be prepared to add value.

2. *Relationship comes first, task second.* Sharon Drew Morgan, author of *Selling with Integrity*, says you can't sell a product unless there is a level of comfort between you and the prospect. She encourages salespeople to take the time to create a level of comfort, rapport, and collaboration that encourages open communication.[40] Placing task before relationship is based on the belief that the salesperson knows more than the customer. Morgan reminds us that "the buyer has the answers; the seller has the questions."[41] These answers will surface only when the buyer–seller relationship is characterized by rapport and trust.

3. *Be honest with yourself and with others.* To achieve excellence in terms of ethical practices, you have to believe that everything you do counts. Tom Peters, in *Thriving on Chaos*, says, "Integrity may be about little things as much as or more than big ones."[42] It's about accuracy in completing your expense account—and resisting the temptation to inflate the expense report for personal gain. It's about avoiding the temptation to stretch the truth, to exaggerate, or to withhold information. Paul Ekman, author of *Telling Lies*, says that withholding important information is one of the primary ways of lying.[43] A complete and informative sales presentation may include information regarding the product's limitations. If you let your character and integrity be revealed in the little things, others will see you as someone who acts ethically in all things. Any violation of honesty, however small, dilutes your ethical strength, leaving you weaker for the big challenges you will face sooner or later.[44]

The Trust Factor

Everyone involved in personal selling must work hard to build relationships based on trust. When the customer and the salesperson trust each other, they will usually find ways to form a productive partnership. Although trust is an essential element of every sale, the meaning of trust changes with the type of sale.[45]

- *Trust in Transactional Sales.* The primary customer focus in this type of sale is trust in the product. Is the product reliable? Is the product priced as low as possible? Can the product be delivered in a timely fashion? The transactional buyer may purchase a product from a salesperson with whom they do not feel totally comfortable if it meets their purchase criteria.

- *Trust in Consultative Sales.* In a consultative sale, the customer focus shifts from the product to the person who sells the product. The consultative buyer is thinking, "Can I trust this salesperson to identify my problem and offer me one or more solutions?" Customers involved in a consultative sale usually do not separate the product from the person selling it. They want to do business with a salesperson who displays such positive qualities as warmth, empathy, genuineness, competence, and integrity.

- *Trust in Strategic Alliance Sales.* The strategic alliance buyer wants to do business with an institution that can be trusted. This buyer looks beyond the well-qualified salesperson and assesses the entire organization. The strategic alliance customer will not feel comfortable partnering with a company whose values differ greatly from their own. Ethical accountability will greatly influence the way a partner is judged and valued.

Although trust is intangible, it is at the very core of all meaningful relationships. Trust is quickly lost and slowly won.[46]

Ethical and Legal Issues in International Business

Ethical and legal issues that are quite complex on the domestic scene become even more complicated at the international level. International business is growing and Canada is deeply involved in the global marketplace. Thomas Friedman, author of the bestselling book *The World Is Flat: A Brief History of the Twenty-First Century*, says today's highly competitive and global marketplace is flattening the world of international business. Our companies must adopt a more aggressive global focus in order to compete with China, India, and other dynamic economies.[47]

Cultural Issues

Today's global marketplace reflects a kaleidoscope of cultures, each with its own unique qualities. **Culture** is the sum total of beliefs, values, knowledge, ethnic customs, and objects that people use to adapt to their environment. Cultural barriers can impede acceptance of products in foreign countries and weaken interpersonal relationships. When the salesperson understands the cultural background of the foreign customer, communication problems are less likely. Many people from Asia, Arab countries, and much of Africa prefer a more indirect style of communication and therefore value harmony, subtlety, sensitivity, and tact more than brevity.[48] The customer who seems to be agreeing with everything you say may have no intention of buying your product. This person may simply be displaying polite and tactful behaviours.

culture The sum total of beliefs, values, knowledge, ethnic customs, and objects that people use to adapt to their environment.

Perceptions of time differ from country to country. Canadians value promptness, but businesspeople from other countries often approach meetings in a more relaxed manner. Arriving late for a meeting may not be viewed as a problem. Many companies are spending thousands of dollars to make sure that employees sent abroad are culturally prepared. Eastman Chemical Company, for example, has developed a highly successful orientation program for employees who have accepted overseas assignments.[49]

Legal Issues

Doing business in the global marketplace continues to be an ethical minefield. Illegal demands for bribes, kickbacks, or special fees may stand in the way of successful transactions. Canadian and U.S. governments have enacted legislation that prohibits companies from using bribes or kickbacks to influence foreign officials. But monitoring illegal activities throughout the world is a very difficult task.[50] Motorola, for example, uses software to analyze invoices and payments in order to uncover possible payoffs. Gifts from suppliers to Canadian and U.S. companies can also be a problem. United Technologies sends a letter to foreign suppliers each year saying, "We don't want gifts."[51]

Canadian and U.S. businesses acknowledge that it is difficult to compete with organizations from other countries that are not bound by our laws. However, the International Business Ethics Institute (**www.business-ethics.org**) believes our companies have been a very positive role model for the rest of the business world. As noted previously in this chapter, high ethical standards depend on strong leadership provided by management personnel at all levels of the organization. Integrity starts at the top.

REVIEWING KEY CONCEPTS

- Describe how ethical decisions influence relationships in selling.

  Character and integrity strongly influence relationships in personal selling. Unethical sales practices will ultimately destroy relationships with customers. These practices undermine trust, which is at the very core of all meaningful relationships.

- Discuss factors that influence character development.

  Many colleges and universities are playing a more active role in character development. Character education is often integrated into courses that focus on ethics. Character is composed of personal standards of behaviour, so all of us can do things that build character. Keeping our commitments to others provides just one example of how character is built.

- Describe the factors that influence the ethical conduct of sales personnel.

  Salespeople can benefit from the stabilizing influence of good role models. Although top management personnel are usually far removed from day-to-day selling activities, they can have a major impact on salespeople's conduct. Dishonesty at the top of an organization can cause an erosion of ethical standards at the lower echelons. Sales managers provide another important role model. They interpret company policies and help establish guidelines for acceptable and unacceptable selling practies.

- Discuss guidelines for developing a personal code of ethics.

  Salespeople must establish their own standards of personal conduct. They must decide how best to serve their company and build strong partnerships with their customers. The pressure to compromise one's ethical standards surfaces almost daily. The primary deterrent is a strong sense of right and wrong. Three general guidelines that can serve as a foundation for a personal code of ethics are:

  a. Personal selling must be viewed as an exchange of value.

  b. Relationship comes first, task second.

  c. Be honest with yourself and with others.

- Describe ethical and legal issues in international business.

  At the international level, ethical and legal issues can be very complex. The global marketplace reflects a great number of cultures, each with its unique qualities. Coping with illegal activities throughout the world is also very challenging. Illegal demands for bribes, kickbacks, or special fees can serve as a barrier to business transactions.

Key Terms

business ethics **173**

contract **184**

cooling-off laws **184**

culture **187**

reciprocity **177**

values **182**

Review Questions

1. What is the definition of *business ethics*? Why is this topic receiving so much attention today?

2. Carefully review Figure 9.1, the CPSA Sales Institute Code of Ethics. Select the three standards you feel would present the greatest challenge to salespeople. Explain your choices.

3. How does business slander differ from business libel?

4. What major factors help influence salespeople's ethical conduct?

5. What are cooling-off laws? How do they protect consumers?

6. Why must a salesperson's ethical sense extend beyond the legal definition of what is right and wrong?

7. Explain why the sales manager plays such an important role in influencing the ethical behaviour of salespeople.

8. A company policy on ethics will usually cover several major areas. What are they?

9. Is it ever appropriate to give gifts to customers? Explain.

10. List and describe three guidelines used as a foundation of a self-imposed code of business ethics.

Application Exercises

1. You find that you have significantly overcharged one of your clients. The error was discovered when you received payment. It is unlikely that the customer or your company will become aware of the overcharge. Because of this error, the company realized a high net profit on the sale. Your commissions are based on this profit. What, if anything, will you do about the overcharge?

2. Access the Canadian Professional Sales Association Web site at **www.cpsa.com**. Click on the Sales Certification link and the Apply Today link to examine the steps to becoming a certified sales professional (CSP). Review the CPSA Sales Institute Code of Ethics printed in this chapter (or through the link on this Web site). Discuss your views on the impact professional certification has on the ethical behaviour of salespeople. Do you think the designation CSP would affect the impression a customer might have of a salesperson?

3. You work for a supplier of medical equipment. Your sales manager informs you that he wants you to capture a certain hospital account. He also tells you to put on your expense account anything it costs to secure the hospital as a client. When you ask him to be more specific, he tells you to use your own judgment. Up to this time you have never questioned your sales manager's personal code of ethics. Make a list of the items you feel can be legitimately charged to the company on your expense account.

4. For some time your strongest competitor has been making untrue derogatory statements about your product and about you as a salesperson. You know for a fact that her product is not as good as yours, yet hers has a higher price. Several of your best customers have confronted you with these charges. Describe how you plan to answer them.

5. Sales managers must approve expense reports turned in by members of the sales force. Assume the role of sales manager for a sales force that includes 12 salespeople who travel frequently and average about two overnight trips each week. Recently you noticed that the expense reports turned in by two of your salespeople seem quite high. You suspect that these salespeople are padding their expense reports. What steps should you take to determine if cheating is occurring? How can a sales manager prevent the padding of expense reports?

ROLE-PLAY EXERCISE

This morning you met with a customer who has purchased office supplies from you for almost three years. You are quite surprised when she says, "I am prepared to place an order worth $10 500, but you must match an offer I received from a competitor." She then explains that the competitor is offering new customers a seven-day all-expenses-paid trip to Quebec City if they place an order for more than $10 000. What would you do?

Prepare to role play your response with another student. Review the material in this chapter, paying special attention to ways you can add value and build long-term relationships with ethical decision making.

CRM Application Exercise   Preparing Mailing Lists with CRM

Log on to the Salesforce.com system. Go to the Reports tab and select the Park Inn Mailing List report. Choose the printable view. The mailing information for each contact will be displayed on the screen. Select File, Print and print this list.

A friend of yours is a salesperson with a firm that installs the cables used to connect network components, a service that your company does not offer. Your friend wants to know if you will share the customer list that you just printed. What should be your response?

Case Problem

Dana Davis dropped into the receiving department of Regina Steel Fabricators, one of the company's oldest and best accounts. Dana had been called by Tyler Hensman, their senior purchasing person, to inspect the last shipment of structural tubing sold to them. According to Tyler, when the tubing was sheared to the lengths required, the shear dimpled the ends of the tubes, and the dimples had not been removed as requested. The tubes were, therefore, not perfectly round, and the casters that were to fit into the ends would not do so without considerable effort. Davis was puzzled by the quality control problem. The company has a long-standing policy of not shipping a product to a customer unless it has passed inspection by the quality control staff.

Dana arrived just after lunch, and while waiting for Gary Anderson, the store's supervisor, noticed that there was a large shipment of stainless steel bolts and nuts sitting in the store's receiving area. They were marked type 304 stainless steel, one of the cheaper grades. Dana was curious because a price quotation had been given to Tyler Hensman the previous week on the same material in type 316 stainless steel, a much more expensive grade.

Dana Davis approached a young clerk who was working in the receiving area. "Where did that shipment come from?"

"Quality Distribution," the young man replied, without looking directly at Dana.

"What was the cost of the material?" Dana inquired.

"Don't know. My copy of the order doesn't show a cost, nor does the packing slip that came in the shipment," the young man said as he shrugged his shoulders.

"Is it supposed to be type 304 or type 316?" Dana persisted.

"It just says stainless steel bolts and nuts on my copy of the purchase order," replied the clerk. "And the packing slip just says stainless steel as well. There's no mention of type of stainless. If you want to find out more, you'll have to contact Tyler Hensman in our purchasing department. This order was placed by him."

Dana Davis was getting more curious about the shipment from Quality Distribution. Upon returning to the office, Dana decided to call Tyler Hensman and ask for the order. A decision was made not to mention what was seen in the store's receiving area. "Tyler, I'm calling about that price quotation I gave you last week for 316 stainless steel bolts and nuts. Will you give us an order?"

"Sorry. I placed the order with Quality Distribution last week because their price was better," Tyler replied. "You'll have to sharpen your pencil if you want our business."

Dana Davis knew there was no way Quality Distribution could compete on price because it was basically a small jobber firm that really wasn't in the stainless steel business. But Dana didn't want to say that to Tyler Hensman. "How much sharper?"

"Just a bit, but you know it wouldn't be honest for me to tell you," Tyler laughed.

After they talked for a few more minutes Dana Davis promised to check pricing options and determine if the next price could be more competitive. After hanging up the phone, Dana sat at his desk, staring at the wall. Davis realized a careful approach was needed. There was something wrong and the issue needed to be resolved quickly. This was an important long-term account for his company, and he couldn't afford to lose it.

Questions

1. Has Dana Davis's behaviour been ethical? Why or why not?

2. Has Tyler Hensman's behaviour been ethical? Why or why not?

3. What should Dana Davis do?

PART II

ROLE-PLAY EXERCISE
Developing a Relationship Strategy

SCENARIO

You are an experienced sales representative employed by Canadian Steel Processing, a company that has been in business for nearly 70 years. Your company is an ISO 9002–certified manufacturing company that has earned many accolades, including three consecutive J. D. Power & Associates awards for customer satisfaction. Over the years the company has invested heavily in automation technology as a means of ensuring consistent manufacturing quality. The Canadian Steel Processing sales force understands that the company will not be the lowest bidder in most sales situations because the highest quality can never be obtained at the lowest price.

CUSTOMER PROFILE

Tyler Hensman has held the position of senior purchasing agent at Regina Steel Fabricators for several years. Throughout this period, Tyler has negotiated over a dozen purchase agreements with Dana Davis, senior account representative with Canadian Steel Processing. Tyler takes pride in purchasing quality steel products at the best price.

SALESPERSON PROFILE

Dana Davis began working for Canadian Steel Processing Company about four years ago. After completion of an extensive sales training program, Dana was assigned to a territory in Saskatchewan. After three successful years, Dana was promoted to senior account representative.

PRODUCT

Canadian Steel Processing sells a wide range of steel products. Many of the orders filled are for high stress steel beams, stainless steel bolts and nuts, and structural tubing used in commercial building construction. Most orders specify a certain quality of steel.

INSTRUCTIONS

For this role play you will assume the role of Dana Davis, senior account representative employed by Canadian Steel Processing. To prepare for the role play, you should carefully read the case problem at the end of Chapter 9. This information will help you understand the issues that need to be addressed.

During the early stages of the role play, you will want to obtain more information from the customer and resolve any misunderstandings. You want to obtain an order for type 316 stainless steel bolts and nuts, and maintain a good relationship with this important customer. Keep in mind that ethical decisions can greatly influence the relationship between a salesperson and the customer. Reflect on the important information covered in Chapter 9 prior to your meeting with Tyler Hensman.

Chapter 10
Creating Product Solutions

Figure 10.1 Companies such as Lowe's Canada communicate their core values to customers, suppliers, employees, and other stakeholders.

KNOW YOUR COMPETITION

Acquiring knowledge of your competition is another important step toward developing complete product knowledge. Salespeople who have knowledge of their competitors' strengths and weaknesses are better able to emphasize the benefits they offer and add value. Prospects often raise specific questions concerning competing firms. If you cannot provide answers or if your answers are vague, the sale may be lost.

Your Attitude toward Your Competition

Regardless of how impressive your product is, the customer will naturally seek information about similar products sold by other companies. Therefore, you must acquire facts about competing products before the sales presentation. It has never been easier to obtain information about competing products. Check the competitor's Web site, annual reports, press releases, and marketing material. Once armed with this information, you will be more confident in your ability to handle questions about the competition.

The attitude you display toward your competition is of the utmost importance. Every salesperson should develop a set of basic beliefs about the best way of dealing with competing products. Here are a few helpful guidelines:

1. *In most cases, do not refer to the competition during the sales presentation.* This shifts the focus of attention to competing products, which is usually not desirable.

2. *Never discuss the competition unless you have all your facts straight.* Your credibility will suffer if you make inaccurate statements. If you do not know the answer to a specific question, simply say, "I do not know."

3. *Never criticize the competition.* You may be called on to make direct comparisons between your product and competing products. In these situations, stick to the facts and avoid emotional comments about apparent or real weaknesses.

4. *Be prepared to add value.* The competition may come to your prospect with a comparative advantage in price, delivery, or some other area. Be prepared to neutralize the competitor's proposal with a value-added approach. If your competitor has slow delivery, encourage the customer to talk about why prompt delivery is important.[28]

Customers appreciate an accurate, fair, and honest presentation of the facts. They generally resent highly critical remarks about the competition. Avoid mudslinging at all costs. Fairness is a virtue that people greatly admire.

Become an Industry Expert

Salespeople need to become experts in the industry they represent. In many cases this means moving beyond the role of product specialist and becoming a business analyst. Staying current and developing an understanding of business processes takes time and may require additional education.[29] If your clients work in the banking industry, read the appropriate trade journals and become active in professional associations that serve bankers' needs.

SOURCES OF PRODUCT INFORMATION

THERE ARE SEVERAL SOURCES OF PRODUCT INFORMATION AVAILABLE TO SALESPEOPLE. Some of the most common include: (1) product literature, catalogues, and online resources developed by the company, (2) plant tours, (3) internal sales and sales support team members, (4) customers, (5) the product, and (6) trade and technical publications.

Product Literature, Catalogues, and Online Resources Developed by the Company

Most companies prepare materials that provide a detailed description of their product. This information is usually quite informative, and salespeople should review it carefully. If the company markets a number of products, a sales catalogue is usually developed. To save salespeople time, many companies give them computer software that provides a constantly updated, online product catalogue. Advertisements, promotional brochures, and audio cassettes or compact discs can also be a valuable source of product information. Mitsubishi Caterpillar Forklift America presents its basic product information online, so it's available to dealer representatives in the privacy of their homes, hotel rooms, or wherever else they bring their laptops. Each of the seven product information courses takes about an hour. To reinforce basic product knowledge, the company offers advanced instructor-led courses.[30] Some companies are using interactive distance learning (delivered via satellite) to present different types of sales training.

Plant Tours

Many companies believe that salespeople should visit the manufacturing plant and see the production process first-hand. Such tours not only provide valuable product information but also increase the salesperson's enthusiasm for the product. A new salesperson may spend several days at the plant getting acquainted with the production process. Experienced personnel within the organization can also benefit from plant tours.

Internal Sales and Sales Support Team Members

Team selling has become popular, in part, because many complex sales require the expertise of several sales and sales support personnel. Expertise in the areas of product design, finance, or transportation may be needed to develop an effective sales proposal. Pooled commissions are sometimes used to encourage team members to share information and work as a team.

Customers

Persons who actually use the product can be an important source of information. They have observed its performance under actual working conditions and can provide an objective assessment of the product's strengths and weaknesses. Some companies collect testimonials from satisfied customers and make this persuasive information available to sales staff. Wabi Iron and Steel Corp. in New Liskeard, Ontario, manufactures components for machinery that must operate under adverse conditions. The company keeps ahead of its

Surveys indicate that product knowledge training should be a basic element of any sales training program.

Customer Relationship Management with Technology

Starting Fast with CRM

New salespeople can be overwhelmed by the amount of information they need to master. This includes information about the company and its processes, products, and customers. Companies can now make learning easier with information technology. Information about the company and its processes can be stored on the company's network, on its virtual private network (VPN), or on CD-ROM discs. Computer-based training (CBT) permits new employees to learn at their own pace about a product's specifications, features, benefits, uses, and selling points.

Companies can now provide salespeople with software that they can use to accurately and effectively create product solutions. Electronic configuration software allows salespeople to select the components necessary to assemble a custom-tailored solution to meet their prospects' needs. This software guides users through the product selection process while ensuring that the components will be compatible with one another.

Companies can deliver to new salespeople a rich body of customer information through a strong commitment to the use of customer relationship management (CRM) software. The salesperson who carefully records his or her business and relationship contacts with customers and prospects will, over time, accumulate a valuable store of information. A new salesperson taking over these accounts can quickly "come up to speed" with these people and their needs. (See the exercise Finding Product Information in CRM on page 210 for more information.)

competitors by systematically developing and testing improved alloys in close cooperation with one of its major customers. It has been able to develop components exclusively for this customer, and its success has given Wabi the profile it needs to compete in new markets. In recognition of its sales success, Wabi won an Ontario Global Traders Award.[31]

Salespeople employed by semiconductor manufacturer Intel Corporation are expected to take the company's business customers from the conceptual stage of their purchase all the way to delivery of the finished product. Dialogue with customers begins very early in the sales cycle when customers need help designing their end product.[32] This approach requires the empowerment of the sales force with greater depth and breadth of product information.

Product

The product itself should not be overlooked as a source of valuable information. Salespeople should closely examine and, if possible, use each item they sell to become familiar with its features. Investigation, use, and careful evaluation of the product will provide a salesperson with additional confidence.

Trade and Technical Publications

Trade and technical publications such as *Canadian Grocer* and *Advertising Age* provide valuable product and industry information. Popular magazines and the business section of the newspaper also offer salespeople considerable information about their products and their competition. Publications such as *Consumer Reports* test products extensively and report the findings in nontechnical language for the benefit of consumers. These reports are a valuable source of information.

Word of Caution

Is it possible to be overly prepared? Can salespeople know too much about the products and services they sell? The answer to both questions is generally no. Communication problems can arise, however, if the salesperson does not accurately gauge the prospect's level of understanding. There is always the danger that a knowledgeable salesperson will overwhelm the potential buyer with facts and figures. This problem can be avoided when salespeople adopt the feature–benefit strategy.

ADDING VALUE WITH A FEATURE–BENEFIT STRATEGY

FREDERICK W. SMITH, FOUNDER OF FEDERAL EXPRESS, FIRST PROPOSED THE CONCEPT of overnight delivery in a paper that he wrote as an undergraduate at Yale University. The now-famous paper was given a C by his professor. Many years later Smith said, "I don't think that we understood our real goal when we first started Federal Express. We thought that we were selling the transportation of goods; in fact, we were selling peace of mind."[33]

Throughout this chapter we emphasize the importance of acquiring information on the features of your product, company, and competition. Now it is important to point out that successful sales presentations translate product features into benefits that meet a specific need expressed by the customer. The "peace of mind" that Frederick W. Smith mentioned is a good example of a buyer benefit. Only when a product feature is converted to a buyer benefit does it make an impact on the customer.

Distinguish between Features and Benefits

To be sure we understand the difference between a product feature and a buyer benefit, let us define these two terms.

A **feature** is data, facts, or characteristics of your product or service. Features often relate to craftsmanship, design, durability, and economy of operation. They may reveal how the product was developed and manufactured. Product features are often described in the technical section of the written sales proposal and in the literature provided by the manufacturer.

A **benefit** is whatever provides the consumer with personal advantage or gain. It answers the question, "How will I benefit from owning or using the product?" If you mention to a prospect that a certain tire has a four-ply rating, you are talking about a product feature. If you go on to point out that this tire will provide greater safety, last longer, and improve gas mileage, you are pointing out benefits.

feature Anything that a customer can feel, see, hear, taste, smell, or measure to answer the question, "What is it?" Features often relate to craftsmanship, durability, design, and economy of operation.

benefit Something that provides the customer with personal advantage or gain to answer, for the customer, the question, "How will the customer benefit from owning or using the product?"

General versus Specific Benefits

Neil Rackham, author of *The SPIN Selling Fieldbook*, says that a statement can only be a benefit if it meets a specific need expressed by the buyer. When you link a benefit to a buyer's expressed need, you demonstrate that you can help solve a problem that has been described by the customer. A general benefit shows how a feature can be helpful to a buyer, but it does not relate to a specific need expressed by the buyer. Here are two examples of specific benefits:

"Our water purification system meets the exact specifications you have given us for environmental compliance."

"Our XP400 model meets the safety criteria you've spelled out."

Rackham says that benefit statements linked to the customer's expressed need are especially effective in large and complex sales.[34]

Some sales training programs suggest that salespeople need to include advantages in the sales presentation. Advantages are characteristics of the product (i.e., features) that can be used or will help the buyer. Consider the following statement:

"Prior to shipping, all of our containers are double wrapped. This means that our product is completely free from contamination when it arrives at your hospital."

Some salespeople develop an advantage statement for each important product feature. Unfortunately, these advantages are often included in the sales presentation even when the buyer has not expressed a need for this information. When this happens, the advantage can be described as a general benefit.

Successful salespeople focus on specific benefits that relate to a need explicitly expressed by the customer. Less successful salespeople take the position that the best way to create value is to present as many benefits as possible. They use a "shotgun" approach to benefits, assuming that more benefits create higher volume. High-performance salespeople work hard to discover which benefits the customer really cares about. Today's customer measures value by how well your product benefits fit their needs.[35]

Use Bridge Statements

We know that people buy benefits, not features. One of the best ways to present benefits is to use a bridge statement. A **bridge statement** is a transitional phrase that connects a statement of features with a statement of benefits. This method permits customers to connect the features of your product to the benefits they will receive. A sales representative for a food wholesaler, for example, might use a bridge statement to introduce a new snack food:

> "This product is nationally advertised, *which means* you will benefit from more presold customers."

Some companies prefer to state the benefit first and the feature second. When this occurs, the bridge statement may be a word such as "because."

> "You will experience faster turnaround and increased profits *because* the first order includes point-of-purchase advertising materials that focus on the Valentine's Day promotion you have planned."

Identify Features and Benefits

A careful analysis of the product will help identify both product features and customer benefits. Once all the important features have been identified, arrange them in logical order. Then write beside each feature the most important benefit the customer will derive from that feature. Finally, prepare a series of bridge statements to connect the appropriate features and benefits. Using this three-step approach, a hotel selling conference and convention services and a manufacturer selling electric motors used to power mining equipment developed feature–benefit worksheets (see Tables 10.1 and 10.2). Notice how each feature is

Table 10.1 Convert Product Features to Benefits

Salespeople employed by a hotel can enhance the sales presentation by converting product features to benefits.

Feature	Benefit
Facilities	
Our hotel conference rooms were recently redecorated.	Which means all your meetings will be held in rooms that are attractive and comfortable.
Our rooms were completely redecorated this year and many are now designated non-smoking.	Which means your people will find the rooms clean and attractive. In addition, those who wish can select a non-smoking room.
Food Services	
We offer four different banquet entrées prepared by our executive chef, who was recently selected Chef of the Year by the Canadian Federation of Chefs and Cooks.	Which means your conference will be enhanced by delicious meals served by a well-trained staff.
Our hotel offers 24-hour room service.	Which means your people can order food or beverages at their convenience.

Table 10.2 Convert Company Features to Benefits

Here we see company features translated into customer benefits.

Feature	Benefit
Our company has the largest selection of motors in the area.	Which means you will have an excellent choice of models to interface with your equipment.
We hire only certified service technicians.	Which means your equipment will be kept running in peak condition by well-qualified service personnel.
Our company has an inventory of all major spare parts.	Which means you will have less equipment downtime and will make higher profits.

translated into a benefit that would be important to someone purchasing these products and services. Table 10.2 reminds us that company features can be converted to benefits.

Avoiding Information Overload

Knowing your product has always been essential to good selling, but concentrating on product alone can be a serious mistake. Salespeople who love their products and possess vast product knowledge about them may overload their customers with product data they neither need nor want. This practice is sometimes described as a "data dump." With the aid of specific types of questions (see Chapter 14), the customer's needs can be identified.

Selling Today

Customer Needs Determine New Product Sales Success

When Xerox introduced the 9200 mega-copier, sales were far below expectations. Buyers initially interested in the copiers became more resistant as sales presentations proceeded—a finding that surprised company officials. A questionnaire administered to the sales force found a negative correlation between enthusiasm and sales. That is, salespeople who were less enthusiastic sold more copiers than those who had higher enthusiasm—another surprising finding. When researchers made sales calls with Xerox salespeople, they discovered two differences between how salespeople tried to sell the new copiers and how they sold more established products.

First, they asked 40 percent fewer questions. Second, they provided three times as many product details. Instead of being customer-centred and asking questions to discover customer needs, the salespeople were product-centred, performing "feature dumps." One theory was that salespeople would introduce new products to customers the same way the prod-

ucts were introduced to them. That is, if management described all the "bells and whistles" to the salespeople, the sales representatives would do the same to customers.

To test this theory, researchers intervened in a new product launch for a Kodak blood analyzer. Researchers described to 12 randomly chosen salespeople how the product solved customer problems, without describing any of the product's "bells and whistles." The salespeople were further coached to avoid describing product features and to ask questions that uncovered needs. After one year, the salespeople in the experimental group achieved sales 54 percent higher than a matched group who had experienced the company's standard product launch—one with all the "bells and whistles." This finding supports David Milliken's views. The national director of business development at Deloitte & Touche says, "Any minute you spend talking about a product or feature that doesn't connect to an explicit need is a minute wasted."[b]

Once the customer's needs are known, the salesperson can develop a customized sales presentation that includes selected features that can be converted to specific benefits.

Elaine Parker used questions to engage the customer and identify his problem. She also provided answers to questions raised by the customer:

Questions related to the product
What product is best for our type of operation?
Does the product meet our quality standards?
Given the cost of this product, will we maintain our competitive position in the marketplace?

Questions related to the company
Does this company provide the most advanced technology?
What is the company's reputation for quality products?
What is the company's reputation for standing behind the products it sells?

Questions related to the salesperson
Does the salesperson possess the knowledge and experience needed to recommend the right product?
Can the salesperson clearly communicate specific buyer benefits?
Can the salesperson serve as a trusted adviser?
Will this salesperson provide support services after the sale?

Salespeople who are knowledgeable in all areas of the product-selling model are better able to position a product. Knowledge helps you achieve product differentiation, understand the competition, and prepare an effective value proposition. The competitive analysis worksheet (Table 10.3) can help you discover ways to position your product as the superior choice over your competition.

A Word of Caution

Because many of today's information-age products are very complex, product differentiation must be handled with care. Salespeople are sometimes tempted to use technical lingo—real and invented—to impress the buyer. This problem often surfaces in a situation in which the salesperson is not sure how to describe the value-added features of the product. Robert Notte, technology chief for travel outfitter Backroads, says that during the telecom boom, salespeople representing WorldCom (now MCI) and other firms babbled endlessly, using industry jargon that was often unintelligible. "They wanted you to be impressed," Robert Notte says. Some customers were so intimidated they were afraid to ask questions—or make a buying decision.[13]

PRODUCT-POSITIONING OPTIONS

Product positioning is a concept that applies to both new and existing products. Given the dynamics of most markets, it may be necessary to reposition products several times during their lifespan, because even a solid popular product can lose market position quickly. Salespeople have assumed an important and expanding role in positioning products. To succeed in our information-drenched society, marketers must use a more direct

Table 10.3 Competitive Analysis Worksheet

A value-added product-selling strategy is enhanced when salespeople analyze product, company, and salesperson attributes of the competition in relation to benefits they offer. This information helps the salesperson create value within the sales process.

	My Company	Competitor A	Competitor B
Product Attributes			
Quality			
Durability			
Reliability			
Performance			
Packaging flexibility			
Warranty			
Brand			
Company Attributes			
Reputation			
Industry leadership			
Facilities			
Ease of doing business			
Distribution channels			
Ordering convenience			
Returns, credits, etc.			
Salesperson Attributes			
Knowledge/Expertise			
Responsiveness			
Pricing authority			
Customer orientation			
Honesty/Integrity			
Follow-through			
Presentation skills			

and personalized form of communication with customers. Advertising directed toward a mass market will often fail to position a complex product.

Throughout the remainder of this chapter we discuss specific ways to use various product-positioning strategies. We explain how salespeople can (1) position new and emerging products versus mature and well-established products, (2) position products with price strategies, and (3) position products with value-added strategies.

Selling New and Emerging Products versus Mature and Well-Established Products

product life cycle Stages of a product from the time it is first introduced to the market until it is taken off the market, including the stages of introduction, growth, maturity, and decline.

Products, like human beings, are born, grow up, mature, and grow old. In marketing, this process is known as the **product life cycle**; it includes the stages a product goes through from the time it is first introduced until it is discontinued. As the product moves through its cycle, the strategies relating to competition, promotion, pricing, and other factors must be evaluated and possibly changed. The nature and extent of each stage in the product life cycle are determined by several factors, including:

1. The product's perceived advantage over available substitutes;
2. The product's benefits and the importance of the needs it fulfills;
3. Competitive activity, including pricing, substitute product development and improvement, and effectiveness of competing advertising and promotion; and
4. Changes in technology, fashion, or demographics.[14]

As you develop a product-selling strategy, you must consider where the product is positioned within its life cycle. The sales strategy used to sell a new and emerging product will be much different from the strategy used to sell a mature, well-established product (see Fig. 10.2).

Selling New and Emerging Products

Selling strategies used during the new and emerging stage are designed to develop a new level of expectation, change habits, and in some cases establish a new standard of quality (see Fig. 10.2). The goal is to build desire for the product. Highly talented and resourceful salespeople are needed during the product initiation phase. Salespeople must be resourceful, possess information regarding every aspect of the product, and be able to present a convincing value proposition.[15]

When Brother International Corporation introduced its line of Multi-Function Centre (MFC) machines, the goal was to convince buyers that one machine could replace

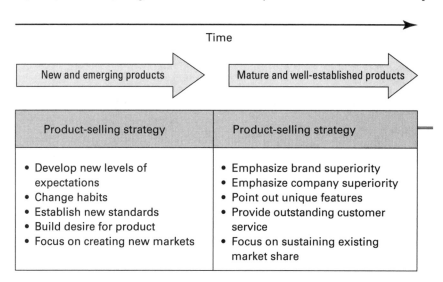

Figure 10.2 Product-selling strategies for positioning new and emerging products versus mature and well-established products

Managing New Product Information with CRM

Today, salespeople are challenged to manage a steady stream of information about customers' needs and products or solutions. From this stream of information, the sales professional must select product information that will be relevant to a specific customer and deliver the information in a manner that the customer can understand. Customer relationship management (CRM) assists the busy salesperson by providing tools that can collect information and link it to those who need it. Most CRM systems can receive and organize information from e-mail, from Web sites, and from the files of reference material that are kept within a company's information system. Sales professionals can add value to this information by summarizing, combining, and tailoring the information to meet a customer's needs.

When new product information is received, databases of customer data can be quickly searched to find those customers who might have an interest. The new product information can be merged into an e-mail, fax, or letter to that customer, along with other information (e.g., benefits) that help the customer assess its value. Later, the CRM system can display a follow-up alert, reminding the sales professional of the information that was shared with the customer.

five separate machines. However, before buyers would give up their copy machine, fax machine, laser printer, and other machines, they asked some hard questions. Is a multifunction machine reliable? Does the quality match that of the current machines? Finding the best machine for each customer is challenging because Brother offers more than 10 different MFC models to choose from.

In some cases the new product is not a tangible item. Several years ago IntraLinks closed its first big sale, a $50 000 contract, with J. P. Morgan. The company got its start providing the financial services industry with the secure transmission of highly confidential information across the Internet. Patrick Wack and his business partners convinced J. P. Morgan and other financial firms that they did not need to rely on an army of foot messengers and FedEx trucks to deliver sensitive documents. They were not only selling a new product, they were selling a vision that included new levels of expectations. The value proposition focused on faster, more secure document transfer, which, in the customer's mind, translated into improved customer service and cost savings. Today Patrick Wack is selling this document transfer concept to customers in a variety of business communities.[16]

Selling Mature and Well-Established Products

Mature and well-established products are usually characterized by intense competition as new brands enter the market. Customers who currently buy your product will become aware of competing products. With new and emerging products, salespeople may initially have little or no competition and their products may dominate the market. However, this condition may not last long.

Sun Life Financial regularly provides its agents with new products. Yet the company finds that competing insurance companies quickly copy them. When competing products enter the market, Sun Life sales agents must adopt new strategies. One positioning strategy Sun Life uses is to emphasize the company's history of superior service to policyholders for nearly 150 years and its undeniable financial strength. It is a growth-focused company, headquartered in

Canada but with offices in 22 countries. Agents often describe Sun Life as a supportive company that gives high priority to service after the sale, and a stable organization that will be around to service future needs.[17] The objective is to create an awareness in the customer's mind that Sun Life is a solid company with a long history of good service to policyholders.

The relationship strategy is often critical in selling mature and well-established products. To preserve market share and ward off competitors, many salespeople work hard to maintain a strong relationship with the customer. At Sun Life, salespeople have found that good service after the sale is one of the bestselling strategies because it builds customer loyalty.

Selling Products with a Price Strategy

Product, promotion, distribution, and price are the four elements that make up the marketing mix. Pricing decisions must be made at each stage of the product life cycle. Therefore, setting the price can be a complex process. The first step in establishing price is to determine the firm's pricing objectives. Some firms set their prices to maximize their profits; they aim for a price as high as possible without causing a disproportionate reduction in unit sales. Other firms set a market share objective; management may decide that the strategic advantage of an increased market share outweighs a temporary reduction in profits. Many of the new companies doing business on the Internet have adopted this approach.

Pricing strategies often reflect the product's position in the product life cycle. When large high-definition flat screen televisions were in the new and emerging stage, customers who wanted this innovative product were willing to pay $5000 or more for a unit.

Transactional Selling Tactics That Emphasize Low Price

Some marketers have established a positioning plan that emphasizes low price and the use of transactional selling tactics. These companies maintain a basic strategy that focuses on meeting competition. If the firm has meeting competition as its pricing goal, it makes every effort to charge prices that are identical or close to those of the competition. Once this positioning strategy has been adopted, the sales force is given several price tactics to use. Salespeople can alter (i.e., lower) the base price through the use of discounts and allowances. Discounts and allowances can take a variety of forms. A few of the more common ones are:

quantity discount A price reduction made to encourage a larger volume purchase than would otherwise be expected.

The **quantity discount** allows the buyer a lower price for purchasing in multiple units or above a specified dollar amount.

seasonal discount Adjusting prices up or down during specific times to spur or acknowledge changes in demand.

With **seasonal pricing**, the salesperson adjusts the price up or down during specific times to spur or acknowledge changes in demand. Lower off-season travel and lodging pricing is an example.

promotional allowance A price reduction given to a customer who participates in an advertising or sales support program.

A **promotional allowance** is a price reduction given to a customer who participates in an advertising or a sales support program. Many salespeople give supermarkets promotional allowances for advertising or displaying a manufacturer's products.

trade or **functional discount** A discount given to channel intermediaries to cover the cost of the services they provide.

Channel intermediaries, such as wholesalers, often perform credit, storage, or transportation services. A **trade** or **functional discount** covers the cost of these services.[18]

Another option available to salespeople facing a buyer with a low-price buying strategy is to "unbundle" product features. Let's assume that a price-conscious customer wants to

The age of information has created many career opportunities for people who want to sell professional services. Strong demand for professional services has surfaced in such diverse fields as telecommunications, banking, computer technology, training, and health care. When Gary Svoboda resigned his position as vice president at the Canadian Innovation Centre—where he worked for 18 years—he started his own consulting business, Adventus Research (**www.adventusresearch.com**). It specializes in new product application identification and research, primarily in technology and industrial markets. Like thousands of other professional service providers, Gary had to decide how much to charge for his service. Should he price his service on an hourly basis or on a project basis? Here are some things to consider when determining fees:

- *Experience:* In the case of Gary Svoboda, new clients benefit from what he learned during his many years at the Canadian Innovation Centre.

- *Exclusivity:* If you are one of only a small number of people with a particular capability, you may be able to charge more. Specialists often charge higher fees than generalists.

- *Target Market:* Some markets are very price-sensitive. If you are selling your services to large corporations that are accustomed to paying high fees, you may be able to set your fees higher. If you are providing your services to small business clients, expect resistance to high fees.

- *Value:* How important is your service to the client? Some service providers charge higher fees because they create greater value for their customers.[b]

schedule a conference that will be accompanied by a buffet-style meal. To achieve a lower price, the salesperson might suggest a cafeteria-style meal, thereby eliminating the need for servers. This product configuration involves less cost to the seller, and the cost savings can be passed on to the buyer. Timken Company, a century-old bearing maker, has adopted bundling as a way to compete with other manufacturers around the world. The company now surrounds its basic products with additional components in order to provide customers with exactly what they need. These components can take the form of electronic sensors, lubrication systems, castings, or installation and maintenance. Giving customers bundling options has given Timken a big advantage over foreign competitors who often focus on the basic product. Salespeople who represent Timken have flexible pricing options.[19]

These examples represent only a small sample of the many discounts and allowances salespeople use to compete on the basis of price. Price discounting is a competitive tool available to large numbers of salespeople. Excessive focus on low prices and generous discounts, however, can have a negative impact on profits and sales commissions.

Consequences of Using Low-Price Tactics

Pricing is a critical factor in the sale of many products and services. In markets where competition is extremely strong, setting a product's price may be a firm's most complicated and important decision. The authors of *The Discipline of Market Leaders* encourage business firms to pick one of three disciplines—best price, best product, or best service—and then do whatever is necessary to outdistance the competition. However, the authors caution us not to ignore the other two disciplines: "You design your business to excel in one direction, but you also have to strive to hit the minimum in the others."[20] Prior to using low-price tactics, everyone involved in sales and marketing should answer these questions:

"WE HAVE QUALITY AND WE HAVE LOW PRICES...
WHICH DO YOU WANT ?"

Agency Sales Magazine from the Manufacturing Agent National Association (MANA)

■ *Are you selling to high- or low-involvement buyers?* Some people are emotionally involved with respected brands, such as BMW, Sony, and BlackBerry. A part of their identity depends on buying the product they consider the best. Low-involvement buyers care mostly about price.[21]

■ *How important is quality in the minds of buyers?* If buyers do not fully understand the price–quality relationship, they may judge the product by its price. For a growing number of customers, long-term value is more important than short-term savings that result from low prices.

■ *How important is service?* For many buyers, service after the sale is a critical factor. Even online customers, thought to be very interested in price, rate quality of service very highly. This is especially true in business-to-business sales. A survey conducted by Accenture reported that 80 percent of nearly a thousand corporate buyers rate a strong brand and reliable customer service ahead of low prices when deciding which companies to do business with online.[22]

Influence of Electronic Business on Pricing

Companies large and small are racing to discover new sales and marketing opportunities on the Internet. Products ranging from personal computers to term insurance can now be purchased from various Web sites. Salespeople who are involved primarily in transactional selling and add little or no value to the sales transaction will often not be able to compete with online vendors. To illustrate, consider the purchase of stocks online from one of Canada's many discount brokers. At the present time it's possible to make an online purchase for a fraction of the cost of using a full-service broker. A well-informed buyer, willing to visit several Web sites, can make decisions based on online information and investing tools that were considered to be beyond the understanding of the average investor only a few years ago. Persons who need little or no assistance buying stocks can visit Canada's largest discount broker, TD Waterhouse Discount Brokerage, or one of the many others, including E*Trade Canada, RBC Action Direct, and CIBC Investor's Edge, to name only a few of the many choices available to informed consumers. The person who wants help selecting a stock can turn to a full-service broker such as BMO Nesbitt Burns or Scotia McLeod. Full-service brokers can survive and may prosper as long as they can add value to the sales transaction. The new economy is reshaping the world of commerce, and every buyer continues to have more choice.

Selling Your Product with a Value-Added Strategy

value-added strategies
Relationship, product, or service strategies that a company uses to add value for the customer.

Many progressive marketers have adopted a market plan that emphasizes **value-added strategies**. Companies add value to their product with one or more intangibles, such as better-trained salespeople, increased levels of courtesy, more dependable product deliveries,

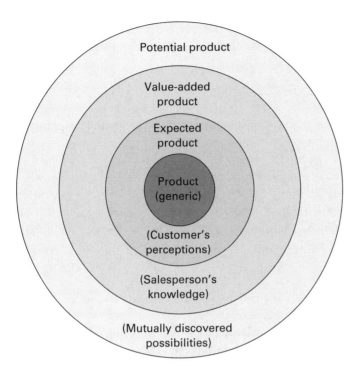

Figure 10.3 The total product concept. An understanding of the four possible products is helpful when the salesperson develops a presentation for different customers.

better service after the sale, and innovations that truly improve the product's value in the eyes of the customer. In today's highly competitive marketplace these value-added benefits give the company a unique niche and a competitive edge. Companies that don't make selling and delivering high-value solutions a high priority will consistently lose sales to competitors.[23]

To understand fully the importance of the value-added concept in selling, and how to apply it in a variety of selling situations, it helps to visualize every product as having four dimensions. The total product is made up of four possible products: the generic product, the expected product, the value-added product, and the potential product (see Figure 10.3).[24]

Generic Product

The **generic product** is the basic, substantive product you are selling. Generic product describes only the product category—for example, life insurance, rental cars, clothing, hotels, or personal computers. Every Ritz-Carlton hotel offers guest rooms, food and beverage service (i.e., restaurants, bars, and banquet space), meeting rooms, guest parking, and other basic services. For customers who visit Tilley Endurables, the generic product is the men's and women's travel and adventure clothing and accessories they find there. The generic products at a bank are money that can be loaned to customers and basic chequing account services. The capability of delivering a generic product gives the mar-

generic product The basic, substantive product being sold.

keter the right to play in the game, to compete in the marketplace.[25] Generic products, even the lowest-priced ones, often cannot compete with products that are expected by the customer.

Expected Product

Every customer has minimal purchase expectations that exceed the generic product itself.[26] Ritz-Carlton must offer not only a comfortable guest room, but also a clean one. Some customers expect a "super" clean room. The **expected product** is everything that represents the customer's minimal expectations. The customer at Tilley Endurables will expect quality products, a good selection, fashionable accessories, and well-informed salespeople.

The minimal purchase conditions vary among customers, so the salesperson must acquire information concerning the expected product that exists in the customer's mind. When the customer expects more than the generic product, the product can be sold *only* if those expectations are met. Every customer perceives the product in individualized terms, which a salesperson cannot anticipate.

Determining each customer's expectations requires the salesperson to make observations, conduct background checks, ask questions, and listen to what the customer is saying. You are attempting to discover both feelings and facts. Top salespeople encourage the customer to think more deeply about the problems they face and discover for themselves the value of a solution. They *avoid* offering solutions until the needs are clearly spelled out. If the buyer says, "The average gas mileage for our fleet of delivery trucks is only 17 miles per gallon," the salesperson might respond with this question: "How does this low mileage rate affect your profitability?" To move the customer's attention from the expected product to a value-added product, you need to keep the customer focused on solutions.[27]

Research reported in the *Harvard Business Review* indicates that it is very difficult to build customer loyalty if you are selling only the expected product. Customer satisfaction and loyalty do not always move in tandem. The customer who purchases the services of Ernst & Young Consulting may feel satisfied after the project is completed but may never do business with the company again. Customer loyalty is more likely to increase when the purchase involves a value-added product.[28]

Value-Added Product

The **value-added product** exists when salespeople offer customers more than they expect. When you make a reservation at one of the Ritz-Carlton hotels and request a special amenity such as a tennis lesson, a record of this request is maintained in the computer system. If you make a reservation at another Ritz-Carlton at some future date, the agent will inform you of the availability of a tennis court. The guest who buys chocolate-chip cookies in the gift shop at one location may find some waiting in the room for his or her next stay weeks later. The hotel company uses modern technology to surprise and delight guests.[29] Tilley Endurables provides many things to enhance customers' shopping experiences. At their retail store locations, customers get free cookies, shop in an engaging environment, and can have alterations to clothing done in minutes. Even at its online location, the company adds value for its customers. It provides information on its products, service, and guarantees, and even provides travel information on almost anywhere in the world customers might be travelling. Among the most important factors that contribute to the value-added product is the overall quality of

---

expected product Everything that represents the customer's minimal expectations.

value-added product Product that exists when salespeople offer the customer more than they expect.

employees with whom the customer has contact. Sales and sales support staff who display enthusiasm and commitment to the customer add a great deal of value to the product.[30]

Potential Product

After the value-added product has been developed, the salesperson should begin to conceptualize the **potential product**—what may remain to be done; that is, what is possible.[31] As the level of competition increases, especially in the case of mature products, salespeople must look into the future and explore new possibilities.

potential product What may remain to be done to a product—that is, what is possible.

In the highly competitive food services industry, restaurant owners like to do business with a distribution sales representative (DSR) who wants to help make the business profitable. The DSR who assumes this role becomes a true partner and looks beyond the customer's immediate and basic needs. The potential product might be identified after a careful study of the restaurant's current menu and customer base. To deliver the potential product, a salesperson must discover and satisfy new customer needs, which requires imagination and creativity.

Steelcase Incorporated, a leading manufacturer of office furniture, has developed the "Think" chair, which is 99 percent recyclable and can be disassembled with basic hand tools in about five minutes. This $900 chair meets a growing demand for products made of parts that can be recycled several times and manufactured in ways least harmful to the environment. Steelcase developed this "potential product" after learning that customers are increasingly seeking environmentally safe products and are sometimes willing to pay a premium for them.[32]

The potential product is more likely to be developed by salespeople who are close to their customers. Many high-performing salespeople explore product possibilities with their customers on a regular basis. Potential products are often mutually discovered during these exchanges.

Every indication points toward product-selling strategies that add value becoming more important in the future. New product life cycles are shrinking, so more companies are searching for ways to add value during the new and emerging stage. Some companies that have experienced low profits selling low-priced products are reinventing those products. They search for product features that provide benefits customers think are worth paying for. Maytag Corporation developed the expensive environment-friendly Neptune washing machine for customers who will pay more for a washer that uses less water. Tilley Endurables continues to create value for customers by regularly adding new and better products to its product lines.

VALUE CREATION INVESTMENTS FOR TRANSACTIONAL, CONSULTATIVE, AND STRATEGIC ALLIANCE BUYERS

In most cases, investments in value creation during the transactional sale are minimal. With such sales, salespeople usually place emphasis on finding ways to eliminate any unnecessary costs and on avoiding delays in processing the order. Technology investments can sometimes play a big role in improving efficiencies.[33] For example, customers may be encouraged to order products online.

A considerable amount of value creation takes place in consultative sales. Higher investments in value creation are permitted because companies need to invest in developing a good understanding of the customer's needs and problems. This is especially true in large complex sales where creating custom-tailored solutions and delivering more real benefits to the customer provides the opportunity for higher margins. If your company is selling mobile autonomous robots, the sales cycle will be quite long, and investments will be quite high. Sales representatives may take several weeks to study the applications of this product in a hospital, a manufacturing plant, or a large warehouse facility. The use of these robots may eventually result in significant cost savings for the customer.[34]

Value creation investments in strategic alliance sales are the highest. As noted in Chapter 5, strategic alliances represent the highest form of partnering. Creating value often requires leveraging the full assets of the company, so that investments go well beyond the sales force. Alliances are often developed by a team of specialists from such areas as finance, engineering, and marketing. A proposed alliance may require investments in new technology, manufacturing facilities, and warehouses.[35]

CRM Application Exercise Finding Product Information in CRM

Providing immediate access to product information can increase a salesperson's efficiency and responsiveness to customer requests. Computers excel at the task of quickly providing information. An example can be found in the Salesforce.com CRM case study software. Basic information about networks is available in the Documents section. After logging on to Salesforce.com, select the Documents tab, then the Product Information folder. Choose any of the available documents by clicking on View, then Open. Print the document. Using the same e-mail procedure in the CRM Application Exercise "Preparing Letters with CRM" from Chapter 3, page 146, attach this document to a new e-mail. After revising the e-mail template, click on the Attach File button. In the drop-down list, select the Product Information folder, then choose the document you want to send. Click Attach, then Done. After reviewing your e-mail, press Send.

Reality Selling Today Video Case Problem

Texas Monthly is a regional magazine covering politics, business, and culture, but focusing largely on leisure activities and events in Texas. The magazine has a large real estate advertising section, as well as classified sections in which nearly all advertisers are Texas-based businesses appealing to a prospective buyer who is interested in connecting with Texas history and culture. It also has a large, loyal reader base all over Texas, mostly urban, well-educated, and affluent, and the magazine's salespeople pride themselves on their ability to find creative solutions for their customers.

Today, Amy Vandaveer, a sales representative for *Texas Monthly*, is meeting with the marketing director for the Woodlands Town Center, a major community development organization. The Woodlands is a planned community outside of Houston and the recently added Woodlands Town Center includes restaurants, shops, and a hotel and convention centre.

The marketing director's goal is to make the Woodlands Town Center a destination for Houston residents, rather than another area serving people who already live in the Woodlands. Up to this point, the Woodlands Town Center has mostly relied on word of mouth and the positive publicity that it received after winning awards to attract visitors; now, the marketing director is interested in using more print advertising and has scheduled this meeting with Amy to learn more about the possibilities of advertising with *Texas Monthly*.

As a rule, Amy uses relatively informal presentations on her sales calls. The most significant part of her presentation is a copy of *Texas Monthly*; showing potential customers a recent issue gives them the opportunity to see the magazine's overall look and feel, and gives them a good look at the context in which their ads would appear. Over the course of the informal presentation, Amy also shows the customer statistics on the reader base of *Texas*

Monthly and the ways in which they respond to ads in the magazine, as well as a price sheet for various types of ads.

After listening to what the Woodlands Town Center needs, Amy proposes a four-page colour ad, which can also be printed separately from the magazine for use as a brochure. Although the price depends on the number of stand-alone brochures that are ordered, she estimates that the cost of the ad would be about $50 000. She and the marketing director agree on a timeline for a more formal proposal that can be shared with the rest of the Woodlands Town Center board, and Amy moves on to the rest of her day. (See chapter opener on page 238 and Reality Selling Today Role-Play 3 in Appendix 1 on page 409 on for more information.)

Questions

1. Explain how Amy Vandaveer can use the three prescriptions for a product-selling strategy in preparing and presenting product solutions.

2. What are the major benefits that Amy incorporates into her presentation?

3. What are the most likely objections that the marketing director might raise?

4. In addition to the actual product strategy, how important will information about *Texas Monthly* (its history, mission, past performance, etc.) be in closing the sale?

Partnership Selling: A Role Play/Simulation

Visit the role play simulation materials provided in the Student Resources section of your companion Web site at **www.pearsoned.ca/manning**. *A Contents page lists appropriate page references for the activities.*

Read *Employment Memorandum 1* (p. 105), which introduces you to your new training position with the Hotel Convention Centre. You should also study the product strategy materials that follow the memo to become familiar with the company, product, and competitive knowledge you will need in your new position.

Read *Customer Service/Sales Memorandum 1* and complete the two-part customer/service assignment provided by your sales manager. In item 1, you are to configure a price-product sales proposal; in item 2, you are to write a sales cover letter for the sales proposal. Note that the information presented in the price–product sales proposal will consist of product facts or features, and the information presented in your sales cover letter should present specific buyer benefit statements. These forms should be custom-fitted to meet your customer's— B. H. Riveras—specific needs. All the product information you will need is in the product strategy materials provided as enclosures and attachments to *Employment Memorandum 1*.

Chapter 11
The Buying Process and Buyer Behaviour

Learning Objectives

After studying this chapter, you should be able to

1 Discuss the meaning of a customer strategy

2 Explain the difference between consumer and business buyers

3 Understand the importance of alignment between the selling process and the customer's buying process

4 Understand the buying process of the transactional, consultative, and strategic alliance buyer

5 Discuss the various influences that shape customer buying decisions

 Reality Selling Today Video Series

The past decade has witnessed a major power shift in the direction of the customer. Today's customers have greater access to information that lets them make more informed decisions. They are more demanding, and salespeople must work harder to meet their needs. Every sales call must begin with the customer as the central focus of attention. Tom Peters, noted author and consultant, says we must "Become one with the customer."[1] The customer focus must encompass the buying process—how people buy—and buyer behaviour—why people buy.

We know that new products must satisfy the customer's needs, but identifying these needs can be very challenging. No one understands this challenge better than Justin Bremer (see page 213), a financial advisor at Wealth Design Group (**www.wealthdesigngroup.net**). An integral part of Bremer's job is to work closely with his clients to custom-design comprehensive and innovative financial plans to help them achieve and sustain long-term success. Since financial services of this nature are intangible yet highly personal, Justin Bremer must understand each customer's complex buying process. Prior to making a sales call, for example, he must perform pre-call planning and research. Is the client a business or an individual?

What type of information will the client need to make a decision? What will make the client be open with Bremer about his or her financial situation? Understanding buyer behaviour and the buying process helps create effective selling strategies.

DEVELOPING A CUSTOMER STRATEGY

THE GREATEST CHALLENGE TO SALESPEOPLE IN THE AGE OF INFORMATION IS TO improve responsiveness to customers. In fact, a growing number of sales professionals believe that the customer has supplanted the product as the driving force in sales today. This is especially true in those situations in which the products of one company in an industry are becoming more and more similar to those of the competition. Jerry Acuff, author of *Stop Acting Like a Seller And Start Thinking Like a Buyer*, encourages salespeople to think like buyers. In order to think like a buyer salespeople must understand the buying process and focus on what the customer is looking for.[2]

Adding Value with a Customer Strategy

A **customer strategy** is a carefully conceived plan that will result in maximum customer responsiveness. One major dimension of this strategy is to achieve a better understanding of the customer's buying needs and motives. Information has become a strategic resource. When salespeople take time to discover needs and motives, they are in a better position to offer customers a value-added solution to their buying problem.

customer strategy
A carefully conceived plan that will result in maximum customer responsiveness.

Every salesperson who wants to develop repeat business should figure out a way to collect and systematize customer information. The authors of *Reengineering the Corporation* discuss the importance of collecting information about the unique and particular needs of each customer:

> "Customers—consumers and corporations alike—demand products and services designed for their unique and particular needs. There is no longer any such notion as the customer; there is only this customer, the one with whom a seller is dealing at the moment and who now has the capacity to indulge his or her own personal tastes."[3]

The first prescription for developing a customer strategy focuses on the customer's buying process (see Fig. 11.1). Buying procedures and policies can vary greatly from one buyer to

Strategic/Consultative Selling Model	
Strategic step	**Prescription**
Develop a personal selling philosophy	✓ Adopt marketing concept ✓ Value personal selling ✓ Become a problem solver/partner
Develop a relationship strategy	✓ Adopt win-win philosophy ✓ Project professional image ✓ Maintain high ethical standards
Develop a product strategy	✓ Become a product expert ✓ Sell benefits ✓ Configure value-added solutions
Develop a customer strategy	• Understand the buying process • Understand buyer behaviour • Develop prospect base

Figure 11.1 Today, one of the greatest challenges to salespeople is to improve responsiveness to customers. A well-developed customer strategy is designed to meet this challenge.

another. This is especially true in business-to-business selling. If a salesperson fails to learn how the buyer plans to make the purchase, then he or she may find the selling process out of alignment with the customer's buying process. Keith Eades, author of *The New Solution Selling*, says: "If we haven't defined how our buyers buy, then we make assumptions that throw us out of alignment with our buyers. Misalignment with buyers is one of selling's most critical mistakes."[4]

The second prescription focuses on why customers buy. This topic will be discussed in detail later in this chapter. The third prescription for developing a customer strategy emphasizes building a strong prospect base, which is discussed in Chapter 12.

Complex Nature of Customer Behaviour

The forces that motivate customers can be complex. Arch McGill, a former vice president of IBM, reminds us that individual customers perceive the product in their own terms, and that these may be "unique, idiosyncratic, human, emotional, end-of-the-day, irrational, erratic terms."[5] Different people doing the same thing—such as purchasing a personal computer—may have different needs that motivate them, and each person may have several motives for a single action. With the proliferation of market research studies, public opinion polls, surveys, and reports of "averages," salespeople might easily fall into the trap of thinking of the customer as a number. The customer is a person, not a statistic. Companies that fully accept this basic truth are likely to adopt a one-to-one marketing strategy based on a bedrock concept: *Treat different customers differently*.[6]

consumer buyer behaviour
Buying behaviour of individuals and households who buy goods and services for personal consumption.

business buyer behaviour
Buying behaviour of organizations that buy goods and services for use in the production of other products and services or for the purpose of reselling or renting them to others at a profit.

buying centre A cross-functional team of decision makers who often represent several departments.

CONSUMER VERSUS BUSINESS BUYERS

CONSUMER BUYER BEHAVIOUR REFERS TO THE BUYING BEHAVIOUR OF INDIVIDUALS AND households who buy goods and services for personal consumption. The Canadian consumer market consists of more than 33 million people who purchase many billions of dollars' worth of goods and services each year. **Business buyer behaviour** refers to the buying behaviour of organizations that buy goods and services for use in the production of other products and services that are sold, rented, or supplied to others.[7] In many business buying situations, several people work together to reach a decision. The **buying centre** is a cross-functional team of decision makers who often represent several departments. Each team member is likely to have some expertise needed in a particular purchase decision. Salespeople must continually identify which individuals within a firm will be members of the buying centre.[8]

It is not uncommon for salespeople to sell products and services to both consumer and business buyers. A well-established interior decorating firm will likely work with homeowners as well as commercial clients who own hotels, restaurants, and art galleries. A salesperson employed by an automobile dealership will often sell to corporate customers who maintain a fleet of cars or trucks as well as to consumers who buy vehicles for personal use.

There are some similarities between consumer markets and business markets. Both involve people who assume the role of buyer and make purchase decisions to satisfy needs. These two markets differ, however, in some important areas. Figure 11.2 provides a brief review of some of these differences. A business purchase is likely to involve more participants in the decision making who may be well trained. Most purchasing agents spend time learning how to buy better.[9]

Consumer Buyers	Business Buyers
Purchases made for individual or household consumption	Purchases made for some purpose other than personal consumption
Decisions usually made by individuals	Decisions frequently made by several people
Purchases often made based on brand reputation or personal recommendations with little or no product expertise	Purchases often made according to precise technical specification based on product expertise
Purchases based primarily on emotional responses to product or promotions	Purchases based primarily on rational criteria
Individual purchasers may make quick decisions	Purchasers may engage in lengthy decision process
Products are consumer goods and services for individual use	Products are often complex; classified by how organizational customers use them

Figure 11.2 Differences between Consumer and Business Buyers.

Source: Adapted from Michael R. Solomon and Elnora W. Stuart, *Marketing: Real People, Real Choices*, Third Edition (Upper Saddle River, NJ: Prentice Hall 2003), p. 193.

Types of Business Buying Situations

There are three major types of business buying. The amount of time and effort organizational buyers spend on a purchase usually depends on the complexity of the product and how often the decision must be made.[10] At one extreme is the *new-task buy*, which may require extensive research. At the other extreme is the *straight rebuy*, which is a fairly routine decision. In the middle is the *modified rebuy*, which will require some research.[11]

New-Task Buy A first-time purchase of a product or service is a **new-task buy**. Depending on the cost and complexity of this purchase, the buying decision may require several weeks for information gathering and the involvement of numerous participants. In some cases, a buying committee is formed to consider the new product's quality, price, and service provided by suppliers. Salespeople who are involved in new-task buying situations must rely heavily on consultative selling skills.

new-task buy A first-time purchase of a product or service.

Straight Rebuy A **straight rebuy** is a routine purchase of items needed by a business-to-business customer. Let's assume you have decided to open a new restaurant and need a steady supply of high-quality cooking oil. After talking to several restaurant suppliers

straight rebuy A routine purchase of previously purchased goods or services.

and testing several oils, you select one that meets your needs. Your goal now is to simplify the buying process with the use of a straight rebuy plan. As long as the supplier continues to meet your criteria for price, quality, service, and delivery, future purchases will be routine. Organizations use the straight rebuy approach for such items as cleaning supplies, copy paper, and cartridges for computer printers. Salespeople must constantly monitor every straight rebuy situation to be sure the customer is completely satisfied. A competing supplier will be quick to exploit any sign of dissatisfaction by the customer.

Modified Rebuy The tide of change is a powerful force in the world of business. From time to time, your customers may wish to modify product specifications, change delivery schedules, or renegotiate prices. Several years ago, the North American automobile manufacturers—faced with greater competitive pressures from China, Germany, Japan, Korea, and other nations—turned to their suppliers and demanded price reductions. Suppliers were required to become involved in a **modified rebuy** or risk loss of the account. A modified rebuy often requires the involvement of several participants. Well-trained professional salespeople work hard to provide outstanding service after the sale and anticipate changes in customer needs. Some salespeople regularly ask their customers what they value most about the existing buying situation and how improvements can be made in this area.

Building Strategic Alliances In Chapter 5, we described strategic alliances as the highest form of partnering. Alliances are often formed by companies that have similar business interests and believe the partnership will help them gain a mutual competitive advantage. Large companies often form several alliances. Some strategic alliances take the form of systems selling. **Systems selling** appeals to buyers who prefer a packaged solution to a problem from a single seller, thereby avoiding all the separate decisions involved in a complex buying situation.[12]

Several years ago, Kinko's reinvented itself as a document solutions provider for business firms of all sizes. Full-service Kinko's stores began offering the buyer networks of computers equipped with popular software, ultra-fast colour printers, high-speed Internet connections, and, of course, a variety of document preparation services. After Kinko's was purchased by FedEx, a network of 1200 digitally connected FedEx Kinko's locations began offering a wider selection of customized, needs-based document solutions. One large financial institution consolidated the services of 13 vendors by forming an alliance with FedEx Kinko's.[13] Systems selling efforts at FedEx Kinko's have become an important strategy for winning and holding accounts.

Types of Consumer Buying Situations

As noted previously, consumer buying behaviour refers to purchases of products for personal or household use. The amount of time consumers devote to a purchasing decision can vary greatly depending on the cost of the product, familiarity with the product, and the importance of the item to the consumer. Few buyers invest much effort in selecting a tube of

modified rebuy Purchasing when the buyer wants to reconsider product specifications, prices, or suppliers.

systems selling A type of selling that appeals to buyers who prefer a packaged solution to a problem from a single seller, thereby avoiding all the separate decisions involved in a complex buying situation.

toothpaste, but most will devote extensive time to decision making over the purchase of a new automobile or a home. Consumer buying can fall into one of three categories depending on the degree of consumer involvement: habitual, variety-seeking, or complex buying.

Habitual Buying Decisions

A **habitual buying decision** usually requires very little consumer involvement and brand differences are usually insignificant.[14] For frequently purchased, low-cost items such as shampoo or paper towels, consumer involvement in the decision-making process is very low. Supermarket shoppers often display habitual buying behaviour as they select items.

habitual buying decision A consumer buying decision that requires very little involvement and in which brand differences are usually insignificant.

Variety-Seeking Buying Decisions

A **variety-seeking buying decision** is also characterized by low customer involvement, but also by important perceived brand differences.[15] Brand switching is not uncommon for such decisions because buyers can be influenced by advertising appeals, coupons, or lower prices to try a new brand. Brand switching is usually motivated by the desire for variety rather than product dissatisfaction.

variety-seeking buying decision A consumer buying decision motivated by the desire for variety rather than by product dissatisfaction.

Complex Buying Decisions

A **complex buying decision** is characterized by a high degree of involvement by the customer. Consumers are likely to be highly involved when the product is expensive, purchased infrequently, and highly self-expressive.[16] The purchase of a vacation home, a long-term care insurance policy, an expensive boat, or a costly piece of art would require a complex buying decision. The learning process for some purchases can be very lengthy.

complex buying decision An often lengthy consumer buying decision characterized by a high degree of involvement.

ACHIEVING ALIGNMENT WITH THE CUSTOMER'S BUYING PROCESS

THE FOUNDATION OF A SUCCESSFUL SALES EFFORT IS KNOWING HOW BUYERS BUY. If salespeople don't know what the customer's decision-making process is and they proceed according to their own agenda, they risk losing the sale. If salespeople have not defined how buyers buy, then they make assumptions that throw their sales process out of alignment with the buyer's buying process.[17] Too often salespeople rely on generalizations about the buyer's decision-making process rather than acquiring specific information.

The **buying process** is a systematic series of actions, or a series of defined, repeatable steps, intended to achieve a result.[18] Organizational purchasing structures and buying procedures can vary greatly from company to company, so we need to be clear on how decisions are being made within each account. In some cases, the steps in the buying process have been clearly defined by the organization and this information is available to any potential supplier. However, this information may not tell us the whole story. Salespeople need to obtain answers to these types of questions:

buying process The stages a buyer goes through when making a buying decision.

How urgent is my proposal to the buyer? When will the buying decision be made?

Will "political" factors within the organization influence how the decision is made?

Has the money needed to purchase my product been allocated?

Which person or persons in the buying organization will actually use or supervise the use of the product I am selling?[19]

Customers make buying decisions in many ways, so understanding each individual buyer's decision-making process is central to success in personal selling. Some buyers will have multiple buying processes. Buying decisions involving a straight rebuy, for example, will likely differ from buying decisions involving a new-task buy.[20]

Steps in the Typical Buying Process

The term "process" brings to mind a set formula that applies to every situation. But buying decisions are made in different ways, so it would be inappropriate to view the buying process as a uniform pattern of decision making. However, there is a model, a form of decision making that buyers usually apply to their unique circumstances. Figure 11.3 shows the typical stages in the buying-decision process: need awareness, evaluation of solutions, resolution of problems, purchase, and implementation. This model is especially helpful in understanding organizational buying decisions and large consumer acquisitions. Consumers who make habitual buying decisions often skip or reverse some of these stages.[21]

Need Awareness Need awareness is the first stage in the buying process. The buyer recognizes that something is imperfect or incomplete. The need for energy conservation technology may surface when oil prices rise to higher levels. The need for a customer service training program may become evident when surveys show a decline in customer satisfaction. Salespeople can create value at this stage of the buying process if they can help determine the magnitude of the customer's problem and identify a solution. For example, a sales representative may be able to help the buyer estimate the cost of poor customer service and recommend a way to improve service. Customers need help in determining whether they have a problem large enough to justify the cost of a proposed solution.[22]

Evaluation of Solutions Buyers who experience need awareness usually begin searching for information that will help them evaluate possible problem solutions. They realize, at this point, that the problem they face is amenable to some type of solution. In some cases, there are several solutions that the customer needs to study. Salespeople can add value at this stage by providing useful information that helps the customer make an informed choice. In some cases, the value justification can be presented in

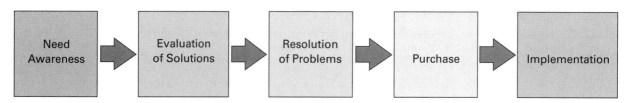

Figure 11.3 Steps in the typical buying-decision process.

terms of cost reduction or increased revenue. In other cases, the value justification may be intangible, such as customer satisfaction, improved security, or reduced stress. In business-to-business selling situations, value justification that can be measured is usually the most powerful.

To establish a true partnership with the customer, you need to be sure that you are offering them information that will help them achieve their objectives. If you possess a good understanding of the customer's buying process, you will know what they are trying to accomplish.[23]

Resolution of Problems   At this stage of the buying process, the customer is aware of a need and has evaluated one or more solutions. While the customer has decided to do something, he or she is likely to have issues that must be resolved before moving ahead. This is especially true in the case of complex sales.[24]

Some customers will want the proposed solution in writing. Competitors may be invited to submit written proposals. A well-written proposal is one way to add value. Customers may request specific information that can only be provided by the supplier's engineers or accountants. Customers may insist on visiting the supplier's manufacturing plant so that they can see the production process first-hand. Buyers often need help to overcome obstacles that prevent them from moving to the purchase stage of the buying process.

Purchase   Once the customer has, with the help of the salesperson, overcome all obstacles and concerns, he or she can make the purchase decision. Professional salespeople create value in many ways at this stage of the buying process. First, they can make sure the purchase is "hassle free." This may mean working with the customer to arrange the best financing, or supervising delivery and installation of the product. Salespeople can add value by becoming a "customer advocate" within their own organization. This may mean negotiating with various departments to expedite the order. Buyers want to work with salespeople who are able to quickly solve any order fulfillment problems.[25]

Implementation   The first sale is only the beginning of the salesperson's relationship with the buyer. Repeat sales occur when your company as supplier has demonstrated the ability to add value in various ways after the sale. Value creation can take the form of timely delivery, superior installation, accurate invoicing, follow-up contacts by the salesperson, or anything else that is important to the customer.

UNDERSTANDING THE BUYING-DECISION PROCESS FOR TRANSACTIONAL, CONSULTATIVE, AND RELATIONSHIP SELLING

THE NEXT STEP IN UNDERSTANDING THE CUSTOMER'S BUYING PROCESS IS TO DISCUSS three value creation selling approaches that appeal to certain types of customers. We will now discuss when to work effectively with each type of buyer.[26]

Transactional Process Buyer

Transactional buyers are well aware of their needs and usually know a great deal about the products or services they intend to purchase. In a truly transactional sale, buyers will become frustrated if the salesperson attempts to use needs assessment, problem solving, or relationship building. They are not looking for new information or advice from the salesperson. Most transactional buyers have conducted their own research and, in most cases, have decided which product best meets their needs. They don't want hand-holding and they don't want the salesperson to waste their time.[27]

How can a salesperson add value to a transactional sale? If the buyer is already aware of his or her needs, has evaluated solutions, and has no issues or concerns that need to be resolved, then the salesperson needs to focus on the purchase stage of the five-part buying process model (see Fig. 11.3). Do whatever is necessary to facilitate a convenient and "hassle-free" purchase. Eliminate any unnecessary costs or delays in processing the order. The transactional buyer may quickly turn to a competitor if he or she experiences unnecessary costs or delays.

Consultative Process Buyer

Consultative selling, a major theme of this text, was described in Chapter 5. This sales approach appeals to buyers who lack needs awareness or need help evaluating possible solutions. Some buying decisions require assistance from a consultative salesperson because the product is very complex and/or the cost of the product is very high. The purchase of a new home provides a good example in the consumer arena. Home buyers usually seek the assistance of an experienced realtor. For business buyers, the purchase of Internet phone-calling equipment provides a good example where consultative selling is beneficial. Organizations that are considering such a purchase might seek answers to such questions as: Can we keep a portion of our traditional phone network? Will the new system provide the same voice quality as our traditional system? Internet phone-calling equipment is available from several suppliers, including Avaya Incorporated and Cisco Systems Incorporated. Some customers will need help comparing the technology available from these and other suppliers.[28]

Successful consultative salespeople focus a great deal of attention on needs awareness, which is step one in the buying process model (see Fig. 11.3). This is where salespeople can create the most value by helping customers to gain an understanding of their problems and creating solutions that correct these problems.[29] Many customers seek help defining needs and solutions, but avoid dealing with sales representatives who simply want to sell a product.

Consultative selling encompasses the concept that salespeople should conduct a systematic assessment of the prospect's situation. This usually involves collecting as much information as possible prior to the sales call, and using a series of carefully worded questions to obtain the customer's point of view during the sales call. Two-way communication will provide for a mutual exchange of ideas, feelings, and perceptions.

The consultative salesperson will help the customer evaluate solutions and help resolve any problems that surface prior to the purchase stage. Consultative salespeople also work hard to add value at the implementation stage of the sales process. This may involve supervising product delivery and installation, servicing warranties, and providing other services after the sale.

Strategic Alliance Process Buyer

As noted previously, the goal of strategic alliances is to achieve a marketplace advantage by teaming up with another company. Alliances are often formed by companies that have similar business interests and seek to gain a mutual competitive advantage. Dell Computer, for example, formed a partnership with Microsoft and Intel to provide customized e-business solutions. In the highly competitive global market, going it alone is sometimes more difficult.[30]

Step one in building an alliance is a careful study of the proposed partner. This research is often coordinated by senior management and may involve persons working in the areas of sales, marketing, finance, and distribution. At some point, representatives from both companies will meet and explore the mutual benefits of the alliance. Both parties must be prepared to explain how they will add value once the alliance is formed.

The Buyer Resolution Theory

Several theories explain how customers arrive at a buying decision. One traditional point of view is based on the assumption that a final buying decision is possible only after the prospect has answered five logical questions (see Fig. 11.4). This is called the

Buyer resolution theory recognizes that a purchase is made only after the prospect has made five buying decisions that result from specific, affirmative responses to the five key questions.	
Why should I buy?	Realistically, it is difficult to provide prospects with an answer to this question. In many cases, salespeople fail to help customers become aware of a need. Therefore, large numbers of potential customers are not sufficiently persuaded to purchase products that will provide them with genuine buyer benefits.
What should I buy?	If a prospect agrees that a need does exist, then a sales representative is ready to address this buying decision. He or she must convince the prospect that the product being offered will satisfy the need. In most cases, the buyer can choose from among several competing products.
Where should I buy?	As products become more complex, customers are giving more attention to "source" decisions. In a major metropolitan area someone who wants to buy a LaserJet 3160 or a competing product will be able to choose from several sources.
What is a fair price?	Today's better-educated and -informed consumers are searching for the right balance between price and value (i.e., buyer benefits). They are better able to detect prices that are not competitive or that do not correspond in their minds with the product's value.
When should I buy?	A sale cannot be closed until a customer has decided when to buy. In some selling situations, the customer will want to postpone the purchase because of reluctance to part with the money.

Figure 11.4 Buyer resolution theory. This theory, sometimes referred to as "The 5 Ws Theory," focuses attention on questions the customer may need answers to before making a purchase decision. The absence of an answer to any of these questions will likely result in a customer objection.

Figure 11.5
Developing a customer strategy model. This model illustrates the many factors that influence buying decisions. It can serve as a guide for developing a highly responsive customer strategy.

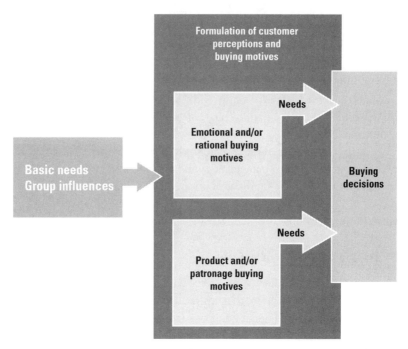

buyer resolution theory. One strength of this buying theory is that it focuses the salesperson's attention on five important factors that the customer is likely to consider before making a purchase: need, product, source, price, and time. Answers to these five questions provide valuable insights about the customer's buying strategy. One important limitation of this theory is that a salesperson cannot always anticipate which of the five buying decisions might be most difficult for the prospect to make. If the selling process does not mesh with the buying process, a sale is less likely. There is no established sequence in which prospects make these five decisions, so a highly inflexible sales presentation would not be effective.

UNDERSTANDING BUYER BEHAVIOUR

WHILE EVERY CUSTOMER IS UNIQUE, SALESPEOPLE NEED TO UNDERSTAND THE important social and psychological influences that tend to shape customer buying decisions. We will review concepts that come from the fields of psychology, sociology, and anthropology. Figure 11.5 illustrates the many forces that influence buying decisions.

Basic Needs That Influence Buyer Behaviour

Basic human needs have changed little throughout our economic history. However, the ways in which needs are fulfilled have changed greatly in the age of information.[31] The starting point for developing an understanding of the forces influencing buying decisions is a review of the individual needs that shape the customer's behaviour. To gain insights into customer behaviour motivated by both physiological and psychological needs, it is helpful to study the popular hierarchy of needs developed by Abraham Maslow.

Selling to Couples

There are many situations where salespeople sell to a couple, rather than to an individual: real estate, mutual funds, cars, wedding rings, insurance. These situations can pose additional challenges for salespeople. Each person in a couple may, for example, bring hidden agenda to the purchase. An unseasoned salesperson risks alienating or offending one partner and, perhaps as a result, losing the sale.

According to Marilyn Powers, a practising therapist, couples exhibit one of three communications stages: a fusion stage, a power struggle stage, or an independent stage. Couples in the fusion stage think and feel alike, and try to avoid conflict. As a result, they make hasty decisions, often without providing adequate information to the salesperson. This may result in the sale being cancelled, or in after-sale customer dissatisfaction. To prevent this, the salesperson needs to ask sufficient questions during the need discovery stage of the sales process to be sure he or she fully understands the couple's needs.

Couples in the power struggle stage actively seek a win-lose solution, where one partner's "win" over the other partner is more important than the actual purchase decision. Here, the salesperson needs to slow the sales process and craft a "win-win" solution for the couple. The best way to do this is to focus on each person, being sure to establish and understand each individual's needs. Through active listening—paraphrasing and restating each participant's comments—the salesperson may be able to defuse the emotional situation, keeping the communication lines open and establishing some common ground. Unfortunately, there will be instances where it is apparent that one key decision maker will win the power struggle. Here, some salespeople argue that it is best to align with that person as it will be impossible to keep both participants happy; other salespeople argue that it is best to remain impartial and to avoid getting involved in the power struggle.

Couples in the independent stage often have different opinions about what they should buy, but they are willing to continue their search for a third solution that may be better than either of their independent solutions. A salesperson who encounters this situation may need to give the couple additional time to communicate with each other, and should not try to close the sale too quickly.

Judith C. Tingley and Lee E. Robert, authors of *GenderSell: How to Sell to the Opposite Sex*, suggest some tips to use, depending on whether the salesperson is a man or a woman. They suggest that male salespeople must be careful to avoid being patronizing or condescending toward women when trying to sell to a mixed-gender couple. A male salesperson should greet the woman first, keep her involved throughout the sales process, and be careful to use gender-neutral language. Female salespeople need to build credibility quickly, be more rational and less emotional in their selling style, and treat both partners with equal respect.[a]

Maslow's Hierarchy of Needs According to Abraham Maslow, basic human needs are arranged in a hierarchy according to their strength (Fig. 11.6). His theory rests on the assumption that as each lower-level need is satisfied, the need at the next level demands attention.

Physiological Needs. Sometimes called primary needs, **physiological needs** include the needs of food, water, and sleep. Maslow placed our physiological needs at the bottom of the pyramid. He believed that these basic needs tend to be strong in the minds of most people.

Security Needs. After physiological needs have been satisfied, the next need level that tends to dominate is safety and security. **Security needs** represent our desire to be free from danger and uncertainty. The desire to satisfy the need for safety and security

physiological needs Primary or physical needs, including food, water, air, warmth, and sleep.

security needs These represent our desire for protection from the elements and to be free from danger and uncertainty; buying decisions to support these needs could include clothing, shelter, and insurance.

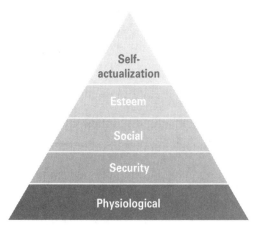

Figure 11.6 The forces that motivate customers to make specific buying decisions are complex. This model illustrates Maslow's hierarchy of needs.

social needs Needs that reflect a person's desire for affection, identification with a group, and approval from others.

esteem needs The desire to feel worthy in the eyes of others, to develop a sense of personal worth and adequacy or a feeling of competence and importance.

often motivates people to purchase such items as medical and life insurance or a security alarm for their home or business.

Social Needs. The need to belong, or **social needs**, reflects our desire for identification with a group and approval from others. These needs help explain our continuing search for friendship, social acceptance among one's peers, and long-term business relationships.

Esteem Needs. At the fourth level of Maslow's needs hierarchy are **esteem needs**, which reflect our desire to feel worthy in the eyes of others. We seek a sense of personal worth and adequacy, a feeling of competence.

Self-Actualization. Maslow defined the term **self-actualization** as a need for self-fulfillment, a tapping of one's full potential. It is the need to "be all that you can be," to have mastery over things you are doing. One goal of consultative selling is to help the customer experience self-actualization in terms of the relationship with the salesperson.

The five-level needs hierarchy model developed by Maslow is somewhat artificial in certain circumstances. At times, several of our needs interact simultaneously. Consider the business lunch where you are not only conducting business with a client but are also satisfying your need to consume food and beverages, to engage in social activities, and perhaps to seem important in your own eyes and, you hope, the eyes of your customer. However, the model does provide salespeople with a practical way of understanding which need is most likely to dominate customer behaviour in certain situations.

Group Influences That Influence Buying Decisions

As noted earlier, the people around us influence our buying decisions. These **group influences** can be classified into four major areas: (1) role, (2) reference groups, (3) social class, and (4) culture and microcultures[32] (Fig. 11.7). Salespeople who understand these roles and influences can develop the type of insight customers view as being valuable.

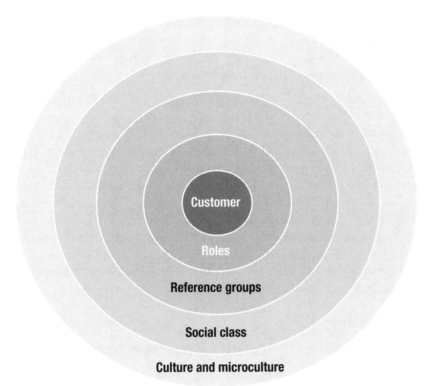

Figure 11.7 To gain additional insights into customers' motivations, sales-people can study group influences that affect buying decisions.

Role Influence   Throughout our lives we occupy positions within groups, organizations, and institutions. Closely associated with each position is a **role**—a set of characteristics and expected social behaviours based on the expectations of others. All the roles we assume (e.g., student, member of the school board, our position at work) influence not only our general behaviour but also our buying behaviour. In today's society, for example, a woman may assume the role of mother at home and purchasing manager at work. In the manager's role, she may feel the need to purchase a conservative wardrobe, enroll in a leadership training course, or join a professional association.

Reference Group Influence   A **reference group** consists of the categories of people that you see yourself belonging to, and with which you habitually compare yourself. Members of a reference group tend to influence the values, attitudes, and behaviours of one another.[33] The reference group may act as a point of comparison and a source of information for the individual member. In the business community, the Canadian Professional Sales Association may be a reference group for its members. As a member of a reference group, each of us may observe other people in the group to establish our own norms; these norms may become a guide for our purchasing activities.

Social Class Influence   A **social class** is one of society's relatively permanent and ordered divisions whose members share similar values, interests, and behaviours.[34] The criteria used to rank people according to social class vary from one society to another. In

self-actualization The need for self-fulfillment; a tapping of one's full potential to meet a goal; the need to be everything one is capable of being.

group influences Forces that other people exert on customers' buying behaviour.

role A set of characteristics and expected social behaviours based on the expectations of others. All the roles we assume may influence our buying behaviour.

reference group Two or more people who have well-established interpersonal communications and tend to influence the values, attitudes, and buying behaviours of one another. They act as a point of comparison and a source of information for a prospective buyer.

social class A group of people who share similar values, interests, and behaviours.

some societies, land ownership allows entry into a higher social class. In other societies, education is a major key to achieving upper-class status. Social class, in most cases, is not determined by a single factor. It is determined by a combination of such factors as income, education, occupation, and accumulated wealth.

culture The values, beliefs, institutions, transmitted behaviour patterns, and thoughts of a people or society.

Cultural Influence **Culture** can be defined as the accumulation of values, rules of behaviour, forms of expression, religious beliefs, and transmitted behaviour patterns for a people or society that shares a common language and environment. Culture tends to encourage or discourage particular behaviours and mental processes.[35] We maintain and transmit our culture chiefly through language. Culture has considerable influence on buying behaviour. Today, culture in Canada is getting more attention because of rapid increases in immigration. As cultural diversity increases, companies must re-examine their sales and marketing strategies. Within most cultures are groups whose members share value systems based on common life experiences and situations. We call such a group a **microculture**. Some microcultures, such as mature consumers, Blacks, Southeast Asians, and Aboriginal Canadians, are important market segments.

microculture Value systems shared by communities based on common life experiences and situations that differ from those of the dominant society's culture.

Perception—How Customer Needs Are Formed

perception A process through which sensations are interpreted, using our knowledge and experience.

Perception is the process through which sensations received through sight, hearing, touch, taste, and smell are interpreted, using our knowledge and experience. Buyer behaviour is often influenced by perception.[36] When Volkswagen announced that it would build an ultra-luxury car that would sell for more than $100 000, many people questioned the merits of this decision. Could the maker of the Beetle and the Golf compete in the market segment dominated by Lexus, Mercedes Benz, Jaguar, and BMW? So far, sales of the Volkswagen Phaeton have been slow even though most automobile journalists view it as a truly luxury car.[37] Is perception the barrier to sales growth?

We tend to screen out or modify stimuli, a process known as *selective attention*, for two reasons. First, we cannot possibly be conscious of all inputs at one time; just the

Customer Relationship Management with Technology

Managing Multiple Contacts with CRM

Salespeople often find that groups of their contacts have common interests and buying motives. Customers and prospects may be segmented into groups by buying influences, by the products they purchase, by the industries in which they are involved, or by their size. Customer relationship management software can enable the salesperson to easily link contacts as groups and "mass produce" information that is custom-fitted to the needs of people in a specific group. For example, each owner of a specific product may receive a telephone call, personalized letter, or report that describes the benefits of a new accessory available from the salesperson. (See the exercise Managing Multiple Contacts with CRM on page 232 for more information.)

commercial messages we see and hear each day are enough to cause sensory overload. Second, we are conditioned by our social and cultural background, and by our physical and psychological needs, to use selectivity.

Buyers may screen out or modify information presented by a salesperson if it conflicts with their previously learned attitudes or beliefs. The business buyer who feels the new office furniture designs that combine individual work space will only encourage impromptu employee chitchat is apt to use selective attention when the salesperson begins discussing product features. Salespeople who can anticipate this problem of selective attention should acquire as much background information as possible before meeting with the prospect. During the first meeting with the customer, the salesperson should make every effort to build a strong relationship so that the person opens up and freely discusses personal perceptions. Salespeople who do this have accepted one of the great truisms in sales and marketing: "Facts are negotiable. Perception is rock solid."

Buying Motives

Every buying decision has a motive behind it. A **buying motive** can be thought of as an aroused need, drive, or desire that stimulates purchasing behaviour intended to satisfy the aroused need. Our perceptions influence or shape this behaviour. An understanding of buying motives provides the salesperson with the reasons why customers buy. Unfortunately, some buyers will not or cannot tell you their buying motives. A company may be planning a new product launch and wants to keep this initiative a secret. In some cases revealing important information may make the customer feel vulnerable. And some customers may not be aware of one or more buying motives that will influence the purchase decision.[38]

As you might expect, some buying decisions are influenced by more than one buying motive. The buyer of catering services may want food of exceptional quality served quickly so that all the guests can eat together. This customer may also be quite price-conscious. In this situation, the caterer should attempt to discover the **dominant buying motive (DBM)**. The DBM will have the greatest influence on the buying decision.[39] If the customer is anxious to make a good impression on guests who have discriminating food tastes, then food quality may be the dominant buying motive. Successful salespeople have adopted a product strategy that involves discovery of the buying motives that influence the purchase decision. In Chapter 14, we describe a need identification process that can be used to discover customers' buying motives.

Emotional versus Rational Buying Motives

A careful study of buyer perceptions and behaviour reveals that people make buying decisions based on both emotional and rational buying motives. An **emotional buying motive** is one that prompts the prospect to act because of an appeal to some sentiment or passion. When customers buy expensive Harley-Davidson motorcycles, they are paying for much more than a high-flying "hog"; they are purchasing entry into a community of like-minded enthusiasts who share a passion for all things Harley.[40] Emotions can be powerful and often serve as the foundation of the dominant buying motive. A **rational buying motive** usually appeals to the prospect's reason or judgment based on objective thought processes. Some common rational buying motives include quality, price, and availability of technical assistance.

buying motive An aroused need, drive, or desire that initiates the buying-decision process.

dominant buying motive The motive that has the greatest influence on a customer's buying decision.

emotional buying motive A motive that prompts the prospect to act as a result of an appeal to some sentiment or passion.

rational buying motive A motive that prompts the prospect to act because of an appeal to the prospect's reason or better judgment such as price, quality, and availability of technical assistance. Generally these result from an objective review of available information.

This Trimark Investments ad appeals to a customer's emotional buying motives.

Emotional Buying Motives A surprising number of purchases are guided by emotional buying motives. Recent research indicates that buying is a lot more emotional than most marketers thought. Many buyers are guided more by feelings than by logic.[41] Even technology firms sometimes rely on emotional appeals as part of their marketing strategy. Doing business in Canada, or anyplace else in the world, is never purely a rational or logical process. Recognize that there is an emotional component to every sale and tune in to the emotional cues such as body language, tone of voice, and emotive words. With the power of empathy you can get on the same page, emotionally, as your customer.[42]

Rational Buying Motives A purchase based on rational buying motives is generally the result of an objective review of available information. The buyer closely examines product or service information with an attitude that is relatively free of emotion. Business buyers are most likely to be motivated by such rational buying motives as on-time delivery, financial gain, competent installation, saving of time, increased profits, reduced costs, or durability. Business buyers representing large firms, such as Research In Motion, Air Canada, and Canadian National Railways, rely on a buying process that is more formalized than the consumer buying process. Purchases made by these companies usually call for detailed product specifications, written purchase orders, and formal approval. The business buyer and the salesperson work closely during all stages of the buying process, which begins with a precise definition of the customer's problem. Salespeople who sell to business buyers spend a great deal of time gathering, interpreting, and disseminating customer-specific information.[43]

This Samsung Electronics Canada ad appeals to a customer's rational buying motives.

Patronage versus Product Buying Motives Another way to help explain buyer perceptions and behaviour is to distinguish between patronage and product buying motives. Patronage buying motives and product buying motives are learned reasons for buying. These buying motives are important because they can stimulate repeat business and referrals.

Patronage Buying Motives A **patronage buying motive** is one that causes the prospect to buy products from one particular business. The prospect has usually had prior direct or indirect contact with the business and has judged this contact to be beneficial. In those situations where there is little or no appreciable difference between two products, patronage motives can be highly important. At a time when look-alike products are very common, these motives take on extra importance. Some typical patronage buying motives are superior service, complete selection of products, competence of sales representatives, and ability to buy online.

patronage buying motive A motive that causes the prospect to buy a product from one particular company rather than another. Typical patronage buying motives include superior service, attractive decor, product selection, and competence of the salesperson.

Product Buying Motives A **product buying motive** is one that leads a prospect to purchase one product in preference to another. Interestingly enough, this decision is sometimes made without direct comparison between competing products; the buyer simply feels that one product is superior to another. Numerous buying motives trigger prospects to select one product over another, including brand, quality, price, and design or engineering preference.

product buying motive A motive that causes the prospect to buy one particular product brand or label over another. Typical product buying motives include brand, quality, price, and design or engineering preference.

It is hard to imagine how salespeople can create value for customers unless they understand the customer's buying motives. Figure 11.8 provides various examples of how salespeople can put this understanding into creating value at different stages of the buying process.

Strategic Initiatives Identified	Need Awareness	Evaluation of Solutions	Resolution of Problems	Purchase	Implementation
Present and/or design unique strengths that fit the strategic initiative.	Partner with customers to understand unique needs in new and improved ways.	Configure or adapt superior solutions to unique needs.	Provide assistance and advice to overcome problems and provide solutions.	Adapt and suggest effective methods to purchase and enjoy solutions.	Assist and/or train customers in maximum satisfaction from purchase.

Figure 11.8 Creating Value Throughout the Buying Process Model.
A sample list of methods for creating value throughout each of the steps in the buying process. Specific methods should be created after arriving at a careful understanding of the unique needs of the individual customer.

REVIEWING KEY CONCEPTS

- Discuss the meaning of a customer strategy.

  The importance of developing a *customer strategy* was introduced in this chapter. This type of planning is necessary to ensure maximum customer responsiveness. Buying procedures and policies can vary greatly from one buyer to another. If a salesperson does not learn how the buyer plans to make the purchase, then there is the strong possibility that the selling process will be out of alignment with the customer's buying process.

- Explain the difference between consumer and business buyers.

  Business buyer behaviour was compared to consumer buyer behaviour. Three types of business buying situations were described: straight rebuy, new-task buy, and the modified rebuy. Systems selling, a common business buying strategy, was also described. Three types of consumer buying situations were defined: habitual buying decisions, variety-seeking buying decisions, and complex buying decisions.

- Understand the importance of alignment between the selling process and the customer's buying process.

  Customers make buying decisions in many ways, so it would be inappropriate to view the buying process as a uniform pattern of decision making. However, there is a common decision-making model that most buyers

apply to their unique circumstances. The typical stages in the buying decision process are needs awareness, evaluation of solutions, resolution of problems, purchase, and implementation.

- Understand the buying process of the transactional, consultative, and strategic alliance buyer.

  Three value-creation selling approaches that appeal to certain types of customers were discussed: the transactional process buyer, the consultative process buyer, and the strategic alliance process buyer. The consultative process buyer offers the greatest challenge to most salespeople.

- Discuss the various influences that shape customer buying decisions.

  We noted that buyer behaviour is influenced in part by individual (physical and psychological) needs. Maslow's popular model ranks these needs. There are also a number of group influences that shape our psychological needs to various degrees. Buyer behaviour is influenced by the roles we assume, reference groups, social class, and culture. *Perception* was defined as the process of selecting, organizing, and interpreting information inputs to produce meaning. We discussed *emotional* and *rational buying motives* and compared patronage and product motives.

Key Terms

Review Questions

1. According to the Strategic/Consultative Selling Model, what are the three prescriptions for the development of a successful customer strategy?

2. List and describe the three most common types of business buying situations.

3. Describe the five major steps in the typical buying process.

4. List and describe three value-creation selling approaches that appeal to various types of customers.

5. According to the buyer resolution theory, a purchase is made only after the prospect has made five buying decisions. What are they?

6. Explain how Maslow's hierarchy of needs affects buyer behaviour.

7. Describe four group influences that affect buyer behaviour.

8. What is meant by the term *perception*?

9. Distinguish between emotional and rational buying motives.

10. J. D. Power, founder of J. D. Power and Associates, says, "We define quality as what the customer wants." Do you agree or disagree with his observations? Explain your answer.

Application Exercises

1. Select several advertisements from a trade magazine. Analyze each one, and determine which rational buying motives the advertiser is appealing to. Explain whether these advertisements also appeal to emotional buying motives. Then select a magazine that is aimed at a particular consumer group—for example, *Chatelaine*, *Canadian Business*, or *Better Homes and Gardens*. Study the advertisements and determine what buying motives they appeal to.

2. The $100 000 Volkswagen Phaeton is a far cry from the Volkswagen Beetle. VW's new flagship model is designed to challenge Lexus, Mercedes Benz, and BMW. The Phaeton, like the original Lexus LS400, is positioned as another choice in the luxury-car market. Do you think potential customers accept the Phaeton as a truly luxurious car? Will customer perceptions play a role in the acceptance of this new model? Explain your reasoning.

3. J. D. Power and Associates is a global marketing information services firm that helps businesses and consumers make better decisions through credible customer-based information. The company provides an unbiased source of marketing information based on opinions of consumers. Visit **www.jdpower.com** and become familiar with the type of information services offered. View some of the studies done on Canadian consumer satisfaction and be prepared to discuss interesting findings in class.

4. Assume your college or university is considering buying 100 new PCs for student labs throughout the campus. Describe who you think will be involved in the buying centre (by role), and what you think the motives might be for each of them.

5. Assume your college or university is considering replacing its mainframe computer. Its current mainframe computer is now 15 years old and has been creating problems for some time. The cost of a modern replacement is estimated at between $1.5 and $2 million. Will this be a new task buy, a modified rebuy, or a straight rebuy? If you were a salesperson selling mainframe computers, how would you treat this opportunity? Explain.

ROLE-PLAY EXERCISE

In this role play, you will assume the role of a salesperson working at a clothing store. The inventory includes a wide range of business professional clothing such as suits, sport coats, dress shirts, and accessories; the store also offers a full range of business casual clothing. A member of your class will assume the role of a customer who visits your store for the purpose of buying clothing for work. He or she is about to graduate and will start work at a new job in approximately two weeks. In addition to clothing, your store offers complete alteration services and credit plans. During the role play, you should develop a relationship with the customer using strategies discussed in previous chapters and determine the customer's needs with questions, attentive listening, and observation.

CRM Application Exercise   Managing Multiple Contacts with CRM

The Salesforce.com database identifies four architectural firms. You can look up these firms and arrange to contact them. Start by selecting the Accounts tab. In the Account list click on the "Industry" field to sort the list by industry. Select the first architecture firm. Then, on the Account Detail screen, select any one of the contacts for that firm. Using the same procedure as the exercise in Chapter 7, page 146, send an e-mail to this contact. Use the "Architecture Calls" template. After sending the e-mail and returing to the Contact Screen, select the e-mail you just sent from the Activity History section. Click on "Create Follow Up Task." On the Task screen select Phone Call as the type, and enter Architecture Calls as the subject. Enter "next Monday" as the date. Change the reminder time to 9:00 a.m., the time you want to schedule these calls. Click Save. Repeat this process for all four architecture accounts.

Verify that these architecture calls have been scheduled for next Monday by returning to your home screen. The calls will be in the My Tasks section.

Reality Selling Today Video Case Problem

Justin Bremer, the financial advisor featured at the beginning of this chapter, is continuously developing new accounts, servicing existing accounts, and introducing new products and services. The major challenge of selling financial advice is undoubtedly clients' information privacy. Referral from existing customers, therefore, is important. This positive word of mouth can only come naturally from satisfied customers. Even so, Justin understands that creating a good impression when he meets a potential client for the first time is a job half done.

Individuals and businesses do not want to talk about the details of their existing financial plans to strangers, much less to new financial advisors. In addition, switching from one financial services company to another creates exorbitant costs, both in terms of time and money. Consequently, clients want to buy financial products and services from companies that not only help them balance risks and gains but also provide outstanding services over the long run. Finally, the market for financial services is quite competitive.

Wealth Design Group's competitive advantage is its ability to offer comprehensive yet innovative financial solutions to its clients. When Justin meets with a prospect, he asks several questions to determine the client's needs and buying motives. He realizes that in some cases several motives may influence the purchase decision. He also knows that buying behaviour is influenced by perception, so he must probe to find out what prospects are really thinking by asking clarifying questions at the right time. He proactively goes after information that is relevant to making the sales without appearing intrusive. In short, he always makes sure that he spends enough time with his clients in the very first encounter to understand their needs and concerns. Then he works closely with his team to come up with solutions that are customized to those specific needs. At the same time, he must make it clear to the clients about how his company stands out in the highly competitive market and provide them with in-depth analysis of their current financial health to speed up buyers' decision-making processes.

Questions

1. Does it appear that Justin Bremer has built his customer strategy on the three prescriptions featured in the Strategic/Consultative Selling Model? Explain.

2. What aspects of the need–satisfaction theory has Justin incorporated into his approach to customers? Explain.

3. As an individual looking for long-term financial solutions, would you be more influenced by rational or emotional buying motives? Explain.

4. What steps has Justin taken to initiate a long-term partnership with his customers?

Chapter 12
Developing and Qualifying a Prospect Base

Learning Objectives

After studying this chapter, you should be able to

1   Discuss the importance of developing a prospect base

2   Identify and assess important sources of prospects

3   Describe criteria for qualifying prospects

4   Explain common methods of collecting and organizing prospect information

5   Describe the steps in managing a prospect base

When Greyhound Courier Express (GCX), the courier division of Greyhound Canada Transportation, had a need to increase the access and visibility of customer information throughout its organization, it chose Salesforce.com. GCX salespeople—some of whom manage as many as 3000 clients—were using stand-alone contact management tools and even paper-based day planners. GCX now uses Salesforce.com to effectively and efficiently maintain complete and accurate prospect information. Customized data fields allow GCX salespeople to access and monitor important sales information, and the user-friendly Web interface is convenient for the many diverse users within the company. Customers receive better service as salespeople receive alerts that remind them when important activities must be performed.[1]

Account-based software vendors such as Salesforce, NetSuite, and Oracle Siebel are helping companies develop effective customer relationship management (CRM) systems. These systems are at the heart of every successful one-to-one marketing initiative. Success in selling depends on one's ability to identify prospects, gain insight into a prospect's needs, and develop an accurate picture of the prospect's value.[2]

PROSPECTING—AN INTRODUCTION

prospecting A systematic process of identifying potential customers.

prospect A potential customer who meets the qualification criteria established by you or your company.

GERHARD GSCHWANDTNER, EDITOR OF *SELLING POWER*, SAYS, "THE MAIN PURPOSE of a salesperson is not to make sales, but to create customers."[3] Identifying potential customers is an important aspect of the customer strategy. In the terminology of personal selling, this process is called **prospecting**. A potential customer, or **prospect**, is someone who meets the qualification criteria established by you or your company.

Finding prospects who can make the decision to purchase is not as easy as it sounds. This is especially true in business-to-business sales. In many situations, the salesperson must make the sales presentation to multiple decision makers. One of these decision makers might be the technical expert who wants an answer to the question: "Does the product meet the company's specifications?" Another decision maker may be the person who will actually use the product. The employee who will use the forklift truck you are selling may be involved in the purchase decision. Of course, there is often a "purse-string" decision maker who has the ultimate authority to release funds for the purchase. During periods of economic uncertainty, the decision-making process often moves upward. It is sometimes difficult to make connections with upper-level executives. One solution is to plan a joint sales call involving a higher-level executive from your own company.[4]

The goal of prospecting is to build a qualified **prospect base** made up of current customers and potential customers. Building a prospect base involves the use of CRM software to monitor movement of the customer through the sales process. Many successful companies find that current customers account for a large percentage of their sales. Every effort is made to devise and implement a customer strategy that builds, fosters, nurtures, and extends relationships with established customers.[5]

prospect base A list of current and potential customers.

Importance of Prospecting

Every salesperson must cope with customer attrition—that is, the inevitable loss of customers over a period of time, which can be attributed to a variety of causes. Unless new prospects are found to replace lost customers, a salesperson will eventually face a reduction in income and possible loss of employment. Paul Tindall of Toronto-based Coaching Works says, "Top performers prospect consistently. Low performers don't."[6] To better understand the significance of prospecting, let us examine a few common causes of customer attrition.

1. *The customer may move to a new location outside the salesperson's territory*. The Canadian population is very mobile. This cause of attrition is especially common in the retail and service industries.

2. *A firm may go out of business or merge with another company*. In some areas of business, the failure rate is quite high. In recent years we have witnessed a record number of mergers, which has caused massive changes in purchasing plans.

3. *A loyal buyer or purchasing agent may leave the position because of promotion, retirement, resignation, or serious illness*. The replacement may prefer to buy from someone else.

4. *Sales are lost to the competition*. In some cases, the competition offers more value. The added value may take the form of better quality, a better price, a stronger relationship, better service, or some combination of these factors.

Some studies reveal that the average company loses 15 to 20 percent of its customers every year. Depending on the type of selling, this figure might be higher or lower. Clearly, many customers are lost for reasons beyond the salesperson's control. If salespeople want to keep their earnings at a stable level, they will need to develop new customers.

Joe Girard, once recognized by the *Guinness Book of Records* as the world's greatest salesperson, used the "Ferris wheel" concept to illustrate the relationship between prospecting and the loss of customers due to attrition.[7] As people (i.e., customers) get off the Ferris wheel, the operator (i.e., salesperson) fills their seats one at a time, moves the wheel a little, and continues this process until all the original riders have left the wheel and new ones have come aboard (Fig. 12.1). In reality, of course, established customers do not come and go this fast. With the passing of time, however, many customers will be replaced.

Prospecting Requires Planning

Prospecting should be viewed as a systematic process of locating potential customers. Some prospecting efforts can be integrated easily into a regular sales call. Progressive marketers do three things to improve the quality of their prospecting effort:

1. *Increase the number of people who board the Ferris wheel.* You want to see a continuous number of prospects board the Ferris wheel because they are the source of sales opportunities. If the number of potential prospects declines sharply, the number of sales closed will also decline.

2. *Improve the quality of the prospects who board the Ferris wheel.* Companies often establish quality standards that ensure a steady supply of prospects with high profit potential. For example, some companies focus their prospecting efforts on consultative process buyers. These are prospects who often lack need awareness and need help evaluating possible solutions.

3. *Shorten the sales cycle by quickly determining which of the new prospects are qualified prospects—qualified as to need, authority to buy, ability to pay, and willingness to purchase the product.* Gerhard Gschwandtner says, "Time is the ultimate scorekeeper in the game of selling." He points out that many salespeople do not meet their sales goals because they do not quickly qualify new prospects.[8] Later in this chapter we will examine qualifying practices and discuss how to shorten the sales cycle with sales force automation methods.

Selling in Action
Prospecting with Your Partners

When Megan Michael sees a new office building going up, she stops her car and makes inquiries about who is to occupy the building. As a sales representative for an office furniture supplier, BKM Total Office, she needs to be aware of new office space. However, this approach is not her most important prospecting method. She has found the telephone to be her most effective prospecting tool. Megan speaks regularly with her customers to find out if they know companies that might need BKM's products. Architects, designers, and builders who have previously worked with Megan have proved to be good sources of referrals. The key to her prospecting success is maintaining a strong relationship with her existing customers. She realizes that you must be an effective partner before you can ask for help.[a]

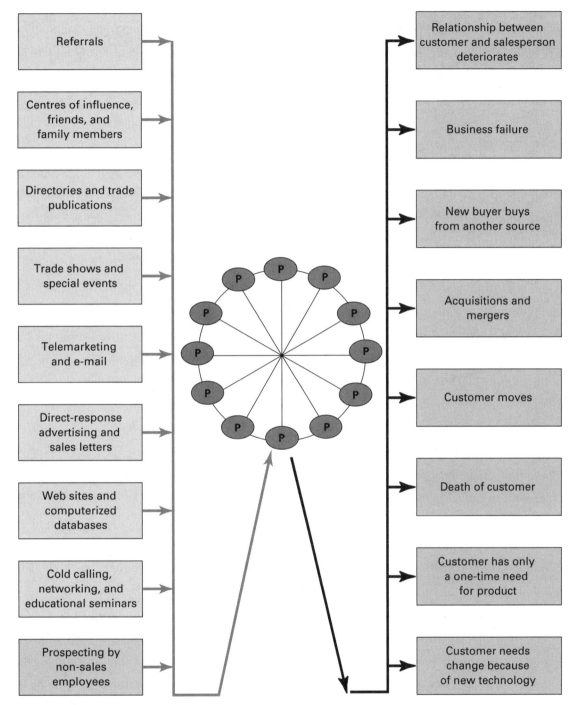

Figure 12.1 The Ferris wheel concept illustrates the resupply of an ongoing list of prospects to combat customer attrition. It is part of the customer strategy of Joe Girard, world sales record holder.

Using the Same CRM Software as Cisco Systems

Cisco Systems, Inc. has deployed the Salesforce.com CRM solution to 15 000 users, from North America and India to Dubai and Dublin. Ultimately, there will be 25 000 users. Salesforce.com provides Cisco with effective prospect management tools, namely dashboards, account planning, and partner/distributor reports.

- Dashboards track metrics such as opportunities, lead conversion rates, number of account plans, and top accounts for sales reps and managers. Individual sales people create their own reports to help chart their progress.
- Account planning, which had previously been difficult to institute, is increasingly leveraged with Salesforce.
- Partners are part of Cisco's customer "eco-system." Overall productivity and effectiveness are improved by extending leads to partners and tracking conversion to opportunity and ultimately to a sale.

You have the opportunity to use a demonstration version of the solution, Salesforce.com, used by Cisco. Just like a Cisco salesperson, you will be assigned a number of prospect accounts and given individual and company information about each account's contact person in Salesforce. Your participation in the CRM case study and exercises will give you hands-on experience with the strategic development of a prospect base using modern sales technology. Not only will you be using the same software used by thousands of salespeople, you will also be working with data derived from authentic selling challenges. (See the CRM case study Reviewing the Prospect Database on p. 260 for more information.)

Prospecting Plans Must Be Assessed Often

In today's dynamic, ever-changing marketplace, prospecting plans must be monitored continuously. Some prospecting techniques that worked well in the past may become ineffective because of changing market conditions. Midwest Training Institute, a firm that helps companies improve their production and sales efficiency, experienced a dramatic sales decline during the first quarter of the year. This decline came after years of steady sales increases. Joel Pecoraro, president of the company, initiated a thorough investigation and discovered that his sales staff were relying primarily on one prospecting approach that was no longer successful: the salespeople were calling established customers. Pecoraro designed an incentive program that rewarded salespeople who adopted new prospecting techniques, such as attending an association meeting where the salesperson could meet potential prospects or speaking at a meeting attended by persons who might need the services offered by Midwest Training Institute.[9]

SOURCES OF PROSPECTS

EVERY SALESPERSON MUST DEVELOP A PROSPECTING SYSTEM SUITED TO A PARTICULAR selling situation. There are several sources of prospects, and each should be carefully examined.

- Referrals
- Centres of influence, friends, and family
- Directories

- Trade publications
- Trade shows and special events
- Telemarketing and e-mail
- Direct response advertising and sales letters
- Web sites
- Computerized databases
- Cold calling
- Networking
- Educational seminars
- Prospecting by non-sales employees

Referrals

The use of referrals as a prospecting approach has been successful in a wide range of selling situations. In most cases, referral leads result in higher close rates, larger sales, and a shorter sales cycle. A **referral** is a prospect who has been recommended by a current customer or by someone who is familiar with the product. Satisfied customers, business acquaintances, and even prospects who do not buy can often recommend the names of persons who might benefit from purchasing the product. Customers are more likely to give a referral if they perceive value in the product you sell. When you build value into your sales process, you increase the odds that the customer will give you a referral. Jim Domanski, CEO of Teleconcepts Consulting of Kanata, Ontario, says that when you have a referral, there is an explicit or implicit endorsement of you, your company, and your product by the source.[10]

referral A prospect who has been recommended by a current customer or by someone who is familiar with the product or service.

Endless Chain Referrals   One approach to obtaining referrals, called the endless chain referral, is easy to use because it fits naturally into most sales presentations. A salesperson selling long-term health care insurance might ask, "Miss Chen, who do you know who might be interested in our insurance plan?" This open-ended question gives the person the freedom to recommend several prospects and is less likely to be answered with a "no" response. Be sure to use your reference's name when you contact the new prospect, as in this example: "Mary Chen suggested that I call you."

Referral Letters and Cards   Another approach, a variation of the endless chain technique, is the referral letter. In addition to requesting the names of prospects, the salesperson asks the customer to prepare a note or letter of introduction that can be delivered to the potential customer. The correspondence is an actual testimonial prepared by a satisfied customer. Some companies use a referral card to introduce the salesperson. The preprinted card has a place for your customer to sign the new prospect's name and his or her own name, and can be used as part of the sales presentation.

Within the field of personal selling, there is not complete agreement regarding the timing of the referral request. Some sales training programs encourage salespeople to request the referral immediately after closing the sale. Others point out that if you are working with a new customer, it takes time to earn the customer's trust. The customer may feel there is a risk involved in giving you referrals. Once you have built a strong, trusting relationship with the customer, referral requests are more likely to receive a positive response.[11]

Referral Organizations Some salespeople have found that membership in a referral organization is an effective way to obtain good leads. BNI (Business Network International) is one of the largest business networking organizations, with over 3600 chapters worldwide (**www.bni.com**). BNI offers its members the opportunity to share ideas, contacts and referrals.[12] In addition, some local clubs offer referrals as a member benefit.

Centres of Influence, Friends, and Family Members

The centre-of-influence method involves establishing a relationship with a well-connected, influential person who is willing to provide information about potential prospects. This person may not make buying decisions but has influence on other people who do. To illustrate, consider the challenge facing Gary Schneider, creator of a powerful software product that would help small farmers optimize their crop selection. After spending several years developing the product, Gary and his wife began selling the product one copy at a time. During one cold call on a major crop insurer, Gary met a senior researcher who immediately saw the benefits of his product. This respected researcher was in a position

Scott's Directories are good sources of prospects for salespeople.

to influence buying decisions at his company and to provide prospect information for other crop insurers.[13]

A person who is new to the field of selling often uses friends and family members as sources of information about potential customers. It is only natural to contact people we know. In many cases these people have contacts with a wide range of potential buyers.

Directories

Directories can help salespeople search out new prospects and determine their buying potential. A list of some of the more popular national directories is provided here.

Canadian Business Resource, published by Canadian Newspaper Services International, maintains a database of 2500 of Canada's largest firms, and all firms listed on the TSX and TSX Venture exchanges. It also maintains more than 40 000 contact names that are downloadable to your contact management software.

Canadian Key Business Directory, available from Dun & Bradstreet Canada—in print form or on CD—lists and profiles more than 20 000 of Canada's largest companies and maintains more than 60 000 key contact names.

Canadian Trade Index, published by Canadian Manufacturers & Exporters, is available in print, on CD-ROM, and online; it lists more than 30 000 manufacturers, distributors, and industrial service companies and features nearly 100 000 product listings under 20 000 headings.

Frasers.com provides a comprehensive online directory and search tool for Canadian manufacturers, industrial distributors, and their products and services. It also lists international companies that sell in the Canadian marketplace. A separate Web site lists trade shows in Canada and the United States.

Scott's Directories publishes separate directories for corporate (140 000 manufacturers, distributors, banks, law firms, construction companies, etc.), medical (100 000 doctors, dentists, hospitals, etc.), government (federal, provincial, and municipal), associations (10 000 listings), schools (various types), and residential (12 million listings, available by segment). Directories are available in print, on CD-ROM, or online.

Polk city directories provide detailed information on the citizens of a specific community. Polk, in business for nearly 140 years, publishes about 1100 directories covering 10 000 communities in Canada and the United States. Each directory can usually be obtained from your local government or chamber of commerce. Polk directories are available in print, on CD-ROM, and online.

There are hundreds of additional directories covering national, regional, and local business and industrial firms. Some directories are free, while others must be purchased for a nominal fee. One of the most useful sources of free information are telephone directories, most of which have a classified section that groups businesses and professions by category (e.g., Yellow Pages).

If you are involved in the sale of products in international markets, International Trade Canada offers several services to assist you, such as the Canadian Trade Commissioner Service. Canada has trade commissions in more than 125 cities throughout the world, which can provide such essential services as market intelligence and identification of potential customers, suppliers, or distributors and agents. Another valuable resource is the Export Development Corporation, a Crown corporation that helps Canadian exporters compete throughout the world. The corporation provides a wide range of financial and risk management services, and country and market information on most countries where Canadians sell. On its Web site (**www.edc.ca**), you can also view Canadian export performance data by country, and view country economic and credit summaries.

Trade Publications

Trade publications provide a status report on every major industry. If you are a sales representative employed by one of the huge food wholesalers that supply supermarkets, then you will benefit from a monthly review of *Canadian Grocer* magazine. Each month, this trade publication reports on trends in the retail food industry, as well as new products, problems, innovations, and related information. Trade journals such as *Women's Wear Daily*, *Home Furnishings*, *Pulp & Paper Canada*, *Purchasing b2b*, *Industrial Distribution*, and *Canadian Underwriter* are examples of publications that might help salespeople identify prospects.

Trade Shows and Special Events

A trade show is a large exhibit of products that are, in most cases, common to one industry, such as electronics or office equipment. The prospects walk into the booth or exhibit and talk with those who represent the exhibitor. In some cases, sales personnel invite

Trade shows are very effective for prospecting. Barry Siskind has helped many North American companies benefit from trade show participation.

existing customers and prospects to attend trade shows where they will have an opportunity to demonstrate their newest products.

Research studies indicate that it is much easier to identify good prospects and actually close sales at a trade show. In most cases, fewer sales calls are needed to close a sale if the prospect was qualified at a trade show. Once a trade show contact has been identified and judged to be a qualified lead, information regarding the lead should be carefully recorded. When a prospect enters a Xerox Corporation booth, a salesperson uses a few questions to qualify the lead and types the answers into an on-screen form. Xerox uses software developed by NewLeads to record and process data obtained from prospects.[14] Special events—such as a hockey game, a golf tournament, a reception for a dignitary, or a charity event—are also great sources for prospects. Bentley Motor Cars invited a number of potential clients to the famous Le Mans 24-hour endurance race, where prospects watched the Bentley race car compete while sipping champagne. In Canada, charity events serve as a venue for cultivating wealthy clientele who can afford a Bentley automobile.[15]

Telemarketing and E-mail

Telemarketing is the practice of marketing goods and services through telephone contact. It is an integral part of many modern sales and marketing campaigns. One use of telemarketing is to identify prospects. A financial services company used telemarketing to identify prospects for its customized equipment leasing packages. Leads were given to salespeople for consideration. Telemarketing also can be used to quickly and inexpensively qualify prospects for follow-up. Some marketers use the telephone to verify sales leads generated by direct mail, advertisements, or some other method.

telemarketing The practice of marketing goods and services through telephone contact.

Although the response rate for sales e-mails is quite low, they have proven to be a source of leads for many salespeople. Ideally, sales e-mails should be sent only to existing customers or others who have "opted in" to receive them. When you use *broadcast* e-mails, there is a risk that you will be blocked and end up on a spammer blacklist. Online sales specialist Mac MacIntosh says those who use broadcast e-mails should stay within anti-spam laws by giving recipients the right to opt out of future e-mails.[16]

Putting your company name in the subject line can help get e-mails opened by prospects who are familiar with it. Some salespeople send newsletters to current and prospective customers. Lee Levitt, director of sales for software consultant IDC, sends a monthly newsletter to current IDC clients and professionals at large technology companies. He wants to expose them to services his company can provide. Levitt says, "The key is to offer something of value they can quickly digest and use in day-to-day work."[17]

Direct–Response Advertising and Sales Letters

Many advertisements invite the reader to send for a free booklet or brochure that provides detailed information about the product or service. In the category of business-to-business marketing, advertising has the greatest power to generate inquiries. Some firms distribute postage-free response cards (also known as *bingo cards*) to potential buyers. Recipients are encouraged to complete and mail the cards if they desire additional information. In some cases, the name of the person making the inquiry is given to a local sales representative for further action.

Sales letters, sent by e-mail or by Canada Post, can easily be incorporated into a prospecting plan. The prospecting sales letter is sent to persons who are in a position to make a buying decision. Shortly after the letter has been mailed (i.e., three or four days), the prospect is called and asked for an appointment. The call begins with a reference to the sales letter. To make the letter stand out, some salespeople include a promotional item. All sales letters must be written with care. To get results, sales letters must quickly get the reader's attention.

Web Sites

Web site A collection of Web pages maintained by a single person or organization.

Thousands of companies and businesspeople have established Web sites on the World Wide Web. A **Web site** is a collection of Web pages maintained by a single person or organization. It is accessible to anyone with a computer and a modem. Large firms, such as Century 21, maintain Web sites that feature 20 to 30 Web pages. Web sites frequently offer prospects the opportunity to acquire product information that can help them make a buying decision. Financial services companies describe home financing and refinancing options. The Sun Microsystems Web site provides detailed descriptions of Sun's products and solutions. When someone clicks on a Web page and requests information, they will likely become a prospect. Some Web sites offer an incentive to leave contact information.

Many working professionals are using LinkedIn to build a network of business contacts. This networking Web site is similar to MySpace and Facebook, popular social networking Web sites. LinkedIn can be a valuable prospecting tool for salespeople. There are currently 11 million LinkedIn users and membership is growing at a rate of 15 percent a month. To sign up, visit **www.linkedin.com** and click "Join Now" to open an account. Once you have signed up, the next step is to create a profile that will get the attention of those you wish to network with.[18]

Computerized Databases

With the aid of electronic data processing, salespeople can match product features with the needs of potential customers quickly and accurately. In many situations a firm will develop its own computerized database. In other cases, it is more economical to purchase the database from a company that specializes in collection of such information. One example is Salesgenie, offered by infoCANADA. With the aid of this software, you can easily obtain lead generation and prospect selection information for different market segments. Gary Hand, President of Alliance Security Systems, needs to keep his sales team supplied with plenty of leads. Salesgenie provides him with a list of prospects by geographical location and by the value of each house. Salesgenie handles these two classifications easily and has therefore become a major time saver.[19] Salesgenie can provide salespeople with leads in such diverse market segments as medical services, engineering, architecture, agriculture, and education.

OneSource, another product available through infoCANADA, provides in-depth prospect information needed by sales personnel involved in complex, long-cycle sales. Let's assume you are part of a sales team that wants to do business with a group of companies that appear to be highly qualified. OneSource will provide data needed to make sales projections for a specific geographic area and industry type. The real strength of OneSource comes in high-value sales, where a thorough understanding of prospects is needed for the first sales call.[20]

With the aid of a personal computer (PC), salespeople can develop their own detailed customer files. As newer PCs provide expanded storage capacity at lower prices than in the past, salespeople can accumulate a great deal of information about individual customers and use this information to personalize the selling process. For example, a PC can help an independent insurance agent maintain a comprehensive record for each policyholder. As the status of each client changes (e.g., through marriage or the birth of children), the record can easily be updated. With the aid of an up-to-date database, the agent can quickly identify prospects for various existing and new policy options.

Cold Calling

With some products, cold call prospecting is an effective approach to prospect identification. In **cold calling**, the salesperson selects a group of people who may or may not be actual prospects and then calls—by phone or personal visit—on each one. For example, the sales representative for a wholesale medical supply firm might call on every hospital in a given community, assuming that each one is a potential customer. Many new salespeople must rely on cold calling because they are less likely to get appointments through referrals.

cold calling Method of prospecting in which the salesperson selects a group of people who may or may not be actual prospects, and then calls—by phone or personal visit—on each one.

Edward Jones Corporation, a financial services company, is a strong supporter of cold calling. Sales representatives knock on doors and introduce themselves with a friendly, professional message: "Hi, my name is Brad Ledwith, I represent the Edward Jones Corporation, and we sell financial services. We're a unique firm because we try to do all of our business face-to-face. I just wanted to stop by and let you know that I've opened up a Jones office in the area and to find out if it's okay to contact you when I have an investment idea."[21] Sales representatives such as Brad Ledwith connect personally with members of their communities.

Successful cold calls do not happen spontaneously. Some strategic thinking and planning must precede telephone calls and personal visits. Who do you contact? What do you say during the first few seconds? In order to appear confident and competent, carefully develop your opening remarks. If you appear to be nervous or unprepared, the prospect will assume you lack experience. Many salespeople who make cold-call phone calls prepare a well-polished script. The script helps keep you on message and guarantees you will not leave out important information.[22]

Canadian sales trainer and coach Steven J. Schwartz suggests that cold calls can be turned into hot calls through a telephone contact system that uses good call planning, strategic scripting, and effective script delivery. His book *How to Make Hot Cold Calls* explains his system, and his Web site offers a number of personal diagnostic tools for salespeople. (Visit **www.hotcoldcalls.com** and click on "toolbox.") We will answer more questions related to contacting customers in Chapter 13.

Networking

One of the most complete books on networking is *Dig Your Well Before You're Thirsty* by Harvey Mackay. He says, "If I had to name the single characteristic shared by all the truly successful people I've met over a lifetime, I'd say it's the ability to create and nurture

networking The practice of making and using contacts. It involves people meeting people and profiting from the connections.

*info*CANADA is just one of several companies that maintain databases of consumers and businesses and provide salespeople with an excellent way to prospect for customers.

a network of contacts."[23] Networking skills are of special importance to new salespeople, who cannot turn to a large group of satisfied customers for referrals and leads. Professionals (accountants, lawyers, consultants, etc.), entrepreneurs, managerial personnel, and customer service representatives also must develop networking skills. Networking skills are also of critical importance to job seekers because at any given time about 80 percent of all available jobs are not posted in the classifieds or on Internet job boards.[24]

In simple terms, **networking** is the art of making and using contacts: people meeting people and profiting from the connections. Barry Siskind, an Ontario-based consultant and author of *Making Contact*, sees networking as a three-act process. In act one, you must be able to approach someone and engage them in conversation. Act two is when you "net-chat," a term Siskind uses to describe the technique of collecting and giving information, and finding out as much as you can about the other person in the shortest time possible. Act three is where you disengage. Although networking is one of the premier prospecting methods, some salespeople are reluctant to seek referrals in this manner. In addition, many salespeople do not use effective networking practices. Skilled networkers suggest the following guidelines for identifying good referrals:

1. *Meet as many people as you can.* Networking can take place on an airplane, at a Rotary Club meeting, at a trade show, or at a professional association meeting. Don't make the mistake of limiting your networking activities to business contacts. The term **social network** refers to your set of *direct and indirect contacts*. An indirect contact might be the brother of a close friend. The brother works for a large company and can help you see more clearly into the operation of this firm.[25]

2. *When you meet someone, tell the person what you do.* Give your name and describe your position in a way that explains what you do and invites conversations. Instead of saying, "I am in stocks and bonds," say, "I am a financial planner who helps people make investment decisions." Listen more than you talk.

3. *Do not do business while networking.* It usually is not practical to conduct business while networking. Make a date to call or meet with the new contact later.

4. *Offer your business card.* The business card is especially useful when the contact attempts to tell others about your products or services.

5. *Edit your contacts and follow-up.* You cannot be involved with all your contacts, so separate the productive from the nonproductive. Send a short e-mail message to contacts you deem productive and include business information or brochures—anything that increases visibility.[26] Make sure your materials are professional. Use inexpensive contact management software, such as Salesforce.com, to organize your contact information.

There are three types of networks salespeople should nurture (Fig. 12.2). Every salesperson will be well served by networking within his or her own organization. You never know when someone in finance or shipping will be needed to help solve a problem or provide you with important information. A second form of networking involves establishing contacts inside your industry. Make contact with experts in your field, top performers, leaders, successful company representatives, and even competitors. The third form of

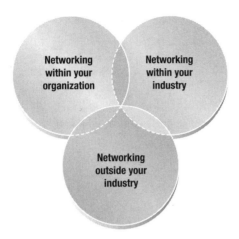

Figure 12.2 Three types of networks. Top-performing salespeople recognize that networking can take place in three areas.

networking involves business contacts with people outside your industry, such as bankers, government officials, developers, and other people in your community. The local golf course may be a good place to make these contacts.[27]

social network Your set of direct and indirect contacts.

Educational Seminars

Many salespeople are using educational seminars as a method of identifying prospects. Seminars provide an opportunity to showcase your product without pressuring prospects to buy. Many banks, accounting firms, wine merchants, and consulting companies use seminars to generate new prospects. Previously we mentioned that Edward Jones's sales representatives often make cold calls on prospects. They also schedule seminars that provide prospects with an opportunity to acquire information regarding the potential benefits of investing in a mutual fund, estate planning, or tax-free investing. A complimentary lunch is usually served before the informative presentation. When inviting prospects, be clear about the seminar's content, and always deliver what you promise.

Prospecting by Non-Sales Employees

Should service technicians, receptionists, bank tellers, and other non-sales personnel be involved in prospecting? For a growing number of firms, the answer is yes. Prospecting need not be the exclusive responsibility of the sales force. Janet Dixon, a UPS sales representative, needed help making contact with an important prospect. This person wouldn't take her calls. She talked to the UPS service provider (a driver), who called on this account and requested his help. He had serviced this company for years and was like part of the family. He knew the prospect personally and persuaded her to accept a call from the salesperson.[28]

The use of educational seminars has become an important prospecting method. You can educate prospective customers with brochures, news releases, catalogues, or your Web site, but educational seminars offer the advantage of face-to-face contact. Barbara Siskind, in her book *Seminars to Build Your Business*, identifies 15 objectives for hosting seminars. Here are a few of the most important.

- *Obtain sales leads.* This is one of the most common objectives for seminars. You can obtain the names of attendees and arrange appointments for future sales calls. Seminars may also help identify actual product users, technical support people, or engineers, who, while they may not be the decision makers, may influence the purchase decision.

- *Promote your place of business.* Your place of business can become a destination for people who might other-

wise not consider visiting it. You have an opportunity to create awareness of your company and develop a positive image for your entire operation and its capabilities.

- *Showcase and demonstrate your expertise.* Seminars allow you to show a carefully targeted group of people that you really know your stuff. Technical experts and others in the organization who can address clients' specific concerns can support salespeople.

Polaroid Canada advertises educational seminars across Canada where imaging specialists assist prospective clients in exploring imaging solutions. Toronto-based Charon Systems, Inc., a systems integrator that deploys networks for organizations, regularly organizes seminars for 80 to 100 technology people from mid-sized firms. President David Fung estimates that 25 percent of prospects become clients.[b]

Combination Approaches

In recent years, we have seen an increase in the number of prospecting approaches used by salespeople. In many cases, success in selling depends on your ability to use a combination of the methods described in this chapter. For example, the large number of prospects identified at a trade show might be used to develop an effective telemarketing program. Prospects are called and an effort is made to set up a personal call. Prospects identified at a trade show or educational seminar might also be sent a sales-oriented newsletter, a sales letter, or an e-mail message inviting prospects to visit your Web page.

QUALIFYING THE PROSPECT

ONE OF THE MOST IMPORTANT KEYS TO SUCCESS IN PERSONAL SELLING IS THE ABILITY to qualify prospects. **Qualifying** is the process of identifying prospects who appear to have a need for your product and should be contacted. Top salespeople use good research and analysis skills to qualify leads effectively.[29]

qualifying The process of identifying prospects who appear to have a need for your product and should be contacted.

The qualifying process is also the first opportunity to consider what the needs of the buyer might be, and how those needs are matched by the characteristics of the product being sold.[30] Some sales organizations link the qualifying process with the need discovery step in the consultative sales process. In most cases, this linkage will depend on the nature and complexity of the prospect's buying process. The more complex the buying process, the more likely these two sales functions will be separate steps in the sales process. We will fully explore the need discovery step in Chapter 14.

Every salesperson needs to establish qualifying criteria. This process involves finding answers to several basic questions.

1. *Does the prospect have a need for my product?* If you sell copy machines, it might appear that every business firm is a prospect. However, a firm that is outsourcing its copy work to FedEx Kinko's may not be a legitimate prospect. Qualifying involves probing for real needs. Let's assume you sell real estate for a large agency. You receive a call from someone who believes that owning a home is a good investment. At this point, it's important to find out what else makes owning a home important for that person. Get permission to ask questions and then determine the person's real needs. In the final analysis, you may decide it would be a waste of your time and the prospect's time to visit several homes that are on the market.[31]

2. *Does the prospect have the authority to buy my product?* Ideally, you should talk to a person who has authority to buy or who can influence the buying decision. Talking to the right person within a large organization may involve collecting information from several sources. Some buying decisions are made by individuals and others are made by a committee. Expensive products often require the approval of a decision maker higher up in the organization.

3. *Does the prospect have the financial resources to buy my product?* It is usually not difficult to obtain credit information for consumers and business buyers. If you are selling products to a business, the *Dun & Bradstreet Reference Book* is an excellent source of credit information. A local credit bureau can provide credit information for a consumer buyer. While the collection of credit information is not difficult, detecting financial instability can be much more complicated. In recent years, we have seen a steady stream of corporate scandals involving accounting irregularities, inflated balance sheets, and outright fraud.[32] Salespeople must be aware of the possibility that a customer may provide incorrect or misleading information.

4. *Does the prospect have the willingness to buy my product?* Rick Page, author of *Hope Is Not a Strategy*, reminds us that many prospects evaluate products but do not buy. When an evaluation stalls, the prospect may have determined that the need is not of great enough magnitude or urgency to make the purchase. Also, in some cases there is not enough support within the company to reach closure. Rather than walk away from this situation, some salespeople move higher in the organization to determine the level of support for the purchase.[33]

A large number of senior executives say they get involved in the sale early in the decision process, yet salespeople have difficulty meeting with high-level decision makers. Most senior executives will not meet with salespeople who are making cold calls. When appointments are granted, the time allocated may be very short; five to ten minutes is not uncommon. How do you establish credibility for yourself and your company in a short time period? Be sure you know a great deal about the company before the appointment and be prepared to demonstrate your knowledge of the company and the industry it serves. Do not propose solutions until you fully understand the buyer's problems. Be sure to communicate value.[34]

This list can be revised to meet the needs of many different types of salespeople. A sales representative for an industrial equipment dealer will see the qualifying process differently from the person who sells commercial real estate. The main consideration is providing accurate answers to each question.

COLLECTING AND ORGANIZING PROSPECT INFORMATION

THE INTERNET AND THE INFORMATION REVOLUTION CONTINUE TO MAKE ACQUIRING and managing sales leads much easier.[35] When it comes to collecting and organizing prospect information, salespeople have a large assortment of computer–based systems available. Companies such as Salesforce.com, Oracle, NetSuite, Sage, and Microsoft all offer software applications designed to collect and organize prospect information. Most of these Sales Force Automation (SFA) Systems or Customer Relationship Management (CRM) Systems, as they are now known, have preset categories or fields that contain sales data on the prospect. This **sales data** is the information seen in most CRM systems, including the contact name, title, address, phone number, e-mail address, etc. It may also include information about what products have been purchased, what sales opportunities exist in the future, who the various members or influencers are in the buying centre, their preferred communication styles (refer to Chapter 8), past sales and forecasted sales volume, and percentage change and date of closing the sale. All of the sales data information about the prospect in a CRM system is presented in the account screen report. Figure 12.3 shows an account screen report for Able Profit Machines. The information in this report, including any notes about previous sales calls, is accessed and studied before the salesperson makes a sales call.

When bringing new prospects into the database, it is expected the salesperson will acquire this sales data and enter it into the records kept on the prospect. This, in some cases, may be done in writing on prospect file cards; however, in most organizations, it is entered on a computer into a shared database in the company's CRM system. The shared

sales data Information available from a company's CRM system.

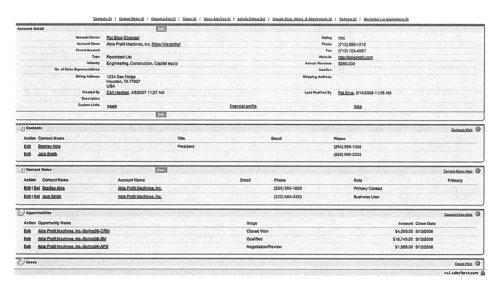

Figure 12.3 The CRM account screen report. This account screen report shows sales data for Able Profit Machines. The sales data, including any notes from previous sales calls, was entered by sales representative Pat Silva of SimNet Systems. Pat Silva has been calling on Able Profit Machines president Bradley Able and on Jack Smith. (For more information on SimNet Systems see the CRM Case Study on p. 260.)

database allows other members of the sales team to access the information and make additions as they work with prospects. In the event a new salesperson takes over an existing prospect database, all of this information can be accessed quickly and used to plan sales strategies to work effectively with prospects.

SALES INTELLIGENCE

IN ADDITION TO COLLECTING SALES DATA, THE COLLECTION OF SALES INTELLIGENCE is necessary when the sale is complex and requires a long closing cycle. Sales intelligence goes beyond data, giving salespeople access to insights into the prospect's marketplace, their firm, their competitors, and even about the prospects themselves. Sales intelligence is needed today over and above sales data because prospects are looking for insights and knowledge from salespeople above and beyond the product features and benefits. In many buying situations today, prospects using advanced search engines have already learned about features and benefits. In terms of sales intelligence, prospects instead expect salespeople to know answers to many of the following questions. Answers to these questions create much of the value that results in successfully turning prospects into long-term customers.

> **sales intelligence** Goes beyond data, giving salespeople access to insights into the prospect's marketplace, their firm, their competitors, and even the prospects themselves.

Do you know me? You need to know more than my name and title. Do you know my role, my goals, how I am evaluated, and how long I have been with the organization? Do you know about the projects I am working on, my style of doing business, and what the requirements are for me to meet my objectives? Do you know about previous dealings I have had with your company? Do I have a favourable opinion of your company and do you know my role and the role of other influencers in the decision–making process?

Do you know my company and my marketplace? Do you know my company mission statement, culture, and vision for the future? Do you know clearly what we are doing, how we are performing in the marketplace, what issues keep us up all night, who our competitors are, and what they are doing? Do you know where we fit into the existing competitive landscape? Are we the leader or are we in the position of having to play catch-up to survive? Can you relate what you sell directly to what we need to accomplish our goals? Do you know who our partners are, or what effect the current economy has on our business?

Do you have any special value-add? You have a product or service you think we need, but what else can you bring to the table? Are there additional resources you can bring to bear to solve my problems or improve my internal business processes? Can you educate me on how you are truly different from the other players in your area of expertise so I can support my recommendation to work with you? Can you help me build a case for return on investment (ROI)?[36]

Answers to these questions come from many sources. CRM suppliers like Salesforce.com, infoCANADA.ca, Sales-i.com, and Vecta.net have programs that supply this kind of sales intelligence to companies and salespeople. OneSource, mentioned earlier in this chapter, is one example of a supplier of sales intelligence. OneSource supplies sales intelligence to Cardinal Logistics Management, a major provider of logistics, transportation, and supply-chain solutions to large retailers, manufacturers, and distribution

Debi Rosati Helps Sell Business Ideas to Investors

Debi Rosati graduated in 1984 from Brock University with an Honours Bachelor of Business Administration and, in 1985, became a chartered accountant. During her career, Debi has held senior finance positions with Tundra, Cognos, and BDO Dunwoody. She was co-founder and chief financial officer for TimeStep Corporation, where she gained financing and operational experience firsthand in a technology start-up company. In 1999, TimeStep was acquired by Newbridge Networks Corporation. Shortly after, Debi joined the venture capital firm Celtic House as a general partner. She was involved in all aspects of venture investing, including evaluating investment opportunities, negotiating deal structures, and guiding operations.

Debi Rosati founded RosatiNet in 2001 as a venture catalyst firm that brings together technology start-up companies and investors. As a venture catalyst, she helps entrepreneurs get the right amount of money, at the right time, with the right investors and the right terms. To recognize both her business success and her long-standing involvement in and commitment to various community events and associations, Debi was awarded the *Ottawa Business Journal* Top 40 under 40 Award in 2001 and the Brock University Faculty of Business Distinguished Graduate Award in 2003. Debi also teaches in the professional programs at Sprott School of Business at Carleton University.

Reflecting on her career, Debi says, "Accounting is an important technical skill that I have used to bring value as a chief financial officer, venture capitalist, business advisor, and board member and community builder. However, my selling skills are equally important to my success as a venture catalyst. I am constantly networking for RosatiNet and its many clients."[c]

companies. Cardinal's salespeople must know each prospect inside and out in order to sell logistics solutions effectively to their 5000 customers. OneSource supplies 24/7, anywhere access to detailed customer profiles, executive contact data and biographies, financial statements, news trade articles, and analyst reports. A special new-alert feature keeps salespeople up-to-date on any and all developments within their customer's company and their industry, including both their customer's customers and their competitors.[37]

Most importantly, this information must be entered into the company's CRM system to get a 360–degree view of the prospect. The information will also be used to move the prospect through the steps in the sales process.

MANAGING THE PROSPECT BASE

HIGH-PERFORMING SALESPEOPLE TODAY ARE FOCUSED ON EFFECTIVELY MANAGING sales activities for all prospects in their database. This means that the size and number of prospects are more carefully considered. Too few prospects in various stages of the sales cycle can quickly signal problems. Alternatively, too many customers can drain a salesperson's resources so that too little effort is focused on prospects with the best opportunities. This is a particular problem when salespeople spend too much effort on prospects that have limited potential. CRM software can help organize customer data into meaningful and easy-to-interpret information, as seen in Figure 12.4.

account analysis An estimate of the sales potential for each account.

To effectively and efficiently manage the prospect base, sales managers and salespeople often conduct an **account analysis** to estimate the sales potential for each prospect. It is a necessary step before deciding how to allocate sales calls across accounts. Portfolio

Action	Account Name	Amount	Close Date	Stage ⌃	Opportunity Name
Edit	Computer Products	$4,500.00	6/24/2008	Qualified	Computer Products-Spring08-APS
Edit	Computer Products	$17,500.00	6/11/2008	Qualified	Computer Products-Spring08-SM
Edit	Quality Builders	$4,500.00	5/13/2008	Qualified	Quality Builders-Spring08-SM
Edit	Ellis Enterprises	$4,500.00	5/13/2008	Qualified	Ellis Enterprises-Spring08-APS
Edit	Lakeside Clinic	$1,855.00	5/13/2008	Qualified	Lakeside Clinic-Spring08-APS
Edit	Johnson and Associates	$750.00	5/13/2008	Qualified	Johnson and Associates-Spring08-APS
Edit	Johnson and Associates	$16,930.00	7/3/2008	Qualified	Johnson and Associates-Spring08-CRM
Edit	International Studios	$4,500.00	5/13/2008	Qualified	International Studios-Spring08-APS
Edit	Landers Engineering	$4,500.00	5/13/2008	Qualified	Landers Engineering-Spring08-APS
Edit	Mercy Hospital	$4,500.00	5/13/2008	Qualified	Mercy Hospital-Spring08-APS
Edit	Murray D'Zines	$4,500.00	5/13/2008	Qualified	Murray D'Zines-Spring08-APS
Edit	Big Tex Auto Sales	$750.00	5/13/2008	Qualified	Big Tex Auto Sales-Spring08-APS
Edit	Excellent Software, Inc.	$4,500.00	5/13/2008	Qualified	Excellent Software,Inc.-Spring08-APS
Edit	Designers Associates	$4,500.00	5/13/2008	Qualified	Designers Associates-Spring08-APS
Edit	Piccadilly Studio	$4,500.00	6/11/2008	Needs Analysis	Piccadilly Studio-Spring08-APS
Edit	General Contractors	$16,745.00	6/12/2008	Needs Analysis	General Contractors-Spring08-CRM
Edit	General Contractors	$1,855.00	6/11/2008	Needs Analysis	General Contractors-Spring08-SM
Edit	Bryan Enterprises	$17,155.00	5/13/2008	Needs Analysis	Bryan Enterprises-Spring08-APS
Edit	Modern Designs	$4,500.00	5/13/2008	Needs Analysis	Modern Designs-Spring08-APS
Edit	Computerized Labs	$4,500.00	7/17/2008	Needs Analysis	Computerized Labs-Spring08-APS
Edit	Media Conglomerate	$4,500.00	7/9/2008	Needs Analysis	Media Conglomerate-Spring08-APS
Edit	Able Profit Machines, Inc.	$16,745.00	5/20/2008	Proposal/Price Quote	Able Profit Machines, Inc.-Spring08-SM
Edit	Murray D'Zines	$16,630.00	6/11/2008	Proposal/Price Quote	Murray D'Zines-Spring08-CRM
Edit	Aeroflot Airlines	$16,520.00	5/13/2008	Proposal/Price Quote	Aeroflot Airlines-Spring08-APS
Edit	Piccadilly Studio	$16,745.00	6/19/2008	Negotiation/Review	Piccadilly Studio-Spring08-CRM
Edit	Able Profit Machines, Inc.	$1,855.00	5/12/2008	Negotiation/Review	Able Profit Machines, Inc.-Spring08-APS
Edit	Bryan Enterprises	$21,020.00	5/13/2008	Negotiation/Review	Bryan Enterprises-Spring08-CRM
Edit	Computer Products	$820.00	5/13/2008	Negotiation/Review	Computer Products-Spring08-CRM

Figure 12.4 The prospect base. This CRM record presents a complete list of salesperson Pat Silva's prospects. Note this list includes information on the forecasted dollar amount of each sale, projected date of close, and what stage of the sales process the prospect is in. In CRM systems like Salesforce, clicking on any of the prospects on this list will allow the user to drill down into detailed contact information and notes supporting these projections.

models and the sales funnel are two popular conceptual tools for performing account analyses and allocating resources to qualified prospects in the database.

PORTFOLIO MODELS

PORTFOLIO MODELS INVOLVE THE USE OF MULTIPLE FACTORS WHEN CLASSIFYING prospects. Figure 12.5 illustrates a typical four-cell model based on two factors: overall account opportunity for the seller and the seller's competitive position; that is, the ability to capitalize on these opportunities.[38]

The overall account opportunity could be a prediction of sales or bookings for a given period. However, it could also be a weighted composite of current sales, growth potential, and gross margin. Competitive position could be an estimate of the share of an account's purchases that are made from the selling firm. However, it could also be a weighted composite of the number and types of relationships the account has with firms that compete with the seller's firm, the account's attitude to the selling firm, how well the selling firm's products meet the account's specific needs, etc. While implementing this type of model can be difficult, one of its real strengths is that it does provide a framework to facilitate communication between salespeople and the various sales support personnel. Teamwork at this stage in the sales cycle can develop improved strategies for working successfully with different accounts and contacts in the prospect base. Portfolio models are most effective where salespeople must understand individual customer needs and where relationship strength is important to sales success.

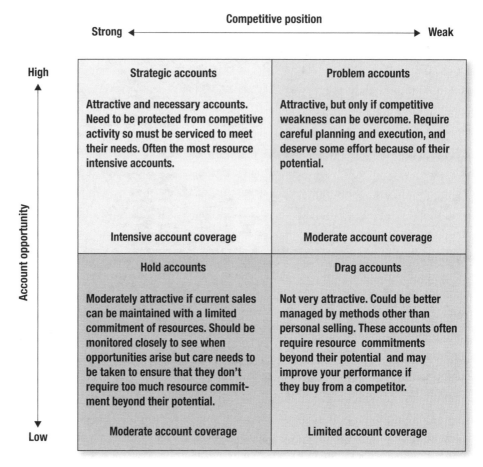

Figure 12.5 The portfolio model. This portfolio model uses account opportunity (forecasted sales) and competitive position (the ability to capitalize on opportunity) to classify how much sales effort should be made on individual accounts in the prospect database. Those prospects listed in the strategic accounts cell (high sales forecast and strong position for closing the sale) will receive the largest amount of sales effort, while those in the drag accounts cell will receive little, if any, attention.

SALES PROCESS MODELS

SALES PROCESS MODELS, ALSO REFERRED TO AS SALES FUNNEL MODELS, CLASSIFY PROSPECTS based on where they are in the sales process. The **sales process model** is the total set of prospects being pursued at any given time. The sales process model is illustrated in Figure 12.6. This five-step model includes qualification, needs analysis, presentation/proposal, negotiations, and order. An account might be simply a qualified prospect, ready for a needs analysis, in serious negotiations with the salesperson, or ready to place an order. In sales process model reports such as the one in Figure 12.6, clicking on any part of the bar graph will drill down into and report all the supporting data on prospects in each stage of the sales process. The position of an account in the sales process has implications for "if and when" the salesperson will be able to close the sale.

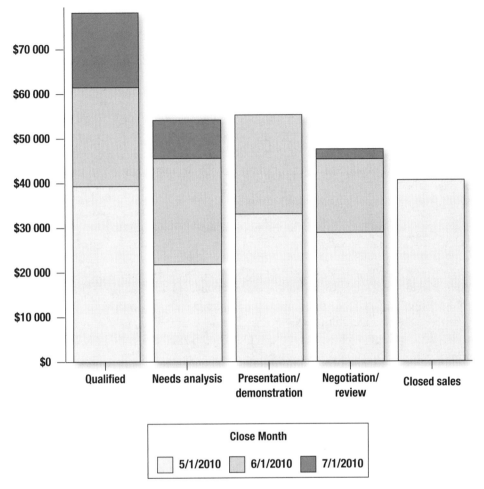

Figure 12.6 The CRM sales process (or funnel) model. The sales process or sales funnel model, as it is frequently called, classifies prospects according to where they are in the sales process. It is important that salespeople balance their portfolio of prospects that are at various stages of the selling process. This enables salespeople to know how many prospects there are and how much revenue is needed at each stage in the sales process to meet sales projections and budgets.

The sales cycle for complex technical sales, such as computer networking installations, might be several months in duration. The number of prospects in the funnel for selling such installations may be small compared to the number for an insurance or real estate salesperson. Insurance salespeople know they need to contact a larger number of people to gain permission to make a smaller number of presentations, to make an even small number of sales. In any selling situation, it is important that salespeople balance their portfolio of prospects that are at various stages of the selling process.[39] A **balanced funnel** enables salespeople to have a sufficiently large number of prospects at each stage in the sales process to meet sales projections and quotas for both the short and the long term.[40] As indicated earlier with Joe Girard's "Ferris wheel" concept, this means that salespeople must ensure that sufficient prospects are regularly added to the funnel to ensure that it does not become empty. In addition to the number of prospects, the quality of the

balanced funnel A portfolio of prospects where there is a sufficiently large number of prospects at each stage in the sales process.

prospects added to the funnel and the ability of the salesperson to manage the sales process will affect the number of sales opportunities that are successfully closed.

Salespeople need to ensure that they "work" the whole funnel so that it is always in balance. They should work on sales opportunities near the bottom of the funnel first; that is, close those that are near the end of the sales process. Then they should work on the top of the funnel; that is, add new prospects. Prospecting is an activity that some salespeople dislike, but if it is not given sufficient attention there is a real danger that the funnel will empty. Finally, salespeople should work on those opportunities that are in the sales process, moving them along through the funnel and ensuring there are regular, predictable sales over time.[41] This process of managing all the prospects in the salesperson's sales funnel to ensure that sales objectives are met is called **pipeline management**.

pipeline management Process of managing all the prospects in the salesperson's sales funnel to ensure that sales objectives are met.

CRM TECHNOLOGY FOR PIPELINE MANAGEMENT

CRM SOFTWARE PROVIDES AN EFFICIENT AND EFFECTIVE TOOL FOR FORECASTING and managing pipelines. Using sales data entered into the account details, contact screens, notes applications, etc., sales forecasts can be updated continually as prospects move through the stages in the sales process. Prospects in the database who are no longer qualified, for whatever reason, can be quickly dropped from the sales funnel. Figure 12.7 shows pipeline dashboards produced by a CRM software suite.

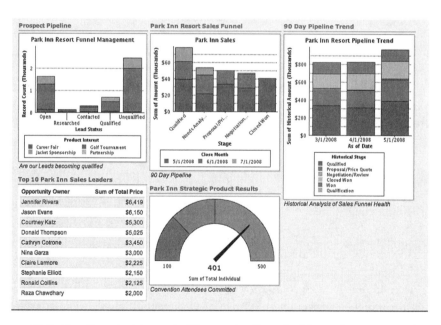

Figure 12.7 Pipeline dashboards. These pipeline dashboards are at-a-glance visualizations that define, monitor, and analyze the relationships existing in the pipeline or funnel. Pipeline analytics exist in most modern CRM systems and are used to produce these important prospect movement reports. The salesperson can quickly and easily access detailed information on specific prospects, and then use this information to plan strategies for moving the prospect to the next stage of the sales process.

Pipeline analytics, defined as the ability to conduct sophisticated data analysis and modelling, are found in most CRM systems. Using pipeline analytics, new reports can be generated regarding the movement of prospects through the sales funnel. These reports can be more clearly presented with the use of dashboards. **Pipeline dashboards** are at-a-glance visualizations that define, monitor, and analyze the relationships existing in the pipeline or sales funnel. Sales team members, including the sales manager, working together from a shared CRM database, can collaborate to create value and enhance the sales strategies to help the salesperson move prospects through the pipeline to a successful sale. CRM pipeline dashboards allow the user to quickly and easily drill down into the reports and records supporting them. This provides for quick updates as prospects move through the sales funnel. Dashboards can also provide insight into the need to add new prospects as existing ones are moved through the sales process.

pipeline analytics Ability to conduct sophisticated data analysis and modelling, allowing salespeople to generate new reports regarding the movement of prospects through the sales funnel.

pipeline dashboards At-a-glance visualizations that define, monitor, and analyze the relationships existing in the pipeline or sales funnel.

REVIEWING KEY CONCEPTS

- Discuss the importance of developing a prospect base.

  Prospect identification has been called the lifeblood of selling. A continuous supply of new customers must be found to replace those lost for various reasons. *Prospecting* is the systematic process of locating potential customers. Prospecting requires careful planning.

- Identify and assess important sources of prospects.

  Analysis of both your product and your existing customers can help to identify, locate, and profile your prospects. Important sources of new customers include referrals (both endless chain referrals and referral letters and cards); centres of influence; friends and family members; directories; trade publications; trade shows and special events; telemarketing and e-mail; direct-response advertising and sales letters; Web sites; computer databases; cold calling; educational seminars; networking; and prospecting by non-sales employees.

- Describe criteria for qualifying prospects.

  Prospecting techniques produce a list of names that must be evaluated using criteria developed by each salesperson. The process of prospect evaluation is called *qualifying*. The qualifying process involves finding answers to several basic questions: Does the prospect have a need for my product? Can the prospect make the buying decision? Can the prospect pay for the purchase? Does the prospect have the willingness to buy my product? An estimate of the volume of sales that could be generated from this prospect and the prospect's credit rating also should be determined.

- Explain common methods of collecting and organizing prospect information.

  Most companies rely on customer relationship management (CRM) systems to keep track of sales data. The collection of sales intelligence beyond sales data enables salespeople to impress their knowledgeable customers with insights that are above and beyond the product and/or service features and benefits.

- Describe the steps in managing a prospect base.

  Salespeople need to allocate their resources wisely to make the most of the prospect base. They do so by conducting account analyses, using either portfolio models or sales funnel models.

Key Terms

Review Questions

1. List and briefly explain the common causes of customer attrition.

2. During periods of economic uncertainty, the decision-making process often moves upward. What basic tips would you give a salesperson who is calling on senior executives?

3. Describe three steps progressive marketers take to improve the quality of their prospecting effort.

4. List the major sources of prospects.

5. Explain how the endless chain referral prospecting method works.

6. Discuss how direct-response advertising and sales letters can be used to identify prospects.

7. What is *networking*? How might a real estate salesperson use networking to identify prospects?

8. What does the term *qualifying* mean? What are the four basic questions that should be answered during the qualifying process?

9. When is sales intelligence important? What are the three most important pieces of sales intelligence a salesperson needs to know?

10. Describe two popular models for performing an account analysis.

Application Exercises

1. Prior to getting involved in networking, it's a good idea to prepare an "elevator" presentation. This is a 30-second pitch that summarizes what you want people to know about you. You might think of yourself as a "product" to be sold to an employer who has a job opening. Make your presentation upbeat and brief. Who are you? What are you currently doing? What type of work are you looking for? Practise the presentation alone in front of a mirror and then present it to one or two class members.

2. You are a sales representative for Xerox Canada, which has just designed a new, less expensive, and better quality copying machine. Make a list of 15 prospects you would plan to call about this machine. From the material in this chapter, identify the sources you would use in developing your prospect list.

3. You are in the process of interviewing for a sales position with Sun Life Financial in Toronto. In addition to filling out an application form and taking an aptitude test, one of the tasks the agency manager requests of you is to develop a list of prospects with whom you are acquainted. He informs you that this list will represent the prospects you will be working with during the first few weeks of employment. The agency manager recommends that you list at least 50 names. Prepare a list of 10 acquaintances you have who would qualify as prospects.

4. Sales automation software is most commonly used in the prospecting phase of selling. New-product releases are continually being developed that provide additional features and benefits to salespeople. The software used in this book is marketed by a leader in the field. Access the **www.salesforce.com** Web site and research the latest version of Salesforce. Click on and examine the latest demonstration copy of this popular sales automation software.

5. Locating companies to work for is a form of prospecting. Assuming you are interested in changing careers, develop a list of 10 companies for which you would like to work. Assign each company a priority according to your interest, from the most desirable (1) to the least (10). Organize your list into six columns showing the company name, telephone number, address, person in charge of hiring, prospect information, and priority. What sources did you use to get this information?

ROLE-PLAY EXERCISE

For this role play, you will assume a sales position at a Lexus dealership. You have just completed a successful sale by signing the papers for the second new Lexus this customer has purchased in the past four years. Because you know your customer has had a very successful experience with his first Lexus, you have decided to use the referral methods described in this chapter. Review the material on referrals and plan what you will say to your customer to build your prospect base. Pair off with another student who will assume the role of your customer. Explain that satisfied customers often know other people who would consider purchasing a Lexus. You might say, "Considering the positive experience you have had as a Lexus owner, you probably know others who appreciate fine automobiles. Is there anyone who comes to mind?" If, after probing, your customer doesn't recall someone immediately, ask permission to call him later to see if anyone has come to mind. Ask this person for actual names, addresses, and other qualifying information about prospective customers he knows. Also ask the customer if he would write a referral note or letter that you could use.

Case Problem

Gary Hanna, Vice President of Sales at Salesforce.com, says, "Once you have a relationship with a customer, maintaining that relationship is a lot more profitable than finding a new customer." A growing number of salespeople are using Salesforce.com or one of its competitors to improve service to customers. Mark Golden, sales force administrator at Ceva Logistics, the world's largest provider of logistics and freight management services, is giving Ceva's customers added value with Salesforce.com. Like most other salespeople, CEVA account managers like Darrin Marks are trying to cope with expanded duties, a faster work pace, and customers with high expectations. Salesforce.com helps in the following ways:

Customer Profiles: All relevant customer information is available in one centralized place. In addition to name, phone, and e-mail, he can include detailed personal information such as hobbies, interests, role in the organization, and who each contact reports to. Past activities such as e-mails, meetings, and conference calls, as well as opportunities that this contact is related to can be noted for a complete 360–degree view of the contact.

Organization and Planning: Darrin can plan and manage his time using the calendar management features available in the Salesforce.com tool. By simply looking at his homepage, Darrin can view all upcoming appointments and activities. Phone calls, customer meetings, and conference calls can be scheduled and recorded with reminder alerts throughout the day. When conference calls are required, managing the invitee list can be accomplished through the tool by picking the appropriate contacts to include. An added feature the tool provides is the ability for Darrin to share his calendar with fellow colleagues in order to better collaborate.

Correspondence: Salesforce.com can be used to manage all correspondence between Darrin and his customers, including e-mails, marketing brochures, and company newsletters. Darrin just needs to navigate to the customer he wants to communicate with, click the "Send an E-mail" button, and pick the type of correspondence he wishes to send. In addition to sending individual e-mails, features such as mass e-mail, mass stay in touch, and mass add to campaign allow Darrin to request updates from all of his contacts or communicate important company information to all of his contacts at once.

Questions

1. If your goal is to maintain long-term partnerships with each of your customers, what features of Salesforce.com are most helpful?

2. Let us assume you are selling copy machines in a city with a population of 100 000 people. Your territory includes the entire city. What features of Salesforce.com would you use most frequently?

3. Some salespeople who could benefit from the use of Salesforce.com or a competing product continue to use a Rolodex or note cards to keep a record of the customers they call on. What are some barriers to the adoption of this type of technology?

4. Examine the Salesforce.com contact screen presented in Appendix 2.

   a. What is Bradley Able's position within the company?

   b. What is the expected "close date" date for Bradley Able's sales opportunity?

   c. What is the forecasted dollar amount of this potential sale?

CRM Case Study Reviewing the Prospect Database

Becky Kemley is the sales manager in the Dallas, Texas, office of SimNet Systems, which sells network products and services. The productivity and the critical mission of Becky's customers can be considerably enhanced by selecting and using the correct LAN (local area network), WAN (wide area network), or VPN (virtual private network) systems. Becky's company is called a value-added reseller (VAR) because its people help customers maximize the value of the products bought through SimNet.

Becky's sales and technical support people may spend several months in the sales process (sales cycle). Salespeople telephone and call on prospects to determine whether they qualify for SimNet's attention. Time is taken to study the customers' needs (i.e., needs identification). The expert opinion of SimNet's technical people is incorporated into a sales proposal that is presented to the prospective customer. The presentation may be made to a number of decision makers in the prospect's firm. The final decision to purchase may follow weeks of consideration within the firm and negotiations with SimNet. Once a decision is made by a customer to buy from SimNet, Becky's people begin the process of acquiring, assembling, and installing the network system; they then follow through with appropriate training, integration, and support services.

Becky's company must carefully prospect for customers. SimNet may invest a significant amount of time helping a potential customer configure the right combination of products and services. This means that only the most serious prospects should be cultivated. Further, Becky's people must ascertain that if time has been invested in a prospective customer, the prospect will follow through with purchases from SimNet.

Becky is responsible for assuring that prospect information is collected and used effectively. The network salespeople use Salesforce.com to manage their prospect information. The system allows salespeople to document and manage their sales efforts with each prospect.

Becky has just hired you to sell for SimNet beginning June 1. Becky has given you the files of Pat Silva, a salesperson who has just been promoted to SimNet's corporate headquarters. Becky has asked you to review the status of Pat's 20 prospect accounts. Pat's customers have been notified that Pat is leaving and that a new salesperson, you, will be contacting them. Becky wants you to review each prospect's record. You are to meet with Becky next Monday. Be prepared to answer the following questions.

Refer to Appendix 2 in the back of your book for instructions on how to access and review the 20 Salesforce.com prospect records of Pat Silva. If you haven't already done so, view the Salesforce video demo at **www.salesforce.com**.

Questions

1. Which contact can you ignore immediately *as a prospect* for making a potential purchase?

2. Referring only to the *date close* category, which four prospects would you call immediately?

3. Referring only to the *dollar amount of sales forecasted* category, which four accounts would you call first?

Does the *likelihood of closing* percentage category have any influence on decisions concerning which prospects to call first? Why?

4. According to information on the records, what sources did Pat Silva use most to find new prospects? Give examples.

PART IV

ROLE-PLAY EXERCISE
Developing a Customer Strategy

SCENARIO

You are a sales representative employed by Park Inn International Hotel and Convention Centre. One of your primary responsibilities is to identify prospects and make sales calls that result in the development of new accounts. During each of these calls, you plan to build a relationship with the customer and describe selected value-added guest services and amenities offered by the Park Inn. You also try to learn as much as possible about the customer's buying process.

CUSTOMER PROFILE

Gabriela Ansari is the founder and Chief Executive Officer of Cantrol Security Inc., a growing high-tech firm with more than 100 employees. The company manufactures and sells security systems for use in residential homes, retail stores, and commercial buildings. According to a recent article in the *Globe and Mail*, Cantrol Security is poised to grow very rapidly in the next year. The article described Gabriela Ansari as a workaholic who usually works 80 hours each week. Delegation does not come easily to this personable, hard-charging entrepreneur.

SALESPERSON PROFILE

You have just completed the Park Inn sales training program and now want to develop some new accounts. In addition to taking care of established customers, you plan to call on at least four new prospects every week.

PRODUCT

Park Inn International is a full-service hotel and convention centre located in Toronto, Ontario. The hotel recently completed a $2.8 million renovation of its meeting and banquet rooms.

INSTRUCTIONS

For this role-play activity, you will meet with Gabriela Ansari, role played by another student, who appears to be a good prospect. During the first sales call, plan to learn more about Gabriela as an individual and acquire more information about Cantrol Security. This meeting will provide you with the opportunity to begin building a long-term partnership. During the first meeting with a prospect, you like to present a limited amount of important product information. In this case, the length of the appointment is 15 minutes, so you should not try to cover too much information. To prepare for the first sales call, read *Employment Memorandum Number 1* in "Partnership Selling: A Role Play/Simulation" online in the Student Resources section at **www.pearsoned.ca/manning**. This memo describes the value-added guest services and amenities offered by Park Inn. For the purpose of this role play, Gabriela Ansari should be considered a consultative process buyer. You can assume that she will need help identifying and evaluating possible solutions. As you prepare for the first call, think about what may take place during future calls. Review the steps in the typical buying process (see Fig. 11.3). Keep in mind that today's more demanding customers are seeking a cluster of satisfactions.

Chapter 13
Approaching the Customer with Adaptive Selling

Learning Objectives

After studying this chapter, you should be able to

1   Describe the three prescriptions that are included in the presentation strategy

2   Discuss the two-part preapproach process

3   Describe team presentation strategies

4   Explain how adaptive selling builds on four broad strategic areas of personal selling

5   Describe the six main parts of the presentation plan

6   Explain how to effectively approach the customer

7   Describe seven ways to convert the prospect's attention and arouse interest

 Reality Selling Today Video Series

The worldwide Hilti Group (**www.hilti.com**) specializes in providing leading-edge technology to the global construction industry. With some 20 000 employees in more than 120 countries around the world, Hilti actively pursues a value-added orientation in all of its activities.

As part of this orientation, Hilti puts its new salespeople through a rigorous training curriculum that includes one month of pre-training on Hilti products and services, three weeks of intensive training in product and services sales, and two weeks on software applications. In addition, these salespeople also ride along with experienced sales managers to get hands-on experience. Furthermore, the company offers refresher courses to keep its salespeople updated on Hilti's products and services, the construction market, and corporate strategy. Equipped with this in-depth knowledge and the value orientation that is deeply rooted in the corporate culture, salespeople like Alim Hirani (on the right in the photo at the top of the next page) are always well-prepared to approach customers to make sales presentations, demonstrate and explain Hilti's products and services, and show the customers both the tangible and intangible benefits that Hilti can offer.

With a direct sales model, Hilti relies heavily on its salespeople to make the connection and deliver its values to its global customers. Alim is a strong believer that he and his sales team are the face of the company. His credibility is embedded in Hilti's credibility

and vice versa. He always makes sure that his sales presentations are well prepared in advance. More importantly, he builds and maintains rapport with his customers from the very beginning of the business relationship because such partnership mentality motivates the customers to disclose their actual concerns. In the end, customers only value solutions that address their actual needs, and Alim—as a Hilti salesperson—knows that very well.

DEVELOPING THE PRESENTATION STRATEGY

THE PRESENTATION STRATEGY COMBINES ELEMENTS OF THE RELATIONSHIP, PRODUCT, AND customer strategies. Each of the other three strategies must be developed before a salesperson can develop an effective presentation strategy.

The **presentation strategy** is a well-conceived plan that consists of three prescriptions: (1) establishing objectives for the sales presentation, (2) developing the presale presentation plan needed to meet these objectives, and (3) renewing one's commitment to provide outstanding customer service (Fig. 13.1).

The first prescription reminds us that we need to establish one or more objectives for each sales call. High-performance salespeople like Alim Hirani understand that it is often possible to accomplish several things during a single call. A common objective of sales calls is to collect information about the prospect's needs. Another common objective is to develop, build, or sustain a relationship with those who will make the buying decision.

A carefully prepared presentation plan ensures that salespeople will be well organized during the sales presentation and prepared to achieve their objectives. A six-step presentation plan is introduced later in this chapter. Establishment of objectives for the sales presentation and preparation of the presale presentation plan must be guided by a strong desire to offer outstanding customer service. Achieving excellence is the result of careful needs analysis, correct product selection, clear presentations, informative demonstrations, win-win negotiations, and flawless service after the sale. Salespeople who are committed to doing their best in each of these areas will be richly rewarded.

presentation strategy
A well-conceived plan that consists of three prescriptions: establishing objectives for the sales presentation, preparing the presale presentation plan needed to meet these objectives, and renewing one's commitment to provide outstanding customer service.

Strategic/Consultative Selling Model*	
Strategic step	Prescription
Develop a personal selling philosophy	✓ Adopt marketing concept ✓ Value personal selling ✓ Become a problem solver/partner
Develop a relationship strategy	✓ Adopt win-win philosophy ✓ Project professional image ✓ Maintain high ethical standards
Develop a product strategy	✓ Become a product expert ✓ Sell benefits ✓ Configure value-added solutions
Develop a customer strategy	• Understand the buying process • Understand buyer behaviour • Develop prospect base
Develop a presentation strategy	• Prepare objectives • Develop presentation plan • Provide outstanding service
* Strategic/consulative selling evolved in response to increased competition, more complex products, increased emphasis on customer needs, and the growing importance of long-term relationships.	

Figure 13.1 The Strategic/Consultative Selling Model provides the foundation for a value-added consultative presentation strategy.

Presentation Strategy Adds Value

How does precall planning add value? Value is added when you position yourself as a resource—not just a vendor. You must prove that you have important ideas and advice to offer.[1] A well-planned presentation adds value when it is based on carefully developed sales call objectives and on a presentation plan created to meet those objectives. Good planning ensures that the presentation is customized and adapted to meet the needs and time constraints of the prospect. Increasingly, customers' time is very limited and they want a concise and thoughtful presentation. Careful planning is the key to delivering more value and increasing your sales productivity.[2]

Salespeople need to be aware of the changing needs of their customers or risk losing out to their competition. Some salespeople do not pay enough attention to how they conduct business with their established customers. Without a precall plan, it's easy to miss opportunities to increase your knowledge of the customer's business, sell new products, or discover ways to improve service.[3]

PLANNING THE PREAPPROACH

Preparation for the actual sales presentation is a two-part process. Part one is referred to as the **preapproach**. The preapproach involves preparing presale objectives and developing a presale presentation plan. Part two is called the **approach** and involves making a favourable first impression, securing the prospect's attention, and transitioning to need identification (Fig. 13.2). The preapproach and approach, when handled correctly, establish a foundation for an effective sales presentation.

The preapproach should be viewed as a key step in preparing for each sales presentation. Professional salespeople complete the preapproach for every presentation whether it involves a new account or an established customer. Top salespeople often spend two or three hours planning for a 25-minute sales call. The preapproach includes the first two prescriptions for developing a presentation strategy: establishing objectives and creating a presale presentation plan.

Establishing Presentation Objectives

Preparation for a sales call is part research, part planning, and part critical thinking. Sales representatives employed by Nalco Chemical Company prepare for each sales call by filling out a 13-point precall planner. One section of this form requires the salesperson to identify the objectives of the call. Nalco is a company that emphasizes professionalism, long-term partnerships, and staying focused on customer needs.[4]

In Chapter 11, we introduced the five stages of the typical buying process (see Fig. 11.3). When you are calling on a *consultative* or *strategic alliance* buyer, you will usually not cover all of these stages during a single sales call. Multi-call sales presentations are especially common in complex sales. Therefore, it's best to develop presentation objectives suitable for each stage of the buying process. During the first stage—need awareness—prospects may or may not be aware of their needs or problems. The need awareness stage is the "investigation" stage. Uncovering and clarifying needs will require the use of appropriate questions (covered in detail in Chapter 14). The following presentation objectives would be appropriate during the first call on a new prospect:

▦ Establish rapport and begin building a relationship with the prospect.

▦ Obtain permission to ask need identification questions.

▦ Obtain personal and business information to establish the customer's profile.

During stage two of the buying process—evaluation of solutions—the customer is ready to consider possible solutions. In some cases, there may be several solutions that must be evaluated. Presentation objectives for stage two might include the following:

▦ Involve the customer in a product demonstration.

▦ Provide value justification in terms of cost reduction and increased revenues.

▦ Compare and contrast the features of, for example, a truck fleet lease plan with a fleet purchase plan.

Every sales call should have an **action objective**. An action objective is something that you want the customer to do during the sales presentation: provide specific financial information; schedule a visit to your manufacturing plant; agree to a trial use of your

preapproach Activities that precede the actual sales call and set the stage for a personalized sales approach, tailored to the specific needs of the prospect. This involves the planning necessary for the actual meeting with a prospect.

approach The first contact with the prospect, either face-to-face or by telephone. The approach has three objectives: to build rapport with the prospect, to capture the person's full attention, and to generate interest in the product you are selling.

action objective Something that you want the customer to do during the sales presentation.

Approaching Prospects in Relationship-Focused Countries

In most countries of the world, business is conducted through established relationships and social networks. People in relationship-focused countries—including most of Africa, Central and South America, Arab countries, and the Asia/Pacific region—prefer to do business after personal relationships and trust have been established. It is often difficult to approach prospects directly in these countries, so, if you are trying to make new contacts, you may need a third-party introduction to help bridge the relationship gap. You may use trade associations, chambers of commerce, banks, or even consultants who specialize in arranging introductions in some countries. Attending international trade shows is one of the best ways to make foreign contacts—people attend these shows expressly to make business connections. Another increasingly popular method is to participate in a trade mission. In recent years, trade missions have been supported by governments at all levels: federal, provincial or territorial, and municipal. The City of Toronto participated in a 23-person trade mission to China in 2008. Many business-people from the Atlantic provinces participated in a trade mission to India in 2008 to promote their region as a gateway for trade between Asia and Canada.[a]

product; agree to a follow-up meeting; or place an order. An action objective brings a sharp focus to the sales presentation.[5]

Once you have an appointment with the prospect and the presentation objectives have been established, consider sending a fax or e-mail message that outlines the agenda for the meeting. This will confirm the appointment and clarify the topics to be discussed.[6]

Multi-call sales presentations are common in many areas, including the retail field. The sale of recreational vehicles, leased automobiles, boats, and quality sound systems for home or business typically require more than one sales call. Some clothing stores and independent tailors make office calls to sell tailored clothing. One example is Mitchells/Richards, a progressive retailer with a reputation for superior customer service. Its salespeople will make office calls on request. Working with a customer at his office usually requires more than one sales call.[7]

Team Presentation Strategies

In today's ever-changing business environment, team selling has surfaced as a major development. Team selling is ideally suited to organizations that sell complex or customized products and services that require direct communication between customers and technical experts. Sales teams can often uncover problems, solutions, and sales opportunities that an individual salesperson working alone might not discover.[8] In some situations, the involvement of technical experts can shorten the selling cycle. The team approach often results in more precise need identification, improved selection of the product, and more informative sales presentations.

Team sales presentations require a more detailed precall plan than individual sales calls. Each team member must have a clear understanding of the role he or she will play during the sales call. Sales presentation objectives should be clearly stated. Team members should share detailed information about the customer, understand the basics of a consultative sales presentation, and be prepared to add value.[9]

Technical Staff Assume Sales Role

Reggie Daniel, CEO of Scientific & Engineering Solutions, says, "The company culture is to have every employee bringing in business." His three full-time salespeople and a selected group of 15 non-sales personnel get paid commissions or bonuses based on the profitability of sales they help close. Steve Newcomb, a technical staff member, helped close a sale that resulted in a $700 000 contract. He not only collected the commission on the sale, he also received a trip to the Super Bowl. Daniel wants his technical staff to have access to the business world because sales opportunities often surface when staff are involved in technical problem solving.[b]

Companies that have moved to team sales have discovered that this approach is not easily executed. At Hickok Cole Architects, team selling is the primary approach used to obtain new accounts. However, the team selling process was not easily mastered by staff members. Determining who would communicate when, and determining how presentations would fall into place seamlessly, took months of practice among the company's teams, which often consisted of six or more people. Without sufficient practice, the staff at Hickok Cole discovered that team presentations were sometimes disorganized.[10]

A variation of the team approach to selling is used by some marketers. Salespeople are trained to seek the assistance of another salesperson or to actually turn the customer over to another salesperson when problems surface. The other salesperson may bring to the selling situation a greater ability to identify the customer's needs or to select the appropriate product. Salespeople who have well-prepared presale objectives know when to seek assistance from another professional.

Selling to a Buying Team

In some cases, salespeople must address and satisfy both the individual and collective concerns of each participant in a multi-buyer situation. The decision makers may be members of a well-trained buying team, a buying committee assembled for a one-time purchase, or a board of directors.

As in any type of selling situation, the salesperson should attempt to determine the various buying influences. When possible, the role of each decision maker, the amount of influence he or she exerts, and each decision maker's needs should be determined before the presentation. Careful observation during the presentation can reveal who may use the product, who controls the finances, and who can provide the expertise necessary to make the correct buying decision.

When you make a group selling presentation, make sure all parties feel involved. Any member of the group who feels ignored could prevent you from closing the sale. Be sure to direct questions and comments to all potential decision makers in the group. As early as possible, identify the most powerful influences.

Find out if there are any silent team or committee members. A silent member is one who will influence the buying decision but does not attend the presentation. Silent members are usually senior managers who have a major influence on the buying decision. If a silent member does exist, you must find a way to communicate, directly or indirectly, with this person.[11]

Rick Page's bestselling trade book *Hope Is Not a Strategy* emphasizes the need for strategic planning during the preapproach. His six keys to winning the complex sale in the age of information help salespeople move to the next level of selling.

ADAPTIVE SELLING BUILDS ON FOUR STRATEGIC AREAS OF PERSONAL SELLING

AT THE VERY HEART OF *ADAPTIVE SELLING* IS THE BELIEF THAT EVERY SALES CALL MUST BE tailored to the unique needs, wants, and concerns of the customer. Adaptive selling involves altering sales behaviours in order to improve communication with the customer. To better identify and respond to the customer's needs frequently requires complex behavioural adjustments before and during the sales call. These adjustments are based on the relationship needs and product needs of the customer. Salespeople today must develop a broader repertoire of selling strategies and apply more effective information-acquisition skills.[12]

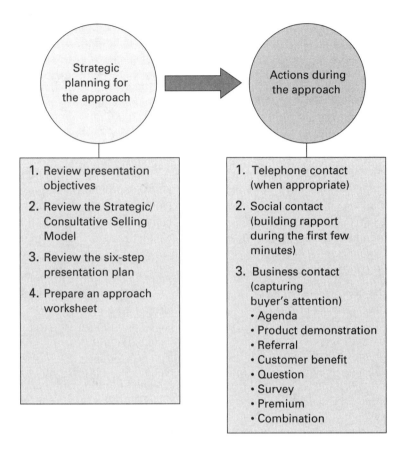

Figure 13.2 Preparing for the presentation involves planning for the activities that will occur before meeting the prospect and for the first few minutes of actual contact with the prospect.

The strategic planning that takes place during the preapproach can greatly enhance the adaptive selling process. This plan includes *strategies* that you use to position yourself with the customers and *tactics* you will use when you are face-to-face with a customer. Planning the approach involves consideration of how the *relationship, product,* and *customer* strategies can enhance the sales presentation (see Figure 13.2).

Review the Relationship Strategy

As noted in Chapter 7, salespeople need to think of everything they say or do in the context of their relationship with the customer. Customers want a quality product and a quality relationship. Building and nourishing a long-term partnership with the customer often begins with attention to many small details. Confirming an appointment with a brief e-mail message and arriving for the appointment a few minutes early sends a positive message to the customer before the first face-to-face meeting.

The first contact between a salesperson and a prospect is very important. A positive or negative first impression can be formed in a matter of seconds. The customer is receiving a variety of verbal and nonverbal messages that can either facilitate or distract from the sales call. Your behaviours and appearance create an image that others observe and remember. Identification of the customer's preferred communication style should be given a high priority during the initial contact. Once you are in the presence of the customer, absorb the many clues that will help you with style identification. Then use *style flexing* to accommodate the needs of that person.

Review the Product Strategy

During the preapproach, you will learn some new things about the potential customer. You will no doubt acquire information that did not surface during the prospecting stage. If this is the case, it pays to take another look at your product. Now it will be easier to identify features with special appeal to the person you are calling on. In addition, you can more accurately identify questions that the prospect might raise.

Product knowledge, combined with knowledge of the customer, builds confidence. Salespeople who are confident in their ability alter the sales approach as needed are much better prepared to engage in adaptive selling.[13] Customers today are anxious to do business with salespeople who have developed "expert power."

Review the Customer Strategy

Personal selling provides us with the opportunity to apply the marketing concept during every contact with the customer. All energies can be directed toward an individual who is likely to think and act differently from anyone else. Customers today have become increasingly sophisticated in their buying strategies. They have higher expectations for value-added products and long-term commitments. A customer strategy focuses on understanding the customer's needs, wants, and buying conditions. With this understanding, adaptive selling strategies are formulated to meet both the relationship and product needs of the customer.

DEVELOPING THE SIX-STEP PRESENTATION PLAN

Once you have established objectives for the sales presentation, the next step (prescription) involves developing the presentation plan. This plan helps you achieve your objectives. Today, with increased time constraints, fierce competition, and rising travel costs, the opportunity for a face-to-face meeting with customers may occur less frequently. The few minutes you have with your customers may be your only opportunity to win their business, so careful planning is more critical than ever.

Planning the Presentation

six-step presentation plan
Preparation involving consideration of those activities that will take place during the sales presentation.

Once you have sufficient background information, you are ready to develop a "customized" presale presentation plan. Preparing a customized sales presentation can take a great deal of time and energy. Nevertheless, this attention to detail gives you added confidence and helps you avoid delivering unconvincing hit-or-miss sales talks. The plan is developed after a careful review of the **six-step presentation plan** (Fig. 13.3). In most cases, the sales process includes the following activities.

The Six-Step Presentation Plan

Step One: APPROACH	○ Review Strategic/Consultative Selling Model ○ Initiate customer contact
Step Two: PRESENTATION	Determine prospect needs Select solution Initiate sales presentation
Step Three: DEMONSTRATION	Decide what to demonstrate Select selling tools Initiate demonstration
Step Four: NEGOTIATION	Anticipate buyer concerns Plan negotiating methods Initiate win-win negotiations
Step Five: CLOSE	Plan appropriate closing methods Recognize closing clues Initiate closing methods
Step Six: SERVICING THE SALE	Follow-through Follow-up calls Expansion selling

Service, retail, wholesale, and manufacturer selling.

Figure 13.3 The six-step presentation plan. A presale plan is a logical and orderly outline that features a salesperson's thoughts from one step to the next in the presentation. Each step in this plan is explained in Chapters 13 to 17.

1. *Approach.* Preparation for the approach involves making decisions concerning effective ways to make a favourable first impression during the initial contact, to secure the prospect's attention, and to develop the prospect's interest in the product. The approach should set the stage for an effective sales presentation.

2. *Presentation.* The presentation is one of the most critical parts of the selling process. If the salesperson is unable to discover the prospect's buying needs, select a product solution, and present the product in a convincing manner, the sale may be lost. Chapter 14 covers all aspects of the sales presentation.

3. *Demonstration.* An effective sales demonstration helps verify parts of the sales presentation. Demonstrations are important because they provide the customer with a better understanding of product benefits.

4. *Negotiation*. Buyer resistance is a natural part of the selling–buying process. An objection, however, does present a barrier to closing the sale. For this reason, all salespeople should become skillful at negotiating resistance. Chapter 15 covers this topic.

5. *Close*. As the sales presentation progresses, there may be several opportunities to close the sale. Salespeople must learn to spot closing clues. Chapter 16 provides suggestions on how to close sales.

6. *Servicing the sale*. The importance of developing a long-term relationship with the prospect was noted in previous chapters. This rapport is often the outgrowth of post-sale service. Learning to service the sale is an important aspect of selling. Chapter 17 deals with this topic.

Adapting the Presentation Plan to the Customer's Buying Process

A truly valuable idea or concept is timeless. The six parts of the presale presentation plan checklist have been discussed in sales training literature for many years; therefore, they might be described as fundamentals of personal selling. These steps are basic elements of most sales and frequently occur in the same sequence. However, the activities included in the six-step presentation plan must be selected with care. Prior to developing the sales call plan, the salesperson must answer one very important question: Do these activities relate to the customer's buying process? As noted in Chapter 11, purchasing structures and buying procedures can vary greatly from company to company. In some cases, the steps in the buying process have been clearly defined by the organization and this information is available to vendors. Selling steps are of little value *unless* they are firmly rooted in your customer's buying process.[14]

THE APPROACH

After a great deal of preparation, it is time to communicate with the prospect, either by face-to-face contact, by telephone, or by some other appropriate method of communication. We refer to the initial contact with the customer as the *approach*. All the effort you have put into developing relationship, product, and customer strategies can now be applied to the presentation strategy. If the approach is effective, you will be given the opportunity to make the sales presentation. If, however, the approach is not effective, the chance to present your sales story may be lost. You can be the best-prepared salesperson in the business but, without a good approach, there may be little chance for a sale.

The approach has three important objectives. First, you want to build rapport with the prospect. Second, you want to capture the person's full attention. Never begin your sales story if the prospect seems preoccupied and is not paying attention. Third, you want to transition to the need discovery stage of the sales presentation.

In some selling situations the first contact with the customer is a telephone call. The call is made to schedule a meeting or, in some cases, to conduct the sales presentation.

The sales presentation should be a model of good two-way communication.

The face-to-face sales call starts with the social contact and continues with the business contact. The telephone contact, social contact, and business contact are discussed in this section.

Establish Your Credibility Early

Thomas A. Freese, author of *Secrets of Question Based Selling*, says credibility is critical to your success in sales. Credibility is an impression that people form of you very early in the sales process.[15] Sometimes little things can erode your credibility before you have a chance to prove yourself. Arriving late for an appointment, spending 45 minutes with the prospect when you said you would need only 15 minutes, or failure to send the prospect information that was promised can quickly weaken a relationship. Failure to be well prepared for the sales call will also undermine your credibility. Credibility grows when the customer realizes you are a competent sales representative who can add value throughout the sales process.

The Telephone Contact

A telephone call provides a quick and inexpensive method of scheduling an appointment. Appointments are important because many busy prospects will not meet with a salesperson who drops in unannounced. When you schedule an appointment, the prospect knows about the sales call in advance and can therefore make the necessary preparations.

Some salespeople use the telephone exclusively to establish and maintain contact with the customer. As noted in Chapter 6, inside salespeople rely almost totally on the telephone for sales. **Telesales**—not to be confused with *telemarketing*—includes many of the same elements as traditional sales: gathering customer information, determining needs, prescribing solutions, negotiating buyer concerns, and closing sales. Telesales calls are usually unscripted, as opposed to the scripted calls widely used in telemarketing.

telesales Using the telephone to acquire information about the customer, determine needs, suggest solutions, negotiate buyer concerns, and close the sale.

In some situations, telesales calls are as dynamic and unpredictable as face-to-face sales calls.

In Chapter 7 we examined some of the factors that influence the meaning we attach to an oral message from another person. With the aid of this information we can see that communication via telephone is challenging. Since the person who receives the call cannot see our facial expressions, gestures, or posture, he or she must rely wholly on the sound of our voice and the words used. The telephone caller has a definite handicap.

The telephone has some additional limitations. A salesperson accustomed to meeting prospects in person may find telephone contact impersonal. Some salespeople try to avoid using the telephone because they believe it is too easy for the prospect to say no. It should be noted that these drawbacks are more imagined than real. With proper training a salesperson can use the telephone effectively to schedule appointments. When you make an appointment by telephone, use the following practices:

1. *Plan what you will say.* It helps to use a written presentation plan as a guide during the first few seconds of the conversation. What you will say is determined by the objectives of the sales call. Have a calendar available to suggest and confirm a date, time, and place for the appointment. Be sure to write it down.

2. *Politely identify yourself and the company you represent.* Set yourself apart from other callers by using a friendly tone and impeccable phone manners. This approach helps you avoid being shut out by a wary gatekeeper (secretary or receptionist).

3. *State the purpose of your call and explain how the prospect can benefit from a meeting.* In some cases, it is helpful to use a powerful benefits statement that gets the prospect's attention and whets the person's appetite for more information. Present only enough information to stimulate interest.

4. *Show respect for the prospect's time by telling the person how long the appointment will take.* Once the prospect agrees to meet with you, say, "Do you have your appointment calendar handy?" Be prepared to suggest a specific time: "Is Monday at 9:00 a.m. okay?"

5. *Confirm the appointment with a brief note, e-mail message, or letter with the date, time, and place of your appointment.* Enclose your business card and any printed information that may be of interest to the prospect.[16]

You should anticipate resistance from some prospects. After all, most decision makers are very busy. Be persistent and persuasive if you genuinely believe a meeting with the prospect can be mutually beneficial.

Effective Use of Voice Mail

The growing popularity of voice mail presents a challenge to salespeople. What type of message sets the stage for a second call or stimulates a return call? It's important to anticipate voice mail and know exactly what to say if you reach a recording. The prospect's perception of you is based on what you say and on voice quality. The following message almost guarantees that it will be ignored: "Ms. Simpson, I am Paul Watson and I am with Elliott Property Management Services. I would like to visit with you about our services. Please call me at 862-1500."[17] Note that this message provides no compelling reason for the prospect to call back. It offers no valid information that would stimulate interest. The

Wall Street Journal, March 10, 1999, p. A–23. From the *Wall Street Journal* by permission of Cartoon Features Syndicate.

"I don't think of myself as the Jenkins Doolittle & Bloom gatekeeper. I rather prefer lead blocker."

In some cases a secretary, assistant, or receptionist will screen incoming telephone calls. Be prepared to convince this person that your call is important. Always treat the gatekeeper with respect and courtesy.

voice-mail message should be similar to the opening statement you would make if you had face-to-face contact with the prospect. For example:

> Ms. Simpson, my name is Paul Watson and I represent Elliott Property Management Services. We specialize in working with property managers. We can help you reduce the paperwork associated with maintenance jobs and provide an easy way to track the progress of each job. I would like the opportunity to visit with you and will call back in the morning.[18]

Note that this message is brief and describes benefits that customers can receive. If Paul Watson wants a call back, then he needs to give the best time to reach him. He should give his phone number slowly and completely. It's usually best to repeat the number. If you are acting on a referral, be sure to say who referred you and why.

Effective Use of E-Mail

Many prospects and established customers like the convenience of e-mail correspondence and prefer it to telephone contact. Your challenge is to make it easy for your correspondents to read and handle your e-mail. Always use a meaningful, specific subject line. People who receive large amounts of e-mail may selectively choose which ones to read by scanning the subject lines and deleting those of no interest. An e-mail with a subject line titled "Action Steps from Our 9/28 Meeting" is more likely to be read than a subject line like "Meeting Notes."[19]

The e-mail message should tell the reader what you want and then encourage a response. Identify the main point of your e-mail within the first or second paragraph. Format the e-mail so it's easy to read. This may require the use of headings (with capitals or boldface print) to identify the main elements of the memo. Proofread all e-mails for proper grammar, punctuation, and spelling.[20] Always use the grammar and spell check tools. Messages that contain errors may misrepresent your competence. Finally, use a signature file—a small block of text that automatically follows each e-mail you send.

A typical signature file includes your full name, title, affiliation, and phone number, and in some cases a slogan.

The Social Contact

According to many image consultants, "First impressions are lasting impressions." This statement is essentially true, and some profitable business relationships never crystallize because some trait or characteristic of the salesperson repels the prospective customer. Sales personnel have only a few minutes to create a positive first impression. Susan Bixler, author of *The New Professional Image*, describes the importance of the first impression this way:

> Books are judged by their covers, houses are appraised by their curb appeal, and people are initially evaluated on how they choose to dress and behave. In a perfect world this is not fair, moral, or just. What's inside should count a great deal more. And eventually it usually does, but not right away. In the meantime, a lot of opportunities can be lost.[21]

Building rapport leads to credibility, which leads to trust. Once trust is established, the prospect is likely to open up and share information. This information will provide clues regarding ways to create value. To be certain that your first impression is appropriate, review the material in Chapter 7. The information in this chapter is timeless and will serve you well today and in the future.

Developing Conversation

The brief, general conversation during the social contact should hold the prospect's attention and establish a relaxed and friendly atmosphere for the business contact that is to follow. As mentioned in Chapter 7, there are three areas of conversation that should be considered in developing a social contact:

1. *Comments on "here and now" observations.* These comments may include general observations about the victory of a local athletic team, an article in the *Globe and Mail*, or specific comments about awards on display in the prospect's office. Janis

---

Customer Relationship Management with Technology

Planning Personal Visits

Personally visiting prospects and customers helps build strong relationships, yet travelling is expensive and time consuming. A salesperson is challenged to plan visits that will optimize the investment represented by each trip. Access to customer relationship management (CRM) prospect records helps salespeople quickly identify all the accounts in a given geographic area.

CRM empowers salespeople to rapidly review and compare an area's prospects on the basis of position in sales cycle, potential size of account or purchase, likelihood of sale, and the contribution that the visit could make to information gathering and relationship building. A well-managed CRM database will provide salespeople with appropriate business and social topics to discuss when calling selected prospects for an appointment. (See the exercise Planning Personal Visits on page 285 for more information.)

Taylor, sales representative with Trugreen Chemlawn, likes to start each new appointment by seeking "common ground" with her prospects. She looks for such items as a picture of the prospect's children or a trophy.[22]

2. *Compliments.* Most customers will react positively to sincere compliments. Personal items in the prospect's office, achievements, or efficient operation of the prospect's business provide examples of things that can be praised. A salesperson might say, "I learned recently that your company is ranked number one in customer satisfaction by J. D. Power and Associates."

3. *Search for mutual acquaintances or interests.* Discovering that you have mutual friends or interests can serve as the foundation for a strong social contact. Most people enjoy talking about themselves, their hobbies, and their achievements. Debra Fine, author of *The Fine Art of Small Talk*, says, "Small talk isn't stupid. It's the appetizer for all relationships."[23]

Communication on a personal basis is often the first step in establishing a common language that can improve communication between the salesperson and the prospect. How much time should be devoted to the social contact? There is no easy answer to this question. The length of the conversation will depend on the type of product or service sold, how busy the prospect appears to be, and your awareness of topics of mutual interest (see Selling in Action on page 278). In many cases, the conversation will take place over lunch or dinner. Many successful sales have been closed during or after a meal. This explains why some companies enroll their sales staff and other customer contact personnel in dining etiquette classes.

The Business Contact

Converting the prospect's attention from the social contact to the business proposal is an important part of the approach. When you convert and hold your prospect's attention, you have fulfilled an important step in the selling process. Furthermore, without this step, the door has been closed on completing the remaining steps of the sale.

Some salespeople use a carefully planned opening statement or a question to attract the customer's attention to the sales presentation. A statement or question that focuses on the prospect's dominant buying motive is, of course, more likely to achieve the desired results. Buyers must like what they see and hear, and must be made to feel that it will be worthwhile to hear more.

Converting the Buyer's Attention and Arousing Interest

Throughout the years, salespeople have identified and used a number of effective ways to capture the prospect's attention and arouse interest in the presentation. Seven of the most common will be explained in the following material:

- Agenda approach
- Product demonstration approach
- Referral approach

- Customer benefit approach
- Question approach
- Survey approach
- Premium approach

We also discuss combining two or more of these approaches.

Agenda Approach One of the most effective ways to move from the social contact to the business contact is to thank the customer for taking time to meet with you and then review your goals for the meeting. You might say, "Thank you for meeting with me this morning. I would like to accomplish three things during the time you have given me." This statement shows you value the person's time and you have preplanned a specific agenda. Always be open to changing the agenda based on suggestions from the customer.[24]

Product Demonstration Approach Sales representatives who sell copy machines, photographic equipment, automobiles, construction equipment, office furniture, and many

---

Selling in Action

The Social Contact

The social contact should be viewed as effective communication on a personal basis. This brief conversation establishes the foundation for the business contact, so it should be viewed as a significant part of the presentation strategy. The following guidelines can help you develop the skills needed to make good social contact.

1. *Prepare for the social contact.* Conduct a background check on topics of interest to the person you are contacting. This includes reviewing information in the prospect database, reading industry reports, and searching the Internet. Once you arrive at the customer's office, you will discover additional information about the person's interests. Most people communicate what is important to them in the way they personalize their work environment.

2. *Initiate social contact.* The most effective opening comments should be expressed in the form of an open-ended question, such as "I understand you have just been elected president of the United Way." You can improve the possibility of a good response to your verbal question by applying nonverbal communication skills. Appropriate eye contact, voice inflections that

communicate enthusiasm, and a warm smile will increase the customer's receptivity to your opening comments.

3. *Respond to the customer's conversations.* When the customer responds, it is imperative that you acknowledge the message both verbally and nonverbally. The verbal response might be "That is really interesting" or any other appropriate comment. Let the customer know you are listening and that you want him or her to keep talking.

4. *Keep the social contact focused on the customer.* Because you cannot control where a conversation might go, you may be tempted to focus the conversation on topics with which you are familiar. A response such as "Several years ago I was in charge of our company's United Way campaign and we had a difficult time meeting our goal" shifts the focus of the conversation back to you. Continue to focus the conversation on topics that are of interest to the customer. Dale Carnegie said that one of the best ways to build a relationship is to encourage others to talk about themselves.

other products use this straightforward method of getting the prospect's attention. If the actual product cannot be demonstrated, salespeople can use appropriate audiovisual technology such as computer-generated graphics, CDs, and DVDs. Trish Ormsby, a sales representative who sells security systems, uses her portable computer to create a visual image of systems that meet the customer's security needs.[25]

Referral Approach Research indicates that another person will be far more impressed with your good points if these points are presented by a third party rather than by you. The referral approach is quite effective because a third party—a satisfied customer—believes the prospect will benefit from your product. This type of opening statement has universal appeal among salespeople from nearly every field. When you use the referral approach, your opening statement should include a direct reference to the third party. Here is an example: "Mrs. Follett, my name is Kurt Wheeler, and I represent the Cross Printing Company. We specialize in printing all types of business forms. Mr. Ameno—buyer for Raybale Products, Incorporated—is a regular customer of ours, and he suggested I mention his name to you."

Customer Benefit Approach One of the most effective ways to gain a prospect's attention is to immediately point out one benefit of purchasing your product. Try to begin with the most important issue (or problem) facing the client. When using this approach, the most important buyer benefit is included in the initial statement. For example, the salesperson selling a portable Sony projector might open with this statement:

> "The Sony VPL-CS4 lightweight projector strikes a balance between cost, size, brightness, and convenience. It's a good choice for a quick business trip or for a work-at-home presentation."

Another example taken from the financial services field follows:

> "When you meet with a Scotia McLeod investment specialist, you can obtain advice on a family of 48 professionally managed no-load mutual funds."

The key to achieving success with the customer benefit approach is preparation. Prospects are annoyed when a salesperson cannot quickly communicate the benefits of meeting with them. Bruce Klassen, sales manager for Do All Industrial Supply, says, "Our salespeople begin the sales process by researching the prospect and the company. We need to be sure that our product line is going to benefit that prospect before we make even an initial sales approach."[26]

Question Approach The question approach has two positive features. First, a question almost always triggers prospect involvement. Very few people will avoid answering a direct question. Second, a question gets the prospect thinking about a problem that the salesperson is prepared to solve.

Molly Hoover, a sales training consultant, conducts training classes for sales managers and car dealers who want to better understand the subtleties of selling to the female car buyer. She suggests an approach that includes a few basic questions such as:

> "Is the vehicle for business or pleasure?"

> "Will you be buying within the next week or so?"[27]

These opening questions are not difficult to answer, yet they get the customer mentally involved. Some of the best opening questions are carefully phrased to capture attention. The authors of *The Sales Question Book* offer some good examples:

> "Are you aware that we just added three new services to our payroll and accounting package? Could I tell you about them?"

> "We are now offering all our customers a special service that used to be reserved for our largest accounts. Would you be interested in hearing about it?"[28]

Once you ask the question, listen carefully to the response. If the answer is yes, proceed with an enthusiastic presentation of your product. If the answer is no, then you may have to gracefully try another approach or thank the prospect for their time and depart.

Survey Approach Larry Short, a financial advisor with RBC Dominion Securities and a winner of the Atlantic Canada Award of Distinction by the Investment Dealers Association of Canada, frequently uses the survey approach as part of his customer strategy. He has new clients fill out a detailed questionnaire before he sees them for a first appointment.[29] He studies the completed questionnaire and other documents before making any effort to find a solution to any of the customer's financial planning needs. Data collection through the survey is an important part of the problem-solving philosophy of selling. It is often used in selling office machines, business security systems, insurance, and other products where need cannot be established without careful study.

The survey approach offers many advantages. It is generally a non-threatening way to open a sales call. You are simply asking permission to acquire information that can be used to determine the buyer's need for your product. Because the survey is tailor-made for a specific business, the buyer is given individual treatment. Finally, the survey approach helps avoid a premature discussion of price. Price cannot be discussed until the survey is completed.

Premium Approach The premium approach involves giving the customer a free sample or an inexpensive item. A financial services representative might give the customer a booklet that can be used to record expenses. Product samples are frequently used by persons who sell cosmetics. Creative use of premiums is an effective way to get the customer's attention.

The agenda, product demonstration, referral, customer benefit, question, survey, and premium approaches offer the salesperson a variety of ways to set the stage for the presentation strategy. With experience, salespeople learn to select the most effective approach for each selling situation. Table 13.1 provides examples of how these approaches can be applied in real-world situations.

Combination Approaches

A hallmark of consultative selling is flexibility. Therefore, a combination of approaches sometimes provides the best avenue to need identification. Sales personnel who have adopted the consultative style will, of course, use the question and survey approaches most frequently. Some selling situations, however, require that one of the other approaches be used, either alone or in combination with the question and survey

Table 13.1 Business Contact Worksheet

This worksheet illustrates how to prepare effective real-world approaches that capture the customer's attention.

Method of Approach	What will you say?
1. Agenda	1. (Office supply) "Thank you for meeting with me, Ms. Zhou. During the next 45 minutes, I plan to accomplish three things."
2. Product demonstration	2a. (Retail clothing) "We have just received a shipment of new fall sweaters from Braemar International."
	2b. (Business forms manufacturer) "Our plant has just purchased a $300 000 Harris Graphics composer, Mr. Reichart. I would like to show you a copy of your sales invoice with your logo printed on it."
3. Referral	3. (Food wholesaler) "Paula Doeman, procurement manager for St. Joseph's Hospital, suggested that I provide you with information about our computerized 'Order It' system."
4. Customer benefit	4. (Real estate) "Mr. and Mrs. Stuart, my company lists and sells more homes than any other company in the area where your home is located. Our past performance would lead me to believe we can sell your home within two weeks."
5. Question	5. (Hotel convention services) "Mrs. McClaughin, will your 2011 Annual Franchisee Meeting be held in April?"
6. Survey	6a. (Custom-designed computer software) "Mr. Pham, I would like the opportunity to learn about your accounts receivable and accounts payable procedures. We may be able to develop a customized program that will significantly improve your cash flow."
	6b. (Retail menswear) "May I ask you a few questions about your wardrobe? The information will help me better understand your clothing needs."
7. Premium	7. (Financial services) "I would like to give you a publication entitled *Guaranteed Growth Annuity*."

approaches (see Fig. 13.4). An example of how a salesperson might combine referral and question approaches follows:

Salesperson: Carl Hamilton at Simmons Modern Furniture suggested that I visit with you about our new line of compact furniture designed for today's smaller homes. He believes this line might complement the furniture you currently feature.

Customer: Yes, Carl called me yesterday and mentioned your name and company.

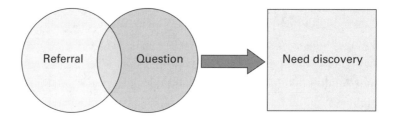

Figure 13.4 Combination approaches provide a smooth transition to the need discovery part of the consultative-style presentation.

> **Salesperson:** Before showing you our product lines, I would like to ask you some questions about your current product mix. First, what do you currently carry in the area of bedroom furniture?

Coping with Sales Call Reluctance

The transition from the preapproach to the approach is sometimes blocked by sales call reluctance. Fear of making the initial contact with the prospect is one of the biggest obstacles to sales success. For new salespeople, the problem can be career-threatening. **Sales call reluctance** includes thoughts, feelings and behavioural patterns that conspire to limit what a salesperson is able to accomplish. It is an internal, often emotional, barrier to sales success. Sales call reluctance can be caused by several different thought patterns:[30]

- Fear of taking risks
- Fear of group presentations
- Lack of self-confidence
- Fear of rejection

Regardless of the reasons for sales call reluctance, you can learn to deal with it. Here are some suggestions:

- *Be optimistic about the outcome of the initial contact.* It is better to anticipate success than to anticipate failure. Martin Seligman, professor of psychology at the University of Pennsylvania and author of the bestselling book *Learned Optimism*, says that success in selling requires a healthy dose of optimism.[31] The anticipation of failure is a major barrier to making the initial contact.

- *Practise your approach before making the initial contact.* A well-rehearsed effort to make the initial contact increases your self-confidence and reduces the possibility that you may handle the situation badly.

- *Recognize that it is normal to feel anxious about the initial contact.* Even the most experienced salespeople experience some degree of sales call reluctance and this reluctance can surface anywhere in the sales process.

- *Develop a deeper commitment to your goals.* Abraham Zaleznik, professor emeritus at the Harvard Business School, says, "If your commitment is only in your mind, then you'll lose it when you encounter a big obstacle. If your commitment is in your heart *and* your mind, you'll create the power to break through the toughest obstacles."[32]

sales call reluctance Fear of making the initial contact with the prospect.

Selling to the Gatekeeper

Many decision makers have an assistant or secretary who manages their daily schedule. This person is commonly referred to as the "gatekeeper." If you want to reach the decision maker, work hard to align yourself with the person who schedules this person's appointments. Rule number one is to treat the gatekeeper with respect. Learn his or her name and what he or she does. Keep in mind that this person can be an important source of information. For example, the gatekeeper can tell you how the buying process works and provide information regarding new developments in the company. This person may be able to help you make a preliminary qualification before you reach the decision maker. When you treat this person as an expert by soliciting his or her views, you establish a relationship that can pay big dividends today and in the future.[33] When possible, use personal referrals from someone the prospect knows. If you have met the prospect previously, describe the meeting and tell the gatekeeper why you feel a second meeting would be beneficial.

REVIEWING KEY CONCEPTS

- Describe the three prescriptions that are included in the presentation strategy.

  Developing a presentation strategy involves preparing presale objectives, developing a presale presentation plan, and providing outstanding customer service. The presentation strategy combines elements of the relationship, product, and customer strategies.

- Discuss the two-part preapproach process.

  Preparation for the sales presentation is a two-part process. Part one is referred to as the *preapproach* and involves preparing presale objectives and developing a presale presentation plan. It's best to develop presentation objectives for each stage of the buying process. Part two is called the *approach* and involves making a good first impression, securing the prospect's attention, and transitioning to need identification.

- Describe team presentation strategies.

  In recent years, team selling has surfaced as a major development. Sales teams can often uncover problems, solutions, and sales opportunities that no individual salesperson could discover working alone. Team sales presentations require a more detailed precall plan than individual sales calls. Without careful planning and extensive practice (rehearsal), team presentations are likely to be delivered in a disorganized manner.

- Explain how adaptive selling builds on four broad strategic areas of personal selling.

  Adaptive selling involves altering sales behaviours in order to improve communication with the customer. Salespeople today are challenged to develop a broader repertoire of selling strategies. Salespeople skilled in adaptive selling consider how the relationship, product, and customer strategies can enhance the sales presentation.

- Describe the six main parts of the presentation plan.

  After collecting background information, salespeople need to create a customized presale presentation plan. The plan is developed after careful study of the six-step presentation plan that includes approach, presentation, demonstration, negotiation, close, and servicing the sale.

- Explain how to effectively approach the customer.

  The approach may involve face-to-face contact, telephone contact, or some other appropriate method of communication. If the approach is effective, the salesperson will be given an opportunity to make the sales presentation. A major goal of the *social contact* is to make a good first impression, build rapport, and establish credibility. The *business contact* involves converting the prospect's attention from the social contact to the sales presentation.

- Describe seven ways to convert the prospect's attention and arouse interest.

    Over the years, salespeople have identified several ways to convert the prospect's attention and arouse interest in the presentation. Some of the most common ways include the agenda approach, product demonstration approach, referral approach, customer benefit approach, question approach, survey approach, and premium approach.

Key Terms

action objective **265**

approach **265**

preapproach **265**

presentation strategy **263**

sales call reluctance **282**

six-step presentation plan **270**

telesales **273**

Review Questions

1. What is the purpose of the preapproach? What are the two prescriptions included in the preapproach?

2. Explain the role of objectives in developing the presale presentation plan.

3. Why should salespeople establish multiple-objective sales presentations? List four possible objectives that would be appropriate for stage one and stage two of the buying process.

4. Compare and contrast team sales presentations and individual sales calls.

5. Describe the major steps in the presentation plan. Briefly discuss the role of adaptive selling in implementing the presentation plan.

6. What are the major objectives of the approach?

7. Review the Selling in Action boxed feature on page 278. Briefly describe the four guidelines that can help you make a good social contact.

8. What are some rules to follow when leaving a message on voice mail? On e-mail?

9. What methods can the salesperson use to convert the prospect's attention to the sales presentation?

10. Discuss why combination approaches are considered an important consultative-selling practice. Provide one example of a combination approach.

Application Exercises

1. Assume that you are a salesperson who calls on retailers. For some time, you have been attempting to get an appointment with the head buyer for one of the best retailers in the city to persuade her to carry your line. You have an appointment to see her in 90 minutes. You are sitting in your office now and it will take you about 30 minutes to drive to your appointment. Outline what you should be doing between now and the time you leave to meet your prospect.

2. Tom Nelson has just graduated from Algonquin College with a major in marketing. He has three years of experience in the retail grocery business and has decided he would like to work as a salesperson for the district office of Procter & Gamble. Tom has decided to telephone and set up an appointment for an interview. Write out exactly what Tom should *plan* to say during his telephone call.

3. Concepts from Dale Carnegie's *How to Win Friends and Influence People* can help you prepare for the social contact. Access the Dale Carnegie Training Web site (**www.dalecarnegie.com**) and examine the courses offered. Search for the Sales Advantage Course. Read the course description and review the two main things you will learn in this program. View the online Sales Action System demo video at **http://sas.infoally.com/sas/index.asp** to learn how Dale Carnegie's Web-based

coaching program enhances what is learned in the course. (Click on the Overview link on the right side of the page where you are invited to "Learn More.")

4. Canadian author and sales trainer Steven J. Schwartz is internationally known for his expertise in helping salespeople get appointments. Visit his Web site at **www.hotcoldcalls.com** and hit "Toolbox." One of the items here is a 24-question self-assessment tool that can help you identify initial mistakes you might make when initially contacting prospects by telephone. Complete the survey and assess how well you did. Continue until you get all answers correct.

5. You are being interviewed for a sales position with a national electronics retailer. The job is very important to you as it will help pay your living expenses while you complete your studies. During the interview, the manager says, "We are known for honesty and outstanding service, and we expect any salesperson we hire to sell only products that meet customer needs. Please take 10 minutes and write five questions that you would ask a customer who approaches you in our store and wants to buy a digital camera. I will also want to know why you have chosen the questions you have chosen." What questions will you ask? Defend your choice.

ROLE-PLAY EXERCISE

Research the new computer that you would like to purchase in the future or that you have just purchased. Strategically, prepare to meet a prospect who has been referred to you by a friend and who would like to purchase a similar computer. Using Table 13.1, prepare four different business contact statements or questions you could use to approach your prospect. Review the material in this chapter and then pair off with another student, who will assume the role of your prospect. First, role play the telephone contact and set up an appointment to get your prospect into your store to meet with you and look at the computer. Second, role play the approach you will use when the prospect actually comes into the store. Afterward, review how well you made the approach.

CRM Application Exercise   Planning Personal Visits

CRM software allows trip planners to examine the status of prospects in the geographic area to be visited. Log on to Salesforce.com. Assume that you wish to visit prospects in the city of Bedford, Texas. Using Salesforce.com, find all the prospects in Bedford. Select the Reports tab. Select the Contact by Location report. In the Generated Report section, edit the filter to include only those accounts in Bedford. Sort the resulting report by ZIP code to plan your route by clicking on the Zip Code field. After arranging by phone to visit these people, the salesperson can print the information contained in these records and take them along. Click Printable View and print the report. You should now have printed information about all customers in Bedford. Salespeople today use the Internet to schedule trip transportation and lodging, and to check the weather forecast. Using the Search bar, search for any one of the accounts in Bedford. Select the account record for that account from the search results. Click on the "Map" link to find this account on an Internet map.

Reality Selling Today Video Case Problem

The global construction industry is a lucrative market, with customer needs ranging from measuring products to sophisticated construction solutions. Hilti, the company featured in the vignette at the start of this chapter, provides its customers around the world with leading-edge construction products and services with outstanding added value. Hilti prides itself on its direct sales model, which allows its salespeople and service teams to work directly *with* and *for* the customers.

Alim Hirani, an account manager for Hilti, adopts the relationship marketing approach in his selling strategy. He often starts his sales calls, which have been carefully planned, with ice breakers such as asking about the customer's family rather than making the sale immediately. His sales presentations may take place in clients' offices or even at construction sites. Consequently, he must always plan well in advance the best way to make his sales presentations for specific sales calls. At all times, he must attempt to establish his own and his company's credibility by demonstrating the premium value that Hilti's products and services can offer his clients. Whenever possible, Alim tries to get the customer involved in product demonstration "because, after all, 'seeing is believing.'" Once the customers see for themselves the benefits of Hilti's product features, moving the customers from the investigation and evaluation stages to the action stage is just a formality.

Alim sells not only individually but also as part of a team. For major clients who require a complete package of building/construction, mechanical/electrical, telecom, and interior finishing products and services, Alim works closely with his team members to make sure the information he acquires from the customer during initial contacts is made available to other salespeople and technical personnel of the team. In the construction industry, closing the sale is—most of the time—just the beginning. Well-trained product application specialists join Alim to offer customers after-sales services, technical support, and training.

Questions

1. Why should Alim Hirani adopt the three prescriptions for the presentation strategy?

2. Salespeople are encouraged to establish multiple-objective sales presentations. What are some objectives Alim Hirani should consider when he calls on construction foremen at the construction site?

3. What are some special challenges Alim Hirani faces when he makes his sales presentations in a non-office setting?

4. Put yourself in the position of a construction salesperson. Can you envision a situation when you might combine different ways to convert the prospect's attention and interests into action? Explain.

CRM Case Study Establishing Your Approach

Becky Kemley, your sales manager at SimNet Systems, has notified Pat Silva's former prospects by letter that you will be calling on them soon. She wants to meet with you tomorrow to discuss your preapproach to your new prospects. Review the records in the Salesforce.com database.

Questions

1. Becky wants you to call on Robert Kelly. Describe what your call objectives will be with Mr. Kelly.

2. Describe a possible topic of your social contact with Mr. Kelly and how you would convert it into a buying contact.

3. Becky has given you a reprint of a new article about using networks for warehouse applications. Which of your prospects might have a strong interest in this kind of article? How would you use this article to make an approach to that prospect?

Partnership Selling: A Role Play/Simulation

Developing a Relationship Strategy

Visit the role play/simulation materials provided in the Student Resources section of your companion Web site at **www.pearsoned.ca/manning**. *A Contents page lists appropriate page references for the activities.*

Read *Employment Memorandum 2*, which announces your promotion to account executive. In your new position you will be assigned by your instructor to one of the two major account categories in the convention centre market. You will be assigned to either the *association accounts market* or the *corporate accounts market*. The association accounts market includes customers who are responsible for planning meetings for their association or group. The corporate accounts market includes customers who are responsible for planning meetings for the company they represent. You will remain in the account category for the rest of the role plays.

Note the challenges you will have in your new position. Each of these challenges will be represented in the future *sales memoranda* you will be receiving from your sales manager.

Read *Sales Memorandum 1* for the account category you are assigned. (Note that "A" means association and your customer is Erin Adkins, and "B" means corporate and your customer is Leigh Combs.) Follow the instructions in the sales memorandum and strategically prepare to approach your new customer. Your call objectives will be to establish a relationship (social contact), share an appealing benefit, and find out if your customer is planning any future conventions (business contact).

You will be asked to assume the role of a customer in the account category that you are not assigned as a salesperson. Your instructor will provide you with detailed instructions for correctly assuming this role.

Chapter 14
Creating the Consultative Sales Presentation

Learning Objectives

After studying this chapter, you should be able to

1 Describe the characteristics of the consultative sales presentation

2 Discuss the use of questions to determine needs

3 Select solutions that match customer needs

4 List and describe three types of need-satisfaction presentation strategies

5 Present general guidelines for creating value-added presentations

 Adaptive Selling Today Training Video Series

The effective use of questions is the starting point of the consultative sales presentation. Questions are also used in building adaptive-style selling relationships, and understanding and adapting product solutions that meet the needs of customers. Questions span the entire sales process and are also used to successfully negotiate, close, and service a sale.

Questions, Questions, Questions,[1] the second video in our Adaptive Selling Today Training Video Series, introduces and shows how to use the four adaptive selling today questions described in this chapter. A top-producing Internet telephone systems sales representative, featured in the video, learns one of his largest accounts may be going with another supplier.

Our salesperson's company has brought in a new sales training program on how to use questions effectively, and our salesperson is the first to learn the system. With his newly acquired knowledge and skill on the use of questions, our salesperson schedules another call to see if he can, with the use of questions, re-establish his relationship and salvage the sale.

In this follow-up call, we find out how well he has learned to adapt and use questions to discover and better understand the customer's needs, create value, and solve the customer's buying problem. Throughout the three part video, our salesperson learns about the following questions and what these questions reveal during the sales presentation.

In the Adaptive Selling Today Training Video, Johnny, our Internet telephone systems salesperson, finds out he may be losing one of his top accounts. After learning about the strategic use of questions throughout the sales process, he schedules another appointment to apply what he has learned and hopefully better meet his customer's needs.

SURVEY questions	*reveal*	CUSTOMER PROBLEMS
PROBING questions	*reveal*	CUSTOMER PAIN
NEED-SATISFACTION questions	*reveal*	CUSTOMER PLEASURE
CONFIRMATION questions	*reveal*	MUTUAL UNDERSTANDING

The use of an effective questioning strategy, so important to the consultative sales process, is one of the greatest challenges facing salespeople.

THE CONSULTATIVE SALES PRESENTATION

A GROWING NUMBER OF SALESPEOPLE, LIKE JOHNNY, OUR INTERNET TELEPHONE systems salesperson pictured above, have adopted the consultative sales presentation (Fig. 14.1). Consultative selling, as introduced in Chapter 5, involves meeting customer needs by asking the right questions, listening to customers, understanding—and caring about—their problems, selecting the appropriate solution, and following through after the sale. Consultative selling focuses on identification of the customer's problem and finding a solution. This approach is very different from product-oriented selling. As one author noted, "Product-oriented selling can easily lapse into product evangelism . . ." Product-oriented selling is usually inefficient and ineffective.[2] Key concepts related to creating the consultative sales presentation are featured in Figure 14.2. This approach can be used effectively in all types of selling: service, retail, wholesale, and manufacturing. It results in increased customer satisfaction, more sales, fewer cancellations and returns, more repeat business, and more referrals.

The Six-Step Presentation Plan

Step One: APPROACH	☑ Review Strategic/Consultative Selling Model ☑ Initiate customer contact
Step Two: PRESENTATION	◯ Determine prospect needs ◯ Select solution ◯ Initiate sales presentation
Step Three: DEMONSTRATION	◯ Decide what to demonstrate ◯ Select selling tools ◯ Initiate demonstration
Step Four: NEGOTIATION	◯ Anticipate buyer concerns ◯ Plan negotiating methods ◯ Initiate win-win negotiations
Step Five: CLOSE	◯ Plan appropriate closing methods ◯ Recognize closing clues ◯ Initiate closing methods
Step Six: SERVICING THE SALE	◯ Follow-through ◯ Follow-up calls ◯ Expansion selling
Service, retail, wholesale, and manufacturer selling.	

Figure 14.1 Creating the sales presentation. A consultative sales presentation involves adding value by accurately determining the prospect's needs, selecting an appropriate product or service, and initiating an effective sales presentation.

TRANSITIONING FROM THE APPROACH

As we noted in Chapter 13, an effective approach sets the stage for the sales presentation. Once you have established rapport with the prospect and captured their full attention, you are ready to transition from the approach to need identification. There is no set formula to follow during the transition, but there are two tactics commonly used by salespeople. One is to state (or restate) the purpose of your sales call: "I want to determine if your company might benefit from an innovative truck leasing plan we have developed." The second tactic involves getting permission to ask questions. You might say, "Before I describe our leasing plan, would it be all right if I ask a few questions about your current truck fleet operation?"

To be most effective, the salesperson should think of the presentation as a four-part process. The consultative sales presentation guide (Fig. 14.2) features these four parts.

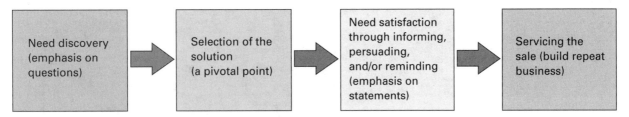

Figure 14.2 The consultative sales presentation guide. To be most successful, the salesperson should think of the sales presentation as a four-part process.

Part One—Need Discovery

A review of the behaviours displayed by high-performance salespeople helps in understanding the importance of precise need discovery. They have learned how to skillfully diagnose and solve the prospect's problems better than their competitors can. This problem-solving capability translates into more repeat business and referrals, and fewer order cancellations and returns.[3]

Unless the selling situation requires mere order taking (i.e., from customers who know exactly what they want), need discovery is a standard part of the sales presentation. It may begin during the approach, if the salesperson uses questions or a survey during the initial contact with the customer. If neither is used during the approach, need discovery begins immediately after the approach.

The pace, scope, depth of inquiry, and time allocated depend on a variety of factors, including the sophistication of the product, the selling price, the buyer's knowledge of the product, the product applications, and, of course, the time available for dialogue between the salesperson and the prospect. Each selling situation is different, so a standard set of guidelines for need discovery is not practical. Additional information on need discovery is presented later in the chapter.

Part Two—Selection of the Solution

The emphasis in sales and marketing today is on determining buyer needs and then selecting or configuring custom-fitted solutions to satisfy these needs. Therefore, an important function of the salesperson is product selection and recommendation. The salesperson must choose the product or service that will provide maximum satisfaction. When making this decision, the salesperson must be aware of all product options, including those offered by the competition.

Salespeople who have the ability to conduct an effective value-added needs analysis can achieve the status of trusted adviser. Mary is a personal shopper who works in a large department store and helps customers update their wardrobes. When asked what her days are like, she says, "It starts and ends with being a good listener." She promises her customers that she will never let them walk out of the store with clothing that does not look right.[4]

Part Three—Need Satisfaction through Informing, Persuading, or Reminding

The third part of the consultative sales presentation consists of communicating to the prospect, both verbally and nonverbally, the satisfaction that the product or service will provide. The salesperson places less emphasis on the use of questions and begins making

The sales presentation can inform, persuade, or remind.

statements. These statements are organized into a presentation that informs, persuades, or reminds the prospect of the most suitable product or service. Later in this chapter, and in several of the remaining chapters, we discuss specific strategies used in conjunction with the demonstration, negotiating buyer concerns, and closing the sale.

Part Four—Servicing the Sale

Servicing the sale is a major way to create value. These activities, which occur after closing the sale, ensure maximum customer satisfaction and set the stage for a long-term relationship. Service activities include expansion selling, making credit arrangements, following through on assurances and promises, and dealing effectively with complaints. Servicing the sale is covered in detail in Chapter 17.

In those cases where a sale is normally closed during a single sales call, the salesperson should be prepared to go through all four parts of the Consultative Sales Presentation Guide. However, when a salesperson uses a multi-call approach, preparation for all the parts is usually not practical. The person selling computer systems or investments, for example, will almost always use a multi-call sales presentation. Need discovery (part one) is the focus of the first call.

NEED DISCOVERY ACTIVITIES THAT CREATE VALUE

A LAWYER DOES NOT GIVE THE CLIENT ADVICE UNTIL THE LEGAL PROBLEM HAS BEEN carefully studied and confirmed. A doctor does not prescribe medication until the patient's symptoms have been identified. In like manner, the salesperson should not recommend purchase of a product without thorough need identification. You start with the assumption that the prospect's need or problem is not known. The only way to determine

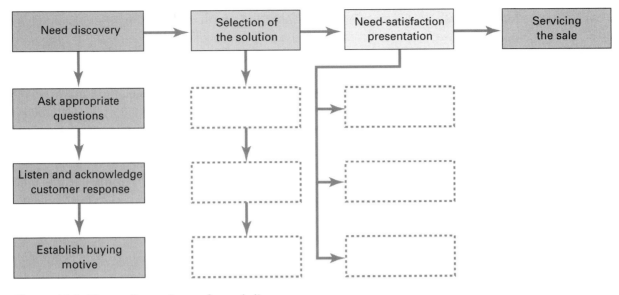

Figure 14.3 Three dimensions of need discovery

and confirm the need or problem is to get the other person talking. You must obtain information to properly clarify the need and propose either a single solution or a range of solutions.

Customers may not realize that they actually have a problem. Even when they are aware of their need, they may not realize that your company has a solution to their problem.

Need discovery (sometimes called *need analysis*) begins with precall preparation, when the salesperson is acquiring background information on the prospect. It continues once the salesperson and the prospect are engaged in a significant dialogue. Through the process of need discovery, the salesperson establishes two-way communication by asking appropriate questions and listening carefully to the prospect's responses. These responses will usually provide clues concerning the prospect's dominant buying motive (see Fig. 14.3).

need discovery The salesperson establishes two-way communication by asking appropriate questions and listening carefully to the customer's responses.

Asking Questions

The effective use of questions to achieve need identification and need satisfaction is the single greatest challenge facing most professional salespeople. The types of questions you ask, the timing of those questions, and how you pose them will greatly affect your ability to create customer value. According to research on over 35 000 salespeople by Neil Rackham, author of *Spin Selling*, mastering the use of questions can increase one's success in sales by 17 percent.[5] Questions help clarify the exact dimensions of the problem, help the customer evaluate a range of solutions, and assist the customer in evaluating the potential outcome of the solution that is implemented.[6]

In every selling situation we want the prospect to be actively thinking, sharing thoughts, and asking questions. Until the person begins to talk freely, the salesperson will have difficulty diagnosing and solving the customer's problems. A well-planned sales

Table 14.1 Types of Questions Used in Conjunction with Consultative Selling

(*Note:* Salesperson selling fractional ownership of a jet aircraft to a well-known golf professional on the Professional Golf Association (PGA) Tour who is currently using commercial air travel)

Type of Question	Definition	When Used	Example
Survey	Discovers basic facts about buyer's existing situation and problem	Usually at the beginning of a sale	"Can you describe the problems you experience travelling to each of the pro golf tournaments?"
Probing	Designed to uncover and clarify the prospect's buying problem and the circumstances surrounding the problem	When you feel the need to obtain more specific information to fully understand the problem	"Are the travel problems affecting your concentration when you are preparing for the event?"
Confirmation	Used throughout the sales process to verify the accuracy and assure a mutual understanding of information exchanged by the salesperson and buyer	After important information has been exchanged	"So, you think the uncertainty associated with commercial air travel is having some effect on your game?"
Need-Satisfaction	Designed to move the sales process toward commitment and action	When you change the focus from the problem to a discussion of the solution	"With fractional ownership of your own jet, what personal benefits would this bring to your performance in the 30 tournaments you play each year?"

presentation includes a variety of preplanned questions (Table 14.1) and questions that are formulated spontaneously during the sales presentation. We describe the four most common types of questions used in the field of personal selling.

Survey Questions Reveal Problems

At the beginning of most sales presentations, there is a need to collect information about the buyer's existing situation and problem. A **survey question**—or *information-gathering question*, as survey questions are sometimes called—is designed to obtain this knowledge. To accomplish this, there are two types of survey questions: general and specific.

A **general survey question** can help the salesperson discover facts about the buyer's existing situation and are often the first step in the partnership-building process. Here is a sampling of general information-gathering questions that can be used in selected selling fields:

"I understand that your regional facilities don't necessarily use the same delivery carriers, is that correct?" (*Shipping service*)

"Tell me about the challenges you are facing in the area of data storage." (*File server*)

survey question A question used to help the salesperson collect information about the buyer's existing situation and problem.

general survey question A question used early in the sales presentation to help the salesperson discover facts about the buyer's existing situation.

"What is your current rate of employee turnover?" (*Customer service training*)

"Can you provide me with information on the kinds of meetings and conventions you plan for your clients and employees?" (*Hotel convention services*)

"Can you describe the style of home furnishings you prefer?" (*Retail home furnishings*)

In most selling situations, general survey questions are followed by specific survey questions.

A **specific survey question** is designed to give prospects a chance to describe in more detail a problem, issue, or dissatisfaction from their point of view. These questions, sometimes referred to as *problem questions*, give you an opportunity to delve more deeply into the customer's buying situation. Five examples of specific survey questions follow:

"Has it occurred to you that by not consolidating your shipping with one carrier, you're likely spending more than is really necessary?" (*Shipping service*)

"How do you feel about installing another server to your system?" (*File server*)

"To what extent is employee turnover affecting your customer service?" (*Customer service training*)

"What meal function features are most important to your guests?" (*Hotel convention services*)

"Are you looking for an entertainment centre that blends in with the existing furniture you have?" (*Retail home furnishings*)

Survey questions, general or specific, should not be used to collect factual information that can be acquired from other sources prior to the sales call. The preapproach information-gathering effort is especially important when the salesperson is involved in a large or complex sale. These buyers expect the salesperson to do his or her homework and to not waste the buyer's time discussing basic factual information that is available from other sources.

Although survey questions are most often used at the beginning of the sales presentation, they can also be used at other times. Information gathering may be necessary at any time during the sales presentation. We present the four types of questions in a sequence that has proven to be effective in most selling situations. However, it would be a mistake to view this sequence as a *rigid* plan for every sales presentation.

A good salesperson and a good doctor have one thing in common: They encourage questions.

Table 14.2 Need Discovery Worksheet

Preplanned questions—sometimes used in conjunction with preprinted forms—are often used in service, retail, wholesale, and manufacturer selling. Salespeople, such as Johnny in the *Questions, Questions, Questions* video, who use the consultative approach frequently record answers to their questions and use this information to correctly select and recommend solutions in subsequent calls in their multi-call sales situations. Open and closed questions used in the area of financial services appear in the following list.

Preplanned Questions to Discover Buying Motives	Customer Response
1. "Now, as I understand it, you're currently pursuing an Internet phone system to offset your high cellular costs?"	*(Closed/General Survey)*
2. "Are you aware that with the system you are currently using, your brokers may have to keep their laptops on in order to make and receive Internet calls?"	*(Closed/Specific Survey)*
3. "So what happens if, say, your broker is waiting for an important return call and then inadvertently logs off his or her laptop without a way to roll over the client's return call into a centralized system?"	*(Open/Probing)*
4. "Let's see if WE understand this—the brokers won't support the system you're considering because it doesn't include instant messaging? And since the brokers would be the primary users of the new system, you're concerned that the system will fail without their support. Is that correct?"	*(Closed/Summary-Confirmation)*
5. "What if we could develop a communications system for you that included I.M. and met the SEC requirements? What positive impact could that have on your situation?"	*(Open/Need-Satisfaction)*

High-performing salespeople spend time strategically preparing questions that might prove useful before they make the sales call. The worksheet in Table 14.2 provides some examples of planned questions. Note that both open and closed questions are listed. An **open question** requires the prospect to go beyond a simple yes or no response. A **closed question** can be answered with yes or no or with a brief response.

Open questions are very effective in certain selling situations because they provoke thoughtful and insightful answers. The specific survey question "What are the biggest challenges you face in the area of plant security?" focuses the prospect's attention on problems that need solutions. Closed questions, however, can be equally effective when the sales conversation needs to be narrowed or focused on a specific issue. The question "Is your security concern primarily in the area of inventory control?" narrows the focus to a more specific problem.

Probing Questions Reveal Customer's Pain

Early in the sales process, the salesperson should make every effort to fully understand the buying problem and the consequences surrounding the problem. This is especially important when the problem is difficult to describe, the solution is complex, or the potential impact of a wrong decision is enormous.[7] A **probing question** helps you to uncover and

open question A question that requires the prospect to respond with more than just a yes or no response.

closed question A question that can be answered with yes or no or a brief response.

probing question A question that helps the salesperson to uncover and clarify the prospect's buying problem and the circumstances surrounding the problem.

clarify the prospect's buying problem and the circumstances surrounding the problem. Probing questions are used more frequently in large, complex sales. They often uncover the current level of customer concern, fear, or pain related to the problem. The following probing questions, sometimes referred to as *implication* questions in Rackham's *Spin Selling* (see Selling Today on page 300), are more focused than the survey questions presented earlier:

> "But doesn't every incorrect label cost you to ship to an incorrect address, then cost you again to have it shipped back to you?" (*Shipping service*)

> "What would the consequences be if you choose to do nothing about your current server situation?" (*File server*)

> "How does senior management feel about employee turnover and the related customer service problem?" (*Customer service training*)

> "Is poor service at the meal function negatively affecting the number of people returning to your seminar?" (*Hotel convention services*)

> "Is it important that you have easy access for connecting your DVD, TiVo, and wireless LAN network? (*Retail home furnishings*)

Probing questions help the salesperson and the prospect reach a mutual understanding of *why* a problem is important. Asking appropriate specific probing questions requires extensive knowledge of your company's capabilities, detailed insight into your customer's buying problem, and a great deal of practice.

The best sales presentations are characterized by active dialogue. As the sales process progresses, the customer becomes more open and shares perceptions, ideas, and feelings freely. A series of appropriate probing questions stimulates the prospect to discover things that he or she has not considered before.

Confirmation Questions Reveal Mutual Understanding

A **confirmation question** can be used throughout the sales process to verify the accuracy and assure a mutual understanding of information exchanged by the salesperson and the buyer (see Table 14.1). These questions help determine if there is mutual understanding of the problems and circumstances the prospect is experiencing. Throughout the sales process there is always the potential for a breakdown in communication. Perhaps the language used by the salesperson is too technical. Maybe the prospect is preoccupied and has not listened closely to what has been said. Many confirmation questions are simple and to the point.

> "If I understand you correctly, the monitoring system must be set up at both your corporate headquarters and the manufacturing operation. Is that correct?" (*File server*)

> "I want to be sure I am clear that you feel there is a direct relationship between employee turnover and the problem that exists in customer service." (*Customer service training*)

> "Did you say your seminar attendance dropped 12 percent last year?" (*Hotel convention services*)

> "So you want a new entertainment centre that blends with your current light-coloured oak furniture?" (*Retail home furnishings*)

confirmation question A question used throughout the sales process to verify the accuracy and assure a mutual understanding of information exchanged by the salesperson and the buyer.

buying condition A qualification that must be available or fulfilled before the sale can be closed.

The length of the sales process can vary from a few minutes during a single-call presentation to several weeks in a complex multi-call sales presentation. As the sales process progresses, the amount of information available to the salesperson and the customer increases. As the need discovery progresses, the customer's buying criteria or conditions surface. A **buying condition** is a qualification that must be available or fulfilled before the sale can be closed. The customer may buy only if the product is available in a certain colour or can be delivered by a certain date. In some selling situations, product installation and service after the sale are considered important buying conditions by the customer. In a large, complex sale, several buying conditions may surface. The salesperson has the responsibility of clarifying and confirming each condition.

summary confirmation question A question used to clarify and confirm buying conditions.

One of the best ways to clarify and confirm buying conditions is with a **summary confirmation question**. To illustrate, let us consider a situation in which Laura Feng, sales manager at a major hotel, has interviewed a prospect who wants to schedule a large awards banquet. After a series of survey, probing, and confirmation questions, Laura feels confident she has collected enough information to prepare a proposal. However, to be sure that she has all the facts and has clarified all of the important buying conditions, she asks the following *summary confirmation question*:

> "Let me summarize the major items you have mentioned. You want all of the banquet attendees served within an eight-minute time frame after the opening speaker has finished his speech? And you need a room that will comfortably seat 60 persons banquet-style, and 10 of these persons will be seated at the head table. Is this correct?"

Once all the buying conditions are confirmed, Laura can prepare a proposal that reflects the specific needs of her customer. The result is a win-win situation for the customer and the salesperson. The chances of closing the sale greatly improve. In multi-call sales processes, it is wise to begin subsequent calls with summary confirmation questions that re-establish what was discussed during the previous call(s):

> "Let me begin by going over what we discussed in our last visit. Your current shipper gives you a 50 percent discount and provides their own custom label printer?"

If the customer responds in the affirmative, the salesperson continues with another summary-confirmation question.

> "You also have to buy fairly expensive custom labels, and at around $90 a pack, you're spending over $20 000 just on labels, is that still correct?"

This enables the salesperson to verify that the previously discovered buying conditions have remained the same and not changed since the last meeting.

Need-Satisfaction Questions Reveal Pleasure

need-satisfaction question A question designed to move the sales process toward commitment and action by helping to clarify the problem in the prospect's mind and by building a desire for your solution.

The fourth type of question used in the sales process is fundamentally different from the other three. A **need-satisfaction question** is designed to move the sales process toward commitment and action. These are helpful questions that focus on the solution. The chances of closing the sale greatly improve because *need-satisfaction questions*—or, as they are sometimes called, *solution* or *pleasure* questions—focus on specific benefits and build desire for a solution.

Survey, probing, and confirmation questions focus on understanding and clarifying the customer's problem. Need-satisfaction questions help the prospect see how your product or service provides a solution to the problem you have uncovered. The opportunity to close the sale greatly improves because you have cast the solution in a pleasurable light.

In most cases, need-satisfaction questions are used after the salesperson has created awareness of the seriousness of the buyer's problem. The questions you ask will offer relief from his or her current levels of concern, pain, or frustration with pleasurable thoughts about a solution. The following examples provide insight into the use of need-satisfaction questions:

> "And if I told you that I can offer you cost savings of at least 5 percent over your current shipping expenses, would that be meaningful?" (*Shipping service*)

> "Tests on similar applications show a new file server can increase data storage by 30 to 40 percent. How much do you feel you would achieve?" (*File server*)

In many selling situations a product demonstration is an essential stage in the sales process. In this case, the salesperson might use the following need-satisfaction question:

> "What benefits would you see if we provided a demonstration of one of our training modules to senior management so they can understand what you and I have discovered about reducing employee turnover?" (*Customer service training*)

Once the prospect's needs are clearly identified, need-satisfaction questions can be valuable closing tools. Consider these examples:

> "Considering the benefits we have summarized and agreed on, and noting the fact that our staff will deliver an outstanding meal function, would you like to sign this confirmation so we can reserve the rooms and schedule the meals that you need?" (*Hotel convention services*)

This real estate salesperson, with the help of a computerized database of homes, is using probing and confirmation questions to clarify the needs of the customer.

Questions, Questions, Everywhere

The use of questions to discover needs and present solutions is discussed in several popular personal selling books. For comparison purposes, the approximate equivalents to the four types of questions described in this chapter are listed.

Selling Today by Manning, Reece, Ahearne, and MacKenzie	The Spin Selling Fieldbook by Rackham	The New Solution Selling by Eades	The New Conceptual Selling by Heiman, Sanchez, with Tuleja	Secrets of Question Based Selling by Freese
Survey	Situation	Open	Confirmation	Status
Probing	Problem	Control	New Information	Issue
Confirmation	Implication	Confirming	Attitude	Implication
Need-Satisfaction	Need-Payoff		Commitment	Solution
			Basic Issue	

The questions above are listed in the sequence presented by the authors. To determine the exact definition of each type of question, check the source.

Need-satisfaction questions, such as the previous examples, are very powerful because they build desire for the solution and give ownership of the solution to the prospect. When the prospect understands which parts of the problem(s) your solution can solve, you are less likely to invite objections. In some cases, you may identify problems that still need to be clarified. When this happens, you can use survey, probing, or confirmation questions to obtain more information.

At this point you have received only a basic introduction to the four most common types of questions used during the selling process. (For more insight into the application of questions to the sales process, view the three videos in the "Questions, Questions, Questions" series referred to in this chapter's opening vignette. Also refer to the video role-play exercises on pages 313–314.) We will revisit these important sales tools later in this chapter and in Chapters 15, 16, and 17.

Listening to and Acknowledging the Customer's Response

To fully understand the prospect, a salesperson must listen closely to and acknowledge every response. The authors of *First Impressions* offer these words of advice to salespeople who use questions as part of the need discovery process: "What you do after you ask a question can reveal even more about you than the questions you ask. You reveal your true level of interest in the way you listen."[8] Most of us are born with the ability to hear, but we have to learn how to listen. The starting point is developing a listening attitude. Always regard the prospect as worthy of your respect and full attention.

Selling a Product That Doesn't Exist

Some creative entrepreneurs start selling their product before it even exists. Greg Gianforte wanted to start an Internet-software company in the late 1990s. He noted that no one seemed to be making a good product that would help companies respond to e-mail from customers. Armed with a product feature sheet, Gianforte started trying to sell a nonexistent product. He called customer-support managers at hundreds of companies. After reviewing the product features, he explained that the product would be ready in 90 days. Some of these potential customers mentioned features he had not thought of. This input helped him develop a better product. After two weeks of cold calls, he knew exactly what customers wanted and began the development of RightNow software. It was ready for customer use in 90 days. He then hired his first three employees—all of them salespeople. Gianforte says, "Sales is really the most noble part of the business because it's the part that brings the solution together with the customer's need." Today, more than 1200 organizations worldwide use RightNow solutions.[a]

Once you have made a commitment to becoming a good listener, develop active listening skills.

Developing Active Listening Skills

Active listening is the process of feeding back to the prospect what you as a listener think the person meant, in terms of both content and feelings. Active listening requires intense involvement as you concentrate on what you are hearing, exhibit your listening attitude through your nonverbal messages (see Chapter 7), and feed back to the prospect what you think he or she meant.[9] Developing active listening skills involves three practices that can be learned by any salesperson willing to make the commitment:

active listening The process of feeding back to the prospect what you as a listener think the person meant, in terms of both content and feelings. It involves taking into consideration and exhibiting both verbal and nonverbal messages.

- *Focus your full attention.* This is not easy because the delivery of the messages we hear is often much slower than our capacity to listen. Thus, we have plenty of time to let our minds roam, to think ahead, and to plan what we are going to say next. Our senses are constantly feeding us new information while someone is trying to tell us something. Staying focused is often difficult and involves use of both verbal and nonverbal messages.[10] To show that you are paying attention, lean toward the prospect while murmuring "uh-huh," "okay," or "I understand," and nod in agreement when appropriate. Avoid nodding rapidly or saying "uh-huh" loudly or frequently because this will communicate impatience or a desire to turn the conversation back to yourself.[11]

    During every sales presentation there will be times when silence should be welcomed. Use silence to control the flow of information and draw out the customer. Customers are often inclined to fill silence by talking. Throughout an effective sales presentation the customer should be talking more than the salesperson.[12]

- *Paraphrase the prospect's meaning.* After the prospect stops talking, pause for two or three seconds and then state in your own words what you think the person meant. This technique not only helps ensure understanding but also is an effective relationship-building strategy. The prospect feels good knowing that not only are you listening to what has been said but you are making an effort to ensure accuracy. In addition to

In many selling situations, note-taking will demonstrate a high level of professionalism.

paraphrasing the content, use questions to dig for full understanding of the customer's perceptions.[13] The use of survey or probing questions is appropriate any time you need to clarify what is being said by the prospect.

- *Take notes.* Although note-taking is not necessary in every sales presentation, it is important in complex sales where the information obtained from the prospect is critical to the development of a buying solution. Taking notes is a good way to demonstrate to the prospect that you are actively listening. When you take notes, you increase your memory of what was heard. Your notes should be brief and to the point.[14] If the information you receive from the customer is too technical or unfamiliar, do not hesitate to ask for clarification of information you don't understand.

Customer Relationship Management with Technology

Reviewing Account Status

Salespeople regularly review the status of their prospects' records in their CRM databases. In some cases, this is done on the computer screen. In other situations, a printed copy of the records can enhance the process.

Salespeople review their files to ascertain at what phase in the Consultative Sales Presentation Guide each prospect is in the sales cycle. Then they will decide which action to take to help move the prospect to the next phase. Sales managers can be helpful with this process, especially for new salespeople. Managers can help salespeople evaluate the available information and suggest strategies designed to move to the next phase.

Even experienced salespeople count on their sales managers to help plan presentations. Managers can help salespeople evaluate their prospects' needs, select the best solution, and plan a presentation most likely to succeed. (See the exercise Printing the Customer Database on page 314 for more information.)

Establishing Buying Motives

The primary goal of questioning, listening, and acknowledging is to uncover prospect needs and establish buying motives. Our efforts to discover prospect needs will be more effective if a salesperson focuses his or her questioning on determining the prospect's primary reasons for buying. When a prospect has a definite need, it is usually supported by specific buying motives.

The greatest time investment in personal selling is on the front end of the sales process. First you must plan the sales call and then, once you are face-to-face with the customer, you can begin the need-discovery stage. It is during the early stage of the sales process that you can create the greatest value for the customer.[15]

SELECTING SOLUTIONS THAT ADD VALUE

THE SECOND PART OF THE CONSULTATIVE SALES PRESENTATION CONSISTS OF SELECTING OR creating a solution that satisfies the prospect's buying motives. After identifying the buying motives, the salesperson carefully reviews the available product options. At this point, the salesperson is searching for a specific solution to satisfy the prospect's buying motives. Once the solution has been selected, the salesperson makes a recommendation to the prospect (see Fig. 14.4).

If the sale involves several needs and the satisfaction of multiple buying motives, selection of the solution may take several days or even weeks and involve the preparation of a detailed sales proposal. A company considering the purchase of automated office equipment would likely present this type of challenge to the salesperson. The problem needs careful analysis before a solution can be identified.

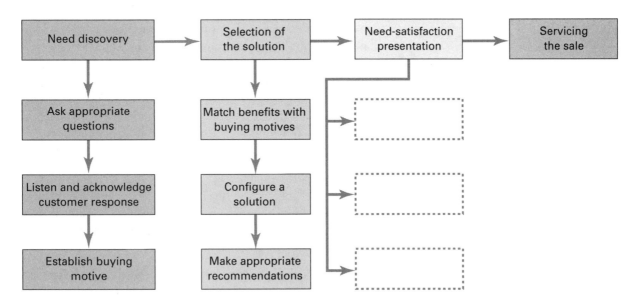

Figure 14.4 Three dimensions of product selection

Match Specific Benefits with Buying Motives

As we noted in Chapter 10, products and services represent problem-solving tools. People buy products when they perceive that they fulfill a need. We also noted that today's more demanding customers seek a cluster of satisfactions that arise from the product itself, from the company that makes or distributes the product, and from the salesperson who sells and services the product. Tom Reilly, author of *Value-Added Selling*, says "Value-added salespeople sell three things: the product, the company, and themselves. This is the three-dimensional bundle of value."[16] When possible, the salesperson should focus on benefits related to each dimension of value. Of course, it is a mistake to make benefit statements that do not relate to the specific needs of the customer. High-performance salespeople present benefits that are precisely tailored to the customer's needs. Benefits that are not relevant to the customer's needs waste time and may invite objections.[17]

Configure a Solution

Most salespeople bring to the sale a variety of products or services. Salespeople who represent food distributors can offer customers a mix of several hundred items. Most pharmaceutical sales representatives can offer the medical community a wide range of products. Best Buy, a large retailer of electronics, offers customers a wide range of audio and visual entertainment options. The customer who wants to purchase a sound system, for example, can choose from many combinations of receivers, speakers, and other equipment.

Make Appropriate Recommendations

The recommendation strategies available to salespeople are similar to those used by a doctor who must recommend a solution to a patient's medical problem. In the medical field, three possibilities for providing patient satisfaction exist. In situations in which the patient easily understands the medical problem and the appropriate treatment, the doctor can make a recommendation and the patient can proceed immediately toward well-being. If the patient does not easily understand the medical problem or solution, the doctor may need to discuss thoroughly with the patient the benefits of the recommended treatment. If the medical problem is not within his or her medical specialty area, the doctor may recommend a specialist to provide the treatment. In consultative selling, the salesperson has these same three counselling alternatives.

Recommend Solution—Prospect Buys Immediately　The selection and recommendation of a product to meet the prospect's needs may occur at the beginning of the sales call, such as in the product approach; during the presentation, just after the need discovery; or near the end, when minor resistance has been negotiated. At any of these three opportunities, presentation of a solution that is well matched to the prospect's needs may result in an immediate purchase.

Recommend Solution—Salesperson Makes Need-Satisfaction Presentation　This alternative requires a presentation of product benefits, including demonstrations and negotiating resistance, before the sale is closed. In this situation, the prospect may not be totally aware of a buying problem, and the solution may not be easily

CARQUEST Auto Parts (**www.carquest.ca**) promises to deliver what customers need. To achieve this lofty goal, the company enrolled its 1200 outside sales force members in *Action Selling*. A major objective of this sales training program is to help salespeople become trusted business consultants. They learned that asking—not telling—is the key to sales success. Emphasis throughout the course is placed on asking more and better questions. Duane Sparks, who developed *Action Selling*, says "The success rate of sales calls rises significantly when more than two specific customer needs are uncovered by questioning."[b]

understood or apparent. The salesperson will need to make a detailed presentation to define the problem and communicate a solution to the customer.

Recommend Another Source   Earlier in this book, we indicated that professional salespeople may recommend that a prospect buy a product or service from another source, maybe even a competitor. If, after a careful needs assessment, the salesperson concludes that the products represented will not satisfy the customer's needs, the consultative salesperson should recommend another source.

Paul Roos, a sales representative for Hewlett-Packard, once met with a customer who wanted to buy a newly introduced HP product for an application where it would not work. Paul explained why the product was unsuitable and then took time to configure a competing product to meet the customer's needs. He lost that sale to a competitor, but the assistance provided confirmed his integrity and made a lasting impression on the customer. That customer later became a high-value account.[18]

NEED SATISFACTION—SELECTING A PRESENTATION STRATEGY

DECISIONS CONCERNING WHICH PRESENTATION STRATEGY TO EMPHASIZE HAVE become more complex because of several factors discussed in previous chapters: longer sales cycles, multiple buying influences, emphasis on repeat sales and referrals, greater emphasis on custom-fitting solutions, and building of long-term partnerships. Conducting business in the new economy, which is based on the assets of knowledge and information, requires that we think about ways to improve the sales presentation. Here is how one author described this challenge:

> "As we move from the rutted byways of the Industrial Age to the electronic thoroughfares of the Information Age, business presentations become a measure of our ability to adapt to new surroundings. The most successful and forward-thinking companies already have assigned presentations a new, fundamental and strategic importance."[19]

The need-satisfaction strategy involves assessing the prospect's needs; selecting the solution; and deciding whether to use an informative, persuasive, or reminder presentation (Fig. 14.5).

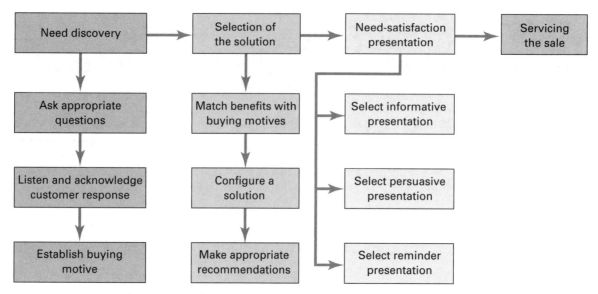

Figure 14.5 The three strategies to use in developing an effective need-satisfaction presentation

Informative Presentation Strategy

To be informative, a message must be clearly understood by the prospect. Of course, clarity is important in any presentation, but it needs special attention in a presentation in which the primary purpose is to inform. The **informative presentation** emphasizes factual information typically taken from technical reports, company-prepared sales literature, or written testimonials from persons who have used the product. This strategy emphasizes clarity, simplicity, and directness. Salespeople need to keep in mind the "less is more" concept. Too often the prospect is given far too much information and detail.[20]

Persuasive Presentation Strategy

Many salespeople believe that when a real need for their product exists, the stage is set for a persuasive presentation. The major goals of the **persuasive presentation** are to influence the prospect's beliefs, attitudes, or behaviour, and to encourage buyer action. Persuasive sales presentations include a subtle transition stage where the dialogue shifts from an intellectual emphasis to an emotional appeal. Every buying decision is influenced by both reason and emotion, but the amount of weight given to each of these elements during the decision-making process can vary greatly depending on the prospect.[21]

In the field of personal selling, persuasion is an acceptable strategy once a need has been identified and a suitable product has been selected. When it is clear that the buyer will benefit from ownership of the product or service, an enthusiastic and persuasive sales presentation is usually appropriate. The persuasive presentation strategy requires a high level of training and experience to be effective, because a poorly planned and delivered persuasive presentation may raise the prospect's anxiety level. The persuasive presentation, when handled properly, does not trigger fear or distrust.

Reminder Presentation Strategy

Studies show that awareness of a company's products and services declines as promotion is stopped. This problem represents one of the reasons many companies employ *missionary* salespeople to maintain an ongoing awareness of and familiarity with their product lines. Other types of salespeople also use this strategy by delivering a **reminder presentation** (sometimes called a *reinforcement presentation*). Route salespeople rely heavily on reminder presentations to maintain their market share. They know that if they do not make frequent calls and remind customers of their products, customers may turn to the competition.

The reminder presentation is sometimes a dimension of service after the sale (see Chapter 17). Sales personnel working with repeat customers are in a good position to remind them of products or services offered in their own department or another department located in some other area of the business. Some products require special care and maintenance. Busy customers may need to be reminded of the maintenance services offered by your company. In some cases, the service department is a major profit generator, so reminder calls need to be given a high priority.

Some customers get used to the great quality and service you provide and begin to view your product as a commodity. Once this happens, the customer may ask for a price reduction. To keep customers focused on value rather than price, remind them (from time to time) of the value-added services you provide.[22]

DEVELOPING A PERSUASIVE PRESENTATION THAT CREATES VALUE

THERE ARE MANY WAYS TO INCORPORATE PERSUASION INTO A SALES PRESENTATION. In this section we review a series of guidelines that should be followed during preparation of a persuasive presentation.

Place Special Emphasis on the Relationship

Throughout this book we have emphasized the importance of the relationship strategy in selling. Good rapport between the salesperson and the prospect establishes a foundation for an open exchange of information. Robert Cialdini, writing in the *Harvard Business Review*, says the science of persuasion is built on the principle of liking: *People like those who like them.* Establish a bond with the prospect early by uncovering areas of common interest, using praise when it's appropriate, and being completely trustworthy.[23] Don't forget to adapt your communication style to accommodate the needs of the customer (see Chapter 8).

Sell Specific Benefits and Obtain Customer Reactions

People do not buy things; they buy what the things will do for them. They do not buy an auto battery; they buy a sure start on a cold morning. Office managers do not buy laser printers; they buy better-looking letters and reports. Every product or service offers the prospect certain benefits. The benefit might be greater comfort, security, a feeling of confidence, or economy.

If you are selling Allstate insurance, for example, you should become familiar with the service features. One feature is well-trained employees, and another is the convenient location of Allstate offices throughout Canada. The benefit to customers is greater peace of mind in knowing that they will receive good service at a nearby location. Allstate salespeople understand the importance of selling the company, the product, and themselves.

After you state the feature and convert it into a buyer benefit, obtain a reaction from the customer by using confirmation or need-satisfaction questions (refer to Table 14.1). You should always check to see if you are on the right track and if your prospect is following the logic of your presentation. Here are some examples:

Feature	Benefit	Question
Seven-hour battery life*	Fewer work interruptions when travelling	"Battery life is important to you, isn't it?" (*Confirmation question*)
Automatic climate control system for automobile	Temperature in car not varying after initial setting	"Would you like the luxury of setting the temperature and then not worrying about it?" (*Need-satisfaction question*)

*Feature of Fujitsu Lifebook laptop

The feature–benefit–reaction (FBR) approach is used by many high-performance salespeople. Involving the customer with appropriate questions helps you maintain two-way communication.

Minimize the Negative Impact of Change

As we noted earlier, salespeople are constantly threatening the status quo. They sell people the new, the different, and the untried. In nearly all selling situations, the customer is being asked to consider change of some sort and, in some cases, it is only natural for the person to resist change. Whenever possible, salespeople should try to help the prospect view change in a positive and realistic way. Change is more acceptable to people who understand the benefits of it and do not see it as a threat. Always anticipate the one question (spoken or unspoken) that every buyer asks: "How will this product benefit me?" To minimize the impact of change, be sure to personalize the benefit with a specific reference to the customer's need.

Place the Strongest Appeal at the Beginning or End

Research indicates that appeals made at the beginning or end of a presentation are more effective than those given in the middle. A strong appeal at the beginning of a presentation will, of course, get the prospect's attention and possibly generate interest. Made near the end of the presentation, the appeal sets the stage for closing the sale.

Target Emotional Links

emotional link A connector that links a salesperson's message to the customer's emotions and increases the chances of closing a sale—for example, quality improvement, on-time delivery, service, innovation.

An **emotional link** is a connector between your messages and the prospect's emotions.[24] Some common emotional links in the business community are quality improvement, on-time delivery, increased market share, innovation, customer service, and reduction of operating expenses. Targeting just a few emotional links can increase your chances of closing the sale. When you target emotional links, use persuasive words such as *proven*, *efficient*, *save*, *convenient*, *world-class*, *new*, and *improved*. Also use the terminology to which your prospect is accustomed. Do not hesitate to present important information in a dramatic way.

Use Metaphors, Stories, and Testimonials

Metaphors, sometimes referred to as *figurative language*, are highly persuasive sales tools. Metaphors are words or phrases that suggest pictorial relationships between objects or ideas. With the aid of metaphors, you can paint vivid pictures for prospects that will command their attention and keep their interest. The success of the metaphor rests on finding common ground (i.e., shared or well-known experiences) so that your message gets a boost from a fact already known or believed to be true. A salesperson presenting Cobalt boats, a line of high-quality runabouts selling for $30 000 to $300 000, might refer to his products as "the Steinways of the runabout class."[25] Stories not only help you sell more products, they also help you enrich relationships with your customers. A good story focuses the customer's attention and can effectively communicate the value of a product or service as well. The story should be appropriate to the customer's situation, short, and told with enthusiasm.[26]

Many salespeople find it beneficial to quote a specific third party. Third-party testimonials from satisfied customers can help a prospect feel confident about using your product.

GENERAL GUIDELINES FOR CREATING VALUE-ADDED PRESENTATIONS

THERE ARE MANY WAYS TO MAKE ALL THREE NEED-SATISFACTION PRESENTATION strategies more interesting and valuable. A more effective presentation can be developed using the following general guidelines. Each of these guidelines will be discussed in more detail in Chapters 15 to 17.

Strengthen the Presentation Strategy with an Effective Demonstration

The need-satisfaction presentation can be strengthened if the salesperson preplans effective demonstrations that clarify product features and benefits. Many salespeople encounter doubt or skepticism during the sales presentation. The prospect often wants some kind of assurance or proof. If the demonstration is convincing and removes doubt from the customer's mind, you have created value.

Product itself	Graphs, charts, and test results
Models	Laptop computers and demonstration software
Photos, illustrations, and brochures	Bound paper presentations
Portfolios	Catalogues
Testimonials and case histories	
Reprints	

Preplan Methods for Negotiating and Closing the Sale

Salespeople who make the most efficient use of time are adding value. To make your presentation as concise and to the point as possible, you should preplan methods for negotiating misunderstandings or resistance that might surface during the presentation. You need to bring some degree of urgency to the selling environment by presenting focused solutions. In most cases, the focus of the negotiation is on one of the following areas:

- *Need awareness* is vague or nonexistent.
- *Price* does not equal perceived value.
- The buyer is satisfied with his or her present *source*.
- *Product* does not meet the buyer's perceived requirement.
- The *time* is not right.

Methods used to negotiate buyer resistance in each of these areas are introduced in Chapter 15. It also is important to preplan closing and confirming of the sale. This planning should include a review of closing clues that may surface during the sales presentation and methods of closing the sale. These and other topics are discussed in Chapter 16.

Preplan Customer Service Methods That Add Value

Customer service, in its many forms, provides an opportunity to add value. Very often prospects want a preview of the customer service options during the sales presentation. And, in some cases, customer service is the key to closing the sale. Consider the purchase that must be financed and where the customer expects you to be familiar with various credit options. You can add value with timely delivery of the product, proper installation, and follow-up to ensure customer satisfaction. Customer service will be discussed in detail in Chapter 17.

Keep Your Presentation Simple and Concise

The best way to achieve conciseness is to preplan your sales call. Think ahead of time about what you are going to say and do. Anticipate questions and resistance the prospect may voice, and be prepared with accurate information and concise answers.

Preplanning also involves time allocation. Figure 14.6 illustrates an ideal breakdown of time allocation between the salesperson and the prospect during all three parts of the sales presentation. In terms of involvement, the prospect assumes a greater role during the need discovery stage. As the salesperson begins the product selection process, the prospect's involvement decreases. During the need-satisfaction stage, the salesperson is doing most of the talking, but note that the prospect is never totally excluded.

In addition to preplanning the sales presentation, consider rehearsing in front of your colleagues. A less threatening approach might be to practise your presentation for your spouse or a close friend. Videotaping the rehearsal can help you see how you really look.

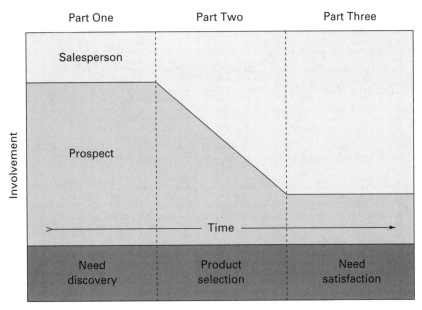

Figure 14.6 Time used by both the salesperson and the prospect during each part of the consultative sales presentation

Do you appear too stiff and motionless? Do you talk too fast or too slow? It's a good idea to practise presentations with specific customers in mind.[27]

The Consultative Sales Presentation and the Transactional Buyer

Throughout this chapter, you have been given a comprehensive introduction to the consultative sales presentation. It is important to keep in mind that the fundamentals of consultative selling must be customized to meet the individual needs of the customer. For example, some of the guidelines for developing an effective presentation must be abandoned or greatly altered when you are working with a transactional buyer. In most cases, transactional buyers understand what product they need and when they need it. The Internet has armed many transactional buyers with a great deal of information, so the salesperson who spends time asking survey questions or making a detailed informative presentation may be wasting the customer's time. Most of these buyers simply want the salesperson to configure a product solution that focuses on pricing and delivery issues.[28]

Planning and Execution—Final Thoughts

The importance of strategic planning and the execution of the sales presentation is explained in this chapter. Figure 14.7 summarizes the key concepts that must be considered during the planning and execution process. This approach can be used effectively in the four major employment settings: service, retail, wholesale, and manufacturing. It results in increased customer satisfaction, more sales, fewer cancellations and returns, more repeat business, and more referrals.

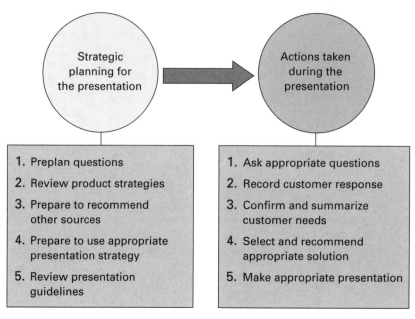

Figure 14.7 Salespeople who truly represent value to their customers plan ahead strategically for the actions taken during the presentation.

REVIEWING KEY CONCEPTS

- Describe the characteristics of the consultative sales presentation.

  A well-planned and well-executed consultative sales presentation is an important key to success in personal selling. To be most effective, the presentation should be viewed as a four-part process: need discovery; selection of the solution; need-satisfaction through informing, persuading, or reminding; and servicing the sale.

- Discuss the use of questions to determine needs.

  The most effective sales presentation is characterized by two-way communication. It should be encouraged with survey, probing, confirmation, summary-confirmation, and need-satisfaction questions. Beware of assuming information about the prospect, and be sure the language of your presentation is clearly understood. Listen attentively as the prospect responds to your questions or volunteers information. Develop active listening skills.

- Select solutions that match customer needs.

  After making a good first impression during the approach and getting the customer's full attention, the salesperson begins the presentation. The salesperson's ability is tested during this part of the sale because this is where the prospect's buying motives are established and a solution is configured.

- List and describe three types of need-satisfaction presentation strategies.

  Once you have selected a solution that matches the customer's needs, you must decide which presentation strategy to emphasize. Need satisfaction can be achieved through informing, persuading, or reminding. The salesperson can, of course, use a combination of these presentation strategies in some cases.

- Present general guidelines for creating value-added presentations.

  Effective presentations require a great deal of preplanning. Effective demonstrations, methods of negotiating and closing the sale, and customer service methods should be preplanned.

Key Terms

active listening **301**

buying condition **298**

closed question **296**

confirmation question **297**

emotional link **308**

general survey question **294**

informative presentation **306**

need discovery **293**

need-satisfaction question **298**

open question **296**

persuasive presentation **306**

probing question **296**

reminder presentation **307**

specific survey question **295**

summary confirmation question **298**

survey question **294**

Review Questions

1. List and describe the four parts of the Consultative Sales Presentation Guide.

2. List and describe the four types of questions commonly used in the selling field.

3. Define the term *buying conditions*. What are some common buying conditions?

4. Describe the process of active listening, and explain how it will improve the listening efficiency rate.

5. Discuss the dimensions of need discovery.

6. Distinguish among the three types of need-satisfaction presentation: informative, persuasive, and reminder.

7. What are the guidelines to follow when developing a persuasive sales presentation?

8. What are some advantages of using the feature–benefit–reaction (FBR) approach?

9. What is a metaphor? Why is the use of metaphors considered a persuasive sales tool?

10. Discuss how time is used by the salesperson and the customer as the consultative sales presentation proceeds.

ROLE-PLAY APPLICATION EXERCISES FOR "QUESTIONING" VIDEO SERIES

Most sales skill development exercises used in the classroom are product-oriented. As noted on page 289, "Product-oriented selling can easily lapse into product evangelism." This three-part video series on questioning focuses on the customer's buying process, consultative selling, and building high-quality partnerships.

The goal of this series is the identification and clarification of the customer's problem and finding a solution. The first video focuses on the appropriate use of survey and confirmation questions to identify the customer's problem. Video two introduces the use of probing and need-satisfaction questions. Probing questions examine and clarify the potential issues surrounding the customer's problem, while need-satisfaction questions focus the sales process on the appropriate solution. The third video demonstrates the use of these questions in a challenging, yet typical, contemporary sales setting.

The role-play exercises presented below challenge the participant to understand, apply, and integrate questioning skills presented in this chapter and in the video series. Product information for these exercises is found in "Partnership Selling: A Role Play/Simulation" online in the Student Resources section at **www.pearsoned.ca/ manning**. See pages 105 to 117. Customer information will be found in the B. H. Rivera Contact Report presented on page 117 (disregard any other information on this page). You will assume the role of a newly hired salesperson as described in the Position Description on page 105. Refer to the questioning material and examples presented on pages 292–299. Use a need discovery worksheet like the one on page 296 for developing your questions.

After viewing the video *Questions—Discovering and Confirming Customer Problems*, review the online role play/simulation material, pages 105 to 117. Refer to the

Contact Report on page 117 (as noted, disregard any other information on this page). Assume you were assigned to this account and you are meeting B. H. Rivera to inquire about additional information regarding when the meeting will be held and what audiovisual equipment might be needed. Prepare a list of general survey and specific survey questions that reveal when, during the next month, the meeting will be held and what, if any, audiovisual equipment (see pages 113–114) might be needed. Plan to use a summary-confirmation question to verify the existing four items on the Contact Sheet. Using the questions you have created, role play this part of the need-discovery process.

After viewing the video *Questions—Discovering Pain and Pleasure* and reviewing the information you prepared in the role play above, prepare three probing questions. These questions should clarify and reveal a mutual understanding of issues and consequences regarding food service, facility design, and audiovisual equipment. Also, using the information on pages 105 to 117, prepare five need-satisfaction questions that reveal how the features of your convention centre provide a solution to the buying situation. Select appropriate proof devices

to demonstrate these specific benefits. Using these questions, meet again with B. H. Rivera and role play this part of the questioning process. Prepare and use confirmation questions as the need arises.

After viewing the video *Questions—Getting it Right* and using the information in the first two role plays, prepare a need-satisfaction presentation to Cameron Rivera, a new meeting planner just hired at Graphic Forms. Cameron, a cousin of B. H., was previously employed as a training coordinator at West College. Due to extensive growth in the company, B. H. has turned all meeting planning over to Cameron. Cameron will make the final selection of a facility for the meeting described on page 117, plus 11 more identical meetings to be scheduled in the next 12 months. You have also been informed that the Marriott and Sheraton hotels will be making presentations (note the comparative room, parking, and transportation rates). You will travel to Graphic Forms to make your presentation. Prepare appropriate survey, probing, confirmation, and need-satisfaction questions and presentation strategies that will help secure this important account—then role play this presentation.

CRM Application Exercise   Printing the Customer Database

Sales managers regularly help salespeople review the status of their accounts. These strategic account review meetings often involve examining all of the information available on the salespeople's most promising prospects. The sales manager and salesperson will each have a copy of all information currently available

for the accounts either on their computer screens or on paper. To produce a paper record of the information contained in Salesforce.com, click the reports tab and select the Account Master report. Click on printable view and print the report.

Case Problem

When Deborah Karish wakes up in the morning, she does not have to worry about a long commute to work. Her office is in her home. As an Amgen (**www.amgen.com**) pharmaceutical sales representative, Deborah spends most of her day visiting hospitals, medical clinics, and doctors' offices. She spends a large part of each day serving as a consultant to doctors, head nurses, pharmacists, and others who need information and advice about the complex medical products available from her company.

As might be expected, she also spends a considerable amount of time conducting informative presentations designed to achieve a variety of objectives. In some situations, she is introducing a new product, and in other cases she is providing up-to-date information on an existing product. Some of her presentations are given to individual health care professionals, and others are given to a group. Each of these presentations must be carefully planned.

Deborah uses informative and reminder presentations almost daily in her work. Informative presentations are given to doctors who are in a position to prescribe her products. The verbal presentation often is supplemented with audiovisual aids and printed materials. Reprints of articles from leading medical journals are often used to illustrate the success of her products in treating patients. These articles give added credibility to her presentations. Some of her informative presentations are designed to give customers updates on the prescription drugs she sells. Reminder presentations are frequently given to pharmacists who must maintain an inventory of her products. She has found it necessary to periodically remind pharmacists of product delivery procedures and policies, and of special services available from Amgen. She knows that without an occasional reminder, a customer can forget information that may be important.

In some cases, a careful needs analysis is required to determine if her products can solve a specific medical problem. Each patient is different, so generalizations concerning the use of her products can be dangerous. When doctors talk about their patients, Deborah must listen carefully and take good notes. In some cases, she must get additional information from company support staff. If a customer needs immediate help with a problem, she gives the person a toll-free 1-800 number to call for expert advice. This line is an important part of the Amgen customer service program.

Deborah's career in pharmaceutical sales has required continuous learning. In the beginning she had to learn the meaning of dozens of medical terms and become familiar with a large number of medical problems. If a doctor asks, "What is the bioavailability of Neutogen?" she must know the meaning of the medical term and be knowledgeable about this Amgen product.

Deborah also spends time learning about the people with whom she works. She recently said, "If I get along with the people I work with, it makes my job a lot easier." When meeting someone for the first time, she takes time to assess his or her communication style and then adapts her own style to meet his or her needs. She points out that in some cases the competition offers a similar product at a similar price. In these situations, a good relationship with the customer can influence the purchase decision.

Questions

1. If you become a pharmaceutical sales representative, how important is it to adopt the three prescriptions for a presentation strategy? Explain.

2. Deborah Karish spends a great deal of time giving individual and group presentations. Why is it essential that she be well prepared for each presentation? Why would a "canned" presentation, one that is memorized and delivered almost word for word, be inappropriate in her type of selling?

3. Salespeople are encouraged to establish multiple-objective sales presentations. What are some objectives that Deborah might achieve during a sales presentation to doctors who are not currently using her products?

4. What are some special challenges faced by Deborah when she makes a group presentation? How might she enhance her group presentations?

5. Put yourself in the position of a pharmaceutical sales representative. Can you envision a situation in which you might combine the elements of an informative, persuasive, and reminder presentation? Explain.

CRM Case Study Planning Presentations

Becky Kemley, your sales manager at SimNet Systems, wants to meet with you this afternoon to discuss the status of your accounts. It is common for prospects to have several contacts with SimNet before ordering a network system. These multi-call contacts, or *sales cycle phases*, usually include getting acquainted and prequalifying, need discovery, proposal presentation, closing, and account maintenance. Becky wants to know what phase each account is in and, particularly, which accounts may be ready for a presentation.

Questions

1. Which five accounts have already had a need discovery? Which two accounts are scheduled for a need discovery? Which six accounts are likely to buy but have not yet had a need discovery?

2. Which two accounts have had a need discovery and now need a product solution to be configured?

3. Which three accounts do not now have a network and appear to be ready for your sales presentation?

4. For those accounts listed next that are ready for your sales presentation, which strategy would you use for each: informative, persuasive, or reminder?

   | Able Profit Machines | International Studios |
   | Big Tex Auto Sales | Lakeside Clinic |

5. Which accounts appear to be planning to buy without a need discovery or product configuration/proposal? What risks does this pose?

 ## Partnership Selling: A Role Play/Simulation

Visit the role play/simulation materials provided in the Student Resources section of your companion Web site at **www.pearsoned.ca/manning**. *A contents page lists appropriate page references for the activities.*

Understanding Your Customer's Buying Strategy

Read *Sales Memorandum 2* ("A" or "B" depending on the account category you were assigned in Chapter 13). Your customer has called you back because you made such a good approach in call 1, and wants to visit with you about a convention recently assigned. In this call, you are to use the information gathered in sales call 1 to re-establish a good relationship, discover your customer's convention needs, and set an appointment to return and make a presentation.

Follow the instructions carefully and prepare survey questions prior to your appointment. Keep your survey questions general and attempt to get your customer to share information openly. Use specific survey questions later during the appointment to gain more insight. Be careful about doing too much of the talking. In the need discovery, your customer should do most of the talking, with you taking notes and using them to ask confirmation and summary confirmation questions in order to check the accuracy of your perceptions concerning what the customer wants. After this meeting, you will be asked to prepare a sales proposal using the information you have gathered.

Your instructor may again ask you to assume the role of a customer in the account category that you are not assigned as a salesperson. If so, you will receive detailed customer instructions, which you should follow closely. This will provide you with an opportunity to experience the strategic/consultative/partnering style of selling from a customer's perspective.

Chapter 15
Negotiating Buyer Concerns

Learning Objectives

After studying this chapter, you should be able to

1 Describe the principles of formal negotiations as part of the win-win strategy

2 Describe common types of buyer concerns

3 Discuss specific methods of negotiating buyer concerns

4 Outline methods for creating value in formal negotiations

5 Describe how to work with buyers who are trained in negotiation

 Reality Selling Today Video Series

Marriott International Inc. (**www.marriott.com**) is a world-renowned company with approximately 8500 salespeople and 3000 lodging properties around the world—more than 50 of them in Canada.[1] One of its properties is the Marriott Houston Hobby, which is located within a mile of the Hobby Airport in Houston, Texas. Apart from accommodation, the hotel offers comprehensive meeting facilities complemented by expert catering and audiovisual resources. Corporate catering manager Heather Ramsey, in the photo at the top of the next page, is in charge of convention and meeting sales at the Marriott Houston Hobby. She always has a ready response when customers raise concerns about prices and the tranquility of an airport hotel. She emphasizes the value to the customers by describing the state-of-the-art meeting and conference facilities offered by the hotel, its convenience to travellers, as well as other unique features not offered by the competition. Sometimes customers do not communicate openly about their needs and concerns to Heather. She often must work hard to identify their actual needs to offer them the best value and bring benefits to the hotel as well. Her negotiation process with new customers will normally involve identifying their actual needs, and then listening to, clarifying, and overcoming concerns that the customers express.

NEGOTIATING BUYER CONCERNS AND PROBLEMS

MANY SALES PROFESSIONALS ARE VERY PROFICIENT IN NEED DISCOVERY AND selecting the right solution, but are weak in the area of negotiating an agreement that is favourable both to the customer and to the salesperson's firm. Some salespeople fail to

anticipate buyer concerns and plan negotiating methods (Fig. 15.1). A recent poll reports that as many as 83 percent of sales executives from 25 industries said they generally enter negotiations with no formal strategy![2] Another common mistake is making last-minute concessions in order to close the sale.[3] In this chapter, we describe effective strategies for anticipating and negotiating buyer concerns.

We have noted previously that the heaviest time investment in value-added selling is on the front end of the sale. This is especially true for large, complex sales that require a long sales cycle. Identifying the customer's needs and developing the best solution can be very time consuming. However, when you do these things effectively, you are creating value in the eyes of the customer. When you build value on the front end of the sale, price becomes less of an issue on the back end of the sale.[4]

Formal Integrative Negotiation—Part of the Win-Win Relationship Strategy

Frank Acuff, negotiations trainer and author of *How to Negotiate Anything with Anyone, Anywhere Around the Globe,* says, "Life is a negotiation."[5] Negotiating skills have application almost daily in our personal and professional lives. Some of the more traditional personal selling books discuss how salespeople should "handle" buyer objections. The message communicated to the reader was that personal selling was a "we versus they" process resulting from distributive negotiations: Somebody wins, and somebody loses. The win-win solution, where both sides win, was not offered as an option. In this chapter, we focus on integrative negotiations that are built on joint problem-solving, trust, and rapport to achieve win-win situations.

Ron Willingham, author of two books on selling with integrity, says: "When trust and rapport are strong, negotiation becomes a partnership to work through customer concerns. But when trust and rapport are weak, almost any negotiation becomes too combative."[6] Trust and rapport must be established on the front end of the sale and maintained throughout the sales process. High-performance salespeople, like Heather Ramsey, take

The Six-Step Presentation Plan	
Step One: APPROACH	☑ Review Strategic/Consultative Selling Model ☑ Initiate customer contact
Step Two: PRESENTATION	✓ Determine prospect needs ✓ Select solution ✓ Initiate sales presentation
Step Three: DEMONSTRATION	✓ Decide what to demonstrate ✓ Select selling tools ✓ Initiate demonstration
Step Four: NEGOTIATION	○ Anticipate buyer concerns ○ Plan negotiating methods ○ Initiate win-win negotiations
Step Five: CLOSE	○ Plan appropriate closing methods ○ Recognize closing clues ○ Initiate closing methods
Step Six: SERVICING THE SALE	○ Follow-through ○ Follow-up calls ○ Expansion selling
Service, retail, wholesale, and manufacturer selling.	

Figure 15.1 Negotiating customer concerns and problems.

time to discover the customer's needs and try to recommend the best possible solution. And always keep in mind that any agreement that leaves one party dissatisfied will come back to hurt the other party later, sometimes in ways that cannot be predicted.[7]

What is **negotiation**? One definition is "working to reach an agreement that is mutually satisfactory to both buyer and seller." It involves resolving the problems or concerns that prevent people from buying.[8] As we noted in Chapter 5, the salesperson increasingly serves as a consultant or resource, and provides solutions to buyers' problems. The consultant seeks to establish and maintain long-term relationships with customers. The ability to negotiate problems or concerns is one of the most effective ways to create value for the customer. Figure 15.2 outlines the steps a salesperson can take to anticipate and negotiate problems.

negotiation Working to reach an agreement that is mutually satisfactory to buyer and seller.

Negotiation Is a Process

By definition, negotiations seek to move polarized parties into the realm of common interests.[9] Negotiations can take place before the sales call or at any time during the sales presentation. Early negotiations may involve the meeting location, who will attend the sales presentation, or the amount of time available for the first meeting. Salespeople sometimes

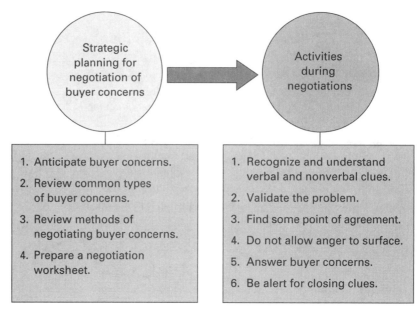

Strategic planning for negotiation of buyer concerns	Activities during negotiations
1. Anticipate buyer concerns. 2. Review common types of buyer concerns. 3. Review methods of negotiating buyer concerns. 4. Prepare a negotiation worksheet.	1. Recognize and understand verbal and nonverbal clues. 2. Validate the problem. 3. Find some point of agreement. 4. Do not allow anger to surface. 5. Answer buyer concerns. 6. Be alert for closing clues.

Figure 15.2 Salespeople today must be prepared to anticipate and negotiate buyer concerns and problems.

make early concessions to improve the relationship. This approach, however, may set a costly precedent for later in the sale.[10] Some concessions can have a negative influence on the sales presentation.

In most cases, you can anticipate that the most important negotiations will take place during stage three of the buying process (see Fig. 11.3). Resolution of problems can sometimes

Negotiation is defined as "working to reach an agreement that is mutually satisfactory to both buyer and seller." It involves building relationships instead of making one-time deals.

be time consuming. Establishing a strategic alliance, described in Chapter 5 as the highest form of partnering, requires lengthy negotiations that may extend over weeks, months, or even years. Once the alliance is finalized, negotiations continue when concerns voiced by one party or the other surface.

PLANNING FOR FORMAL NEGOTIATIONS

PROFESSIONAL BUYERS ARE WELL-TRAINED NEGOTIATORS. TO NEGOTIATE WITH THEM effectively, salespeople first need to engage in detailed planning. Ironically, one of the most common mistakes negotiators make is not doing their homework in advance.[11]

Gather Information before the Negotiation

"Exhaustive preparation is more important than aggressive argument."[12] Robert H. Schuller offers invaluable advice in this crucial step.[13] First, a salesperson should prepare from both counterparts' points of view by identifying the similarities and differences of the goals and objectives of both sides. Then, information should be gathered from a number of sources, including business associates, buyers' Web sites, or even previous vendors for the same buyers. The salesperson should bear in mind that negotiation is an information game: the more, the better.[14]

Decide Team versus Individual Negotiations for Both Seller and Buyer

The next logical step in this preparatory stage is to decide who will be in the negotiations. In a business-to-business selling context, it is not unusual to send a cross-functional team (a team consisting of individuals from many business functions throughout the organization) to the meeting with the buying centre at the buyer's premises. Other situations might call for senior managers or "the big dogs." If teams are involved, make sure there is a leader and establish guidelines for information exchange among the team members.

Understand the Value of What You Are Offering

It is important that we know what is of real value to the customer and not consider value only in terms of purchase price. The real value of what you are offering may be a value-added intangible such as superior product knowledge, good credit terms, prompt delivery, or a reputation for honest dealings. An important aspect of the negotiation process is discovering what is of utmost importance to the buyer (see Table 15.1). The focus of personal selling today should be the mutual search for value. Some salespeople make the mistake of offering a lower price the moment buyer concerns surface. In the customer's mind, however, price may be of secondary importance compared with the quality of service after the sale. Detailed tactics for creating values in formal negotiations appear at the end of the chapter.

Table 15.1 Negotiating Buyer Concerns

Objections are often requests for more information to justify the buying decision. Objections can tell us a lot about the real source of hesitation and what type of information the customer is seeking.

Buyer's Concern	Source of Hesitation	Request For
"Price too high."	Perceived cost vs. benefit	Value articulation
"Think about it."	Afraid to make a bad decision	Comfort, proof
"Talk to boss."	Unable to justify decision	Risk reduction, benefit review
"Need more quotes."	Unsure you're the best option	Targeted solutions, value
"Set with current supplier."	Doesn't see benefit of change	Differentiation
"Bad history."	Past experience is affecting current review	Proof of change

Determine Your Goals and Financial Objectives

BATNA Best Alternative to Negotiated Agreement.

ZOPA Zone of Posible Agreement.

Two important concepts should be mentioned. First is **BATNA** (Best Alternative to Negotiated Agreement), defined as "what alternative(s) will be acceptable to you if your negotiation does not succeed."[15] You will likely make concessions in formal negotiations; therefore, you must assess both your own and your customer's BATNA. The second important concept is **ZOPA** (Zone of Possible Agreement), defined as the space between the seller's walk-away point and the buyer's highest willingness to pay.[16] The walk-away point represents the lowest offer a party would be willing to accept and is also called the "reservation value." For example, if your walk-away point is $42.65M and the highest price the buyer is willing to pay is $48M, your ZOPA is any offer that falls within this range, or a zone of $5.35M ($48M − $42.65M).[17]

Prepare an Agenda

An agenda outlines what will and will not be discussed and in what sequence. As the seller, you want to achieve "small wins" to create goodwill before dealing with tough issues. Therefore, you want to prioritize these items on your proposed agenda. Experienced buyers, however, also come to the meeting table with a detailed agenda. Negotiations might start with a discussion about the agenda itself.

Review Adaptive Selling Styles

The successful negotiation of buyer concerns is based in large part on understanding human behaviour. This knowledge, coupled with a good measure of common sense, helps us overcome most buyer concerns. In one-on-one negotiations, adaptive selling styles are useful (see Chapter 9). The Platinum Rule of negotiating is, "Do unto others as they want done unto them."[18] When negotiations are conducted in teams, the situation gets more complicated. The role of the negotiation leader is to maintain smooth information exchange despite different communication styles.

THE NEGOTIATIONS WORKSHEET

YOUR PLANNING MUST BE SYSTEMATICALLY ORGANIZED. IT HELPS TO PREDICT AND classify possible resistance with the aid of a negotiations worksheet. To illustrate how this form works, let us review an example from the food industry. Mary Turner is a salesperson for Durkee Famous Foods. She represents more than 350 products. Mary calls on supermarkets daily and offers assistance in the areas of ordering and merchandising. Recently, her company decided to offer retail food stores an allowance of $1 per case of olives if the store purchased 15 or more cases. Prior to talking with her customers about this offer, Mary sat down and developed a negotiations worksheet, shown in Fig. 15.3. We cannot

Negotiations Worksheet		
Customer's concern	Type of concern	Possible response
"Fifteen cases of olives will take up valuable space in my receiving room. It is already crowded."	Need	**Combination direct denial/superior benefit** "You will not have to face that problem. With the aid of our merchandising plan you can display 10 cases immediately on the sales floor. Only 5 cases will become reserve stock. You should move all 15 cases in about two weeks."
"This is a poor time of the year to buy a large order of olives. People are not buying olives at this time."	Time	**Combination indirect denial/third-party testimony** "I agree that it has been a problem in the past, but consumer attitudes seem to be changing. We have found that olives sell well all year long if displayed properly. More people are using olives in the preparation of omelets, pizza, and other dishes. Of course, most relish trays feature olives. We will supply you with point-of-purchase material that provides kitchen-tested ways to use this high-profit item."
"I have to stay within my budget."	Price	**Superior benefit** "As you know, olives represent a high-profit item. The average margin is 26 percent. With the addition of our $1.00 per case allowance, the margin will rise to about 30 percent. This order will give you a good return on your investment."
"I am very satisfied with my present supplier."	Source	**Combination question/trial order** "What can I do to get you to take just a trial order?"

Figure 15.3 Before the presentation, it is important to prepare a negotiations worksheet.

Negotiating Across Cultures

Negotiations in the global economy vary from one country to another because of cultural differences. German buyers are more apt to look you in the eye and tell you what they do not like about your product. Japanese buyers, on the other hand, do not want to embarrass you and, therefore, bury their concerns beneath several layers of courtesy. In China, now one of the most important markets for Canadian businesses, negotiations are more straightforward. People who have been doing business in China for many years suggest a very direct approach to negotiations.

However, do not become antagonistic or discourteous. Do get involved in Chinese business rituals that are intended to create a friendly atmosphere.

When you enter into negotiations in foreign countries, it is important to understand and accommodate the customer's culture. You may not get every detail exactly right, but you win respect by trying. Selling in certain cultures often requires more time spent bonding and building rapport. Several meetings may be needed to lay the groundwork for the actual sale.[a]

anticipate every possible problem, but it is possible to identify the most common problems that are likely to arise. The negotiations worksheet can be a useful tool.

Conducting the Negotiation Session

During the formal negotiation session, it is beneficial to master the skills presented throughout this book, i.e., good social contact, asking good questions, listening actively, using proof devices, and applying methods of negotiating objections. There are a number of golden rules that a salesperson should internalize to be successful in formal negotiations.

Many salespeople have learned to anticipate certain problems and forestall them with a well-planned and well-executed presentation.

These include understanding the problem, creating alternative solutions, periodically recapitulating what has been agreed, and making wise concessions in a timely manner.

Understand the Problem

David Stiebel, author of *When Talking Makes Things Worse!*, says we need to understand the difference between a misunderstanding and a true disagreement. A *misunderstanding* is a failure to accurately understand the other person's point. For example, the salesperson believes the customer is primarily interested in price, but the customer's primary need is on-time delivery. A *disagreement*, in contrast, is a failure to agree that would persist despite the most accurate understanding.[19] Be certain that both you and the prospect are clear on the true nature of what needs to be negotiated. When the prospect begins talking, listen carefully and then listen some more. With *probing questions*, you can fine-tune your understanding of the problem.

Create Alternative Solutions That Can Add Value

When the prospect finishes talking, it is a good practice to validate the problem using a *confirmation question*. This helps to isolate the true problem and reduce the chance of misunderstanding. The confirmation question might sound like this: "I think I understand your concern. You feel the warranty does not provide you with sufficient protection. Is this correct?" By taking time to ask this question you accomplish two important objectives. First, you are giving personal attention to the problem, which pleases the customer. Second, you gain time to think about the best possible response.

The best possible response is very often an alternative solution. In formal negotiations, this is often referred to as "**logrolling**."[20] Many of today's customers do not want to hear that there is only one way to do things, or a single solution. In the age of information, people have less time to manage their work and their personal lives, so they expect new levels of flexibility. When negotiations are focused only on price, the salesperson can introduce other issues that can create value for the customer, and possibly for the seller. Some additonal issues the salesperson should consider include delivery dates, financing, contract length, quality, exclusivity clauses, levels of service support, and warranties.

logrolling Offering an alternative solution.

Periodically, Review Acknowledged Points of Agreement

Negotiating buying problems is a little like the art of diplomacy: It helps to know what points of agreement exist. This saves time and helps establish a closer bond between you and the prospect. At some point during the presentation, you might summarize by using a *summary-confirmation question*: "Let us see if I fully understand your position. You think our product is well constructed and will provide the reliability you are looking for. Also, you believe our price is fair. Am I correct on these two points?"

Once all the areas of agreement have been identified, there may be surprisingly few points of disagreement. The prospect suddenly sees that the advantages of ownership far outweigh the disadvantages. Now that the air is cleared, both the salesperson and the customer can give their full attention to any remaining points of disagreement.

The business environment is sometimes turbulent. Hence, it might be advisable in negotiations to "pack a reserve parachute." To avoid buyers' frustration when things do not go as agreed upon, lay the groundwork for the unexpected and be open about backup plans with the buyers.[21]

Do Not Make Concessions Too Quickly

Give away concessions methodically and reluctantly, and always try to get something in return. A concession given too freely can diminish the value of your product. Also, giving a concession too easily may send the signal you are negotiating from a position of weakness. Neil Rackham, author of several books on spin selling, says, "Negotiate late, negotiate little and never let negotiation become a substitute for good selling."[22]

Timing and the Pareto Law

Time plays a critical role in negotiations. Most often, negotiations will conclude in the final 20 percent of the time allowed. In negotiations, experience with the Pareto Law reveals that 80 percent of your results are generally agreed upon in the last 20 percent of your time. Since influence tactics are more likely to exert an effect when their target is under time pressure, negotiators should use time as a strategic weapon by buying more time to fully consider concessions or giving a deadline to speed up agreement.[23]

Know When to Walk Away

For many reasons, salespeople must sometimes walk away from a potential sale. If the customer's budget doesn't allow the purchase of your product, don't press the issue. If the customer's best offer is not favourable for your company, don't continue to waste your time. If the buyer is only interested in the lowest possible price, and you represent a marketer committed to a value-added sales strategy, consider withdrawing from negotiations. If you discover that the prospect is dishonest or fails to keep his word, discontinue negotiations. Be aware of how much flexibility (your BATNA and ZOPA) you have in terms of price, specifications, delivery schedules, and so forth, and know when you have reached your "walk-away" point.[24]

Finally, when appropriate, document negotiated settlements in writing. These will be helpful when formal contracts are drawn up. Negotiation minutes will also serve as a control tool for follow-up actions.

COMMON TYPES OF BUYER CONCERNS

WHEN SALESPEOPLE ARE AWARE OF PATTERNS OF BUYER RESISTANCE, THEY CAN THEN anticipate that certain concerns may arise during the sales call and be better prepared for each meeting with a customer. The majority of buyer concerns fall into five categories: need, product or service, source, time, and price.

Concerns Related to Need for the Product

If you have carefully completed your precall planning, then the prospect will likely have a need for your product. You can still expect, however, that the initial response may be,

"I do not need your product." This might be a conditioned response that arises nearly every time the prospect meets with a sales representative. It may also mask the real reason for not buying, which might be lack of funds, lack of time to examine your proposal carefully, or some other reason. Sincere need resistance is one of the greatest challenges that face a salesperson during the early part of the sales process. Think about it for a moment. Why would any customer want to purchase a product that does not seem to provide any real benefits? Unless we can create need awareness in the prospect's mind, there is no possible way to close the sale.

If you are calling on business prospects, the best way to overcome need resistance is to prove that your product is a good investment. Every business hopes to make a profit. Therefore you must demonstrate how your product or service can contribute to that goal. Can your product increase sales volume? Can it reduce operating expenses? If the owner of a hardware store says, "I already carry a line of high-quality tools," point out how a second line of less expensive tools will appeal to another large segment of buyers. With the addition of the new line, the store will be in a better position to compete with other stores (e.g., discount merchandise stores and supermarkets) that sell inexpensive tools.

Concerns about the Product or Service

You will recall from Chapter 11 that consultative process buyers may lack needs awareness or need help evaluating possible solutions. Therefore, the product (solution) often becomes the focal point of buyer resistance. When this happens, try to discover specific reasons why the prospect has doubts about your product or service. Often you may find that one of the following factors has influenced the buyer's attitude:

1. *The product or service is not well established.* This is a common form of buyer resistance if you are selling a new or relatively new product. People do not like to take risks. They need plenty of assurance that the product is dependable. Use laboratory test results, third-party testimonials from satisfied users, or an effective demonstration to create value.

2. *The present product or service is satisfactory.* Change does not come easily to many people. Purchasing a new product may mean adopting new procedures or retraining employees. In the prospect's mind the advantages do not outweigh the disadvantages, so buyer resistance surfaces. To overcome this resistance, a salesperson must build a greater amount of desire in the prospect's mind. Concentrate on superior benefits that give your product a major advantage over the existing product, or reconfigure the product and offer customized services to better meet the customer's needs.

Concerns Related to Source

Concerns related to source can be especially challenging when the prospect is a relationship buyer. The buyer may already have well-established partnerships with other companies. If the prospect feels genuine loyalty to his or her present supplier, you will have to work harder to establish a relationship and begin the need discovery process.

When dealing with the loyalty problem, it is usually best to avoid direct criticism of the competing firm. Negative comments are apt to backfire because they damage your professional image. It is best to keep the sales presentation focused on the customer's problems and your solutions.

There are positive ways to cope with the loyalty concern. Here are some suggestions:

1. *Work harder to identify problems your company can solve with its products or services.* With the help of good questions, you may be able to understand the prospect's problems better than your competitors do.

2. *Point out the superior benefits of your product or company.* The logic of your presentation may override the emotional ties that may exist between the prospect and the present supplier.

3. *Work on recruiting internal champions to build more support for your message.* Use referrals whenever possible.[25]

4. *Try to stay visible and connected.* Every contact with the prospect is one more step in building a relationship. David Haslam, President of Toronto-based Presidential Plumbing Ltd., devotes time to a number of community projects. He says, "I believe in community involvement, but I'm also gaining invaluable experience, getting contacts."[26]

Concerns Related to Time

stall Resistance related to time.

If a prospect says, "I want time to think it over," you may be encountering concerns related to time. Resistance related to time is often referred to as the **stall**. A stall usually means the customer does not yet perceive the benefits of buying now. In most cases the stall indicates that the prospect has both positive and negative feelings about your product. Consider using *probing questions* to determine the negative feelings: "Is it my company that concerns you?" "Do you have any concerns about our warranty program?"

It is all right to be persuasive if the prospect can truly benefit from buying now. If the price may soon rise, or if the item may not be available in the future, then you should provide this information. You must, however, present this information sincerely and accurately. It is never proper to distort the truth in the hope of getting the order.

Renewing a contract also calls for renegotiations. In these cases, be up front and explain the benefits in precise terms as to what additional values the new price will bring to the client. Sometimes it is advisable to offer a break in the payment schedule to overcome the client's adverse feelings about the price hike.[27] To enhance the relationship with long-term business partners, the seller sometimes has to look at the market to re-evaluate what is really fair pricing and voluntarily renegotiate with the buyer to lower the price before the buyer asks for it.[28]

Concerns Related to Price

Price objections are one of the biggest obstacles salespeople have to conquer.[29] There are two important points to keep in mind concerning price resistance. First, it is one of the most common forms of buyer resistance in the field of selling. Therefore, you must learn to negotiate skillfully in this area. Second, it may be nothing more than an excuse. If you are selling a product or service to a transactional buyer, price may be the primary barrier to closing the sale. When people say, "Your price is too high," they probably mean, "You have not sold me yet." In the eyes of most customers value is more important than price.

Always try to position your product with a convincing value proposition. Customers who perceive added value are less likely to choose a competing product simply on the basis of price. We will present specific tactics to deal with this issue shortly.

SPECIFIC METHODS OF NEGOTIATING BUYER CONCERNS

THERE ARE EIGHT SPECIFIC METHODS OF NEGOTIATING BUYER CONCERNS. In analyzing each buyer concern, we should try to determine which method can be most effective. Sometimes, using a combination of methods is appropriate.

Direct Denial

Direct denial involves refuting the opinion or belief of a prospect. The direct denial of a problem is considered a high-risk method of negotiating buyer concerns. Therefore, you should use it with care. People do not like to be told they are wrong. Even when the facts prove the prospect is wrong, resentment can build if we fail to handle the situation properly.

When a prospect offers buyer resistance that is not valid, we sometimes have no option other than to openly disagree. If the person is misinformed, we must provide accurate information. For example, if the customer questions the product's quality, meet the concern head-on with whatever proof seems appropriate. It is almost never proper to ignore misinformation. High-performance salespeople counter inaccurate responses from the prospect promptly and directly.

The manner in which you state the denial is of major importance. Use a win-win approach. Be firm and sincere in stating your beliefs, but do not be offensive. Above all, do not patronize the prospect. A "know-it-all" attitude can be irritating.

direct denial Involves refuting the prospect's opinion or belief. The direct denial of a problem is considered a high-risk method of negotiating buyer concerns.

Indirect Denial

Sometimes the prospect's concern is completely valid or at least accurate to a large degree. This method is referred to as the **indirect denial**. The best approach is to bend a little and acknowledge that the prospect is at least partially correct. After all, if you offered a product that is objection-proof, you would likely have no competitors. Every product has a shortcoming or limitation.[30] The success of this method is based in part on the need most people have to feel that their views are worthwhile. For this reason the indirect denial method is widely used. An exchange that features the use of this approach follows. The salesperson is a key account sales representative for Tele-Direct Atlantic.[31]

indirect denial Often used when the prospect's concern is completely valid, or at least accurate to a large degree. The salesperson bends a little and acknowledges that the prospect is at least partly correct.

Salesperson: The total cost of placing your one-quarter-column ad in the yellow pages of the five different directories you have chosen is $32 000.

Prospect: As a builder I want to reach people who are planning to build a home. I am afraid my ad will be lost among the hundreds of ads featured in your directories.

Salesperson: Yes, I agree the yellow pages in our directories do feature hundreds of ads, but the section for general contractors features less than 30 ads. Our design staff can prepare an ad that can be highly visible and can set your company apart from ads placed by other contractors.

Note that the salesperson used the words, "Yes, I agree . . ." to reduce the impact of denial. The prospect is less likely to feel her point of view has been totally disproved. One note of caution: Avoid the "Yes . . . but" response. When you use the word *but*, it invalidates anything preceding it. A more effective response would be, "I understand your concerns, Ms. Thomas, however there is another way to view this issue."[32]

Feel–Felt–Found

Successful salespeople are sensitive to clues that indicate the client feels something is wrong. One way to empathize with the client's concerns is to use the "feel–felt–found" strategy. Here is how it works. George Hutchison, Chairman and CEO of North Bay, Ontario–based Equisure Financial Network Inc., is an ace negotiator who regularly uses this method. When someone raises a major concern, he will often say to the person, "I know how you *feel*. Others have *felt* the same way. However, we've *found* that. . . ." Hutchison says that, besides offering empathy, this method reassures the person that others have successfully overcome the same concerns.[33]

Questions

Throughout this chapter, we have described several situations where probing or confirmation questions can enhance the negotiation process. We must also keep in mind the important role of need-satisfaction questions. In Chapter 14, we noted that *need-satisfaction questions* are designed to move the sales process forward toward commitment and action. These questions focus on the solution.[34] Consider the following exchange that involves a price concern:

> **Buyer:** It would be difficult for our human resources department to absorb the cost of your psychological tests.

> **Seller:** What would a 10 percent reduction in employee turnover save your company?

In these examples, the questions are designed to get the customer's attention focused on the solution. These questions also give ownership of the solution to the prospect. See Chapter 14 for more examples of the need-satisfaction question.

Superior Benefit

Sometimes the customer raises a problem that cannot be answered with a denial. For example: "Your television commercial proposal does not include payroll costs for actors who will be used during the shoot. This means we must cover this expense." You should acknowledge the valid objection and then discuss one or more superior benefits: "Yes, you are correct. We do conduct the talent search and coach the actors throughout the development of the commercial. In addition, if you are not happy with the performance of the actors, we will conduct a second search for new actors and remake the commercial at no additional cost to you." A **superior benefit** is a benefit that in most cases outweighs the customer's specific concern.

superior benefit A benefit that will, in most cases, outweigh the customer's specific concern.

Demonstration

If you are familiar with your product as well as that of your competition, this method of negotiating buyer resistance is easy to use. You know the competitive advantages of your product and can discuss these features with confidence.

The product demonstration is one of the most convincing ways to overcome buyer skepticism. With the aid of an effective demonstration, you can overcome specific concerns.

Sometimes a second demonstration is needed to overcome buyer skepticism. This demonstration can provide additional proof. High-achieving sales personnel know when and how to use proof devices to overcome buyer resistance.

Trial Offer

A **trial offer** involves giving the prospect an opportunity to try the product without making a purchase commitment. The trial offer (especially with new products) is popular with customers because they can get fully acquainted with your product without making a major commitment. Assume that a buyer for a large restaurant chain says, "I am sure you have a good cooking oil, but we are happy with our present brand. We have had no complaints from our managers." In response to this comment you might say, "I can understand your reluctance to try our product. However, I do believe our oil is the finest on the market. With your permission, I would like to ship you 30 gallons of our oil at no cost. You can use our product at selected restaurants and evaluate the results. If our oil does not provide you with superior results, you are under no obligation to place an order."

Third-Party Testimony

Studies indicate that the favourable testimony of a neutral third party can be an effective method of responding to buyer resistance. Let us assume that the owner of a small business states that he can get along without the services of a professional landscaper. The salesperson might respond in this manner: "Some business owners feel the way you do. However, once they contract for our service, they do not regret the decision. Mark Williams, owner of Williams Hardware, says our service completely changed the image his

Customer Relationship Management with Technology

Automated Sorting and Productivity

The notes of a busy salesperson can soon become extensive. Paper notes make it difficult, if not impossible, to cross-reference important information within those notes. The notes in a customer relationship management (CRM) system give salespeople immediate access to records containing needed words or phrases. This offers users many advantages, including a method of quickly finding information about buyers with similar interests or concerns. (See the exercise Finding Keywords in a CRM Database on p. 340 for more information.)

business projects to the public." Third-party testimony provides a positive way to solve certain types of buying problems. The positive experiences of a neutral third party almost never trigger an argument with the prospect.

Postpone Method

Today's customers are well informed and may want to engage in negotiations early in the sales process. The customer may raise concerns that you would prefer to respond to later in the presentation. Let's assume you are calling on an office manager who is interested in well-equipped cubicles for eight employees. Soon after you present some product information, the customer says, "How much will eight well-equipped cubicles cost us?" Using the **postpone method**, your response might be, "I would prefer to answer that question in a few minutes. Once I learn what features you prefer, I can calculate a cost estimate." Every customer concern should be taken seriously. Always try to explain why you want to postpone the response.

postpone method A method salespeople use to delay a response when a customer raises a concern that would be better handled later in a sales presentation.

Aramark lists several industries in this ad in which it serves major customers, a form of third-party testimony.

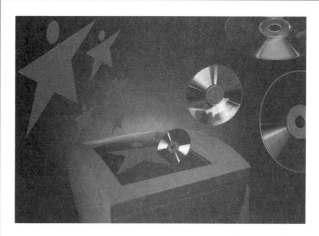

WHO'S GOT THE SOLUTIONS FOR MORE EFFICIENT OFFICE SYSTEMS?

We're ARAMARK Office Services and while our name is new, we bring our clients years of experience in providing total office management solutions. Our point of difference lies in our approach to your business, which is solutions based supported by technology and equipment, not the other way around.

Our range of services includes on-site print on demand, copy centre, mail centre management, Electronic Document Management Systems, distribution, fulfilment and stationery and forms control. ARAMARK provides you with the most advanced equipment available with dedicated specialists in each area.

In addition, ARAMARK's unique "Unlimited Partnership" culture offers a wide range of managed services from food service to cleaning to office coffee. All designed for cost effectiveness and to save you time, time that can be focused on your core business.

Now isn't that the best solution of all.

ARAMARK
Managed Services, Managed Better.
FORMERLY VERSA SERVICES

ARAMARK₀ Managed Services for Business, Education, Healthcare, Sports & Entertainment, Offshore and Remote, and Government: Food, Refreshment, Office Management, and Facility Services. Visit us at www.aramark.ca

Combination Methods

As noted previously, consultative selling is characterized by flexibility. A combination of methods sometimes proves to be the best way to deal with buyer resistance. For example, an indirect denial might be followed by a question: "The cost of our business security system is a little higher than that of the competition. The price I have quoted reflects the high-quality materials used to develop our system. Wouldn't you feel better entrusting your security needs to a firm with more than 25 years of experience in the business security field?" In this situation, the salesperson also might consider combining the indirect denial with an offer to arrange a demonstration of the security system.

A salesperson might attempt to turn the objection into a **trial close** by concluding the sale without prejudicing the opportunity to continue the selling process with the buyer should they refuse to commit themselves. This might take the form of, "If I can address this final concern of yours, will you buy it?[35] See Figure 15.3 on p. 323 for more examples of combination methods.

CREATING VALUE DURING FORMAL NEGOTIATIONS

The challenge a salesperson faces in almost every negotiation is to sell products and services as unique value propositions, not simply on the basis of price. "If salespeople rely on price only to capture and retain business, they reduce whatever they're selling to a commodity. Once that happens, there is no customer loyalty.[36] In this section, we focus on how a salesperson can tactfully create value for buyers during formal negotiations without compromising profits.

THE PITFALLS OF PAYING TOO LITTLE

It's unwise to pay too much. But it's worse to pay too little.

When you pay too much, you lose a little money, that is all.

When you pay too little you sometimes lose everything, because the thing you bought was incapable of doing the thing it was bought to do.

The common law of business balances prohibits paying a little and getting a lot. It can't be done.

If you deal with the lowest bidder, it is well to add something for the risk you run.

—*John Ruskin, British Writer*

How to Deal with Price Concerns

As we have noted, price resistance is common, so we must prepare for it. There are some important "dos and don'ts" to keep in mind when price concern surfaces.

Do Clarify Price Concerns with Questions When you are confronted with a price objection, determine what the customer is really saying. You will recall from

Chapter 13 that *specific survey questions* encourage the customer to give you more details. The following questions might be used when price concerns surface:

"When you say our prices are higher, could you be more specific, please?"

"What did you anticipate the price to be?"

When the customer says budget is the primary reason for delaying the purchase, you might ask, "If you had the budget, would you buy?" Questions can help you determine what the customer is really thinking.[37]

Do Add Value with a Cluster of Satisfactions As noted in Chapter 10, a growing number of customers are seeking a cluster of satisfactions that includes a good product, a salesperson who is truly a partner, and a company that stands behind its products. Many business firms are at a competitive disadvantage when the price alone is considered. When you look beyond price, however, it may become obvious that your company offers more value for the dollar.

Stephen Smith, senior account manager for Bell Atlantic, says that price is like the tip of the iceberg—it is often the only feature the customer sees. Salespeople need to direct the customer's attention to the value-added features that make up the bulk of the iceberg that is below the surface (Figure 15.4).[38] Do not forget to sell yourself as a high-value

Figure 15.4 A sales proposal is sometimes like an iceberg. The customer sees the tip of the iceberg—the price—but does not see the value-added features below the surface.

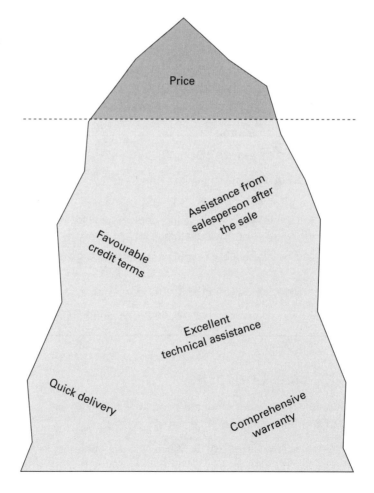

element of the sales proposal. Emphasize your commitment to customer service after the sale. Also, listen carefully to identify and reconfirm what intangibles in addition to the product or service the customers *actually* value.[39]

Do Not Make Price the Focal Point of Your Sales Presentation You may need to discuss price, but do not bring it up too early. The best time to deal with price is after you have reviewed product features and discussed buyer benefits. You increase the chances for a win-win outcome by increasing the number of issues you can resolve. If you negotiate price along with delivery date, support services, or volume purchases, you increase the opportunities for a trade-off so you and the customer both win something of value.[40]

Do Not Apologize for the Price When you do mention price, do so in a confident and straightforward manner. Do not have even a hint of apology in your voice. Convey to the prospect that you believe your price is fair and make every effort to relate price to value. Many people fear paying too much for a product or service. If your company has adopted a value-added strategy, point out this fact to the prospect. Then discuss how you and your company add value.

Do Point Out the Relationship between Price and Quality In our highly competitive, free enterprise economy there are forces at work that tend to promote fair pricing. The highest quality can never be obtained at the lowest price. Quality comes from the Latin word *qualitas*, meaning, "What is the worth?" When you sell quality, price is more likely to be secondary in the prospect's mind. Always point out the value-added features that create the difference in price. Keep in mind that cheap products are built down to a price rather than up to a standard.[41]

Do Explain and Demonstrate the Difference between Price and Cost Price represents the initial amount the buyer pays for the product. Cost represents the amount the buyer pays for a product as it is used over a period of time. The price–cost comparison is particularly relevant with a product or service that lasts a long time or is particularly reliable. Today, airlines are comparing the price and cost of small regional jets manufactured by Bombardier of Canada and Embraer of Brazil with large jets sold by Boeing and Airbus. Figure 15.5 compares the CRJ200 offered by Bombardier with the A320 offered by Airbus. Sales representatives at Bombardier point out the fast speed (534 MPH) and low fuel consumption of the CRJ200.[42]

	CRJ200	A320
Passengers (seats)	50	150
Cost of aircraft	$21.0 million	$48.2 million
SHORT TRIP (925 km)		
Cost per seat per km	3.34¢	2.85¢
Total cost of trip	$961	$2460
LONG TRIP (1850 km)		
Cost per seat per km	2.79¢	2.16¢
Total cost of trip	$1604	$3722

Figure 15.5 The Winner in the Short Run. Airlines are comparing the price and cost of small regional jets with large jets sold by Boeing and Airbus. The cavernous Airbus leads on seat cost per kilometre, but the much lower price per trip of the CRJ200 makes it a winner in the minds of some buyers.

Adapted from *Fortune*, 9/4/00 © 2000 Time Inc. All rights reserved.

NEGOTIATING PRICE WITH A LOW-PRICE STRATEGY

As noted in Chapter 10, some marketers have positioned their products with a price strategy. The goal is to earn a small profit margin on a large sales volume. Many of these companies have empowered their salespeople to use various low-price strategies such as quantity discounts, trade discounts, seasonal discounts, and promotional discounts. Some salespeople are given permission to match the price of any competitor. Many *transactional buyers* are primarily interested in price and convenience during negotiations, so consider eliminating features that contribute to a higher selling price.

Working with Buyers Who Are Trained in Negotiation

In recent years, we have seen an increase in the number of training programs developed for professional buyers. Some salespeople are also returning to the classroom to learn negotiation skills. Learning how to negotiate is one of the linchpins of effective selling."[43] SalesForce Training & Consulting is a Canadian sales training and consulting company with 25 years of experience. It offers a number of 45- to 90-minute workshops, one being "Handling Genuine Objections." It also offers a half-day workshop, "Handling the Dreaded Price (*and Other*) Objections." These help salespeople handle many of the negotiating techniques that salespeople need to know. The Canadian Professional Sales Association offers a popular course, "Effective Negotiating Strategies," which is designed to provide salespeople with the keys to successful negotiations.

Professional buyers often learn to use specific tactics in dealing with salespeople. Homer Smith, author of *Selling through Negotiation*, provides these examples:

Budget Limitation Tactic.[44] The buyer may say, "We like your proposal, but our budget for the convention is only $8500." Is the buyer telling the truth, or is the

Selling in Action
Apply Negotiation Skills in the Job Market

Chester L. Karrass, creator of the Effective Negotiating seminar, says, "In business, you don't get what you deserve; you get what you negotiate." This is good advice for the job seeker. Most employers will not propose the highest wage possible at the beginning of the offer. If you want a higher starting wage, you must ask for it. Employers often have a predetermined range for each position and the highest salary is reserved for the applicant who brings something extra to the job. To prepare for a productive negotiation, you must know your own needs and you must know something about the worth of the position. Many employers will tell you the salary range prior to the interview. The Internet can be a good source of salary information for certain types of jobs. In terms of your needs, try to determine what you care about the most: Interesting work? Future promotion? A flexible work schedule? If you are willing to negotiate, you can increase your pay by hundreds or even thousands of dollars. Be prepared to sell yourself, negotiate the salary you feel is appropriate, and achieve a win-win solution in the process.[b]

person testing your price? The best approach in this instance is to take the budget limitation seriously and use appropriate negotiation strategies. One strategy is to reduce the price by eliminating features or items, sometimes described as **unbundling**. In the case of a truck fleet sale, the salesperson might say, "We can deliver the trucks with a less powerful engine and, thus, meet your budget figure. Would you be willing to purchase trucks with less powerful engines?"

Take-It-or-Leave-It Tactic.[45] How do you respond to a buyer who says, "My final offer is $3300, take it or leave it"? A price concession is, of course, one option. However, this is likely to reduce profits for the company and lower your commission. An alternative strategy is to confidently review the superior benefits of your product and make another closing attempt. Appealing to the other person's sense of fairness also may move the discussion forward. If the final offer is totally without merit, consider calling a halt to the negotiation to allow the other party to back down from his or her position without losing face.[46]

Let-Us-Split-the-Difference Tactic.[47] In some cases, the salesperson may find this price concession acceptable. If the buyer's suggestion is not acceptable, then the salesperson might make a counteroffer.

"If . . . Then" Tactic. This approach involves the buyer saying something like, "Unless you agree immediately to a price reduction of 20 percent, we'll have to look elsewhere for a supplier." In this situation the consequence could be serious. The correct response depends upon the outcome of the assessment of the balance of power conducted during the preparation. If the buyer does have a number of options, all of which offer the same kind of benefits as yours, then you may have to concede. If your product offers clear advantages over the competition, then you may be able to resist the challenge.

"Sell Low Now, Make Profits Later" Tactic. In this situation, also referred to as the "Reward in Heaven Tactic," the buyer may say something like, "If you can reduce the price another $500 on this job, I will give you all my future work." This may be a genuine statement, and in fact may meet your own objective of gaining a foothold in your buyer's business. You might respond with "Because of the price I have quoted, I am unable to discount this job. However, if you do give me this job and your future jobs, I will discount your future work." This negotiation approach can actually create value for both you and your customer.

These tactics represent only a sample of those used by professional buyers. To prepare for these and other tactics, salespeople need to plan their negotiating strategies in advance and have clear goals. Decide in advance on the terms you can and cannot accept. It is important that you have the authority to set prices. Buyers want to do business with someone who has decision-making authority. Daniel Skarlicki, a specialist in organizational behaviour at the University of British Columbia, says, "Simply put, negotiations are won or lost in the planning and preparation, not at the negotiating table. Don't wing it."[48]

unbundling Eliminating features or items that contribute to a higher selling price.

Renting Pandas

Ron Barbaro, chairman of The Brick Group Income Fund and former chairman and CEO of the Ontario Lottery and Gaming Corporation, says that when he first started in sales, he was not a good salesperson but he had determination and was a good worker. It was this determination and hard work that enabled him to sell more than $1 million worth of insurance in his first year. He went on to become president of Prudential Insurance Company of America's Canadian and worldwide operations. His determination—and undoubtedly the negotiating and problem-solving skills he learned while selling—helped him close what he refers to as his toughest, but most rewarding, sale.

When Ron Barbaro was chairman of the board for the Metro Toronto Zoo, he was instrumental in bringing the first Giant Panda exhibit to Canada from Asia. "They wouldn't give the pandas to us, nor would they sell them to us," says Ron. He eventually succeeded in negotiating a panda exhibit rental.[c]

REVIEWING KEY CONCEPTS

- Describe the principles of formal negotiations as part of the win-win strategy.

  Negotiations play a central role in the selling profession. Generic principles of formal integrative negotiations include preparing for negotiations, knowing the value of what you are offering, understanding the problem, creating alternate solutions, finding some point of agreement, and knowing when to walk away. If a salesperson uses a negotiations worksheet, then it can be much easier to plan systematically.

- Describe common types of buyer concerns.

  Sales resistance is natural and should be welcomed as an opportunity to learn more about how to satisfy the prospect's needs. Buyers' concerns often provide salespeople with precisely the information they need to close a sale. These concerns fall into five broad categories: need, product or service, source, time, and price. Whatever the reasons, the salesperson should *negotiate* sales resistance with the proper attitude, never making too much or too little of the prospect's concerns.

- Discuss specific methods of negotiating buyer concerns.

  We describe seven specific methods of negotiating buyer concerns: direct denial, indirect denial, need-satisfaction questions, superior benefits, demonstration, trial offer, testimony, and postpone method. The use of these methods and combinations thereof varies depending on the particular combination of salesperson, product, services, and prospect.

- Outline methods for creating value in formal negotiations.

  We have described several specific methods for creating value in formal negotiations, but you should remember that practice in applying them is essential and that there is room for a great deal of creative imagination in developing variations or additional methods. With careful preparation and practice, negotiating buyer concerns about price should become a stimulating challenge to each salesperson's professional growth.

- Describe how to work with buyers who are trained in negotiation.

  Buyers who are trained in negotiations resort to a number of tactics that a salesperson should be prepared for. In any case, the ultimate goal of formal integrative negotiations is to achieve win-win solutions by offering buyers the value they appreciate without compromising the sellers' benefits.

Key Terms

BATNA **322**

direct denial **329**

indirect denial **329**

logrolling **325**

negotiation **319**

postpone method **332**

stall **328**

superior benefit **330**

trial offer **331**

unbundling **337**

ZOPA **322**

Review Questions

1. Explain why a salesperson should welcome buyer concerns.

2. List the common types of buyer concerns that might surface in a presentation.

3. How does the negotiations worksheet help the salesperson prepare to negotiate buyer concerns?

4. Explain the value of using *probing* and *confirmation* questions when negotiating buyer concerns.

5. List eight specific strategies for negotiating buyer resistance.

6. John Ruskin says that it is unwise to pay too much when making a purchase, but it is worse to pay too little. Do you agree or disagree with this statement? Explain.

7. What is usually the most common reason prospects give for not buying? How can salespeople deal effectively with this type of concern?

8. Professional buyers may have learned to use specific negotiation tactics in dealing with salespeople. List and describe two tactics that are commonly used today.

9. When a customer says, "I want time to think it over," what type of resistance is the salesperson encountering? Suggest ways to overcome this type of buyer concern.

10. Discuss the merits of using need-satisfaction questions to negotiate buyer concerns.

Application Exercises

1. When conducting negotiations with a customer, take into consideration their communication style. Select two of the four communication styles (Emotive, Directive, Reflective, or Supportive) and prepare guidelines for negotiating with each one. Review the material in Chapter 8 before completing this exercise.

2. During an interview with a prospective employer, the interviewer raises a concern that you are not qualified for the job for which you are applying. On the basis of your observation, you do not believe the interviewer fully understands the amount of experience you have or that you really have the ability to perform the job requirements. Write how you would overcome the concern the interviewer has raised.

3. Assume you have decided to sell your own home. During an open house, a prospect you are showing through the house begins to criticize every major selling point about your home.

   a. You have taken excellent care of your home, believe it to be a good home, and have done a lot of special projects to make it more enjoyable. What will be your emotional reaction to this prospect's criticisms? Should you express this emotional reaction?

   b. You think this prospect is really interested in buying your home, despite this surface criticism. How would you negotiate the sales resistance that he or she is showing?

4. The Canadian Professional Sales Association (**www .cpsa.com**) is a leading supplier of sales training programs. One of its most popular two-day courses is Effective Negotiating Strategies. Access the CPSA home page and click on the "sales training" link. Click on "effective negotiating strategies" and review the information on this course. Report your findings.

5. You sell high-quality, energy-saving air purifiers for residential customers. Your have noticed that your success rate is much higher when you complete your presentation than when the prospect interrupts your presentation early wanting to know the price. Some customers will not let you continue once you give them a price, and some customers will continue to ask you for a price each time you stall them. Describe the best alternatives for handling this situation without insulting or angering the prospect.

ROLE-PLAY EXERCISE

You work for the sales department of an apparel manufacturing company. Montreal Fashions, a company that you met with during a recent trade show, is going to visit your facilities next week. You understand that this company wants to "buy low" but normally places large orders. However, you want to "sell high." Your company might not be able to deliver very large orders unless you invest in new facilities. Montreal Fashions says it will send over a team of three people: the vice-president of marketing, the purchasing manager, and a designer. They are interested in developing a collection for the next season and going over a "price exercise" with you. In addition, they are interested in placing a trial order at the price of a bulk order (i.e., large order). Delivery of the order is to be made in two weeks. Unfortunately, this trial order is well below the minimum quantity you're willing to accept,

and your company normally needs one month to fill a new order.

(1) How do you convey this information to the other departments within your company to prepare for this meeting? Will you invite your boss to the meeting? Why?

(2) Using a negotiations worksheet, plan your response to the following statements made by the purchasing manager: (a) We are concerned that you will not be able to meet our quality requirements, (b) Your price is too high, (c) Either take this trial order or we will look for another vendor. Decide at what point in the negotiations on price and delivery date you will turn down or accept the offer. Role play your response to each of these statements.

CRM Application Exercise Finding Keywords in a CRM Database

During sales training this week, your sales manager, Becky Kemley, led a discussion about negotiating buyer resistance and managing their concerns. The discussion included methods of identifying and responding to price concerns. You intend to identify those prospects that have a price objection so that you can better prepare to work with them. Using Salesforce.com, access all records containing the word "price" by going to the "Reports" tab and selecting "Opportunity Pipeline Report." This report lists all your opportunities. Customize this report to limit it to opportunities where price is an objection by adding the criteria "Description Contains Price." This report now contains three records where price is an issue. This report also contains the primary contact information for the opportunities at these three companies. To find contact information for all the contacts in the Salesforce.com database for these opportunities, click on the "Opportunity" link in each record.

Reality Selling Today Video Case Problem

Each year, public and private organizations send thousands of employees to meetings held at hotels, motels, convention centres, conference centres, and resorts. These meetings represent a multimillion-dollar business in Canada and the United States. Airport hotels such as the Marriott Houston Hobby, introduced at the beginning of this chapter, are a good example of the venues typically selected for these meetings The Marriott Houston Hobby is conveniently located only one mile from the Hobby Airport in Houston, Texas. It has a

competitive edge over its competition because it lies outside of the flight path. In addition to convenience and tranquility, the goal of the hotel is to provide guests with outstanding meeting and conference services. The hotel offers 235 deluxe guest rooms, 52 suites, 13 soundproof meeting rooms with state-of-the-art audiovisual technology, and continuous break service that can accommodate any agenda. Lavish customized meal events from a wide variety of international cuisines are a specialty of the Marriott Houston Hobby.

In an ideal situation, Heather Ramsey, corporate catering manager at the hotel, tries to get prospects out for an inspection of the property. Prospects might also sample hors d'ouvres or lunch during a site tour. This tour, in some ways, fulfills the function of a sales demonstration. Throughout the tour, Heather describes special amenities and services offered by the hotel. She also uses this time to get better acquainted with the needs of the prospect. Once the tour is complete, she escorts the prospect back to her office and completes the needs assessment. Next, she prepares a detailed sales proposal or, in some cases, a contract. The proposal needs to contain accurate and complete facts because when signed, it becomes a legally enforceable sales contract.

For big events, the sales proposal is rarely accepted without modification. Professional meeting planners are experienced negotiators and press hard for concessions. Some have completed training programs developed for professional buyers. The concessions requested may include a lower guest room rate, lower meal costs, complimentary suites, or a complimentary event such as a wine and cheese reception. It might take as long as two months to reach an agreement with sophisticated buyers.

Of course, some buyer resistance is not easily identified. Heather Ramsey says that she follows four steps in dealing with buyer concerns:

1. *Identify the actual needs of the prospects.* To achieve win-win deals, Heather spends time asking specific questions about the customer's needs, such as the audience for the event, the size and timing of the event, and the customer's budget. The prospects normally focus on negotiating details of food menu, group rates for room rental, and audiovisual facilities.

2. *Locate the resistance.* Some prospects are reluctant to accept the offer, but the reason may be unclear. Heather has discovered that asking open-ended questions goes a long way in understanding the actual resistance. Once the reason for resistance is uncovered, Heather knows how to deal with it.

3. *Clarify the resistance.* If a prospect says, "I like your facilities, but your prices are a little high," then the salesperson must clarify the meaning of this objection. Is the prospect seeking a major price concession or a small price concession?

4. *Overcome the objection.* Heather says, "You must be prepared for negotiations by understanding both your flexibility and the customer's needs." The hotel must earn a profit or publicity, so concessions can be made only after careful consideration of the bottom line and other intangible benefits.

Heather has discovered that the best way to negotiate buyer concerns is to make sure both the prospect and the resort feel like winners once the negotiations are finalized. If either party feels like a loser, a long-term relationship will not be possible. During peak seasons, Heather might also need to negotiate the schedule of events with prospects to minimize opportunity costs for the hotel while keeping the customers happy by offering off-season concessions. Refer to the opening vignette of this chapter for more information.

Questions

1. If you were selling convention services for a hotel located in a large city, what types of buyer concerns would you expect from a new prospect?

2. Let us assume that you are representing the Marriott Houston Hobby and you are meeting with a new prospect at the hotel for a site tour. This prospect is planning to host an important event at your hotel for 200 guests. List the questions that you might ask the prospect to identify her actual needs. In doing so, be specific about the alternatives (e.g., high-end, medium, or regular packages) that you can offer the prospect and the order of presenting them to the prospects.

3. If you meet with a professional buyer who is trained in negotiation, what tactics can you expect the person to use? How would you respond to each of these tactics?

4. What subtle questions will you ask to ascertain that the negotiator is the decision maker without hurting her feelings? What actions will you take if you find out she is not the decision maker?

CRM Case Study   Negotiating Resistance

 Becky Kemley has asked you to review Pat Silva's former prospect accounts. She wants you to look for accounts with which you might anticipate buyer concerns during a presentation.

Questions

1. Which account might voice a time concern and say, "We want to put off our decision for now." How would you propose dealing with this buyer concern?

2. Which account is most likely to try to get you to agree to a lower price and how would you respond?

3. Which account might you anticipate would use the phrase "We want to shop around for a good solid supplier"? What would be your response?

Partnership Selling: A Role Play/Simulation

Visit the role play/simulation materials provided in the Student Resources section of your companion Web site at **www.pearsoned.ca/manning**. A *Contents page lists appropriate page references for the activities.*

Developing a Sales Presentation Strategy—Negotiating

Refer to *Sales Memorandum 3* and strategically plan to anticipate and negotiate any buyer concerns that may arise during your presentation. You should prepare a negotiations worksheet to organize this part of your presentation.

The instructions for item 2e direct you to prepare negotiations for time, price, source, and product concerns. You will note that your price is approximately $200 more than your customer budgeted for this meeting.

You will have to be very effective in negotiating a value-added strategy because your convention centre is not a low-price supplier. (See Chapter 10 on value-added product strategies.)

During the presentation, you should use proof devices from the product strategy materials provided in *Employment Memorandum 1* to negotiate concerns you anticipate. You may also want to use a calculator to negotiate any financial arrangements, such as savings on parking or airport transportation. Place these materials in the front pocket of your three-ring binder (portfolio) for easy access during your presentation. You may want to ask another person to be your customer, instructing him or her to voice the concerns you have anticipated, and then respond with your negotiation strategies. This experience will provide you with the opportunity to rehearse your negotiation strategies.

Chapter 16
Adapting the Close and Confirming the Partnership

Learning Objectives

After studying this chapter, you should be able to

1   Describe the proper attitude to display toward closing the sale

2   List and discuss selected guidelines for closing the sale

3   Explain how to recognize closing clues

4   Discuss specific methods of closing the sale

5   Explain what to do when the buyer says yes and what to do when the buyer says no

 Adaptive Selling Today Training Video Series

Ask For the Order, or **AFTO** as it is also called, is the third training video in the Adaptive Selling Today Training Video Series. The video begins with a salesperson who has a fear of closing the sale. Research shows that many sales are lost because salespeople fear asking for the order, and that even when they do, it is not unusual to have to ask three or four times. Along with many successful examples of how to ask for the order, AFTO presents a three-dimensional approach to overcoming any fear one may have of asking.

AFTO presents many closing methods, described in this chapter, that illustrate the importance of adapting your closing questions to the customer's particular buying situation. Specific methods of asking for the order are clearly presented in dramatic sequences, representing a wide variety of selling situations.

AFTO presents a system to use throughout the sales process to gain a better understanding of your customer's needs, and ultimately help your customers make sound buying decisions.

ADAPTING THE CLOSE—AN ATTITUDE THAT ADDS VALUE

Susan Minns, vice-president of client services at Event Spectrum in Toronto, looks at closing from the prospect's point of view. Although the special event plan she has prepared may seem perfect, she realizes that the customer may have a different point of view. A special event for her company may involve a national sales conference, a corporate executive retreat, a new product launch, or even a client appreciation event for large or small companies that want to recognize and thank their important customers. She must try to see the actual event through the eyes of the Event Spectrum customer and, from this insight, use adaptive closing questions to confirm the sale and begin to build a long-term partnership. Susan believes that relationship-building skills must be applied at every step of the sales process. If she is continuously adding value throughout the sales presentation, closing a sale and getting a contract will be much easier. This is especially true in those cases in which price might be a barrier to closing.[1]

CLOSING THE SALE—YESTERDAY AND TODAY

THROUGHOUT THE EVOLUTION OF PERSONAL SELLING, WE HAVE SEEN MAJOR changes in the way closing is perceived. Prior to the introduction of consultative selling and the partnering era, closing was typically presented as the most important aspect of the sales process. The early sales training literature also presented closing methods that encouraged manipulation of the customer. Use of any closing method that is perceived by the customer as pushy or manipulative will damage your chances of building a long-term partnership.

Figure 16.1 Effective closing methods require careful planning.

The Six-Step Presentation Plan	
Step One: APPROACH	☑ Review Strategic/Consultative Selling Model ☑ Initiate customer contact
Step Two: PRESENTATION	✔ Determine prospect needs ✔ Select solution ✔ Initiate sales presentation
Step Three: DEMONSTRATION	✔ Decide what to demonstrate ✔ Select selling tools ✔ Initiate demonstration
Step Four: NEGOTIATION	✔ Anticipate buyer concerns ✔ Plan negotiating methods ✔ Initiate win-win negotiations
Step Five: CLOSE	○ Plan appropriate closing methods ○ Recognize closing clues ○ Initiate closing methods
Step Six: SERVICING THE SALE	○ Follow-through ○ Follow-up calls ○ Expansion selling
Service, retail, wholesale, and manufacturer selling.	

Closing should not be viewed as a strategy to win at the expense of the customer. The proper attitude should be "If this is the best solution for the customer, I should help her make the correct decision."[2] Once the best solution is determined, *asking for the order* is the next logical step.

We take the position that in many selling situations, the salesperson needs to assume responsibility for obtaining commitment from the customer. Some closing methods can move the customer from indecision to commitment. When these methods are used effectively, the prospect will not feel pressured. In some cases, we need to simply replace defence-arousing language—such as "This is the lowest price available anywhere"—with a positive *need-satisfaction question,* such as "Wouldn't this new software help you achieve more efficient inventory control?"

Asking for the order is less difficult if the salesperson is strategically prepared for the close. Preparation for the close involves understanding customer needs, custom-fitting solutions, and planning appropriate closing methods. Throughout the sales presentation, the salesperson should recognize closing clues and be prepared to use effective closing methods (Fig. 16.1).

REVIEW THE VALUE PROPOSITION FROM THE PROSPECT'S POINT OF VIEW

CLOSING THE SALE IS USUALLY EASIER IF YOU LOOK AT THE *VALUE PROPOSITION* from the prospect's point of view. Have you effectively summarized the mix of key benefits? Will your proposal fulfill the customer's needs? Is your proposal strong enough to win over a customer who is experiencing buying anxieties?

Gene Bedell, author of *3 Steps to Yes*, reminds us that buying often causes emotional stress. The following buying anxieties help explain why some customers are reluctant to make a commitment to your proposal.[3]

> *Loss of options.* If the customer agrees to purchase a $5000 design proposal, then that money will not be available for other purchases or investments. Agreeing to purchase a product or service often means that some other purchase must be postponed. Anxiety and stress build as the customer thinks about allocating limited resources.

> *Fear of making a mistake.* If the customer believes that agreeing with a closing request may be the wrong thing to do, he or she may back away just when the decision seems imminent. Fear of making a mistake can be caused by lack of trust in the salesperson.

> *Social or peer pressures.* Some customers make buying decisions with an eye on the opinions and reactions of others. A business buyer may have to justify a purchase to her boss or to employees who will actually use the product. Be prepared to deal with these anxieties as you get closer to closing the sale. Sometimes a little gentle persuasion will help the anxious customer make a decision.

Closing the Sale—The Beginning of the Partnership

Tom Reilly, in his book *Value-Added Selling*, says, ". . . you don't close sales; you build commitment to a course of action that brings value to the customer and profit to the seller."[4] This building process begins with an interesting approach and need discovery. It continues with effective product selection and presentation of benefits, which build desire for the product. After a well-planned demonstration and after negotiating sales resistance, it is time to obtain commitment. Closing ought to be a natural conclusion to the selling process.

GUIDELINES FOR CLOSING THE SALE

A NUMBER OF FACTORS INCREASE THE ODDS THAT YOU WILL CLOSE THE SALE (see Fig. 16.2). These guidelines for closing the sale have universal application in the field of selling.

Focus on Dominant Buying Motives

Most salespeople incorporate the outstanding benefits of their product into the sales presentation. This is only natural. They are, however, alert to the *one* specific benefit that generates the most excitement. The buying motive that is of greatest interest deserves special attention. Vince Peters, director of sales training and development for Wyeth-Ayerst International, tells his 8000 pharmaceutical salespeople that the key to closing "is to find out exactly what a prospect is looking for."[5] Throughout the need discovery stage, pay close attention to the buyer's interests. Focus your closing efforts on the point of greatest interest and give the prospect a reason for buying.

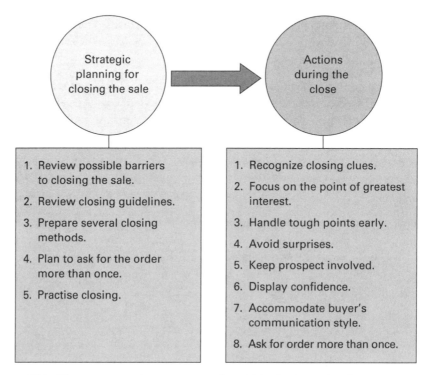

Figure 16.2 The presentation strategy should include reviewing these guidelines for closing and confirming the sale.

Longer Selling Cycles and Incremental Commitments

Longer selling cycles have become a fact of life in many industries. One reason for this change is that more decision makers are involved in purchasing some products. A survey of 1300 companies by sales analysis firm CSO Insights indicates that increased competition, more complex buying processes, and higher buyer workloads are also adding time to the sales cycle. The buying cycle for many products can be measured in months and some buying cycles can be measured in years.[6]

When you are working on a large, complex sale, you should try to achieve **incremental commitment** throughout the sales process. Some form of incremental commitment should be obtained during each step in a multi-call sales presentation. At the conclusion of the first sales call, for example, you may obtain commitment to an agenda for the second call. At the second call, you might obtain commitment for the prospect to tour your company facilities. Each commitment should move the sale forward toward a signed order.

In some cases, the best way to shorten a sales cycle is to create an entirely new way to locate and approach customers. The customer base for Telegraph Hill Robes is upscale hotels and spas. When Maria Spurlock assumed the duties of CEO, the typical sales cycle was six months to two years. Most Telegraph Hill Robes clients were large established hotels, and decisions regarding the purchase of robes often involved the general manager and the head of housekeeping. Spurlock decided to focus more sales efforts on hotels still under construction. The key decision maker for a hotel under construction was often just one person, the interior designer. By working with designers, she reduced the sales cycle to three months or less.[7]

incremental commitment
Gradually moving the customer to total commitment (i.e., closing on a purchase) by gaining cumulative commitment with each sales call.

Negotiate the Tough Points before Attempting the Close

Many products have what might be thought of as an Achilles heel—in other words, the product is vulnerable or appears to be vulnerable in one or more areas. Negotiate a win-win solution to the tough points before you attempt to close the sale. Such factors can lose the sale if you ignore them. The close should be a positive phase of the sales presentation. This is not the time to deal with a controversial issue or problem.

In the case of Rolex watches, Lexus automobiles, or Banff Springs Hotel conference facilities, for example, the Achilles heel may be price. Each of these products may seem expensive in comparison with competing ones. People who sell them find ways to establish the value of their product before attempting the close.

Avoid Surprises at the Close

Some salespeople make the mistake of waiting until the close to reveal information that may come as a surprise to the prospect. For example, the salesperson quotes a price but is not specific concerning what the price includes. Let us assume that the price of a central air-conditioning unit is $4000. The prospect believes that the price is competitive in relation to similar units on the market and is ready to sign the order form. Then the salesperson mentions casually that the installation charge is an extra $975. The prospect had assumed that the $4000 price included installation. Suddenly the extra fee looms as a major obstacle to closing the sale.

The surprise might come in the form of an accessory that costs extra, terms of the warranty, customer service limitations, or some other issue. Do not let a last-minute surprise damage the relationship with the buyer and threaten the completion of a sale.

"Tough-Mindedness"—Display a High Degree of Self-Confidence at the Close

Do you believe in your product? Do you believe in your company? Have you identified a solution to the customer's problem? If you can answer yes to each of these questions, then there is no need to display timidity. Look the prospect in the eye and ask for the order. Do not be apologetic at this important point in the sales presentation. The salesperson who confidently asks for the sale is displaying the boldness that is so effective in personal selling.

Ask for the Order More Than Once

Too often, salespeople make the mistake of not asking for the order or asking just once. If the prospect says no, they give up. Michael LeBoeuf, author of *How to Win Customers and Keep Them for Life*, reports that almost two-thirds of all sales calls conclude without the salesperson asking for the order. He also says that a majority of customers say no several times before saying yes.[8] Some of the most productive salespeople ask for the order three, four, or even five times. A surprising number of yes responses come on the fourth or fifth attempt. Of course, not all these closing attempts necessarily come during one call. Determination is a virtue if your product solution solves the customer's problem.

Recognize Closing Clues

closing clue An indication, either verbal or nonverbal, that the prospect is preparing to make a buying decision.

As the sales presentation progresses, you need to be alert to closing clues (sometimes called *buying signals*). A **closing clue** is an indication, either verbal or nonverbal, that the prospect is preparing to make a buying decision. It is a form of feedback, which is so important in selling. When you detect a closing clue, it may be time to attempt a close.

Many closing clues are quite subtle and may be missed if you are not alert. This is especially true in the case of nonverbal buying signals. If you pay careful attention—with your eyes and ears—many prospects will signal their degree of commitment.[9] As we noted earlier in this text, one of the most important personality traits salespeople need is empathy, the ability to sense what the other person is feeling. In this section we will review some of the most common verbal and nonverbal clues.

Verbal Clues Closing clues come in many forms. Spoken words, or verbal clues, are usually the easiest to perceive. These clues can be divided into three categories: (1) questions, (2) recognitions, and (3) requirements.

Questions One of the least subtle buying signals is the question. You might attempt a trial close after responding to one of the following questions:

Do you have a credit plan to cover this purchase?

What type of warranty do you provide?

How soon can our company get delivery?

Recognitions A recognition is any positive statement concerning your product or some factor related to the sale, such as credit terms or delivery date. Some examples follow:

> We like the quality control system you have recommended.
>
> I have always wanted to own a boat like this.
>
> Your delivery schedule fits our plans.

Requirements Sometimes customers outline a condition that must be met before they will buy. If you are able to meet this requirement, it may be a good time to try a trial close. Here are some requirements that the prospect might voice:

> We will need shipment within two weeks.
>
> Our staff will need to be trained in how to use this equipment.
>
> All our equipment must be certified by the plant safety officer.

In some cases, verbal buying clues will not jump out at you. Important buying signals may be interwoven into normal conversation. Listen closely whenever the prospect is talking.

Nonverbal Clues Nonverbal buying clues will be even more difficult to detect. Once detected, this type of signal is not easy to interpret. Nevertheless, you should be alert to body movement, facial expression, and tone of voice. Here are some actions that suggest that the prospect may be prepared to purchase the product.[10]

- The prospect's facial expression changes. Suddenly the person's eyes widen and genuine interest is clear in the facial expression.
- The prospect begins showing agreement by nodding.
- The prospect leans forward and appears to be intent on hearing your message.
- The prospect begins to examine the product intently or study the sales literature.

When you observe or sense one of these nonverbal buying clues, do not hesitate to ask for commitment. There may be several opportunities to close throughout the sales presentation. Important buying signals may surface at any time. Do not miss them.

SPECIFIC METHODS FOR CLOSING THE SALE

THE SALES PRESENTATION IS A PROCESS, NOT A SINGLE ACTION. EACH STEP DURING the process should create another layer of trust and move the customer closer to making a commitment. Throughout the sales process, you are positioning yourself as a valued resource.[11]

There is no *best* closing method. Your best bet is to preplan several closing methods and adapt the ones that seem appropriate to each customer (see Fig. 16.3). Given the complex nature of many sales, it is often a good idea to be prepared to use a combination of closing methods. Do keep in mind that your goal is not only to close the sale but also to develop a long-term partnership.

Trial Close

A **trial close**, also known as a *minor point close*, is a closing attempt made at an opportune time during the sales presentation to encourage the customer to reveal either readiness

trial close A closing attempt made at an opportune time during the sales presentation to encourage the customer to reveal either readiness or unwillingness to buy.

Closing Worksheet		
Closing clue (prospect)	**Closing method**	**Closing statement (salesperson)**
"That sounds fine."	Direct appeal close	"Good. May I get your signature on this order?"
"What kind of financing do you offer?"	Multiple options close	"We have two financing methods available: 90-day open credit or two-year long-term financing. Which of these do you prefer?"
"Well, we don't have large amounts of cash available at this time."	Assumptive close	"Based on your cash position, I would recommend you consider our lease–purchase plan. This plan allows you to pay a very small initial amount at this time and keep the cash you now have for your everyday business expenses. I will be happy to write up your order on the lease–purchase plan."
The prospect completes a careful reading of the proposal, then looks satisfied (a nonverbal clue).	Combination summary-of-benefits/direct appeal close	"That solution surpasses your quality requirements, meets your time deadlines, and provides your accounting department with the details it requested. Can you get your chief financial officer's signature on the order?"

Figure 16.3 Preparing for the close requires the preplanning of several closing methods. Research indicates that in many selling situations several closing attempts will be necessary.

or unwillingness to buy. When you are reasonably sure that the prospect is about to make a decision but is being held back by natural caution, the trial close may be appropriate. It is a good way to test the buyer's attitude toward the actual purchase. The trial close can also be effectively adapted to achieving incremental commitment in more complex multi-call sales. A trial close is often presented in the form of a probing or confirmation question. Here are some examples:

We can arrange an August 1 shipment. Would this date be satisfactory?

Would you rather begin this plan on July 1 or July 15?

Is the timing right to do a presentation to the executive committee?

Will a $2000 down payment be possible at this time?

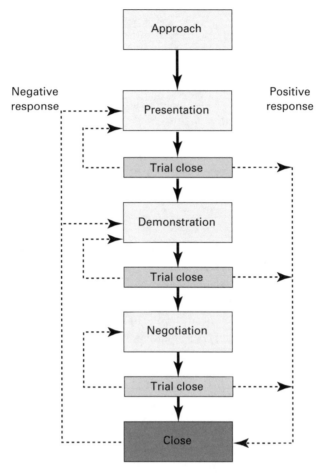

Figure 16.4 The trial close should be attempted at an opportune time during the sales presentation. It is appropriate to initiate a trial close after steps two, three, or four of the six-step presentation plan.

Some salespeople use the trial close more than once during the sales presentation. After the salesperson presents a feature, converts that feature to a buyer benefit, and confirms the prospect's agreement that the benefit is important, it is appropriate to use a trial close.

In broader terms, it would be appropriate to attempt a trial close after steps two, three, or four of the six-step presentation plan (see Fig. 16.4).

Direct Appeal Close

The **direct appeal close** has the advantages of clarity and simplicity. This close involves simply asking for the order in a straightforward manner. It is the most direct closing approach, and many buyers find it attractive. Realistically, most customers expect salespeople to ask for the sale.

direct appeal close Involves simply asking for the order in a straightforward manner.

The direct appeal should not, of course, come too early. It should not be used until the prospect has displayed a definite interest in the product or service. The salesperson must also gain the prospect's respect before initiating this appeal. Once you make the direct appeal, stop talking. John Livesay, a magazine ad director, says being patient at the close is his "secret weapon." He remains silent after asking the customer to buy. He avoids asking more questions or making additional statements. This approach gives the customer time to think about the proposal.[12]

A variation of the direct appeal close involves using a question to determine how close the customer is to making a buying decision. The question might be "How close are we to closing the sale?" This direct question calls for a direct answer. The customer is encouraged to reflect on the progress of the sale.[13]

Assumptive Close

The **assumptive close**—sometimes called *take-it-for-granted* close—asks for a minor decision, assuming that the customer has already decided to buy.[14] This closing approach comes near the end of the planned presentation. If you have identified a genuine need, presented your solutions in terms of buyer benefits, presented an effective sales demonstration, and negotiated buyer concerns satisfactorily, it may be natural to assume the person is ready to buy. Noted sales consultant Jeffrey Gitomer says the assumptive close is appropriate when the salesperson has removed perceived risks and the prospect has confidence in the salesperson.[15] The assumptive close usually takes the form of a question that focuses on a minor point. Here are some examples:

If you feel the Model 211 gives you the major benefits you are looking for, let's schedule delivery for next Tuesday.

Since our production systems provide you with the order fulfillment flexibility you require, let's go ahead and place your order.

The assumptive close asks for a minor decision, assuming that the customer has decided to buy.

Most customers will view either of these statements as the natural conclusion of the events that preceded it. Assumptive closes often include a benefit with your request for action.[16] This is a subtle way to ask for a decision when you are quite certain the customer has already decided to buy. You are only bringing the selling–buying process to a close.

Summary-of-Benefits Close

Let us assume that you have discussed and demonstrated the major benefits of your product and you detect considerable buyer interest. However, you have covered a great deal of material. There is a chance that the prospect will not be able to put the entire picture together without your help. At this point, you should provide a concise summary of the most important buyer benefits. Your goal in the **summary-of-benefits close**—also referred to as the *step-by-step close*—is to re-emphasize the benefits that will help bring about a favourable decision. This closing statement gives you the opportunity to restate how the benefits will outweigh the costs.[17]

Let us see how this closing method works in the management education industry. Foster Zanuto, representative for Brock University's Management Development Centre, recently called on Ray Busch, director of marketing for a large corporation. Near the end of the sales presentation, Foster summarized the major benefits in this manner:

> Mr. Busch, we can provide you with a state-of-the-art seminar room that will seat 30 people comfortably and four smaller rooms for the workshops you have planned. Our staff will serve a noon lunch. The cost will be $295 per person, including the instructor's fees. Finally, we will see that each of your employees receives a pad of paper, a pen, and a copy of the workshop program. Today I can reserve these facilities for November 24, which is your first preference for a meeting date. Can I go ahead and enter your reservation into our computer?

Notice that the salesperson has reviewed all the important elements of the value proposition and then asked a *need-satisfaction question*. This question is designed to move the sales process toward commitment and action.

Special Concession Close

The **special concession close** offers the buyer something extra for acting immediately. A special inducement is offered if the prospect will agree to sign the order. The concession may be part of a low-price strategy such as a sale price, a quantity discount, a more liberal credit plan, or an added feature that the prospect did not anticipate.

You should use this closing approach with care, because some customers are skeptical of concessions. This is especially true when the concession comes after the salesperson has made what appears to be the final offer.

Nicholas Graham, founder and chairman of Joe Boxer Corporation, spends considerable time presenting his novelty underwear line to retailers. Graham recalls that one of his most difficult sales involved Saks Fifth Avenue, the prestigious department store. He wanted the company to carry Joe Boxer underwear and suggested a Daniel Boone–inspired boxer with a detachable raccoon tail. Graham says, "They had never seen anything so absurd in their life." To close the sale, he let the store take 24 pairs on consignment. "They sold out in one hour," Graham says. Saks has been a committed customer ever since.[18]

Multiple Options Close

multiple options close When the salesperson gives the prospect several options to consider and tries to assess the prospect's degree of interest in each.

In many selling situations, it is a good idea to provide the prospect with options regarding product configuration, delivery, and price. This is especially true when you are dealing with the price-conscious *transactional buyer*. As noted in the previous chapter, today's customer expects new levels of flexibility. In the **multiple options close**, allow the person to examine several different options and try to assess the degree of interest in each one. As you near the point where a close seems appropriate, remove some of the options. This will reduce confusion and indecision.

The multiple options technique is often used in office equipment sales. If a small business owner wants to purchase a copy machine, most vendors will offer several models for consideration. Let us assume that the prospect has examined four models and seems to be uncertain about which one would be the best choice. The salesperson might determine which copier is least appealing and eliminate it as an option. Now the prospect can choose among three copiers. If the prospect seems to favour one copier, it would be appropriate to ask for the order.

When using the multiple options close, follow these simple steps:

1. Configure more than one product solution.
2. Cease showing product options when it appears that the prospect has been given ample selection. Too many choices can result in confusion and indecision.
3. Remove products (or features) that the prospect does not seem genuinely interested in and concentrate on the options the prospect does seem to be interested in.

Balance Sheet Close

balance sheet close A visual way of showing the customer the reasons for making a decision now versus not making a decision now.

The **balance sheet close** appeals to customers who are having difficulty making a decision even though they have been given plenty of information. Let's assume that the customer feels he or she has a choice: Buy now or buy later. The salesperson draws a T on a sheet of paper and writes the captions below on each side of the crossbar.

Reasons for buying now	Reasons for not buying now
1.	1.
2.	2.
3.	3.
4.	4.

To get the process rolling, the salesperson might say, "Let's see how many reasons we can list for buying now." On the left side of the T, the salesperson lists some reasons for buying now. These should be benefits in which the customer has already expressed an interest. On the right side, reasons for not buying now are listed. Throughout the listing process, the salesperson should engage the customer in a dialogue. This closing method will not be effective if the salesperson is doing all the talking.

Once a Salesman . . .

Many of Canada's most successful salespeople have demonstrated their aptitude for selling at an early age. Greg Brophy, President and CEO of Oakville, Ontario–based Shred-it, started a lawn-watering business when he was in elementary school. In high school, he started a driveway-sealing business with his brother and went door-to-door in the evenings selling the service. In university, he bought and sold real estate. Following graduation from McMaster University, Greg Brophy started Shred-it, a company that now employs more than 2600 people at 140 branches in 16 countries on five continents. Shred-it has more than 150 000 customers, including *Fortune* 500 companies, hospitals, banks, and government departments and agencies.

In the early days of the company, Greg was both president and a salesperson. As the company grew, he was able to coach new salespeople on how to sell Shred-it services. Today, Greg Brophy still sees himself fulfilling an important sales role. Greg Brophy says, "I still consider myself very much a salesperson and really enjoy the interaction with potential clients."[b]

Management Close

In previous chapters, we have discussed the merits of involving the sales manager or senior executives in sales calls. To close a major account, salespeople sometimes call on top management for help. This is the **management close**. Ryan Hegman, who works for Hegman Machine Tool Inc., recalls a sale that involved a $1.5 million automated manufacturing system. During the sales process, he brought in the president of the company, the vice-president of sales, and the lead engineer. "Each added value in a separate way," Ryan explains. One important reason to involve management is to make prospects feel that your whole company's resources will be available to support the customer.[19]

management close A close that involves bringing the sales manager or senior management to the sales presentation as a way to help close a sale.

Impending Event Close

The **impending event close**—also known as the *positive/negative technique*—involves making positive use of a negative point. This technique of closing requires that you know the needs of the prospects well enough to turn their objections into your selling points. More often than not, you will need to have a good relationship with your prospects to make the method work.

For example, the salesperson might say, "As you have agreed, our product does have several advantages over the competing offerings. I also want to share with you that we cannot make delivery before the middle of next month (the negative point) due to high demand (the positive point). However, I believe you're not looking for delivery until the end of next month (make sure you know this as a fact), so if you place this order today, delivery will not be a problem."

impending event close Involves making positive use of a negative point.

Combination Close

In some cases, the most effective close is one that combines two or more of the closing methods we have discussed. To illustrate, let us observe Colleen White as she attempts to close a sale in the office of a buyer for a large department store. Colleen represents a firm that manufactures a wide range of leather clothing and accessories. Near the end of her planned presentation, she senses that the prospect is quite interested in her products but seems reluctant to make a decision. This is how she handles the close:

> Ms. Taylor, I have described two benefits that seem especially important to you. First, you agree that this line will be popular with the fashion-conscious shoppers your store caters to. Second, you indicated that the prices I quoted will allow you excellent profit margins and third, if we process your order now, you will have the merchandise in time for the pre-holiday buying period. With this in mind, let's go ahead and process your order today.

Notice that this close starts with a summary of benefits and ends with an assumptive close.

ADAPTING TO THE CUSTOMER'S COMMUNICATION STYLE

IN CHAPTER 8, WE EXAMINED THE CONCEPT OF COMMUNICATION STYLES AND achieving versatility through style flexing. We noted that people with different behaviour styles will make their decisions in very distinct ways. We need to take the prospect's style into consideration when deciding how to approach the close.[20]

Directive Most Directives are goal-oriented individuals who are ready to make quick decisions once they believe your solution meets their needs. They like doing business with salespeople who display confidence that they can give customers the benefits they want. The Directive may reject your trial close just to test your confidence level. The highly assertive Directive will respect persistence and determination.

Emotive The Emotive needs social acceptance, so provide support for their opinions and ideas. Maintain good eye contact and be a good listener. Don't let this buyer's emotional statements throw you off balance. Spontaneous statements, spoken dramatically and impulsively, should be expected.

Supportive You can expect the Supportive customer to be slow in making the buying decision. This buyer is more apt to worry about change or taking risks. It's important to understand his or her perceived risks so you can provide reassurance before asking for a buying decision. Curb the desire to put pressure on the Supportive customer—it may make this buyer more indecisive. Patience is important.

Reflective Before you ask the Reflective customer for a buying decision, make sure you review important factual information. These buyers are less likely to be influenced by emotion. Ask Reflectives, "Is there any other information I can provide before you make a decision?" Never pressure the Reflective customer to make a quick decision.

PRACTISE CLOSING

YOUR SUCCESS IN SELLING WILL DEPEND IN LARGE PART ON LEARNING HOW TO MAKE these eight closing methods work for you. You will not master these approaches in a few days or a few weeks, but you can speed up the learning process with preparation and practice. Role playing is the best-known way to experience the feelings that accompany closing and to practise the skills needed to close sales. To prepare the role play, anticipate various closing scenarios and then prepare a written script of the drama.[21] Find someone (e.g., your sales manager, friend, or spouse) to play the role of the customer and give that person a script to act out. Practise the role play in front of a video recorder, and then sit back and observe your performance. The video monitor provides excellent feedback. Use the closing worksheet (see Fig. 16.3) to prepare for practice sessions.

CONFIRMING THE PARTNERSHIP WHEN THE BUYER SAYS YES

CONGRATULATIONS! YOU HAVE CLOSED THE SALE AND HAVE ESTABLISHED THE beginning of what you hope will be a long and satisfying partnership with the customer. Before preparing to leave, be sure that all details related to the purchase agreement are completed. Check everything with the buyer, and then ask for a signature if necessary.

Once the sale has been closed, it is important to take time to reassure the customer. This is the **confirmation step** in closing the sale. Before you leave, reassure the customer by pointing out that he or she has made the correct decision, and describe the satisfaction that will come with ownership of the product. The reason for doing this is to resell the buyer and to prevent buyer's remorse. **Buyer's remorse** (sometimes called *cognitive dissonance*) is an emotional response that can take various forms such as feelings of regret, fear, or anxiety.[22] It's common to wonder whether we have made the right decision. Compliment the customer for making a wise choice. Once the sale is closed, the customer may be required to justify the purchase to others. Your words of reassurance will be helpful.

Before leaving, thank the customer for the order. This is very important. Everyone likes to think that a purchase is appreciated. No one should believe that a purchase is taken for granted. Even a small order deserves words of appreciation. In many cases, a follow-up thank-you letter is appropriate.

In several previous chapters we said that a satisfied customer is one of the best sources of new prospects. Never hesitate to ask, "Do you know anyone else who might benefit from owning this product?" or a similar question. Some customers may even agree to write an introductory letter on your behalf.

confirmation step Reassuring the customer after the sale has been closed, pointing out that he or she has made the correct decision. This may involve describing the satisfaction of owning the product.

buyer's remorse Feelings of regret, fear, or anxiety that a buyer may feel after placing an order.

WHAT TO DO WHEN THE BUYER SAYS NO

HIGH-PERFORMANCE SALESPEOPLE LEARN TO MANAGE DISAPPOINTMENT. A STRONG display of disappointment or resentment is likely to close the door to future sales. Losing a sale may be painful, but it can also be a valuable learning opportunity. Doing some analysis of what went wrong can help you change the outcome of future sales. Here are some things you should do after a lost sale.[23]

1. *Make sure the deal is really dead.* There is always a chance that the prospect's decision can be changed. You might want to mount a last-ditch effort and reopen the presentation.

2. *Review the chain of events.* When you experience a no-sale call, try to benefit from the experience. If you were part of a sales team, get each member's reaction. Soon after the prospect has said no, schedule a debriefing session. If you worked alone, engage in honest self-analysis. If you carefully look at your performance during every aspect of the sales process, you may be able to identify weaknesses that can be corrected.

When the customer says yes, take a few moments to express appreciation and to congratulate the person for making a wise decision.

3. *Interview the customer.* Obtaining feedback requires a delicate approach. If you probe too aggressively, you may appear argumentative. If your approach is too passive, and the client's comments are general, you will not know how to improve. The key is to couch your questions in neutral terms. Rather than asking, "Why didn't we get the order?" try this approach: "Thank you for considering our company. We hope to do business with you at some time in the future. Would you mind helping me understand any shortcomings in our sales proposal?"

Always keep the door open for future sales. Tell the prospect you would love to work with him or her at some time in the future. Then put this person back on your prospect list, record any new information you have learned about the prospect, and continue to keep in touch. Marvin Gottlieb, president of The Communication Project, recalls the loss of a very large piece of business from a large IT firm. This company decided to begin doing its own training rather than outsource it to Gottlieb's company. Rather then give up hope, Gottlieb continued to maintain relationships with key people at the IT firm. After four years, he was invited to present information on a needed service. He closed a $50 000 sale in less than a month.[24]

Prepare the Prospect for Contact with the Competition

Some prospects refuse to buy because they want to take a close look at the competing products. This response is not unusual in the field of selling. You should do everything possible to help the customer make an intelligent comparison. It is always a good practice to review your product's strong points one more time. Give special emphasis to areas in which your product has a strong competitive advantage. Make it easy for the person to buy your product at some future date.

Adding and Deleting Prospects

Prospect and customer databases are continually changing. Promotions, transfers, mergers, and many other events require additions to and deletions from a salesperson's automated data. Most customer relationship management (CRM) software makes this an easy process and warns users against the inadvertent removal of an account. (See the exercise Changing Prospect Information on page 361 for more information.)

REVIEWING KEY CONCEPTS

- Describe the proper attitude to display toward closing the sale.

  The early sales training literature presented closing methods that sometimes encouraged manipulation of the customer. Use of any closing method that is perceived by the customer as pushy or manipulative will damage your chances of building a long-term partnership. Closing should not be viewed as a strategy to win at the expense of the customer. Once the customer's need has been confirmed, salespeople should determine the most ethical and effective method of moving the buyer from indecision to commitment.

- List and discuss selected guidelines for closing the sale.

  Long sales cycles require multiple commitments. These commitments need to be obtained from the prospect throughout a multi-call sales presentation. The buying motive that is of greatest interest deserves special attention at the close. Always negotiate tough points before attempting the close, display a high degree of confidence, and ask for the order more than once.

- Explain how to recognize closing clues.

  The salesperson must be alert to *closing clues* from the prospect. These clues fall into two categories: verbal and nonverbal. Verbal clues are the easiest to recognize, but they may be subtle as well. Again, it is important to be an attentive listener. The recognition of nonverbal clues is more difficult, but careful observation helps in detecting them.

- Discuss specific methods of closing the sale.

  Several closing methods may be necessary to get the prospect to make a buying decision; therefore, it is wise for the salesperson to preplan several closes. These closing methods should be chosen from the list provided in this chapter and then customized to fit the product and the type of buyer with whom the salesperson is dealing. In some selling situations, the use of *combination closes* is very effective. Flexing to the customer's communication style is important.

- Explain what to do when the buyer says yes and what to do when the buyer says no.

  The professional salesperson is not discouraged or offended if the sale is not closed. Every effort should be made to be of further assistance to the prospect— the sale might be closed on another call. Continue to keep in touch. Even if the sale is lost, the experience may be valuable if it is analyzed in order to learn from it.

Key Terms

assumptive close (take-it-for-granted close) **352**

balance sheet close **354**

buyer's remorse **357**

closing clue **348**

confirmation step **357**

direct appeal close **351**

impending event close **355**

incremental commitment **347**

management close **355**

multiple options close **354**

special concession close **353**

summary-of-benefits close
(step-by-step close) **353**

trial close (minor point close) **349**

Review Questions

1. List some aspects of the sales presentation that can make closing and confirming the sale difficult to achieve.

2. Describe three buying anxieties that sometimes serve as barriers to closing the sale.

3. What guidelines should a salesperson follow for closing the sale?

4. Why is it important to review the value proposition from the prospect's point of view?

5. Define the term *incremental commitment*. Why is it important to achieve incremental commitments throughout the sale?

6. Explain how the multiple options close might be used in the sale of men's and women's suits.

7. Is there a best method to use in closing the sale? Explain.

8. What is meant by a trial close (the minor point close)? When should a salesperson attempt a trial close?

9. Explain the summary-of-benefits close (step-by-step close).

10. What confirming steps should a salesperson follow when the customer says yes? What should be done when the customer says no?

Application Exercises

1. Which of the following statements, often made by prospects, would you interpret as buying signals?

   a. "How much would the payments be?"

   b. "Tell me about your service department."

   c. "The company already has an older model that seems good enough."

   d. "We do not have enough cash flow right now."

   e. "How much would you allow me for my old model?"

   f. "I do not need one."

   g. "How does that switch work?"

   h. "When would I have to pay for it?"

2. You are an accountant who owns and operates an accounting service. You have been contacted by the president of an advertising agency about the possibility of having you audit her business on a regular basis. The president has indicated that she has investigated other accounting firms and thinks that they price their services too high. With the knowledge you have about the other firms, you know you are in a strong competitive position. Also, you realize her account would be profitable for your firm. You would really like to capture this account. How will you close the deal? List and describe two closing methods you might use in this situation.

3. Zig Ziglar, Brian Tracy, and Tom Reilly are well-known authors and speakers on the subject of closing the sale. Access each of their Web sites and research the books, courses, and videos they have available for companies and individuals to purchase and learn more about closing the sale. Prepare a summary of what you find available. Does the material in this chapter parallel the kind of information these individuals present?

   www.zigziglar.com

   www.briantracy.com

   www.tomreillytraining.com

4. If the prospect is ready to buy before you have presented all of your selling points, should you make an effort to complete your sales presentation? Explain your answer.

5. Books have been written explaining hundreds of different closes that salespeople can use. One close that some salespeople commonly use is called the impending doom close. This is one of many closing techniques we would never recommend in our book. Using your search engine, find out how this particular close works. Explain why you would never expect to see this close recommended in our book.

ROLE-PLAY EXERCISE

Examine the superior benefits of the convention centre identified in "Partnership Selling: A Role Play/Simulation" online in the Student Resource section at **www.pearsoned.ca/manning**. Specifically, research the qualities of the "five-star" executive chef, the award-winning renovation of the facility, the cost of parking and transportation to and from the airport, and the easy highway access to and from the facility. You should assume the role of director of sales and, with this information, prepare a closing worksheet on the combination of summary-of-benefits and direct appeal closes for a prospective customer. Also, using the information from the audiovisual presentation guide, prepare a special concession close, allowing free use of the laser pointer and wireless microphone with a value of $107.50 for a group presentation to the 23 people who will be staying in single rooms at the hotel. Role play the close of a sale using these closing methods to another student role playing a prospect who is seriously considering using one of your competitors.

CRM Application Exercise Changing Prospect Information

Adding new contacts and changing existing contact information is easy with Salesforce.com, as it is with most CRM software. Create a contact record for B. H. Rivera by selecting "Contact" from the "Create" drop-down list on the left side of the Salesforce.com home screen. This displays a blank record that can be completed by selecting fields with the mouse or by using the tab key to move from field to field. In the company field, type "Graphic Forms" and type 3195556194 (no hyphens) into the phone field. "2134 Martin Luther King" is the address, and the city, state, and Zip code are Atlanta, GA, and 61740.

Most CRM software permits you to save time and avoid errors by selecting field data from menus. For example, point at the lead source field and click the drop-down list. A menu of choices should appear. From this menu, select Cold Call as the status for the B. H. Rivera record.

You have just added a new record to Salesforce.com. Generally, most CRM applications discourage deleting records that have a customer. Deleting these records could also delete important historical information that is useful for analysis and understanding of the customer. The alternative is to make the contact inactive. This will remove them from most reports and transactions. To make a contact inactive, search for the contact record (B. H. Rivera) using the Salesforce.com search bar. Under "Action" on the search results screen, press edit. Tab to the inactive field and click the box. B. H. Rivera is now an inactive contact in Salesforce.com.

Case Problem

The team at Event Spectrum can help make your dreams come true. The team can help you plan a special event—large or small—in almost any venue. If you want to show appreciation to your chief executive officer, who is retiring, the Event Spectrum team will make sure the party is truly special. They can help organize employee reward and recognition programs, strategy planning retreats for executives, or even corporate team-building events. One special event involved approximately 850 employees of Unilever Canada who were brought to Las Vegas over a two-week period to launch a new company vision.

Susan Minns, vice-president of client services, enjoys working with customers. Her customers vary greatly in terms of age, education, income, and social class. The key to working effectively with all of these people is relationship building. Once she builds rapport with clients and establishes a foundation built on trust, they are more likely to open up and discuss their needs. Event planners have at their disposal a wide range of planning tools, including facilities and event production expertise, but customer needs guide the use of these resources.

Susan finds that if the sales presentation is well planned and delivered, closing the sale and confirming a contract is easier. She believes that good listening skills and careful probing can help uncover dominant buying motives. For example, the client who wants an event with a special theme may have difficulty expressing her thoughts. Susan must probe and listen closely in order to understand the customer's desires. She must also create value throughout the presentation in order to set the stage for the close. A special event can cost anywhere from a few thousand dollars to—at the other extreme—several million dollars, so price can be a barrier to closing.

Questions

1. What closing clues should Susan look for?
2. What trial closes would be appropriate?
3. What tough points should be negotiated before attempting to close?
4. Can you visualize a situation in which Susan might use a multiple options close? Explain.
5. Assume that a large corporation wants to schedule a recognition event for 40 people. This event will begin with cocktails and appetizers and end with a served meal. Special entertainment will precede the meal. What items might be included in a summary-of-benefits close?

CRM Case Study Forecasting the Close

You are interested in discovering what your commissions may be for the next few months, just from examining Pat Silva's former accounts. To do this, you review the Opportunity Pipeline report. There are five fields on this report that will help you forecast your performance for the next three months: Probability, Close Date, Dollar Amount, Expected Amount, and Stage. When working on these opportunities, Pat entered the information found in each of these fields. Pat maintained the Opportunity Stage field so that at any point in time this field accurately reflects where each opportunity is in the sales process. The Probability field is calculated by Salesforce.com based on this opportunity stage. In the Probability field, Pat estimated the percentage of possibility that the account might place an order. The Dollar Amount field refers to how much Pat thought the account would spend, and the month Pat believed the account would order is in the Close Date field. The Expected Amount field is calculated based on a formula SimNet believes is accurate. In this case, it is simply the probability times the amount.

The total for each month is calculated on this report. For an estimate of your commission income, multiply each month's forecast by 10 percent.

Pat did not show that any forecasted sales were 100 percent. Pat recognized that the sales might not close, the amount anticipated (Dollar Amount) might not be achieved, and the close might not take place during the month projected. Pat knew that these prospects would not close themselves; certain steps would have to be taken to increase the probability that the prospect would place an order. To collect your commissions, you will have to discover the steps most likely to close these sales.

Questions

1. What would your commission income be for all of Pat's accounts if you closed them as Pat forecasted?
2. What kind of special concession might be necessary to close the sale with Quality Builders?
3. What kind of close may be necessary to get an order from Computerized Labs?
4. What kind of close would be appropriate for the Lakeside Clinic?

Partnership Selling: A Role Play/Simulation

Visit the role play/simulation materials provided in the Student Resources section of your companion Web site at **www.pearsoned.ca/manning**. *A Contents page lists appropriate page references for the activities.*

Developing a Sales Presentation Strategy—Closing the Sale

Refer to *Sales Memorandum 3* and strategically plan to close the sale with your customer. To consider the sale closed, you will need to secure the signature of your customer on the sales proposal form. This will guarantee your customer the accommodations listed on the form. These accommodations may change depending on the final number of people attending your customer's convention.

This is an important point to keep in mind when closing the sale; however, you still must get the signature to guarantee the accommodations.

Follow the instructions carefully, and prepare a closing worksheet listing at least four closes using the methods outlined in this chapter. Two of these methods should be the summary-of-benefits and the direct appeal. Remember that it is not the policy of your convention centre to cut prices, so your methods should include value-added strategies.

Use proof devices to make your closes more convincing, and place them in the front pocket of your three-ring binder/portfolio for easy access during your presentation. You may want to ask another person to be your customer and practise the closing strategies you have developed.

Chapter 17
Servicing the Sale and Building the Partnership

Learning Objectives

After studying this chapter, you should be able to

1   Explain how to build long-term partnerships with customer service

2   Describe current developments in customer service

3   List and describe the major customer service methods that strengthen the partnership

4   Explain how to add value with expansion selling

5   Explain how to deal effectively with complaints

customer service All the activities that enhance or facilitate the sale and use of a product.

Windsor Factory Supply (WFS) is one of Canada's largest general-line industrial distributors. The company started as a two-man operation in Windsor, Ontario, in 1955. Jerry Slavik and Cliff Cretney, both 22 years old, decided to leave another distributor and begin their own company. They had $500 between them, and raised an equal amount from relatives. Joe Sobocan joined the company a few months later, and Cliff soon left for personal reasons. Jerry and Joe began an employee profit-sharing plan as the company grew, with the intention that it would someday become 100 percent employee-owned. This occurred in 1995, shortly after Jerry and Joe retired. WFS now has six Canadian branches in Windsor, Leamington, Sarnia, Wallaceburg, London, and Mississauga, a warehouse near Detroit, Michigan, and a branch in South Carolina. Currently, there are more than 220 WFS employees. Sales are approaching $100 million, far beyond the first-year sales of approximately $50 000. How has it achieved its tremendous growth? The company has a strong internal culture and a healthy business philosophy. The company's foundation is built on *quality*, *satisfaction*, and *dependability*, and it is known for outstanding **customer service**. President Rick Thurston describes the company philosophy as one based on the belief that being able to service existing customers is more important than gaining new customers, since a large amount of incremental business comes from the current customer base. He says, "Our business is built on relationships. Of course, we are always looking for opportunities, but we know that sometimes it is important to curb growth so that quality service to existing customers is not compromised. A great example is our most recent expansion into the United States. We had been asked on many occasions to open up more facilities to support customer growth there, but we recognized that our successful Canadian approach would not necessarily be a fit for all U.S. markets. After many years of fine-tuning our relationship with one key customer, we decided to open a South Carolina branch in 2008."[1]

The Six-Step Presentation Plan

Step One: APPROACH	☑ Review Strategic/Consultative Selling Model ☑ Initiate customer contact
Step Two: PRESENTATION	✓ Determine prospect needs ✓ Select solution ✓ Initiate sales presentation
Step Three: DEMONSTRATION	✓ Decide what to demonstrate ✓ Select selling tools ✓ Initiate demonstration
Step Four: NEGOTIATION	✓ Anticipate buyer concerns ✓ Plan negotiating methods ✓ Initiate win-win negotiations
Step Five: CLOSE	✓ Plan appropriate closing methods ✓ Recognize closing clues ✓ Initiate closing methods
Step Six: SERVICING THE SALE	Follow-through Follow-up calls Expansion selling

Service, retail, wholesale, and manufacturer selling.

Figure 17.1 Servicing the sale involves three steps: follow-through, follow-up calls, and expansion selling.

Servicing the sale encompasses a variety of activities that take place during and after the implementation stage of the buying process (Fig. 11.3). In this chapter, we present servicing the sale as a three-part process: follow-through on assurances and promises; follow-up with ongoing communication after the sale; and expansion selling, which involves the identification of additional needs and providing solutions (Figure 17.1). Each of these strategies can add value and build the partnership.

BUILDING LONG-TERM PARTNERSHIPS WITH CUSTOMER SERVICE

IN A WORLD OF INCREASED GLOBAL COMPETITION AND NARROWING PROFIT MARGINS, customer retention through value-based initiatives can mean the difference between increasing or eroding market share. Progressive marketers are searching for ways to differentiate their service from that of competitors and build emotional loyalty through value.[2]

A sales organization that can develop a reputation for servicing each sale is sought out by customers who want a long-term partner to help them with their buying needs.

Satisfied customers represent an "auxiliary" sales force—a group of people who will recommend customer-driven organizations to others. If customers are pleased with the service they receive after the sale, be assured that they will tell other people. Recent research shows that when someone has a good customer service experience, he or she tells an average of six people; when someone experiences outstanding customer service, he or she tells twice as many.[3]

Achieving Successive Sales

In Chapter 5, we defined *partnering* as a strategically developed, long-term relationship that solves the customer's problem. A successful partnering effort results in successive sales and referrals (Fig. 5.4).

Many of today's large companies want to partner with suppliers who sell and deliver quality products and services that continually improve their processes and profits. The first sale is only the beginning of the relationship—an opportunity to earn a repeat sale. Repeat sales come after the supplier demonstrates the ability to add value in various ways.[4] This value may take the form of timely delivery, superior installation, accurate invoicing, technical know-how, social contacts, or something else that is important to the customer. In business-to-business sales, the relationship should intensify as the supplier delivers extensive postsale support. Taking the customer's point of view and acting in the customer's interest, often described as *customer advocacy*, is a major factor underlying repeat business.[5]

Responding to Increased Postsale Customer Expectations

According to Ted Levitt, author of *The Marketing Imagination*, people buy expectations, not things. They buy the expectations of the benefits you promised. Once the customer buys your product, expectations increase. Levitt points out that after the sale is closed, the buyer's attitude changes. The buyer expects the salesperson to remember the purchase as a favour bestowed on him or her by the buyer. Nitin Nohria, business professor and co-author of *What Really Works: The 4-2 Formula for Sustained Business Success*, says, "Customers are enormously punishing when companies don't meet their expectations."[6]

Increased customer expectations after the sale is closed require a strategic plan for servicing the sale. Certain aspects of the relationship, product, and customer strategies can have a positive influence on the customer's heightened expectations. In most business-to-business sales, the salesperson cannot service the sale alone. To manage the account properly, the salesperson will need assistance from shipping, technical support, engineering, and other departments. Customer service is increasingly a team effort.[7]

How do you respond to a customer who has increased expectations?

- *First, you should be certain your customer strategy is on target.* You must fully understand the needs and wants of the customer. What is the customer trying to accomplish, and how can you help him or her do it better?

- *Second, you should focus like a laser beam on follow-through and follow-up activities.* Throughout every sales presentation, the salesperson will offer assurances and make some promises. The salesperson's credibility will be tarnished if any of these commitments are ignored.

Job Searches Require Widening the Net

You have a good education but you don't have a job. This scenario is playing out in the lives of thousands of people throughout Canada. Before you send out another thousand resumes via the Internet or spend more time searching for employment opportunities, consider the results of a study conducted by Drake Beam Morin (DBM), a workplace-consulting firm. Networking is the top tactic for landing a job, outpacing other strategies such as the Internet and newspaper ads. The report indicates that 66 percent of DBM clients found new jobs via networking, whereas just 6 percent found employment through the Internet. Don't overlook the value of personal contact that gives you the opportunity to sell yourself.[a]

■ *Third, you should re-examine your product strategy.* In some cases, you can enhance customer satisfaction by suggesting related products or services. If the product is expensive, you can follow through and offer assistance in making credit arrangements. If the product is complex, you can make suggestions concerning use and maintenance. Each of these forms of assistance may add value to the sale.

High Cost of Customer Attrition

Financial institutions, public utilities, airlines, retail stores, restaurants, manufacturers, and wholesalers face the problem of gaining and retaining the patronage of clients and customers. These companies realize that keeping a customer happy is a good strategy. To regain a lost customer can be four to five times more expensive than keeping a current customer satisfied.[8]

There is no longer any doubt that poor service is the primary cause of customer attrition. Surprisingly few customers (12 to 15 percent) are lost because of product dissatisfaction. No more than 10 to 15 percent of lost customers leave because of price considerations. Some studies have found that from 50 to 70 percent of customer attrition is because of poor service.[9] A carefully developed strategic plan to reduce customer defection will pay big dividends.

Larry Rosen, now chairman and CEO of Harry Rosen Inc., fully embraces the customer-for-life philosophy of doing business. The company's obsession with quality products and outstanding customer service has enabled it to expand to 16 locations across Canada. Larry Rosen says, "We don't look at a person that walks into our store as an immediate sale. We look at him with a potential lifetime value."[10]

CURRENT DEVELOPMENTS IN CUSTOMER SERVICE

IN HIS BOOK *BUSINESS @ THE SPEED OF THOUGHT*, BILL GATES PREDICTS THAT IN THIS millennium, customer service will become the primary value-added function.[11] He recognizes that customer service is the primary method of building and extending the partnership. Customer service, in its many forms, nourishes the partnership and keeps it alive.

Salespeople are in a unique position to enhance *customer satisfaction* and *trust*, the two major contributors to relationship quality. With adequate orientation and training, members of the sales force can build long-term, profitable customer relationships. Recent research indicates that the building process involves five important service behaviours that are especially important in the context of business-to-business selling.[12]

- **Diligence** Diligence combines two types of service behaviours: responsiveness and reliability. In today's highly competitive, time-starved business environment, salespeople must provide service in a timely manner. Service behaviours that demonstrate both reliability and responsiveness include following up on commitments, returning phone calls, fulfilling customer requests, and being available when needed.

- **Information communication** This service behaviour involves regularly relaying product information to the customer in a clear and concise manner. Communicating information must encompass the entire sales process. Early on, this may involve drawing objective comparisons between your product and competitive offerings, and continually reiterating a clear case for your product. After the sale is closed, information communication often involves providing updated information on product usage.

- **Inducements** This service behaviour is aimed at personalizing the relationship with the customer. In Chapter 7 we noted that the manner in which salespeople establish, build, and maintain relationships is not an incidental aspect of personal selling. Some service behaviours provide the customer with an incentive, or an inducement, for maintaining the relationship with the salesperson. Becoming genuinely interested in the customer, talking in terms of the customer's interests, or doing special favours can strengthen the relationship with the customer.

- **Empathy** As the information age unfolded and the global economy heated up, we learned that it takes more than quick and accurate information communicated through advanced technology to retain customers. Empathy is one of those high-touch abilities that mark the fault line between salespeople who are highly productive and those who are average or below average in terms of productivity.[13] Salespeople who display a strong willingness to help customers and make an effort to understand them are demonstrating empathetic behaviour.

- **Sportsmanship** This service behaviour can be defined as a salesperson's willingness to tolerate setbacks and disappointments without displaying negativism. It means demonstrating good social judgment and professionalism during all customer inter-actions. If you have a 10:00 a.m. appointment with a customer but are required to wait until 10:30 a.m. for the meeting to begin, how will you handle this disappointment?

Computer-Based Systems

Customer-friendly computer-based systems are frequently used to enhance customer service. Computers give both the salesperson and the customer ready access to information and problem-solving alternatives. Nantucket Nectars provides a good example of a company that has enhanced customer service with computer-based systems. The 150 distributors can log on to **www.juiceguys.com** to place and check orders. Nantucket Nectars' 85 field salespeople can log on to NectarNet, a dedicated company Web site, from their homes to check on the status of customer orders and determine inventory levels.[14]

The sales staff at Harry Rosen Gentlemen's Apparel, the highly successful clothing retailer mentioned earlier in this chapter, use technology to establish a more personal relationship with the customer. In a matter of seconds, salespeople can review a customer's complete buying history, his or her birthday and anniversary, clothing sizes, favourite colours, children's names, or any other information that the customer has willingly provided. With this information salespeople are better able to bond with their customers. Maggie Chung, a sales manager in the Vancouver store, says, "At Harry Rosen, I've really learned the value of customer relationships. I have some customers who visit me almost monthly."[15]

CUSTOMER SERVICE METHODS THAT STRENGTHEN THE PARTNERSHIP

CUSTOMER SERVICE ENCOMPASSES ALL ACTIVITIES THAT ENHANCE OR FACILITATE the sale and use of one's product or service. The skills required to service a sale are different from those required prior to the sale (Fig. 17.2). High-performance sales personnel do not abdicate responsibility for delivery, installation, and warranty interpretation, or other customer service responsibilities. They continue to strengthen the partnership with follow-through, follow-up, and expansion selling.

Maggie Chung, a sales manager at Harry Rosen in Vancouver, uses a customer relationship management system to help manage relationships with customers.

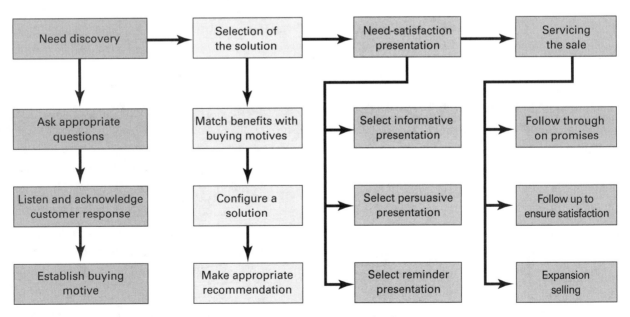

Figure 17.2 The complete consultative sales presentation guide illustrates the ways in which high-performance salespeople use value-added strategies to service the sale and build repeat business and referrals. Customer service provides many opportunities to strengthen the partnership.

Adding Value with Follow-Through

A major key to an effective customer service strategy is follow-through on assurances and promises that were part of the sales presentation. Did your sales presentation include claims for superior performance; promises of speedy delivery; assistance with credit arrangements; or guaranteed factory assistance with installation, training, and service?

Most sales presentations are made up of claims and promises that the company can fulfill. However, fulfillment of these claims will depend to a large degree on after-sale action. Postsale follow-through is the key to holding that customer you worked so hard to develop. The first sale can be the beginning of a long-term partnership or it can be the last sale. The following services can help ensure a second sale and successive sales.

A follow-up phone call to thank the customer and find out if he or she is pleased with the product will strengthen the relationship after the sale.

Make Credit Arrangements Credit has become a common way to finance purchases. This is true of industrial products, real estate, automobiles, home appliances, and many other products. Closing the sale will often depend on your ability to develop and present attractive credit plans to the customer. Even if you do not get directly involved in the firm's credit and collection activities, you must be familiar with how the company handles these matters. Salespeople need to establish a relationship with the credit department and learn how credit analysts make their decisions.[16]

Making credit decisions gets a lot tougher when you are conducting business in foreign countries. Overseas transactions can be complex, and in some cases there is little recourse if a customer does not pay. Doron Weissman, president of Overseas Brokers, a freight forwarder and export brokerage firm, says, "When I sell my services, I automatically qualify the account to make sure they're financially able to meet my demands. If not, I move on."[17]

Schedule Deliveries Many organizations are adding value with on-time deliveries. A late delivery can be a problem for both the supplier and the customer. To illustrate, let us assume that the supplier is a manufacturer of small appliances and the customer is a department store chain. A late delivery may mean lost sales because of out-of-stock conditions, cancellation of the order by the department store, or loss of future sales.

The causes of late delivery may be beyond your control. It is your responsibility, however, to keep the customer informed of any delays. You can also take steps to prevent a delay. Check to be sure your order was processed correctly. Follow up to see if the order was shipped on time. Always remember: "Every time an order is handled, the customer is handled. Every time an order sits unattended, the customer sits unattended."[18]

Be Present During Delivery When the first delivery is made, be there to be sure the customer is comfortable with the purchase. Check to determine if the order is complete and be available to offer assistance.[19]

Monitor Installation Buyer satisfaction is often related to proper installation of the product. This is true of consumer products such as security systems, central air-conditioning, solar heating systems, and carpeting. It is also true of industrial products such as electronic data processing equipment and air-quality control systems. Some salespeople believe it is to their advantage to supervise product installation; they are then able to spot installation problems. Others make it a practice to follow up on the installation to be sure no problems exist.

Offer Training in the Use or Care of the Product For certain industries, it is essential that users be trained in how to use the new product. This is true of factory equipment, electronic cash registers, farm implements, and a host of other products. Technology has become so complex that many suppliers must provide training as part of the follow-up to ensure customer satisfaction. Most organizations that sell computers and other types of electronic equipment for office use now schedule training classes to ensure that customers can properly use and care for the products. These companies believe that users must be skilled in handling their equipment.

Provide Price Change Information Price changes need not be a serious problem if they are handled correctly. The salesperson is responsible for maintaining an up-to-date price list. As your company issues price changes, record them accurately. Customers expect you to quote the correct price the first time.

Prevent Postsale Problems There are ways to prevent postsale problems. The key is conscientious follow-up to be sure everything has been handled properly. Get to know the people who operate your shipping department. They are responsible for getting the right products shipped on time, and it is important that they understand your customers' needs.

Become acquainted with people in the credit department. Be sure that they maintain a good, businesslike relationship with your customers. This is a delicate area; even small mistakes—a "pay now" notice sent too early, for example—can cause hurt feelings. If your company uses customer support staff to resolve postsale problems, be sure to get acquainted with the people who provide this service.

Schedule regular account reviews to determine the level of customer satisfaction. The focus of these reviews should be key decision makers. Are there lingering service-type issues that make you vulnerable to the competition? You want to be certain there are no open doors for your competitors. If you discover a problem, act quickly to resolve it. In some cases these formal account reviews will uncover opportunities to improve customer service. You will also become more of a consultant in the eyes of the customer.[20]

Adding Value with Customer Follow-Up

Customer follow-up methods usually have two major objectives. One is to express appreciation for the purchase and, thus, to enhance the relationship established during the sales presentation. You no doubt thanked the customer at the time the sale was closed, but appreciation should be expressed again a few days later. The second purpose of the follow-up is to determine whether the customer is satisfied with the purchase. Both of these methods will strengthen the buyer–seller relationship and build a partnership that results in additional sales.

In survey after survey, poor service and lack of follow-up after the sale are given as primary reasons people stop buying from a particular supplier. Most customers are sensitive to indifferent treatment by the sales representative. With this fact in mind, you should approach follow-up in a systematic and businesslike way. There are five follow-up methods.

Personal Visit This is usually the most costly follow-up method, but it may produce the best results. It is the only strategy that allows face-to-face, two-way communication. When you take time to make a personal visit, the customer knows that you really care.

Use the personal follow-up to keep the customer informed of new developments, new products, or new applications. This information may pave the way for additional sales. Use the personal visit to reassess where you stand with the account. The reassessment process should involve something more than a "How's it going?" question. If you want the customer to see you as a partner, ask the tough questions: "Are there any problems that I need to address?" "Can you suggest any ways we can better serve your business?" Tom Reilly, author and sales trainer, says, "Your perceptions of your performance are meaningless. It's the customer's perceptions that count."[21]

value reinforcement
Reinforcing to the customer the value they are getting from their purchase.

Personal visits provide a wonderful opportunity to engage in **value reinforcement**. Value reinforcement means getting credit for the value you create for the customer. You might review all of your follow-through activities so the customer realizes the many ways you have added value. Whenever possible, document your value-added services and point out any benefits that the customer has received. In some cases, positive bragging is an effective value reinforcement technique.[22]

Telephone Call The telephone provides a quick and efficient way to follow up a sale. A salesperson can easily make 10 or 12 phone calls in a single hour, and the cost will be minimal. If you plan to send a thank-you card or letter, follow it up with a thank-you call. The personal appeal of the phone call will increase the effectiveness of the written correspondence. The telephone call has one major advantage over written correspondence: It allows for a two-way exchange of information. Once an account is well established, you may be able to obtain repeat sales by telephone.

E-mail Message In many cases it is a lot quicker to send an e-mail message than to make a phone call. Salespeople report that they waste a lot of time playing "phone tag." Some customers prefer e-mail messages and may become irritated if you do not adhere to their wishes. If you know that a customer is not in the habit of checking their e-mail all that often, use the telephone as a back-up method. When in doubt, use parallel channels of communication.

Letter or Card Written correspondence is an inexpensive and convenient way to thank the customer for the order and to promise continued service. Some companies encourage their salespeople to use a formal letter typed on company stationery. Other

To: Walt Higgins, service engineer
From: Diane Ray, sales representative

Action Promised: Visit the bank's Ottawa location within the next week to check on installation of our security system.

Assistance Needed: System B-420 was installed at the bank's main

Ottawa branch on October 24. As per our agreement, you should make a follow-up call to check the installation of the system and provide bank personnel with a Form 82 certification checklist. The form should be given to Mr. Sandeep Khosla, the branch manager.

Copies to: Mr. Sandeep Khosla

Figure 17.3 The call report

companies have designed special thank-you cards, which are signed and sent routinely after a sale is closed. The salesperson may enclose a business card. These thank-you cards do have one major limitation: They are mass-produced and, therefore, lack the personal touch of handwritten cards and envelopes. Personalized notes, birthday cards, and anniversary cards can make a positive impression.

Call Report The **call report** is a form that serves as a communications link with persons who can assist with customer service. The format varies, but generally it is a simple form with only four or five spaces. The sample call report form that appears in Figure 17.3 is used by a company that installs security systems at banks and other financial institutions.

A form such as this is one solution to the problem of communication between company personnel and the customer. It is a method of follow-through that triggers the desired action. It is simple, yet businesslike.

Follow-up programs can be as creative or ingenious as you wish. Every sales organization competes on value, so you must continually think of new ways to add value. Creative use of your interpersonal communication skills can keep your messages fresh and personalized. Keep in mind that people buy both from the head and from the heart. Let customers know how much you care about their business.[23] You can use these five methods independently or in combination. Your main consideration should be some type of appropriate follow-up that (1) tells customers you appreciate their business, and (2) determines whether they are satisfied with the purchase.

> **call report** A written summary that provides information on a sales call to people in the sales organization so that follow-up action can be taken as necessary.

Adding Value with Expansion Selling

Personal selling is the process of identifying and filling the customer's needs. As the salesperson learns more about the customer and establishes a relationship based on trust and mutual respect, opportunities for expansion selling will arise. Expansion selling can take three forms: full-line selling, cross-selling, and upselling.

Full-Line Selling Sometimes called *suggestion selling*, **full-line selling** is the process of recommending products or services that are related to the main item sold to the customer. The recommendation is made when, in the salesperson's judgment, the product or service can provide additional satisfaction. To illustrate, let's look at the sale of new houses. Many

> **full-line selling** The process of suggesting products or services that are related to the main item being sold to the customer.

Confirming Immediately

Close-up and personal information sharing creates a core on which successful relationships may be built and sustained. Friends have long supplemented their personal visits with notes, letters, and telephone calls.

Contemporary technology offers new ways to save time in addition to enhancing and extending relationship-rich communications. Enlightened salespeople use the fax, phone and e-mail as fast, thus effective, methods to give information to their customers. E-mail can be particularly useful to quickly convey temporary messages such as those that confirm, affirm, or verify. (See the CRM case study Servicing the Sale with CRM on p. 383 for more information.)

contractors offer customers who want to differentiate their home a variety of options, including marble in the entryway, granite countertops, gourmet kitchen appliances, or Jacuzzi-like tubs for the bathroom. Customization is an important value-added service for many customers.[24]

Full-line selling is no less important when selling services. For example, a travel agent has many opportunities to suggest related products. Let us assume that a customer purchases a two-week vacation in Ireland. The agent can offer to book hotel reservations or schedule a guided tour. Another related product would be a rental car. Sometimes, a new product is simply not "right" without related merchandise. A new business suit may not look right without a new shirt and tie. An executive training program held at a fine hotel can be enhanced with a refreshment break featuring a variety of soft drinks, fresh coffee, and freshly baked pastries.

Customers will view full-line selling as a form of value-added service when it is presented correctly. There is a right way and a wrong way to make recommendations. Here are some guidelines to follow:

1. *Plan for full-line selling during the preapproach step.* Before meeting with the customer, develop a general plan that includes your objectives for this important dimension of selling. Full-line selling is easier when you are prepared.

2. *Make recommendations after you have satisfied the customer's primary need.* While there are some exceptions to this rule, it's usually best to meet the primary need first. In the case of a new home purchase, for example, the customer should first select the model home and then make decisions regarding the upgrades.

3. *Make your suggestions thoughtful and positive.* "We just received a new order of silk ties that would go well with your new shirt. Let me show you the collection." Avoid questions like, "Can we ship anything else?" This question invites a negative response.

4. *When appropriate, demonstrate the suggested item or use sales tools to build interest.* If you have suggested a shirt to go with a new suit, allow the customer to see it next to the suit. In industrial selling, show the customer a sample, or at least a picture if the actual product is not available.

Full-line selling is a means of providing value-added service. When you use it correctly, customers will thank you for your thoughtfulness and extra service. It is also a proven sales-building strategy.

Cross-Selling We have seen an increase in the use of cross-selling to grow sales volume. **Cross-selling** involves selling products that are not directly associated with products that you have sold to an established customer. A bank customer who has a home equity loan might be contacted and asked to consider purchase of a mutual fund. The customer who has purchased a townhouse might be a candidate for a security service. One financial services company, Quick & Reilly, has trained its 600 customer service representatives to use cross-selling when customers call regarding their current investments. By completing the cross-selling training programs, the representatives learned how to assess the caller's financial goals and develop a tailored proposal of products and services. Quick & Reilly achieved a 35 percent sales increase after developing the cross-selling program.[25]

More and more companies use cross-selling to discover additional sources of business within established accounts. Buyers generally welcome cross-selling efforts because they are searching for ways to consolidate purchases. They like the convenience of buying several items from the same source.[26]

Salespeople who have a good understanding of the customer's needs and have earned the customer's respect will face less resistance when recommending a product or service. To achieve success with cross-selling, you need to use *survey questions* and *probing questions* (see Chapter 14). A general survey question such as "Can you tell me more about your expansion plans?" may uncover information needed to position your cross-selling sales strategy. However, you will likely need to use probing questions to uncover and clarify a buying problem that may open the door to a cross-selling opportunity. Keep in mind that cross-selling has to be a well-thought-out part of your strategy and process.[27]

> **cross-selling** Selling to an established customer products that are not directly related to products the customer has already bought.

Upselling The effort to sell better-quality products is known as **upselling**. It is an important selling method that often adds customer value. Mike Weber, sales manager at Young Electric Sign Company, offers us two important tips on upselling. First, you need a well-established relationship with the customer—a relationship built on trust. Second, you need to continually qualify the prospect throughout the buying process. As you hear customers tell you more about their needs, you may see an opportunity to upsell. Weber says his salespeople usually engage in upselling at the design stage. The customer is shown a rough sketch of the desired sign and another rendition of something better. The added value of the more expensive option will become obvious to the customer.[28] In many selling situations, such factors as durability, comfort, or operating economy help justify the higher-priced product. A professional salesperson explains to the customer why it is in his or her best interest to spend "just a little more" and get the best value for the dollar. Most customers are more concerned with making the right purchase than they are with making the least expensive purchase.[29]

> **upselling** Effort to sell better-quality products.

Preplan Your Service Strategy

Servicing the sale is a very important dimension of personal selling, so a certain amount of preplanning is essential. It helps to preplan your service strategy for each of the three areas we have discussed: follow-through, follow-up, and expansion selling. You cannot anticipate every aspect of the service, but you can preplan important ways to add value once the sale is implemented. Develop a servicing-the-sale worksheet, like the one shown in Figure 17.4, prior to each sales presentation.

Figure 17.4 Servicing the sale worksheet. Follow-through on assurances and promises, customer follow-up, and expansion selling must be carefully planned. Use of this worksheet will help you preplan ways to add value.

Servicing the Sale Worksheet

Method of Adding Value	What You Will Say or Do
Follow-Through Set up a secure Web site or Extranet so the client can track the production and delivery of custom-engineered seed research equipment.	Set up the secure Web site in a timely manner and then contact the customer when it is operational. Explain how to access the Web site and review the benefits of using this source of assistance.
Schedule training for persons who will be using the new technology.	Send training schedule to customer and confirm the dates with a follow-up call.
Follow-Up Send a thank-you letter to each member of the team who made the purchase decision.	Express sincere appreciation for the purchase and explain the steps you will take to ensure a long-term partnership.
Check to be certain that the training was effective.	Visit the customer's research facility and talk with the employees who completed the training. Answer questions and provide additional assistance as needed.
Expansion Selling *Full-line selling.* Recommend Simonize System 5 paint protection program to a new car buyer.	Explain that this paint protection program—with Teflon Surface Protector—protects the vehicle's good looks and resale value for five years.
Cross-selling. A vacation home rental and real estate company contacts a customer who has rented a vacation home for more than 10 years. The customer is given information regarding vacation home ownership and construction services.	Discuss vacation home ownership as an investment opportunity. Describe lot selection, home design options, and finance plans.
Upselling. A large consulting firm wants to replace the commercial grade carpet in its office complex. Suggest the company purchase a high-grade carpet that will be more crush- and mat-resistant.	Explain and demonstrate with samples how a tight yarn twist, a short nap, and more stitches per centimetre will make the carpet more crush- and mat-resistant.

PARTNERSHIP-BUILDING STRATEGIES SHOULD ENCOMPASS ALL KEY PEOPLE

SOME SALESPEOPLE DO A GREAT JOB OF COMMUNICATING WITH THE PROSPECT BUT ignore other key people involved in the sale. To illustrate how serious this problem can be, let us look at the approach used by Jill Bisignano, a sales representative for a major restaurant supply firm. Jill had called on Bellino's Italian Restaurant for several years. Although she was always very friendly to Nick Bellino, she treated the other employees with nearly total indifference. One day she called on Nick and was surprised to learn that he was retiring and had decided to sell his restaurant to two long-time employees. As you might expect, it did not take the new owners long to find another supplier. Jill lost a large account because she had failed to develop a good personal relationship with other key employees. It pays to be nice to everyone.

Here is a partial list of people in your company and in the prospect's company who can influence both initial and repeat sales:

1. *Receptionist.* Some salespeople simply do not use common sense when dealing with the receptionist. This person has daily contact with your customer and may schedule most or all calls. To repeatedly forget this individual's name or display indifference in other ways may cost you dearly.

2. *Technical Personnel.* Some products must be cleaned, lubricated, or adjusted on a regular basis. Take time to get acquainted with the people who perform these duties. Answer their questions, share technical information with them if necessary, and show appreciation for the work they are doing.

3. *Stock Clerks or Receiving Clerks.* People who work in the receiving room are often responsible for pricing incoming merchandise and making sure that these items are stored properly. They may also be responsible for stock rotation and processing damage claims.

4. *Management Personnel.* Although you may be working closely with someone at the departmental or division level, do not forget the person who has the final authority and responsibility for this area. Spend time with management personnel occasionally and be alert to any concerns they may have.

This is not a complete list of the people you may need to depend on for support. There may well be other key people who influence sales. Always look beyond the customer to see who else might have a vested interest in the sale.

PARTNERING WITH AN UNHAPPY CUSTOMER

WE HAVE LEARNED THAT UNHAPPY CUSTOMERS GENERALLY DO NOT INITIATE A verbal or written complaint. This means that postsale problems may not come to the attention of salespeople or other personnel within the organization. We also know that unhappy customers do share their negative experiences with other people. A dissatisfied customer will typically tell eight to ten people about their problem.[30] A double loss occurs when the customer stops buying your products and takes steps to discourage other people from buying your products. When complaints surface, salespeople should view the

When to Say Goodbye to a Customer

Today's salespeople often find that they must devote considerable time to establish and build partnering relationships with important customers. Some salespeople are recognizing that they often have too many customers—or even some wrong customers—and are deciding to reduce their customer base selectively. Too many customers drain precious sales resources and endanger a salesperson's ability to serve his or her most important accounts. Wrong customers often demand customized products and services at prices so low they cannot be served profitably. Further, they frequently complain or demand a level of service that is unjustified for their current sales or future sales potential.

Jeff Multz, director of sales and marketing at FirstWave Technologies, found he was serving too many customers. He relates an example that occurred when he owned his own consulting business. He realized that 80 percent of his customers were a drain on his business, so he called 3000 of them to explain he could no longer serve them. Partly as a result, his sales increased by 50 percent the next year, but his profit increased by 50 percent in just five months.

David Sutcliffe, CEO of Richmond, B.C.–based Sierra Wireless, found he was serving the wrong customers. He discovered the value of not focusing on price-sensitive customers who typically buy small quantities but demand special attention. He says, "I give them a competitor's name, phone number or e-mail address. I know they're thinking I'm out of my mind. But if your competitors are so busy choking on those small orders, you can focus on and win the more profitable opportunities."

There is a growing trend today for salespeople to focus more on territory profit than simply on sales.[c]

problem as an opportunity to strengthen the business relationship. To achieve this goal, follow these suggestions:

1. *Give customers every opportunity to disclose their feelings.* Companies noted for outstanding customer service rely heavily on telephone systems, such as toll-free hotlines, to ensure easy access. At Federal Express, Cadillac Division of General Motors, and IBM—to name a few companies—specially trained advisers answer the calls and offer assistance. When a customer purchases a Ford vehicle, the salesperson introduces the customer to service staff who provide a key role in providing postsale service. The goal is to personalize the relationship with another member of the service team. Ford has discovered that after-sale contact builds a perception of value.[31] When customers do complain, by telephone or in person, encourage them to express all their anger and frustration. Do not interrupt. Do not become defensive. Do not make any judgments until you have heard all the facts as the customers see them. If they stop talking, try to get them to talk some more. How you deal with anger is very important. Encourage the angry customer to vent his or her feelings. By asking questions and listening carefully to the response, you can encourage the person to discuss the cause of the anger openly. After venting feelings and discussing specific details, the angry customer will expect a response. Briefly paraphrase what seems to be the major concern and express a sincere desire to find ways to solve the problem.[32]

2. *Keep in mind that it does not really matter whether a complaint is real or perceived.* If the customer is upset, you should be polite and sympathetic. Do not yield to the temptation to say, "You do not really have a problem." Remember, problems exist when customers perceive they exist.[33]

3. *Accept responsibility.* Avoid the temptation to blame the shipping department, the installation crew, or anyone else associated with your company. Never tear down the company you work for. The problem has been placed in your hands, and you must accept responsibility for handling it. "Passing the buck" will only leave the customer with a feeling of helplessness.

4. *Politely share with the customer your point of view concerning the problem's cause.* At least explain what you think happened. The customer deserves an explanation. At this point a sincere apology is usually appropriate.

5. *Decide what action must be taken to remedy the problem.* Take action quickly and offer a value-added atonement. Don't just do what is expected; delight the customer by exceeding their expectations. Winning customer loyalty today means going beyond making it right.[34]

The value of customer complaints can emerge in two forms. First, complaints can be a source of important information that may be difficult to obtain by other means. Second, customer complaints provide unique opportunities for companies to prove their commitment to service. Loyalty builds in the customer's mind if you do a good job of solving his or her problem.[35]

A Word of Caution

When you are dealing with major or minor customer service problems and an apology is necessary, do not use e-mail. When a minor problem surfaces, call the customer personally. Do not delegate this task to someone else in your organization. If you need to apologize for a major problem that has occurred, meet with the customer in person. Schedule the meeting as soon as possible.[36]

REVIEWING KEY CONCEPTS

- Explain how to build long-term partnerships with customer service.

  Servicing the sale is a major dimension of the selling process, with the objectives of providing maximum customer satisfaction and establishing a long-term partnership. Servicing the sale encompasses a variety of activities that take place during and after the buying process. In this chapter, we present servicing the sale as a three-part process: follow-through on assurances and promises, follow-up with ongoing communication after the sale, and expansion selling.

- Describe current developments in customer service.

  In the new millennium, customer service has become a primary value-added function. Salespeople are in a

unique position to enhance customer satisfaction and trust by displaying five important service behaviours: diligence, information communication, inducements, empathy, and sportsmanship.

- List and describe the major customer service methods that strengthen the partnership.

  A major key to an effective customer service strategy is follow-through on assurances and promises that were part of the sales presentation. Follow-through services may involve making credit arrangements, scheduling deliveries, monitoring installation, training in the use or care of the product, providing product updates, and similar services. Salespeople can also add value with a sincere expression of appreciation. Follow-up methods include personal visits, telephone calls, e-mail messages, letters, or call reports.

A salesperson depends on the support of many other people in servicing a sale. Maintaining good relationships with support staff members who help service your accounts is well worth the time and energy required.

- Explain how to add value with expansion selling.

As the salesperson learns more about the customer, opportunities for expansion selling will arise.

Expansion selling can take three forms: full-line selling, cross-selling, and upselling.

- Explain how to deal effectively with complaints.

Dealing effectively with an unhappy customer should be thought of as an opportunity to strengthen the business relationship. Always give the customer every opportunity to disclose feelings. Encourage the angry customer to vent his or her feelings and listen closely to what is said. Briefly summarize what seems to be the major concern and express a sincere desire to find ways to solve the problem.

Key Terms

call report **373**
cross-selling **375**
customer service **364**

full-line selling (or suggestion selling) **373**
upselling **375**
value reinforcement **372**

Review Questions

1. You are currently a sales manager employed by a company that sells long-term care insurance. Tomorrow you will meet with five new sales trainees. Your major goal is to explain why it is important to service the sale. What important points will you cover?

2. Define *customer service*. List the three major activities associated with this phase of personal selling.

3. Explain how full-line selling fits into the definition of customer service. How does *full-line selling* differ from *cross-selling*?

4. List and describe five service behaviours that are especially important in the context of business-to-business selling.

5. Adding value with follow-through can involve several postsale services. List five possible services.

6. How does credit become part of servicing the sale?

7. This chapter describes the value of the lifetime customer. Is it realistic to believe that people will become lifetime customers in our very competitive marketplace?

8. Define *upselling* and explain how it can add value.

9. What types of customer service problems might be prevented with the use of a call report?

10. What are five things you should do when trying to re-establish a partnering relationship with a dissatisfied customer?

Application Exercises

1. You are a salesperson working in the paint department at a Canadian Tire store. A customer has just purchased 75 litres of house paint. Assume that your store carries everything in the painting line, and list as many items as you can think of that could be used for expansion selling. Explain how your suggestions of these items could be a service to the customer.

2. You work as a wholesale salesperson for a plumbing supply company. One of your customers, a contractor, has an open line of credit with your company for $10 000 worth of products. He is currently at his limit; however, he is not overdue. He just received word that he has been awarded a $40 000 plumbing contract at the local airport. The contract requires that he supply

$9000 worth of plumbing products. Your customer does not have the cash to pay for the additional products. He informs you that unless you can provide him with some type of financing, he may lose the contract. He says that he can pay you when he finishes his next job in 60 days. Explain what you will do.

3. You have just interviewed for a job that you would really like to have. You have heard that it is a good idea to follow up an interview with a thank-you note or letter and an indication of your enthusiasm for the position. Select the strategy you will use for your follow-up, and explain why you chose it.

4. Using your search engine, examine the Internet for information on customer satisfaction. Type in "cus-tomer satisfaction" + selling. Are you surprised by the number of queries on this subject? Examine some of the queries related to what customers have said about specific company customer service programs. Be prepared to discuss some of what you find in class.

5. *Buyer remorse* was explained in Chapter 16. It is a common response customers have after making an important purchase. You are a salesperson who has been very successful selling cars to young families. Knowing that buyer remorse is a common response, how can you use this to help service a sale and build a partnership? Explain.

ROLE-PLAY EXERCISE

Visit the role play/simulation materials provided in the Student Resources section of your companion Web site at **www.pearsoned.ca/manning**. A *Contents page lists appropriate page references for the activities.*

An important aspect of personal selling is the need to add value with follow-through and follow-up. Both of these account management activities can be time-consuming, especially if the salesperson is not skilled at setting up appointments that fit into a busy schedule. In this role play, you are to set up three follow-through meetings with a customer who has just purchased conference services from the convention centre you represent. First, you must contact your client three days from today to confirm the availability of the Revolving Platform Room for the meeting of 300 people. Second, you must contact this same client a week from today to get approval on the number of chicken Wellington banquet-style dinners needed (see Partnership Selling, p. 107, and Guarantees on p. 117). And, third, because your client isn't sure about the need for a microphone (see Partnership Selling, pp. 112–114), you need to call your client the day before the meeting, which is scheduled four weeks from today, to verify whether you or your client will supply a microphone.

Equipped with a calendar, you should establish dates and times when your client will be available to talk or meet with you. Before you meet with your client, plan to recommend at least two times of the day that fit into your schedule for each of your meetings. If your client cannot meet at either of these times, ask your client to recommend a time. Do not start out by asking when your client is available because this could conflict with your busy schedule. Write the agreed-on times and dates in your calendar, suggesting your client do the same, so there will be no misunderstandings. Because these dates are deadlines, suggest that your client call you back if, for some reason, the schedule changes. Inform your client that you will plan to be at the hotel when the client's meeting starts and that you will be available to make sure everything is properly scheduled. Give your client your phone number and e-mail address and ask him or her to contact you if there are any questions between now and the meeting date. Have another student role play the customer and, after the role play, assess your customer service.

Case Problem

Windsor Factory Supply Limited (WFS), introduced in the opening vignette, is one of Canada's most respected industrial distributors. Many customers remain loyal to WFS because they value outstanding service, a broad range of industrial, automotive, and construction products, and a supplier that will work closely with them to solve their buying problems. The success of WFS can be traced to a number of factors:

- A *desire to build as many relationships and the strongest relationships possible with all customers.* WFS frequently moves employees to new positions within the company: a warehouse person may become an outside salesperson and, later, be transferred to inside sales; an outside salesperson may be transferred to purchasing, or back to inside sales. (Rick Thurston, now president, began as a driver/delivery person at the Leamington branch in 1984.) This creates maximum flexibility within the company but, more importantly, means that inside salespeople know the difficulties that outside salespeople face, and they often have personal contacts within customer firms. It also means that outside salespeople have had the benefit of training and learning while in the warehouse and on the inside sales desk. As a result, customers frequently have strong relationships with and trust in several WFS employees who they know can help them.

- A *strong belief that work should be rewarding for all employees.* "Employee happiness is very important to us. Happy employees help build positive relationships with customers," says Rick Thurston. Employees share many experiences, from going to major sporting events to having company parties and picnics. Twice, for example, all of the employees shared an expense-paid trip to Las Vegas. The company also sponsors many community events and encourages volunteerism among its employees. There is an excellent employee benefits package, which includes education and recreation allowances. This employee investment has been rewarded many times over. At one point, the company had gone four years without a single absentee day. Employees even provide important input on management. In fact, a management committee, including the president, is elected each year.

- An *investment in customer service and a strong service culture.* The company has invested in computer equipment and programming and is able to tell customers immediately how much inventory it has and where that inventory is located. Purchasing, payables, invoicing, receivables, account profiles, sales and other financial reports, and vehicle maintenance schedules are all computerized. Employees are empowered to make decisions whenever customer service is an issue. On one occasion, two employees took a company van and left Windsor to get some material in Pittsburgh, Pennsylvania, for a customer who urgently needed it, and they returned immediately with the material. If a customer calls to order something that is urgently needed but the delivery truck has left for the day, the customer is never told to wait for the next delivery. Someone else within the company will see that the order gets delivered.

- A *willingness to experiment and grow to meet changing customer needs.* In 2008, Windsor Factory Supply acquired Keep Industrial Supply, which will continue to operate under its own name. However, it provides three new locations, and its customer relationships and business solutions will complement those of WFS. With the addition of the South Carolina operation, the company now has 10 branches and numerous on-site customer integrated-supply agreements. Many WFS customers now check inventory, place orders, or check order status online. The company has also established commodity management programs with its best customers, whereby it manages all of the general supply items for these companies. WFS is always willing to add items to its inventory for customers who will buy them, and an increasing number of customers are taking advantage of this service.[37]

Questions

1. How might a Windsor Factory Supply salesperson add value with full-line selling? Cross-selling?

2. What types of follow-through activities and follow-up calls should Winsdor Factory Supply salespeople be prepared to initiate? How can inside salespeople be used to help maintain value-added customer relationships?

3. How can commodity management programs and other special inventory management programs be

used to add value for Windsor Factory Supply? How can such programs contribute to the company's long-term success?

4. Assume that you have just received a phone call from an important customer who says, "We just received a shipment that is needed urgently, but there are some problems with it. We need you to take some action fast." What will you do? Be specific. How might you partner with this unhappy customer?

CRM Case Study   Servicing the Sale with CRM

You have taken over a number of accounts of another salesperson, Pat Silva. Most of these accounts are leads, which means that they have not yet purchased from SimNet. Two accounts did purchase networks from Pat: Ms. Karen Murray of D'Zines, and Ms. Judith Albright, owner of Piccadilly Studio. You now want to be sure that these sales are well serviced.

Questions

1. Whom should you speak with, within SimNet, before following through and contacting each of the owners? What would you need to discover?

2. What will be your follow-up strategy for each customer?

3. Does the fact that these customers initiated their orders (they were not sold the products, they bought them) influence your follow-up strategy?

4. List and describe five important service behaviours that are especially important in the context of business-to-business selling.

5. Do you see any expansion-selling opportunities with these two accounts? Which *suggestion-selling* methods should you consider?

Partnership Selling: A Role Play/Simulation

Visit the role play/simulation materials provided in the Student Resources section of your companion Web site at **www.pearsoned.ca/manning**. A *contents page lists the appropriate page references for the activities.*

Developing a Sales Presentation Strategy—Servicing the Sale

Refer to *Sales Memorandum 3*, and strategically plan to service the sale with your customer. After closing the sale—getting the customer's signature—there are several steps to take in order to add value and build customer confidence and satisfaction. These steps are important to providing total quality customer service, and should provide for repeat sales and a list of referred customers.

Following the instructions in item 2g of your presentation plan, you need to schedule a future appointment to telephone or personally call and confirm the number of people attending the convention, and final room and menu needs (see the convention centre policies). Also during this conversation you might suggest beverages for breaks, audiovisual needs, and any other items that will make this an outstanding convention for your customer.

You should have your calendar available to suggest and write down dates and times for this future contact. Any special materials, such as a calendar, can be placed in the back pocket of your portfolio. You may want to ask another person to be your customer and practise the customer service strategies you have prepared.

At this point you should be strategically prepared to make the presentation to your customer as outlined in *Sales Memorandum 3*. Your instructor will provide you with further instructions.

PART V

ROLE-PLAY EXERCISE
Developing a Presentation Strategy

SCENARIO

This role play is a continuation of the Part IV role-play exercise. You recently met with Gabriela Ansari, founder and chief executive officer of Cantrol Security Inc. The purpose of the first sales call was to begin the relationship-building process and present selected value-added guest services and amenities offered by the Park Inn International Hotel and Convention Centre. You also obtained some information regarding the customer's buying process. For this role play, you will prepare a persuasive presentation for a second sales call to Gabriela Ansari, during which you must elicit information you need to prepare a formal sales proposal.

CUSTOMER PROFILE

Prior to starting Cantrol Security, Gabriela Ansari spent 12 years working in sales and sales management at General Electric Corporation (GE), described by *Fortune* magazine as America's most admired company. Working for GE was a great learning experience for Gabriela, who is trying to apply the GE success formula to Cantrol Security. She is the classic extrovert, a person who combines high sociability and high dominance.

SALESPERSON PROFILE

You are new to the field of selling, but you are a quick learner. The first visit with Gabriela Ansari went well, and now he is preparing for the second sales call. Gabriela is planning a large banquet to recognize her employees but has not yet selected a location for this event. While working for GE, Gabriela attended more than 25 business conferences and was disappointed by many of them. Too often, they were held at look-alike hotels that served bland food typically served by poorly trained waiters who

displayed little enthusiasm. You took notes throughout the meeting and will address these concerns during the second sales call.

PRODUCT

The Park Inn is a full-service hotel and convention centre. After completion of a recent $2.8 million renovation, the Park Inn received the Excellence in Renovation Design Award from the Ontario Architectural Association.

INSTRUCTIONS

The first sales call was basically an informative presentation. Near the end of the visit, Gabriela Ansari did disclose her plans for a large recognition banquet to be held on October 25, the company's second anniversary. No other information was provided, but Gabriela agreed to a second meeting to be held the following week.

Based on the information collected during the first call, you are now planning a persuasive presentation that will involve the first three steps of the six-step presentation plan (see Fig. 13.3). At the office of Gabriela Ansari—to be role played by another student—you will need to re-establish the relationship and then initiate the agenda approach (see Chapter 13). Begin the presentation with appropriate survey, probing, and confirmation questions. These questions should be preplanned using information found in Chapter 14.

As the need-discovery phase of the presentation progresses, the customer's buying criteria or buying conditions should surface. Prior to the second sales call, you should also select and be prepared to demonstrate appropriate selling tools (i.e., proof devices). A variety of selling tools suitable for reproduction can be found in "Partnership Selling: A Role Play/Simulation" online in the Student Resource section at **www.pearsoned.ca/manning**. Ensure that you preplan feature–benefit selling statements that appeal to Gabriela Ansari's needs. The importance of selling specific benefits and obtaining customer reactions cannot be overemphasized (see Chapter 14).

A major objective of the second sales call is to move the sale forward by convincing Gabriela Ansari that the Park Inn offers an outstanding combination of value-added guest services and amenities and is prepared to meet her needs. The sale will not be closed during the second call, but you will try to obtain a commitment to prepare a formal sales proposal to be presented to Gabriela Ansari within 48 hours. (See Partnership Selling, on your companion Web site for a sample sales proposal form.)

Chapter 18
Opportunity Management: The Key to Greater Sales Productivity

Learning Objectives

After studying this chapter, you should be able to

1 Discuss the four dimensions of opportunity management

2 List and describe time management strategies

3 Explain factors that contribute to improved territory management

4 Identify and discuss common elements of a records management system

5 Discuss stress management practices

Many of the best salespeople we know had no intention to pursue a career in sales, but had experiences early in their lives that helped them develop personality traits and abilities that have certainly contributed to their success. During her school years, Paula Shannon acted in plays, practised public speaking, and participated in a number of competitive sports, most notably gymnastics. She spent a year studying in Belgium, where she learned to adapt to another culture and social setting, and learned a third language. Paula now speaks six languages.

Paula credits managing a large paper route at a young age with helping to teach her about responsibility. Later, she worked as a waitress, did some interpretation on a tour bus, sold clothing and other items at retail, and spent a summer in customer service for a large commercial waste management firm. In Europe, Paula worked as a management trainee for Berlitz International. This program helped give her a solid grounding in general business: operations, finance, accounting, human resources, and sales. Following her management training, Paula Shannon began to handle sales for several Berlitz language centres. Paula says her belief and confidence in the product she was selling was evident. She credits her boss at the time, Anita Komlos, whom she describes as "one of the most natural and effective salespeople I have ever known," with helping her learn how to probe effectively and when to "shut up."

Paula Shannon has managed to learn something of value from everything she has done. She is clearly focused on managing herself and her career. Today, Paula Shannon is senior vice-president and chief sales officer for Boston-based Lionbridge Technologies, Inc. She manages its global sales force of 70 from her home office in Montreal.[1]

OPPORTUNITY MANAGEMENT—
A FOUR-DIMENSIONAL PROCESS

WHAT MAKES A SALESPERSON SUCCESSFUL? SOME PEOPLE BELIEVE THE MOST important factor is hard work. This is only partly true. Some people work hard but do not accomplish much. They lack purpose and direction. This lack of organization results in wasted time and energy. Hard work must be preceded by careful planning. Every moment spent planning, according to some experts in self-management, saves three or four moments in execution.[2]

Wasting time and energy is the slippery slope to failure in the age of information. Many salespeople are drowning in information and the flood of messages each day leaves little time to think and reflect. Sales and sales support personnel, like most other knowledge workers, are working under tighter deadlines. The response time to customer inquiries has been shortened and customers are less tolerant of delays.

As pressures build, it's easy to overlook opportunities to identify prospects, make sales, and improve service to customers. The ability to perceive opportunities and seize them is an important characteristic of high-achieving salespeople.[3] **Opportunity management** should be viewed as a four-dimensional process consisting of the following components:

opportunity management A four-dimensional process consisting of time, territory, records, and stress management.

1. *Time management.* There are only about 250 business days per year. Within each day there is only so much time to devote to selling. Selling hours are extremely valuable. When salespeople are asked to evaluate the major challenges they face in their work, "Not enough time" is often rated number one. Dealing with information overload and achieving balance in life are also major challenges.

2. *Territory management.* A **sales territory** is a group of customers and prospective customers assigned to a single salesperson. Every territory is unique. Some territories consist of one or two cities or counties, while others encompass several provinces. The number of accounts within each territory will also vary. Today, territory management is becoming less of an art and more of a science.

sales territory A group of customers and prospective customers assigned to a single salesperson.

3. *Records management.* Every salesperson must maintain a certain number of records. These records help to "systematize" data collection and storage. A wise salesperson never relies on memory. Some of the most common records include planning calendars, prospect forms, call reports, summary reports, and expense reports.

4. *Stress management.* A certain amount of stress comes with any selling position. Some salespeople have learned how to take stressful situations in stride. Others allow stress to trigger anger and frustration. Learning to cope with various stressors that surface in the daily life of a salesperson is an important part of the self-management process.

TIME MANAGEMENT

A SALESPERSON CAN INCREASE SALES VOLUME IN TWO MAJOR WAYS. ONE IS BY improving selling effectiveness, and the other is by spending more time in face-to-face selling situations. The latter objective can best be achieved through improved time and territory management.

Improving the management of both time and territory is a high priority in the field of selling. These two closely related functions represent major challenges for salespeople.

Let us first look closely at time management. There is definitely a close relationship between sales volume and number of customer contacts made by the salesperson. You have to make calls to get results.

Time-Consuming Activities

Some salespeople who have kept careful records of how they spend their time each day are surprised to learn how little they spend in face-to-face selling situations. A national survey of 1500 salespeople from 13 industries found that on average, salespeople spend 60 percent of their time on administrative duties or travel.[4] Administrative duties can include such things as completion of sales records and time spent on customer follow-through and follow-up. Salespeople need to examine carefully each of these activities and determine whether too much or too little time is spent in any area. One way to assess time use is to keep a time log. This involves recording, at the end of every hour, the activities in which you were engaged during that time.[5] At the end of the week, add up the number of minutes spent on the various activities and ask yourself, "Is this the best use of my time?" Once you have tabulated the results of your time log, it should be easy to identify the "time wasters." Pick one or two of the most wasteful areas, and then make plans to correct the problem. Set realistic goals that can be achieved. Keep in mind that wasting time is usually a habit. To manage your time more effectively, you need to form new habits. Changing habits is hard work, but it can be done.[6]

Time Management Methods

Sound time-management methods can pave the way to greater sales productivity. The starting point is forming a new attitude toward time conservation. You must view time as a scarce resource not to be wasted.[7] The time-saving strategies presented here are not new, nor are they unique. Time-conscious people in all walks of life are using them.

Develop a Series of Personal Goals According to Alan Lakein, author of *How to Get Control of Your Time and Your Life*, the most important aspect of time management is knowing what your goals are. He is referring to all goals—career goals, family goals, and life goals. People who cannot or do not sit down and write out exactly what they want from life lack direction. Brian Tracy, who developed the "Law of Direction" says, "Your ability to set clear, specific goals will do more to guarantee you higher levels of success and achievement than any other single skill or quality."[8]

The goal-setting process requires that you be clear about what you want to accomplish. If your goal is too general or vague, progress toward achieving that goal is difficult to observe. Goals such as "I want to be a success" or "I desire good health" are much too general. The major principles that encompass goal setting are outlined in Table 18.1.

Goals have a great deal of psychological value to people in selling. Sales goals, for example, can serve as a strong motivational force. To illustrate, let us assume that Mary Paulson, sales representative for a cosmetic manufacturer, decides to increase her sales by 15 percent over the previous year. She now has a clear goal to aim for and can begin identifying specific steps to achieve the new goal.

Mary Paulson has established a long-term goal as part of a yearly plan. Some goals require considerable time and should be part of a one-year plan. Next, Mary should set aside an hour or so at the end of each month to decide what she wants to accomplish during the coming month. Weekly planning is also important. Once a week—Friday is a good time—set goals for the next week and develop a plan for reaching them. Finally, Mary should develop a daily plan.[9]

Prepare a Daily To-Do List Sales professionals who complete the time management course offered by FranklinCovey are encouraged to engage in event control. This involves planning and prioritizing events every day.[10] Start each day by thinking about what you want to accomplish. Then write down the activities (Fig. 18.1). Putting your thoughts on paper (or in your computer) forces you to clarify your thinking. Investment firm regional director Heather Gardner records her daily planned activities in her BlackBerry and Microsoft Outlook calendar. On a typical day, the BlackBerry will show entries for every

Figure 18.1 A daily list of activities can help a salesperson set priorities and save time.

half hour. Gardner works through her detailed to-do list by adhering to one unshakable rule: Avoid nonpaying activities during working hours.[11]

Now you should prioritize your "to-do" list; do not let outside distractions interfere with your plan. Begin each day with the highest-priority task.

Vancouver-based Priority Management offers an online quiz to help you assess whether you are efficient or effective and a number of online articles to help you manage time and tasks better (**www.prioritymanagement.com**).

Maintain a Planning Calendar Ideally, a salesperson needs a single place to record daily personal and business appointments, deadlines, and tasks. Dennis Heinzlmeir, who teaches time management at Mount Royal College in Calgary, says, "Our brains are very poor organizers." The solution is to create systems "to relieve our overburdened minds."[12] Unfortunately, many salespeople write daily tasks and appointments on any slip of paper they can find: backs of envelopes, business cards, napkins, or Post-it notes. Hyrum W. Smith, author of *The 10 Natural Laws of Successful Time and Life Management*, calls these pieces of paper "floaters." They just float around until you either follow through on them or lose them. It's a terribly disorganized method for someone who wants to gain greater control of his or her life.[13] The use of floaters often leads to the loss of critical information, missed appointments, and lack of focus. Select a planning calendar design (the FranklinCovey Day Planner is one option) that can bring efficiency to your daily planning efforts. You should be able to determine at a glance what is coming up in the days and weeks ahead (Fig. 18.2).

Many salespeople are using **personal digital assistants** (PDA) to organize information. Small, pocket-size PDAs, such as those available from Palm or BlackBerry, offer many of the features common to laptop computers. The salesperson can send and receive e-mails or text messages and download important customer information. Salespeople can also input their customer notes immediately after a sales call. The PDA also serves as an electronic memo pad, calendar, expense log, address book, and more. These organizers can be used to keep track of appointments and serve as a perpetual calendar.

Organize Your Selling Tools You can save valuable time by finding ways to organize sales literature, business cards, order blanks, samples, and other items needed during a sales call. You may waste time on a callback because some item was not available during your first call. You may even lose a sale because you forgot or misplaced a key selling tool.

If you have a great deal of paperwork, invest in one or more file cabinets. Some salespeople purchase small, lightweight cardboard file boxes to keep their materials organized. These boxes can easily be placed in your car trunk and moved from one sales call to another. The orderly arrangement of selling tools is just one more method of time conservation.

The key to regular use of the four time-saving techniques already described is *commitment*. Unless you are convinced that efficient time management is important, you will probably find it difficult to adopt these new habits. A salesperson who fully accepts the "time is money" philosophy will use these techniques routinely.

Saving Time with Meetings in Cyberspace and Other Methods of Communication

As the cost of travel increases, more and more salespeople are asking the question, "Is this trip necessary?" Instead of travelling to a customer's office, some salespeople schedule a telephone conference call. A modern alternative to this type of conference call is a meeting

personal digital assistant
A small, personal device that stores information and provides many of the features common to laptop computers.

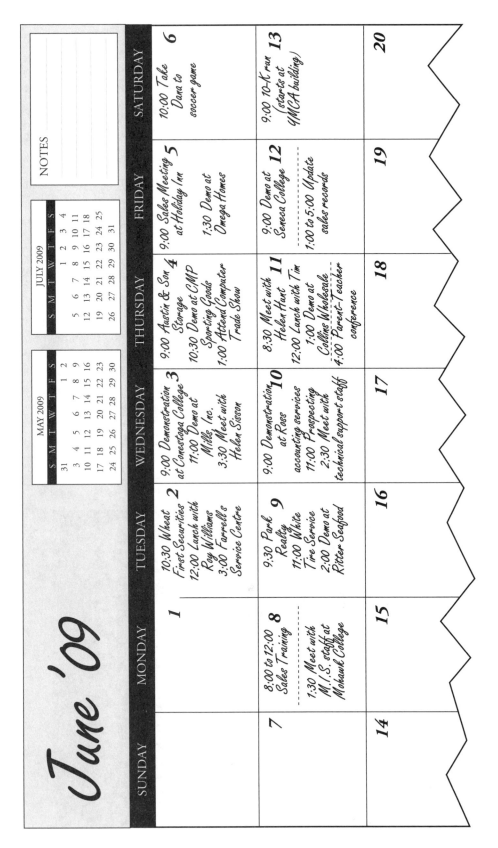

Figure 18.2 Monthly planning calendar sample. Shown are 11 days of a monthly planning calendar for a computer service sales representative. Monthly planning calendars such as this one are now a key function of most CRM systems.

in cyberspace. The voice of each meeting participant travels over a phone line and attendees view visuals—PowerPoint presentations—on their desktop computers. Nerac Inc., an information-services company, often schedules Web conferences for potential customers. The sales representative can bring online a Nerac researcher who presents an introduction to the company's closely guarded databases. Clients get to watch the researcher at work over the Internet.[14]

Some customers actually prefer telephone contact for certain types of business transactions. Here are some situations in which the phone call is appropriate.

- Call the customer in advance to make an appointment. You will save time, and the customer will know when to expect you.

- Use the telephone to keep the customer informed. A phone call provides instant communication with customers at a low cost.

- Build customer goodwill with a follow-up phone call. Make it a practice to call customers to thank them for buying your product and to determine if the customer is satisfied with the purchase.

Some customers prefer to be contacted by e-mail, and it would be a mistake to ignore their preference. Busy people often discourage telephone calls to minimize interruptions.

Voice-mail automated telephone systems are now being used by companies of all sizes. These systems not only answer the phone and take messages but also provide information-retrieval systems that are accessible by telephone. This technology is especially useful for salespeople who need to exchange information with others. For many salespeople, the cellular telephone has become a convenient and time-saving sales tool. A pager also can be used to facilitate communication with customers and the main office.

The cell phone and laptop have become convenient and time-saving sales tools.

The fax machine takes telecommunication a step further. With the aid of a fax machine, salespeople can send and receive documents in seconds using standard public or cellular telephone lines. Detailed designs, charts, and graphs can be transmitted across the country or around the world.

TERRITORY MANAGEMENT

MANY MARKETING ORGANIZATIONS HAVE FOUND IT HELPFUL TO BREAK DOWN THE total market into manageable units called sales territories. As noted earlier, a *sales territory* is the geographic area where prospects and customers reside. While some firms have developed territories solely on the basis of geographic considerations, a more common approach is to establish a territory on the basis of classes of customers. Territories are often classified according to sales potential. Some marketers assign sales representatives to key industries. The *Ottawa Citizen* newspaper divides its customer base into major business lines, such as real estate and automotive.[15] Regardless of how the sales territory is established, it is essentially a specific number of present and potential accounts that can be called on conveniently and economically.

What Does Territory Management Involve?

To appreciate fully the many facets of territory management, it will be helpful to examine a typical selling situation. Put yourself in the shoes of a salesperson who has just accepted a position with a firm that manufactures a line of high-quality tools. You are responsible for a territory that covers Manitoba and Saskatchewan, which includes 88 auto supply firms that carry your line of tools. It also includes 38 stores that do not carry your tools. On the basis of this limited information, how would you carry out your selling duties? To answer this question, it will be necessary to follow these steps:

Step 1: Classify All Customers. Salespeople often divide their territory by area code, by industry, by product, or by projected sales volume. Always divide your territory in a way that makes sense.[16] If you classify customers according to potential sales volume, then you must answer two questions: What is the dollar amount of the firm's

---

Customer Relationship Management with Technology

Islands of Information

Companies often use many different software programs that contain information about customers. The firm may have customer purchase and payment history in its accounting system. Customer service problems may be recorded in the service department's software. A help-desk program may be used by people in customer support.

The company's salespeople may be using one software program to manage their contacts with customer personnel, another program to prepare quotes, and yet another for correspondence with customers. To reduce these "islands" of customer information, more companies are finding ways to merge this information or to acquire software that performs more than one of these functions. Some customer relationship management (CRM) systems are combining a number of these functions into one integrated package.

current purchases? What amount of additional sales might be developed with greater selling effort? Store A may be purchasing $3000 worth of tools each year, but potential sales for this firm amount to $5000. Store B currently purchases $2000 worth of tools a year, and potential sales amount to $2500. In this example, store A clearly deserves more time than store B.

It is important to realize that a small number of accounts may provide a majority of the sales volume. Many companies get 75 to 80 percent of their sales volume from 20 to 25 percent of their total number of customers. The problem lies in accurately identifying which accounts and prospects fall into the top 20 to 25 percent category. Once this information is available, you can develop customer classification data that can be used to establish the frequency of calls. Jennifer Kline, a pharmaceutical salesperson employed by Schering-Plough's animal care division, gives a high priority to loyal customers. Kline says, "The people who are writing for you will continue to write for you if you serve them well.[17]

Step 2: Develop a Routing and Scheduling Plan. Many salespeople have found that travel is one of their most time-consuming nonselling activities. A great deal of time can also be wasted just waiting to see a customer. The primary objective of a sales routing and scheduling plan is to increase actual selling by reducing time spent travelling between accounts and waiting to see customers.

If a salesperson called on only established accounts and spent the same amount of time with each customer, routing and scheduling would not be difficult. In most cases, however, you need to consider other variables. For example, you may be expected to develop new accounts on a regular basis. In this case, you must adjust your schedule to accommodate calls on prospects. Another variable involves customer service. Some

Balancing Career and Family

Women today know that they will probably be working for pay for part or all of their adult lives. Most will also perform multiple roles that can be stressful and tiring. Many women who work full-time in sales also assume the responsibilities of wife and mother. Ellyn Foltz, vice-president of sales and marketing for Dataline Incorporated, maintains a fully equipped personal computer (PC) and Internet hookup at her home. She gets up early and usually spends about 90 minutes on her work while family members are eating breakfast. In the evening, she logs on and completes two or three hours of work after her son is in bed. Foltz has structured her life so that she does not have to make "impossible choices" between work and family. She turned down a high-profile job that would have required constant travel.

Jill Doran, director of national accounts for National Car Rental, says that her employer gives her the tools and support she needs to maintain balance in her life. She took maternity leave for each of her children and now has the freedom to work from her home part of each week. When she is at home, Doran checks her voice mail and e-mail frequently to be sure she is responsive to each of her national accounts. She records everything in her daytimer to avoid work–family conflicts.

As women struggle to balance career and family choices, many employers are doing more to help. Women, as well as men, who work in sales, often have the option of spending part of every week working from home.[b]

salespeople devote considerable time to adjusting warranty claims, solving customer problems, and paying goodwill visits.

There are no precise rules to observe in establishing a sales routing and scheduling plan, but the following guiding principles apply to nearly all selling situations:

1. Obtain or create a map of your territory and mark the location of present accounts with pins or a marking pen. Each account might be colour-coded according to sales potential. This will give you a picture of the entire territory. Many companies are using mapping software to create a territory picture that can be viewed on the computer screen. With the aid of TerrAlign mapping software, salespeople can align sales territories by account size or geography, analyze sales information, generate maps and reports, and produce territory recommendations.[18]

Mapping software such as eMap allows companies to instantly communicate up-to-date territory maps and reports to field salespeople.

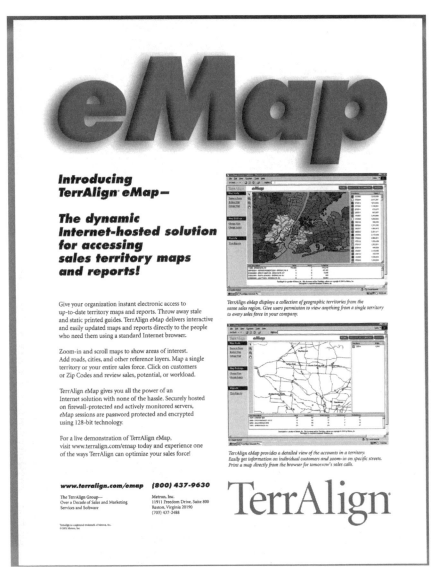

Mapping software such as eMap allows companies to instantly communicate up-to-date territory maps and reports to field salespeople.

2. If your territory is geographically quite large, consider dividing it into smaller areas. Postal codes provide one option. You can then plan work in terms of several trading areas that make up the entire territory.

3. Develop a routing plan for a specific period of time. This might be a one- or two-week period. Once the plan is firm, notify customers of your anticipated arrival time by telephone, letter, or e-mail.

4. Develop a schedule that accommodates your customers' needs. Some customers appreciate getting calls on a certain day of the week or at a certain hour of the day. Try to schedule your calls in accordance with their wishes.

Figure 18.3 Sales call plan

Sales Call Plan

Salesperson _____   For week ending _____

Territory _____   Days worked _____

Planned Calls	**Total Completed Calls**

Number of planned calls _____   Number of calls only _____

Number of planned presentations _____   Number of presentations _____

Number of planned telephone calls _____   Number of telephone calls _____

Account Category Planning   Number of orders _____

A. Account calls _____   Total km travelled _____

B. Account calls _____   A. Account calls _____

C. Account calls _____   B. Account calls _____

          C. Account calls _____

Companies called on	Address	Date	Customer rating	Comments about call

5. Think ahead, and establish one or more tentative calls in case you have some extra time. If your sales calls take less time than expected or if there is an unexpected cancellation, you need optional calls to fill the void.

6. Decide how frequently to call on the basis of sales potential. Give the greatest attention to the most profitable customers. Many salespeople use the 80/20 rule. They spend 80 percent of their time calling on the most productive customers and 20 percent calling on smaller accounts and prospects.[19]

Sales Call Plans

You can use information from the routing and scheduling plan to develop a **sales call plan**. This proposal is a weekly action plan, usually initiated by the sales manager. Its primary purpose is to ensure efficient and effective account coverage.

The form most sales managers use is similar to the one shown in Figure 18.3. One section of the form is used to record planned calls. A parallel section is for completed calls. Additional space is provided for the names of firms called on.

The sales manager usually presents the sales call plan to individual members of the sales staff. The plan's success depends on how realistic the goals are in the eyes of the sales staff, how persuasive the sales manager is, and what type of training accompanies the plan's introduction. It is not unusual for members of the sales force to respond with comments such as, "My territory is different," "Do not put me in a procedural straitjacket," or "My territory cannot be organized." The sales manager must not only present the plan in a convincing manner but also provide training that helps each salesperson implement the plan successfully.

sales call plan A plan developed with information taken from the routing and scheduling plan. The primary purpose of the plan is to ensure efficient and effective account coverage.

RECORDS MANAGEMENT

Although some salespeople complain that paperwork is too time-consuming and reduces the amount of time available for actual selling, others recognize that accurate, up-to-date records actually save time. Their work is better organized, and quick accessibility of information usually makes it possible to close more sales and improve customer service.

A good record-keeping system gives salespeople useful information with which to check their own progress. For instance, an examination of the sales call plan at the end of the day provides a review of who was called on and what was accomplished. The company also benefits from complete and accurate records. Reports from the field help management make important decisions. A company with a large sales force operating throughout a wide geographic area relies heavily on information sent to the main office.

Common Records Kept by Salespeople

A good policy is never to require a record that is not absolutely necessary. The only records worth keeping are those that provide positive benefits to the customer, the salesperson, or the personnel who work in sales-supporting areas of the company. Each record should be brief, easy to complete, and free of requests for useless detail. Where possible, the format should provide for the use of check marks as a substitute for written responses. Completing sales record forms should not be a major burden.

What records should you keep? The answer to this question will vary depending on the type of selling position. Some of the records most commonly kept by salespeople are described in this section.

Customer and Prospect Files Most salespeople find it helpful to keep records of customers and prospects. Each of these files has space for name, address, telephone and fax numbers, and e-mail address. Other information recorded might be the buyer's personal characteristics, the names of people who might influence the purchase, or appropriate times to make calls. Most salespeople have replaced their card files with computerized record systems.

Call Reports The call report (also called an *activity report*) is a variation of the sales call plan described earlier in this chapter. It is used to record information about the people on whom you have called and what took place. The call report is one of the most basic records used in the field of selling. It provides a summary of what happened during the call and an indication of what future action is required. The call reports (daily and weekly) featured in Figure 18.4 are typical of those used in the field.

We are seeing less emphasis on call reports that require only numbers (e.g., calls made each day, number of proposals written). With increased interest in customer relationship management and customer databases, companies are putting more emphasis on collecting information that will expand the customer's profile and provide knowledge on current buying behaviour and short- and long-range buying plans.

Expense Records Both your company and the government agencies that monitor business expenses will require a record of selling expenses. These usually include such items as meals, lodging, travel, and, in some cases, entertainment expenses. Several expense-reporting software packages are now available to streamline the expense-reporting process. Automated expense reports save the salesperson a great deal of time and allow expenses to be reimbursed while the salesperson is still on the road.

Sales Records The records used to report sales vary greatly in design. Some companies require daily reports, others weekly ones. As you would expect, one primary use of the sales report is to analyze salespeople's performance.

You can take certain steps to improve a reporting system. Charley Cohon, president of Prime Devices, wanted his salespeople to turn in sales call reports each Monday. However, sales representatives often delayed writing these reports until well after the calls were made. His salespeople were anxious to call on prospects, but not eager to write reports. To improve his reporting system, Cohon offered his salespeople a dedicated phone number just to receive and retrieve voice mail. Sales reps could call in their reports, which would be transcribed by a clerk in the office.[20]

Some records should be completed right away, while you can easily recall the information. Accuracy is always important. It can be embarrassing to have an order sent to the wrong address simply because you have transposed a figure. Take time to proofread forms and use a spell checker.

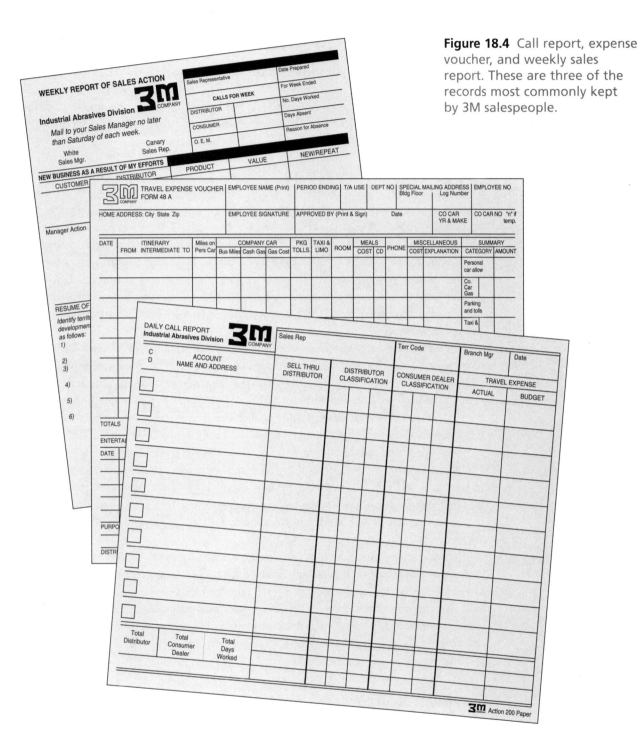

Figure 18.4 Call report, expense voucher, and weekly sales report. These are three of the records most commonly kept by 3M salespeople.

You should re-examine your territory management plan continually. Update it often so it reflects the current status of your various accounts. When possible, use a portable computer or PDA and appropriate software to improve your records management system. Computers can help you achieve increased selling time and enhance customer service.

Maintaining Perspective

Personal selling is often characterized by emotional highs and lows. It's easy to lose perspective and drift into an emotional low during what seems like a sales slump. Carefully prepared records can serve as a reality check. For example, you may be upset by low first quarter sales. A check of your records, however, could indicate that first quarter sales were low during the previous year.[21]

STRESS MANAGEMENT

PERSONAL SELLING PRODUCES A CERTAIN AMOUNT OF STRESS, IN PART FROM THE non-routine nature of sales work. Each day brings a variety of new experiences, some of which may cause stress. Prospecting, for example, can be threatening to some salespeople. Long hours on the job, the loss of leisure time, and too little time for family members can also be stressful. While "variety is the spice of life," there is a limit to how much diversity one can cope with. One of the keys to success in selling is learning how to bring order to the many facets of the job. We also must be physically and mentally prepared to handle work-related stress.

stress Refers to two simultaneous events: an external stimulus called a stressor, and the physical and emotional responses to that stimulus.

Stress refers to two simultaneous events: an external stimulus called a stressor, and the physical and emotional responses to that stimulus (anxiety, fear, muscle tension, surging heart rate, and so on). Negative, threatening, or worrisome situations accumulated over time can cause depression and burnout, and make you sick.[22] In personal selling, too much negative stress hurts relationships and productivity. Some stress is beneficial because it helps keep us motivated, but too much stress can be unhealthy if left unchecked.

Stress might be caused by trying to figure out ways to meet a sales quota or schedule travel throughout a sales territory. Missed appointments, presentations before large groups, and lack of feedback concerning your performance also can create stress. Ironically, some of the time-saving tools used by salespeople (e.g., fax machines, cellular phones, and e-mail) make it difficult for them to escape the pressures of their job. Many salespeople feel they are on call 24 hours a day.

Information surplus has replaced information scarcity as an important new problem in the age of information. Increasingly, knowledge workers report tension with colleagues, loss of job satisfaction, and strained personal relationships as a result of information overload. Too much information also crowds out quiet moments needed for reflection and to restore balance in our lives.[23] It is not possible to eliminate stress from your life, but you can adopt stress management strategies that can help you cope with it. Four stress management strategies are discussed next.

Develop a Stress-Free Home Office

Many salespeople maintain a home office. With a little effort, it's possible to create a less stressful home office environment. Install a business line for phone, e-mail, and fax that rings only in the office. It's not professional to have other family members answering business calls. If your office is not an appropriate meeting space, meet with clients at their office or at a restaurant. Establish set hours. Try not to let work hours extend into evenings and weekends. Let your neighbours and friends know you keep office hours and cannot be disturbed during "working" hours.[24]

Made in China, Sold in Japan—from Canada

Richard Li does most of his work from his home office. While that is becoming more common today, Richard's case is somewhat special. Richard is the president of a manufacturing company in China and he manages the company's relationships with its key customers. Richard's company employs approximately 150 people manufacturing more than 3000 different component parts that are used in the manufacture of other products. What's so special? Richard's home office is in Vancouver, where he resides with his wife Shirley, his son Sean (age 6), and his daughter Sherlee (born in July 2008). Richard's customers are all in Japan.

How is this possible? Richard travels two or three times each year to see his customers in Japan, and otherwise manages his relationships via the Internet. His most important customer places orders with two weeks' advance notice: one week for manufacturing and one week for shipping product from China to Japan. This is because this customer operates "just-in-time." That means it wants shipments to arrive at its plant just when they are needed in its own manufacturing process. The strong relationship that has developed between the two companies has created a co-dependence, so that they are each very important to the other.[c]

Maintain an Optimistic Outlook

Optimistic thoughts give rise to positive attitudes and effective relationships with customers. According to Martin Seligman, professor of psychology and author of *Learned Optimism*, optimists are more likely to view problems merely as temporary setbacks. They focus on their potential success rather than on their failures. Pessimists, in contrast, tend to believe bad events will last a long time and tend to give up more easily when faced with a challenge.[25]

Seligman reminds us that optimism is a learned behaviour. For example, you can spend more time visualizing yourself succeeding. If you want to succeed at something, picture yourself doing it successfully. The visualization process needs to be repeated over and over again.[26]

Passion Group Ltd. is one of many newer, Canadian technology-based companies concerned with providing a work environment where employees can have fun and feel comfortable. One of its employees, Rufus, is a five-year-old Jack Russell terrier. Rufus has been "employed" for three years and shares under-the-desk space with a six-month-old Border terrier named Oliver. His official position is mascot; he is responsible for "promoting a positive attitude in the office."[27]

Practise Healthy Emotional Expression

When stress occurs, you may undergo physiological and psychological changes. Your heartbeat quickens, your blood pressure rises, and tension builds. To relieve the pressure you may choose a *fight* or a *flight response*. With a fight response, you might unleash an avalanche of harsh words or ignore a person with whom you are dealing. These reactions, of course, are not recommended. This behaviour may damage relationships with team members, customers, or customer support personnel.

A flight response is running away from the problem: Rather than face the issue squarely, you decide to turn your back on it. Flight is usually not satisfactory, as the problem will seldom go away by itself. If you feel stress from an impractical quota, for example, talk to

Table 18.2 Five-Minute Stress Busters
▨ Take five minutes to identify and challenge unreasonable or distorted ideas that precipitated your stress. Replace them with ideas that are more realistic and positive.
▨ Take a five-minute stress-release walk outdoors. Contact with nature is especially beneficial.
▨ Enjoy stress relief with a gentle five-minute neck and shoulder massage.
▨ Spend five minutes visualizing yourself relaxing at your favourite vacation spot.
▨ Take a five-minute nap after lunch.
▨ Spend five minutes listening to a recording featuring your favourite comedian.

Source: Barry L. Reece and Rhonda Brandt, *Effective Human Relations: Personal and Organizational Applications* (Boston: Houghton Mifflin Company, 2008). Reprinted by permission of the publisher.

your sales manager and try to get the quota reduced. Don't just give in to the feeling of being overwhelmed. If you are spending too much time away from family, take a close look at your territory management plan and try to develop a more efficient way to make sales calls. It is not possible to eliminate those elements that cause us stress, but we can find ways to cope with daily stressors. There are stress management activities that can be used during brief pauses in your day (see Table 18.2).

Maintain a Healthy Lifestyle

An effective exercise program—jogging, tennis, golf, racquetball, walking, or some other favourite exercise—can counter the harmful chemicals that build up in your bloodstream

Exercise is an excellent way to moderate stress.

after a prolonged period of stress. Toronto-based IT consulting company Burntsand Inc. provides a recreation room to help employees de-stress.[28]

The food you eat can also play a critical role in helping you manage stress. Health experts agree that the typical Canadian diet—high in saturated fats, refined sugars, additives, caffeine, and even too much protein—is the wrong menu for coping with stress. Employees of Husky Injection Molding Systems Ltd. in Bolton, Ontario, enjoy fresh, healthy food at the company cafeteria. The company's wellness centre sponsors programs for weight management, fitness instruction, physical therapy, and smoking cessation.[29]

Leisure time can provide you with the opportunity to relax and get rid of work-related stress. One of the most effective strategies for managing the negative aspects of stress is getting enough quality sleep. The number of hours of sleep required for good health varies from person to person, but seven or eight hours seems to be about right for most people. The critical factor is whether you feel rested in the morning and prepared to deal with the day's activities. In many respects, salespeople must possess the same self-discipline as professional athletes. Sales work can be physically demanding. Lack of proper rest, poor eating habits, excessive drinking, and failure to exercise properly can reduce one's ability to deal with stress and strain.

REVIEWING KEY CONCEPTS

- Discuss the four dimensions of opportunity management.

  All salespeople can learn more about their products and improve their selling skills. However, there is no way to expand time. Our only option is to find ways to improve in the four dimensions of opportunity management discussed in this chapter: time management, territory management, records management, and stress management.

- List and describe time management strategies.

  Effective time management methods can pave the way to greater sales productivity. To achieve greater time conservation, salespeople should adopt the following timesaving strategies: Develop a series of personal goals; prepare a daily "to-do" list; maintain a planning calendar; organize your selling tools; and save time with meetings in cyberspace and other methods of communication.

- Explain factors that contribute to improved territory management.

  The first step in territory management is the classification of all customers according to sales volume or some other appropriate criteria. You should normally spend the most time with accounts that have the greatest sales potential. The second step requires developing

a routing and scheduling plan. This plan should reduce time spent travelling between accounts. Salespeople are often guided by a *sales call plan*.

- Identify and discuss common elements of a records management system.

  A good record-keeping system provides many advantages. Accurate, up-to-date records can actually save time because work is better organized. The company also benefits because sales reports provide an important communication link with members of the sales force. Today, computers are used to develop more efficient record-keeping systems. Common records kept by salespeople include customer and prospect files, call reports, expense records, and sales records.

- Discuss stress management practices.

  There is a certain amount of stress associated with sales work. This is due in part to the non-routine nature of personal selling. Salespeople must learn to cope with factors that upset their equilibrium. Stress management strategies include developing a stress-free home office, maintaining an optimistic outlook, practising healthy emotional expression, and maintaining a healthy lifestyle.

Appendix 1

Reality *Selling Today* Role-Play Scenarios

 The eight role-play scenarios in this appendix are all extensions of the Reality *Selling Today* videos presented throughout the text. Using the information presented in the chapter opening vignettes, case problems, and videos, and the information presented in this section, you will have available the most detailed and realistic setting for selecting, preparing, and presenting a mock role play.

As you discovered in the videos and related material, these are real salespeople in real selling situations, enjoying successful and rewarding careers in the profession of selling. In these Reality *Selling Today* role-play scenarios, you also assume these same responsibilities by selecting a similar position in the same office as the sales professionals presented in the videos. Just like the evolution of their careers, you will need to learn about your new company, its products, and, specifically, the customer you will be calling on.

Detailed information is presented in each of the scenarios. Web sites are presented to provide more information about the company, its products, and the industry. Reference is made to reviewing the chapter opening vignettes and corresponding case problems for learning more about your new company and selling responsibility.

The role plays presented in this appendix are also specifically designed to prepare for professional selling role-play competition at the annual college and university competitive event conventions (refer to http://coles.kennesaw.edu/ncsc/ and www.deltaepsilonchi.org/compevents/SRP.html for more information).

The following companies, sales positions, and customer types are presented:

- Liberty Mutual, Marcus Smith, www.libertymutual.com, Financial Services—See Chapter 5.

- CB Richard Ellis, Susannah Rosas, www.cbre.com, Commercial, Real Estate Services—See Chapter 7.

- *Texas Monthly*, Amy Vandaveer, www.texasmonthly.com, Advertising and Sales Promotion—See Chapter 10.

- Wealth Design Group, Justin Bremer, www.wealthdesigngroup.net, Financial Services—See Chapter 11.

- CRM Software, Salesforce.com, www.salesforce.com On-line CRM Software—See Chapter 12.

- Hilti Corporation, Alim Hirani, www.hilti.com, Construction Products and Services—See Chapter 13.

- Marriott International, Heather Ramsey, www.marriott.com, Meeting and Convention Services—See Chapter 15.

Using the sales information you have learned throughout the book and the sales worksheets presented, prepare to make your sales call.

Reality Selling Today Role-Play 1: Liberty Mutual

Marcus Smith
Liberty Mutual

(This mock sales call role-play scenario was created exclusively for use with the *Selling Today: Creating Customer Value* text book.)

Your Role at Liberty

You will be an independent insurance broker for Liberty International Underwriters (www.libertyiu.com), working out of the same office as Marcus Smith, featured in the Chapter 5 Reality *Selling Today* video. Liberty International Underwriters is a division of Liberty Mutual Group, a company that operates in both personal and commercial insurance markets. Liberty Mutual's personal insurance products include auto, home, life, and personal liability. In addition, it also offers a wide range of products and services for business. Property insurance, including ocean cargo insurance, represents one of its important lines of business. Liberty International Underwriters was formed in 1999 as a global specialty business with an emphasis on niche insurance products distributed through the independent broker network. (Refer to the Chapter 5 opening vignette and case problem and review the Chapter 5 Reality *Selling Today* video for more information.)

Your Customer: Farris Footwear Inc.

You will meet with Pat Stanley, the import director at Farris Footwear Inc. Founded in 1980 in Los Angeles, California, this large import–export company serves as a one-stop shop for its customers for a wide variety of footwear, from beach slippers, indoor slippers, sports sandals, sports shoes, and ladies' shoes, to cowboy boots. Although its customer base includes retail shoe stores, department stores, and discount stores, the company is shifting its focus to the premium market, where profit margins are higher. Farris Footwear Inc. imports footwear from a number of countries in Asia, Europe, and Latin America. Imports are generally bought under FOB (free on board) terms of trade, according to which Farris Footwear, rather than the seller, arranges insurance of the goods. Most shipments are made by sea. Monthly imports might reach $1 million during peak seasons. Every two years, Farris Footwear reviews its relationship with its insurance and forwarding agents.

Ocean Cargo Insurance

As globalization sweeps across nations, U.S. imports have risen some 40 percent over the past five years. So has the U.S. ocean cargo insurance market.

The basic ocean cargo policy covers perils of the sea (e.g., stranding, sinking, fire, and collision) and perils on the sea (e.g., heavy weather and theft). Other risks such as war risk and civil commotion might be added to the policy. For shipments that involve multiple modes of transportation, such as a combination of marine transportation and inland transit, additional insurance coverage is required. The client normally signs a contract (called a policy) with an insurance broker, who will then work with insurance company underwriters. Big players in the market are members of the American Institutes of Marine Underwriters (www.aimu.org).

The insurance premium (i.e., price) is a function of the sums insured, market conditions, loss experience, and other factors such as risks idiosyncratic to the country of departure. Under an open cargo policy, all goods shipped during the year will be covered, with a maximum amount per shipment.

Quick Facts About Farris Footwear Inc.'s Needs

- Farris Footwear Inc. currently uses two insurance companies, Mandarin Insurance Company for all of its imports from Asian countries, and Sasser Insurance Company for its imports from the other countries. Mandarin has been working with Farris for six years, while Sasser signed its contract with Farris two years ago.

- Farris Footwear Inc. receives shipments year round, although peak seasons are from October to February. The main warehouse is located in its headquarters in California due to its proximity to the port of Long Beach, but it also owns two other transit warehouses in Houston, Texas, and New Jersey.

- Footwear is normally packed in carton boxes, with a small sachet of anti-mold chemical, especially for leather shoes.

- Because of the competitive nature of the ocean cargo insurance market, insurance premiums tend to be similar across companies. Farris Footwear Inc. is more interested in value-added services such as shipment tracking, claim resolution, risk management resources, and training.

- Most Farris Footwear Inc. imports are from the People's Republic of China, Indonesia, Vietnam, Italy, and Brazil.

Your Call Objectives

In your meeting with Pat Stanley, you hope to identify the decision maker of the insurance agent review process, which will start in a month. You also want to know more about Farris's insurance needs. In addition, you hope to convince Pat that your company can offer outstanding services that go beyond basic ocean cargo insurance.

Reality Selling Today Role-Play 2: CB Richard Ellis

Susannah Rosas
CB Richard Ellis

(This mock sales call role-play scenario was created exclusively for use with the *Selling Today: Creating Customer Value* text book.)

Your Role at CB Richard Ellis

You will be a sales representative for CB Richard Ellis (www.cbre.com), working out of the same office as Susannah Rosas, featured in the Chapter 7 Reality *Selling Today* video. The company offers a variety of premium real estate services, both commercial and industrial. Headquartered in Los Angeles, California, the company has a network of more than 400 branch offices worldwide, with some 30 000 well-trained employees. (Refer to the Chapter 7 opening vignette and case problem and review the Chapter 7 Reality *Selling Today* video for more information.)

Your Customer: Norman Flooring Company

You will meet with Kerry Nelson, the owner of Norman Flooring Company. The company was established in 1996, specializing in flooring solutions for both residential and industrial markets in Texas. Despite the slowdown of the U.S. economy, Norman Flooring has been enjoying a healthy annual growth rate in revenue of 10 percent in the past few years. In its headquarters in Houston, Texas, the company has two warehouses that are rented on a short term of six months to a year. Each warehouse also has an office where administrative staff control inventory, deliver flooring materials to subcontractors, and handle other clerical issues. The company realizes that with the current growth rate, it will soon see itself constrained by its somewhat limited warehousing facilities. As a result, it is actively looking for larger industrial properties at locations that are not only easily accessible from highways and ports but also close to major developing residential areas.

The Industrial Property Market

Surprisingly, the U.S. industrial property market has not been strongly influenced by the recent U.S. economic slowdown. The three major industrial property markets include distribution hubs, port facilities, and high-tech centres. Last year, rent growth was greatest in the latter two markets, standing at roughly 3 percent, and the lowest in the former market, at about 0.5 percent. The industrial property market is no exception to the supply and demand rule. Net absorption, defined as the balance between increasing demand and new supply, has been very healthy in markets such as Houston, where availability has been falling. Warehousing represents the largest segment of the industrial property sector. About 25 percent of this warehousing segment was new supply. The industrial market outlook is optimistic, with rent growth expected to remain positive over the next few years.

Quick Facts About Norman Flooring Company's Needs

- The company is looking for industrial warehousing facilities that are in very good condition, with little to no deferred maintenance. The area should be at least 16 000 square feet.

- The location should be easily accessible from the Houston port, in an area that is known to be free from flooding risks.
- The initial lease term will be one year, with the possibility of rent-to-own.
- Preferably, the property site should offer available space for expansion.
- The office building is preferably attached to the warehouse.
- The property should have digital surveillance and perimeter fencing with computer-controlled keypad entry access.

Your Call Objectives

In your meeting with Kerry Nelson, you hope to identify the company's warehousing needs. In addition, you hope to convince Kerry that your company can offer outstanding value-added services, such as nationwide property maintenance consulting.

Reality Selling Today Role-Play 3: *Texas Monthly*

Amy Vandaveer
Texas Monthly

(This mock sales call role-play scenario was created exclusively for use with the *Selling Today: Creating Customer Value* text book.)

Your Role at *Texas Monthly*

You are a sales representative for *Texas Monthly* magazine (www.texas monthly.com), working out of the same office as Amy Van der Veer featured in the Chapter 10 Reality *Selling Today* video. Your magazine covers politics, business, and culture, but focuses largely on leisure activities and events in Texas; it has a large real estate advertising section, as well as classified sections in which nearly all advertisers are Texas-based businesses appealing to a prospective buyer who is interested in connecting with Texas history and culture. Through you, your potential customers have access to a large, loyal reader base all over Texas, mostly urban, well educated, and affluent. (Refer to the Chapter 10 opening vignette and case problem and review the Chapter 10 Reality *Selling Today* video for more information.)

Your Customer: Roger Linville Properties

You will meet with Kim Pratt, the marketing director at Roger Linville Properties, a property management company. Kim was referred to you by a family friend, who told you that although Roger Linville Properties has reached most of its residents through simple word-of-mouth publicity, it is now considering increasing its magazine advertising. According to your friend, who met Kim through their daughters' Girl Scout troop, Kim's career began at an advertising agency specializing in real estate, then moved to the client side. In all, Kim has 15 years of experience in the marketing of high-end real estate.

Roger Linville Properties started selling units in its first condo building in 1987 and now has 12 upscale high-rise condo buildings in Houston and Galveston. Each property has a sales manager and a marketing manager, and the individual properties do some advertising controlled by those managers, but Kim is ultimately in control of the company's marketing and advertising strategy.

Your supervisor at *Texas Monthly* has some connections to Roger Linville Properties, and he was able to tell you more about its current advertising situation. According to him, Roger Linville Properties does the majority of its advertising in magazines available for free in the Houston area. You've seen these glossy magazines in the waiting areas of restaurants and hotels; they cater to an affluent readership with society pages, event news, and ads for upscale products and services. The company also uses some billboards, and individual properties use direct mail and well-publicized open houses to attract prospective residents.

The majority of the Roger Linville buildings are within the city of Houston. You've learned from their Web site that there are several buildings in the Galleria area, surrounded by luxury shopping and restaurants, and one near the Rice Village shopping arcade in West University. They also have buildings in the downtown theatre district, which has recently become an increasingly popular location for luxury lofts and condos. In Galveston, they have one building in the historic Strand area and several resort-like condos on the beachfront. Judging by the prices and the amenities they offer, such as concierge service and in-building spas, you can tell that their prime market is affluent people looking for a low-maintenance home that they will rarely have to leave. Most of the properties are advertised as second homes, particularly the Galveston condos, which are promoted as the perfect local vacation home.

While on the Web site, you noticed that the company is currently in the process of building two new properties: one in the River Oaks area, Houston's most exclusive residential neighbourhood, and one in the Woodlands, an affluent master-planned community north of Houston. They will begin pre-selling units in these two properties in the next few months. In addition, your supervisor has heard rumours recently that Roger Linville has been negotiating to acquire land in the Dallas area, suggesting that the company may be planning expansion there as well.

Your Call Objectives

In your meeting, you hope to convince Kim Pratt that magazine advertising can be more successful than it has been so far, and that *Texas Monthly* is the magazine to use. Hopefully, you will close a deal by the end of the meeting.

Reality Selling Today Role-Play 4: Wealth Design Group

Justin Bremer
Wealth Design Group

(This mock sales call role-play scenario was created exclusively for use with the *Selling Today: Creating Customer Value* text book.)

Your Role at Wealth Design Group

You will be a sales representative for Wealth Design Group (www.wealthdesigngroup.net), working out of the same office as Justin Bremer, featured in the Chapter 11 Reality *Selling Today* video. The company offers custom-designed financial solutions for its clients. Its current products and solutions include life insurance, retirement plans, investing solutions, education funding, estate planning, and special services for professional athletes. Although a client can select to use a specific financial product, Wealth Design Group representatives can also work closely with clients to develop comprehensive services as a personal financial advisor. (Refer to the Chapter 11 opening vignette and case problem and review the Chapter 12 Reality *Selling Today* video for more information.)

Your Customer: Jesse Bowers

You will meet with Jesse Bowers, who is 40 years old. Jesse is widowed, with two children, ages 10 and 12. As an upper–middle-class American, Jesse had not been paying much attention to financial planning until recently, when the U.S. economy began showing signs of slowing down. Jesse prefers working through a financial advisor who can take care of all of his financial issues.

Selling Personal Financial Services

As a personal financial advisor, a broker has to go through several steps in identifying the client's needs. In a typical initial meeting with a client, the broker has to appear as professional and knowledgeable as possible to build trust. In the end, financial information is sensitive information that individuals are unwilling to share with strangers. Once trust is established, the broker delves deeper into the information provided by the client to identify his or her needs before offering financial advice and services. At this stage, a needs analysis is necessary. This step requires the broker to gather all of the relevant information about the client, such as income, age, savings, family situation, lifestyle, medical conditions, and debt situation.

Quick Facts About the Client's Needs

- Jesse, whose spouse is deceased, currently has a bank savings account of $50 000.
- Jesse plans to send both children to a decent state college because a good education can open more doors of opportunity.
- Although Jesse prefers working through a financial advisor, he is interested in knowing what advantages this option has compared with working directly with a financial company.

Your Call Objectives

Last month, you met Jesse at a conference, where you had only very sketchy information about this client. In your second meeting with Jesse Bowers, you hope to follow up on where you left off in your first meeting. More specifically, you hope to get more detailed information about Jesse's needs and his current financial situation. In addition, you hope to convince him that your company can offer outstanding services that are not available anywhere else. There's also an opportunity for cross-selling.

Reality Selling Today Role-Play 5: Salesforce.com

salesforce.com   (This mock sales call role-play scenario was created exclusively for use with the *Selling Today: Creating Customer Value* text book.)

Your Role at Salesforce.com

You are a sales representative for Salesforce.com (www.salesforce.com). Your company is the world leader in on-demand customer relationship management (CRM) services. Unlike most CRM applications, companies that use your services store customer and sales data on Salesforce.com. One of the benefits of on-demand CRM services is that customers incur neither up-front capital investment nor on-site administration costs. Your company also offers solutions that are customized to specific customer needs, such as creating different interfaces for different departments and work groups, and providing limited access to data for specific authorized work groups.

Your Customer: Rename Clothing Company

You will meet with Jesse Golden, the marketing director at Rename Clothing Company. A family-owned business in Garden Grove, California, the company is expanding at a fast pace not only in the United States, but also in Latin American markets that the company entered into two years ago. The company currently has a sales force of 20 people, and out-sources its selling activities for overseas operations to local firms. Each salesperson is responsible for three to four customers. While outsourcing has the advantages of capital-izing on market knowledge of local partners, the company realized it does not have full control over their selling efforts. Domestically, the company has strong relationships with its buyers, but there have been signs of work overload among the sales force. While Rename has three in-house brands that it distributes using its own channel, it does pro-vide sourcing solutions to mid- and high-end department stores under their private labels. Rename works closely with its suppliers in more than five countries, mainly in Europe and Asia. It also has a small manufacturing facility in California for sample development and small-batch order production.

Quick Facts About Rename Clothing Company's Needs

The apparel industry is a sophisticated, fast-moving industry with several designs launched every season, and repeat orders must be met as fast as possible before end-users change their tastes. As a company that operates in middle- to high-end markets, Rename positions itself as a sourcing company with a fast turnaround for its customers. The nature of the industry requires salespeople to be highly diligent in market information gathering, processing, and dissemination across geographic areas and departments.

At present, the in-house salespeople use spreadsheets for almost all of their selling activities, such as recording sales calls, reporting to sales managers, and tracking delivery of orders, to name just a few. Jesse joined the company two months ago and realized the current system showed clear signs of overload. Mistakes have started to occur more often, and the company has received quite a few complaints about shipment delays, wrong labeling on products, and wrong packaging. As marketing director, Jesse spent several days making sense of disparate information about Rename's domestic sales and has heard mixed reports about its overseas operation. Jesse's secretary lamented that the spreadsheets provided by the sales force are not in a uniform format, making it difficult to consolidate the database. Meanwhile, salespeople claim that their customers are not all the same, and they need to customize their spreadsheets so that they can keep track of things more easily.

With high pressure for growth, Rename is looking for an efficient way to consolidate and manage its customer database. Jesse is also in the process of establishing a branch office in Mexico and will staff three local salespeople to manage Rename's business in this growing market. In overseas markets, the focus is more on customer acquisition and lead management, while in domestic markets, Jesse is more concerned with keeping Rename's existing customers happy.

Your Call Objectives

In your meeting with Jesse Golden, you hope to convince him that Salesforce.com is the right CRM solution for Rename. You can do this by providing him with interesting facts and benefits Salesforce.com can offer (see more information at www.salesforce.com). Hopefully, you will close a deal by the end of the meeting.

Reality Selling Today Role-Play 6: Hilti Corporation

Alim Hirani
Hilti Corporation

(This mock sales call role-play scenario was created exclusively for use with the *Selling Today: Creating Customer Value* text book.)

You will be a sales representative for Hilti (www.hilti.com), working out of the same office as Alim Hirani, featured in the Chapter 13 Reality *Selling Today* video. The company provides the global construction industry with innovative products and services. In addition to a wide variety of high-end products such as measuring systems, drilling and demolition, installation systems, foam systems, and screw fastening systems, the company also offers its customers customized training programs and consulting services. Hilti sales representatives work directly with customers rather than through intermediary parties. (Refer to the Chapter 13 opening vignette and case problem and review the Chapter 13 Reality *Selling Today* video for more information.)

Your Customer: Ellis Exhibition Inc.

You will meet with Casey Smith, procurement manager for Ellis Exhibition Inc. The company owns a 100 000-square-foot exhibition centre that hosts several local and regional events in Atlanta, Georgia. Some of these events have become a must-see for the local business community. Depending on the theme and the products being showcased, Ellis Exhibition offers exhibitors outstanding display services that include floor plans, display solutions, display installation, and booth dismantlement. After an event, the installation systems are reused, while installation accessories are generally discarded. Casey Smith believes that by buying the right type of installation accessories, Ellis can save a lot of money, and therefore offer its exhibitor customers more competitive prices.

Quick Facts About Ellis Exhibition Inc.'s Needs

- Ellis Exhibition Inc. spends about $500 000 a year on installation accessories. These accessories are galvanized, but they can also be painted to match the colour theme stipulated by exhibitors.

- Ellis uses a wide variety of installation accessories, from hexagon nuts and head screws to distance holders.

- Ellis does not want to stock these accessories. Exhibitors who want to use Ellis display services are required to place their order three months in advance. Then, an Ellis accountant will calculate the necessary accessories needed for each event.

- Ellis is extremely concerned with the quality of all of its installation systems and accessories.

Your Call Objectives

In your meeting with Casey Smith, you hope to identify the specific types and the expected quantity of installation accessories. You also want to know about delivery requirements. In addition, you might be able to cross-sell other Hilti products and services, such as sprinkler systems.

Reality Selling Today Role-Play 7: Marriott International, Inc.

Heather Ramsey
Marriott International Inc.

(This mock sales call role-play scenario was created exclusively for use with the *Selling Today: Creating Customer Value* text book.)

Your Role at Marriott

You will be a sales representative for Marriott International Inc. (www.marriott.com), working out of the same hotel as Heather Ramsey, featured in the Chapter 15 Reality *Selling Today* video. Founded in 1927 by J. Willard and Alice S. Marriott, Marriott has grown from a root beer stand to a multinational company with more than 3000 lodging properties located in some 70 countries around the world. Apart from luxurious hotel accommodation under several well-managed brands, the company also offers outstanding services for meetings and events. From weddings to corporate meetings, Marriott's clients know that they are always in good hands. (Refer to the Chapter 15 opening vignette and case problem and review the Chapter 15 Reality *Selling Today* video for more information.)

Your Customer: Hiroshi Watanabe/Chris Scott

You will meet with Chris Scott, personal secretary to Mr. Hiroshi Watanabe, owner of a chain of high-end tailor stores in California. Mr. Watanabe and his wife were married 25 years ago in a simple wedding ceremony. The couple immigrated to the U.S. with only five dollars between them. They worked very hard to make ends meet, and their fate took a turn when both were hired full-time for the first time by a small tailor shop, Mr. Watanabe as a deliveryman and his wife as a helper.

With strong entrepreneurial spirit and incessant learning, they soon opened their own business using their meager savings. Initial clients were mainly friends, but they soon found a niche in the market by combining traditional Japanese garment making with American contemporary fashion. Before they knew it, celebrities started knocking on their door, asking for custom-made evening gowns and suits. A couple of years later, they opened their first concept store under the name Watanabe, and positioned it as a high-end custom-made tailor house. They also provided customers with a full range of custom-designed accessories.

Their two sons soon joined the team, managing stores and franchisees in prime locations in Los Angeles and San Francisco, California. As their silver wedding anniversary is approaching, Mr. Watanabe asks Chris to organize something very special for his wife to make up for the years of hard work the couple has been through.

Event Planning

More information on event planning is available at www.marriott.com. You should also be able to get more information on anniversary party ideas from the Internet.

Quick Facts About the Clients' Needs

- The anniversary has to be formal as many celebrities will be invited.
- The menu has to be as bountiful and sumptuous as possible.
- Costs are not a major concern. However, Chris should be shopping for the best offer.

- Chris is in charge of information gathering and screens offers from three major hotels. Chris already has an offer from a Marriott competitor.

- The goal is not only to impress the guests but also Mrs. Watanabe.

- The highlight of the anniversary is a recount of the couple's happy marriage.

Your Call Objectives

In your meeting with Chris Scott, you hope to identify Mr. Watanabe's needs. In addition, you hope to convince him that you provide the best event planning services, which your competitor cannot offer. In doing so, you should be prepared to offer Chris a number of creative ideas to make the event both formal and memorable.

Appendix 2

Use of the Salesforce.com Customer Relationship Management (CRM) System

Students—A Special Opportunity

salesforce.com *Selling Today* now offers you a unique opportunity to learn the reason modern software is helping to redefine sales and marketing. The software you will be using in this application is referred to as Customer Relationship Management (CRM) software. CRM systems include functions necessary to automate and support the sales force, commonly known as sales force automation (SFA) functions. There are two types of SFA software—account based and contact based. Contact-based software, such as the popular ACT! Contact Management Software, features an individual contact or customer as the method for navigating the application.

As customer accounts have become larger, with multiple buyers involved in the purchasing decision, contact-based software proved inadequate, and most sales and marketing departments have moved to an account-based software. Account-based software such as the on-line Salesforce.com application featured in this exercise, allows for capturing information on each of the buyers that influence buying within an account. (See Chapter 12 for additional types of CRM software available for managing the prospect database.)

Using the log on instructions below, you can access the Salesforce/Selling Today CRM software and customer database. Salesforce.com is the leading Internet-hosted CRM application in the world. Internet-hosted applications are also known as SaaS, or "Software as a Service." The Salesforce/Selling Today application is easy to use and includes information about more than 20 customers. You can experience firsthand how salespeople gain the sales advantage with this category of software.

Beginning in Chapter 5, you will find the first **Customer Relationship Management with Technology** insight. These insights, along with the **CRM Application Exercise** at the end of each chapter, are simple, easy-to-follow instructions on using Salesforce.com to store and access a wide variety of business and personal information about your customers. You will discover the convenience of using this software to stay in touch with people.

Salesforce.com includes important customer information that you will use in your **CRM Case Study** assignments for Chapters 12 through 17. You will access this information to approach, present, demonstrate, negotiate, close, and service more than $1.2 million worth of sales.

Effectively using information technology, especially customer relationship management software, will give you a career advantage in today's highly competitive workplace. After mastering the exercises provided, you can report your CRM experience on your résumé.

Instructions for Using the Customer Relationship Management (CRM) Software

The software that you will be using is a demonstration version of Salesforce.com, the leading SaaS CRM software. This demonstration version is limited to only 25 accounts and 50 contacts that may be entered. The full version of Salesforce.com is more robust and can manage thousands of customers, contacts, leads, and opportunities.

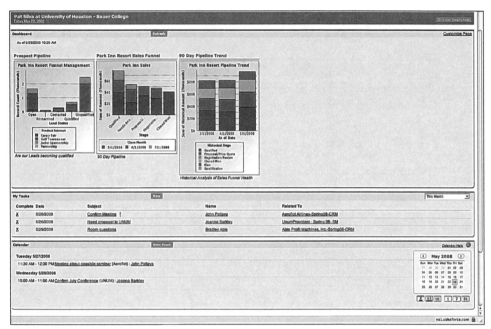

Figure A2.1 Sample Home Screen

The Home Screen presents dashboards that remind the user of the status of their prospecting and selling activities within their entire prospect database. It provides a quick view of progress toward achieving the sales forecast.

Source: Courtesy of Salesforce.com.

Running the Software

Start your Internet browser and go to **www.pearsoned.ca/manning**. Click the Using Salesforce.com link and follow the instructions for your initial log on. After logging on, the first screen that you see is your home page (see Figure A2.1).

Using the Software

Salesforce.com is a browser-based program and uses standard Internet browser features. Navigation—moving around the application—is accomplished by mouse-clicking on tabs and hot links. *Hot links* are underlined fields or words on the screen. A set of *tabs* is always at the top of the Salesforce screen. Pressing one of these tabs takes you to the section of Salesforce that is the main screen for that important object or type of information, like Account, Contact, or Opportunities. When you click a hot link, the application takes you to that object (for example, a "lead") or performs that action (for example, "edit"). Therefore, when you need to do something within the application, you click a hot link or a tab.

The screen that displays the information about a customer is referred to as the Account screen. There are seven sections on the Salesforce.com Account screen. First is the Account Detail screen. This screen contains basic information about the account, such as name, address, and main phone number. If you scroll down the Account screen past the detail section, you will see the six related list sections. These sections contain additional information, or records, related to the account, such as contacts, planned activities, activity history, notes, and document attachments. There is a related list for each of the sales opportunities we will be working on for this account. The first concept to master about Salesforce.com is that everything is organized around accounts: You can see that clearly from this Account screen. (See Figure A2.2.)

You can get to any of the information on the related list simply by clicking any of the hot links on that list. Clicking the first contact name on the Contact list takes you directly to all the information about that contact. Clicking "Opportunity" takes you directly to that sales opportunity. (See Figure A2.3.)

Three tools on the left side of every Salesforce.com screen make it easy and fast to use the application. First is the Search bar. Use this search capability to enter and go directly to

Figure A2.2 Sample Account Screen

The Account (or Sales Opportunity) Screen provides information on each of the accounts in your prospect database. Note the tabs across the top of the screen. Pressing any of these tabs automatically takes you to that object or type of information. The first thing to master about Salesforce.com is that everything is organized around accounts.

Source: Courtesy of Salesforce.com.

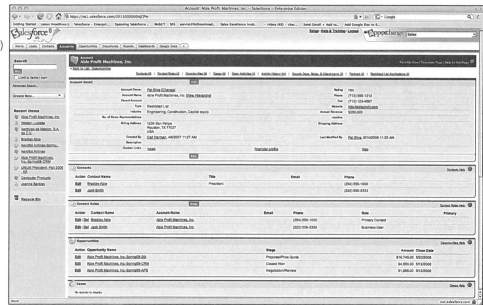

any item in the database: Accounts, Contacts, Leads, Opportunities, Products, and so forth. Second is the "Create New" drop-down list. If you click this button, you will be able to create a new item for the Salesforce database. Salesforce will even help by pre-populating the new item with as much information as possible. For example, if you are looking at the Account Detail screen for Able Profit Machines and click "Create New . . . Contact," Salesforce will already have the account name, address, and phone number. The third tool is the "Recent Items" list. Salespeople tend to work on the same 10 or 15 items over and over again until they have completed a major task. Salesforce always remembers the most recent 10 items and puts them on this list. Just click the hot link to take you directly to that object. You will be surprised how useful and efficient all three of these tools are.

Figure A2.3 Sample Contact Screen

The Contact Screen provides detailed information on each of the individuals within the account that may have influence on the sale process. Often referred to as members of the buying group, the individuals on these screens are accessed and used when strategically planning a sales call. Note the tools on the left side of the contact screen for gaining more detailed information and insight into planning effective sales strategies.

Source: Courtesy of Salesforce.com.

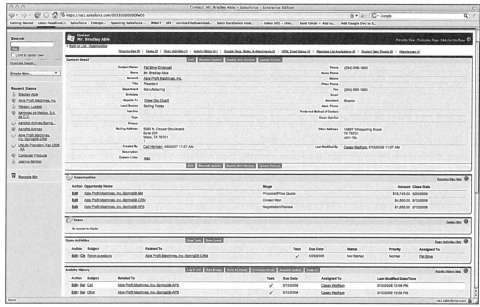

Notes

Chapter 5

1. Michael R. Solomon, Greg W. Marshall, Elnora W. Stuart, *Marketing: Real People, Real Choices*, 5th Ed. (Upper Saddle River, N.J: Prentice Hall, 2008), p. 445.
2. Lucy McCauley, "Voices: The State of the New Economy," *Fast Company*, September 1999, p. 124.
3. Stan Davis and Christopher Meyer, *Blur: The Speed of Change in the Connected Economy* (New York: Addison-Wesley Publishers), 1998, p. 9.
4. David Shenk, *Data Smog: Surviving the Information Glut* (New York: HarperEdge, 1997), pp. 27–29.
5. Michael R. Solomon, Greg W. Marshall, Elnora W. Stuart, *Marketing: Real People, Real Choices*, 5th Ed., ibid.
6. Michael Hammer, *The Agenda* (New York: Random House, 2001), p. 6.
7. Gary L. Frankwick, Stephen S. Porter, AND Lawrence A. Crosby, "Dynamics of Relationship Selling: A Longitudinal Examination of Changes in Salesperson-Customer Relationship Status," *Journal of Personal Selling and Sales Management*, Spring, 2001, p. 135.
8. Greg Ip, "Why High-Flyers, Built on Big Ideas, Are Such Fast Fallers," *Wall Street Journal*, April 4, 2002, p. A1.
9. For a comprehensive description of the distinct stages in the evolution of personal selling, see Thomas R. Wotruba, "The Evolutionary Process of Personal Selling," *Journal of Personal Selling and Sales Management*, Summer 1991, p. 4.
10. Phillip Kotler and Gary Armstrong, *Principles of Marketing*, 12th Ed., (Upper Saddle River, NJ: Prentice Hall, 2008), p. 10.
11. Louis E. Boone and David L. Kurtz, *Contemporary Marketing*, 11th Ed. (Mason, OH: Southwestern Publishing, 2004), p. 11.
12. Norihiko Shirouzu, Gregory L. White, and Joseph B. White, "Beyond Explorer Woes, Ford Misses Key Turns in Buyers, Technology," *Wall Street Journal*, January 14, 2002, p. A–1.
13. Malcolm Fleschner, "World Wide Winner–The UPS Story," *Selling Power*, November/December 2001, p. 58; "50 Best Companies to Sell For," *Selling Power*, November/December 2004, pp. 94–95.
14. "America's 25 Best Sales Forces," *Sales & Marketing Management*, July 2000, p. 59; "The 25 Best Service Companies to Sell For," *Selling Power*, November/December 2004, p. 95.
15. Gary Armstrong and Philip Kotler, *Marketing—An Introduction*, 7th Ed. (Upper Saddle River, NJ: Prentice Hall, 2005), p. 57.
16. Gerhard Gschwandtner, "The Power of the Selling Profession," *Selling Power*, October 2003, p. 10; Gerhard Gschwandtner, "SP 500 Salespeople Drive the Economy," *Selling Power*, October 2004, p. 59.
17. Robert M. Peterson, George H. Lucas, and Patrick L. Schul, "Forming Consultative Trade Alliances: Walking the Walk in the New Selling Environment," *NAMA Journal*, Spring 1998, p. 11; Beth Belton, "Technology Is Changing Face of U.S. Sales Force," *USA Today*, February 9, 1999, p. 2A.
18. Charles Gottenkieny, "Proper Training Can Result in Positive ROI," *Selling*, August 2003, p. 9.
19. Thomas R. Wotruba, "The Evolutionary Process in Personal Selling," *Journal of Personal Selling & Sales Management*, Summer 1991, p. 4.
20. Christian Homburg, Nicole Koschate, and Wayne D. Hoyer, "Do Satisfied Customers Really Pay More? A Study of he Relationship between Customer Satisdfaction and Willingness to Pay More," *Journal of Marketing*, April 2005, pp. 84–96.
21. Michael R. Solomon, Greg W. Marshall, Elnora W. Stuart, *Marketing—Real People, Real Choices*, 4th Ed. (Upper Saddle River: New Jersey, Prentice Hall, 2006), p. 35.
22. Robert E. Miller and Stephen E. Heiman, *Strategic Selling* (New York: Warren Books, 1985), p. 26.
23. Jack Snader, "Is It Consultative Selling or Detailing?" *Newspost*, Fall 1999, pp. 21–32; Patricia Seybold, *The Customer Revolution* (New York: Random House, 2001), p. 1.
24. Fernando Jaramillo, William B. Locander, Paul E. Spector, and Eric G. Harris, "Getting the Job Done: The Moderating Role of Initiative on the Relationship between Intrinsic Motivation and Adaptive Selling," *Journal of Personal Selling & Sales Management*, Winter 2007, pp. 59–74.
25. Keith M. Eades, *The New Solutions Selling* (New York: McGraw-Hill, 2004), pp. ix–x.
26. Marvin A. Jolson, "Broadening the Scope of Relationship Selling," *Journal of Personal Selling & Sales Management*, Fall 1997, p. 77.
27. Keith M. Eades, *The New Solutions Selling*, ibid., pp. 102–104.
28. Patricia Seybold, *The Customer Revolution* (New York: Random House, 2001), p. 1.
29. Jagdish Sheth and Reshma H. Shah, "Till Death Do us Part . . . . But Not Always: Six Antecedents to a Customer's Relational Preference in Buyer-Seller Exchanges," *Industrial Marketing Management*, June 2003, pp. 627–631.
30. Erin Strout, "Fast Forward," *Sales & Marketing Management*, December 2001, pp. 37–38.
31. Geoffrey Brewer, "The Customer Stops Here," *Sales & Marketing Management*, March 1998, pp. 31–32.
32. Gary Armstrong and Philip Kotler, *Marketing—An Introduction*, 7th Ed., ibid., p. 23.
33. Jenex Corporation, "The Jenex Corporation Grants Worldwide License to Distribute and Sell Thermapik Device," news release, February 28, 2007, www.jenexcorp.com/pressreleases.asp?ID=109, accessed May 18, 2008.
34. See Cy Charney, "Choose Your Partners," *Value-Added Selling 21*, December 16, 2003, p. 3.
35. For a discussion of strategic selling alliances that involves the sales representatives from two or more organizations, see J. Brock Smith and Donald W. Barclay, "Selling Partner Relationships: The Role of Interdependence and Relative Influences," *Journal of Personal Selling & Sales Management*, Fall 1999, pp. 21–40.

36. Gary Armstrong and Philip Kotler, *Marketing: An Introduction*, 7th Ed., ibid., p. 16.
37. Michael Hammer, *The Agenda* (New York: Random House, 2001), pp. 38–39.

SOURCES FOR BOXED FEATURES

a. Philip Kotler, Neil Rackham, and Suj Krishnaswamy, "Ending the War Between Sales & Marketing," *Harvard Business Review*, July/August 2006, pp. 68–78.; Dave Stein, "Sales and Marketing Alignment, Take 2," *Sales & Marketing Management*, January/February 2007, p. 9.
b. Robert Kreitner, *Management*, 8th ed. (Boston: Houghton Mifflin, 2001), pp. 3–4.

Chapter 6

1. Würth Canada web site, www.wurthcanada.com and BlueSky Personnel Solution Web site. www.blueskypersonnel.com, both accessed June 28, 2008.
2. Stanley Marcus, "Sales School," *Fast Company*, November 1998, p. 105.
3. Thomas A. Stewart, "Knowledge, the Appreciating Commodity," *Fortune*, October 12, 1998, p. 18.
4. John Naisbitt, *Megatrends* (New York, NY: Warner Books, 1982), p. 18
5. Dennis Jenkins, "Entrepreneurial Endeavors for Sales & Marketing Professionals," *American Salesman*, August 2007.
6. Beth Belton, "Technology Is Changing Face of U.S. Sales Force," *USA Today*, February 9, 1999, p. A2.
7. Brian Tracy, *The 100 Absolutely Unbreakable Laws of Business Success* (San Francisco, CA: Berrett-Koehler Publishers, Inc., 2000), p. 192.
8. Linda Corman, "Look Who's Selling Now," *Selling*, July/August 1996, pp. 46–53; "Everyone's a Seller," *Sales & Marketing Management*, March 2003, p. 12.
9. Paul Grescoe, *The Mavericks* (Toronto, ON: McGraw-Hill Ryerson, 1999), p. 122.
10. Ibid.
11. Harry Beckwith, *Selling the Invisible* (New York: Warner Books, 1997), p. 38; See Norm Brodsky, "Street Smarts," *Inc.*, June 2004, pp. 53–54.
12. Gabrielle Birkner, "Who Says Titles Don't Matter," *Sales & Marketing Management*, July 2001, p. 14.
13. Jay Somerset, "The Compensation Challenge," *Contact*, Spring 2008, pp. 18–24.
14. Michele Marchetti, "What a Sales Call Costs," *Sales & Marketing Management*, September 2000, pp. 80–81.
15. Theodore B. Kinni, "Fast Track to the Top: How to Start Out in Sales and End Up as CEO," *Selling Power*, July/August, pp. 56–61.
16. Carol Hymowitz, "Women Put Noses to the Grindstone, and Miss Opportunities," *Wall Street Journal*, February 3, 2004, p. B1.
17. Bonnie Harris 2007, "Wanted: Women in Finance, Why: Client Base Changing," *The Des Moines Register*, Monday, Jan 29, 2007, p. 4D.
18. Brett A. Boyle, "The Importance of the Industrial Inside Sales Force: A Case Study," *Industrial Marketing Management*, September 1996, p. 339.
19. See Louis E. Boone, David L. Kurtz, H. F. (Herb) MacKenzie, and Kim Snow, *Contemporary Marketing*, Second Canadian Edition (Toronto, ON: Nelson Canada, forthcoming).
20. Canadian Bankers Association, "Your Guide to Financial Services," www.cba.ca/eng/Tools/Brochures/tools_financialservices2.htm and www.cba.ca/eng/Tools/Brochures/tools_financialservices2.htm, downloaded April 18, 2002.
21. Erin Munro and Samantha Cheuk, personal interviews, July 24, 2008.
22. Pearl Paul, personal interview and correspondence, July 29, 2008.
23. Michael Davidson, personal correspondence, January 4, 2005.
24. Gerald L. Manning and Barry L. Reece, Intelecom Video Library, *Selling Today* 9/e.
25. Ibid.
26. Ibid.
27. Chris Mckee, personal interview, July 28, 2008; The Hitch House Web site, www.thehitchhouse.com, accessed July 27, 2008.
28. Donna Harris, "Asbury Sells College Graduates on Auto Retail," *Automotive News*, January 26, 2004, p. 26.
29. Direct Sellers Association of Canada, personal correspondence from Joan Lee, Director of Operations, July 25, 2008.
30. Heather Johnson, "Field of Sales," *Training*, July 2004, p. 34.
31. Gerhard Gschwandtner, "Rendezvous with a Rainmaker," *Selling Power*, May 2001, pp. 98–100.
32. David Munro, personal correspondence, February 13, 2000.
33. Kristine Ellis, "Deal Maker or Breaker?" *Training*, April 2002, pp. 34–37; Michele Marchetti, "Sales Training Even a Rep Could Love," *Sales & Marketing Management*, June 1998, p. 70.
34. Terry Loe in Henry Canaday, "You Can Do It", *Selling Power*, January/February 2007, pp. 23–26.
35. Henry Canaday, "In the Trenches," *Selling Power*, March 2007, pp. 25–27.
36. Alex Pettes, correspondence and personal interviews, November 2004–March 2008.

SOURCES FOR BOXED FEATURES

a. CBC News, "A Criminal Mind: The Life and Times of Eddie Greenspan," aired January 20, 2005, www.cbc.ca/lifeandtimes/greenspan.html, accessed June 13, 2005; "My Greatest Sale," Eddie Greenspan, interviewed by Laura Pratt, *Profit*, May 2005, p. 36.
b. Betsy Cummings, "Selling Around the World," *Sales & Marketing Management*, May 2001, p. 70; Jan Yager, *Business Protocol* Second Edition (Stamford, CT: Hannacroix Books, 2001), pp. 120–21.
c. Kali Pearson, "The Good, the Bad and the Ugly," *Profit*, February–March 2002, pp. 48–50; Brian Ziegler, "Your Business Card Can Be a Powerful Tool," *Des Moines Register*, August 2, 1999, B17.

Chapter 7

1. Daniel Goleman, *Working with Emotional Intelligence* (New York: Bantam Books, 1998), pp. 24–28, 317; Geoffrey James, "Use Emotional Intelligence to Improve Sales," *Selling Power*, January/February 2005, p. 43–45.
2. Daniel Goleman, *Emotional Intelligence* (New York: Bantam Books, 1995), p. 34; Cary Cherniss and Daniel Goleman (eds.), *The Emotionally Intelligent Workplace*, (San Francisco, CA: Jossey-Bass, 2001), pp. 22–24. For more information on social competence, see Daniel Goleman, *Working With*

Emotional Intelligence (New York: Bantam Books, 1998), pp. 24–28.

3. L. B. Gschwandtner and Gerhard Gschwandtner, "Balancing Act," *Selling Power*, June 1996, p. 24.

4. Ron Willingham, *Integrity Selling For The 21st Century* (New York: Currency Doubleday, 2003), p. 11.

5. Daniel H. Pink, *A Whole New Mind*, New York: Riverhead Books, 2005, pp. 48–63.

6. Ilan Mochari, "In a Former Life," *Inc.*, April 2001, p. 100.

7. J. D. Power Consumer Center, www.jdpower.com, accessed May 4, 2002.

8. *Partnering: The Heart of Selling Today*. VHS (Des Moines, IA: American Media Incorporated, 1990).

9. Paul S. Goldner, "How to Set the Playing Field," *Selling*, April 1998, p. 9.

10. Larry Wilson, *Selling in the 90s* (Chicago, IL: Nightingale Conant, 1988), p. 35.

11. William Keenan, Jr. "Customer Satisfaction Builds Business," *Selling*, March 1998, p. 12.

12. Tim Sanders, *Love Is the Killer App* (New York: Crown Business, 2002), p. 23.

13. Malcolm Fleschner, "World Wide Winner—The UPS Story," *Selling Power*, November/December 2001, p. 58.

14. Neil Rackham and John R. DeVincentis, *Rethinking the Sales Force* (New York: McGraw-Hill, 1999), pp. 79–83.

15. Phillip C. McGraw, Self Matters, New York: Simon & Schuster, 2001, pp. 69–70.

16. Sharon Begley, "Follow Your Intuition: The Unconscious You May Be the Wiser Half," *Wall Street Journal*, August 30, 2002, P. B1: Sharon Begley, "How Do I Love Thee? Let Me Count the Ways-and Other Bad Ideas," *Wall Street Journal*, September 6, 2002, P. B1

17. Phillip C. McGraw, "Dr. Phil: Know Your Goal, Make a Plan, and Pull the Trigger," *The Oprah Magazine*, September 2001, pp. 60–61; See Barry L. Reece and Rhonda Brandt, *Effective Human Relations—Personal and Organizational Applications* (Boston: Houghton Mifflin Company, 2005), pp. 95–102.

18. McGraw, Self-Matters, p. 73.

19. Stephen E. Heiman and Diane Sanchez, *The New Conceptual Selling* (New York: Warner Books, 1999), pp. 48–49. See Stephen R. Covey, "Win-Win Strategies," Training, January 2008, p. 56.

20. David Mayer and Herbert M. Greenberg, "What Makes a Good Salesman" *Harvard Business Review*, July-August 2006, p. 166. For information on how empathy training helps sales representatives improve see Cliff Edwards, "Death of a Pushy Salesman," *Business Week*, July 3, 2006.

21. Ibid.

22. Shoshana Zuboff, "A Starter Kit for Business Ethics," *Fast Company*, January 2005, p. 91.

23. Carol Hymowitz, "Management Missteps in '04 Hurt Companies, Endangered Customers," *Wall Street Journal*, December 21, 2004, p. B1; "Edward Jones Agrees to Settle Host of Charges," *Wall Street Journal*, December 21, 2004, p. C1; John Hechinger, "Putnam May Owe $100 million," *Wall Street Journal*, February 2, 2005, p. C1; Erin McClam, "Witness Tells of Coverup," *News & Observer*, January 29, 2005, p. 3D.

24. Nathaniel Branden, *Self-Esteem at Work*, p. 35.

25. Barbara Killinger, *Integrity: Doing the Right Thing for the Right Reason* (Montreal & Kingston: McGill-Queen's University Press, 2007), p. 13.

26. Eli Jones, Jesse N. Moore, Andrea J. S. Stanaland, and Rosalind A. J. Wyatt, "Salesperson Race and Gender and the Access and Legitimacy Paradigm: Does Difference Make a Difference?" *Journal of Personal Selling and Sales Management*, Fall 1998, p. 74; "Danielle Sacks, The Accidental Guru," *Fast Company*, January 2005, pp. 65–71.

27. Barry L. Reece and Rhonda Brandt, *Effective Human Relations—Personal and Organizational Applications*, 9th ed. (Boston, MA: Houghton Mifflin, 2005), p. 35–37.

28. Roy M. Berko, *Andrew D. Wolvin, and Darlyn R. Wolvin, Communicating*, 8th ed. (Boston: Houghton Mifflin Company, 2001), p. 45.

29. Ibid., p. 50.

30. Susan Bixler, *The Professional Image* (New York: Putnam Publishing Group, 1984), p. 216.

31. Barbara Pachter and Marjorie Brody, *Complete Business Etiquette Handbook* (New York: Prentice Hall, 1995), p. 14.

32. Adapted from Leonard Zunin, *Contact: The First Four Minutes* (New York: Nash Publishing, Ballantine Books, 1972), p. 109; and Jerry La Martina, "Shake It, Don't Crush It," *San Jose Mercury News*, June 25, 2000, p. 4PC.

33. Deborah Blum, "Face It!" *Psychology Today*, September/October 1998, pp. 32–69; See Julia Chang, "Selling in Acting," *Sales & Marketing Management*, May 2004, p. 22.

34. Barbara Pachter and Mary Brody, *Complete Business Etiquette Handbook* (Englewood Cliffs, NJ: Prentice Hall, 1995), p. 27; "The Eyes Have It," *Sales & Marketing Management*, January 2002, p. 20.

35. Appropriate clothing for work is discussed in Christina Binkley, "Case Study: Dressing for the Naked CEO," *Wall Street Journal*, August 23, 2007, p. D8.

36. Melinda Ligos, "Does Image Matter?" *Sales & Marketing Management*, March 2001, p. 52–55.

37. Margaret Webb Pressler, "Camouflage for the Cubicles," *News & Observer*, April 25, 2004, p. 4-E.

38. Susan Bixler and Nancy Nix-Rice, *The New Professional Image* (Adams Media Corporation, 1997), p. 11–15; Barbara Pachter and Marjorie Brody, *Complete Business Etiquette Handbook*, p. 72.

39. Paul Galanti, "Talking Motivates—Communication Makes Things Happen," *Personal Selling Power*, November–December 1995, p. 88.

40. Susan Berkley, "Hone Your Sharpest Sales Weapon," *Sales & Field Force Automation*, July 1997, p. 24.

41. Joann S, Lublin, "To Win Advancement, You Need to Clean up Any Bad Speech Habits," *Wall Street Journal*, October 5, 2004, p. B.1.

42. David E. Weliver, "My Fair CEO," *Inc.*, October 30, 2001, p. 112.

43. "Is Etiquette a Core Value?" *Inc.*, May 2004, p. 22.

44. Tim Sanders, *Love Is the Killer App* (New York: Crown Business, 2002), p. 18.

45. Steven Covey, *The 7 Habits of Highly Effective People* (New York: Simon & Schuster, 1989), pp. 240–41.

46. L. B. Gschwandtner, "Mary Lou Retton," *Personal Selling Power*, Fifteenth Anniversary Issue, 1995, p. 99.

47. Jack Canfield, *The Success Principles* (New York: Harper Collins, 2005), pp. 342–343.

48. Colleen DeBaise, "Offbeat Hobbies May Help Build Relationships with Some Clients," *Wall Street Journal*, February 9, 2005, p. B2.

49. Anne Murphy Paul, "Self-Help: Shattering the Myths," *Psychology Today*, March/April 2001, p. 64; Arnold A. Lazarus and Clifford N. Lazarus, *The 60-Second Shrink* (San Luis Obispo, CA: Impact Publishers, 1997), pp. 3–4.
50. Phillip C. Mc Graw, *Self Matters* (New York: Simon & Shuster, 2001), pp. 69–76.
51. Rick Saulle, "Honor Diversity," *Selling Power*, May 2004, p.54.

SOURCES FOR BOXED FEATURES

a. Brenda Lockyer, personal correspondence, January 4, 2005.
b. Adapted from "Secrets of Power Persuasion for Salespeople," by Roger Dawson. See Roger Dawson, "And Your Name was Again?" *Value-Added Selling 21*, July 16, 2007, p. 2.
c. Andrew S. Gallan, "Bringing CARE to Your Customers," *Sales & Marketing Management*, May 2004, p. 72.

Chapter 8

1. Mike McNamee and Christopher Schmitt, "The Chainsaw Al Massacre," *Business Week*, May 28, 2001, p. 48; Dennis K. Berman and Joann S. Lublin, "Restructuring, Personality Clashes Led to Lucent Executive's Exit," *Wall Street Journal*, May 17, 2001, p. B1; Charles Fishmann, "Jeff Bezos," *Fast Company*, February 2001, pp. 80–82.
2. Douglas A. Bernstein, Louis A. Penner, Alison Clarke-Stewart, and Edward J. Roy, *Personality*, 6th ed. (Boston: Houghton Mifflin, 2003), p. 518.
3. Robert Bolton and Dorothy Grover Bolton, *People Styles at Work* (New York: AMACOM, 1996), p. 10.
4. Fernando Jaramillo, William B. Locander, Paul E. Spector, and Eric G. Harris, "Getting the Job Done: The Moderating Role of Initiative on the Relationship Between Intrinsic Motivation and Adaptive Selling," *Journal of Personal Selling & Sales Management*, Winter 2007, pp. 59–74.
5. David W. Merrill and Roger H. Reid, *Personal Styles and Effective Performance* (Radnor, PA: Chilton Books, 1981), p. 1.
6. For a more complete description of *The Versatile Salesperson* training program visit the Wilson Learning Corporation Web page, www.wilsonlearning.com, accessed January 20, 2005.
7. Robert J. Sternberg, *Thinking Styles* (New York: Cambridge University Press, 1997), p. 8.
8. Robert Bolton and Dorothy Grover Bolton, *People Styles at Work* (New York, AMACOM, 1996).
9. Geoff James, "Inside the Psychology of Selling," *Selling Power*, January/February 2004, pp. 25–28.
10. The dominance factor was described in an early book by William M. Marston, *The Emotions of Normal People* (New York: Harcourt, 1928). Research conducted by Rolfe LaForge and Robert F. Suczek resulted in the development of the Interpersonal Checklist (ICL), which features a dominant–submissive scale. A person who receives a high score on the ICL tends to lead, persuade, and control others. The Interpersonal Identity Profile, developed by David W. Merrill and James W. Taylor, features a factor called "assertiveness." Persons classified as being high in assertiveness tend to have strong opinions, make quick decisions, and be directive when dealing with people. Persons classified as being low in assertiveness tend to voice moderate opinions, make thoughtful decisions, and be supportive when dealing with others.
11. David W. Johnson, *Reaching Out—Interpersonal Effectiveness and Self-Actualization*, Eighth Edition (Boston, MA: Allyn and Macon, 2003), p. 83.

12. The research conducted by LaForge and Suczek resulted in identification of the *hostile–loving continuum*, which is similar to the *sociability continuum*. Their Interpersonal Checklist features this scale. L. L. Thurstone and T. G. Thurstone developed the Thurstone Temperament Schedule, which provides an assessment of a "sociable" factor. Persons with high scores in this area enjoy the company of others and make friends easily. The Interpersonal Identity Profile developed by Merrill and Taylor contains an objectivity continuum. A person with low objectivity is seen as attention seeking, involved with the feelings of others, informal, and casual in social relationships. A person who is high in objectivity appears to be somewhat indifferent toward the feelings of others. This person is formal in social relationships.
13. Sam Deep and Lyle Sussman, *Close the Deal* (Reading, MA: Perseus Books, 1999), p. 157.
14. Len D'Innocenzo and Jack Cullen, "Chameleon Management," *Personal Selling Power*, January–February 1995, p. 61.
15. "A Global Profiling Tool," Wilson Learning Corporation, Eden Prairie, MN. 1999.
16. Tom Ritchey, *I'm Stuck, You're Stuck*, San Francisco, CA: Berrett-Koehler, Inc. 2002, p. 5.
17. Ron Willingham, *Integrity Selling for the 21st Century* (New York: Currency Doubleday, 2003), pp. 20–21.
18. Stuart Atkins, *How to Get the Most from Styles-Based Training* (Beverly Hill, CA: Stuart Atkins, 1996), p. 1.
19. Gary A. Williams and Robert B. Miller, "Change the Way You Persuade," *Harvard Business Review*, May 2002, p. 65.
20. Robert Bolton and Dorothy Grover Bolton, *People Styles at Work*, p. 65.
21. David Merrill and Roger Reid, *Personal Styles and Effective Performance* (Radnor, PA: Chilton Books, 1981), p. 2.
22. Roger Wenschlag, *The Versatile Salesperson* (New York, NY: John Wiley & Sons, 1989), pp. 165–171.
23. Nina Munk, "How Levi's Trashed a Great American Brand," *Fortune*, April 12, 1999, p. 85.
24. "The Top 25 Managers of the Year," *Business Week*, January 14, 2002, p. 65.
25. Stuart Atkins, *How to Get the Most from Styles-Based Training*, p. 3.
26. Ron Willingham, *Integrity Selling* (New York: Doubleday, 1987), pp. 21–23.
27. Eric F. Douglas, *Straight Talk* (Palo Alto, CA: 1998), p. 92.
28. Ron Willingham, *Integrity Selling*, p. 37.
29. David W. Merrill and Roger H. Reid, *Personal Styles and Effective Performance*, pp. 134, 135.
30. Stuart Atkins, *The Name of Your Game* (Beverly Hills, CA: Ellis & Stewart, 1981), p. 51.

SOURCES FOR BOXED FEATURES

a. Correspondence with Dr. Steve Bajura dated April 14, 2002.
b. Christopher Caggiano, "*Psychopath, Inc.*, July 1998, p. 83.
c. "The Platinum Rule, www.platinumrule.com, accessed May 4, 2008.

Chapter 9

1. Leslie Scism, "Some Agents 'Churn' Life Insurance Policies, Hurt Their Customers," *Wall Street Journal*, January 3, 1995, p. 1.
2. Betsy Cummings, "Keeping Your Sales Force Clean," *Sales & Marketing Management*, June 2007, p. 10; Phil Hirschkorn,

"Another Suspension in Student Loan Probe," www.cbsnews.com, accessed April 9, 2007.

3. O. C. Ferrell, John Fraedrich and Linda Ferrell, *Business Ethics*, 5th ed. (Boston: Houghton Mifflin Company, 2002), p. 6. The importance of character at the leadership level is described in Noel M. Tichy and Warren G. Bennis, "Making the Tough Call," *Inc.*, November 2007, pp. 36–38.

4. Stephen R. Covey, *The Seven Habits of Highly Effective People* (New York: Simon & Schuster, 1989), pp. 18, 92. See Adam Hanft, "The New Lust for Integrity," *Inc.*, February 2004, p. 104.

5. Jan Yager, *Business Protocol* (Stamford, CT: Hannacroix Creek Books, 2001), pp. 199–200.

6. Sharon Begley, "A World of Their Own," *Newsweek*, May 8, 2000, pp. 53–56; Jaren Sandberg, "Office Sticky Fingers Can Turn the Rest of Us into Joe Fridays," *Wall Street Journal*, November 19, 2005, p. B1.

7. John A. Byrne, "How to Fix Corporate Governance," *Business Week*, May 6, 2002, pp. 69–78.

8. Josh Freed, "Investigators: Drug Salesman Foiled Pharmacist," *The News & Observer*, August 26, 2001, p. 12A.

9. Robert Simons, Henry Mintzburg, and Kunal Basu, "Memo to CEOs," *Fast Company*, June 2002, pp. 117–21.

10. Marjorie Kelly, "Waving Goodbye to the Invisible Hand," *Business Ethics*, March/April 2002, p. 4. For a somewhat different point of view, see George Stalk, "Warm and Fuzzy Doesn't Cut It," *Wall Street Journal*, February 15, 2005, p. B2.

11. Yochi J. Dreazen, "Pressure for Sales Fostered Abuses at WorldCom," *Wall Street Journal*, May 16, 2002, p. B1. See Norm Kamikow, "Ethics & Performance," *Workforce Performance Solutions*, March 2006, p. 4.

12. Beth Schultz, "Ethics under Investigation," *Network World Framingham*, April 26, 2004, pp. 72–74.

13. Robert Simons, *et al.*, "Memo to CEOs," pp. 120–21.

14. Patrick Smith, "You Have a Job, But How About a Life?" *Business Week*, November 16, 1998, p. 30.

15. Mitchell Pacelle, "Citigroup Works on Reputation," *Wall Street Journal*, February 17, 2005, p. C3.

16. Patricia B. Gray, "Business Class," *Fortune*, April 17, 2006, p. 336; Margery Weinstein, "Survey Says: Ethics Training Works," *Training*, November 2005, p. 15; "ERC Survey & Benchmarking," www.ethics.org, accessed October 8, 2007.

17. Patricia Gray, "Business Class," *Fortune*, April 17, 2006, p. 336; Philip Kotler and Gary Armstrong, *Principles of Marketing*, 12th ed. (Upper Saddle River, NJ: Prentice Hall, 2008), p. 568.

18. Alan M. Webber, "Are All Consultants Corrupt?" *Fast Company*, May 2002, pp. 130–134.

19. Brenda Bouw, "In praise of an ethical education," *Globe and Mail*, March 18, 2002, p. C1.

20. Gary Armstrong and Philip Kotler, *Marketing*, 6th ed. (Upper Saddle River, NJ: Prentice Hall, 2003), p. 619.

21. Betsy Cummings, "Ethical Breach," *Sales & Marketing Management*, July 2004, p. 10.

22. Sun Life Financial website, www.sunlife.com, and "Code of Business Conduct," accessed June 26, 2008.

23. Michele Krebs, "All the Marketing Men," *Autoweek*, February 16, 1998, p. 11.

24. Ken Brown and Gee L. Lee, "Lucent Fires Top China Executives," *Wall Street Journal*, April 7, 2004, p. A8;

Carl F. Fey, "How to Do Business in Russia," *Wall Street Journal*, October 27, 2007 p. R4.

25. Steven Sack, "Watch the Words," *Sales & Marketing Management*, July 1, 1985, p. 56.

26. Patricia S. Eyres, "Steps for Staying Out of Court and Trouble," *Selling*, April 2002, p. 10.

27. Michael Schrage, "Internet: Internal Threat?" *Fortune*, July 9, 2001, p. 184.

28. Rob Zeiger, "Sex, Sales & Stereotypes," *Sales & Marketing Management*, pp. 52, 53.

29. Barry L. Reece and Rhonda Brandt, *Effective Human Relations—Personal and Organizational Applications*, Tenth Edition (Boston, MA: Houghton Mifflin, 2008), p. 110.

30. Betsy Cummings, "Do Customers Hate Salespeople?" *Sales & Marketing Management*, June 2001, pp. 50–51.

31. Ron Willingham, *Integrity Selling for the 21st Century* (New York: Currency Doubleday, 2003), p. 1.

32. Ron Willingham, "Four Traits All Highly Successful Salespeople Have in Common," (audiotape presentation), Phoenix, AZ, 1998.

33. Price Pritchett, *The Ethics of Excellence* (Dallas, TX: Pritchett & Associates, Inc., n.d.), p. 14.

34. Robert Kreitner, Barry Reece, and James P. O'Grady, *Business*, Second Edition (Boston, MA: Houghton Mifflin, 1990), pp. 647–48.

35. Karin Schill Rives, "Workers Find Clause Has Teeth," *News & Observer*, July 29, 2001, p. E1.

36. Dawn Marie Driscoll, "Don't Confuse Legal and Ethical Standards," *Business Week*, July/August 1996, p. 44.

37. Nancy Henderson Wurst, "Who's Afraid of Ethics?" *Hemisphere Magazine*, November 2006, pp. 120–123.

38. Carol Wheeler, "Getting the Edge on Ethics," *Executive Female*, May/June 1996, p. 47.

39. Ron Willingham, *Integrity Selling for the 21st Century, ibid.*, p. 11.

40. Sharon Drew Morgan, *Selling with Integrity*, (San Francisco, CA: Berrett-Koehler Publishers, Inc., 1997), pp. 25–27.

41. Ibid., pp. 27–28.

42. Tom Peters, *Thriving on Chaos* (New York: Alfred A. Knopf, 1988), p. 521.

43. Gerhard Gschwandtner, "Lies and Deception in Selling," *Personal Selling Power*, Fifteenth Anniversary Issue, 1995, p. 62.

44. Price Pritchett, *The Ethics of Excellence* (Dallas, TX: Pritchett & Associates, Inc., [n.d.]), p. 18.

45. Neil Rackham and John R. DeVincentis, *Rethinking the Sales Force* (New York: McGraw-Hill, 1999), pp. 83–84. A discussion of the trust factor is included in Jacqueline Durett, "A Matter of Trust," *Sales & Marketing Management*, January/February 2007, pp. 36–37.

46. Geoffrey Colvin, "The Verdict on Business: Presumed Guilty," *Fortune*, November 15, 2004, p. 78.

47. "The World Is Flat: A Brief History of the Twenty-First Century," www.thomaslfriedman.com, accessed October 10, 2007.

48. Matthew McKay, Martha Davis, and Patrick Fanning, *Messages: The Communication Skills Book* (Oakland, CA: New Harbinger, 1995), p. 108.

49. O. C. Ferrell, John Fraedrich, and Linda Ferrell, *Business Ethics: Ethical Decision Making and Cases*, 5th ed. (Boston: Houghton Mifflin Company, 2002), p. 208.

50. Barry L. Reece and Rhonda Brandt, ibid., pp. 125–26.
51. William M. Pride, Robert J. Hughes, and Jack R. Kapoor, *Business*, 7th ed. (Boston: Houghton Mifflin Company, 2002), p. 40.

SOURCES FOR BOXED FEATURES

a. Beth Schultz, "Ethics under Investigation," *Network World*, April 26, 2004, pp. 72–73; "Living the Values: A Guide to Ethical Business Practices at Nortel Networks. www.nortelnetworks.com/corporate/community/ethics/collateral/code_of_conduct_ nolinks.pdf, downloaded December 30, 2004.
b. Renee Houston Zemanski, "When the Competition Gets Tough," *Selling Power*, April 2006, pp. 17–19.

Chapter 10

1. Interview with Amy Vandaveer on April 13, 2007. For additional information regarding *Texas Monthly* magazine, visit www.texasmonthly.com.
2. Keith M. Eades, *The New Solution Selling* (New York: McGraw-Hill, 2004), pp 4–5.
3. Geoffrey James, "Solution Selling," *Selling Power*, May 2006, pp. 45–48. This article is based on an interview with Keith Eades, author of *The New Solution Selling*.
4. Michael R. Solomon and Elnora W. Stuart, *Marketing: Real People, Real Choices*, Third Edition (Upper Saddle River, NJ: Prentice Hall, 2008), p. 237.
5. "Strategic Vista International Inc. Introduces a Revolution in Safety and Security Protection to Consumers," Canada NewsWire, Ottawa, July 28, 2004, p. 1.
6. "Loki Management Systems Is Selected as Finalist in Microsoft 2004 Impact Awards," Canada NewsWire, Ottawa, October 29, 2004, p. 1.
7. Neil Rackham and John R. DeVincentis, *Rethinking the Sales Force* (New York: McGraw-Hill, 1999), p. 79.
8. Department of Finance Canada. www.fin.gc.ca/toce/2002/cmfi_e.html, accessed May 6, 2002.
9. Karen E. Starr, "Simple Solutions," *Selling Power*, July/August 2001, p. 22.
10. Christopher Whittier, "Quotation Management: The Revolution is Here to Stay," www.resultsonline.com, accessed August 27, 2007.
11. John Fellows, "A Decent Proposal," *Personal Selling Power*, November/December 1995, p. 56.
12. Adapted from John Fellows, "A Decent Proposal," *Personal Selling Power*, November–December 1995, p. 56. See Neil Rackham, "Seven Rules for Creating Winning Sales Proposal's," *Value-Added Selling 21*, December 16, 2003, p. 20.
13. "Feeling under the Gun? Check Your Proposal," *Selling*, October 2001, p. 3.
14. Neil Rackam, "Seven Rules for Creating Winning Sales Proposals," *Value-Added Selling 21*, December 16, 2003, p. 20.
15. "What Kind of Rep Is Most Trustworthy?" *Sales & Marketing Management*, February 2001, p. 90.
16. Tom Peters, *Re-Imagine! Business Excellence in a Disruptive Age* (London: Dording Kindersley Limited, 2003), p. 224.
17. Reimer Express news release, "Reimer Express and Its Parent Roadway Express Receive System Wide ISO 9002 Certification," www.reimerexpress.com/news/reimerpressers/2000-04-04.html, accessed June 29, 2008.

18. Betsy Cummings, "Welcome to the Real Whirled," *Sales & Marketing Management*, February 2001, pp. 87–88.
19. Ian Gelenter, "Build Satisfaction with a Service Contract," *Selling*, May 1998, p. 7.
20. Tom Reilly, "Should You Set Prices?" *Selling*, August 2000, pp. 1, 14.
21. Gerhard Gschwandtner, "ROI Selling," *Selling Power*, November/December 2004, p. 10.
22. William M. Pride, Robert J. Hughes, and Jack R. Kapoor, *Business*, Eighth Edition (Boston, MA: Houghton Mifflin, 2005), pp. 456–57.
23. Working.canada.com, "*Financial Post*'s 10 Best Companies to Work For," available at http://working.canada.com/profiles/rim/profile.html, accessed June 29, 2008.
24. Michael L. Askew, "What I Know Now," *Fast Company*, November 2005, p. 108.
25. Michael R. Williams and Jill S. Attaway, "Exploring Salespersons' Customer Orientation as a Mediator of Organizational Culture's Influence on Buyer-Seller Relationships," *Journal of Personal Selling & Sales Management*, Fall 1996, pp. 33–52.
26. "Dealer Merchandising Portfolio," *Views: The Inner Circle News*, Winter 2000, p. 10.
27. "Grassroots Problem Solving," *Inc.*, March 1996, p. 92.
28. See Brian Tracy, "Analyzing the Competition," *Value Added Selling 21*, September 16, 2003, p. 2.
29. Jim Dickie, "Lowest Price Isn't the Answer," *Selling*, August 2000, p. 14.
30. Bob Mundson, "A Personal Blend," *Training*, February 2004, p. 11.
31. "Ontario Global Traders Awards," *Profit*, September 2001, Advertising Supplement.
32. Margery Weinstein, "Selling Points," *Training*, June 2007, p. 51.
33. Jill Rosenfeld, "Unit of One," *Fast Company*, April 2000, p. 98.
34. Neil Rackham, *The SPIN Selling Fieldbook* (New York: McGraw-Hill, 1996), pp. 149–52; *Value-Added Selling 21*, December 26, 2006, p. 4.
35. Gary Hamil, *Leading the Revolution* (Boston, MA: Harvard Business School Press, 2000), p. 87; Neil Rackham, "Improve This Skill and Boost Sales up to 27%," *Value-Added Selling 21*, March 2, 2004, p. 1; *Value-Added Selling 21*, December 26, 2006, p. 4.

SOURCES FOR BOXED FEATURES

a. Rhea Seymour, "Ideas That Work," *Profit*, June 2002, p. 69.
b. Robert G. Cooper, *Product Leadership* (Reading, MA: Perseus Books, 1998), p. 12; Neil Rackham, "What's New," *Selling Power*, January/February 1999, pp. 90, 92–93.

Chapter 10 cont.

1. Peter Egan, "The Best of All Worlds Bunch," *Road & Track*, July 2002, pp. 52–78. "2005 Geneva: Lexus Finesses Next IS Sport Sedan," www.autoweek.com, accessed March 1, 2005. Greg Kable, "Audi A4 Debuts at Frankfurt," *Autoweek*, September 3, 2007, p. 10. Joe Rusz, "Saab 9-3 & XWD" *Road & Track*, October 2007, p. 60.
2. Neal E. Boudette, "The Luxury-Car Market Gets More Crowded," *Wall Street Journal*, March 3, 2005, p. D1;

J. P. Vettraino, "2006 BMW 3 Series: Technology Update," www.autoweek.com, accessed March 1, 2005.

3. Michael R. Solomon, Grey W, Marshall, and Elnora W. Stuart, *Marketing: Real People, Real Choices*, 5th ed. (Upper Saddle River, NJ: Pearson Education, 2008), p. 220.

4. D. Lee Carpenter, "Return on Innovation—the Power of Being Different," *Retailing Issues Letter*, May 1998, p. 3.

5. Brian Tracy, "Keeping the Customers You Make," *Selling*, November 2003, pp. 1, 4.

6. Tom Reilly, "You Must Differentiate to Win," *Selling*, April 2001, pp. 1, 10.

7. Gary Armstrong and Philip Kotler, *Marketing: An Introduction*, 7th ed. (Upper Saddle River, NJ: Prentice Hall, 2005), p. 12.

8. Tom Leverton, "Five Questions," *Sales & Marketing Management*, July 2004, p. 13.

9. Theodore Kinni, "The Value Proposition," *Selling Power*, July/August 2005, p. 75.

10. Michael Arndt, "Built for the Long Haul" *Business Week*, January 30, 2006, p. 66.

11. Carl K. Clayton, "Sell Quality, Service, Your Company, Yourself," *Personal Selling Power*, January/February 1990, p. 47.

12. Elaine Parker, "How I Made the Sale," *Value-Added Selling 21*, June 17, 2003, pp. 1–2.

13. Suein L Hwang, "It Was a WOMBAT for the Meatware, But It Was a Good Sell," *Wall Street Journal*, May 15, 2002, p. B1.

14. J. Thomas Russell and W. Ronald Lane, *Kleppner's Advertising Procedure* (Englewood Cliffs, NJ: Prentice-Hall, 1996), pp. 46–47.

15. Mark Leslie and Charles A. Holloway, "The Sales Learning Curve," *Harvard Business Review*, July/August 2006, p. 121.

16. Jess McCuan, "Reeling In the Big One" *Inc.*, August 2004, pp. 43–44; "What Is IntraLinks?" www.Intralinks.com, accessed March 2, 2005.

17. Sun Life Financial Web sites, www.sunlife.ca and www.sunlife.com, accessed July 4, 2008.

18. Michael R. Solomon and Elnora W. Stuart, *Marketing: Real People, Real Choices* Fourth Edition (Upper Saddle River, NJ: Prentice Hall, 2006), pp. 347–48.

19. Carlos Tejada, "The Allure of Bundling," *Wall Street Journal*, October 7, 2003, p. B 1.

20. Michael Treacy, "You Need a Value Discipline—But Which One?" *Fortune*, April 17, 1995, p. 195.

21. Robert Shulman and Richard Miniter, "Discounting Is No Bargain," *Wall Street Journal*, December 7, 1998, p. A30.

22. Andy Cohen, "Survey Says: Service Beats Price Online," *Sales & Marketing Management*, July 2002, p. 18.

23. Geoffrey James, "Solution Selling," *Selling Power*, May 2006, p. 46.

24. Adapted from a model described in "Marketing Success through Differentiation—of Anything," *Harvard Business Review*, January/February 1980.

25. Joanna Johnson, "A New Perspective on Marketing," *Construction Dimensions*, April 1990, p. 14.

26. Ted Levitt, *Marketing Imagination* (New York: Free Press, 1983), p. 80.

27. Neil Rackham, "Boost Your Sales 20% by Improving This Skill," *Value-Added Selling 21*, June 17, 2003, pp. 1–2.

28. Thomas A. Stewart, "A Satisfied Customer Isn't Enough," *Fortune*, July 21, 1997, pp. 112–13.

29. "Business Bulletin," *Wall Street Journal*, September 24, 1998, p. A1.

30. "Study: What Really Matters to Your Customers," *Value-Added Selling 21*, February 14, 2005, p. 4.

31. Ted Levitt, *Marketing Imagination*, P. 84.

32. Rebecca Smith, "Beyond Reycling: Manufacturers Embrace 'C2C' Design," *Wall Street Journal*, March 3, 2005, p. B1.

33. Neil Rackham and John R. DeVincentis, *Rethinking the Sales Force* (New York: McGraw-Hill, 1999), p. 89.

34. Ibid., pp. 89–90.

35. Ibid., p. 90.

36. Francy Blackwood, "The Concept That Sells," *Selling*, March 1995, pp. 34–36; *Systems Furniture Overview*, Steelcase Incorporated, November 1995, pp. 48–50. Rebecca Smith, "Beyond Recycling: Manufacturers Embrace 'C2' Design," *Wall Street Journal*, March 3, 2005, p. B1.

SOURCES FOR BOXED FEATURES

a. Malcolm Fleschner, "Chief Sales Executives," *Selling Power*, April 2002, pp. 58–59.

b. Personal interview with Gary Svoboda, June 3, 2002.

Chapter 11

1. Tom Peters, *Re-imagine! Business Excellence in a Disruptive Age* (London, UK: Dorling Kindersley, 2003), pp. 309–10.

2. "Nighttime Reading for Daytime Success," *Sales & Marketing Management*, May 2007, p. 44.

3. Michael Hammer and James Champy, *Reengineering the Corporation: A Manifesto for Business Revolution* (New York: Harper Business, 1993), p. 18.

4. Keith M. Eades, *The New Solution Selling* (New York: McGraw-Hill, 2004), pp. 32–33.

5. Tom Peters and Nancy Austin, *A Passion for Excellence* (New York: Random House, 1985), p. 71.

6. "How Well Do You Know Your Customers?" *Sales & Field Force Automation*, January 1999, p. 141.

7. Gary Armstrong and Philip Kotler, *Marketing: An Introduction*, Sixth Edition (Upper Saddle River, NJ: Prentice Hall, 2003), pp. 191–92, 215.

8. Michael R. Solomon and Elnora W. Stuart, *Marketing: Real People, Real Choices*, Third Edition (Upper Saddle River, NJ: Prentice Hall, 2003), pp. 200–202.

9. Gary Armstrong and Philip Kotler, *Marketing: An Introduction*, Seventh Edition (Upper Saddle River, NJ: Prentice Hall, 2005), p. 169.

10. Michael R. Solomon and Elnora W. Stuart, *Marketing: Real People, Real Choices*, 2008, p. 182.

11. Ibid., pp. 182–183.

12. Philip Kotler and Gary Armstrong, *Principles of Marketing*, Twelfth Edition (Upper Saddle River, NJ: Prentice Hall, 2008), pp. 163–166.

13. www.fedex.com, accessed December 16, 2004.

14. Philip Kotler and Gary Armstrong, *Principles of Marketing*, Twelfth Edition, pp. 146–147.

15. Ibid., p. 147.

16. Ibid., pp. 145–146.

17. Keith M. Eades, *The New Solution Selling*, pp. 32–33. Betsy Cummings, "Proving the Sale Process," *Sales & Marketing Management*, June 2006, p. 12.

18. Keith M. Eades, *The New Solution Selling*, p. 31.

19. Stephen E. Heiman and Diane Sanchez, *The New Conceptual Selling* (New York: Warner Books, 1999), pp. 190–91.
20. Research reported in Tom Atkinson and Ron Koprowski, "Sales Reps' Biggest Mistakes," *Harvard Business Review,* July-August 2006. p. 1, indicates that 26 percent of the business-to-business buyers say salespeople "don't follow my company's buying process."
21. Gary Armstrong and Philip Kotler, *Marketing,* Seventh Edition, p. 160.
22. Neil Rackham and John R. DeVincentis, *Rethinking the Sales Force* (New York: McGraw-Hill, 1999), p. 66.
23. Bill Stinnett, "Reverse-Engineer the Buying Process," *Selling,* December 2004, p. 16.
24. Neil Rackham and John DeVincentis, *Rethinking the Sales Force,* p. 68.
25. Ibid., p. 69.
26. Neil Rackham and John DeVincentis provide extensive coverage of these three selling modes in *Rethinking the Sales Force.* See also Neil Rackham and John R. DeVincentis, "Let the Customer Define Value—and Sales Will Rise," *Value-Added Selling 21,* January 13, 2004, pp. 1–2.
27. Neil Rackham and John R. DeVincentis, "Let the Customer Define Value—and Sales Will Rise," pp. 1–2.
28. Ken Brown, "Little-Known Avaya Tackles Cisco in Internet Calling Gear," *Wall Street Journal,* October 26, 2004, p. B1.
29. Neil Rackham and John DeVincentis, *Rethinking the Sales Force,* p. 74.
30. Philip Kotler and Gary Armstrong, *Principles of Marketing,* 10th Ed. (Upper Saddle River, NJ: Prentice Hall, 2004), p. 28.
31. Stan Davis and Christopher Meyer, *Blur: The Speed of Change in the Connected Economy* (New York: Addison-Wesley Publishers, 1998), p. 16.
32. William M. Pride and O.C. Ferrell, *Marketing,* Tenth Edition (Boston, MA: Houghton Mifflin, 1997), pp. 143–148.
33. Douglas A. Bernstein, Alison Clark-Stewart, Edward J. Roy, and Christopher D. Wickens, *Psychology,* Sixth Edition (Boston, MA: Houghton Mifflin, 2003), p. 648.
34. Gary Armstrong and Philip Kotler, *Marketing: An Introduction,* Seventh Edition, pp. 147–148.
35. Douglas A. Bernstein, et al., *Psychology,* Fourth Edition, p. 21.
36. Louis E. Boone and David L. Kurtz, *Contemporary Marketing,* Eleventh Edition (Mason, OH: Southwestern Publishing, 2004), p. 267.
37. Roger Hart, "Luxury, VW's Way," *AutoWeek,* December 27, 2004, pp. 18–19; Tom Reilly, "All Sales Decisions are Emotional for the Buyer," *Selling,* July 2003, p. 13.
38. Roy Chitwood, "Hidden Buyer Motives: Handle Them With Care," *Value-Added Selling 21,* April 2, 2007, p. 4.
39. Phil Kline, "Dominant Buying Motive Is the Result of Strong Emotions," *Marketing News,* May 24, 1993, p. 4.
40. Stan Davis and Christopher Meyer, *Blur,* p. 52.
41. Robert McGarvey, "The Buyer's Emotional Side," *Selling Power,* April 2006, p. 35.
42. Ibid., p. 36.
43. Gary Armstrong and Philip Kotler, *Marketing,* Sixth Edition, p. 216; Sid Chadwick, "New Twists in Price vs. Perceived Value," *Sales and Marketing Advisory Magazine,* July/August 2001, p. 6.

SOURCES FOR BOXED FEATURES

a. Judith C. Tingley and Lee E. Robert, *GenderSell: How to Sell to the Opposite Sex* (New York: Simon & Schuster, 1999).
b. Dave Stein, "Selling Across Generation Gaps," *Sales & Marketing Management.* October 2007, p. 9.

Chapter 12

1. Salesforce.com Web site, www.salesforce.com/customers/travel-transportation/greyhound.jsp, accessed July 5, 2008;
2. Don Peppers, Martha Rogers, and Bob Dorf. "Is Your Company Ready for One-to-One Marketing?" *Harvard Business Review,* January/February 1999, pp. 151–54.
3. Gerhard Gschwandtner, "Thoughts to Sell By," *Personal Selling Power,* Fifteenth Anniversary Issue, 1995, p. 122.
4. Dorothy Leeds, "Where Are the Real Decision Makers?" *Personal Selling Power,* March 1993, p. 62; Gerhard Gschwandtner, "Getting Squeezed," *Selling Power,* May 2002, p. 10.
5. Terry Hill, "How Do You Sustain And Grow Your Customer Relationships," *American Salesman,* October 2007, p. 26.
6. Paul Tindall, "Prospecting: It Separates the Best from the Rest," *Sales Exchange,* November 17–23, 2003.
7. For additional information on Joe Girard see "Joe Girard on Becoming The World's Greatest Salesperson," *Harvard Business Review,* July–August 2006, p. 25.
8. Gerhard Gschwandtner, "The Funnel Concept," *Personal Selling Power,* May/June 1993, p. 23.
9. Joel R. Pecoraro, "Panning for Gold," *Sales & Marketing Management,* November 2004, p. 56.
10. Jim Domanski, "Referrals: The Easy Way to Prospect," in *Top Dog Sales Secrets,* Michael Dalton Johnson, ed. (Carlsbad, CA: Penny Union, 2007), pp. 13–15.
11. Geoffrey James, "How to Earn Customer Referrals," *Selling Power,* July/August 2004, pp. 25–28.
12. BNI-International Web site, www.bni.com, accessed February 14, 2005.
13. Thomas Petzinger, Jr., "Selling a 'Killer App' Is a Far Tougher Job Than Dreaming It Up," *Wall Street Journal,* April 3, 1998, p. B1.
14. Daniel Tynan, "Tricks of the Trade Show," *Sales & Marketing Management,* January 2004, p. 27.
15. Ron Donoho, "Steering New Sales," *Sales & Marketing Management,* November 2001, pp. 31–35.
16. Henry Canaday, "Carefully Composed," *Selling Power,* May 2007, pp. 44–46.
17. Ibid., pp. 45–46.
18. Sue Stock, "Are You Linked," *News & Observer,* July 8, 2007, pp. E1 and E6.
19. Henry Canaday, "Zeroing In On Prospects," *Selling Power,* March 2006, p. 82.
20. Ibid., pp. 84–85.
21. Andy Cohen, "Man About Town," *Sales & Marketing Management,* June 2000, p. 29.
22. John Boe, "Selling is a Contact Sport: Keys to Effective Phone Calling." *American Salesman,* January 2008, p. 26. For more information on cold calls see Scott Stears, "Cold Calls Have Yet to Breathe Their Last Gasp," *Wall Street Journal,* December 14, 2006, p. D2.

23. Maxwell Maltz, Dan S. Kennedy, William T. Brooks, Matt Oechsli, Jeff Paul, and Pamela Yellen, *Zero-Resistance Selling* (Paramus, NJ: Prentice-Hall, 1998), p. 167.
24. Stacy L. Bradford, "Ten Job-Networking Tips," *The News & Observer*, January 30, 2005, p. E7.
25. Tuba Üstüner and David Godes, "Better Sales Networks," *Harvard Business Review*, July–August 2006, pp. 102–112.
26. Michele Marchetti, "Do You Have the Knack for Networking?" *Sales & Marketing Management*, January 1996, p. 30; Deb Haggerty, "Successful Networking Begins as a State of Mind," *Selling*, December 2004, p. 13.
27. Maxwell Maltz, et al., pp. 179–180.
28. Steve Atlas, "Trouble Connecting?" *Selling Power*, September 2001, p. 27.
29. "Are You Generating and Using Quality Leads?" *Value-Added Selling 21*, September 16, 2003, p. 4.
30. Thomas R. Watruba, "The Evolution of Selling," *Journal of Personal Selling and Sales Management*, Summer 1991, p. 7.
31. This example was adapted from "Skills Workshop" by William F. Kendy, *Selling Power*, January/February 2000, p. 26.
32. Mitchell Pacelle, "Former SEC Chairman Levitt Decries Business Ethics in the U.S.," *Wall Street Journal*, June 17, 2002, p. C7; Shoshana Zuboff, "A Starter Kit for Business Ethics," *Fast Company*, January 2005, p. 91.
33. Rick Page, *Hope Is Not a Strategy* (Atlanta, GA: Nautilus Press, 2002), pp. 69–71.
34. "Senior Execs Share Insider Tips," *Selling*, March 2000, pp. 1, 14; Tom Reilly, "Selling to Mr. Big Is Tough, But . . . ," *Selling*, February 2001, pp. 1, 12.
35. Henry Canada, "Fishing for Big Ones", Personal Selling Power, Source Book 2008, p. 46.
36. Jim Dickie and Barry Trailer, "Proactive Sales Intelligence: The New Requirement for Getting Into the Game," Salesforce.com 2007.
37. Ibid., pp. 46–47.
38. H. F. (Herb) MacKenzie, *Sales Management in Canada* (Toronto, ON: Pearson Education Canada, 2008), p. 140.
39. Tony Parinello, "Keeping Track of Prospects," www.entrepreneur.com/article/0,4621,306013,00.html, January 13, 2003, downloaded February 14, 2008.
40. Don Thomson, *Keeping the Funnel Full* (French Creek, BC, Mardon Publishing, 2004), p. 7.
41. H. F. (Herb) MacKenzie, ibid., p. 141.

SOURCES FOR BOXED FEATURES

a. Sarah Lorge, "The Best Way to Prospect," *Sales & Marketing Management*, January 1998, p. 80.
b. Interview with Gene Chahley, Polaroid Canada Inc., May 19, 1997; Barbara Siskind, *Seminars to Build Your Business* (North Vancouver, BC: Self-Counsel Press, 1998), pp. 9–12; Sheldon Gordon, "Punch Up Your Profits," *Profit*, May 1999, pp. 17–22.
c. Debi Rosati, personal correspondence, October 27, 2004.

Chapter 13

1. Malcolm Fleschner, "Too Busy to Buy," *Selling Power*, March 1999, p. 36.
2. Gina Rollins, "Prepped to Sell," *Selling Power*, September 2006, pp. 74–77.
3. Bradford Agry, "Every Client Meeting Provides a Dynamic New Opportunity," *Selling*, April 2002, pp. 1, 4.
4. Malcolm Fleschner, "Anatomy of a Sale," *Selling Power*, April 1998, p. 76; Gina Rollins, "Prepare for the Unknown," *Selling Power*, July/August 2003, pp. 26–30.
5. Tom Reilly, "Prepare Like a Pro," www.TomReillyTraining.com, accessed April 8, 2007.
6. "Set the Agenda," *Personal Selling Power*, May/June 1995, p. 79.
7. Donna Fenn, "Because His Family Business Makes an Art of Customer Service," *Inc.*, April 2005, p. 94; Telephone interview with Pamela Miles, staff member at Mitchells/Richards, March 22, 2005.
8. Philip Kotler and Gary Armstrong, *Principles of Marketing*, Tenth Edition (Upper Saddle River, NJ: Prentice Hall, 2004), p. 531.
9. Rick Page, *Hope Is Not a Strategy* (Atlanta, GA: Nautilus Press, 2002), p. 25.
10. Betsy Cummings, "Group Dynamics," *Sales & Marketing Management*, January/February 2007, p. 8.
11. James F. O'Hara, "Successful Selling to Buying Committees," *Selling*, February 1998, p. 8.
12. George R. Franke and Jeong-Eun Park, "Salesperson Adaptive Selling Behavior and Customer orientation: A Meta –Analysis" *Journal of Marketing Research*, November 2006, pp. 693–702; Leroy Robinson, Jr., Greg W. Marshall, William C. Moncrief, and Felicia G. Lassk, "Toward a Shortened Measure of Adaptive Selling," *Journal of Personal Selling & Sales Management*, Spring 2002, pp. 111–119.
13. The role of confidence in adaptive selling is discussed in Leroy Robinson, Jr., Greg W. Marshall, William C. Moncrief, and Felicia G. Lassak, "Toward a Shortened Measure of Adaptive Selling," *Journal of Personal Selling & Sales Management*, Spring 2002, pp. 111–119.
14. Neil Rackham and John R. Vincentis, Rethinking the Sales Force (New York: McGraw-Hill, 1999), p. 217.
15. Thomas A. Freese, *Secrets of Question Based Selling* (Naperville, IL: Sourcebooks, 2003), p. 114.
16. John Fellows, "Your Foot in the Door," *Selling Power*, March 1996, pp. 64–65.
17. Adapted from Art Sobczak, "Please, Call Me Back!" *Selling*, March 1999, p. 12.
18. *Ibid.*
19. Deborah Dumaine, "Managing Customers with E-Mail," *Selling Power*, March 2004, p. 94.
20. Rachel Zupek, "Reply all and Other Email Gaffes," *Business.com*, September 2007, p. 26.
21. Susan Bixler and Nancy Nix-Rice, *The New Professional Image* (Holbrook, MA: Adams Media Corporation, 1997), p. 3.
22. Steve Atlas, "How to Cultivate New Turf," *Selling Power*, January/February 2003, p. 26.
23. Maxine Clayton, "60 Seconds on Small Talk," *Fast Company*, November 2004, p. 43.
24. Dean A. Goettsch, "Make Your First Meeting Count," *Selling*, July 2004, pp. 1, 4.
25. Melissa Campanelli, "Sound the Alarm," *Sales & Marketing Management*, December 1994, pp. 20–25.
26. Carolee Boyles, "Prewarm Cold Calls," *Selling Power*, July/August 2001, p. 30.
27. Abner Little, "Selling to Women Revs Up Car Sales," *Personal Selling Power*, July/August 1990, p. 50.

28. "Six Great Upselling Questions," *Personal Selling Power*, April 1993, p. 44.
29. Interview with Larry Short, June 9, 1997.
30. Theodore Kinni, "How to Identify and Remove the Problems Underlying Call Reluctance," *Selling Power*, November/December 2004, pp. 69–71; "Types of Call Reluctance," *Value-Added Selling 21*, February 14, 2005, p. 4.
31. Alan Farnham, "Are You Smart Enough to Keep Your Job?" *Fortune*, January 15, 1996, pp. 34–42.
32. "The Disappointment Trap," *Selling Power*, January/February 1999, p. 14.
33. Roy Chitwood, "Still Trying to Slip Past Gatekeepers? Forget It!" *Value-Added Selling 21*, December 16, 2003, pp. 1–2.

SOURCES FOR BOXED FEATURES

a. Richard R. Gesteland, *Cross-Cultural Business Behavior* (Copenhagen: Handelshøjskolens Forlag, Copenhagen Business School Press, 1999), pp. 19–23; Bill Schiller, "Miller Declares China Mission 'An Eye-opener,'" *Toronto Star*, April 20, 2008, p. A10; David Shipley, "N.B. Business Leaders Encouraged by India Trip," *Telegraph-Journal* (Saint John), February 23, 2008, p. C1.
b. Susan Creco, "Sales: What Works Now," *Inc.*, February 2001, p. 56.

Chapter 14

1. *Questions, Questions, Questions,* produced by Art Bauer, West Des Moines, IA, 2006.
2. Louise E. Boone and David L. Kurtz, *Contemporary Marketing*, 11th Ed. (Mason, Ohio: Southwestern Publishing, 2004), p. 576; Geoffrey James, "Consultative Selling Strategies," *Selling Power*, April 2004, pp. 17–20.
3. Duane Sparks, *Questions-The Answer to Sales*, The Sales Board: Minneapolis, MN 2005, p. vii.
4. Rose A. Spinelli, "Listening: A Priority in Shopping for Others," *Chicago Tribune*, November 30, 2003, p. 55.
5. Neil Rackham, *Spin Selling* (New York, NY: McGraw-Hill, 1988).
6. Geoffrey James, "Driving the High-Stakes Sales," *Selling Power*, May 2007, p. 51.
7. Ibid.
8. Ann Demarais and Valerie White, *First Impressions—What You Don't Know About How Others See You* (New York: Bantam Books, 2004), pp. 68–69.
9. Barry L. Reece and Rhonda Brandt, *Effective Human Relations: Personal and Organizational Applications*, 10th edition (Boston, MA: Houghton Mifflin, 2008), p. 40.
10. Ibid.
11. Demarais and White, *First Impressions*, p. 70.
12. William F. Kendy, "The Silence Play," *Selling Power*, July/August 2007, pp. 29–30.
13. Matthew McKay, Martha Davis, and Patrick Fanning, *Message: The Communication Skills Book* (Oakland, CA: New Harbinger, 1995), p. 15; Susan Scott, *Fierce Conversations* (New York: Viking Penguin, 2002), p. 157.
14. William F. Kendy, "How to Be a Good Listener," *Selling Power*, April 2004, p. 43.
15. Tom Reilly, *Value-Added Selling* (New York, NY: McGraw-Hill, 2003), p. 130.

16. Ibid., pp. 17, 167.
17. Kerry L. Johnson, "The Things Dales Masters Do," *Value-Added Selling 21*, April 16, 2007, p. 3.
18. Paul F. Roos, "Just Say No," *Selling Power*, October 2003, p. 50.
19. "Presentation-Wise, We've Lost Our Tails," *Sales & Field Force Automation*, July 1999, p. 4.
20. Dean A. Goettsch, "Guidelines for Rethinking Sales Presentations," *Selling*, October 2001, p. 14.
21. Gary A. Williams and Robert B. Miller, "Change the Way You Persuade," *Harvard Business Review*, May 2002, p. 6; Renee Houston Zemanski, "Subtlety Can Sell," Selling Power, January/February 2007, pp. 42–44.
22. Mike Coyne, "How I Made the Sale," *Value-Added Selling 21*, August 12, 2003, pp. 1 and 4.
23. Robert B. Cialdini, "Harnessing the Science of Persuasion," *Harvard Business Review*, October 2001, p. 74.
24. Stephanie G. Sherman and V. Clayton Sherman, *Make Yourself Memorable* (New York: AMACOM, 1996), pp. 58–59.
25. John Grossmann, "Location, Location, Location," *Inc.*, August 2004, p. 83.
26. Rich Mesch, "Spinning Yarns—Seven Tips for Using Stories to Enhance Simulations and Learning," *SPBT Focus*, Spring 2007, pp. 42–46.
27. Chad Kaydo, "Lights! Camera! Sales!" *Sales & Marketing Management*, February 1998, p. 111.
28. Neil Rackham and John DeVincentis, *Rethinking the Sales Force* (New York: McGraw-Hill, 1999), p. 17.

SOURCES FOR BOXED FEATURES

a. Emily Barker, "Start with . . . Nothing," Inc. February 2002, pp. 67–73. "About Right Now Technologies," www.rightnow.com, accessed April 4, 2005.
b. Duane Sparks, *Questions—The Answer to Sales*, The Sales Board, Minneapolis, MN. 2005, p. vi; "CARQUEST Cares," www.carquest.com, accessed November 7, 2007.

Chapter 15

1. Bill Marriott, www.blogs.marriott.com/default.asp?item =580243, accessed July 4, 2008.
2. *Selling Power*, June 2007, p. 32.
3. Geoff James, "The Art of Sales Negotiation," *Selling Power*, March 2004, pp. 25–28.
4. Tom Riley, *Value-Added Selling* (New York: McGraw-Hill, 2003), p. 17.
5. Hal Lancaster, "You Have to Negotiate for Everything in Life, So Get Good at It," *Wall Street Journal*, January 27, 1998, p. B1.
6. Ron Willingham, *Integrity Selling for the 21st Century* (New York: Currency Doubleday, 2003), p. 154.
7. Brian Tracy, *The 100 Absolutely Unbreakable Laws of Business Success* (San Francisco, CA: Berrett-Koehler Publishers, 2000), p. 235.
8. Ron Willingham, *Integrity Selling for the 21st Century*, p. 153.
9. Brenda Goodman, "The Art of Negotiation," *Psychology Today*, January/February 2007, pp. 64–65.
10. Gregg Crawford, "Let's Negotiate," *Sales & Marketing Management*, November 1995, pp. 28–29.
11. Michael Soon Lee, *The American Salesman*, August 2007, pp. 25–28.

12. Rob Walker, "Take It or Leave It: The Only Guide to Negotiating You Will Ever Need," *Inc.*, August 2003, p.81.
13. Robert H. Schuller, "Preparing to Negotiate," in *The Only Negotiating Guide You'll Ever Need: 101 Ways to Win Every Time in Any Situation* by Peter B. Stark and Jane S. Flaherty, Chapter 10, pp. 81–85.
14. Deepak Malhotra and Max H. Bazerman, *Negotiation Genius* (New York: Random House, 2007), p. 102.
15. Peter B. Stank and Jane Flaherty, *The Only Negotiating Guide You'll Ever Need* (New York: Broadway Books, 2003), p.84.
16. Deepak Malhotra and Max H. Bazerman, ibid., pp. 20–23.
17. Ibid.
18. Peter B. Stank and Jane Flaherty, ibid., p. 79.
19. David Stiebel, *When Talking Makes Things Worse!* (Dallas, TX: Whitehall & Norlton, 1997), p. 17.
20. For details, see Deepak Malhotra and Max H. Bazerman, ibid., pp. 59–64, p. 82.
21. Don Maruska, *Value Added Selling 21*, April 30, 2007, p. 2.
22. Joseph Conlin, "Negotiating Their Way to the Top," *Sales & Marketing Management*, April 1996, p. 62; Neil Rackham, "Winning the Price War," *Sales & Marketing Management*, November 2001, p. 26.
23. Deepak Malhotra and Max H. Bazerman, ibid., p. 175.
24. Lain Ehman, "Not a Done Deal," *Selling Power*, November/ December 2003, pp. 42–44; "Negotiate the Right Price Despite Customer Pressure," *Selling*, July 2004, p. 2.
25. William F. Kendy, "Solving the 'Friendship Buying' Problem," *Selling Power*, November/December 2001, pp. 40–44.
26. Steven J. Schwartz, *How to Make Hot Cold Calls*, revised edition (Toronto, ON: Stoddart Publishing, 2001), p. 42.
27. Marc Freeman, "Say It and Sell It," *Sales & Marketing Management*, November/December 2006, p. 13.
28. William F. Kendy, "The Price Is Too High," *Selling Power*, April 2006, pp. 30–33.
29. Ibid.
30. Jeff Keller, "Objections? No Problem," *Selling Power*, September 1996, pp. 44–45.
31. Adapted from Nanci McCann, "Irate over Rates," *Selling*, July–August 1996, p. 25.
32. Tom Reilly, ibid., p. 189.
33. Rick Kang, "Management by Defiance," *Profit*, June 1999, pp. 63–64.
34. See Neil Rackham, *The New SPIN Selling Fieldbook*, (New York: McGraw-Hill, 1996), pp. 127–45.
35. David Jobber and Jeff Lancaster, *Selling and Sales Management*, 7th ed. (Prentice Hall/Financial Times, 2006), p. 261.
36. William F. Kendy, ibid., p. 30.
37. Tom Reilly, ibid., p. 191–92.
38. Joseph Conlin, "Negotiating Their Way to the Top," *Sales & Marketing Management*, April 1996, p. 58.
39. William F. Kendy, ibid., pp. 30–33.
40. Sam Deep and Lyle Sussman, *Close the Deal: Smart Moves for Selling* (Reading, MA: Perseus Books, 1999), p. 225.
41. Roland M. Sandell, "Five Sure-Fire Methods to Overcome Objections to Price," *American Salesman*, October 1976, p. 38.
42. Alex Taylor, "Little Jets Are Huge," *Fortune*. September 4, 2000, pp. 275–278.
43. William F. Kendy, "Negotiation Tactics," *Selling Power*, September 2006, p. 31.
44. Homer Smith, "How to Cope with Buyers Who Are Trained in Negotiation," *Personal Selling Power*, September 1988, p. 37.
45. Ibid.
46. Robert Adler, Benson Rosen, and Elliot Silverstein, "Thrust and Parry," *Training & Development*, March 1996, p. 47.
47. Homer Smith, ibid.
48. Laura Pratt, "Everyone's a Winner," *Profit*, November 2001, p. 47.

SOURCES FOR BOXED FEATURES

a. "Getting to Yes, Chinese Style," *Sales & Marketing Management*, July 1996, pp. 44–45; Sam Deep and Lyle Sussman, *Close the Deal: Smart Moves for Selling* (Reading, MA: Perseus Books, 1999), pp. 279–81; James K. Sebenius, "Six Habits of Merely Effective Negotiators," *Harvard Business Review*, April 2001, p. 90.
b. Hal Lancaster, "You Have to Negotiate for Everything in Life, So Get Good At It," *The Wall Street Journal*, January 27, 1998, p. B1; Amy Lindgren, "Want a Raise? Don't Daydream; Polish Your Negotiating Skills," *Des Moines Register*, April 26, 1998, p. 1L.
c. Mary Klonizakis, "A Class Act," *Contact*, September 2000, p. 18.

Chapter 16

1. Susan Minns, vice-president of client services, Event Spectrum, Personal interview and correspondence, July 9, 2008.
2. Ron Willingham, *Integrity Selling for the 21st Century*, New York: Currency Doubleday 2003, p. 179.
3. Gene Bedell, *3 Steps to Yes* (New York: Crown Business, 2000), pp. 72–80.
4. Tom Reilly, *Value-Added Selling* (New York: McGraw-Hill, 2003), p. 176.
5. Andy Cohen, "Are Your Reps Afraid to Close?" *Sales & Marketing Management*, March 1996, p. 43.
6. Michele Marchetti, "Make Process a Sales Priority," *Sales & Marketing Management*, September 2006, p. 16. See John Graham, "How to Profit From Customer Buying-Cycle Basics," *The American Salesman*, May 2007, pp. 19–23.
7. Susan Creco, "The Need for Speed—How to Rev up Your Sales Cycle," *Inc. Magazine*, April 2007, p. 38.
8. Graham Denton, "The Single Biggest Closing Mistake," Graham Denton Skills Center (Web page) May 4, 1999, p. 1.
9. Ray Dreyfock, "Is the Buyer Ready?" *Selling Power*, January/ February 2002, p. 52.
10. "The Closing Moment," *Personal Selling*, October 1995, p. 48; Lain Ehman, "How to Read Hidden Signals," *Selling Power*, June 2004, pp. 36–38.
11. Ron Karr, "Expert Advice—The Titan Principle," *Selling Power*, October 2001, p. 32.
12. Jenny McCune, "Closing Sales with a Splash," *Selling*, September 2004, p. 15.
13. "Selling Tips," *Selling*, May 1999, p. 13.
14. Ron Willingham, *Integrity Selling* (New York: Doubleday, 1987), p. 133.
15. Jeffrey Gitomer, "Did You Get the Order? If You Didn't, Here's Why," *Business Record*, May 7, 2007, p. 36.
16. Tom Reilly, ibid., p. 179.
17. Ron Willingham, *Integrity Selling for the 21st Century* (New York: Currency Doubleday, 2003), p. 184.

18. Jenny C. McCune, "The Brief Story of Underwear's Stupendous Success," *Selling*, March 2000, p. 15.
19. Joan Leotta, "The Management Close," *Selling Power*, November/December 2001, pp. 26–28. See Megan Sweas, "Heavyweights on Call," *Sales & Marketing Management*, December 2003, p. 14.
20. Ron Willingham, *Integrity Selling for the 21st Century*, ibid., pp. 185–187.
21. Mel Siberman, *Active Training* (Toronto, ON: Maxwell Macmillan Canada, 1990), pp. 96–99.
22. T. J. Becker, "That Queasy Feeling," *Chicago Tribune*, July 21, 2002, p. W1.
23. Betsy Wiesendanger, "When a Sale Goes South," *Selling Power*, November/December 2003, pp. 65–67.
24. Betsy Cummings, "Done Deal—How One Sales Pro Closed a Big Customer," *Sales & Marketing Management*, September 2006, p. 13.

SOURCES FOR BOXED FEATURES

a. "Ask for the Order" (West Des Moines, IA: Video Learning, LLC, 2004).
b. Securit Web site, www.securit.com, accessed July 8, 2008; Interview with Greg Brophy, February 19, 1997; correspondence from Judy Robson, August 26, 1999; correspondence from Bonnie Shettler, May 2005.

Chapter 17

1. Windsor Factory Supply Web site, www.wfsltd.com, accessed August 4, 2008; Rick Thurston, personal interview, August 5, 2008.
2. Bob Johnson, "Loyalty Lessons from the Pros," *Customer Support Management*, July/August 1999, p. 115; Ranjay Gulati and James B. Oldroyd, "The Quest for Customer Focus," *Harvard Business Review*, April 2005, pp. 92–97.
3. Ibid.
4. Gary Armstrong and Philip Kotler, *Marketing: An Introduction*, Sixth Edition (Upper Saddle River, NJ: Prentice Hall, 2003), p. 553.
5. Don Peppers and Martha Rogers, "Customer Loyalty: A Matter of Trust," *Sales & Marketing Management*, June 2006, p. 22.
6. Theodore Levitt, *The Marketing Management* (New York: Macmillan, 1983), pp. 117–18; Tahl Raz, "The '4 + 2 Formula' for Success," *Inc.*, August 2003, p. 42.
7. See Tom Reilly, "Value Added Service is a Team Sport," Tom Reilly Training, www.tomreillytraining.com, accessed April 8, 2007.
8. Geoffrey Brewer, "The Customer Stops Here," *Sales & Marketing Management*, March 1998, pp. 31–32; See Ron Zemke and Chip Bell, *Service Magic* (Chicago: IL: Dearborn Trade Publishing, 2004).
9. "Why Customers Leave," *Sales & Marketing Management*, May 1998, p. 86; Tom Peters, *The Circle of Innovation* (New York: Vintage Books, 1997), pp. 138–39.
10. Max Morden, "Service with a Smile," *In Touch* (Richard Ivey School of Business, Fall 1999), p. 37.
11. Bill Gates, *Business @ the Speed of Thought* (New York: Warner Books, 1999), p. 67.
12. Michael Ahearne, Ronald Jelinek, and Eli Jones, "Examining the Effect of Salesperson Service Behavior in a Competitive Context," *Journal of the Academy of Marketing Science*, December 2007, pp. 603+.
13. See Daniel H. Pink, *A Whole New Mind* (New York, NY: Riverhead Books, 2005), pp. 48–53.
14. Steve Ham, "Oracle—Why It's Cool Again," *Business Week*, May 8, 2000, pp. 115–119.
15. Maggie Chung, personal interview, July 25, 2008.
16. Chad Kaydo, "An Unlikely Sales Ally," *Sales & Marketing Management*, January 1999, p. 69.
17. Sally J. Silberman, "An Eye for Finance," *Sales & Marketing Management*, April 1996, p. 26.
18. Benson P. Shapiro, V. Kasturi Rangon, and John Sviokla, *Harvard Business Review*, July/August 2004, p. 162.
19. Daryl Allen, "Relationship Selling Is Key to Success," *Selling*, March 2002, p. 12.
20. Dave Kahle, "Protecting Your Good Accounts," *The American Salesman*, June 2007, p. 12.
21. Tom Reilly, "Create Satisfied Customers: Always Be Sure to Exceed Their Expectations," *Selling*, January 2001, p. 3; Mary Salafia. "Reassessment Planning," *Selling Power*, May 2004, p. 56.
22. Tom Riley, *Value-Added Selling* (New York: McGraw-Hill, 2003), p. 117.
23. Andrea Nierenberg, "Eight Ways to Stay Top of Mind," *Selling*, April 1998, p. 7.
24. Queena Sook Kim, "For Sale: Super-Model Home," *Wall Street Journal*, August 6, 2002, p. D-1.
25. Melinda Ligos, "The Joys of Cross-Selling," *Sales & Marketing Management*, August 1998, p. 75.
26. Tom Riley, *Value-Added Selling*, pp. 124–25.
27. William F. Kendy, "Add-Ons Add Up," *Selling Power*, January/February 2007, p. 30.
28. William F. Kendy, "Skills Workshop," *Selling Power*, June 2000, pp. 33–34.
29. Jo Ann Brezette, "Smart Answers to Clients' Questions," *Window Fashions Design & Education Magazine*, September 2001, p. 120; Lain Ehman, "Upsell, Don't Oversell," *Selling Power*, January–February 2004, pp. 30–32.
30. "Inspirations from Michele," *Inspiring Solutions*, February 1999, p. 3.
31. Bob Johnson, "Loyalty Lessons from the Pros," *Customer Support Management*, July/August 1999, p. 115.
32. Barry L. Reece and Rhonda Brandt, *Effective Human Relations: Personal and Organizational Applications*, Tenth Edition. (Boston, MA: Houghton Mifflin Company, 2008), p. 215.
33. Bradley E. Wesner, "From Complaint to Opportunity," *Selling Power*, May 1996, p. 62
34. Gerald A Michaelson, "When Things Go Wrong, Make It Right," *Selling*, March 1997, p. 12.
35. Michael Abrams and Matthew Paese, "Winning and Dining the Whiners," *Sales & Marketing Management*, February 1993, p. 73.
36. "How to Diffuse a Customer Problem," *Sales & Marketing Management*, May 2000, p. 14.
37. Rick Thurston, ibid.; Windsor Factory Supply Web site, ibid.

SOURCES FOR BOXED FEATURES

a. Jeff Barbian, "It's Who You Know," *Training*, December 2001, p. 22.

b. "Relationships with Customers Must Be Job Number 1," *Food-Service Distributor*, July 1989, p. 74; Joan O. Fredericks and James M. Salter II, "Beyond Customer Satisfaction," *Management Review*, May 1995, pp. 29–32.

c. Betsy Cummings, "You're Outta Here, "*Sales & Marketing Management*, June 2001, pp. 65–66; Rhea Seymour, "Ideas That Work," *Profit*, June 2002, pp. 66–70; Betsey Cummings, "The Perfect Plan," *Sales & Marketing Management*, February 2002, p. 53.

Chapter 18

1. Paula Shannon, personal correspondence, May 2005 and November 30, 2007.

2. Renee Houston Zemanski, "A Matter of Time," *Selling Power*, October 2001, p. 82.

3. Eugene Greissman, "Seven Characteristics of High-Achieving Salespeople," *Value-Added Selling* 21, March 16, 2004, p. 4.

4. Betty Cummings, "Increasing Face Time," *Sales & Marketing Management*, January 2004, p. 12.

5. Barry J. Farber, "Not Enough Hours in the Day," *Sales & Marketing Management*, July 1995, pp. 28–29.

6. If you are interested in how to break bad habits and form good ones, see James Claiborn and Cherry Pedrick, *The Habit Change Workbook* (Oakland, CA: New Harbinger Publications, 2001).

7. See Alison Stein Wellner, "The Time Trap," *Inc.*, June 2004, pp. 42–44.

8. Brian Tracy, *The 100 Absolutely Unbreakable Laws of Business Success* (San Francisco: Berrett-Koehler Publishers, Inc., 2000), pp. 40–47.

9. Charles R. Hall, "Create Excitement, Get Motivated Through Planning," *Selling*, February 2000, p. 13.

10. Ed Brown, "Stephen Covey's New One-Day Seminar," *Fortune*, January 1999, p. 138.

11. Besty Wiesendanger, "Time to Spend," *Selling Power*, November/December 2003, pp. 28–32.

12. Laura Pratt, "Twenty-five Hours a Day," *Profit*, November 2001, p. 41.

13. Hyrum W. Smith, *The 10 Natural Laws of Successful Time and Life Management* (New York: Warner Books, 1994), p. 108.

14. Thomas E. Weber, "Meetings in Cyberspace May Soon Be as Routine as the Conference Call," *Wall Street Journal*, June 4, 2001, p. B1.

15. Michele Marchetti, "Territories: For Optimal Performance, Segment Your Customer Base by Industry," *Sales & Marketing Management*, December 1998, p. 35.

16. Lain Chroust Ehmann, "In the Details," *Selling Power*, September 2007, p. 34.

17. Ibid., p. 36.

18. Alison Smith, "Plan Your Territory," *Selling Power*, March 2003, pp. 37–38.

19. Daryl Allen, "Maximize Your Territory Coverage, Increased Sales and Higher Profits Will Follow," *Selling*, June 2001, p. 10.

20. Henry Canaday, "Automated Reports Boost Sales Productivity," *Selling Power*, June 2007, p. 13.

21. "Maintaining Perspective by Keeping Good Records," *Value-Added Selling 21*, August 20, 2007, p.4.

22. Bruce Cryer, Rollin McCraty, and Doc Childre, "Pull the Plug On Stress," *Harvard Business Review*, July 2003, pp. 1–2.

23. David Shenk, "Data Smog," *Perdid*, Spring 1999, pp. 5–7.

24. "More Useful Tips for Running Your Home Office," *Selling*, January 2001, p. 11; "Home Office Etiquette," *Sales & Marketing Management*, January 2000, p. 74.

25. Patricia Sellers, "Now Bounce Back," *Fortune*, May 1, 1995, p. 57.

26. Martin Seligman, *Learned Optimism*, (New York, NY: Knopf, 2001), p. 4; Annie Murphy Paul, "Self-Help: Shattering the Myths," *Psychology Today*, March/April 2001, p. 64; Arnold A. Lazarus and Clifford N. Lazarus, *The 60-Second Shrink* (San Luis, Obispo CA: Impact Publishers, 1997), pp. 3, 4.

27. "Canada's Fastest Growing Companies 2002," *Profit*, June 2002, p. 36.

28. "Canada's Fastest Growing Companies 2002," *Profit*, June 2002, p. 36.

29. Husky Injection Molding Systems, "Working Together," available www.husky.ca/abouthusky/careers-220-223.html, accessed August 4, 2008.

SOURCES FOR BOXED FEATURES

a. Kip Grant, "Saying 'I Do' to Lifelong Learning," *Contact*, January 2000, p. 9.

b. Michael Adams, "Family Matters," *Sales & Marketing Management*, March 1998, pp. 61–65.

c. Li Shusheng, personal interview, July 24, 2008.

Credits

Figure Credits

Fig. 7.3, p. 133: From the book *The Double Win* by Dennis Waitley (Old Tappan, NJ: Fleming H. Revell Co., 1985). **Fig. 10.3, p. 207:** Adapted and reprinted by permission of *Harvard Business Review*. An exhibit from "Marketing Success through Differentiation of Anything" by Theodore Levitt (Jan/Feb 1980). Copyright © 1980 by the President and Fellows of Harvard College, all rights reserved. **Fig. 18.1, p. 389:** Supplied by author. **Fig. 18.4, p. 399:** Used with the permission of 3M Corp.

Advertisement Credits

p. 192: Courtesy Lowe's Canada. **p. 228:** Courtesy AIM Funds Management Inc. **p. 229:** Reprinted with permission of Samsung Electronics Canada. **p. 240:** Courtesy Scott's Directories. **p. 242:** Courtesy International Training and Management Company. **p. 246:** Reprinted with permission of infoCANADA. **p. 268:** Courtesy of The Complex Sale, Inc. **p. 332:** Aramark. **p. 395:** Courtesy of TerrAlign Group, Inc.

Photo Credits

Note: Cartoon credits appear on page.

p. 124: Supplied by author. **p. 129:** Image Source Black/Almay. **p. 135:** Radius Images/Almay. **p. 143:** David Madison/Stone/Getty Images. **p. 149:** Stan Honda/Agence France Presse/Getty Images. **p. 152:** Bruce Ayres/Stone/Getty Images. **p. 157:** AP/World Wide Photos. **p. 158:** © CORBIS/ Outline. **p. 159:** CP Photo/Larry MacDougal. **p. 160:** © The Copyright Group/SuperStock. **p. 166:** Bruce Ayres/Getty Images Inc.—Stone Allstock. **p. 178:** Steve Niedorf/Image Bank/Getty Images. **p. 182:** Photonica/Getty Images. **p. 183:** © CORBIS. **p. 195:** Image Source/Getty Images. **p. 250:** Courtesy of Salesforce.com. **p. 253:** Courtesy of Salesforce.com. **p. 256:** Courtesy of Salesforce.com. **p. 273:** Asia Images Group/Almay. **p. 292:** Jose L. Pelaez/The Stock Market. **p. 299:** Jeffery Shaw. **p. 302:** © CORBIS/Stock Market. **p. 320:** © Super Stock. **p. 324:** © Digital Vision. **p. 352:** Stockbyte/Almay. **p. 358:** Image Source Pink/Almay. **p. 369:** Supplied by author. **p. 370:** Photographer's Choice/Getty Images. **p. 392:** Michael Paras/Photographic Services. **p. 402:** © moodboard/Corbis.